The Rare Soul Bible
Volume Two

Dave Rimmer
Visit my website at www.soulfulkindamusic.net

Printed in the United Kingdom

First Printing: April 2016

Soulful Kinda Music – The Rare Soul Bible Volume Two

Dedicated To

Margie Rimmer

23rd June 1960 - 29th January, 2010

Introduction

Well it's been fourteen years since the first volume was published, and I'm still getting people asking if there are copies available. I'm afraid there are none left, either with me or with Bee Cool, so you'll just have to trawl the web for a copy

So what's in this book ? Pretty much, more of the same. It's still the aim to produce the most complete discography's of Sixties Soul artists' 45s possible, and set them out in a clear, and easily understood format, and I think that's what has been achieved again.

When the first book was published, the discography's it contained were as complete as I could get them. Of course the very act of publishing them meant that people contacted me and said "You've missed so and so off that discography." Thank you to everyone who did contact me. All the updates are now included on the discography section of the Soulful Kinda Music website. It's the same with this set of artist discography's. They are as complete as I can get them, at the time the book is published.

In addition, this time, there are loads of complete label discography's. I'd always assumed that label discography's would be fairly simple to complete in comparison to an artist discography. You just start at number 1, and finish at the last number. How wrong could I be. Life would be that simple if record companies used a consecutive numbering system. Unfortunately most of them didn't ! So it can be just as frustrating trying to get a listing finished off. All of the discography's in the book are as complete as I can make them. I have consulted as many sources as possible to try and fill in some of the gaps, and whilst on some labels it's just not been possible to fill in all the gaps, I can guarantee, at the time of the book being printed, these discography's are the most complete ones ever published.

The main sources of information that I've consulted are Bosko Asanovic over in Canada, who has probably provided either the complete discography, or an update, to each and every discography in this book, and the members of Soul-Source website, as well as too many individuals to mention. Plus of course a miryad of record lists, and reference books.

Thanks must go to all the people who have given me lifts, booked me as a DJ, played me records, sold me records, and bought me a beer at all the venues I've visited, I couldn't have done it without you all.

Although it's been fourteen years since the first book was published, I started it years ago. My life kind of stopped when my darling wife Margie, passed away on the 29th January, 2010. So this book is dedicated to her memory.

However, the book has finally come to fruition because of the encouragement of my now fiancé, Jessica Wecker, so I have to thank her just as much for her love and encouragement.

Soulful Kinda Music – The Rare Soul Bible Volume Two

Index

All Chapter heading photos were taken by the Author.

Cover photo by Paul Royle

The Accents

The Accents (members Gabe Lapano (vocals and keyboards), Don Beck (saxophone), Tony Johnson (drums), Don Lovas (guitar) and Frank Mannix (bass). This line-up of the San Diego based group played live concerts but made no known recordings.

Sandy & The Cupids (members Sandra "Sandi" Rouse, ...)

CRC Charter 2 - If I Didn't Know Him / Rebel - 1964

The Accents featuring Sandi (members Sandra "Sandi" Rouse (vocals) Gabe Lapano (vocals and keyboards), Doug Myers (saxaphone), Tony Johnson (drums), Don Lovas (guitar) and Frank Mannix (bass).

Commerce 5012 - Better Watch Out Boy / Tell Me - 1964
Challenge 1112 - Better Watch Out Boy / Tell Me - 1964
Charter 1017 - I've Got Better Things To Do / Then He Starts To Cry - 1964

The Accents featuring Sandi and Gabe (members Sandra "Sandi" Rouse, Gabe Lapano, Doug Myers, Tony Johnson, Don Lovas and Frank Mannix.

Challenge 59254 - Better Watch Out Boy / Tell Me - 1964

The Accents featuring Sandi (members Sandra "Sandi" Rouse, Gabe Lapano , Doug Myers , Tony Johnson, Don Lovas and Frank Mannix)

Liberty 55813 - What Do You Want Me To Do / I Really Love You - 1965

The Accents (members Sandra "Sandi" Rouse, Gabe Lapano , Doug Myers , Tony Johnson, Don Lovas and Frank Mannix)

Karate 529 - On The Run / He's The One - 1966 (the group broke up when Doug Myers was drafted)

The Brain Police (members Tony Johnson (drums), Frank Mannix (bass), David Randle (guitar), Rick Randle (vocals, keyboards, harmonica and guitar) - a former member of The Other Four and The Mandells) When he left the group Johnson later became a sought-after live and session drummer, playing with Mary Wells, Junior Walker, Commander Cody, Maria Muldaur and Hoyt Axton among others.

The Brain Police (members David Randle (guitar), Rick Randle (vocals, keyboards, harmonica and guitar), Benny Bennett (percussion), Norman Lombardo (vocals and bass) - a former member of The Other Four, Sid Smith (drums) and Larry Grant (guitar) - a former member of The Other Four and The Mandells)

Soulful Kinda Music – The Rare Soul Bible Volume Two

The Brain Police (members Norman Lombardo (vocals and bass), Sid Smith (drums)
- a former member of The Roosters on A & M 746 and Larry Grant (guitar))

Head X 2002 / 3 - World Of Wax* / Smoking At Windsor Hill - 1969 *same song as on
their demo Lp but different version.

After the above 45 was released Sid Smith accepts an offer to tour with Roy
Head.Rick Randle became a member of Framework just before the group broke
up, later he and Framework's drummer Carl Spiron set up a two man band but never
recorded. Sometime in 1969 Norman Lombardo joined the pair and they formed a
group called The Dry Creek Road Band who are known to have recorded a demo.
Norman Lombardo and Rick Randle were then asked to play in The Dudes a back-up
band that was being formed for Rita Coolidge. This band also included Spooner
Oldham, Randy Bishop and Chris Etheridge. After Rick Randle joined hard rock
groups Bighorn and Child recording and touring with each. He then formed the
Seattle based Randle-Rosburg band which became known as Striker, who released
an album on Arista in 1978)

Beverly Ann

Beverly Ann (Beverly Bremers)

Showcase 9805 - We Got Trouble / The Great Pretender – 1965

Cheryl Ann (Can anyone verify that this is Beverly Bremers)

Patty 52 - I Can't Let Him / Goodbye Baby - ?

Beverly Ann (Beverly Bremers)

RCA Victor 47-9269 - He's Coming Home / He Won't See The Light - 1966
RCA Victor 47-9468 - You've Got Your Mind On Other Things / Until You - 1968

Beverly Bremers

Scepter 12315 - Don't Say You Don't Remember / Get Smart Girl – 1971
Scepter 12332 - When Michael Calls / Toy Girl – 1971
Scepter 12348 - We're Free / Colors Of Love - 1972 (Some Copies Issued With A
Picture Sleeve)
Brut 513 - Let It Play On / I Just Need Some Music -1972 (Promo Issue Only)
Scepter 12363 - I'll Make You Music / I Made A Man Out Of You, Jimmy – 1972
Scepter 12370 - Heaven Help Us All / All That's Left Is The Music – 1973
Scepter 12378 - Run To Her / Baby I Don't Know You – 1973
Scepter 12380 - Daddy's Coming Home / A Little Bit Of Love – 1973
Scepter 12391 - Sing A Happy Song / Get Smart Girl – 1974
Scepter Sdj 12399 - Get Up In The Morning (Mono) / Get Up In The Morning
(Stereo) - 1974 (Written By Deke Richards, Arranged By Deke Richards And Gene
Page)
Scepter 12399 - Get Up In The Morning / One Day At A Time – 1974

Soulful Kinda Music – The Rare Soul Bible Volume Two

Columbia 10180 - What I Did For Love / You're Precious To Me – 1975
Columbia 10451 - The Prisoner / Flight 309 To Tennessee - 1976

Beverley Bremers / John Paul Young

Eric 6003 - Don't Say You Don't Remember / Love Is In The Air* - 1983 *Flip By John Paul Young.

Jigsaw / Beverly Bremers

Collectables Col 033807 - Sky High / Don't Say You Don't Remember - ? *Flip By Beverly Bremers.

Beverly Bremers

Collectables Col 3-10180 - What I Did For Love / You're Precious To Me - ?

Lee Andrews & The Hearts

Lee Andrews & The Hearts (Members: Lee Andrews, Roy Calhoun, Butch Curry ??)

Rainbow 252 - Maybe You'll Be There / Baby Come Back - 1954
Rainbow 256 - White Cliffs Of Dover / Much Too Much - 1954
Rainbow 259 - The Fairest / Bells Of St. Mary - 1954
Riviera 965 - Maybe You'll Be There / Baby Come Back - 1954
Gotham 318 - Bluebird Of Happiness / Show Me The Merengue - 1956
Gotham 320 - Lonely Room / Leona - 1956
Gotham 321 - Just Suppose /It's Me - 1956
Main Line 101 - Try The Impossible / Nobody's Home - 1957
Main Line 102 - Long Lonely Nights / The Clock - 1957
Chess 1665 - Long Lonely Nights / The Clock - 1957
Chess 1675 - Tear Drops / The Girl Around The Corner - 1957
Argo 1000 - Tear Drops / The Girl Around The Corner - 1957
Casino 452 - Try The Impossible / Nobody's Home - 1958
United Artists 123 - Try The Impossible / Nobody's Home - 1958
United Artists 136 Why Do I / Glad To Be Here - 1958
United Artists 151 - Maybe You'll Be There / All I Ask Is Love - 1958
United Artists 162 - Just Suppose / Boom - 1959

The Five Hearts

Arcade 107 - Unbelievable / Aunt Jenny - 1959
Casino 107 - Unbelievable / Aunt Jenny - 1959

Lee Andrews

Casino 110 - I Wonder / Baby Come Back - 1959

Soulful Kinda Music – The Rare Soul Bible Volume Two

The Hearts

Chancellor 1057 - It's Unbelievable / On My Honor - 1960

Lee Andrews

Jordan 125 - A Wise Man Said / If You Only Care - 1960
Swan 4065 - I've Got A Right To Cry / I Miss You So - 1960
Swan 4076 - A Night Like Tonight / You Gave To Me - 1961
Swan 4087 - P.S. I Love You / I Cried - 1961

Lee Andrews & The Hearts

Gowen 1403 - Together Again / My Lonely Room - 1962

Famous Hearts

Guyden 2073 - Aisle Of Love / Momma - 1962

Lee Andrews

Parkway 860 - I'm Sorry Pillow / Gee But I'm Lonesome - 1963
Parkway 866 - Looking Back / Operator - 1963

Lee Andrews & The Hearts

Grand 156 - Teardrops / The Girl Around The Corner - 1963
Grand 157 - Long Lonely Nights / The Clock - 1963
Crimson 1002 - Island Of Love / Oh My Love - 1964
Crimson 1005 - Cold Gray Dawn / All You Can Do - 1964

Lee Andrews

V.I.P. 1601 - You, You, You / Hug-A-Bee (Instrumental) - 1965

Lee Andrews & The Hearts

Lost Nite 1001 - Cold Gray Dawn / All You Can Do - 1965
RCA 47-8929 You're Taking A Long Time Coming Back / Quiet As It's Kept - 1966
Crimson 1009 - Never The Less / Never The Less - 1967 (Promo copy)
Crimson 1009 - Island Of Love / Never The Less - 1967
Crimson 1015 - I've Had It / Little Bird - 1968
Lost Nite 1004 - Oh My Love / Can't Do Without You - 1968
Lost Nite 1005 - Quiet As It's Kept / Island Of Love - 1968

Congress Alley (Members: Lee Andrews.....)

Avco Embassy 4610 - God Bless The Children / Congress Alley - 1973
Avco Embassy 4616 - God Save America / I'm Gonna Prove It - 1973

Soulful Kinda Music – The Rare Soul Bible Volume Two

Lee Andrews & The Hearts

Gotham 323 - Sipping A Cup Of Coffee / Just Suppose (Alt. Take) - 1981
Gotham 324 - Window Eyes / Long Lonely Nights (Alt. Take) - 1981
Gotham 325 - I Miss My Baby/Boom (Alt. Take) - 1981

The Ambers

The Ambers (members Robert Rhoney, Robert Taylor, Billy Chinn, Ozzie Beck and Jerry White)

New Art 104 - Blue Birds / Baby I Need You - 1965
Verve 10436 - Now I'm In Trouble / I Love You Baby - 1966
Smash 2111 - Potion Of Love / Another Love - 1967
Jean 727 - Don't Go / Soul In Room # 401 - ?
Jean 729 - Don't Go / Never Could You Be (My Girl) - ?

Arthur Alexander

The Heartstrings (members Arthur Alexander, ...)

June Alexander (Arthur Alexander)

Judd 1020 - Sally Sue Brown / The Girl That Radiates That Charm* - 1960 *also recorded in 19? by Jimmy Ray Hunter and The Del Rays on Fame Recording Co. 602.

Arthur Alexander (born 10-May-1940 in Florence, Alabama -- died 9-June-1993 in Nasville, Tennessee -- cause: heart attack)

Dot 16309 - You Better Move On / A Shot Of Rhythm And Blues - 1962
Dot 16357 - Where Have You Been (All My Life) / Soldier Of Love - 1962
Dot 16387 - Anna (Go To Him)* / I Hang My Head And Cry - 1962 *covered in 1964 by The Beatles on Vee-Jay (Spec. DJ No. 8) and in 1965 by The Fiestas on Old Town 1178.
Dot 16425 - You're The Reason / Go Home Girl - 1963
Dot 16454 - I Wonder Where You Are Tonight / Dream Girl - 1963
Dot 16509 - Pretty Girls Everyhere / Baby Baby - 1963
Dot 16554 - Where Did Sally Go / Keep Her Guessin' - 1963
Dot 16616 - Black Knight / Ole John Amos - 1964
Dot 16737 - Detroit City / You Don't Care - 1965
Sound Stage 7 2556 - The Other Woman / (Baby) For You* - 1965 *although written by Arthur Alexander the track was credited to Elizabeth A. Barton the maiden name of his ex-wife.
Sound Stage 7 2572 - Turn Around (And Try Me) / Show Me The Road - 1966 (session guitarist Glen Campbell, backing vocals by The Blossoms (members Fanita James, Jean King and Gloria Taylor)

Soulful Kinda Music – The Rare Soul Bible Volume Two

Monument 1060 - I Need You Baby / Spanish Harlem* - 1968 *originally recorded in 1960 by Ben E. King on Atco 6185.
Sound Stage 7 2619 - Set Me Free / Love's Where Life Begins - 1968
Sound Stage 7 2626 - Bye Bye Love* / Another Place, Another Time** - 1969 *originally recorded in 1957 by The Everly Brothers on Cadence 1315. **also recorded in 1967 by Jerry Lee Lewis on Smash 2146.
Sound Stage 7 2652 - Glory Road / Cry Like A Baby* - 1970 *originally recorded in 1967 by The Box Tops on Mala 565.
Warner Bros. 7571 - I'm Comin' Home / It Hurts To Want It So Bad - 1972
Warner Bros. 7633 - Mr. John / You Got Me Knockin' - 1972
Warner Bros. 7658 - Burning Love / It Hurts To Want It So Bad - 1972
Warner Bros. 7676 - Lover Please* / They'll Do It Every Time - 1973 *written by Billy Swan.
Buddah 492 - Every Day I Have To Cry Some* / Everybody Needs Somebody To Love - 1975 *written by Arthur Alexander. Also recorded in 1968 by Lattimore Brown on Sound Stage 7 2616 and in 1970 by Phil Flowers on A & M 1168 plus in 1980 by Debby Boone on Warner Bros. 49652.
Buddah 522 - Sharing The Night Together / She'll Throw Stones At You - 1976
Buddah 602 - Sharing The Night Together / She'll Throw Stones At You - 1978
Music Mill 1012 - Hound Dog Man's Gone Home / So Long Baby - 1977
Collectables Col 033757 - You Better Move On / Anna (Go To Him) - ?

Chris Kenner / Tony Clarke /// Supercharge / Arthur Alexander

Ripete 1032 - Something You Got / This Heart Of Mine /// Red Dress / Everyday I Have To Cry - 1988

Arthur Alexander

Ripete 199 - You Better Move On / Anna (Go To Him) - 1990

Label Listings

Airtown

001 - Tommy Wills (Man With A Horn) - Night Train 66 Style / Honky Tonk II 66 Style
002 - Casinos - That's The Way / Too Good To Be True
003 - Trojans - Talk To Me / We Belong Together
004 - Tommy Wills - Funky Sax / Born To Lose-I Can't Stop Loving You
006 - Virgil Murray's Tomorrow's Yesterday - Summer Dreamin' / I Still Care
007 - Tommy Wills - (Sweet, Sweet Baby) Since You've Been Gone / (Funky) 4 Corners
008 - Soul Finders Inc. - Funky Soul Music / Come On Up
009 - ?
010 - Johnny Holiday - Tormented / Mercy, Mercy, Mercy On Me

Soulful Kinda Music – The Rare Soul Bible Volume Two

011 - Shooting Stars - I Watch The Clock / Donna
012 - Vondels - Hey Girl (How You've Changed) / Soldier Boy
013 - Spoon - You Can't Lose Them All / Don't Know What It Is
014 - Tommy Willis – Since I Fell For You / Lost Dreams

Alpha

1 - Donnels - Johnny Oh / Here Comes The Bride
2 - Jimmy Wallace – Forever / How Did You Destroy
3 - Johnnie Alton – Heartbreaks / Boys Have Feelings Too
4 - Donnels - It's Better / Everybody Don't Know
5 - Ronnie And Joyce - On The Stage Of Love / Yes I'm Falling In Love
6 - Jimmy Wallace - I'll Be Back / Let By Gones Be By Gones
7 - Fluffy Falana - My Little Cottage (By The Sea) / Hangover From Love
8 - Celestrals - Man's Best Friend / Wait For Me

Anna

101 - Voice Masters - Oops I'm Sorry / Hope And Pray – 1959
102 - Voice Masters – Needed / Needed (For Lovers Only) – 1959
1103 - Hill Sisters - Hit And Run Away Love / Advertising For Love – 1959
1104 - Bob Kayli - Never More / You Knows What To Do – 1959
1105 - Wreg Tracey - Take Me Back (I Was Wrong) / All I Want Is You – 1959
1106/ 1107- Paul Gayten - The Hunch / Hot Cross Buns – 1959
1108 - Johnny & Jackey - Lonely & Blue / Let's Go To A Movie Baby - 1960
1109 - Larry Darnell - With Tears In My Eyes / I'll Get Along Somehow - 1960
1110 – Falcons - This Heart Of Mine / Just For Your Love - 1960
1111 - Barrett Strong - Money (That's What I Want) / Oh! I Apologise - 1960
1112 - Paul Gayten - Beatnik Beat / Scratch Back 1960
1113 - Letha Jones - I Need You / Black Clouds - 1960
1114 - Ty Hunter & The Voice Masters - Orphan Boy / Everything About You - 1960
1115 - Herman Griffin & The Mello-Dees - Hurry Up And Marry Me / Do You Want To
See My Baby - 1960
1116 - Barrett Strong - Yes, No, Maybe So / You Knows What To Do - 1960
1117 - Ruben Fort - So Good / I Feel It -1960
1118 - Allan (Bo) Story - Blue Moon / Don't -1960
1119 - Joe Tex - All I Could Do Was Cry (Part 1) / All I Could Do Was Cry (Part 2) -
1960
1120 - Johnnie & Jackie - Hoy Hoy / No One Else But You - 1960
1121 - Bill (Winehead Willie) Murray & George (Sweet Lucy) Copeland - Big Time
Spender (Part 1) / (Part 2) - 1960
1122 - Cap-Tans - Tight Skirts And Crazy Sweaters / I'm Afraid - 1960
1123 - Ty Hunter & Voice Masters – Everytime / Free - 1960
1124 - Joe Tex & The Vibrators - I'll Never Break Your Heart (Part 1) / (Part 2) - 1960

Soulful Kinda Music – The Rare Soul Bible Volume Two

1125 - Lamont Anthony - Let's Talk It Over / Benny The Skinny Man - 1960
1126 - Wreg Tracey - All I Want For Christmas (Is Your Love) / Take Me Back (I Was Wrong) - 1960
1127 - David Ruffin - I'm In Love / One Of These Days - 1961
1128 - Joe Tex - Baby You're Right / Ain't It A Mess – 1961

Arctic

101 - Tifannys - Love Me / Happiest Girl In The World - 1964
102 - Barbara Mason - Come To Me / Girls Have Feelings Too - 1965
103 - Volcanos - Baby / Make Your Move - 1965
104 - Cindy Gibson - Step By Step / Whisper You Love Me Baby - 1965
105 - Barbara Mason - Yes I'm Ready / Keep Him - 1965
106 - Volcanos - Storm Warning / Baby - 1965
107 - Kenny Gamble And The Floaters - Down By The Seashore Part 1/ Part 2 - 1965
108 - Barbara Mason - Come To Me / Sad, Sad Girl - 1965
109 - Herb Johnson - Gloomy Day / Carfare Back - 1965
110 - Lane Relations - Everything On Earth / Cleaning Up Here - 1965
111 - Volcanos - Help Wanted / Make Your Move - 1965
112 - Barbara Mason - You Got What It Takes / If You Don't (Love Me,Tell Me So) - 1965
113 - Light Lunch & Freeloader - How Can I Win Your Love / Inst - 1965
114 - Kenny Gamble & The Romeos - Ain't It Baby Part 1 / Part 2 - 1965
115 - Volcanos - (It's Against The) Laws Of Love / Inst - 1965
116 - Barbara Mason - Don't Ever Want To Lose Your Love / Is It Me - 1965
117 - Mike & Ike - Ya Ya / Sax On The Tracks - 1966
118 - Honey & The Bees - I'm Confessin' / One Time Is Forever - 1966
119 - Brocking Choral Ensemble - How I Got Over Part 1 / Part 2 - 1966
120 - Barbara Mason - I Need Love / Bobby Is My Baby - 1966
121 - Jack & Jill - Take Me For What I Am / There You Go Again - 1966
122 - Kenny Rossi - Don't Lose This Love / Turn On Your Love Light - 1966
123 - Kenny Gamble - Don't Stop Loving Me / The Joke's On You - 1966
124 - Lane Relations - If I Had A Hammer / In The Dark - 1966
125 - Volcanos - Lady's Man / Help Wanted - 1966
126 - Barbara Mason - Poor Girl I'm In Trouble / Hello Baby - 1966
127 - Kenny Gamble - Chains Of Love / (I'll Just) Keep On Smilin' - 1967
128 - Volcanos - Make Your Move / You're Number 1 - 1967
129 - Lane Relations - The Blood Part 1 / Part 2 - 1967
130 - Temptones - Girl I Love You / Good Bye - 1967
131 - Kenny Hamber - Ain't Gonna Cry (Over One Girl) / Anything You Want - 1967
132 - Mary Deloach - Move This Thing Part 1/ Part 2 - 1967
133 - Brockington Choral Ensemble - I Feel The Spirit Moving / He's There - 1967
134 - Barbara Mason - You Can Depend On Me / Game Of Love - 1967
135 - Harold Melvin & The Blue Notes - Go Away / What Can A Man Do - 1967
136 - Temptones - Say These Words Of Love / This Could Be The Start Of Something Good - 1968
137 - Barbara Mason - Oh How It Hurts / Ain't Got Nobody - 1968
138 - Dee Dee Barnes-Do What You Wanna Do / I'm Yours And You're Mine - 1968

Soulful Kinda Music – The Rare Soul Bible Volume Two

139 - Kenny Hamber - Looking For A Love / These Arms Of Mine - 1968
140 - Barbara Mason - Dedicated To The One I Love / Half A Love - 1968
141 - Honey & The Bees - Go Now / Why Do You Hurt The One Who Loves You - 1968
142 - Barbara Mason - Half A Love / Slipping Away - 1968
143 - Teddy & The Fingerpoppers - Soul Groove Part 1 / Part 2 - 1968
144 - Della Humphrey - Don't Make The Good Girls So Bad / Your Love Is All I Need - 1968
145 - Billy Floyd - My Oh My / Time Made You Change - 1968
146 - Barbara Mason - Don't Ever Go Away / I'm So Good For You - 1968
147 - Ambassadors - I Really Love You / I Can't Believe You Love Me - 1969
148 - Barbara Mason - Take It Easy / You Never Loved Me - 1969
149 - Honey & The Bees - Love Addict / I'll Be There - 1969
150 - Ambassadors - Ain't Got The Love Of One Girl / Music Makes You Wanna Dance - 1969
151 - Winfield Parker - Brand New Strat / Shake That Thing - 1069
152 - Honey & The Bees - Sunday Kind Of Love / Baby Do That Thing - 1969
153 - Ambassadors - Storm Warning / I Dig You Baby - 1969
154 - Barbara Mason - You Better Stop It / Happy Girl - 1969
155 - Della Humphrey - Just Like Boys Do / Over The Tracks - 1969
156 - Ambassadors - A.W.O.I. / Can't Take My Eyes Off Of You - 1969
157 - Jimmy Bishop - A Blackman / Mr.Charlie - 1969
158 - Honey & The Bees - Baby,Do That Thing / Sunday Kind Of Love - 1969
159 - Della Humphrey - Will You Love Me Tomorrow / Let's Wait Until Dark - 1969
160 - Royal Five - Ain't No Big Thing (But It's Growing) / Peace Of Mind - 1969
201/202 - Derek Martin - Don't Leave Me / Stoned Out Of My Mind – 1969

Arock

1000 - The Diplomats - Unchained Melody / Cards On The Table - 1963
1001 - Gene Burks - Monkey Man / Can't Stand Your Fooling Around - 1963
1002 - Gene Walker & The Combo - Sophisticated Monkey / Empire City - 1964
1003 - Gary & Gary - I'm Leavin' (For Parts Unknown) / Deuces Wild - 1964
1004 - The Diplomats - Here's A Heart / I Am A Witness - 1964
1005 - The Diplomats - Here's A Heart / He's Got You Now - 1964
1006 - The Mark Fredericks Orchestra - (A Theme For A) Lost Love / Evelyn - 1964
1007 - Gene Burks - Shirley Jean / Take My Hand - 1964
1008 - The Diplomats Accom. By Chet 'Poison Ivey' Band - Help Me / Hey Mr. Taxi Driver - 1964
1009 - The D. C. Playboys - You Were All I Needed / Too Much - 1964
1010 - The Larks - Another Sleepless Night / For The Love Of Money - 1964
1011 - Mark Fredericks His Piano & Orch.- A Boy Ten Feet Tall / Tina's Theme - 1964
1012 - Tutti Hill - He's A Lover / When The Going Gets Rough - 1964
1013 - Joe Bragg - It's A Lovely Thing / Pretty Please – 1964

Atac

Soulful Kinda Music – The Rare Soul Bible Volume Two

101 – Gino Washington - Doing The Popcorn / What Can A Man Do
102 – Gino Washington - I'll Be Around (When You Want Me) / Like My Baby
127 – Gino Washington - Lady Liberty Part 1 / Part 2
1943 – Gino Washington - Sassa Frassa Sue Part 1 / Sassa Frassa Sue
2743 – Gino Washington - It's Winter (But I Have Spring Fever) / Foxy Walk
2828 – Gino Washington & The Davis Sisters - I'm So In Love / Flying High
2829 – Gino Washington - You Got Me In A Whirlpool Part 1 / Part 2
2830 – Gino Washington - (We're In A) Rat Race / Oh Not Me
2878 – Gino Washington - Oh Not Me / Hey I'm A Love Bandit
2930 – Gino Washington - Could It Be I'm Falling / I'm Flying High
2930 – Sir George Washington / Sir George Gino Washington & The Ides Of Time
Band - Could It Be I'm Falling / I'm Flying High
3031 – Gino Washington - (Oh) I'll Never Leave You / (Oh) I'll Never Leave You
7823 – Gino Washington with The Altrasonics and The Versatiles - I'll Be Around
(When You Want Me) / Like My Baby
7824 – Gino Washington – It's Winter (But I Have Spring Fever) / Foxy Walk
7825 – Gino Washington - Doing The Popcorn / What Can A Man Do
7826 – Gino Washington - Girl Here I Am / Do You Have That Soul
7829 - The Soul Agents - Foxy Lady / Instrumental
62743 – Gino The Gamanisist - Heaven Must Have Known / Lovers Interlude
62743 – Gino Washington & The G W Band - Hey I'm A Love Bandit / We Gonna
Make It

Audio Arts

700 - Remarkables - Is The Feeling Still There / Easily Mislead
701 - Incredibles - I Can't Get Over Losing Your Love / Crying Heart
60000 - Remarkables - You Wouldn't Have Anything / I Can't Give it Up
60001 - Incredibles - I'll Make It Easy / Crying Heart
60002 - William & Michael - Our Time Is Running Out / How Can You Do It Baby
60003 - Midnight Mail - I Can't Get It / I Can't Quit
60004 - Cassietta George - Silent Night / (The) Greatest Gift
60005 - ?
60006 - Incredibles There's Nothing Else To Say / Another Dirty Deal
60007 - Incredibles - Heart And Soul / I Found Another Love
60008 - Mongo & McCall - Mongo And McCall / So Help Me, Baby
60009 - Incredibles - Without A Word / Standing Here Crying
60010 - Incredibles - For Sentimental Reasons / I Can't Get Over Losing Your Love
60011 - Carl Gilbert - Crying Heart / Fool Fool Fool
60012 - Cassietta George - Every Day Brings About A Change / Somebody Bigger
Than You And I
60013 - Anita May & Interstate 5 - When It's Dark / Tarnished Angel
60014 - Incredibles - Fool, Fool, Fool / Lost Without You - 1968
60015 - King George & Fabulous Souls - Baby I've Got It / Inst
60016 - Incredibles - Miss Treatment / All Of A Sudden
60017 - Incredibles - Standing Here Crying / All Of A Sudden
60018 - Incredibles - Fool, Fool, Fool / Stop The Raindrops
60019 - King George &The Fabulous Souls- I Need You / Instrumental

Soulful Kinda Music – The Rare Soul Bible Volume Two

60019 - Norfleet - Soul Heaven / Instrumental
60020 - Ron Kenoly - Moving On / The Glory Of Your Love
60021 - Cassietta George - Everything Is Beautiful / Take Him With You
60022 - Cassietta George- Let's Get Together / The Trembler
60023 - Cassietta George-The Trembler / Reach Out And Touch
60024 - Al Waples & Incredibles - Moving On / Love Now
60025 - Jerry Kane - Not Enough Love / What Does A Bird Do
60026 - Cassietta George - Somebody's Watching / He Never Left Me Alone
60027 - Cassietta George - Didn't We / Everything Is Beautiful
60028 - Incredibles - I Can't Get Over Losing Your Love / Audio Arts Strings - There's Nothing Else To Say
60029 - Cassietta George - His Eye On The Sparrow / One More Baby Child Born
60030 - ?
60031 - Incredibles - Standing Here Crying / Crying Heart

66778 - Cassietta George - Don't Give Up / In The Garden

Autumn

1 – Bobby Freeman – Come To Me / Let's Surf Again – 1963
2 – Bobby Freeman – C'mon And Swim Part 1 / Part 2 – 1963
3 – Sly Stuart – I Just Learned How To Swim / Scat Swim – 1963
4 – The Upsetters – Autumn's Here / Draggin' The Main – 1963
5 – Bobby Freeman – S-W-I-M / That Little Old Heartbreaker – 1964
6 – Rico & The Ravens – In My Heart / Don't You Know – 1964
7 – The Spearmints – Jo Ann / Little One – 1964
8 – Beau Brummels – Laugh Laugh / Still In Love With You Baby – 1964
9 – Bobby Freeman – Friends / I'll Never Fall In Love Again – 1964
10 – Beau Brummels – Just A Little / They'll Make You Cry – 1964
11 – The Mojo Men – Mama's Little Baby / Off The Hook – 1964
12 – The Dixies – Geisha Girl / He's Got You – 1964
13 – The Carousels – Beneath The Willow / Sail Away – 1964
14 – Sly – Buttermilk Part 1 / Part 2 – 1964
15 – The Vejtables – Anything / I Still Love You – 1964
16 – Beau Brummels – You Tell Me Why / I Want You – 1964
17 – The Chosen Few – I Think It's Time / Nobody But Me – 1964
18 – The Other Tikis – If I'd Been Dreaming / Pay Attention To Me – 1964
19 – The Mojo Men – Dance With Me / Loneliest Boy In Town – 1964
20 – Beau Brummels – Don't Talk To Strangers / In Good Time – 1964
21 – The Casualiers – Just For You / This Is A Mean World – 1964
22 – Charity Shayme – Ain't It Baby / Then You Try – 1964
23 – The Vejtables – The Last Thing On My Mind / Mansion Of Tears – 1964
24 – Beau Brummels – Good Time Music / Sad Little Girl – 1964
25 – Bobby Freeman – Cross My Heart / The Duck – 1964
26 – Sly – Temptation Walk Part 1 / Part 2 – 1965
27 – The Mojo Men – She's My Baby / Fire In My Heart – 1965
28 – The Other Tikis – Bye Bye Bye / Lost My Love Today – 1965

Soulful Kinda Music – The Rare Soul Bible Volume Two

Vickie Baines

Parkway 957 - Losing You / Got To Run - 1965
Parkway 966 - Country Girl / Are You Kidding - 1966
Loma 2078 - We Can Find True Love / Sweeter Than Sweet Things - 1967

The Baltimore and Ohio Marching Band

Jubilee 5592 - Lapland / Condition Red - 1967
Jubilee 5614 - The Baltimore And Ohio Marching Band Song / The Wanderer - 1968
Jubilee 5644 - Sgt. Crunch / Typsy Turvy - 1968
Jubilee 5672 - Little Arrows / Sergeant Crunch - 1969

Jackey Beavers
From Cartersville to Detroit, and back !

Jackey Beavers was born and raised in Cartersville, Georgia, and it was from here that he joined the US Airforce straight from High School. During his stint in the Service he was stationed at Fort Custer in Battle Creek, and it just happened that one of the regular features of the camp club was a talent competition. Whilst Jackey regularly won the competition, the ones he didn't win were won by a gentleman called Johnny Bristol. Recognising an opportunity the two soon joined forces and began performing as a duo, named Johnny & Jackie. Regular appearances at the El Grotto Lounge in Battle Creek (Where the house band was led by Junior Walker) led to them signing for Anna Records, and being managed by Gwen Gordy.

Two releases followed for the label, and although neither were hits, they sold enough copies for Gwen Gordy to retain them as artists when Anna Records closed and Anna started Tri-Phi Records with Harvey Fuqua. Again, several releases followed, and certainly the duo had no problem gaining live work. It was their second release on Tri-Phi that was to have the most impact though, even though it was the duo's biggest hit, but not at the time it was recorded by Johnny & Jackey !

'Someday, We'll Be Together' was written by Johnny Bristol, Jackey Beavers, and Harvey Fuqua, and became a million seller when it was released as the last single Diana Ross recorded with The Supremes.

One further release followed and then the Tri-Phi label closed it's doors with most of the artists transferring to Berry Gordy's Motown label, Johnny Bristol included. Jackey Beavers though decided that he would go back to work for Roquel Davis (Joint owner of Anna Records with Gwen Gordy) who was by this time the Artist and Repertoire Director at Chicago's Checker Records.

Two releases followed in 1965, the first 'Jack-a-Rue' being a moderate hit. Sadly the second failed to make the charts and Checker Records didn't continue with any

Soulful Kinda Music – The Rare Soul Bible Volume Two

further recordings.

Label hopping through the next few years Jackey Beavers achieved very little commercial success as an artist. However, he recorded some wonderful songs that he wrote himself, particularly his solo release for Revilot 'Love That Never Grows Old' which is now recognized as classic Detroit 'Northern Soul'. In total, Jackey Beavers registered in excess of a hundred songs with BMI, and they were recorded by a huge number of different artists.

Moving on, Jackey found himself at Nashville's Sound Stage 7 Records, as not just a recording artist, but also a producer. He also worked at the famed WLAC Radio station.

There was also a period where Jackey joined and toured with The Continental Showstoppers, although no recordings were made during this time.

Eventually though, a lack of commercial success as an artist meant that Jackey moved back to Cartersville.

Originally buying and running a nightclub called the Brothers Three, he gave it away to his brother because he found he actually hated working in this side of the music industry.

Returning to College, Jackey Beavers earned his degree and became an ordained Minister, originally at the New Hope Baptist Church and later at the Glory Harvester Church. It was whilst at the Glory Harvester Church that his interest in music resurfaced and he recorded several Gospel albums on the Glory label in the 1980's.

Throughout this period Jackey also maintained a healthy interest in local politics, and in particular the welfare of prisoners, and worked as Executive Assistant to Joe Frank Harris, the Governor of Georgia, for eight years, Executive Assistant to Bobby Whitworth, the Commissioner of Georgia's Department of Corrections, for three years, and aide to Tom Murphy, Speaker of the Georgia House of Representatives, for seven years.

Jackey Beavers also wrote a column for the Cartersville Daily Tribune News for many years. Sadly, as reported by his own paper, he passed
away in October, 1988.

Discography

Johnny & Jackey (Johnny Bristol and Jackey Beavers)

Anna 1108 - Let's Go To A Movie Baby / Lonely And Blue - 1960
Anna 1120 - Hoy Hoy* / No One Else But You - 1960 *also recorded in 1962 by The Davenport Sisters on Tri-Phi 1008.
Tri-Phi 1002 - Carry Your Own Load* / So Disappointing - 1961 *also recorded in 1970 by Jr. Walker & The All-Stars on Soul 35081.
Tri-Phi 1005 - Someday We'll Be Together* / She Don't Play - 1961 *also recorded in 1969 by Diana Ross & The Supremes on Motown 1156. The male vocal on their

Soulful Kinda Music – The Rare Soul Bible Volume Two

version was supplied by Johnny Bristol who was also the session's producer at a one day session at Hitsville on 13-June-1969.
Tri-Phi 1016 - Do You See My Love (For You Growing)* / Carry Your Own Load - 1962 *also recorded in 1970 by Jr. Walker & The All-Stars on Soul 35081.
Tri-Phi 1019 - Baby Don'tcha Worry* / Stop What You're Saying - 1963 *also recorded in 1966 by Tammi Terrell on Motown 1095.

Jackey Beavers (born Robert L. Beavers 19-June-1937 --- died 28-October-2008 --- cause: following an extended illness)

Checker 1102 - Silly Boy / Jack-A-Rue - 1965
Checker 1119 - Sling Shot / I Want Somebody – 1965
Nation 21765 - Come Back My Love / Understatement Of The Year - 1965

Jackie Beavers

Dade 2041 - Trying To Get You Back Girl (Part 1) / Trying To Get You Back Girl (Part 2) - 1967

Jackey Beavers

Revilot 208 - A Love That Never Grows Old / I Need My Baby - 1967
Grand Land 19,000 - Bring Me All Your Heartaches / Don't Wanna Lose You - 1968

The Soul Continentals (members Jackie Beavers, ...)

Jaber 7110 - Movin' And A Groovin' / ? - 1968

Jackey Beavers

Jaber 7111 - Lover Come Back* / Gee You're A Pretty Thing - 1968 (orange label) *also recorded in 19 by The Camaros on Dar Cha 1151.
Jaber 7111 - Lover Come Back / I Hate To See A Man Cry - 1968 (Blue Label)

The Jackey Beavers Show (members Jackie Beavers, ...)

Jaber 7112 - We're Not Too Young To Fall In Love / ? - 1968 (also released on this number was "Let's Do It Today / Peace" by The "Us")
Jaber 7114 - Hold On / Hey Girl (I Can't Stand To See You Cry) – 1968

The Jackie Beavers Show (members Jackie Beavers, ...)

Mainstream 713 - When Something Is Wrong With My Baby / We're Not Too Young To Fall In Love - 1969

Jackey Beavers

Sound Stage 7 2649 - Hey Girl (I Can't Stand To See You Go) / Hold On - 1969

Soulful Kinda Music – The Rare Soul Bible Volume Two

3355555555

Sound Stage 7 2649 - Hey Girl (I Can't Stand To See You Go) / Singing A Funky Song - 1969
Sound Stage 7 2662 - You Can Have Her / There's A Heartbreak Somewhere - 1970
Sound Stage 7 2662 - You Can Have Her Part 1 / You Can Have Her Part 2 - 1970
Sound Stage 71502 - Someday We'll Be Together / Lover Come Back – 1971
Sound Stage 7 1506 - Hey Girl (I Can't Stand To See You Go) / Singing A Funky Song – 1972

Jackey Beavers & The Fame Gang (members Jackey Beavers, ...)

Sound Plus 2104 - Someone (Bigger Than You Or Me)* / La La La (Can You Feel It) - 1972 *also recorded in 1966 by Sam Baker on Sound Stage 7   2568.

Jackey Beavers

Seventy 7 77-120 - Where Did I Go Wrong / Gee Baby, You're A Pretty Thing - 1973
Seventy 7 77-133 - I Never Found A Girl (To Love Me ...) / Place In The Sun - 1973
Seventy 7 77-133 - Someone (Bigger Than You Or Me) / Place In The Sun - 1972
Seventy 7 2146 - I Want You To Hold On / Hey Girl – 1974
Seventy 7 901 - Ooh, I Love You / That's The Way I Want Our Love - 1974
Seventy 7 904 - Somebody Help The Beggarman / Mr. Bumpman (Give Me A Hand) (Part 2) – 1974

Archie Bell & The Drells

Little Pop & The Fireballs (members Archie Bell, ...)

Formed in the early 1960's there are no known recordings by the group.

Archie Bell & The Drells (Members Archie Bell (born on 1-September-1944 in Henderson, Texas), James Wise, Huey 'Billy' Butler and Joe Cross)

(At various times, including when Archie Bell had been drafted into the Services, the following people became members of the group for Lee Bell, Willie Pernell, L.C. Watts, Cornelius Fuller, Lucious Larkins, and Charles Gibbs)

East West 55102 - She's My Woman, She's My Girl / Yankee Dance - 1966
Ovide 222 - She's My Woman, She's My Girl / Yankee Dance - 1967
Ovide 226 - A Soldiers Prayer / One In One - 1967
Ovide 228 - Tighten Up* / Dog Eat Dog - 1967 *originally an instrumental performed by The T. S. U. Toronados.
Atlantic 2478 - Tighten Up / Dog Eat Dog - 1968 (January)
Atlantic 2478 - Tighten Up (Part 1)* / Tighten Up (Part 2) - 1968 (February) *Track Recorded October-1967.
Atlantic 2534 - I Can't Stop Dancing / You're Such A Beautiful Child - 1968
Atlantic 2559 - Do The Choo Choo / Love's Gonna Rain On You - 1968
Chess 2048 - She's My Woman, She's My Girl / Yankee Dance - 1968

Soulful Kinda Music – The Rare Soul Bible Volume Two

Atlantic 2583 - (There's Gonna Be A) Showdown* / Go For What You Know - 1968 *Recorded 1-November-1968.
Atlantic 2612 - Just A Little Closer / I Love My Baby - 1969
Atlantic 2644 - Girl You're Too Young / Do The Hand Jive - 1968
Atlantic 2663 - My Balloon's Going Up / Giving Up Dancing - 1969
Atlantic 2693 - Here I Go Again* / A World Without Music - 1969 *Recorded 16-May-1969 In Philadelphia, Pa.
Atlantic 2721 - Don't Let The Music Slip Away / Houston, Texas - 1970
Atlantic 2744 - I Wish / Get It From The Bottom - 1970
Atlantic 2768 - Wrap It Up / Deal With Him - 1970
Atlantic 2793 - Love At First Sight / I Just Want To Fall In Love - 1970
Atlantic 2829 - Archie's In Love / Let The World Know - 1971
Atlantic 2855 - I Can't Face You Baby / Green Power - 1971
Glades 1707 - Dancing To Your Music / Count The Ways - 1973
Glades 1711 - You Never Know What's On A Woman's Mind / Ain't Nothing For A Man In Love - 1973
Glades 1718 - Girls Grow Faster Than Boys / Love's Gonna Rain On You - 1974
T. S. O. P. 4767 - I Could Dance All Night / King Of The Castle - 1975
T. S. O. P. 4774 - The Soul City Walk / The King Of The Castle - 1975
T. S. O. P. 4775 - Let's Groove (Part 1) / Let's Groove (Part 2) - 1976
Portrait 7254 - Don't Let Go / Where Will You Go When The Party's Over - 1976
Philadelphia International 3605 - Right Here Is Where I Want To Be / Nothing Comes Easy - 1976
Philadelphia International 3615 - Everybody Have A Good Time / I Bet I Can Do That Dance - 1977
Philadelphia International 3632 - There's No Other Like You / Glad You Could Make It - 1977

The Philadelphia International All Stars (Lou Rawls, Billy Paul, Teddy Pendergrass, The O'Jays, Archie Bell and Dee Dee Sharpe) / MFSB

Philadelphia International 3636 - Let's Clean Up The Ghetto / Let's Clean Up The Ghetto* - 1977 *flip by MFSB.

Archie Bell & The Drells

Philadelphia International 3637 - I've Been Missing You / It's Hard Not To Like You - 1977
Philadelphia International 3651 - Old People / On The Radio - 1978
Philadelphia International 3710 - Strategy / We Got 'Em Dancing - 1979
Philadelphia International 3731 - How Can I / Sho Me How To Dance - 1979

Archie Bell

Becket 4 - Anytime Is Right / Without You - 1981
Becket Records 501 - Anytime Is Right / ? - 1981 (12" Release)
Columbia/WMOT 03057 - Touchin' You (Part 1) / Touchin' You (Part 2) - 1982

Archie Bell & The Drells

Soulful Kinda Music – The Rare Soul Bible Volume Two

Playhouse - 1984 (12" Release)
Achievement 10008 - Look Back Over Your Shoulder / Instrumental - 1988
Prt Mare16 - Look Back Over Your Shoulder / ? - 1988 (12" Release)
? - Glad You Could Make It / There's No Other Like You - ? (12" Release)
Collectables Col 046287 - Let's Groove (Part 1 & 2) / The Soul City Walk - ?

Cody Black – A Journeyman Of Detroit Soul.

Cody Black was born in Cincinnati in March, 1939, and grew up in the city not far from Sid Nathan's King records. In fact by the time he was twelve years old his parents had moved to a house on Brewster, which was only two blocks away from the recording studio. Given his interest in music it was only natural that the inquisitive twelve year old would soon become a regular visitor to the King Records offices and recording studios.

He started singing with local Vocal group 'The Echoes' in 1955, but by 1956 had left them to join The Victorials with whom he recorded the Johnny Pate produced 'I Get The Feeling / Prettiest Girl In The World' single for Imperial records. The record failed to make any impact on the charts and in 1956 Cody was drafted for a three year tour in the US Air Force. By the time he returned to Cincinnati in 1959 most of the other group members had married and lost interest in the music scene. The group reformed for a short while, and performed locally, but eventually, by 1960 they broke up completely.

Whilst performing with The Victorials, and later as a single artist, Cody had bumped into Mickey Stevenson, and Clarence Paul, from Motown on several occasions. They had both encouraged him to relocate to Detroit, but in 1961 he was keen to remain in Cincinnati because he had managed to get a record deal with local label Pamela Records.

One release ensued: 'Come To Me (Girl) / Stranger Than A Fairy Tale', but with a spectacular lack of promotion, again sank without trace. A further deal with Universe Records produced another single: 'The Camel Walk / Joreen (She's Something Else)', in 1962. Credited to Cody Black & The Celestrials on the 'Camel Walk' side and Cody Black & His Girls on the 'Joreen' side.

It is likely, because of the typeface, and location of the recording being in Cincinnati, that this was a custom press in Cincinnati, done by King Records in 1962.

As this record had failed to make any noise in the charts Cody decided to relocate to Detroit. Allegedly, the receptionist at Motown refused to let Cody speak to Mickey Stevenson, so he walked out (I wonder if it was Martha Reeves ?), and managed to get work as a house painter.

He did of course eventually become involved in the burgeoning music scene in Detroit, and consequently met Mike Hanks, owner of the D-Town label, at The Phelps Lounge. A friend recommended Cody as a singer to Mike Hanks, who insisted that he

Soulful Kinda Music – The Rare Soul Bible Volume Two

get up on stage and sing for him. Cody obliged, singing a cover of Ray Charles 'Drown In My Own Tears'.

Mike Hanks obviously liked what he heard, but surprisingly didn't sign Cody as an artist, he offered him a job as an A & R Executive with the D-Town label. It took another year, during which Cody acted as a songwriter for the label as well as his A & R duites, before he was offered the chance to record for the label.

The resulting single, released in 1964, 'Move On / These Chains Of Love' on D-Town 1032 was significant only because it contained the original release of the song later covered by J J Barnes, 'These Chains Of Love'. The next single to be released also failed to create any chart action for Cody when it was released, but it certainly created a stir on the Northern Soul scene some twenty years later: D Town 1057 - Mr. Blue / You Must Be In Love – 1965.

Shortly after the release of this single one of Cody's friends approached him about a track that he had recorded on another singer. Grant Burton was the friend, and the track was 'I'm Slowly Molding'. Unhappy with the vocal, Grant and Cody went down to Cincinnati and dubbed Cody over the backing. Cody then approached his old friend Sid Nathan at King records for a one off release on King Records.

One more release came on D-Town, but despite the input of some money into the label by Roosevelt Greer, who had been singing and recording long before he became a professional American Football player, very little happened with the single.

Cody was becoming disenchanted with the exposure that the label was able to get him. He was still happy working at D-Town with Mike Hanks, Rudy Robinson, and Grant Burton, but wanted his own career to start moving as a singer, so he left the label and had a one off release for Wheelsville Records: Wheelsville 1071 - I Will Give You Love / I Am Particular.

Another two one-off releases on different labels quickly followed: Gig 201 - It's Our Time To Fall In Love / (Keep Your Baby Home Or) You'll Be Sorry, in 1966, and Groove City 960 - Because You First Loved Me / The Night A Star Was Born in early 1967.

The Groove City release was a Rudy Robinson, Grant Burton, and Cody Black composition which should really have been a hit, but like all his previous releases didn't exactly set the charts alight.

A move to yet another label at the beginning of 1967 saw Cody recording for the Ram-Brock label, and it looked like he was finally going to have a hit with his first release for them. 'Going Going Gone' on Ram-Brock 2002 started to sell well in the Detroit area, and although the hit never really materialised, there was enough success to ensure that Ram-Brock released two further singles from him. In addition the record was enough of a local hot to ensure that Cody was able to work live for several years to come in the Detroit area.

The following two singles failed to capitalise on the success of 'Going Going Gone' though, but Cody was, because of his raised profile, becoming a regular opening act for some of the star names who performed in Detroit, Gladys Knight and the Pips, and Aretha Franklin to name but two.

As a result of this Cody was signed by Ted White, Aretha's husband, to a brand new

Soulful Kinda Music – The Rare Soul Bible Volume Two

label that he had just set up.

In addition to having connections at a high level in the music industry, through his marriage to Aretha Franklin, Ted White also had connections at Capitol Records, who signed a distribution deal with Ston-Roc Records. Two releases by Cody Black were issued as a result of this deal, and both were on Capitol labels, using the Capitol numbering system, that also bore the logo of Ston-Roc Records.

One further release in 1971, Ston-Roc 3378 – 'I Still Love You / Ice Cream Song' came after capitol declined to renew the distribution deal (This single is often seen listed as a 1969 release, however the RCA Custom matrix numbers place it as a 1971 release).

The live work was still healthy, and that's how Cody earned his livelihood for the next six years, touring and performing in clubs and as the opening act for larger tours. He also continued to write and record his own songs, but failed to get a contract to release them.

In 1977, fed up with trying to get others to release his recordings Cody decided to set up his own label, Renaissance Records. In a way, it was the perfect solution, Cody wrote, produced, arranged, and sang on all four sides of the two releases. Unfortunately, without the backing of one of the majors, the records lacked the promotional push to become hits, and they were the last ever vinyl releases by him.

Not deterred by the lack of success Cody still continued to record, and in 2000 was rewarded with the release of his first CD on Mustang Sally Records (The label was owned by Detroit stalwart Mack Rice). A mixture of Blues and Soul music, the CD is still available on Amazon.

In 2004 Cody made his first visit to the UK, and performed an outstanding show at the Prestatyn Northern Soul Weekender which featured many of his Sixties Detroit recordings.

The Bobbettes

The Harlem Queens (members Emma Pought (born 28-April-1942 in New York City), Jannie Pought (born 11-January-1944 in New York City ~ died 1980 in New Jersey), Reather Dixon (born 1-May-1945 in New York City), Helen Gathers (born 18-March-1943 in New York City), Laura Webb (born 1943 ~ died 8-January-2001,cause: complications from colon cancer), ?, ? and ?) 1955 line-up.

The Bobbettes (members Emma Pought, Jannie Pought, Reather Dixon, Helen Gathers and Laura Webb)

Atlantic 1144 - Mr. Lee / Look At The Stars – 1957
Atlantic 1159 - Speedy / Come-A, Come-A – 1957
Atlantic 1181 - Zoomy / Rock And Ree-Ah-Zole – 1958
Atlantic 1194 - The Dream / Um Bow Wow – 1958
Atlantic 2027 - Don't Say Goodnight / You Are My Sweetheart – 1959

Soulful Kinda Music – The Rare Soul Bible Volume Two

Triple-X 104 - I Shot Mr. Lee / Billy – 1960
Atlantic 2069 - I Shot Mr. Lee / Untrue Love – 1960
Triple-X 106 - Have Mercy Baby* / Dance With Me Georgie - 1960 *also recorded in 1953 by The Dominoes On Federal 12068.
Galliant 1006 - Oh My Papa / I Cried - 1960

The Bobbettes (members Emma Pought, Jannie Pought, Reather Dixon and Laura Webb)

End 1093 - Teach Me Tonight / Mister Johnny Q – 1961
End 1095 - I Don't Like That (Part 1) / I Don't Like That (Part 2) - 1961 (some copies issued with picture sleeve)
Gone 5112 - I Don't Like That / Mr. Johnny Q - 1961
King 5490 - Oh My Papa / Dance With Me Georgie - 1961
King 5551 - Looking For A Lover / Are You Satisfied (With Your Love) – 1961
King 5623 - My Dearest / I'm Stepping Out Tonight – 1962
Jubilee 5427 - Over There / Loneliness – 1962
Jubilee 5442 - The Broken Heart / Mama Papa - 1962

Johnny Thunder

Diamond 129 - Loop De Loop* / Don't Be Ashamed - 1962 *although uncredited the backing vocals were by The Bobbettes.

The Bobbettes (members Emma Pought, Jannie Pought, Reather Dixon and Laura Webb)

Diamond 133 - Teddy* / Row, Row, Row - 1962 *said to be tribute to groups producer Teddy Vann.
Diamond 142 - Close Your Eyes / Somebody Bad Stole De Wedding Bell – 1963
Diamond 156 - My Mama Said / Sandman – 1964
Diamond 166 - In Paradise / I'm Climbing A Mountain – 1964
Diamond 181 - You Ain't Seen Nothin' Yet / I'm Climbing A Mountain – 1965
Diamond 189 - Teddy / Love Is Blind – 1965
RCA 47-8832 - Having Fun / I've Gotta Face The World – 1966
RCA 47-8983 - It's All Over / Happy Go Lucky Me - 1966

The Soul Angels (members Mattie LaVette, Reather Dixon and Emma Pought)

Josie 1002 - It's All In Your Mind / The Ladies Choice (Instrumental) - 1969

The Bobbettes (members Emma Pought, Jannie Pought, Reather Dixon and Laura Webb)

Mayhew 712297/98 - All In Your Mind / That's A Bad Thing To Know - 1971 (Some Copies Issued With Picture Sleeve)
Mayhew 37 - Tighten Up Your Own Home / Looking For A New Love – 1972
Mayhew 237 - Tighten Up Your Own Home / Let Your Love Flow – 1972
Mayhew 861/2 - It Won't Work Out / Good Man – 1974
Mayhew 1060 - Happy Go Lucky Me / ? - ?

Soulful Kinda Music – The Rare Soul Bible Volume Two

The Sophisticated Ladies (members Emma Pought, Jannie Pought, Reather Dixon and Laura Webb)

Bareback 532 - Check It Out (Part 1) / Good Man – 1977
Mayhew/Bareback Mbb-12-532 - Check It Out (Part 1) (5:04) / Check It Out (Part 2) - 1977 (12" Release - 33 1/3rpm)
Bareback 353 - Check It Out (Part 1) / Good Man - 1977

The Bobbettes (members Reather Dixon, Emma Pought and Laura Webb) 1981 line up.

Atlantic Dmd-283 - Love Rhythm (Long Version) (8:12) / Love Rhythm (Short Version) (3:40) - 1981 (12" Release Promo Issue Only)
Radio 4816 - Love Rhythm / You Aint Really Down - 1981 (12" Release)
Qit Bc-652 - Love Rhythm (6:33) / Love Theme - 1981 (12" release)

The Bobbettes / The Vibrations

Atlantic Oldies Series 13044 - Mr. Lee / My Girl Sloopy - ? (back to back hits)

The Bobbettes (members Reather Dixon, Emma Pought, Debra Thompson and Pamela Tate) current line up.

Big Maybelle

The Sweethearts Of Rhythm (members Mabel Louise Smith, Tiny Davis, Jackie Glenn and Mattie Watson) late 1930's female group.

Christine Chatman's Orchestra (members Christine Chatman, Mabel Louise Smith, ...)

Decca 8660 - Hurry, Hurry / ? - 1944

The Tiny Bradshaw Band (members Tiny Bradshaw, Mabel Louise Smith, ...) Big Maybelle made three records on the King label with this band - unsure if she is credited on label.

King ? - 1948
King ? - 1948 ~ 1949
King ? - 1949

Big Maybelle (born Mabel Louise Smith in Jackson, Tennessee on 1-May-1924....Died 23-January-1972 cause: died while in a diabetic coma in a Cleveland, Ohio hospital)

Okeh 6931 - Gabbin' Blues / Rain Down Rain - 1952
Okeh 6955 - Way Back Home / Just Want Your Love - 1953
Okeh 6988 - Send For Me / Jinny Mule - 1953

Soulful Kinda Music – The Rare Soul Bible Volume Two

Okeh 7009 - My Country Man / Maybelle's Blues - 1954 (With The Leroy Kirkland Orchestra)
Okeh 7026 - You'll Never Know / I've Got A Feelin' - 1954
Okeh 7042 - My Big Mistake / I'm Gettin' 'Long Alright - 1954
Okeh 7053 - Don't Leave Poor Me / Ain't No Use - 1955
Okeh 7060 - Whole Lotta Shakin' Goin' On / One Monkey Don't Stop No Show - 1955
Okeh 7066 - Such A Cutie / The Other Night - 1956
Savoy 1195 - Candy / That's A Pretty Good Love - 1956 (with The Kelly Owens Orchestra)
Savoy 1500 - Mean To Me / Tell Me Who - 1956
Okeh 7069 - Gabbin' Blues / New Kind Of Mambo - 1956
Savoy 1512 - I Don't Want To Cry / All Of Me - 1957
Savoy 1519 - Rock House / Jim - 1957
Savoy 1527 - So Long / Ring Dang Dilly - 1957

Big Maybelle Smith

Savoy 1536 - Blues, Early, Early (Part 1) / Blues, Early, Early (Part 2) - 1958

Big Maybelle

Savoy 1541 - White Christmas / Silent Night - 1958
Savoy 1558 - Baby, Won't You Please Come Home / Say It Isn't So - 1959
Savoy 1572 - A Good Man Is Hard To Find / Pitiful - 1959
Savoy 1576 - I Understand / Some Of These Days - 1959
Savoy 1583 - I Got It Bad And That Ain't Good / Until The Real Thing Comes Along - 1960
Savoy 1583 - Ramblin' Blues / Until The Real Thing Comes Along - 1960
Savoy 1595 - I Ain't Got Nobody / Going Home Baby - 1961
Brunswick 55234 - Candy / Cry - 1963
Brunswick 55242 - Cold Cold Heart / Why Was I Born - 1963
Brunswick 55256 - Everybody's Got A Home But Me / How Deep Is The Ocean - 1963
Rojac 1003 - Careless Love / My Mother's Eyes - 1964
Scepter 1288 - I Don't Want To Cry / Yesterday's Kisses -1965
Port 3002 - No Better For You / Let Me Go - 1965
Chess 1967 - It's A Man's, Man's, Man's World / Big Maybelle Sings The Blues - 1966
Rojac 1969 - It's Been Raining / Don't Pass Me By - 1966
Rojac 112 - 96 Tears / That's Life - 1967
Rojac 115 - Turn The World Around The Other Way / I Can't Wait Any Longer - 1967
Rojac 116 - Mama (He Treats Your Daughter Mean) / Keep That Man - 1967
Rojac 118 - Quittin' Time / I Can't Wait Any Longer - 1968
Brunswick 55385 - Nobody Knows The Trouble I've Seen / Do Lord - 1968
Rojac 121 - Heaven Will Welcome You, Dr. King / Eleanor Rigby - 1968
Rojac 124 - Old Love Never Dies / How It Lies - 1968
Paramount 0237 - See See Rider / Blame It On Your Love - 1973

Big Maybelle / Ray Bryant

Soulful Kinda Music – The Rare Soul Bible Volume Two

Collectables Col 046247 - Gabbin' Blues / Madison Time (Part 1)* - ? *Flip By Ray Bryant.

Betty Harris as a teenager went to work for Big Maybelle as a maid. Big Maybelle encouraged Betty Harris' talent, and in 1960 she recorded her first single, "Taking Care of Business / Yesterday's Kisses" on Douglas 104.

Marjorie Black

Sue 132 - One More Hurt / You Still Love Her - 1965

Harold Burrage

Decca 48175 - I Need You, Baby / Hi Ya - 1950
Aladdin 3194 - Sweet Brown Gal / Way Down Boogie - 1953

As Harold Barrage

States 144 - Feel So Fine / You're Gonna Cry - 1955

Harold Burrage

Cobra 5004 - One More Dance / You Eat Too Much - 1956
Cobra 5012 - Messed Up / Don't Care Who Knows - 1956
Cobra 5018 - Stop For The Red Light / Satisfied - 1956
Cobra 5022 - She Knocks Me Out / A Heart Filled With Pain - 1956
Cobra 5026 - I Cry For You / Betty Jean - 1958
Vee Jay 318 - What You Don't Know / Crying For My Baby - 1959
Vee Jay 356 - Great Day In The Morning / You K.O'ed Me - 1960
Foxy 009 - I Was Wrong / You Ought To Love Me - 1962
Paso 102 - Fool / Please Love Me - 1961
M-Pac 7201 - Master Key / Faith And Understanding - 1963
M-Pac 7204 - Long Ways Together / I'll Take One - 1963
Vivid 101 - She Knocks Me Out / Heart - 1964
Vivid 102 - I Cry For You / Betty Jean - 1964
M-Pac 7210 - That's A Friend / Everybodys Dancing - 1964
M-Pac 7211 -Baby, I'm Alright / Fifty Fifty - 1964
M-Pac 7222 - Your Friend / Take Me Now - 1965
M-Pac 7223 - You Made Me So Very Happy / Things Ain't What They Used To Be (Since You've Gone) - 1965
M-Pac 7225 - Got To Find A Way / How You Fix Your Mouth - 1965
M-Pac 7229 - More Power To You / A Long Way Together - 1965
M-Pac 7234 - Take Me Now / You Made Me So Happy – 1967

Label Listings

Soulful Kinda Music – The Rare Soul Bible Volume Two

Back Beat

500 - Doug & Josie - I'll Give Love To You / Wine, Dine And Dance
501 - Norman Fox & Rob Roys - Tell Me Why / Audrey
502 - Tics Tocs - Zola / Walking Alone
503 - Original Casuals - So Tough / I Love My Darling
504 - Lorin Dean - Fi Fo Fum / Lonely Avenue
505 - Tony Spade - Life Is A Mystery / What's Gwyne On
506 - Lee Scott And The Windsors - Cool Seabreeze / My Gloria
507 - Bill Bodaford & The Rockets - Little Girl / Teardrops
508 - Norman Fox & Rob Roys - My Dearest One / Dance Girl, Dance
510 - The Original Casuals - Ju Judy / Don't Pass Me By
511 - Dave Atkins - Shake Kum Down / Don't Pass Me By
512 - Billy Kent - Ridin' On A Rainbow / Precious Love
513 - Catalinas - Speechless / Flying Formation
514 - The Original Casuals - Three Kisses Past Midnight / It's Been A Long Time
515 - The La Salles - Chopsticks / Yum Yum
516 - Johnny Spain - I'm In Love / Family Rules
518 - Andy Wilson - Call Her Your Sweetheart / Too Much Of Not Enough
519 - Joe Hinton - I Know / Ladder Of Prayer
520 - Jerry Foster - What Would I Do / Your Love
521 - Morty Marker - Tell Me You Love Me / Tear Down The House
522 - Ronnie Dee - Action Packed / I Make The Love
525 - Doodle Owens - Grapevine / Mary Lou
526 - Joe Hinton - Pretty Little Mama / Will You
527 - Jimmy Duncan - Song Of Love / Doll House
528 - Bobby Doyle - Someone Else Not Me / Pauline
529 - Jerry Foster - My First Love / I'm Here To Tell You
530 - Hank Ayala & The Matadors - Handsome / Betty Joe
531 - Bobby Doyle - Unloved / Hot Seat
532 - Joe Hinton - Thousand Cups Of Happiness / If You Love Me
533 - Tennyson Stephens - Everybody / Rain Rain Rain
534 - Jerry Foster - Lonely One / Romeo
535 - Joe Hinton - Come On Baby / The Girls In My Life
536 - Kate Williams - Texas Is Going To Be Home / Smile
537 - Joe Hinton - You Know It Ain't Right / Love Sick Blues
539 - Joe Hinton - Better To Give Than Receive / There's No In-Between
540 - Joe Hinton - There Oughta Be A Law / You're My Girl
541 - Joe Hinton - Funny / You Gotta Have Love
542 - Lee Lamont - I'll Take Love /The Crying Man
543 - Roy Head - Teenage Letter / Pain
544 - O.V. Wright - Don't Want To Sit Down / Can't Find True Love
545 - Joe Hinton - I Want A Little Girl / True Love
546 - Roy Head - And The Traits Treat Her Right / So Long My Love
547 - Joe Hinton - Everything / Darling Come To Me
548 - O.V. Wright - Monkey Dog / You're Gonna Make Me Cry
549 - Jimmy Washington - You Oughta See My Baby / My One Sin
550 - Joe Hinton - Just A Kid Named Joe / Pledging My Love

Soulful Kinda Music – The Rare Soul Bible Volume Two

551 - O.V. Wright - Poor Boy / I'm In Your Corner
552 - Bobby Adeno - The Hands Of Time / It's A Sad World
553 - The Fanatics - You're Moving Too Fast / Dancing To The Shotgun
554 - Coastliners - Alright / Wonderful You
555 - Roy Head - Apple Of My Eye / I Pass The Day
556 - Jeanette Williams - You Didn't Know Then / A Friend Of Mine
558 - O.V.Wright - Gone For Good / How Long Baby
560 - Roy Head - My Babe / Pain
561 - Tommy Williams - Going Crazy (Over You) / From Me
562 - The Baroque Boys - So Glad Was I / Baroque Au Go-Go
563 - Roy Head - Driving Wheel / Wigglin' And Gigglin'
564 - Lee Lamont - Happy Days / Pleasin' Woman
565 - Joe Hinton - How Long Can I Last / I'm Waiting
566 - The Coastliners - She's My Girl / I'll Be Gone
567 - Shirley Lawson - One More Chance / The Star
568 - Jeanette Williams - All Of A Sudden / Mr. Soft Touch
570 - Commands - Hey It's Love / No Time For You
571 - Roy Head - To Make A Big Man Cry / Don't Cry No More
572 - Gene Goza - These Spurs (Are Made For Riding) / Our Love
573 - The Passions - Baby I Do / Man About Town
575 - Passions - Baby I Do / Man About Town
576 - Roy Head - You're (Almost) Tuff / Tush Hog Inst.
577 - The Coastliners - California On My Mind / I See You
579 - Bobby Adeno - Treat You Like A Queen / I'll Give Up The World
580 - O.V. Wright - Eight Men Four Women / Fed Up With The Blues
581 - Joe Hinton - You've Been Good / Close To Me
582 - Roy Head - A Good Man Is Hard To Find / Nobody But Me
583 - O.V. Wright - Heartaches, Heartaches / Treasured Moments
584 - Fleas - The Flea Part 1 / Part 2
585 - Barbara Favorite - Two-Way Radio / Then I'll Be True
586 - O.V. Wright - What Did You Tell This Girl Of Mine / What About You
587 - Jeanette Williams - Something's Got A Hold On Me / Longing For Your Love
588 - Carl Carlton - Competition Ain't Nothing / Three Way Love
589 - Joe Hinton - Be Ever Wonderful / I'm Satisfied
590 - The Trade Winds - What's Love About / Don't Let My Heart Sag
591 - O.V. Wright - Oh Baby Mine / Working On Your Case
594 - Joe Hinton - Please / Got You On My Mind
595 - The Liberty Bell - Thoughts And Visions / Look For Tomorrow
596 - Eddie Wilson - Shing A Ling Stroll / Don't Kick The Teenager Around
597 - O.V. Wright - I Want Everyone To Know / I'm Gonna Forget About You
598 - Carl Carlton - 46 Drums And 1 Guitar / Why Don't They Leave Us Alone
599 - The Soul Twins - Mr Independent / She's The One
600 - Liberty Belles - Naw Naw Naw / Recognition
601 - Jeanette Williams - Stuff / You Gonna Come Through
602 - Chuck Mcclean - Let Me Hear It From You / My Lover's Vow
603 - Carl Carlton - Look At Mary Wonder / Bad For Each Other
604 - O.V. Wright - Missing You / This Hurt Is Real
605 - Eddie Wilson - Get Out In The Street / It Must Be Love
606 - Oscar Perry - Like I Was Your Only Child / Like It Was The Last Time
607 - O.V. Wright - I'll Take Care Of You / Why Not Give Me A Chance

Soulful Kinda Music – The Rare Soul Bible Volume Two

608 - E.J's Ltd - Black Bull / Rockin' In The Same Old Boat
609 - Jeanette Williams - Hound Dog / I Can Feel A Heartbeat
610 - Carl Carlton - Don't Walk Away / Hold On A Little Longer
611 - O.V. Wright - Love The Way You Love / Blowing In The Wind
613 - Carl Carlton - Drop By My Place / Two Timer
614 - Oscar Perry - Love Me Like Was Last Time / Fool From The Sticks
615 - O.V. Wright - Ace Of Spades / Afflicted
616 - Eddie Simpson - Stone Soul Sister / Stay That Way (Don't Change)
617 - Carl Carlton - You've Got So Much / I Can Feel It

618 – Barry Jones – Turkey Walk / I'm The Great Lover
619 - Carl Carlton - Wild Child / Sure Miss Loving You
620 - O.V. Wright - When You Took Your Love From Me / I Was Born Over
621 - Carl Carlton - Wild Child / Look AT Mary Wonder (How I've Got Over)
622 - O.V. Wright - A Nickel And A Nail / Pledging My Love
623 - Jean Elias - How Long Can I Go On Fooling Myself / You Made Me A Anybody's Woman
624 - Carl Carlton - Where Have You Been / The Generation Gap
625 - O.V. Wright - Don't Let My Baby Ride / He Made Woman For Man
626 - O.V. Wright - Drowning On Dry Land / I'm Gonna Forget About You
627 - Carl Carlton - Why Don't They Leave Us Alone / I Won't Let That Chump Break Your Heart
628 - O.V. Wright - I'd Rather Be Blind / Please Forgive Me
629 - Carl Carlton - I Wanna Be Your Main Squeeze / It Ain't Been Easy
630 - Carl Carlton - Everlasting Love / I Wanna Be Your Main Squeeze
631 - O.V. Wright - I've Been Searching / I'm Going Home (To Live With God)
5103 – O V Wright – I'm In Your Corner / Poor Boy
5104 – Bobby Adeno – Hands Of Time / It's A Sad World
27001 Carl Carlton - I Wanna Be Your Main Squeeze / Everlasting Love

Bamboo

101 - Sylvia Thomas - So Will I / At Last – 1968
102 - ?
103 - The Voice Masters - You've Hurt Me Baby / If A Woman Catches A Fool – 1968
104 - The Profiles - Got To Be Love (Something Stupid) / You Don't Care About Me – 1969
105 - The Voice Masters - Never Gonna Leave You / If A Woman Catches A Fool   - 1969
106 - Mel and Tim - I've Got Puredee (Vocal) / I've Got Puredee (Instrumental) – 1969
107 - Mel and Tim - Backfield In Motion / Do It Right Baby – 1969
108 - The Profiles - Be Careful / I Still Love You – 1969
109 - Mel and Tim - Good Guys Only Win In The Movies / I Found That I Was Wrong – 1970
110 - Lee Charles - Girl You Turned Your Back On My Love / I Never Want To Lose My Sweet Thing – 1970
111 - Lee Charles - Why Do You Have To Go / I Never Want To Lose My Sweet

Soulful Kinda Music – The Rare Soul Bible Volume Two

Thing – 1970

112 - Mel and Tim - Feeling Bad / I've Got Puredee – 1970

113 - The Voice Masters - Dance Right Into My Heart / If A Woman Catches A Fool – 1970

114 - Mel and Tim - Mail Call Time / Forget It, I've Got It – 1970

115 - The Profiles - A Little Misunderstanding / Got To Be Love – 1970

116 - Mel and Tim - We've Got A Groove To Move On / Never On Time – 1970

117 - Lee Charles - You Can't Get Away Girl / You Turned Your Back On Me – 1970

118 - Mel and Tim - I'm The One / Put An Extra Plus To Your Love – 1971

119 - Lee Charles - You Got To Get It For Yourself / Get High On My Baby's Love – 1971

Big Mack

1286 - Edd Henry - Your Replacement Is Here / Crooked Woman

1653 - Ed Prince - Brother In Law / Five

3911 - The Manhattans - The Feeling Is Mutual / Why Should I Cry - 1963

???? - L.Hollis & The Mack-A-Do's - Bui Bui / Monkey Shine Time - 1963

2942 - The Grand Prix's - I See Her Pretty Face / You Drive Me Crazy - 1965 (This is really The Manhattans

6101 - Bob & Fred / The Baha Strings - I'll Be On My Way / I'll Be On My Way (Inst.) - 1966

10010 - The Performers - Mini Skirt Part 1 / The Sleepwalkers   Part 2 - 1968

24221 - The Soul President - Get It Right / Got To Have It - 1969

38849/38850 - Liz Davis - Motherless Child / Standing In The Need Of Love

39349/39350 - Gospel Cavaliers - Ain't It Sweet / How I Got Over

7520 - The Essence - Fever / Inst - 1972

M 7302 - Mae Young - Let's Give Our Love A Try / This Man Puts Sugar In My Soul - 1972

M 7513 - Ms Tyree (Sugar) Jones - If You Feel It / Inst. - 1975

AR 5321 - Oscar Miles - Inside Loving / Going To A Disco

AR 4391 - Vernell Parker - I'm Not The One Pt. 1 / I'm Not The One Pt. 2

Big Wheel

No # - The Falcons – (I'm A Fool) I Must Love You / Love Love Love

1967 – The Falcons – I Can't Help It / Standing On Guard

1968 – Sandy Hollis – I'm Tempted / Tables Will Turn

1969 – Betty Lavette – I'm Holding On / Tears In Vain

1970 – Eddie King – Kindness Love And Understanding / I Talk Too Much

1971 – The Falcons – Love Look In Her Eyes / In Times For The Blues

1972 – The Falcons – Good Good Feeling / Love You Like You've Never Been Loved Before

Soulful Kinda Music – The Rare Soul Bible Volume Two

Blue Cat

101 - Jimmy Justice - Don't Let The Stars Get In Your Eyes / The Guitar Player
102 - The Ad-Libs - The Boy From New York City / Kicked Around - 1965
103 - Little Joseph - The Story Of Christmas / Christmas Jingle
104 - Alvin Robinson - Something You Got / Searchin'
105 - Bruce Forsyth - Real Live Girl / Deep Down Inside
106 - Bessie Banks - Go Now / It Sounds Like My Baby
107 - The Soul Brothers - Keep It Up / I Got A Dream
108 - Alvin Robinson - How Can I Get Over You / I'm Gonna Put Some Hurt On You
109 - ?
110 - Regents - Me & You / Playmates
111 - Ronnie Mitchell - Having A Party / I'm Loving You More Everyday
112 - Sam Hawkins - Hold On Baby / Bad As They Come
113 - Alvin Robinson - Let The Good Times Roll / Bottom Of My Soul
114 - The Ad-Libs - He Ain't No Angel / Ask Anybody
115 - The Bouquets - Welcome To My Heart / Ain't That Love
116 - The Fenways - Hard Road Ahead / The Fight
117 - The Goodies - The Dum Dum Ditty / Sophisticated Boom Boom
118 - Evie Sands - Take Me For A Little While / Run Home To Your Mama - 1965
119 - The Ad-Libs - On The Corner / Oo-Wee, Oh Me Oh My - 1965
120 - Bubbles & Co. - Underneath My Pillow / Just One Girl - 1965
121 - Sam Hawkins - I Know It's Alright / It Hurts So Bad (Drip Drop) - 1965
122 - Evie Sands - I Can't Let Go / You've Got Me Uptight - 1965
123 - The Ad-Libs - I'm Just A Down Home Girl / Johnny My Boy
124 - Newby - I Can't Grow Peaches On A Cherry Tree / Children Sleep
125 - Sidney Barnes - I Hurt On The Other Side / Switchy Walk
126 - Charles Brandy - Without Your Love / I Can't Get Enough Of You
127 - Tiny Tim - April Showers / Little Girl
128 - Linda Jones - Fugitive From Love / You Hit Me Like TNT
129 - Didi Noel - Let The Music Play / No More Tears To Cry
130 - Eddie Jacobs - I'll Be Right Back / Seven Days

Boom

60000 - The Sheep - Hide And Seek / Twelve Months Later - 1966
60001 - Debra Swisher - Thank You And Good Night / You're So Good To Me - 1966
60002 - The Baby Dolls - I Will Do It ('Cause He Wants Me To) / Now That I've Lost You - 1966
60003 - Lee Merril - The Boys From Madrid / Banco Banco - 1966
60004 - Tammy Wayne - Have A Good Time / Kissaway - 1966
60005 - Terry Cashman - Pretty Face / Try Me - 1966
60006 - Cab Calloway - After Taxes / History Repeats Itself - 1966
60007 - The Sheep - Dynamite / I Feel Good - 1966
60008 - ?
60009 - Shep Grant - Animal Party / Goodnight Irene - 1966

Soulful Kinda Music – The Rare Soul Bible Volume Two

60010 - ?
60011 - ?
60012 - Dean Parrish - Tell Her / Fall On Me - 1966
60013 - Lee Merril - Green Hornet / Theme Off The Wall - 1966
60014 - The Last Word - Bidin' My Time / Hot Summer Days - 1966
60015 - The Live Wires - Keep It To Yourself / The Mask   - 1966
60016 - Dean Parrish - Determination / Turn On Your Lovelight - 1966
60017 - Bobby Hebb - Betty Jo From Ohio / Sam Hall Jr. - 1966
60018 - The Quarter Notes - Hey Little Girl / I've Been Loved - 1966
60019 - Gary and The Luvlites - My Heart Just Couldn't Take The Pain / The Shadow Of Your Love - 1966
60020 - Vito and The Salutations - Bring Back Yesterday / I Want You To Be My Baby - 1966
60021 - The Concords - Down The Aisle Of Love / I Feel Love Comin' - 1966
60022 - Giles Strange - Watch The People Dance / You're Goin' Up To The Bottom - 1966
60023 to 60037 were not used.
60038 - Dean Parrish - Skate Part 1 / Skate Part 2 - 1967

Broadway

400 - Johnson Sisters - I Found My Place / You Don't Want Me Anymore
401 - Johnny Burton - Slave Girl / Come On, Dance With Me
402 - Sandra Phillips - You Succeeded / When Midnight Comes
403 - Sandra Phillips - World Without Sunshine / Ok
405 - Thieves - Why Did You Do It To Me / I'm Not The One
406 - Tommy Andre - One More Try / Blueprint
40001 - Ocie Smith - Everybody But Me / Mister Right

Vi Campbell

Vi Campbell

Peacock 1940 - Vi Campbell - Seven Doors / I'm Yours - 1966

Bobby Bland

Duke DLPS-79 - Bobby "Blue" Bland - Soul Of The Man - 1966

Track: Dear Bobby (The Note)* Female part performed by Vi Campbell

Blanch Carter

Blanch Carter

GSF 6881 - Halos Are For Angels / Hello You Again - 1972
RCA 10524 - My Man / Rain - 1975

Blanche Carter (Of The Night People)

TSOB 2005 - Straight Down To The Bone / Straight Down To The Bone (Inst) - 1981

The Casualeers

The Casualeers (members Arnold Davis, Ollie Johnson, Peppy DuBois and Mike Furr)

Roulette 4722 - Dance, Dance, Dance / There's Something About This Girl - 1967
Laurie 3407 - You Better Be Sure / Open Your Eyes - 1967
Laurie 3441 - Come Back To My Arms / When I'm In Your Arms - 1968

Dee Clark

The Golden Tones (Members Cicero Blake, James Harper, Howard Mcclain, Teddy Long And John Carter) 1951 Line-Up.

Red Saunders & His Orch. With Dolores Hawkins & The Hambone Kids (Members Red Saunders, Fip Ricard, Sonny Cohn, Harlan "Booby" Floyd, John Avant, Riley Hampton, Leon Washington, Mckinley Easton, Earl Washington, Jimmy Richardson And ?, Plus Dolores Hawkins. The Hambone Kids Were Delecta "Dee" Clark, Sammy Mcgrier And Ronny Strong)

Soulful Kinda Music – The Rare Soul Bible Volume Two

Okeh 6862 - Hambone / Boot 'Em Up - 1952

The Golden Tones (Members Delecta Clark (Lead), John Mccall (First Tenor), Doug Brown (Second Tenor), Teddy Long (Second Tenor) And John Carter (Bass)) 1953 Line-Up.

The Kool Gents (Members Delecta Clark, John Mccall, Doug Brown, Teddy Long And John Carter)

Vee-Jay 173 - This Is The Night / Do Ya Do - 1956
Vee-Jay 207 - You Know / I Just Can't Help Myself - 1956

The Delegates / Big Jay McNeely

Vee-Jay 212 - The Convention / Jay's Rock* - 1956 *Flip By Big Jay McNeely.

The Delegates (Members Delecta Clark, John Mccall, Doug Brown, Teddy Long And John Carter)

Vee-Jay 243 - Mother's Son / I'm Gonna Be Glad - 1957

Dee Clark (Born Delecta Clark Jr. On The 7-November-1938 In Blytheville, Arkansas - Died 7-December-1990 In Smyrna, Georgia - Cause: Heart Attack)

Falcon 1002 - Gloria / Kangaroo Hop - 1957
Falcon 1005 - Seven Nights / Twenty-Four Boy Friends - 1957
Falcon 1009 - Oh Little Girl / Wondering - 1958
Abner 1019 - Nobody But You / When I Call On You - 1958 (Backup Vocals By The Anita Kerr Singers)
Abner 1026 - Just Keep It Up / Whispering Grass - 1959 (Backup Vocals By The Anita Kerr Singers)
Abner 1029 - Hey Little Girl / It Wasn't For Love - 1959 (Some Copies Issued With Picture Sleeve)
Abner 1032 - How About That* / Blues Get Off My Shoulder - 1959 *Written By Doris (Troy) Higgenson.
Abner (No Number) - Blues Get Off My Shoulder - 1959 (One Sided White Label Promo Issue Only - Noted As "Special D. J. Release From Latest E. P.")
Abner 1037 - At My Front Door (Crazy Little Mama) / Cling-A-Ling - 1960
Vee-Jay 355 - You're Looking Good / Gloria - 1960 (Released In Canada On Delta 3110)
Vee-Jay 372 - Your Friends / Because I Love You - 1961
Vee-Jay 383 - Raindrops* / I Want To Love You - 1961 *Co-Written By Dee Clark And Phillip Upchurch - Also Recorded In 1981 By Kenny Earl On Kik Kik 904.

Dee Clark / Al Smith

Vee-Jay 394 - Gotos Delluvia (Raindrops) / Livin' With Vivian* - 1961 *Flip By Al Smith.

Dee Clark

Soulful Kinda Music – The Rare Soul Bible Volume Two

Vee-Jay 409 - Don't Walk Away From Me / You're Telling Our Secrets - 1961
Vee-Jay 428 - You Are Like The Wind / Drums In My Heart - 1962
Vee-Jay 443 - Dance On Little Girl / Fever - 1962
Vee-Jay 462 - I'm Going Back To School / Nobody But You - 1962
Vee-Jay 487 - I'm A Soldier Boy / Shook Up Over You - 1963
Vee-Jay 532 - How Is He Treating You / The Jones Boy - 1963
Vee-Jay 548 - Walking My Dog / Nobody But Me - 1963
Constellation 108 - Crossfire Time / I'm Going Home - 1963

Red Saunders & His Orch. / Link Wray & The Wraymen.

Okeh 7166 - Hambone / Rumble Mambo* - 1963 (Alternate Take) *Flip By Link Wray & The Wraymen.

Dee Clark

Oldies 45 ? - Raindrops / I Want To Love You - 196?
Oldies 45   65 - When I Call On You / Nobody But You - 1964
Oldies 45   71 - If It Wasn't For Love / Hey Little Girl - 1964

The Kool Gents / The Tokens

Oldies 45   104 - This Is The Night / While I Dream* - 1964 *Flip By The Tokens

Dee Clark / Gladys Knight & The Pips

Oldies 45   113 - You Are Like The Wind / Operator* - 1964 *Flip By Gladys Knight & The Pips.

Dee Clark

Constellation 113 - It's Raining / That's My Girl - 1964
Constellation 120 - Come Closer / That's My Girl - 1964
Constellation 132 - Warm Summer Breeze / Heartbreak - 1964
Constellation 142 - Ain't Gonna Be Your Fool / In My Apartment - 1964

Dee Clark / The Mello Moods

Oldies 45 120 - You Are Like The Wind / Where Are You* - ? *Flip By The Mello Moods.

Dee Clark

Constellation 147 - T. C. B. / It's Impossible - 1965
Constellation 155 - I Can't Run Away / She's My Baby - 1965
Constellation 165 - I Don't Need (Nobody Like You) / Hot Potato - 1966
Constellation 173 - Old Fashion Love / I'm Goin' Home - 1966
Columbia 44200 - In These Very Tender Moments / Lost Girl - 1967

Red Saunders & His Orch. / Link Wray & The Wraymen.

Soulful Kinda Music – The Rare Soul Bible Volume Two

Okeh 7282 - Hambone / Rumble Mambo* - 1967 (Alternate Take) *Flip By Link Wray & The Wraymen.

Dee Clark

Wand 1177 - Nobody But You (Part 1) / Nobody But You (Part 2) - 1968
Liberty 56152 - 24 Hours Of Loneliness / Where Did All The Good Times Go - 1970
United Artists 50759 - You Can Make Me Feel So Good / Old Time Religion - 1971
Rocky / Warner Bros. 7720 - Raindrops '73 / I'm A Happy Man - 1973
Vee-Jay 63-3416/3417 - Walking My Dog / Nobody But Me - ? (Promo Issue)
ABC - 1973
Eric 0168 - Raindrops / Just Keep It Up - 1973
Chelsea 3025 - Ride A Wild Horse / (Instrumental) - 1975
Collectables Col 014597 - Raindrops / I Want To Love You - 1983
MCA - 1984
Solid Smoke - 1984

Gene Chandler / Dee Clark

Original Sound Obg-4507 - Duke Of Earl / Raindrops* - 1984 *Flip By Dee Clark.

Dee Clark / Apollo 100 Featuring Tom Parker.

Ripete R45-220 - Shook Up Over You / Joy* - ? *Flip By Apollo 100 Featuring Tom Parker.

Dee Clark

Collectables Col 030417 - Hey Little Girl / Nobody But You - ?

Dee Clark / Chris Kenner

Collectables Col 035587 - You're Looking Good / I Like It Like That* - ? *Flip By Chris Kenner.

Ep's

Abner 900 - Dee Clark - 1959 Tracks:
Vee-Jay 900 - Dee Clark - 1959 Tracks:

Trivia

The Kool Gents were names after local DJ Herb "Kool Gent" Kent At WGS.

Mitty Collier

The Hayes Ensemble (members Mitty Collier, .) gospel group.

Mitty Collier (born 21-June-1941 in Birmingham, Alabama)

Soulful Kinda Music – The Rare Soul Bible Volume Two

Chess 1791 - I've Got Love / Gonna Get Away From It All - 1961
Chess 1814 - Don't Let Her Take My Baby / I Dedicate My Life To You - 1962
Chess 1856 - Miss Loneliness / My Babe - 1963
Chess 1871 - I'm Your Part Time Love / Don't You Forget It - 1963
Chess 1889 - Let Them Talk / Pain - 1964
Chess 1907 - I Had A Talk With My Man / Free Girl (In The Morning) - 1964
Chess 1918 - No Faith, No Love / Together - 1965
Chess 1934 - Ain't That Love / Come Back Baby - 1965
Chess 1942 - For My Man / Help Me - 1965
Chess 1953 - Sharing You / Walk Away - 1966
Chess 1964 - My Party / I'm Satisfied - 1966
Chess 1987 - Watching And Waiting / Like Only Yesterday - 1967
Chess 2015 - You're The Only One / Do It With Confidence - 1967
Chess 2035 - That'll Be Good Enough For Me / Git Out - 1967
Chess 2050 - Gotta Get Away From It All / Everybody Makes A Mistake Sometime - 1968
Peach Tree 121 - I Can't Lose / You Hurt So Good - 1969
Peach Tree 122 - I'd Like To Change Places / Share What You Got - 1969
Peach Tree 123 - Fly Me To The Moon / True Love Never Comes Easy - 1969
Peach Tree 125 - Lovin' On Borrowed Time / One Heck Of A Lover - 1970
Peach Tree 128 - Your Sign Is A Good Sign / Mama, He Treats Your Daughter Mean - 1970
Entrance 7512 - Is This Our Last Time / I'd Like To Change Places With His Part Time Lover - 1972

The Corsairs / Mitty Collier

Eric 0238 - Smokey Places / I Had A Talk With My Man* - 1978 *flip by Mitty Collier.

Little Milton / Mitty Collier

Chess 129 - Feel So Bad / I Had A Talk With My Man* - ? *Flip By Mitty Collier.

Mitty Collier / Tony Clarke

Collectables Col 034197 - I Had A Talk With My Man / The Entertainer* - ? *flip by Tony Clarke.

The Cooperettes

Dottie & Millie (Members: Dottie Haynes, Millie Weaver.....)

Topper 1014 - Nothing In This World / Talkin' About My Baby - 1966

The Cooperettes (Members: Dottie Haynes, Millie Weaver, ?.....)

Brunswick 55296 - Goodbye School / Goodbye School (Inst) - 1966
Brunswick 55307 - Everything's Wrong / Don't Trust Him - 1966
Brunswick 55329 - Shing-A-Ling / (Life Has) No Meaning Now - 1967

Soulful Kinda Music – The Rare Soul Bible Volume Two

ABC 11156 - Peace Maker / Trouble - 1968
ABC 11197 - Spiral Road / Trouble - 1968
I-D-B 1007 - With All Your Love / Satisfaction - 1971

JoAnne Courcy

Twirl 2020 - Silly Girl / My Poor Broken Heart - 1966
Twirl 2026 - I Got The Power / I'm Gonna Keep You – 1966

So You Want To Run An Allnighter ?

So you want to run an allnighter ?

Well, as anyone who has promoted allnighters knows, it's not easy, very rarely makes a huge amount of money, and causes an enormous amount of stress on the night itself. Believe me, I know, I've been there !

So I thought I'd write a sort of beginners guide to promoting an allnighter.

The Promoters

First off, do you want to take all the work on, on your own ? It's virtually impossible to do it all yourself on the night, so who are you going to recruit ? Husbands, wives, girlfriends, boyfriends, partners are a good source of support (You don't need to pay them), but most people that run allnighters tend to do it with a financial partner who is a mate. It has to be someone you can trust, and usually someone who you would want as a DJ anyway (Because if you're doing a spot yourself, it cuts two DJs off the wages bill in case you make a loss !) Most important of all on the night itself, you have to have someone on the door collecting the money that you can trust, and make sure it's someone who is an absolute dragon when it comes to stopping people sneaking past without paying.

The Finances

Now this might seem a little 'business like' for the Northern scene, but to be honest, you have to know what the whole thing is going to cost you before you start serious planning. You can't just blunder along paying a bit here, and a bit there, and hoping you'll get it all back at the end of the day. You have to know how many paying customers you need through the door to break even, and decide if that is a realistic figure. You also have to take into account, how much you are prepared to lose before the venue either becomes established, or you reach the point where you cannot continue to lose money. I'm not suggesting that the only reason you should run the niter is to make money, but let's be realistic about this: Very few of us, no matter how well off we are, can afford to just throw money away ! So set a budget for the venue, the DJs, the sound system, the advertising, and all the 1001 other things that will crop up. Even allow some in the budget for the phone calls you will be making.

The Venue

Right, that's the team set up. Next on the agenda is a venue. Finding the right venue can be a nightmare in itself. It has to have a dancefloor, a bar, be far enough away from residential property so that the music won't cause problems, and be amenable to running an allnighter (Which in itself can be a battle, try explaining the concept of a load of 40 somethings staying up all night dancing to music that you can't hear on the radio). It gets even more complicated if you want two rooms, it makes it even more difficult finding the right venue. Then you've got to consider is it easily accessible from the motorway network ? Is there enough carparking at the venue ? Is the car parking safe ? What about the cost of hiring the venue itself, is it reasonable ? Do they want to impose any conditions as part of the hire ? These questions all need to be answered before ou even consider signing a contract.

The Local Council

Hmmm, two aspects to this. Firstly, if the venue is owned by the Local Council, it should be a lot simpler, and they will have given implicit approval fror the niter when they agreed to hire the venue to you. If it isn't Council owned, you need to check that the Council will approve the licence application (Assuming the venue applies for one !). It's always advisable to get the Council's support, because they are one of the people who can actually get your venue shut down.

The Date

So, you've found the venue, the owners have agreed to run the allnighters, now you've got to pick a date. And if you thought finding the venue was hard, just look at the calendar, there is hardly a Saturday in the year when there isn't an allnighter on somewhere in the country. So you must talk to other promoters, and if possible try your best not to clash with another niter that has the same music policy as you. Better still, try not to clash with anyone, but if you must, try to ensure as much mileage between your venue and any other that is on the same night.

The Music Policy and DJs

You've now got a venue, and a date booked. You need some DJs don't you. This is where a comprehensive phone book comes in handy. But first you need to make a decision as to what sort of music policy your venue will have, and if you have partners, agree it with them as well. Once you've decided the music policy, several names should suggest themselves, usually guys, who are regular allnighter DJs. Try them first, and then build the rest of your line up around them. If it's going to be a regular thing, do you want several residents and a couple of guests, or a couple of residents to anchor it for you, and all the rest as guests that will change every month. Ah, decisions, decisions.

Almost certainly you won't get the DJs you originally thought of unless you are planning well in advance. For example, I already have over 50 bookings in my diary for 2005. This means that, although a fair number are Fridays, I am already booked to DJ on a lot of Saturday nights. So will a lot of the other busy DJs. Be prepared to draw up a list of names much longer than you will ever need, and then work your way down from the top.

One other thing. Remember if you book a DJ, you are in effect creating a contract between the two of you. You must have enough money available to cover the DJ's fees, even if only ten people turn up. You are the promoter, if the event is a lock out, you make lots of money. The DJ won't ask for more than their agreed fee. If nobody turns up, you are still the promoter, and you have made a loss. The DJ hasn't ! Don't insult the DJ by offering him less money. It's not his fault that people haven't turned up, he has, and will have done the work he was contracted to do, DJ for you, and may well have turned down other work to come and DJ for you.

Record Dealers

To me, a big part of an allnighter (and a Soul night) is whether there are record dealers present. You need to consider two things here. How much space is there available for record dealers. If there isn't much, speak to some of the ones you hope will come and ask them to reserve a table. And secondly, is there enough light for where you are asking them to set up. It's really hard trying to buy and sell records in the dark. Most regular dealers will be able to bring their own lights if they are needed, but they have to be told they are needed.

It's also worth remembering that some Council owned venues actually make an additional charge for people selling merchandise on their premises. As the promoter, you have a choice here. You can negotiate a block booking fee with the Council, and absorb it into your overall costs by paying it yourself. Or you can pass the fee onto the record dealers. Speaking from experience the first option is the preferred one. If you charge record dealers for tables, and they don't sell enough to cover that charge, they won't come back, and that's something you want to avoid.

The Advertising

Flyers, colour post card ones, or the usual black and white ones. It's becoming more common to find printed cards as flyers, ok, it involves more cost up front, but provides a better finished product. Can you do the design work yourself, or do you have to employ someone to do it for you ? Again, it's all questions. Then you've got to consider magazine advertising. The three magazines that are regularly printed these days are this one, Manifesto, and NSoul. Costs rise again if you want to go with an advert in the glossy mags, but 'SKM' is the most reasonably priced of the lot (Plug over). These days, 'On The Scene' is a real necessity as well. If you don't want to run to the cost of an advert, they will still include your venue in the monthly listings, and believe me, a lot of people read 'On The Scene' every month.

Talking of Event listings, it brings into play all the websites that have an events page. Again, I'd recommend Soulful Kinda Music (Well I would, wouldn't I !), but Soul Source also has a very comprehensive listing as well, as do several other sites. You also have to include all the email lists and forums in the deal as well.

Soulful Kinda Music – The Rare Soul Bible Volume Two

Three months before the first allnighter, hopefully, your box of flyers will arrive. You then have to distribute them, and this means getting out and about talking to people. Your DJs will also usually give you a hand distributing flyers, so make sure you have plenty with you whenever you go out.

You also have to consider Radio advertising as well. There are three shows that you should consider: Mark Bicknall on Solar Radio, Kev Roberts on Solar Radio, and Richard Searling on Jazz FM. All three present weekly shows, on commercial stations, and a polite letter or email might well get your allnighter a mention on their show. Almost certainly they will all be happy to accept a paid for advertisement.

The other thing you must think about, is having flyers for the second niter available at the first one. This is always a gamble. If the first one is a disaster, and you can't afford to run a second one, you will have wasted your money on flyers for the second one. But, if it's a great night, you need those flyers to let people know when the second one is going to be. Remember, whilst they are still in the building, they are your customers for your second allnighter. Once they have left the building you have to start the whole process of recruiting them as customers from scratch really.

The Equipment

It's getting close now, so you have to make sure you have the right sound equipment available. Now I know I've gone on about this sort of thing before, but nothing annoys me more than going to a venue to find that the sound system isn't good enough and the end result is crap sound quality. Think about the size of the room, and how long that equipment is going to have to work for. If you haven't got the kit yourself, you will have to hire a sound system. It's much better to hire someone else's sound system rather than just hiring the bit's of kit yourself because if they know what they are doing they will be around all night to tend to their equipment, and will have spares just in case anything should go wrong.

The Security

In a lot of cases you don't have a choice about this these days. You have to have Security staff, and they usually come with the venue. That's not a problem at most places if they have the right attitude and are fairly unobtrusive. Sometimes though they don't realise the crowd they are dealing with is slightly different to most nightclub crowds, and have a really aggressive attitude which is almost unanimously disliked by a Northern crowd. So it pays to just discuss what you want from security with the guy in charge before the night. Occasionally security isn't provided, so you have to consider if you want it. I'd like to say you shouldn't need it at a Northern do, but at the very least these days you need someone on the door who is capable of turning drunk locals away.

Going back to the Local Council side of things, you might also find that they will only grant a licence, if your security staff are registered with them. Something to think about.

Availability

Availability of you that is. It's essential that you make yourself available to any one who wants to contact you, for whatever reason. I've seen flyers that don't give any contact details at all, and think that is absolutely ridiculous. So if you can, give a mobile phone number, and an email address, and when people contact you to ask questions about the event, answer them, no matter how ridiculous their questions are (and you'll get some absolute belters asked.).

Website

If you are going to be running regular niters, a website is an essential tool these days for getting the message across, and for displaying photos of the event, even for putting sound clips of the sounds you will be playing up there. Nearly all of the established clubs these days have their own website, and they vary from all singing and dancing to just one page of information. The one thing you must do though, is to update the bloody thing once it's set up. There is nothing more frustrating to people who surf the web regularly to find that a site isn't updated. To be honest if I find a site hasn't been updated on two visits, I stop looking, and that's a potential customer lost.

If you can't do the website yourself, get someone else to start it off, and then learn how to do it. As long as you are fairly competent on a PC, basic websites are not difficult.

The Week before

Ring everyone concerned, including the DJs, to make sure they know what is happening.

The Night Itself.

You've made it. You've got through the minefield, cleared all the hurdles, and you're just about to open the door. If you've made it this far without upsetting someone, somewhere, you must be an absolute saint, and have the patience of job.

Hopefully, there will be a queue of people waiting to come in, and more will follow them, the equipment will work fine, all the DJs will arrive, in time for their spots, and everyone will have a great night and go home happy, having collected a flyer for the next one on the way out.

If only it worked like that all the time !

You'll find it doesn't, that's why most promoters spend the night running round looking harassed. If they are successful and good problem solvers, nobody will notice any of the potential disasters that crop up through the night, and they will still go home happy having collected a flyer for the next one on the way out.

I won't go into all the potential disasters that could happen on the night, that could fill another couple of pages, but a couple of tips. Get there early, check the sound works, talk to everyone who is going to be working for you, and make sure that they all know their role.

Finally, I'll just add two things: Remember to say thank you to everyone who has been involved in the promotion, and actual night itself.

And the most important of all, remember to keep your wife / girlfriend / boyfriend / partner happy. If you do, they will be great support for you, if you don't it will just add to the stress.

Last of all....................................Good Luck To You

Label Listings

Carla

2526 - Deon Jackson - Love Makes The World Go Round / You Said You Loved Me - 1966
2526 - Deon Jackson - Love Makes The World Go Round / Hello Stranger (Inst) - 1966
2527 - Deon Jackson - Love Takes A Long Time Growing / Hush Little Baby - 1966
2528 - Barbara Paul - Don't Let The Party End / Loving You Baby - 1966
2529 - Excels -   Gonna Make You Mine, Girl / Good Bye Poor Boy - 1966
2530 - Deon Jackson - I Can't Do Without You / That's What You Do To Me - 1966
2531 - Four Pro's - Just Another Girl / There Must Be A Reason - 1966
2532 - Four Pro's - Everybody's Got Some Soul / You Can't Keep A Good Man Down - 1966
2533 - Deon Jackson - Hard To Get Thing Called Love / When Your Love Has Gone - 1966
2534 - Excels - I Wanna Be Free / Too Much Too Soon - 1966
2535 - Jimmy Delphs -I've Been Fooled Before / Almost - 1967
2536 - Excels - California On My Mind / The Arrival of Mary - 1967
2537 - Deon Jackson - Ooh Baby / All On A Sunny Day - 1967
1900 - Deon Jackson - I Need A Love Like Yours / I Can't Go On - 1968
1901 - Excels - Little Innocent Girl / Some Kind Of Fun   - 1968
1902 - Milton Wright & The Terra Shirma Strings - The Gallop (Inst) / Like A Rolling Stone (Inst) - 1968
1903 - Deon Jackson - You Gotta Love / You'll Wake Up Wiser Baby - 1968
1904 - Jimmy Delphs - Dancing A Hole In The World / Dancing A Hole In The World (Inst) - 1968
101 - Riley Hampton - Hello Stranger / My Tune - 1969
103 - Excels - It Isn't So / Run Girl Run - 1970
715 - Richard (Popcorn) Wylie -   Move Over Baby (Here Comes Henry) / Instrumental - 1973
718 - Compacts - Why Can't It Be / That's How My World Began – 1974
201 - Gambrells - I Want To Be Yours / - Pain In My Heart - ?

Soulful Kinda Music – The Rare Soul Bible Volume Two

Correc-Tone

501 - Wilson Pickett - Let Me Be Your Boy / My Heart Belongs To You
502 - James Velvet - Bouquet Of Flowers / When I Need You
503 - Gino Washington - Gino's A Coward / Puppet On A String
1052 - Danny Woods - You Had Me Fooled / My Love Will Never Be The Same
1053 - Theresa Lindsey - It's Love / Good Idea
3178 - Yvonne Vernee - Does He Love Me Anymore / So Much In Love
3476 - Pacesetters - The Monkey Whip / Around The World
3807 - Bobbie Downs - It Won't Be Long / Darling
3810 - Lillian Dorr - The Thrill Is Gone / I Need You
5840 - Theresa Lindsey - Gotta Find A Way / Wonderful One
5841 - Theresa Lindsey - Sugar Mountain / Why Oh Why

Crackerjack

4001 - Spy-Dels - Boll Weevil is Back / We'll Be Together
4002 - Big Daddy Hatfield – Teacher Part 1 / The Teacher Part 2
4003 - Duke Hunter - Nose Trouble / The Bartender
4004 - Elmore Morris - It Seemed Like Heaven To Me / Before I Turned My Back on You
4005 - Linda & The Del-Rios - Come On, Let Me Try / I Don't Want to Be Loved
4006 - Pearl Woods - Lonely Avenue / Don't Tell it All
4007 - Jimmy Merritt - I'll Forget About You / Lonely Battle
4008 - Lyrics - Danger Sign / Lonesomest Time
4009 - Eddie Carlton - Wait / Ko Ko Mo
4010 - Shufflers - Always Be Mine / When The Lights Are Low
4011 - Lyrics - Pick of The Week / Where Have All The Kisses Gone
4012 - Richard Barrett - Let Me Down Easy / Summers Love
4013 - Derek Martin - Daddy Rollin' Stone / Don't Put Me Down Like This
4014 - ?
4015 - Dramatics - Toy Soldier / Hello Summer
4016 - Robin Rice - I've Had It / Wanted
4017 - Chuck Leonard - Nobody But You Girl / Diddley Doo
4018 - Betty Green - Lonely Girl / He's Down on Me

Crimson

1001 – The Camelots – Don't Leave Me Baby / The Letter
1002 – Lee Andrews & The Hearts – Island Of Love / Oh My Love - 1967
1003 – The Moonglows – Gee (But I Wish You Were Here) / My Imagination - 1967
1004 – The Sherwoods – Love You Madly / Moffit's Mess - 1967
1005 – ?
1006 – The Parktowns – That Day Will Never Come / You Hurt Me Inside - 1967
1007 – ?

Soulful Kinda Music – The Rare Soul Bible Volume Two

1008 – The Masters – I Need Your Love / Not Me Baby - 1967
1009 – Lee Andrews & The Hearts – Nevertheless / Island Of Love - 1967
1010 – The Soul Survivors – Expressway To Your Heart / Hey Gyp - 1967
1011 – The Brothers Two – Boogaloo (Soul) Party / You Got It
1012 – The Soul Survivors – Explosion (In Your Soul) / Dathon's Theme - 1968
1013 – Damon Fox – Gotta Get My Baby Back / Black Widow Spider - 1968
1014 – ?
1015 – Lee Andrews & The Hearts – I've Had It / Little Bird - 1968
1016 – The Soul Survivors – Impossible Mission (Mission Impossible) / Poor Man's Dream - 1968
1017 – The Brothers Two – Here I Am In Love Again / Rock And Roll Hall Of Fame - ?
1017 - The Brothers Two - I'm Tired Of You Baby / ? - ?
1018 – The Common Pleas – The Funky Judge / I Wanted More - ?

Don't Become A DJ!

From the number of comments I've received, the article I wrote about not becoming a record dealer was quite well received, and although it was written slightly tongue in cheek, every single thing described in that article actually happened. So on the back of that article, here comes the next one..................

I never really understood why so many people actually want to become DJs. You never make any money at it, you can have one of the most soul destroying hours of your life if nobody dances, and no matter how well the majority of people think you did, there is always one who thought your spot was the worst thing he's ever heard, and he insists on telling you so !

It's not just a case of having the records either, I've heard people with great records do appalling sets, they just have no idea of how to put records together by tempo or musical style, so their set is disjointed and all over the place. I've heard people with great records do an appalling set because they haven't played the records I know they have got and have played a load of complete rubbish. On the other hand, some of the best DJ spots I've heard have come from people who don't have particularly rare records, but have really good taste. I'd far rather hear a good set full of £5.00 records that are quality Soul music than some of the 'played because it's rare rather than good' monstrosities that are around. There also has to be a certain amount of ability in 'reading the dancefloor'. It should be easy, all you've got to do is listen what the DJ's before you play, and make mental notes of what went down well and what didn't. If R & B clears the dancefloor every time it's played, don't play any, same with Oldies and Newies. What is even worse is when a DJ clearly hasn't been listening and starts to play records that have already been played, this just shows they have no real interest in the music or the dancers, or just want to show off by saying "Look I've got one of those as well."

One thing that does contribute to how a DJ's set is received, but in the main is out of his control, is the sound system. Over the years I've used some immaculate sound systems that are really understood by the owners, and set up properly so that the sound is clear, at the right volume, and doesn't vary throughout the night. On the other hand, some systems are so old it seems like they are still using valve amplifiers, or the amplifier is not powerful enough, so it's straining to reach the capacity expected of it, so everything is distorted beyond belief. More common is the promoter who uses his own sound system. I'm sorry, but setting up a sound system is quite a specialist job, and a lot of people just have no idea of how to do it, so please, don't try, use someone who does know how it all works, it really isn't just a case of plugging all the wires into the right holes. Lastly, you get the DJs who are unhappy with the way a system is set up, so alter all the settings, and make it worse. Most common trick here is when they just up the volume until it becomes painful. Think about it please, nobody, but nobody wants the music so loud that it begins to hurt.

Onto the technical skills of the DJ themselves. Cueing a record up is not difficult, so why do so many DJ's records all sound as though they are playing them on a wind up gramophone when they start. Simple, they can't do the job. Using a microphone is another belter. Cheap microphones sound cheap, but even good microphones can sound cheap if the DJ has no idea of how to use it. How many times have you not been able to understand a word the DJ has said ? More than once I'll bet.

I would add that the majority of top DJs these days are perfectly capable of doing things the right way, that's why they remain top DJs. Again it's simple, you can have the right records, but if you can't DJ, very quickly people will discover this and the bookings will stop coming in.

The funny side of being a DJ though is some of the requests you get. I always try and play requests if I've got the record with me, but some people don't even know what record they are asking for, they'll say "Can you play that record you played at wherever three weeks ago" As though I can mystically know which record they are talking about. Or they'll come and ask for a record you've never heard of, and then you play it, only for them to come and say "that's the one". The fact that they had got the artist and title completely wrong appears to be your fault. The other favourite of mine is when you've been DJing for 55 minutes and someone comes and asks for a request, and then gets snotty when you say you haven't got enough time left to play it. Why didn't they come at the beginning of the spot ? Some people come and ask for the most bizarre records anyway, I've been asked to play some Beatles. Chris Anderton, when he was halfway through his spot at one venue was asked if he could "play some Soul music". I found that one really funny because Chris is one of the best DJs around.

Finally onto something that everyone knows is one of my own little hates. If you want to be a Rare Soul DJ, and have the respect of promoters, dancers, collectors, alike, it's simple. If it's not original, don't play it. All the top DJs use original vinyl, they have usually spent a lot of time, energy, and money assembling their collections, and they have usually been booked to DJ because of their abilities and their collection. So why play a bootleg, or a reissue, or a CD even, of a record that you know other DJs have an original of. If we use the analogy of antiques here it becomes easy to understand. Would you want to buy a genuine original antique, or a ten year old copy / fake. Obvious really isn't it. So when you're DJing, use an original, not a ten year old fake, and don't use the excuse the punters don't care, it's not about them in this instance, it's about you, and your credibility as a Rare Soul DJ. Moan over.

The D C Blossoms

The **Tropicals** (members Jacqui Burton, Vicky Burton, Jeanette Talley and Roberta Miller) group founded in 1958.

The **Blossoms** (members Jacqui Burton, Vicky Burton, Jeanette Talley and Roberta Miller)

Okeh 7162 - I'm In Love / What Makes Love - 1962

Soulful Kinda Music – The Rare Soul Bible Volume Two

The D. C. Blossoms (members Jacqui Burton, Vicky Burton and Jeanette Talley)

Shrine 107 - I Know About Her* / Hey Boy** - 1966

Melvin Davis

⊣——————————————————————————————————————

The Jaywalkers (members Melvin Davis, Clyde Wilson, David Ruffin and Tony Newton)

Melvin Davis with The Nite Sounds (members

Fortune 551 - I Won't Be Your Fool / Playboy (Don't You Play In School) - 1962

Melvin Davis (born 29-August-1942 in Milledgeville, Georgia - moved to Detroit at age three)

Jack Pot 3800 - I Don't Want You / About Love - 1963
Ke-Ke 1815 - Wedding Bells / It's No News - 1964
Wheel City 1003 - Find A Quiet Place (And Be Lonely) / This Ain't The Way - ?
Groovesville 1003 - I Must Love You / Still In My Heart - 1966
Mala 590 - Save It (Never Too Late) / This Love Was Meant To Be - 1968
Mala 12009 - Love Bug Got A Bear Hug / Faith - 1968

The 97th Decade (members Melvin Davis, Tony Newton, Lyman Woodard, Leroy Emanuel and Jerry Paul)

8th Day (members Melvin Davis, Tony Newton, Michael Anthony, Carole Stallings, Anita Sherman, Bruce Nazarian, Jerry Paul, Lynn Harter)

Invictus 9087 - She's Not Just Another Woman / I Can't Find Myself - 1971
Invictus 9098 - You've Got To Crawl / It's Instrumental To Be Free (Instrumental)
Invictus 9107 - If I Could See The Light / (Instrumental) - 1971

Melvin Davis

Invictus 9115 -I'm Worried / Just As Long - 1972

8th Day

Invictus 9117 - Rocks In My Head / Eeny-Meeny-Miny-Mo (There's A Crowd) - 1972
Invictus 9124 - I Gotta Get Home (Can't Let My Baby Get Lonely) / Good Book - 1972

Melvin Davis

Invictus 1259 - I'm Worried / You Made Me Over - 1973

Mel Davis

Rock Mill 32484 - Double Or Nothin' / You Can't Run Away - 1976

Soulful Kinda Music – The Rare Soul Bible Volume Two

Rock Mill 32485 - Saving Myself For You / Wacky World – 1983
Rock Mill 6164 - Cash Flow / (Instrumental) - 1985

Melvin Davis

Rock Mill 5238 - Let Love In Your Life / ? - 1991

Charisma (members Melvin Davis, ...)

Rock Mill 8267 - Let Love In Your Life / ? - ?

Mel Davis (Is this the same Mel Davis ?)

Golden State 469 - Just Another Smile / ? - ?

Melvin & Bryan Davis

Rock Mill 1117 - I Need My Baby / Nothings Too Good (For You) - 2005

The Diplomats

If you've been around on the Northern scene for more than a couple of years, almost certainly you will have heard records by The Diplomats, or The Skullsnaps, and they are all the same people. So back to the beginning:

Around 1955, in Salisbury, Maryland, two groups of teenagers were following the time honoured tradition of forming singing groups to give an opening to their talent and artistry (and to attract girls !). One of those groups was called Five Hits and A Miss (The Miss obviously being Norma Lee Trader), and I haven't been able to establish what the other group was called. However, the two groups' paths crossed a few times as they were all in the same High School, and they eventually came together at a Glee Club.

From this meeting a new group evolved called Tiny Tim and The Hits. After singing in local clubs and at beaches on the Maryland shore the group eventually came to the attention of Talbert Caudry, who owned the local movie theatre in Salisbury. He in turn was friends with someone who worked for Roulette Records in New York.

Roulette Records hadn't long been formed, and were on the look out for talent, so an audition was arranged for Tiny Tim and The Hits in New York. The group went along and cut at least four tracks. One of which was released as Roulette 4123 'Wedding Bells / Doll Baby' in 1958. (I've established that one of the other tracks they cut was called 'Golden Moments', but whether it was ever released, and what the flip side was has eluded me.). The record did sell, and although it didn't become a hit, the group should have received some money in terms of royalties.

The Roulette Label was founded in late 1956 or early 1957 by record producer George Goldner and Joe Kolsky in New York City. Morris Levy was installed as president of the label. The partnership was short lived as Billboard announced on

April 6, 1957, "George Goldner has sold his interests in the Roulette, Rama, Gee and Tico labels outright to the Morris Levy combine."

Clockwise from top:
Ervin Waters, Sam Culley, Bill Collier, Tom Price

Morris Levy ran the Roulette label from it's inception. He was born poor in the East Bronx, New York. It was hardly a secret that Levy had many "silent partners" in the Mafia underworld. Levy claimed he was being harassed by the government and had numerous run-ins with the law because of his association with the Genovese family, but he avoided serious prosecution for many years. Consequently, a combination of being young teenagers, and new to the record business, and Morris Levy's reputation meant that if he said there was no money, it meant there was no money ! In fact Levy became notorious for not paying any of his artists throughout the Sixties and Seventies.

That wasn't the point though for the group, they had their first record out, and that's what counted. They weren't totally green though, and they quickly sought more professional help from Sam Cully's Uncle Frank who was a professional musician who had over the years done some recording as well as many live gigs. He recommended they take on a manager called Dr Gilcrest from Newark, New Jersey.

Soulful Kinda Music – The Rare Soul Bible Volume Two

Timothy Wilson at this point decided that a career with the group wasn't for him, and he left the group. It wasn't the end of his musical career though and he went on to record for Veep, Buddah, Blue Rock, and Sky Disc between 1965 and 1972 putting out a total of ten singles over the seven year period.

Dr Gilcrest decided that Tiny Tim And The Hits wasn't the best name the group could go under, and came up with their new name of The Diplomats. He rehearsed them hard, and managed to get them several local gigs, and quite quickly they came to the attention of Wally Roker, a local label owner and record producer. He took them into the studio, and they recorded one of the show standards that Dr Gilcrest had been rehearsing them on 'Unchained Melody', along with a song written by Van McCoy under his pseudonym Allan Davies, called 'Cards On The Table'. Wally Roker was confident that the group would get hits, so he got Al Sears to use the two recordings for the first single on his new Arock label in 1963.

Unfortunately, the group failed to get a hit, but that was to change with the next release 'Here's A Heart'. It entered the Billboard charts in February 1964, and peaked at number 89. For some reason, the record was issued, on the same catalogue number with two different flip sides. One 'I Am A Witness' was a nice group cover version of the recent Tommy Hunt single from 1963. The alternative flipside 'He's Got You Now', which was far more commonly available was a really nice early Soul group sound.

One further single was released on Arock. 'Help Me / Mr Taxi Driver', and it had a very similar sound to the previous release in the hope that it would be a follow up hit. It didn't happen though, and as Wally Roker had left the company to move to Los Angeles, the group also parted company.

They eventually signed for Florence Greenburg's Scepter label and were placed on the Wand subsidiary label. Two singles were released in 1965, 'So Far Away / There's Still A Tomorrow', and 'Love Ain't What It Used To Be / I've Got A Feeling', and although neither troubled the charts significantly all four tracks were solid examples of the mid Sixties group sound that was hitting the charts at the time. Perhaps it was the fact that most of Scepter's, and Wand's promotional budget was focused on The Shirelles, Chuck Jackson, and Dionne Warwick at the time that meant the records never received the support they deserved.

Whatever the reason, the group soon left and made their way to Minit records where just the one single was released 'Honest To Goodness / Don't Bug Me' on Minit 32006 in 1966.

This was the last release for the group as a foursome, and in fact their last release for two years. They weren't idle though. As well as performing as a live act throughout the two year period, they had also developed their writing skills to extend further than their own releases. Through a connection with Bill Curtis, when he started his Fatback record label in 1967, all four members of The Diplomats are credited with writing the 'A' side of the first release on the label 'Stop Pretending' by Mary Davis. Sam Culley is also credited as co=producer on this side.

Soulful Kinda Music – The Rare Soul Bible Volume Two

Then comes one of the long standing misunderstandings on the Northern Scene. That the Four Puzzles were The Diplomats recording under another name. They were totally different groups, although there was a very strong connection between the two groups because the first single on Fatback by The Four Puzzles, 'Especially For You / Right Or Wrong (Good Or Bad) were both written by Sam Cully (on his own for 'Especially For You') and the Diplomats. The next release by the group had their names changed from The Four Puzzles to just The Puzzles, and again both tracks, ' My Sweet Baby / I Need You', were written by the members of The Diplomats (And it's around this time in 1967 when Bill Collier left the group because he isn't included on the writing credits.

The Diplomats own career started up in earnest though in 1968 when they signed to the Dynamo label. The first release was credited to Sam, Erv, and Tom, and whilst it didn't make the charts (In fact none of their future releases would hit the charts from this point on) it started their longest run of releases on one label throughout their career. The following five releases on Dynamo were all credited to The Diplomats, and whilst 'I Can Give You Love' came closest to being a hit, it just failed to reach the chart.

The singles did mean that the group were still managing to get live work, and they even managed to provide the backing vocals to Tony Drake's 'Let's Play House / She's Gone' on Musicor in 1969, although you won't actually find their name on the label. The deal with Dynamo was over by the end of 1970 though and the group were without a recording contract for a short period. Learning to play their own instruments had been a bonus to the group though. Not only did they play on their own recordings, but they backed several of the biggest names around on tour. Acts like The Shirelles, Brook Benton, Little Anthony, and John Lee Hooker, all used the group as backing musicians at some stage.

It was their ability to play their own instruments that got then their next release as well. Buddah Records approached the group to re-record Manu Dibango's hit 'Soul Makossa'. They did, and wrote the flip side as well 'Al's Razor Blade'. For some reason Buddah decided the record would be released credited to All Dyrections. It bombed ! and that was the end of All Dyrections and the Buddah deal.

It was back to The Diplomats for the next release on the small independent label 3rd World. The harmonies were still there as the group crafted an emotion loaded Deep Soul side, which promptly bombed as well. This was the middle of 1970.

In yet another name change in 1973, the group became The Skull Snaps and began recording for the G.S.F. label under the production skills of George Kerr. Several singles resulted, as well as one extremely high demand album. I'm told that there were four singles released on the G.S.F. label, but can only find details of three (And I'm unsure of the legitimacy of one !). Certainly though the group made a huge impression on the Northern Soul scene in 1974 with both 'My Hang Up Is You', and 'I'm Your Pimp'.

The artwork on the album in itself was quite starling, and gave no clue as to the type of music contained in the nine tracks, and if I were to try and describe the style it would have to be closer to Funk than anything else, although certainly the two

Soulful Kinda Music – The Rare Soul Bible Volume Two

'Northern' singles have an uptempo dancer beat rather than a funk beat. I'm confusing myself now, so I'll leave it there on the album !

The album itself has always been rare and hard to find, but regarded as a classic album to the point where it was re-issued in the UK by Charly Records in 1975.

One further release marks the end of The Diplomats recording career, and this was again released as The Skullsnaps (I think), in 1975 and was on another small independent label. Grill 301 – 'Ain't That Loving You', backed with a re-issue of 'Al's Razor Blade'.

By the time the Seventies drew to a close, all three members of the group had left the music industry and taken 'normal' jobs, although all still retained an interest in music through their leisure time interests.

The group had released twenty singles over a sixteen year period, and when they backed other singers had managed to tour the world. Not a bad career really bearing in mind they only hit the charts once. There is one final chapter in the story which was the release in 1996 of the Collectables CD 'Here's A Heart' COL 5733, which I would really recommend anyone to pick up because it contains all of the best of the group's recordings throughout the Sixties with releases from Arock, Wand, Minit, and Dynamo.

Discography

Five Hits & A Miss (members Norma Lee Trader (lead), Howard Harrison "Timothy" Wilson Jr. (born 17-November-1943 in Salisbury, Maryland), Lionel Brown, Orlesto Smith, Thomas Price and William Collier)

Tiny Tim & The Hits (members Timothy Wilson, Lionel Brown, Orlesto Smith, Thomas Price and William Collier)

Roulette 4123 - Wedding Bells / Doll Baby – 1958
Roulette ? - Golden Moments / ? - ?

The Diplomats (members Sam Culley, Ervin Waters, Bill Collier and Thomas Price)

Arock 1000 - Unchained Melody* / Cards On The Table** - 1963 *also recorded in 1955 by Roy Hamilton on EPIC 9102 and in 1963 by Vito & The Salutations on Herald 583.. **written by Allan Davis a pseudonym for Van McCoy.
Arock 1004 - Here's A Heart / I Am A Witness* - 1964 *also recorded in 1963 by Tommy Hunt on Scepter 1261.
Arock 1004 - Here's A Heart / He's Got You Now* - 1964 *also recorded in 1965 as "She's Got You Now" by The Witches on Bang 505.

The Diplomats Accom. by Chet 'Poison' Ivey Band (members Sam Culley, Ervin Waters, Bill Collier, Thomas Price, Chet Ivey, ...)

Arock 1008 - Help Me / Hey Mr. Taxi Driver – 1964

Soulful Kinda Music – The Rare Soul Bible Volume Two

The Diplomats (members Sam Culley, Ervin Waters, Bill Collier and Thomas Price)

Arock - I Really Love You
Arock - Forever
Arock - Don't Ever Go
Arock - Walk With Me
 (Above four tracks unissued until they appeared in the U. K. on a 2004 Kent CD "The Diplomats Greatest Recordings" CDKEND 232.)
Wand 174 - There's Still A Tomorrow / So Far Away - 1965
Wand 195 - Love Ain't What It Used To Be / I've Got A Feeling - 1965
Minit 32006 - Honest To Goodness / Don't Bug Me – 1966
Minit - Perfect Love
Minit - Our Love Has Changed
(Above two tracks unissued until they appeared in the U. K. on a 2004 Kent CD "The Diplomats Greatest Recordings" CDKEND 232.)

Sam, Erv & Tom (members Sam Culley, Ervin Waters and Thomas Price)

Dynamo 116 - Hard To Get / Soul Teacher – 1967

The Puzzles (members Tommy Charles, Leo Wright, Charles Dois and Frank Gibbs)

Fat Back 216 - My Sweet Baby* / I Need You - 1968 *lead Sam Culley as The Puzzles lead singer could not get a "feel" for the song.

Johnny King And Fatback Band (members Johnny King (vocals), Bill Curtis, Gerry Thomas, Sam Culley and Warren Daniel)

BC Project II   101 - Keep On Brother Keep On / Peace, Love Not War - 1968
BC Project II - Peace, Love Not War - 1968 (previously unissued on vinyl alternate version that was released in the U. K. on a 2003 Kent Cd "Fatback's Soul Shop" CDKENM 218)

The Diplomats (members Sam Culley, Ervin Waters and Thomas Price)

Dynamo 122 - I'm So Glad I Found You / I Can Give You Love – 1968
Dynamo 129 - Accept Me / Your Love Is A Shelter – 1969
Dynamo 135 - In My Heart / It's Not How You Make Love – 1969
Dynamo 137 - In The Ghetto / I've Got The Kind Of Love – 1970

Tony Drake (Samuel Garner)

Musicor 1357 - Let's Play House / She's Gone - 1969 (uncredited backing vocals by The Diplomats)

The Diplomats (members Sam Culley, Ervin Waters and Thomas Price)

Dynamo 140 - Here's A Heart / Granny Was Her Name – 1970
3rd World 501 - Sure As The Stars Shine / She's The One – 1970

Soulful Kinda Music – The Rare Soul Bible Volume Two

Johnny King And Fatback Band (members Johnny King (vocals), Bill Curtis, Gerry Thomas, Sam Culley and Warren Daniel)

BC Project II 102 - Put It In / ? – 1971

Tiny Tim & The Hits / Sonny Til & The Orioles

Roulette 13 - Wedding Bells / Crying In The Chapel* - 1971 *flip by Sonny Til & The Orioles

The Skull Snaps (members Sam Culley, Ervin Waters, George Bragg and R. Smith)

GSF - 6891 - My Hang Up Is You / It's A New Day - 1972
GSF 6896 - Didn't I Do It To You / ? – 1973

All Dyrections (members Sam Culley, Ervan Waters and George Bragg)

Buddah 362 - Soul Makossa* / Al's Razor Blade - 1973 *also recorded in 1973 by Manu Dibango on Atlantic 2971.

The Skull Snaps (members Sam Culley, Ervin Waters, George Bragg and R. Smith)

GSF 6902 - I'm Your Pimp / I'm Your Pimp (Long Version) - 1974 (U. K. Bootleg)
Grill 301 - Ain't That Lovin' You / Al's Razor Blade – 1975

Melvin Bliss / The Skull Snaps

Alpha Omega Ao-9501 - Synthetic Substitution / It's A New Day* - 1998 *flip by The Skull Snaps. (12" - 33 1/3 rpm U. K. release)

Lp's

GSF 1011 - The Skull Snaps - 1973
Tracks:

M M R Incorporated ? - ? - ? Tracks: My Hang Up Is You / Having You Around / Didn't I Do It To You / All Of A Sudden / It's A New Day /// I'm Your Pimp / I Turn My Back On Love / Trespassing / I'm Falling Out Of Love.

CD's

The Diplomats

Collectables Vcl 5733 - Here's A Heart - 1996 Tracks: Here's A Heart / He's Got You Now / Unchained Melody / Cards On The Table / Help Me / Hey Mr. Taxi Driver / I'm So Glad I Found You / I Can Give You Love / Accept Me / Your Love Is A Shelter / In My Heart / It's Not How You Make Love / There's Still A Tomorrow / So Far Away / I've Got A Feeling / Love Ain't What It Used To Be / Honest To Goodness.

Soulful Kinda Music – The Rare Soul Bible Volume Two

The Skull Snaps

Charly B00000B8K1 - Skull Snaps - 1999 (U. K. Release)
Tracks:

The Diplomats

Kent Cdkend 232 - The Diplomats Greatest Recordings - 2004 (U. K. Release)
Tracks: Perfect Love (2:14) / Cards On The Table (2:43) / Can't Get You Off My Mind (2:36) / Here's A Heart (2:30) / Accept Me (2:40) / I'm So Glad I Found You (3:01) / Our Love Has Changed (3:08) / Love Ain't What It Used To Be (2:38) / I Really Love You (2:15) / Jerking Time (2:21) / Honest To Goodness (2:05) / Don't Bug Me (2:22) / I Can Give You Love (3:10) / He's Got You Now (2:32) / Help Me (2:29) / Forever (2:31) / Sure As The Stars Shine (3:13) / So Far Away (3:10) / I've Got The Kind Of Love (3:38) / I Am A Witness (2:44) / Don't Ever Go (2:39) / Unchained Melody (2:21) / Walk With Me (2:27) / Hey, Mr. Taxi Driver (2:04) / Soul Teacher - By Sam, Erv & Tom (2:27).

Willie Dixon

Willie Dixon & The Big Wheels (Members: Willie Dixon, Bobby Pointer, James Carr, Sonny Thompson, ?)

Federal 12524 - Our Kind Of Love / Uncle Willie's Got A Thing Going On - 1964

Wyllie Dixon & The Big Wheels (Chy Town) (Members:Willie Dixon, James Carr, Bobby Pointer, Robert Goley

Chitown 101 - Sweet Pea / Sad Times - 1965

Wylliee Dixon

Checker 1164 - How Long Must I Wait / Just Like A Woman - 1966
Toddlin' Town 114 - When Will It End / Gotta Hold On - 1967

Symtec Simmons & Wylie Dixon

Toddlin' Town 4023 - Stay With Me For Better Or Worse / Socking Soul Power - 1969

Bobby Marchan & Willie Dixon / Bobby Marchan

Ace 3008 - God Blessed Our Love / My Day Is Coming - 1975

Wylie Dixon & The Wheels

Jerma 104 - Sad Times / I Guess I Love You - 1976

Soulful Kinda Music – The Rare Soul Bible Volume Two

Willie Dixon

Why 1 - It Don't Make Sense (You Can't Make Peace) / It's In The News - 1982

Johnny Dynamite

Johnny Dynamite (B. John Henry Adams Jr in Milton, Florida)

Format 5001 - Baby (Wish You Were Here) / Midnite Hour
Minaret 141 - The Night They Angels Cried / Everybody's Clown - 1969

Label Listings

DCP

1001 - Crampton Sisters - I Didn't Know What Time It Was / I Cried When I Found You Gone
1002 - Don Costa - Love Theme From Tom Jones / Off Broadway
1003 - Teddy Randazzo - Pretty Blue Eyes / Doo Dah
1004 - Sandy Stewart - Draw Me a Circle / Little Child
1005 - Chantiers - Dear Mr. Clock / Peppermint
1006 - Kathy Keegan - Different Kind of Love / Something Simple
1007 - Ray Allen - He Don't Love You Anymore / Please Make Up Your Mind
1008 - Benny & The Bedbugs - Beatle Beat / Roll Over Beethoven
1009 - Bobby Wilding - I Want to Be a Beatle / Since I've Been Wearing My Hair Like a Beatle
1100 - Don Costa - Main Street / Theme From Golden Boy
1101 - Crampton Sisters - If You Were The Only Boy in The World / It's Gonna Take a Miracle
1102 - Laura Greene - Melancholy Serenade / Sunday, Monday or Always
1103 - Ray Allen - No Top Suit / Yesterday is Sweet
1104 - Little Anthony & The Imperials - I'm on The Outside / Please Go
1105 - Kathy Keegan - When You're Young And In Love / Meditation
1106 - Bobby Wilding - I Want You / Too Young to Fall in Love
1107 - Crampton Sisters - My Guy is Boss / Always
1108 - Teddy Randazzo - Less Than Tomorrow / Lost Without You
1109 - Betty Mabry - Get Ready For Betty / I'm Gonna Get My Baby Back
1110 - Ferraris of Canada - Girls / Please Tell Her
1111 - Jekyll & Hyde - My Baby Loves Monster Movies / Theme From Whodunit
1112 - Gallows Singers - Mama Don't Allow / Long Time Boy
1113 - Bobby Hart - That'll Be The Day / Turn on Your Lovelight
1114 - Simpson Sisters - I Tore Up My Diary / I Don't Wanna Dance

Soulful Kinda Music – The Rare Soul Bible Volume Two

1115 - ?
1116 - Empires - Have Mercy / Love is Strange
1117 - Jesse Young - If You Love Me / Love Me Forever
1118 - ?
1119 - Little Anthony & The Imperials - Goin' Out of My Head / Make It Easy on Yourself
1120 - June Valli - Empty Rooms / I'm Made For Love
1121 - Don Costa - If I Had a Hammer / Put Your Head on My Shoulder
1122 - Sandy Stewart - Yellow And Green Make Me Blue / I;ll Never Go There Anymore
1123 - Mike Scott - Frankie's Angel / Gold Bug
1124 - Don Costa - I Will Wait For You / Pretty Blue Eyes
1125 - Pearlean Gray - For Your Love / Have You Ever Had The Blues
1126 - Jekyll & Hyde - Frankenstein Meets The Beatles / Dracula Drag
1127 - Kathy Keegan - I Want to Be With You / This is The Life
1128 - Little Anthony & The Imperials - Hurt So Bad / Reputation
1129 - Minets of England - My Love is Yours / Wake Up
1130 - Lee Davey - I Won't Stop You / Yeah, Look at This Love
1131 - Donna Fuller - Who Am I / Off Broadway
1132 - Don Costa - Elise / How to Murder Your Wife
1133 - Larry Banks - I Don't Wanna Do It / I'm Comin' Home
1134 - Teddy Randazzo - You Don't Need a Heart / As Long As I Live
1135 - Johnny Cymbal - Go V.W. Go / Sorrow And Pain
1136 - Little Anthony & The Imperials - Take Me Back / Our Song
1137 - Donna Fuller - I Will Wait For You / Again
1138 - ?
1139 - Secrets - No Matter What You Do To Me / Shy Guy
1140 - Ferrari's of Canada - He's Just a Little Boy / Tennessee Waltz
1141 - Nicole Quasee - Someone to Light Up My Life / Watch What Happens
1142 - Bobby Hart - Jealous Feeling / Baby Let Your Hair Down
1143 - Pearlean Gray - Don't Rush Me Baby / Let Them Talk
1144 - Gayle Harris - Ain't Gonna Let It Get Me Down / Here I Go Again
1145 - Rat Pack - Crazy Crazy Love / I Can Do The Mouse Now
1146 - Johnny Cymbal - My Last Day / Summertime's Here at Last
1147 - Kenny & The Impacts - Heartaches / Wishing Well
1148 - Roger Joyce - Because It's All Over Now / No One But The Lonely
1149 - Little Anthony & The Imperials - I Miss You So / Get Out of My Life
1150 - Impacts - Just Because / Pigtails
1151 - Linda Carr - Heart Without Love / I Should Be Happy For Baby
1152 - Bobby Hart - Around The Corner / Cry My Eyes Out
1153 - Teddy Randazzo - You're Not That Girl Anymore / Soul
1154 - Little Anthony & The Imperials - Hurt / Never Again

Dionn

500 - Brenda & The Tabulations - Dry Your Eyes / The Wash - 1966
501 - Brenda & The Tabulations - Stay Together Young Lovers / Who's Lovin You - 1967

Soulful Kinda Music – The Rare Soul Bible Volume Two

502 - Bill Lucas - Cause I Know Your Mine / I Don't Wanna Ever Love Again - 1967
503 - Brenda & The Tabulations - Just Once In A Lifetime / Hey Boy - 1967
504 - Brenda & The Tabulations - When Your Gone / Hey Boy - 1967
505 - The Ordells - Sippin'a Cup Of Coffee / Big Dom - 1967
506 - The Vareeations - The Time / Ssab-Berom - 1968
507 - The Brenda & Tabulations - Baby You're So Right For Me / To The One I Love - 1968
508 - Moses Smith - The Girl Across The Street / Hey Love - 1968
509 - Brenda & The Tabulations - That's In The Past / I Can't Get Over You - 1968
510 - The Vareeations - Foolish One / It's The Loving Season - 1968
511 - Brenda & The Tabulations - A Reason To Live / Hey Boy - 1969
512 - Brenda & The Tabulations - That's The Price You Have To Pay / I Wish I Hadn't Done That - 1968

Drew

1001 - Precisions - Such A Misery / A Lovers Plea - 1966
1002 - Precisions - Why Girl / What I Want - 1967
1003 - Precisions - If This Is Love (I'd Rather Be Lonely) / You'll Soon Be Gone - 1967
1004 - Precisions - Instant Heartbreak (Just Add Tears) / Dream Girl - 1968
1005 - Precisions - A Place / Never Let Her Go - 1968
1006 - Precisions - Sugar Ain't Sweet / What I Want

D-Town

1021 – Ronnie Love – Judy / Show Me What You Got
1022 – Don Heart – They Love To Be Loved / A Telegram With Love
1023 - ?
1024 – Dee Edwards – Too Careless With My Love / He Told Me Lies
1025 – Terri Day – I'm So Glad / Hey Fella
1026 - ?
1027 – Ronnie Love – Deed I Do / Always Be Good
1028 – Armand Kay – The Bigger They Are / My Love My Love
1029 – Lee Rogers – Sad Affair / Doggin' Myself Around
1030 – Don Heart – Don't Give In / I'm Gonna Make A Comeback
1031 – Dee Edwards – Oh What A Party / The Greatest Thrill
1032 – Cody Black – Move On / These Chains Of Love
1033 – The Precisions – My Lover Came Back / I Wanna Tell My Baby
1034 – Dick Kruz & The Fugitives – A Fugitive / (Instrumental)
1035 – Lee Rogers – Our Love Is More / I Want You To Have Everything
1036 – Rudy Robinson Trio – Chicken Scratch Part 1 / Part 2
1037 – Dee Edwards – Happiness Is Where You Find It / What Love Can Do
1038 – The Dimensions – Little Lotta Lou / He's A Lover
1039 – Marco Hammon – Me Boy You Girl / While I'm Away From You
1040 – Ronnie Love – Come Dance With Me / She's Got Love
1040 - The Hesitations / Don Sweet & The Hesitations - Wild Little Willie / Remember

Soulful Kinda Music – The Rare Soul Bible Volume Two

(Two releases on the same number)
1041 – Lee Rogers – You're The Cream Of The Crop / Everybody Else Will
1042 – Chuck Hentley – I'm Gonna Try To Get Over / I Cry Love
1043 – Silky Hargraves – Go On Girl / Hurt By Love
1044 – The Fugitives – On Trial / Let's Get On With It
1045 - ?
1046 - ?
1047 – Ronnie Love – Judy / Detroit Michigan
1048 – Dee Edwards – Tired Of Staying Home / His Majesty My Love
1049 – The Fabulous Peps – Detroit Michigan / Never Had It So Good
1050 – Lee Rogers – Boss Love / Just You And I
1051 – Lillian Dupree – Hide And Seek / (I've Got A) Shield Around My Heart
1052 – Jimmy 'Soul' Clark – That Ain't Cool / You're The Sweetest Thing I Know
1053 - ?
1054 – Romey Rand – Say You're Mine / I'm Coming In
1055 – The Precisions – Mexican Love Song / You're Sweet
1056 - ?
1057 – Cody Black – Mr Blue / You Must Be In Love
1058 – Roosevelt Grier – Pizza Pie Man / Welcome To The Club
1059 – Jackie & The Tonetts – The Proof Of Your Love / Steady Boy
1060 – The Peps – This I Pray / Thinkin' About You
1061 - ?
1062 – Lee Rogers – My One And Only / You Won't Have To Wait Till Christmas
1063 – Dee Edwards – All The Way Home / Love Love Love
1064 – Buddy Lamp – Just A Little Bit Of Lovin' / Next Best Think
1065 – The Fabulous Peps – Speak Your Peace / My Love Looks Good On You
1066 – Cody Black – Would You Let Me Know / Too Many Irons In The Fire
1067 – Lee Rogers – I'm A Practical Guy / Go Go Girl
1068 – De Andre Trio – Batman Theme / Who Can I Turn To
1069 – L'il Soul Brothers – I've Got A Headache / What Can I Be
502 – Lee Rogers – Just You And I / Boss Love
8016 – Lee Rogers – Rockin Skates / It Must Be Love Coming Down On Me
8018 – Jena Johnson – Livin' In Love In New York / ?
8100 – Joey Rubins Jr – Let The Beat Groove You On / Together Again
8108 – Cardella Demillo – Gimmie Whatcha Promised Me / Inst
940 – Coy's Toyz – Come And Get It / ?

Duke

101 – Roscoe Gordon – Hey Fat Girl / Tell Daddy – 1952
102 – Johnny Ace – My Song / Follow The Rule – 1952
103 – Earl Forrest – Rock The Bottle / Baby Baby – 1952
104 – Mighty Dukes – No Other Love / Why Can't I Have You – 1952
105 – Bobby Bland – Lovin' Blues / I O U Blues – 1952
106 – Roscoe Gordon – T Model Boogie / New Orleans Woman – 1953
107 – Johnny Ace – Angel / Cross My Heart – 1953
108 – Earl Forrest & The Beale Streters – Whoopin' & Hollerin' / Pretty Bessie – 1953
109 – Roscoe Gordon – Too Many Women / Wise To You Baby – 1953

Soulful Kinda Music – The Rare Soul Bible Volume Two

110 – St Louis Jimmy – Drinkin' Woman / Why Work – 1953
111 – Bonita Cole & Bill Fort – Life's Like That / Gatemouth's Ghost – 1953
112 – Johnny Ace – The Clock / Ace's High – 1953
113 – Earl Forrest – Last Night's Dream / Fifty Three – 1953
114 – Roscoe Gordon – Rosco's Mambo / Ain't No Use – 1953
115 – Bobby Bland – Army Blues / No Blow No Show – 1953
116 – The 4 Dukes – Crying In The Chapel / I Done Done It – 1953
117 – Google Eyes August – Oh What A Fool / Play The Game – 1953
118 – Johnny Ace – Saving My Love For You / Yes Baby – 1953
119 – The Peacocks – Better Stop – Sad Story – 1954
120 – Little Junior Parker – Dirty Friend Blues / Can't Understand – 1954
121 – Earl Forrest – Out On A Party / Oh Why – 1954
122 – Long John – Crazy Girl / She Used To Be My Woman – 1954
123 – Lester Williams – Good Lovin' Baby / Let's Do It – 1954
124 – Charles Edwins – Bong Gone / I Got Loose – 1954
125 – The Sultans – Good Thing Baby / How Deep Is The Ocean – 1954
126 – Lovey Lewis – Alrighty Baby / Take A Chance With Me – 1954
127 – Little Junior Parker –Sittin' Drinkin' And Thinkin' / Please Baby Please – 1954
128 – Johnny Ace – You've Been Gone So Long / Please Forgive Me – 1954
129 – Roscoe Gordon – Three Can't Love / You Figure It Out – 1954
130 – Earl Forrest – Your Kind Of Love / Ooh Ooh Wee – 1954
131 – Lester Williams – Crazy 'Bout You Baby / Don't Take Your Love From Me – 1954
132 – Johnny Ace – Never Let Me Go / Burley Cutie – 1954
133 – The Sultans – I Cried My Heart Out / Baby Don't Put Me Down - 1954
134 – Google Eyes August – Lead Us On / ? – 1954
135 – The Sultans – What Makes Me Feel This Way / Boppin' With The Mambo – 1954
136 – Johnny Ace – Pledging My Love / No Money – 1955
136 – Johnny Ace – Pledging My Love / Anymore – 1955
137 – Little Junior Parker – Backtracking / I Wanna Ramble – 1955
138 – ?
139 – Junior Ryder – Don't Tell Nobody / Every Star I See – 1955
140 – Jewel Brown – No You Can't Kiss / Where Do I Go From Here – 1955
141 – Bobby Bland – It's My Life Baby / Time Out – 1955
142 – Billy Brooks – Song Of The Dreamer / Mambo Is Everywhere - 1955
143 – Carl Van Moon – Why Does It Have To Be Me / Lonesome Road – 1955
144 – Johnny Ace – Anymore / How Can You Be So Mean – 1955
145 – Billy Brooks – I'm Gone / Donna – 1955
146 – Bobby Bland – You Or None – Woke Up Screaming – 1955
147 – Little Junior Parker – Driving Me / There Better Not Be No Feel – 1955
148 – Johnny Ace – So Lonely -/ I'm Crazy – 1956
149 – Billy Brooks – This Is My Prayer / I Want You Love – 1956
150 – Randy Ship – Am I To Blame / Baby I Need You – 1956
151 – Carl Van Moon – My Love / You're Simply Drivin' Me Mad – 1956
152 – ?
153 – Bobby Bland – You've Got Bad Intentions / I Can't Put You Down – 1956
154 – Johnny Ace – Still Love You So / Don't You Know – 1956
155 – Buddy Ace – What Can I Do / Back Home – 1956
156 – Mr 'Google Eyes' August – Lead Us On / Oh Ho Doddle Lu – 1956

Soulful Kinda Music – The Rare Soul Bible Volume Two

157 – Junior Parker – Mother-In-Law Blues / That's My Baby – 1956
158 – Paul Perryman – Just To Hold My Hand / I'm Crying - 1956
159 – Chuck Edwards – If You Love Me / You Move Me – 1956
160 – Bobby Bland – I Learned My Lesson / I Don't Believe / Lead Us On – 1956
161 – Jo Ann Mitchell – I'll Make It Up / I'm Walking Out On You – 1956
162 – Paul Perryman – Just For Your Call / Yes I Do – 1956
163 – Chuck Edwards – Let's Rock N Roll / I'm Wondering – 1957
164 – Little Junior Parker – My Dolly Bee / Next Time You See Me – 1957
165 – Roscoe Gordon – Keep On Doggin' / Bad Dream – 1957
166 – Leo Baxter – No Nights Without You / No Longer Wanted – 1957
167 – Bobby Bland – Don't Want No Woman / I Smell Trouble – 1957
168 – Little Junior Parker – That's Alright / Pretty Baby – 1957
169 – Paul Perryman – Nobody Loves Me / Long Enough – 1957
170 – Bobby Bland – Farther Up The Road / Sometime Tomorrow – 1957
171 – ?
172 – Brooks & Brown – Sleeping In An Ocean Of Tears / They Call Her Rosalie – 1957
173 – Roscoe Gordon – I've Loved And Lost / Tummer Tee – 1957
174 – Chuck Edwards – Morning Train / Warm My Heart – 1957
175 – El Torros – Yellow Hand / Dance With Me – 1957
176 – Buddy Ace – It Can't Be True / I'm In The Mood – 1957
177 – Little Junior Parker – Peaches / Pretty Little Doll – 1957
178 – The Sultans – My Love Is So High / If I Could Tell – 1957
179 – Capistranos – Now Darling / Po Mary – 1957
180 – Joe Medwick – Never In Love Before / Smile And Say Goodbye – 1958
181 – Paul Perryman – Satellite Fever Asiatic Flu / I'm Walking Out – 1958
182 – Bobby Bland – Bobby's Blues / Teach Me – 1958
183 – Buddy Ace – Whooping And Hollering / Darling It's You – 1958
184 – Little Junior Parker – Wondering / Sitting And Thinking – 1958
185 – Bobby Bland – You Got Me Where You Want Me / Loan A Helping Hand – 1958
186 – Little Sonny – I Gotta Find My Baby / Hear My Woman Calling – 1958
187 – James Davies – What Else Is There To Do / Come To The Rock N Roll – 1958
188 – Five Jades – Without Your Love / Rock And Roll Molly – 1958
189 – Joe Medwick – You Still Send Me / I Have Confidence In You – 1958
190 – Fenton & The Castle Rockers – The Freeze / Double Freeze – 1958
191 – Fenton Robinson – Crazy Crazy Loving – Mississippi Steamboat – 1958
192 – Larry Davies – I Tried / Texas Flood – 1958
193 – Little Junior Parker – Barefoot Rock / What Did I Do – 1958
194 – El Torros – Barbara Jean / You Look Good To Me - 1958
195 – Paul Perryman – Just To Be Close To You / While You Wait – 1958
196 – Bobby Bland – Little Boy Blue – Last Night – 1958
197 – Long Tall Lester – Working Man / All Because Of You – 1958
198 – Miss La-Vell – Teen-Age Love / If I Could Be With You – 1958
199 – Buddy Ace – Beyond The Rainbow / Angel Baby – 1958

Duke Gospel Series were released on catalogue numbers starting 200 to 216

300 – Bobby Bland – You Did Me Wrong / I Lost Sight Of The World – 1959
301 – Junior Parker – Sometimes / Sweet Home Chicago – 1959

Soulful Kinda Music – The Rare Soul Bible Volume Two

302 – Chester McDowall – Baby Don't Leave Me / I Wonder Why – 1959
303 – Bobby Bland – Wishing Well / I'm Not Ashamed – 1959
304 – Ted Taylor – Be Ever Wonderful / Since You're Home – 1959
305 – Paul Perryman – Paul Loves Betty / Teenage Romeo – 1959
306 – Little Junior Parker – Five Long Years / I'm Holding On – 1959
307 – Miss La Vell – Yes I've Been Crying / Stop These Teardrops – 1959
308 – Ted Taylor – Count The Stars / Hold Me Tight – 1959
309 – Little Junior Parker – Stranded / Blue Letter – 1959
310 – Bobby Bland – Is It Real / Someday – 1959
311 – Joe Medwick – Searchin' In Vain / Johnny Brown – 1959
312 – Fenton Robinson – School Boy / As The Years Go By – 1959
313 – Larry Davies – My Little Girl / Angels In Houston – 1959
314 – Bobby Bland – I'll Take Care Of You / That's Why – 1959
315 – Little Junior Parker – Dangerous Woman / Belinda Marie – 1960
316 – Chester McDowall – Tell Me Now / Joy In My Tears – 1960
317 – Little Junior Parker – The Next Time / You're On My Mind – 1960
318 – Bobby Bland – Lead Me On / Hold Me Tenderly – 1960
319 – Peppermint Harris – Ain't No Business / Angel Child – 1960
320 – Roscoe Gordon – Dilly Bop / You'll Never Know – 1960
321 – El Torros – Dance With Me / What's The Matter – 1960
322 – Miss La Vell – Stolen Love / You're The Most – 1960
323 – Ernie Harris – With You / If I – 1960
324 – Little Buck – I'll Follow You / Let It Be Now – 1960
325 – Buddy Ace – Won't You Reconsider / This Little Love Of Mine – 1960#
326 – Little Junior Parker – I'll Learn To Love Again / That's Just Alright – 1960
327 – Bobby Bland – Cry Cry Cry / I've Been Wrong So Long – 1960
328 – Larry Davies – Come Home / Will She Come Home – 1960
329 – Fenton Robinson – Tennessee Woman / You've Got To Pass This Way Again – 1960
330 – Little Junior Parker – Stand By Me / I'll Forget About You – 1960
331 – Jimmy Wilson – My Heart Cries Out For You / Easy Easy Baby – 1961
332 – Bobby Bland - I Pity The Fool / Close To You – 1961
333 – El Torros – Two Lips / You May Say Yes – 1961
334 – Miss La Vell – Just Look At You Fool / Tides Of Love – 1961
335 – Little Junior Parker – Driving Wheel / Seven Days – 1961
336 – Bobby Bland – How Does A Cheating Woman Feel / Don't Cry No More – 1961
337 – Little Buck – Go On With Your Dancing / So Fine So Sweet – 1961
338 – Bobby Bland – Ain't That Loving You / Jelly Jelly Jelly – 1961
339 – Jimmy Wilson – I Don't Care / Patiently – 1961
340 – Bobby Bland – Don't Cry No More / St James Infirmry – 1961
341 – Little Junior Parker – In The Dark / How Long Can This Go One – 1961
342 – Johnny Brown – Suspense / Snakehips – 1961
343 – James Davis – What Else Is There To Do / Come To The Rock N Roll – 1961
344 – Bobby Bland – Who Will The Next Fool Be / You're The One – 1961
345 – Little Junior Parker – Annie Get Your Yo Yo / Mary Jo – 1961
346 - Buddy Ace – What Can I Do / Screaming Please – 1962
347 – Bobby Bland – Who Will The Next Fool Be /Blue Moon – 1962
348 – Clint Gant – Just Like You Like It / All Mine – 1962
349 – Earl Forrest – Memphis Twist / Beale St Popeye – 1962
350 – Willie Mays – My Sad Heart / If You Love Me – 1962

Soulful Kinda Music – The Rare Soul Bible Volume Two

351 – Junior Parker – I Feel Alright Again / Sweeter As The Days Go By – 1962
352 – Bobby Bland – Yield Not To Temptation / How Does A Cheating Woman Feel – 1962
353 – El Torros – Doop Doop A Walla Walla / Mama's Cookin' – 1962
354 – Carl Greenstreet – If You Only Say I Do / The Way The Wind Blows – 1962
355 – Bobby Bland – Stormy Monday Blues / Your Friends – 1962
356 – Otis Rush – Homework / I Have To Laugh – 1962
357 – Junior Parker – Foxy Devil / Someone Somewhere – 1962
358 – C & C Boys – Hey Marvin / You Stole My Heart – 1962
359 – James Davies – I'm Gonna Tell It On Ya / My Precious Darling – 1962
360 – Bobby Bland – Call On Me / That's The Way Love Is – 1962
361 – Buddy Ace – Good Lover / She Will Love – 1963
362 – Junior Parker – It's A Pity / Last Night – 1963
363 – Earl Forrest – The Crown / The Duck – 1963
364 – Junior Parker – If You Don't Love Me / I Can't Forget About You – 1963
365 – Clarence & Calvin – Somebody Better Come Here Quick / I Like It – 1963
366 – Bobby Bland – Sometimes You Gotta Cry A Little / You're Worth It All – 1963
367 – Junior Parker – The Tables Have Turned / Yonsders Wall – 1963
368 – James Davies – Blue Monday / Sing – 1963
369 – Bobby Bland – Ain't It A Good Thing / Queen For A Day – 1963
370 – Bobby Bland – The Feeling Is Gone / I Can't Stop Singing – 1963
371 – Junior Parker – Strange Things Happening / I'm Gonna Stop – 1964
372 – Miss La-Vell – Why Young Men Go Wild / Run To You – 1964
373 – Buddy Ace – It Makes You Want To Cry / You've Got My Love – 1964
374 – James Davis – Chains Around My Heart / Your Turn To Cry – 1964
375 – Bobby Bland – Ain't Nothing You Can Do / After It's Too Late – 1964
376 – Junior Parker – Things I Used To Do / That's Why I'm Always Crying – 1964
377 – Bobby Bland – Share Your Love With Me / After It's Too Late – 1964
378 – Ernie K-Doe – Looking Into The Future / My Mother In Law (Is In My Hair Again) – 1964
379 – C & C Boys – It's All Over Now / My Life – 1964
380 – Brother & Sisters Of Soul – I Don't Like It / Let It Be Me – 1964
381 – Buddy Ace – My Love / True Love Money Can't Buy – 1964
382 – Miss La-Vell – Best Part Of Me / Everybody's Got Somebody – 1964
383 – Bobby Bland – Ain't Doing Too Bad Part 1 / Part 2 – 1964
384 – Junior Parker – I'm In Love / Jivin' Woman – 1964
385 – Bobby Bland – These Hands (Small But Mighty) / Today – 1964
386 – Bobby Bland – Blind Man / Black Night – 1965
387 – Ernie K-Doe – Little Bit Of Everything / Someone – 1965
388 – Clarence & Calvin – Lip Service / You're Gonna Come Down – 1965
389 – Junior Parker – Crying For My Baby / Guess You Don't Know (The Golden Rule) – 1965
390 – Bobby Bland – Ain't No Telling / Dust Got In Daddy's Eyes – 1965
391 – Buddy Ace – Inside Story / Just Hold My Hand – 1965
392 – James Davis – Bad Dream / Ain't It Great – 1965
393 – Bobby Bland – I've Too Far Gone (To Turn Around) / If You Could Read My Mind – 1965
394 – Junior Parker – These Kind Of Blues Part 1 / Part 2 – 1966
395 – Ida Fisher – Bad Understanding / No Request – 1966
396 – Jimmy Outler – It's All Over / Three Little Pigs – 1966

Soulful Kinda Music – The Rare Soul Bible Volume Two

397 – Buddy Ace – Nothing In The World Can Hurt Me (Except You) / It's Gonna Be Me – 1966
398 – Junior Parker – Walking The Floor Over You / Goodbye Little Girl – 1966
399 – Clarence Green & The Rhythmaires – I Saw You Last Night / Keep A Workin' – 1966
400 – Ernie K-Doe – Please Don't Stop / Boomerang – 1966
401 – Buddy Ace – Baby Please Don't Go / Who Can Tell – 1966
402 – Bobby Bland – Good Time Charlie Part 1 / Part 2 – 1966
403 – Riff Ruffin – Peepin' & Hidin' / Thunder & Lightning – 1966
404 – Ernie K-Doe – Little Marie / Somebody Told Me – 1966
405 – ?
406 – Junior Parker – Get Away Blues / Why Do You Make Me Cry – 1966
407 – Bobby Bland – Poverty / Building A Fire With Rain – 1966
408 – Sylvia Maddox – Got To Be Free / Vietnam Blues – 1966
409 – ?
410 – Clarence green & the rhythmaires – I'm wondering / what y'all waiting on me – 1966
411 – Ernie K-Doe – Later For Tomorrow / Dancin' Man – 1966
412 – Bobby Bland – I Ain't Myself Anymore / Back In The Same Old Bag Again – 1966
413 – Junior Palker – Man Or Mouse / Wait For Another Day – 1966
414 – Buddy Ace – Come On In This House / Hold Onto This Old Fool – 1967
415 – ?
416 – Bobby Bland – You're All I Need / Deep In My Soul – 1967
417 – John Roberts & The Hurricanes – The Hurricane / Cold-Hearted Woman – 1967
418 – Willie Mays – My Sad Heart / If You Love Me – 1967
419 – Buddy Ace – I'm Counting On You / Something For These Blues – 1967
420 – Ernie K-Doe – Love Me Like I Wanna / Don't Kill My Groove – 1967
421 – Bobby Bland – Getting Used To The Blues / That Did It – 1967
422 – Augustine Twins – Everyday Of My / My Place – 1967
423 – Ernie K-Doe – Little Marie / Until The Real Thing Comes Along – 1967
424 – Clarence Green – Groundhog / What Happened To Us – 1967
425 – John Roberts – Sockin' 1-2-3-4 / Sophisticated Funk – 1967
426 – Bobby Bland – Shoes / Touch Of The Blues – 1967
427 – The Lamp Sisters – I Thought It Was All Over / Woman With The Blues – 1968
428 – Buddy Ace – Darling Depend On Me / Got To Get Myself Together – 1968
429 – John Roberts – Something Reminds Me / To Be My Girl – 1968
430 – ?
431 – ?
432 – Bobby Bland – Driftin' Blues / You Could Read My Mind / A Piece Of Gold – 1968
433 – Bobby Bland – Honey Child / A Piece Of Gold - 1968
434 – ?
435 – Bobby Bland – Save Your Love For Me / Share Your Love With Me – 1968
436 – John Roberts – I'll Forget You / Be My Baby – 1968
437 – Ernie K-Doe – Gotta Pack My Bag / How Sweet You Are – 1968
438 – Buddy Lamp – I'm Coming Home / Where Have You Been – 1968
439 – The Lamp Sisters – No Cure For The Blues / You Caught Me Napping – 1968
440 – Bobby Bland – Rockin' In The Same Old Boat / Wouldn't You Rather Have Me

Soulful Kinda Music – The Rare Soul Bible Volume Two

– 1968
441 – Buddy Ace – Sweet Little Chocolate Child / Jump Up And Shout – 1969
442 – John Roberts – Baby I Need Somebody / It's All Over – 1969
443 – ?
444 – Fred Ford – Blackeyed Rattlesnake / Last Chance – 1969
445 – ?
446 – ?
447 – Bobby Bland – Gotta Get To Know You / Baby I'm On My Way – 1969
448 – The Lamp Sisters – Sweet Daddy Soul / Today Will Be Yesterday Tomorrow – 1969
449 – Bobby Bland – Chains Of Love / Ask Me 'Bout Nothing (But The Blues) – 1969
450 – Ernie K-Doe – I'm Sorry / Trtying To Make Me Love You – 1969
451 – Paulette Parker – (Gimmie Back) My Love / Should I Let Him Go – 1969
452 – Buddy Ace – Never Let Me Go / She's My Baby – 1969
453 – ?
454 – John Roberts – Pledging My Love / Something Reminds Me – 1970
455 – Paulette Parker – Driving Wheel / I Pity The Fool – 1970
456 – Ernie K-Doe – I'll Make Everything Be Alright / Wishing In Vain – 1970
457 – The Malibus – The Robot / I Just Can't Stand It – 1970
458 – Bobby Bland – If You've Got A Heart / Sad Feeling – 1970
459 – John Roberts – Come Back And Stay Forever / I'll Always Remember – 1970
460 – Bobby Bland – Lover With A Reputation / If Love Ruled The World – 1970
461 – Buddy Lamp – Devil's Gonna Get You / Wall Around Your Heart – 1970
462 – The Lamp Sisters – Ride On / The Way I Love This Man – 1970
463 – Bob Conerly – Little Girls Go Home / A Whole Lot Of Soul Is Gone – 1970
464 – Bobby Bland – Keep On Loving Me (You'll See The Change) / I Just Got To Forget About You – 1970
465 – Marc Antonym – Christmas Together Part 1 / Part 2 – 1971
466 – Bobby Bland – I'm Sorry / Yum Yum Tree – 1971
467 – Hot Chocolates – Keep My Baby Cool / Who Do You Call – 1971
468 – Buddy Lamp – Hen Pecked / If You See Kate – 1971
469 – ?
470 – Eddie Simpson – The Lonely Season – Big Black Funky Slave – 1971
471 – Bobby Bland – Shape Up Or Ship Out / Love That We Share (Is True) - 1971
472 – Bobby Bland – Do What You Set Out To Do / Ain't Nothing You Can Do – 1972
473 – Rhonda Davis – Can You Remember / A Long Walk On A Short Pier – 1972
474 – The Greer Brothers – Let Me Stay A Part Of You / We Don't Dig No Busing – 1973
475 – Jo Ann Garrett – I'm Under Your Control / Sting Me Baby – 1973
476 – Masters Of Soul – I Can See It In Your Eyes / I Hate You – 1973
477 – Bobby Bland – I'm So Tired / If You Could Read My Mind – 1974
478 – Masters Of Soul – Should I Just Read The Signs / I Hate You – 1974
479 – White Family Band – I'm A Little Bit Smarter Now / Miss America Stand Up – 1974
480 – Bobby Bland – I Don't Want Another Mountain To Climb / That's All There Is – 1974
481 – Masters Of Soul – Lovely Little Lassie / Star Child - 1974

Dynamo

Soulful Kinda Music – The Rare Soul Bible Volume Two

101 – Tommy Hunt – Biggest Man / Never Love A Robin
102 – Inez & Charlie Foxx – Tightrope / Baby Take It All
103 – Barbara & Brenda – If I'm Hurt You'll Feel The Pain / Too Young To Be Fooled
104 – Inez & Charlie Foxx – I Stand Accused / Guilty
105 – Tommy Hunt – Words Can Never Tell It / How Can I Be Anything
106 – Kenny Ballard – Down To My Last Heartbreak / There Will Never Be Another You
107 – The Daydreams – Been Ready For A Long Time / Sit Down And Think
108 – Barbara & Brenda – Never Love A Robin / Sally's Party
109 – Inez & Charlie Foxx – Hard To Get / You Are The Man
110 – Tommy Hunt – Complete Man / Searchin' For My Love
111 – Stanley Mitchell – Quit Twisting My Arm / Get It Baby
112 – Inez & Charlie Foxx – (1-2-3-4-5-6-7) Count The Days / A Stranger I Don't Know
113 – Lee Moses – I Need A Woman Of My Own / Your Man
114 – Brooks & Jerry – I Got What It Takes Part 1 / Part 2
115 – Lee Moses – Never In My Life / If Loving You Is Crime
116 – Sam, Erv & Tom – Hard To Get / Soul Teacher
117 – Inez & Charlie Foxx – Undecided / Ain't Going For That
118 – Maskman – The'll Be Some Changes / Never Would Have Made It
119 – Inez & Charlie Foxx – Fellows In Vietnam / Vaya Con Dios
120 – Barbara & Brenda – Don't Wait Uo For Me Mama / Who Put Out The Rumour
121 – The Five O'clock News – Don't Go Angela / Waiting For The Morning
122 – The Diplomats – I Can Give You Love / I'm So Glad I Found You
123 – Billy Clark – The Maskman – Soul Party Part 1 / Part 2
124 – Tommy Hunt – Born Free / Justa Little Taste (Of Your Sweet Lovin')
125 – Maskman & Agents – Yaw'll / One Eye Open
126 – Inez & Charlie Foxx – Come On In / Baby Drop A Dime
127 – Inez & Charlie Foxx - Baby Give It To Me / You Fixed My Heartache
128 – The Green Sisters – Thank You Lord Part 1 / Part 2
129 – The Diplomats – Accept Me / Your Love Is A Shelter
130 - ?
131 – Maskman & The Agents – My Wife My Dog My Cat / Love Bandito
132 – Charles Whitehead – How Can I Forget / Story Of Mr Pitiful
133 – Lucille Brown & Billy Clark – Both Eyes Open / Hot Gravy
134 – Inez & Charlie Foxx & Their Mockin' Band – Speed Ticket / We Got A Chance To Be Free
135 – The Diplomats – In My Heart / It's Not How You Make Love
136 – Maskman & The Agents – Get Away Dreams / I Wouldn't Come Back
137 – The Diplomats – In The Ghetto / I've Got The Kind Of Love
138 – Inez Foxx – North Carolina (South Carolina)
139 – Bethea (& Maskman) – Moon Dream / When You Got Honey
140 - ?
141 – Maskman & The Agents – One Eye Dog In A Meat House / Never Would Have Made It
142 - ?
143 – Bethea (Maskman) & The Agents – It's The Thing / I Wouldn't Come Back

Soulful Kinda Music – The Rare Soul Bible Volume Two

144 – Inez Foxx – Live For Today / You Shouldn't Have Set My Soul On Fire
145 – Harmon Bethea – Put On Your Shoes (And Walk) / Never Would Have Made It
146 – The Jackson Five – You Don't Have To Be Over 21 To Fall In Love / Some Girls Want Me For Their Love
147 – Joe Wilson – Sweetness / When A Man Cries
148 – Maskman – Ain't That Some Shame / Ain't That Some Shame
149 – Joe Wilson – Let A Broken Heart Come In / Your Love Is Sweet

The Patti Drew Story

Born in Charleston, North Carolina, on December 29th, 1944, Patti Drew spent her childhood in Nashville, Tennessee. By 1956 though her family had moved to Chicago, Illinois where her mother obtained employment with a Mr Maury Lathowes.

This was a happy coincidence because Maury was the Chicago Manager for Capitol Records, and Mrs Drew's three eldest daughters; Patti, Lorraine, and Erma just happened to have a singing group. In late 1962, an audition was arranged for the girls with Maury Lathowes. He was suitably impressed and took them to his friend Peter Wright who, following a career as a musician, had formed his own production company.

The collaboration resulted in a contract with Capitol Records, and by 1963 the group's first single (Written by Carlton Black who became a member of the group by virtue of his marriage to Erma Drew) was released under the name of The Drew-Vels.

'Tell Him' became an almost overnight success in the Chicago area, prompting the release of a further two singles, which also were very busy in terms of a local hit in the Chicago area. As was the norm, the group obtained a considerable amount of live work in the Chicago area based on the popularity of the three singles. As also happened quite regularly, the pressures of working as a group overcame the desire to succeed in the charts and the group broke up in 1965.

Peter Wright though had recognised the artistry of Patti Drew especially, so he promptly signed her to a recording contract with his own, newly formed, Quill label. Being rather astute, he also reformed The Drew-Vels without Patti, and signed them as well !

Three singles were released, the first one by The Drew-Vels, and then two from Patti. Although none of them were as popular as the previous Capitol releases, Patti's two singles generated enough business for Capitol to come looking for her and sign her to a solo contract in 1967.

Recognising a good thing when they saw it Capitol then had Patti re-record 'Tell Him' as a solo singer. It paid off, the record charted immediately. Unusually for the time Capitol then released an album by Patti entitled, of course 'Tell Him'. Four further singles quickly followed, but chart success eluded Patti until the release of her fifth Capitol single.

'Workin' On A Groovy Thing / Without A Doubt' returned her to the charts with a bang, reaching #34 on the Billboard Chart and it didn't chart just because of it being a localised hot in Chicago either. This single went into the charts all over the States. In a somewhat ironic way it led to the end of her career some three years on, but more of that later. Because of the national chart status of the single it enabled Patti to tour

extensively all across the US, and also enabled her to record her second album for the label, again named after the hit single, 'Workin! On A Groovy Thing'

The follow up, 'Hard To Handle'/ Just Can't Forget About You' also made the charts in late 1968, and gave Capitol enough faith in Patti to enable her to start recording her third album for the label in as many years.

1969 though was the last year that Patti would hit the charts, this time with 'The Love That A Woman Should Give To A Man / Save The Last Dance For Me'. However, her popularity as a live artist continued, and she was touring fairly constantly throughout the next couple of years only taking a break to record her fourth and final album for Capitol: 'Wild Is Love' in 1970

The album in itself was a departure from her previous style of recording because it was much more Jazz flavoured, and aimed at a slightly different market than her three previous albums. It also demonstrated that Capitol still had enormous faith in Patti Drew. Let's face it, she had only had four charting singles in four years, and here she was releasing her fourth album in the same number of years. Given that the Sixties were still part of the '45's first' ethos of record companies for Black artists this was amazing. Not only that, but the fourth album was also apparently released as a picture disk as well as on the normal black vinyl ! Absolutely unheard of at the time, and I have to wonder whether this would have been the first example of a Black artist releasing a picture disk ?

Sadly though, it was all to come to a rather undignified end in 1971. The pressures of touring had led Patti to form a crippling drug habit, which by late 1971 meant she was unwilling to communicate with anyone from Capitol Records, and to a certain degree anyone else. Fortunately for her sake, her manager at Capitol, Phil Wright rescued her from the situation she was in and took her home to Chicago. (So, if she hadn't had the first national hit, would she have spent so much time touring, and would she have resorted to drugs to get her through it ?)

Although her health recovered, Patti never really returned to her music, and there were no more releases on Capitol, so her contract just expired. A couple of re-issue labels kept her name alive on vinyl over the next couple of years until her final release came in 1975 as a collaboration with Carlton Black for Carl Davis' Innovation II label.

The single was a tribute to the famous at the time, but now more infamous, sporting hero O J Simpson. It completely bombed !

The last involvement with music that I can trace is some live work that Patti did, again with Carlton Black, in a group known as Front Line, but no recordings ever took place.

So there you have it, essentially an eight year career that produced some wonderful Soul music whilst it lasted, but just fizzled out due to overwork and the influence of drugs.

Funnily enough, the last releases Patti Drew has had, have been this year (2007) when the UK Stateside label released a couple of 7" 45s with a green & white

Stateside demo label on them to promote the wonderful CD Bob Fisher & Tony Rounce put together for the Stateside label.

The Delcos

The Delcos were from South Bend, Indiana and all attended South Bend Central High where they all knew each other. By 1962 though, they had all graduated from school when they formed the group. The original members were: Peter Woodard (first and second tenor), Pike Miller (first tenor), Richard Greene (second tenor, baritone), and Otis Smith (bass), and James Thomas (Tenor)

After only a few months, however, they decided that Pike Miller wasn't fitting in and he was asked to leave. He was briefly replaced by his brother, Gilbert, who then also left

The group recorded a whole album of songs, but they were not of sufficient quality to be released having been recorded as rehearsals rather than the finished product recorded in a studio. It was then that Glenn Madison, who knew the rest of the group from school joined, at the same time, James Thomas left and was replaced by Ralph Woods.

In October 1962, the Delcos recorded their first release at the studio of radio station WSBT 'Arabia / These Three Little Words'. Their manager, Juanita Henson's formed her own label to release the single; Ebony Records.

Realising that she might have a hit on her hands Juanita Henson went to Monument Records in Nashville with the hope of better promotion for the single. However Monument had other ideas.

They re-cut both tracks with the group backed by the Boots Randolph Orchestra. The new recording was a far more professional effort, but to me lost the magic of the original Released on the Showcase label (A subsidiary of Monument) in February 1963, it was too late. Any impetus gained from the October '62 Ebony release was gone, and although the group had regional hits, and gained a lot of work from the single, it wasn't enough to secure their future.

Incidentally, the Showcase single was released as a white demo, and then on blue, green, and red labels with the title of the flip side changed from 'These Three Little Words' to 'Those Three Little Words'.

A follow up single was released on Showcase, with a final release on Sound Stage (Which was another Monument subsidiary.) A mystery presents itself here though. Sound Stage 7 2501 is listed as 'Arabia / Those Three Little Words'. However, I can find no evidence that this single was ever released, so if you know different get in touch.

The group eventually broke up when Glenn Madison was drafted for Vietnam, and never got back together again.

E

Big Dee Erwin

The Pastels (members DiFosco Ervin (lead), Richard Travis (first tenor), Tony Thomas (second tenor) and Jimmy Willingham (baritone) the brother of Gus Willingham who was one of the original members of The Cadillacs)

Mascot 123 - Been So Long* / My One And Only Dream - 1957 *written by DiFosco Ervin.
Argo 5287 - Been So Long / My One And Only Dream - 1957
Argo 5297 - You Don't Love Me Anymore / Let's Go To The Rock & Roll Ball - 1958
Argo 5314 - So Far Away / Don't Knock - 1958

Dee Erwin (born 4-August-1939 in New York City, New York died 27-August-1995 in Las Vegas, Nevada, cause: heart failure)

Hull 729 - I Can't Help It (I'm Falling In Love) / Rubin Rubin - 1959
Hull 738 - Let's Try Again / 'Tis Farewell - 1960
Hull 745 - Let's Try Again / 'Tis Farewell -1961?

Dee Irwin

Bliss 1003 - Someday You'll Understand Why / Anytime - 1961

Big Dee Irwin

Dimension 1001 - Everybody's Got A Dance But Me / And Heaven Was Here - 1962
Dimension 1010 - Swinging On A Star* / Another Night With The Boys -
1963 *backing vocals Little Eva.
Dimension 1015 - Happy Being Fat* / Soul Waltzin' - 1963 *backing vocals Little Eva.
Dimension 1018 - Skeeter / You're My Inspiration - 1963

Big Dee Irwin with Little Eva

Dimension 1021 - The Christmas Song / I Wish You A Merry Christmas - 1963

Big Dee Irwin

Dimension 1028 - Heigh Ho* / I Want So Much To Know You - 1964 * backing vocals Little Eva
20th Century Fox 418 - Donkey Walk / Someday You'll Understand Why - 1963
Rotate 851 - You Satisfy My Needs / I Wanna Stay Right Here With You - 1965
Rotate 853 - Follow My Heart / Stop Heart - 1965

Dee Erwin

Roulette 4596 - Discotheque / The Sun's Gonna Shine Tomorrow - 1965
Fairmount 1005 - You Really Are Together / Sweet Young Thing Like You - 1966

Dee Ervin / The Pastels

Astra 1024 - I Can't Help It / My One And Only Dream* - 1966 *Flip By The Pastels.

Dee Erwin

Phil-La Of Soul 303 - Better To Have Loved And Lost / Linda - 1967
Cub 9155 - I Only Get This Feeling / Wrong Direction - 1968

Big Dee Irwin & Suzie (Maria Pereboom)

Polydor Bm56715 - Ain't That Loving You Baby / I Can't Get Over You - 1968 (Uk
Record Numbers - Unsure If This Was Ever A USA Release)

Dee Irwin

Imperial 66295 - I Only Get This Feeling / Wrong Direction - 1968

Big Dee Irwin

Imperial 66320 - I Can't Stand The Pain / My Hope To Die Girl - 1968

Big Dee Irwin with Mamie Galore

Imperial 66334 - By The Time I Get To Phoenix / I Say A Little Prayer /// All I Want
For Christmas Is Your Love - 1968
Imperial 66359 - Day Tripper / I Didn't Wanna Do It, But I Did - 1969
Imperial 66420 - Ain't No Way / Cherish - 1969

Difosco

Earthquake 2 - Sunshine Love / You Saved Me From Destruction - 1971

Dee Ervin

Signpost 70009 - Darling, Please Take Me Back (Stereo) / Darling, Please Take Me
Back (Mono) - 1972

The Pastels (members

Chess ? - 1973
Cadet ? - 1970's

Dee Erwin

Redd Coach 9-7 - I Only Get This Feeling / ? - ?

Dee Ervin (Ripple Band Leader)

Soulful Kinda Music – The Rare Soul Bible Volume Two

Hotlanta HI302 - I Love What You're Doin' To Me / Love Is (Good To Me) - 1974

Dee Ervin

Roxbury 2027 - Face To Face / You Broke My Face - 1976
Roxbury 2033 - The I Love You Song / I Can't Get You Off My Mind - 1977

Difosco

20th Century Fox 2382 - The I Love You Song / The I Love You Song - 1978 (Promo Issue)
20th Century Fox 2382 - The I Love You Song / Ship Of Love - 1978

David Williams lead vocals: Dee Ervin

Avi 201 - Soul Is Free / Soul Is Free – 1978

The Esquires

1957 was an important year for both Milwaukee, and the Moorer family, because that's the year that Gilbert, Alvis, and Betty Moorer decided to form their own group, naming it, The Esquires. In fact all three siblings were still at school at the time the group was formed, so could only undertake local shows. Several members passed through the group during the first four years, including Harvey Scales, although no recordings were made in their own name.

By 1961 Sam Pace had joined the group, and they began to gain some good local reviews. In addition they also gained some experience in the recording studio providing backing vocals for Lonnie walker. Betty actually recorded a couple of singles on her own and consequently decided that she wanted to have a career as a solo singer, so left the group in 1965. She was replaced by Shawn Taylor, although the two did both sing with the group for a short while.

By 1966, the group had outgrown their Milwaukee roots and wanted to start their recording career. A move to Chicago soon followed.

Initially auditioning for Curtis Mayfield, the group were turned down for both the Windy C label, and Mayfield Records. This didn't put them off though, and they continued to approach other producers and label owners. It was an approach to Bill

ul Bible Volume Two

'Bunky' Sheppard that first drew results. Hearing the group's demo of 'Get On Up', he decided to use them as backing singers on the Constellation release by Mill Evans 'Things Won't Be The Same / I've Got To Have Your Love' - Constellation 170 in 1965.

Unfortunately Constellation was on the point of collapse at this time, and only a handful of further releases appeared. However, several other tracks were recorded at the same session, and Bill Sheppard was able to sell the finished productions to other labels. Both releases by Mill Evans; King 6084 - Why Why Why / Right - 1967, and Tou-Sea 128 - Trying To Find A Home / When I'm Ready - 1967, contained uncredited backing by The Esquires.

The financial return from the releases was sufficient to encourage Bill Sheppard to establish another label. This was Bunky Records, and the first release was by The Esquires, now bolstered by the inclusion of Mill Edwards in their line-up.

Bunky 7750 - Get On Up / Listen To Me , which was written by Gilbert Moorer, was released in early 1967, and almost immediately became first a local, then a national hit. Distributed by the Scepter label the record hit number 3 on the R & B Charts, and almost made it to the top ten of the Pop Charts, peaking at number 11 !

As a debut single it was an amazing achievement, and it moved The Esquires from playing local theatres into the

big time, even to appearances at the Apollo Theatre in New York. Sometime in 1967 though, Shawn Taylor was sacked from the group for persistently arriving late for live shows.

The foursome were worked hard by Bill Sheppard, but the rewards made it justifiably hard. The second single, Bunky 7752 - And Get Away / Everybody's Laughing (Again

Soulful Kinda Music – The Rare Soul Bible Volume Two

written by Gilbert Moorer) was released in October 1967, and again proved to be a massive national hit for the group (#9 R & B, and #22 Pop) .

This led to the release of the group's only LP, which in it's own right became a hit on the album charts.

Three more singles followed on Bunky through 1968, and although each one made the charts, none could repeat the huge success of the first two releases and at the end of the year the group moved on from Bunky and signed a recording contract with Scepter Records.

Although the group have a single listed in the Scepter catalogue, (Scepter 12232 - You've Got The Power / No Doubt About It), I've never actually seen a copy, and have quite strong suspicions that it was never released. This is supported by the fact that the same two tracks were released when the group was placed on the Wand imprint.

The group's fortunes improved considerably with the release of their first single for Wand. Whilst their last Bunky singles only just made it into the 40's in the R & B Charts, Wand 1193 - You've Got The Power / No Doubt About It, and the second

release Wand 1195 - Part Angel / I Don't Know, both got into the 20's.

Sadly their third release, Wand 12201 - Whip It On Me / It Was Yesterday, also released in 1969, didn't have the same impact and the group were almost at the end of their tenure with Scepter.

I say almost because one final single was released which contained the group singing, even though it didn't credit them on the label. The next release on Wand was by Betty Moorer, and clearly has her brothers' group providing the background harmonies.

Teaming up again with Bill Sheppard, Gilbert Moorer, co-wrote the group's next release, 'Reach Out', which came out on Capitol Records. It failed to restore the group to the upper reaches of the Charts, and Mill Evans left the group in late 1969.

By the beginning of 1970, Shawn Taylor was back singing harmonies with the group, and they released one single on the B & G label. It was later in the same year though that Gilbert Moorer's writing skills provided the group with another chart entry on the Lamarr label (Lamarr 1001 - Girls In The City / Ain't Gonna Give It Up)

Soulful Kinda Music – The Rare Soul Bible Volume Two

Further releases followed for a variety of labels, but it wasn't until 1976 that The Esquires troubled the Chart compilers again. The Ju-Par label released a re-recorded version of the group's first hit, and 'Get On Up '76 / Dancing Disco' on Ju-Par 104 marks the last chart entry for the group.

The group continued to perform regularly though, and moved back to the Milwaukee area where Gilbert and Alvis Moorer formed the group from a variety of members, and although they cut several singles for local labels they never really got close to the big time again. The death of Gilbert Moorer in 1988 saw the end of the group.

So, a ten year apprenticeship, three years in the limelight and fifteen years performing and re-living the glory days. The Esquires may never have become superstars like The Temptation, but they paid their dues, and earned the fame they got with well crafted harmonies, and soulful vocals.

Milwaukee should be proud.

Discography

The Esquires (members Gilbert Moorer (born in Birmingham, Alabama --- died 28-August-2008 --- cause: throat cancer), Alvis Moorer and Betty Moorer) 1957 line-up.

The Esquires (members Gilbert Moorer, Alvis Moorer, Betty Moorer and Harvey Scales) 1960 line-up

The Esquires (members Gilbert Moorer, Shawn Taylor (joined 1965), Alvis Moorer and Sam Pace (joined 1961))

Lonnie Walker (with uncredited backing from The Ambassadors and The Esquires)

Cuca 1111 - I Slipped, I Stumbled, I Fell / Let's Talk About Us - 1962

Betty Moore (Betty Moorer with uncredited backing from The Esquires)

Cuca 1134 - Long Hot Summer / Voo Doo Waltz - ?
Cuca 1467 - Long Hot Summer / Voo Doo Waltz - ?

Mill Evans (Millard Edwards. A former member of The Sheppards with uncredited backing from The Esquires)

Constellation 170 - Things Won't Be The Same / I've Got To Have Your Love – 1965
King 6084 - Why Why Why* / Right Now - 1967 *also recorded in 1970 by Otis Leavill on Dakar 617. Co-written by Karl Tarleton and Gerald Sims.
Tou-Sea 128 - Trying To Find A Home / When I'm Ready – 1967

The Esquires (Members Gilbert Moorer, Shawn Taylor, Alvis Moorer, Sam Pace And Millard Edwards (Became member after collapse of Constellation Records)

Bunky 7750 - Get On Up* / Listen To Me - 1967 *Written By Gilbert Moorer.

The Esquires (Members Gilbert Moorer, Alvis Moorer, Sam Pace And Millard

Soulful Kinda Music – The Rare Soul Bible Volume Two

Edwards)

Bunky 7752 - And Get Away* / Everybody's Laughing - 1967 *Written By Gilbert
Moorer.
Bunky 7753 - You Say / State Fair – 1968
Bunky 7755 - Why Can't I Stop / The Feelings Gone – 1968
Bunky 7756 - I Know I Can / How Could It Be – 1968
Scepter 12232 - You've Got The Power / No Doubt About It – 1968
Wand 1193 - You've Got The Power / No Doubt About It – 1968
Wand 1195 - Part Angel / I Don't Know – 1969
Wand 12201 - Whip It On Me / It Was Yesterday – 1969

Betty Moorer (With uncredited backing from The Esquires)

Wand 12202 - It's My Thing / Speed Up – 1969

The Esquires (Members Gilbert Moorer, Alvis Moorer, Sam Pace And Millard
Edwards)

Capitol 2650 - Reach Out / Listen To Me – 1969

The Esquires (Members Gilbert Moorer, Alvis Moorer, Sam Pace And Shawn Taylor)

B & G 7751 - Ain't No Reason / Ba Ba-Da-Ba-Dop – 1970
Lamarr 1001 - Girls In The City / Ain't Gonna Give It Up* - 1970 *Co-Written By
Gilbert Moorer.
Rocky Ridge 403 - That Ain't No Reason / Dancin' A Hole In The World* - 1971 *also
recorded in 1968 by Jimmy Delphs on Carla 1904.
Hot Line 103 - Henry Ralph / My Sweet Baby - 1972
New World 101 - Let Me Build You A Whole New World / Stay - 1974
Ju-Par 104 - Get On Up '76 / Dancing Disco - 1976

The Esquires (Members Gilbert Moorer, Alvis Moorer, ...)

Lasco 1101 - My Lady / The Fish – 1979
Cigar Man Music 9880 - What Good Is Music / The Show Ain't Over – 1980
New World 101 - Let Me Build You A Whole New World / Stay - ?
Al Bun 6667 - I Can't Get Along Without You Baby / Just Loafin' - ?
Al Bun 70419 - I Can't Get Along Without You Baby / ? - ?

The O'Kaysions **/ The Esquires**

Collectables Col 031297 - Girl Watcher / Get On Up - ?

Candi Staton / Chick Carbo / Zastrow, Christie & Co. / The Esquires

Ripete 1016 - Suspicious Minds / In The Night /// Moonlight Boogie / Girls In The City
- 1988

LPs

Soulful Kinda Music – The Rare Soul Bible Volume Two

Bunky BS-300 - Esquires - Get on Up and Get Away - 1968
Tracks: And Get Away / Listen To Me / How Was I To Know / Groovin' / Everybody's
Laughin' / How Could It Be // Get On Up / My Sweet baby / No Doubt About It /
Woman / When I'm Ready / Things Won't Be The Same

Label Listings

Eastbound

600 - Jimmie Delphs - Country Girl / Mind Going In The Same Direction -
1972
601 - Unique Blend - Old Fashioned Woman / Yes I'm In Love
602 - Freddy Wilson - Promised Land / Where Is She
603 - Donald Austin - Crazy Legs / Nan Zee
604 - Motivations - I Love You / I'm Loving You You're Leaving Me
605 - Randy Horan - Beside You / The Rock Keeps Rolling
606 - Not Assigned
607 - Catfish Hodge - Boogie Man / Stop
608 - Donald Austin - Sex Plot / Can't Understand The Strain
609 - Fantastic Four - I Had This Whole World To Choose From (And I
Chose You) / If You Need Me, Call Me (And I'll Come Running) - 1973
610 - Jimmy Scott - What Am I Gonna Do (About You Baby) / Pair And A
Spare - **1973**
611 - Melvin Sparks - Ain't No Woman (Like The One I've Got) / Judy's
Groove - **1973**
612 - Caesar Frazier - See-F / Make It With You - 1973
613 - Albert Washington - Sad And Lonely / Wings Of A Dove - 1973
614 - A C Tilman - Girl You Thrill Me / I Like To Dream - 1973
615 - Man Faithe - Someone New / Sorrow - 1973
616 - Houston Person - Kittittian Carnival / 'Tain't Nobody's Business If I Do -
1973
617 - Pleasure Web - Music Man Part 1 / Music Man Part 2 - 1973
618 - Silky Vincent - Funky World Part 1 / Funky World Part 2 - 1973
619 - Junie - Tightrope / Walt's Second Trip - 1973
620 - Fantastic Four - I Believe In Miracles (I Believe In You) / I'm Falling In
Love (I Feel Good All Over) - 1973
621 - Catfish Hodge - Colour Tv Blues / Heartbeat Of The Sreet
622 - Houston Person - Mayola / I Like To Love The Love
623 - Fantasy Hill - Unemployment Blues / Long Time
624 - Robert Lowe - Put Your Legs Yo High / Back To Funk
625 - Shorr's Streakers - Streaker '74 / Virgil - 1974
626 - Unique Blend - Does He Treat You Better / Mommy And Daddy - 1974

Soulful Kinda Music – The Rare Soul Bible Volume Two

626 - Unique Blend - Sorrow / Won't Be Needing Someone New - 1974
627 - Spanky Wilson - Home / Shake Your Head - 1974
628 - Melvin Sparks - Get Down With The Get Down / I've Got To Have You - 1974
629 - Junie - When We Do / The Place - 1974
630 - Catfish Hodge - Birmingham / Ten Speed Bike

Eastern

60001 - Johnny Starr - Don't Hold Back / Swingin' Organ
60002 - Duke Daniels - Backfire / This Is The End
600 - Geraldine Jones - Baby, I'm Leaving You / When You Get Tired
601 - Clyde Dickerson & Teardrops - Guess Who / Cool Weekend
602 - Eddie & Ernie - That's The Way It Is / Time Waits For No One
603 - Eddie & Ernie - Turn Here / I'm A Young Man
604 - Tina Britt - Real Thing / Teardrops Fell
605 - Tina Britt - Look / You're Absolutely Right
606 - Eddie & Ernie - I'm Goin' For Myself / Cat
608 - Eddie & Ernie - Outcast / I'm Gonna Always Love You
609 - Eddie & Ernie - Lost Friends / I Can't Do It
610 - Jean Wells - If You've Ever Loved Somebody / Hello Baby, Goodbye, Too
611 - Magnificent 7- Since You've Been Gone So Long / She's Called A Woman

Emerge

1106 - Anthony & The Delsonics - Every Time / Never Had A Girl (So Sweet) - 1964
1107 - Screaming Joe Neal - Don't Quit Me Baby / She's My Baby - 1964
1108 - Jim Pipkins & The Boss Five - Mr C.C. / I'm Just A Lonely Guy - 1964
1109 - ?
1110 - Marcel Strong & The Triad - Trying To Make Up / Time To Pay (You Back) - 1964
1111 - Mal Adams & The Cashmeres - If I Only Knew / Since Man Began - 1964

Era

1000 - The Thunderbirds - Ayuh, Ayuh / Bluberries - 1955
1001 - Bert Convy & The Thunderbirds - C'mon Back / Hop Bop De Bow - 1955
1002 - Buddy Bregman - East Of Eden / Kentuckian Song - 1955
1003 - Gogi Grant - Love Is / Suddenly There's A Valley - 1955
1004 - The Thunderbirds - I'd Be A Fool To Let You Go / Beguine - 1955
1005 - ?
1006 - Buddy Bregman - Dad's Lavie / Someone In Love - 1955
1007 - The Merry Macs - I'm In Clover / (The) Lord Is A Busy Man - 1955
1008 - Gogi Grant - We Believe In Love / Who Are We - 1955

Soulful Kinda Music – The Rare Soul Bible Volume Two

1009 - Chuck Nelson - (The) Green, Green Mountains / Slap Leathers - 1955
1010 - The Merry Macs - Why Can't We Begin Where We Left Off / Good Will - 1956
1011 - Jana Mason - Compromise / A Diamond, A Pearl And An Ermine Wrap - 1956
1012 - Daws Butler - Con-Fidgity-Ential / The $64,000.00 Question - 1956
1013 - Gogi Grant - No More Than Forever / (The) Wayward Wind - 1956
1014 - Billy Strange - Say You're Mine, Porcupine / Buddy's Girl - 1956
1015 - Chuck Nelson - I Can't Be True / Not While I'm Young - 1956
1016 - The Merry Macs - One Happy Family / (The) Erie Canal - 1956
1017 - Johnny Harper - Two Ton Tillie / Little Doggie - 1956
1018 - Russell Arms - I Saw A Star / Is There Heaven - 1956
1019 - Gogi Grant - When The Tide Is High / You're In Love - 1956
1020 - Connie Russell - You And Your Ways / That'll Be The Day - 1956
1021 - The Merry Macs - Whitewall Tires / Bluesville Usa - 1956
1022 - Gale Robbins - Riverman / This Can't Be The End Of Me - 1956
1023 - Rosalinda - Cruel Tower / My Cherie - 1956
1024 - Doyle O'Dell - According To The Evidence / Bow Your Head And Pray - 1956
1025 - Doyle O'dell - According To The Evidence / Bow Your Head And Pray - 1956
1026 - Russell Arms - (The) World Is Made Of Lisa / Cinco Robles - 1956
1027 - Connie Russell - Barefoot Boy / Deep Inside Of Me - 1956
1028 - The Beebee Twins - Haunted / Send Back My Broken Heart - 1956
1029 - The Salmas Brothers - Go, Let Her Go / Greater Love - 1956
1030 - Billy Strange - It Wasn't Much Of A Town / Big Man - 1956
1031 - Gale Robbins - (The) Feeling Of Love / Blue Raindrops - 1956
1032 - Chuck Nelson - If You Grew Tired Of Me / Calling My Love - 1956
1033 - Russell Arms - Evangeline / Share My Love - 1957
1034 - Alis Leslie - He Will Come Back To Me / Heartbreak Harry - 1957
1035 - The Magic Notes - (The) Wrong Door / Never Again - 1957
1036 - Laurie Loman - Saint Christopher, Bring Him Home / Someone To Live For - 1957
1037 - The Villa Singers - Tony At The Carnival / ? - 1957
1038 - The Planets - Stand There Mountain / Never Again - 1957
1039 - Don Deal - Devil Of Deceit / Unfaithful Diane - 1957
1040 - Russell Arms - Where Can A Wanderer Go / (The) Bridge Of San Angelo - 1957
1041 - Lee Lamar - Teenage Pedal Pushers / Sophia - 1957
1042 - Ben Joe Zeppa - Mom And Dad / Topsy Turvy - 1957
1043 - ?
1044 - Bobby Please - Heartache Avenue / Your Driver's Licence, Please - 1957
1045 - Connie Russell - Nobody Plays Piano Like ... / Fools Paradise - 1957
1046 - Vince Howard - Moonlight Mountain / If You Believe, If You Believe - 1957
1047 - Chuck Nelson - And Then I Remember / Green, Green Mountains - 1957
1048 - Russell Arms - I'm Tired Of Pride / I Wonder Where's My Darlin' - 1957
1049 - The Planets - Wild Leaves / Be Sure - 1957
1050 - Lee Lamar - Straight As An Arrow / King Of The Mountain - 1957
1051 - Don Deal - My Blind Date / Even Then - 1957
1052 - The Cruisers - Buoys And Gulls / (A) Ring Around A Chain - 1957
1053 - Gogi Grant - All Of Me / (The) Golden Ladder - 1957
1054 - Fred Darian - Restless / Treasure Hunt - 1957
1055 - Ronnie Deauville - As Children Go / I Concentrate On You - 1957
1056 - Ronnie Deauville - Laura / It Wasn't Much Of A Town - 1957

Soulful Kinda Music – The Rare Soul Bible Volume Two

1057 - Laurie Loman - Leaves In The Wind / Sittin' By The Window - 1957
1058 - Gloria March - Baby Of Mine / Nippon Wishing Well - 1957
1059 - Russell Arms - Walkin' By Your Window / Hasta La Vista - 1957
1060 - Don Deal - You'd Look Good With A Tear In Your Eye / She Was Here But She's Gone - 1957
1061 - Glen Glenn - I'm Glad My Baby's Gone / Everybody's Movin' - 1957
1062 - Gogi Grant - I Don't Want To Walk Without You / I Gave You My Heart - 1957
1063 - The Passions - My Aching Heart / Jackie Brown - 1957
1064 - Art & Dotty Todd - Along The Trail With You / Chanson D'amour - 1957
1065 - The Scooters - (A) Ring Around A Chain / Everybody's Got A Girl - 1957
1066 - Ronnie Deauville - Hong Kong Affair / Crazy, Wonderful - 1957
1067 - Dick Bush - Ezactly / Hollywood Party - 1957
1068 - Mark Anthony - Everlina Lou / Mangy - 1958
1069 - Magnificent Montague - Ta Ta Do Way / (The) Breather - 1958
1070 - Don Deal & Moontars - Sweet Love / The First Teenager - 1958
1071 - Ronnie Deauville - Unfaithful Diane / Around The Corner (From My House) - 1958
1072 - The Scooters - Everybody's Got A Girl / Big Kiss - 1958
1073 - Bill Rase - Prove It / Roses In The Snow - 1958
1074 - Glen Glenn - Laurie Ann / One Cup Of Coffee - 1958
1075 - Tony & Joe - Gonna Get A Little Kissin' Tonight / (The) Freeze - 1958
1076 - Art & Dotty Todd - Der Glockenspeil / Au Revoir Amour - 1958
1077 - Don Deal - Just Thought I'd Call / (A) Chance Is All I Ask - 1958
1078 - Russell Arms - Der Glockenspeil / Blue Hawaii - 1958
1079 - The Dimples Toy Telephone / Gimme Jimmy - 1958
1080 - The Zanies - Do You Dig Me, Mister Pigmy / (The) Blob - 1958
1081 - Don Wyatt - Let Me Be The One / You Ought To Be In The Movies - 1958
1082 - ?
1083 - Tony & Joe - Where Can You Be / Play Something Sentimental, Mister D. J. - 1958
1084 - Barry Gordon - They / Katy - 1958
1085 - The Tigers - Jelly Bean / Don't Bye Bye Baby Me - 1958
1086 - Glen Glenn - Blue Jeans And A Boy's Shirt / Would Ya' - 1958
1087 - Art & Dotty Todd - Pray / Don't You Worry, My Little Pet - 1958
1088 - Art & Dotty Todd - Stand There Mountain / Straight As An Arrow - 1959
1089 - The Naturals - Don't Send Me Away / (The) Mummy - 1959
1090 - Ivory Wimberly - A Cuore Mia / Cry It Out - 1959
1091 - Johnny Bachelor - Mumbly / Arabella Jean - 1959
1092 - Barry Gordon - Rabbit Habit / Bluebird Song - 1959
3000 - Ronnie Height - It's Not That Easy / Portrait Of Linda - 1959
3001 - Art & Dotty Todd - Ayuh, Ayuh / Paradise - 1959
3002 - The Plaids - Around The Corner / He Stole Flo - 1959
3003 - The Continentals - Soap Sudz / Cool Penguin - 1959
3004 - Donnie Brooks - If You're Lookin' / Li'l Sweetheart - 1959
3005 - Ronnie Height - Mister Blue, I Presume / Juvenile - 1959
3006 - Joey Singer - Keep Me In Your Care / For The Love Of You - 1959
3007 - Donnie Brooks - Sway And Move With The Beat / White Orchid - 1959
3008 - Jay Matty - Tall Tale / Janie, My Lover - 1959
3009 - Ronnie Height - (A) Kiss To Build A Dream On / Maybe Tomorrow - 1959
3010 - Ginny Tiu - Ginny's Chop Sticks / Twelfth Street Rag - 1959

Soulful Kinda Music – The Rare Soul Bible Volume Two

3011 = The Rusco Brothers - There's More / Velvet Eyes - 1959
3012 - Dorsey Burnette - Juarez Town / Tall Oak Tree - 1960
3013 - Bob Wilson - Imogene / Two Little Birds - 1960
3014 - Donnie Brooks - How Long / (The) Devil Ain't A Man - 1960
3015 - Marlene Willis - On A Train Going Nowhere / Caesar Loves Me - 1960
3016 - Johnny Drake & Kitten / Johnny Drake - Why Daddy / Often Broke, But Never Poor - 1960
3017 - Ronnie Height - One Finger Symphony / Memories And Habits - 1960
3018 - Donnie Brooks - Do It For Me / Mission Bell - 1960
3019 - Dorsey Burnette - Big Rock Candy Mountain / Hey, Little One - 1960
3020 - Bill Norvas & Val Grund - Midnight Train / You Did Me Wrong - 1960
3021 - The Four Stars - (The) Frog / Blue Dawn - 1960
3022 - The Valley Boys - Winds In The Valley / Strange One - 1960
3023 - Bob Wilson - Tale Of A Donkey / I Went To Your Wedding - 1960
3024 - Larry Verne - Okefenokee Two Step / Mr. Custer - 1960
3025 - Dorsey Burnette - Red Roses / Ghost Of Billy Malloo - 1960
3026 - The Bell Boys - I Love You / Are You For Me - 1960
3027 - Bob Wilson - Jailer, Jailer / And Her Name Was Scarlet - 1960
3028 - Donnie Brooks - Round Robin / Doll House - 1960
3029 - Donnie Bowser - Stone Heart / I Love You, Baby - 1960
3030 - Shelly Dane - How Can You Tell / Guarantee Of Love - 1960
3031 - Ronnie Height - Mister Blue, I Presume / No Date - 1960
3032 - Carol Jarvis - Don't Throw Pebbles / I'm Breakin' In A Brand New Heart - 1960
3033 - Dorsey Burnette - River And The Mountain / This Hotel – 1960
3034 - Larry Verne - Roller Coaster / Mister Livingston – 1960
3035 - Marlene Willis - Sticking Pins In A Dolly / Billy Barr – 1960
3036 - Libby & Sue - (He Had) Pretty Eyes / Bye, Bye, Bye – 1961
3037 - Johnny Rivers - Andersonville / Call Me – 1961
3038 - The Castells - Rome□/ Little Sad Eyes – 1961
3039 - Bobby Hart - Journey Of Love / Girl In The Window – 1961
3040 - The Tingles - Tell Me Now / Rain, Rain – 1961
3041 - Dorsey Burnette - It's No Sin / Hard Rock Mine – 1961
3042 - Donnie Brooks - That's Why / Memphis – 1961
3043 - Carol Jarvis - My Private Dreams / Give Him A Kiss For Me - 1961
3044 - Larry Verne - Tubby Tilly / Abdul's Party - 1961
3045 - Dorsey Burnette - That's Me Without You / Great Shakin' Fever - 1961
3046 - Gogi Grant - (The) Tide Is High / (The) Wayward Wind - 1961
3047 - Comrade X - Spacenik / ? - 1961
3048 - The Castells - I Get Dreamy / Sacred - 1961
3049 - Donnie Brooks - All I Can Give / Wishbone - 1961
3050 - Jack Bedient & The Chessmen - Questions / (The) Mystic One - 1961
3051 - Larry Verne - Pow, Right In The Kisser / Charlie At The Bat - 1961
3052 - Donnie Brooks - How Long / Boomerang - 1961
3053 - Russell Arms - (The) World Is Made Of Lisa / Cinco Roberts - 1961
3054 - Keith Colley - Zing Went The Strings Of My Heart / It's Nice Out Tonight - 1961
3055 - Wendy Hill - Since You Went Away / Without Your Love - 1961
3056 - Vince Howard - Moonlight Mountain / If You Believe, If You Believe - 1961
3057 - The Castells - My Miracle / Make Believe Wedding - 1961
3058 - Allen Richie - Goochie Bamba / Blue Holiday - 1961

Soulful Kinda Music – The Rare Soul Bible Volume Two

3059 - Donnie Brooks - Up To My Ears In Tears / Sweet Lorraine - 1961
3060 - Churchill & Orchestra - Independence Day Hora / Shalom - 1961
3061 - Louis Gray - Dooley, Dooley Baby / You Get The Money - 1961
3062 - Cindy & Sue - Temple Love / Let's Fall In Love - 1961
3063 - Donnie Brooks - Your Little Boy's Gone Home / Goodnight Judy - 1961
3064 - The Castells - Stiki De Boom Boom / (The) Vision Of You - 1961
3065 - Larry Verne - Speck / Beatnik - 1961
3066 - Breezy - Little Brown Jug / Billy Boy - 1961
3067 - Keith Colley - And Her Name Is Scarlet / Put 'Em Down - 1962
3068 - Ketty Lester - I'm A Fool To Want You / Love Letters - 1962
3069 - The Balladeers - Wedding John Doe / (A) Long Way From Home - 1962
3070 - Wendy Hill - (The) Cheat / Won't You Be Good - 1962
3071 - Donnie Brooks - He Stole Flo / My Favorite Kind Of Face - 1962
3072 - Louis Gray - Wobblin' / Up Above Their Knees - 1962
3073 - The Castells - On The Street Of Tears / So This Is Love - 1962
3074 - The Westwoods - King Cricket Goes To Town / King Cricket - 1962
3075 - Larry Verne - I'm A Brave Little Soldier / Hoo La - 1962
3076 - Hrach Yacoubian - Sultan's Harem / Harem Twist - 1962
3077 - Donnie Brooks - Just A Bystander / Oh, You Beautiful Doll - 1962
3078 - Keith Colley - (The) Number / Someone To Take Your Place - 1962
3079 - The Dimples - Toy Telephone / Gimme Jimmy - 1962
3080 - Ketty Lester - Once Upon A Time / But Not For Me - 1962
3081 - Wendy Hill - I Just Happen To Love You / Come On-A My Home - 1962
3082 - The Sentinals - Latin'ia / Torchula - 1962
3083 - The Castells - Stand There Mountain / Oh, What It Seemed To Be - 1962
3084 - Carol Connors - Two Rivers / Big, Big Love - 1962
3085 - The Arpeggios - Like Old Times / Hot Canary - 1962
3086 - The Jubilee Four - Pauline / Riders In The Sky - 1962
3087 - Bruce Cloud - My Book / Lucky Is My Name - 1962
3088 - Ketty Lester - River Of Salt / You Can't Lie To A Liar - 1962
3089 - The Castells - Only One / Echoes In The Night - 1962
3090 - Marie Celia - Walk With Me / Please Don't Let Go - 1962
3091 - Larry Verne - (The) Porcupine Patrol / (The) Coward That Won The West - 1962
3092 - Mike Smith - By The Time You Read This Letter / That's What I Like To Do - 1962
3093 - The Toy Dolls - Fly Away / Little Tin Soldier - 1962
3094 - Ketty Lester - Love Is For Everyone / This Land Is Your Land - 1962
3095 - Donnie Brooks - It's Not That Easy / Cries My Heart - 1962
3096 - Carol Connors - I Wanna Know / Tommy, Go Away - 1962
3097 - The Sentinals - Latin Soul / Christmas Eve - 1962
3098 - The Castells - Eternal Spring, Eternal Love / Clown Prince - 1962
3099 - The Moments - Walk Right In (Instrumental) / Walk Right In - 1963
3100 - Sounds Off - Working Up A Steam / (The) Angry Desert - 1963
3101 - Bruce Cloud - Little Spark Of Fire / I Waited - 1963
3102 - The Castells - Initials / Little Sad Eyes - 1963
3103 - Ketty Lester - Lullaby For Lovers / Fallen Angel - 1963
3104 - The Moments - Big Round Wheel / Homework - 1963
3105 - The Vine Street Boys - That Certain Someone / Come On Over - 1963
3106 - The Towers - Friday Night Date / Alone In The Big Town - 1963

Soulful Kinda Music – The Rare Soul Bible Volume Two

3107 - The Castells - What Do Little Girls Dream Of / Some Enchanted Evening - 1963

3108 - Pat Zill - I Couldn't See My Heart Before My Eyes / Key Is In The Mail Box - 1963

3109 - The Soul Mates - I Get A Feeling / I Want A Boyfriend - 1963

3110 - Ron Ellington - (The) Ballad Of Billy Strong / You Can Take Your Saturday Nights - 1963

3111 - Jim Carter & Blow Hards - Jailer, Jailer / Coming On - 1963

3112 - Sandy & The Sandstorms - Flutterbug / Sand Storm - 1963

3113 - Albert Stone - Not In Vain / Blue Shadow - 1963

3114 - The Moments - Mamu Zey / Surfin' Train - 1963

3115 - Mary Saenz - In Your Arms / He Didn't Even Say Hello - 1963

3116 - The Crescents - Breakout / Pink Dominoes - 1963

3117 - The Sentinal Six - Encinada / Infinity - 1963

3118 - The Composers - You And Yours / I Had A Dream - 1963

3119 - The Pagents - (The) Big Daddy / Enchanted - 1963

3120 - Tal Walton - That's Why / Mother Earth And Father Time - 1964

3121 - Mark Anthony - That's Good Enough For Me / I Believe - 1964

3123 - Jill Jones - Don't Be Mad / Help Me - 1964

3124 - The Pagents - Shake / Glenda - 1964

3125 - The Bermudas - Chu Sen Ling / Donnie - 1964

3126 - Phil Lucas - Charlie Brennan / Mandy Mine - 1964

3127 - The Sci-Fi's - Blues At Sandy Cove / Science Fiction - 1964

3128 - The Moments - Blues At Sandy Cove / In The Phonograph Booth - 1964

3129 - Cathy Brasher - Too Late To Be Lovers / I'll Remember Jimmy - 1964

3130 - Conrad & The Hurricanes - Sweet Love / Hurricane - 1964

3131 - Dan Rogers - No Girl For Me / I'd Be Lost Without You - 1964

3132 - The Beagles - Deep In The Heart Of Texas / Let's All Sing Like The Birdies Sing - 1964

3133 - The Bermudas - Seeing Is Believing / Blue Dreamer - 1964

3134 - The Pagents - Sad And Lonely / Pa-Cha - 1964

3135 - Larry & Mike - Little Ole Love Maker Me / So Long, Little Buddy - 1964

3136 - The Fisher Brothers - By The Time You Read This Letter / Big Round Wheel - 1964

3137 - The Turn-Arounds - Run Away And Hide / Ain't Nothin' Shakin' - 1964

3138 - Ricky Rene / The Fabulous Desires - Ouch / Dance With Me - 1964

3139 - Larry Verne - Running Through The Forest / Return Of Mister Custer - 1964

3140 - The Hunters - Tiger Shake / (The) Angry Desert - 1964

3141 - Jewel Akens - Tic Tac Toe / (The) Birds And The Bees - 1964

3142 - Jewel Akens - Around The Corner / Georgie Porgie - 1965

3143 - The Messengers - You've Got Me Cryin' / Let Me Be Your Man - 1965

3144 - Rainma Kerr - Barbara / Endlessly - 1965

3145 - Chuck Wood - Blind Date / Chocolate Covered Ants - 1965

3146 - The Elites - What's The Password? / Sir Galahad - 1965

3147 - Jewel Akens - It's The Only Way To Fly / You Sure Know How To Hurt A Guy - 1965

3148 - Barry McGuire - Theme From The Tree / (The) Tree - 1965

3150 - Fred & Clipper Whitney - Gypsies Is Here / Barber's March - 1965

3151 - Jimmy Lewis - Wait Until Spring (Again) (Part 2) / Wait Until Spring (Again) (Part 1) - 1965

Soulful Kinda Music – The Rare Soul Bible Volume Two

3152 - Hungry IV - Young Girl / (The) Hustler - 1965
3153 - The Lyrics - So What / They Can't Hurt Me - 1965
3154 - Jewel Akens - I've Arrived / You Don't Need A Crowd - 1965
3155 - The Unbelievables - There's A Little Bit Of Heaven / Ring Rang Roe - 1965
3156 - Jewel Akens - (A) Slice Of Pie / You Better Believe It - 1965
3157 - Tommy Strange - Two Steps Forward / Don't Bug Me, Baby - 1965
3158 - Jimmy Lewis - What Can I Do / One Love - 1965
3159 - Jewel Akens - He Who Hesitates Is Lost / Sniff Sniff, Poo Pah Pah Doo - 1966
3160 - Guy West - Exit Loneliness / Devil Is Her Name - 1966
3161 - The Wizards - I'm Blind / I Want To Live - 1966
3162 - Dee Dee Dorety - To Go Our Separate Ways / If The World Only Knew - 1966
3163 - Bet E. Martin - You've Got To See Mama Every Night / Let It Be Now - 1966
3164 - Jewel Akens - Mama, Take Your Daughter Back / My First Lonely Night - 1966
3165 - No-Na-Mee's - Just Wanna Be Myself / Gotta Hold On - 1966
3167 - Melvin Boyd - Things Are Gettin' Better / Exit Loneliness, Enter Love - 1966
3168 - Ty Wagner - Slander / I Think I Found Love - 1966
3169 - Howlett Smith - Something To Think About / Quiet Stream - 1966
3170 - Lindsay Crosby - Old Friends Of Mine / Christmas Won't Be The Same - 1966
3171 - Outlaw Blues - Mustafa / Non-Stop Blues - 1967
3173 - Harlen Michael - Day Sleeper / Tell Me - 1967
3174 - The Decades - On Sunset / I'm Gonna Dance - 1967
3175 - Howlett Smith - When The World Was Young / Seven-Up - 1967
3177 - Tommy Mosley - Wishing Well / Big Fat Mama From New Orleons - 1967
3178 - New Scene - Little Bit Of Devil / (The) Battle Lands - 1967
3179 - Othello Robertson - Come On Home / So In Luv - 1967
3180 - L. B. J. & The Birds - Beat Bam / Hello, Hello - 1967
3181 - Search - Too Young / Everybody's Searching - 1967
3182 - Tom & Clarence - Don't Smoke The Banana Peel / Come To The Love-In - 1967
3183 - Billy Watkins - (The) Ice-Man / Blue And Lonely - 1967
3184 - Tommy Mosley - So This Is Love / Exit Loneliness, Enter Love - 1967
3185 - Chocolate Tunnel - Ostrich People / Highly Successful Young Rupert White - 1967
3186 - Steve Flanagan - I've Arrived / I Need To Be Loved So Bad - 1967
3187 - New Scene - The Battle Lands / Little Bit Of Devil - 1967
3188 - Tomorrow's World - When It's All Over / Tinkling Glasses - 1967
3189 - Jesse Davis - Gonna Hang On In There, Girl / Albuquerque - 1967
3190 - Johnny Creach - Three In Love / Ode To Danny Boy - 1967
3191 - The Workshop - New Year's Happening / Presidential Christmas Shopping - 1967
3192 - Jesse Davis - Something To Think About / You Don't Need A Crown - 1967
3193 - Lollipop Fantasy - It's A Groovy World / Waiting For A Dream - 1967
3194 - Donnie Brooks - Love Is Funny That Way / Blue Soldier - 1968
3195 - The Toy Dolls - Fly Away / Little Tin Soldier - 1968
3196 - Brothers Le Gard - Night Bloomin' Jasmin / And Her Name Is Scarlet - 1968
3197 - A Thousand Faces - Sweet Little Cup (Of Lovin') / (A) Thousand Faces - 1968
3198 - Certain Scene - Welcome Back Among The Living / So This Is Love - 1968
3199 - Brothers Le Gard - Coo-Ee Call / (The) Land Where Animals Are People - 1968
3200 - Certain Scene - Welcome Back Among The Living / So This Is Love - 1968

Soulful Kinda Music – The Rare Soul Bible Volume Two

3201 - Us - Delicious / Love Is Not As Grand - 1969
3202 - Phil Baugh - Jesse's Theme / Girl Watcher - 1969
3203 - Men In Space - Apollo Eight (Part 2) / Apollo Eight - 1969
3204 - Gabriel Dean - Everybody's Searchin' / Horoscope - 1969
3205 - Dorsey Burnette - (The) Wayward Wind / Suddenly There's A Valley - 1969
3206 - Herb Newman - Cuando Caliente El Sol / Aquarius - 1969
3207 - Jewel Akens - (A) Slice Of The Pie / (The) Land Where Animals Are People - 1969
3208 - Phil Baugh - Those Were The Days / Dizzy - 1969
3209 - Chris Montez - Let's Dance / Some Kinda Fun - 1969
3210 - Keith Green - L.A. City Smog Blues / Fantastic - 1969
100 - Bassie Griffin - That's What My God Is For / Holy Manna - 1969
101 - The Four Saints - Window Of Dreams / ? - 1969
102 - Shad O'Shea - One Step Back / Goober Jam - 1969
103 - The Earth Brothers - Painted Lady / Fantastic - 1969
104 - Jewel Akens - Mississippi Syrup Sopper / Buenos Aires - 1969
105 - Joni Credit - Housewife From L.A. / Exit Loneliness, Enter Love - 1969
106 - Rheiny Gau - Life / Ballad Of Rheiny Gau - 1970
107 - Twenty-First Century - Parachute Song / (A) Hard Act To Follow - 1970
108 - Keith Green - Sergeant Pepper's Epitaph / Country Store - 1970
109 - The Next World - Blown Out Fugue / Kung-Fu In G Minor - 1970
110 - Jerry Ray - Lonely Mansion / Something To Think About - 1970
111 - Bernie (Show) Byrd - You're In California / It's The Only Way To Fly - 1970
112 - Bert Convy - Something To Think About / Just Give Me A Chance - 1970
113 - Apple Pie 'N' Stover - You're Doin' Alright / Blue Shadow - 1970
114 - Clifton Ridgewood - Little Drummer Boy (Part 2) / Little Drummer Boy (Part 1) - 1970
115 - Hot Blood - Sans Dracula / Soul Dracula - 1970
116 - Connexion - Morning Light / I Believe In You - 1970
117 - Clifton Ridgewood - Yankee Doodle Dandy (Part 2) / Yankee Doodle Dandy (Part 1) - 1970
118 - ?
119 - Foundation - Running Away / Parachute Song - 1970
701 - The Four Saints - Window Of Dreams / When I'm With You Again - ?
193 - The Hi-Fives - Cold Wind / Mean Old Woman - 1961
930 - The Spartans - I Don't Need Another Lover / Forget Her Name - 1976

(No #) - Donnie Brooks Night At El Monte Legion Stadium – Mission Bell / Doll House - ? (promo issue only)

EL-20001 - Gogi Grant - Suddenly There's Gogi Grant - 1956
Tracks: Suddenly There's A Valley / I Let A Song Go Out Of My Heart / Love Is The Sweetest Thing / I'll Never Be The Same / The One I Love (Belongs To Somebody Else) / There Will Never Be Another You

EL-20002 - Ronnie Deauville - Smoke Dreams - 1956
Tracks: Smoke Dreams / Something To Remember You By / Wonderful One / Say It Isn't So / I Had The Craziest Dream / Soft Lights And Sweet Music / I Concentrate On You / Love Is Here To Stay / So In Love / I'll Close My Eyes / As Children Do / Easy

Soulful Kinda Music – The Rare Soul Bible Volume Two

To Remember / I Kiss Your Hand Madame

EL-20003 - Bob Florence - Bob Florence and Trio - 1956
Tracks:

EL-20004 - Doye O'dell & Cass County Boys - Doye - 1956
Tracks: It Makes No Difference Now / According To The Evidence / My Mary / San
Antonio Rose / You're The Only Star In My Blue Heaven / Pretty Woman For The
Boss / Bow Your Head And Pray / Oklahoma Hills / Old Shep / It Won't Be Texas To
You / I Left My Gal In The Mountains / Red River Valley

EL-20005 - Jack Millman - Blowing Up a Storm - 1956
Tracks:

EL-20006 - Merry Macs - Something Old, New, Borrowed and Blue - 1956
Tracks: Lord Is A Busy Man / Bluesville USA / Boom I'm In Clover / Sentimental
Journey / Why Can't We Begin / You Made Me Love You / Whitewall Tires / I Get The
Blues When It Rains / Jingle Jangle Jingle / Erie Canal / Dolores / Good Will

EL-20007 - Page Cavanaugh - Carries the Torch - 1956
Tracks: Can't Get Out Of This Mood / That Old Feeling / Mood Indigo / Perfume
Jewels And Curls / But Not For Me / It Used To Be / That'll Be The Day / There She
Goes / Just For Laughs / I'm Lost / Gloomy Sunday / I'm Thru With Love

EL-20008 - David Andrews - One Little Candle - 1957
Tracks: One Little Candle / He / Suddenly There's A Valley / Faith Can Move
Mountains / Over The Rainbow / Walk Hand In Hand / May The Good Lord Bless And
Keep You / Look For A Silver Lining / I Believe / You'll Never Walk Alone / Bless This
House / Nature Boy

EL-20009 - Joe Dolny Orchestra - Italiano - 1957
Tracks: Oh Marie / Isle Of Capri / Mattinata / Anna / Come Back To Sorrento /
Funiculi Funicula / Mambo Italiano / Luna Rossa / Ferryboat Serenade / I Have But
One Heart / Sicilian Tarantella

EL-20010 - Rosa Linda - Will Success Spoil Rock-Maninoff - 1957
Tracks: Will Success Spoil Rock-Maninoff / Prelude In G Minor / 18th Variation On A
Theme Of Paganini / Rhapsody On A Theme Of Paganini / Joe Green Goes To Town
/ HabanBoogie / Carmen Has a Bizet Day / 88 Keys / Dream Or Two / Rachmaninoff
Concerto No. 2 / Samba A La Chopin

EL-20011 - David Andrews - Come To The Sea - 1957
Tracks: When The Tide Is High / Off Shore / Victory At Sea / Sound Of The Sea / My
Ship / I Cover The Waterfront / Ebb Tide / Harbor Lights / Sand And The Sea / La Mer
/ Four Winds And Seven Seas

EL-20012 - ?

EL-20013 - Russell Arms - Where Can A Wanderer Go - 1957
Tracks: Where Can A Wanderer Go / On A Little Street In Singapore / Along The

Soulful Kinda Music – The Rare Soul Bible Volume Two

Colorado Trail / Moon Over Miami / Blue Hawaii / River Seine / Nightingale Sang In Berkeley Square / How Are Things In Glocca Morra / April In Portugal / Autumn In Rome / Bridge Of San Angelo / Home

EL-100 - Danny Gould - Music to Play Checkers By - 1959
Tracks: Clementine / Shenandoah / Frere Jacques / All Though the Night / Londonderry Air / In the Gloaming / Long Long Ago / Greensleeves / Old Folks at Home / Classical Medley / Gay Nineties Medley

EL-101 - Ginny Tiu - All This and Giny Tiu - 1959
Tracks: China Night / El Relicario / Swedish Rhapsody / Turkish March / Little Brown Gal / Moonlight Sonata // Twelfth Street Rag / Bambo Dance / Waltz In A Flat / Inka Dinka Doo / Minuet In G / San Antonio Rose / Fur Elise / Colonel Bogey March / Dialogue / China Night

EL-102 mono - Dorsey Burnette - Tall Oak Tree - 1960
Tracks: Big Rock Candy Mountain / Hey Little One / Hard Working Man / Lucky Old Sun / Suddenly There's A Valley / Lazy Bones // Red Roses / Noah's Ark / Swing Low Sweet Chariot / Wayward Wind / I Got The Sun In The Morning / Tall Oak Tree

ES-700 stereo - Dorsey Burnette - Tall Oak Tree - 1960
Tracks: Big Rock Candy Mountain / Hey Little One / Hard Working Man / Lucky Old Sun / Suddenly There's A Valley / Lazy Bones // Red Roses / Noah's Ark / Swing Low Sweet Chariot / Wayward Wind / I Got The Sun In The Morning / Tall Oak Tree

EL-103 - Burns & Carlin - Burns and Carlin at the Playboy Club - 1960
Tracks:

EL-104 - Larry Verne - Mister Larry Verne - 1960
Tracks: Mister Livingston / Laundromat / Open The Window / Mister Nero / Mister Saki // Beatnik / Roller Coaster / Miss Priscilla / Mister Custer / Tres Dias / Christopher Columbus

EL-105 - Donnie Brooks - The Happiest - 1961
Tracks: That's Why / Memories Are Made Of This / Mission Bell / How Long / The Devil Ain't A Man / Twilight Time // Memphis / P.S. I Love You / All I Can Give / What'd I Say / Doll House / Round Robin

EL-106 - Gogi Grant - The Wayward Wind - 1960
Tracks: The Wayward Wind / I Don't Want To Walk Without You / When The Tide Is High / I Gave You My Heart / We Believe In Love / Who Are We // Golden Ladder / Love Is / It Happens Every Spring / No More Than Forever / You're In Love / Suddenly There's A Valley

EL-107 - ?

EL-108 - Ketty Lester - Love Letters - 1962
Tracks: Love Letters / Once Upon A Time / P.S. I Love You / I'll Never Stop Loving You / Gloomy Sunday / Fallen Angel // Where Or When / I'm A Fool To Want You / Moscow Nights / Porgy, I's Your Woman Now / When I Fall In Love / Goin' Home

Soulful Kinda Music – The Rare Soul Bible Volume Two

ES-108 - Ketty Lester - Love Letters - 1962
Tracks: Love Letters / Once Upon A Time / P.S. I Love You / I'll Never Stop Loving You / Gloomy Sunday / Fallen Angel // Where Or When / I'm A Fool To Want You / Moscow Nights / Porgy, I's Your Woman Now / When I Fall In Love / Goin' Home

ES-109 - Castells - So This Is Love - 1962
Tracks: So This Is Love / I Get Dreamy / Some Enchanted Evening / The Vision Of You / Stikki De Boom Boom / Make Believe Wedding // Oh! What It Seemed to Be / Sacred / Stand There Mountain / Little Sad Eyes / Clown Prince / Dancing In The Dark

ES-110 - Jewel Akens - The Birds and the Bees - 1965
Tracks: Georgie Porgie / Love Potion No. 9 / Sukiyaki / The Birds And The Bees / Michael / So This Is Love // Around The Corner / Dear Heart / Tic Tac Toe / King Of The Road / It's The Only Way To Fly / The Vegetable Love Song

ES-111 - Howlette Smith - Smitty - 1966
Tracks:

F

The Fabulous Apollos

The Fabulous Apollos

Valtone 101 - Determination / The One Alone - 1966 .

The Fabulous Apollos / The Valtone Band

Valtone 102 - It Ain't No Use / (Instrumental)* - 1967 *flip by The Valtone Band.
Valtone 105 - Some Good In Everything Bad* / (Instrumental) - 1967 *lead Tony Daniels. **flip by The Valtone Band.
Valtone 107 - What's So Good To You* / (Instrumental)** - 1968 *lead Joe Matthews. **flip by The Valtone Band.

Darrow Fletcher

DARROW FLETCHER

Margaret Ann Management
Chicago, Illinois
(312) 324-4377

Darrow Fletcher was born on January 23rd 1951 in Inkster, Michigan, on the outskirts of Detroit, but his family moved to Chicago when he was three. His father, Johnny Haygood, wanted his son to have a show business career, so he had Darrow singing at the tender age of six! He schooled at Hirsh, and later South Shore high schools, and begun recording at the grand old age of fourteen, starting off on George Goldner and Cal Rutland's new label, Groovy Records, based at the infamous Brill Building at 1650 Broadway, New York. His initial release, 'The Pain Gets A Little Deeper' (3001), was released during December '65, was penned by Fletcher and Ted Daniels, and produced by Ted and Haygood. It broke out of NYC and made it to #89 on the pop chart and #23 on the soul chart. Its flip-side, 'My Judgement Day' was written by Maurice Simkins, who had a history of singing around Chicago in various doo-wop groups during the 50's, and went on to write many songs for Fletcher over the next few years. This release also gained a second release on Groovy, as the flip to 3009, and more importantly this coupling also gained a UK release at the time on London Records HLU 10024, but it failed to make any kind of impact. Darrow toured quite a few major venues on the back of the success of his initial release, appearing at the Apollo in New York, the Uptown in Philadelphia and the Regal in Chicago, where he shared the bill with Stevie Wonder, The Elgins, Jimmy Ruffin, B.B. King, Lee Dorsey, The Capitols, and the Sharpees.

His three follow-up 45's for Groovy all emerged during '66, starting off with, 'My Young Misery'/' I Gotta Know Why' (3004), but it didn't score on the charts. Apparently while at school Darrow would sing his new material to his classmates for their opinion and they didn't go for this track...maybe he should've taken their advice! 'MYM' was penned by Fletcher and Karl Rudman, whilst the flip side, 'IGKW' was from Simkins, which also appeared as the B.side to 3007. His next release, a cover of The Three Degrees Swan recording, 'Gotta Draw the Line', from the pen of Richie Barrett, was issued on the new green coloured Groovy (3007) label, replacing the old black colour-ed design. Once again this release failed to sell too. His final release for Groovy was, 'That Certain Little Something' (coupled with the second release of 'MJD'), and was written by another prolific artist/producer, Karl Tarleton, but again the record bombed.

Darrow's father felt that the lack of success was due to poor promotion, so he started his own record label, which he named, 'Jacklyn' after one of his daughters. Darrow's first release on Jacklyn was during '66, 'What Have I Got Now' (1002), written by Simkins and produced by Ted Daniels. The song sold well in the Chicago area allegedly shifting 25,000 copies, yet it failed to break out of the area with blame pointing towards distribution. The flip side is a Fletcher/Haygood ballad, 'Sitting There That Night'. His next release from '67 was a Simkins/Fletcher composition, 'Infatuation' (1003), backed with the ballad, 'Little Girl' from Fletcher/Haygood. This track also featured as the B.side to his following release in '67 for Jacklyn, 'What Good Am I Without You' (1006).

By now Darrow was 18 years old, and frustrated with distribution problems in the past, his father took him to Revue Records, which was owned by M.C.A. with its well-established distribution systems. Three singles were released during '68 and '69, all penned by Maurice Simkins: 'The Way Of A Man'/'I Like The Way I Feel' (R11008); 'Gonna Keep Loving You'/'We Can't Go On This Way' (R11023); 'Those Hanging Heartaches'/'Sitting There That Night' (R11035). 'STITN' was originally the flip side to his initial Jacklyn label release, and was used for a third time on the flip side to his next release, which appeared on the Congress label.

'I Think I'm Gonna Write A Song' (Congress 6011) reached # 71 in the Blues & Soul charts and #47 in the soul charts in March '70. It was written by Detroit legend Don Mancha, who had co-written 'What Good Am I'.

In July '70 Darrow moved to another MCA subsidiary, the Uni label where he had another minor hit with, 'When Love Calls'/'Changing By The Minute' (55244), which made it to # 43 in the soul charts. His next single for Uni the following year, 'What Is This'/'Dolly Baby' (55270) reached #64 in the Blues & Soul chart, and was to be his final assault on the chart.

The next label he graced was on Jacklyn's sister label, Genna Records, with 'Now is the time for Love parts 1&2' (1002), which did nothing leaving Darrow out in the cold until '75 when he emerged on Ray Charles', Crossover label, with two 45's, 'Try Something New' / 'It's No Mistake' (980) and 'We've Got An Understanding' / 'This Time I'll Be The Fool' (983). However, once again a lack of promotion meant another release wouldn't do anything sales-wise. The following year he released, 'Improve'/'Let's Get Together' (7083) on the mighty Atco label, and during '79, 'Rising Cost Of Love'/' Honey, Can I' on its parent label, Atlantic (3600), but neither sold through.

Discography

Darrow Fletcher (born 23-January-1951 in Inkster, Michigan - Rose Battiste's cousin)

Groovy 3001 - The Pain Gets A Little Deeper / My Judgement Day - 1966
Groovy 3004 - My Young Misery / I Gotta Know Why – 1966
Groovy 3007 - Gotta Draw The Line* / I Gotta Know Why - 1966 *also recorded in 1965 by The Three Degrees on Swan 4224.
Groovy 3009 - That Certain Little Something / My Judgement Day – 1966
Jacklyn 1002 - What Have I Got Now / Sitting There That Night - 1966
Jacklyn 1003 - Infatuation / Little Girl - 1967
Jacklyn 1006 - What Good Am I Without You / Little Girl - 1967
Revue 11008 - The Way Of A Man / I Like The Way I Feel – 1968
Revue 11023 - Gonna Keep Loving You / We Can't Go On This Way – 1968
Revue 11035 - Those Hanging Heartaches / Sitting There That Night - 1969
Congress 6011 - I Think I'm Gonna Write A Song / Sitting There That Night - 1970
Uni 55244 - When Love Calls / Changing By The Minute – 1970
Uni 55270 - What Is This / Dolly Baby – 1971
Genna 1002 - Now Is The Time For Love (Part 1) / Now Is The Time For Love (Part 2) - 1971
Crossover 980 - Try Something New / It's No Mistake – 1975
Crossover 983 - We've Got An Understanding / This Time I'll Be The Fool – 1976
Atco 7083 - Improve / Let's Get Together – 1978
Atlantic 3600 - Rising Cost Of Love / Honey, Can I - 1979

James Fountain

Soulful Kinda Music – The Rare Soul Bible Volume Two

Peachtree 124 – My Hair Is Nappy / Burning Up For Your Love – 1969
Peachtree 127 – Malnutrition / Seven Day Lover - 1969

Carolyn Franklin

Carolyn Franklin ((Born 13-May-1944 In Memphis, Tennessee. Died 25-April-1988 In Bloomfield Hills, Michigan - Cause: Cancer) Daughter Of Rev. Cecil L. Franklin And His Wife Barbara. Carolyn Was One Of Six Children, Sister Of Erma Franklin (Born 1939 In Shelby, Mississippi, Died 7-September-2002 - Cause: Cancer) And Aretha Franklin (Born 25-March-1942 In Memphis - Raised In Buffalo And Detroit))

RCA-Victor 47-9734 - The Boxer / I Don't Want To Lose You – 1969
RCA-Victor 74-0188 - Reality / It's True I'm Gonna Miss You – 1969
RCA-Victor 74-0289 - Ain't That Groovy / All I Want Is To Be Your Woman – 1969
RCA-Victor 74-0314 - Everybody's Talkin' / Chain Reaction – 1970
RCA-Victor 74-0373 - You Really Didn't Mean It / All I Want Is To Be Your Woman – 1970
RCA-Victor 74-0783 - As Long As You're There / I Want To Be With You – 1972
RCA-Victor Apbo-022 - You Are Everything / If You Want Me – 1973
RCA-Victor Pb-10688 - I Can't Help My Feeling So Blue / If You Want Me – 1976

Erma Franklin

The Cleo-Patretts (members Erma Franklin, ...)

J. V. B. 23 - Say, Would You, Babe / No Other Love - 1953

Erma Franklin (younger sister of Aretha Franklin)

Epic 9468 - Don't Blame Me / What Kind Of Girl - 1961
Epic 9488 - Hello Again / It's Over - 1962
Epic 9511 - Each Night I Cry / Time After Time - 1962
Epic 9516 - Dear Mama / Never Again - 1962
Epic 9559 - Don't Wait Too Long / Time After Time - 1962
Epic 9594 - Have You Ever Had The Blues / I Don't Want No Mama's Boy - 1963
Epic 9610 - Abracadabra / Love Is Blind - 1963

The Lloyd Price Orchestra (Erma Franklin was the Orchestra's featured vocalist between her next solo recording contract)

Erma Franklin

Shout 218 - Big Boss Man / Didn't Catch The Dog's Bone - 1967
Shout 221 - Piece Of My Heart / Baby What You Want Me To Do - 1967
Shout 230 - Open Up Your Soul / I'm Just Not Ready For Love - 1967

Soulful Kinda Music – The Rare Soul Bible Volume Two

Shout 234 - Right To Cry / I'm Just Not Ready For Love - 1968
Brunswick 55403 - Gotta Find Me A Lover (24 Hours A Day) / Change My Thoughts From You - 1969
Brunswick 55415 - Savng My Love / You've Been Cancelled - 1969
Brunswick 55424 - I Just Don't Need You (At All) / It Could've Been Me - 1969
Brunswick 55430 - Whisper's (Gettin' Louder)* / (I Get The) Sweetest Feeling** - 1970

Label Listings

Fairmount

610 - The Taffys - Key To My Heart / Everybody South Street
611 - The Tempos - Oh Play That Thing / Monkey Do
612 - The Dreamers - Daydreamin' Of You / The Promise
613 - Frankie Brunson - Boys Have Feelings Too / Move Baby Move
614 - Guy Maurice - Don't Look For Me / You've Got To Move
1001 - Tari Stevens - False Alarm / A Bad Boy
1002 - Lonnie Youngblood - Gogo Shoes / Gogo Place
1003 - Irma And The Larks - Don't You Cry / Without You Baby
1004 - Dee Dee Sharp - The Love I Feel For You / Willyam Willyam
1005 - Big Dee Irwin - A Sweet Young Thing Like You / You Really Are Together
1006 - Sonny Richards Panic - Rock With Me Baby / I Got Love
1007 - Billy Leonard - Tell Me Do You Love Me / Tears Of Love
1008 - Jo Ann King - Let Them Love And Be Loved / Don't Play With Fire
1009 - Eddie Jones - Let's Stop Fooling Ourselves / Give Me Good Lovin'
1010 - Shirley Vaughn - Climb Every Mountain / You Don't Know
1011 - Oscar Wright - Leave Me Alone / Fell In Love
1012 - Frankie Beverley - She Kissed Me / Don't Cry Little Sad Boy
1013 - Ray Lewis - Getting Over You / Give My Love A Try
1014 - King Coleman - Freedom(Vocal) / Freedom(Inst.)
1015 - ?
1016 - Lonnie Youngblood - The Grass(Will Always Sing For You) / Wooly Bully
1017 - Frankie Beverley - Because Of My Heart / I Want To Feel I'm Wanted
1018 - Gene Waiters - Shake And Shingaling Part 1 / Part 2
1019 - Daddy Rae & Yvonne - Eleven Commandments Of Woman / Shug ?
1020 - ?
1021 - Damon Fox - Boney Maroney / Packing Up
1022 - Lonnie Youngblood - Soul Food / Goodbye Bessie Mae
1023 - Shirley Vaughn - Stop And Listen / Doesn't Everybody
1024 - Bonnie & Lee - I Need Ya / The Way I Feel About You

Fury

Soulful Kinda Music – The Rare Soul Bible Volume Two

1000 - Lewis Lymon & The Teenchords - I'm So Happy (Tra La La La La La) / Lydia
1001 - The Miracles - Your Love (Is All I Need) / I Love You So
1002 - Hal Paige & The Whalers - Don't Have To Cry No More / Pour The Corn
1003 - Lewis Lymon & The Teenchords - Honey Honey (You Don't Know) / Please Tell The Angels
1004 - Little Bobby Rivers & The Hemlocks - Cora Lee / Joys Of Love
1005 - The Federals - While Our Hearts Are Young / You're The One I Love
1006 - Lewis Lymon & The Teenchords - I'm Not Too Young To Fall In Love / Falling In Love
1007 - The Kodaks With Pearl McKinnon - Teenager's Dream / Little Boy And Girl
1008 - Bobby & Buddy - What's The Word - Thunderbird / I Cried
1009 - The Federals - Dear Loraine / She's My Girl
1010 - The Emotions - Candlelight / It's Love1011 - The Du Mauriers - All Night Long / Baby I Love You
1012 - The Velvets - Dance Honey Dance / I - I - I (Love You So - So - So)
1013 - The Duals - Wait Up Baby / Forever And Ever
1014 - Sherman & Darts - Remember (It's Only You And I) / Rockin' At Midnight
1015 - The Kodacks - Oh Gee Oh Gee / Make Believe World
1016 - Tarheel Slim - Number 9 Train / Wildcat Trainer
1017 - The Southwinds - Build Me A Cabin / They Call Me Crazy
1018 - Curtis Carrington - I'm Gonna Catch You / You Are My Sunshine
1019 - The Kodaks - Kingless Castle / My Baby And Me
1020 - The Kodaks - Run Around Baby / Guardian Angel
1021 - The Channels - My Love Will Never Die / Bye Bye Baby
1022 - The Vibra-Harps - The Only Love Of Mine / Be My Dancing Partner
1023 - Wilbert Harrison - Kansas City / Listen My Darling
1024 - Hal Paige & The Whalers - Going Back To My Home Town / After Hours Blues
1025 - Gino - Catastrophe / Right From The Start
1026 - The 3 Emotions - Night We Met / The Girl I Left Behind
1027 - Wilbert Harrison - Cheating Baby / Don't Wreck My Life
1028 - Wilbert Harrison - 1960 / Goodbye Kansas City
1029 - The Premiers - I Pray / Pigtails Eyes Are Blue
1030 - June Bateman - Believe Me Darling / Come On Little Boy
1031 - Wilbert Harrison - C C Rider / Why Did You Leave
1032 - Clarence "Junior" Lewis - Cupid's Little Helper / Half A Heart
1033 - Gil Hamilton - Much Obliged / Pretty Baby
1034 - The Starlites - Valarie / Way Up In The Sky
1035 - Sammy Myers - You Don't Have To Go / Sad Sad Lonesome Day
1036 - The Scarlets - Truly Yours / East Of The Sun
1037 - Wilbert Harrison - Since I Fell For You / Little School Girl
1038 - Delmar - Depending On You / Lizzie Mae
1039 - Little Junior Lewis - Come On Back Where You Belong / And That's All I Need
1040 - Little Junior - Can She Give Me Fever / Your Heart Must Be Made Of Stone
1041 - Wilbert Harrison - The Horse / Da-De-Ya-Da (Anything For You)
1042 - Helen Bryant - That's A Promise / I've Learned My Lesson
1043 - Riff Ruffin - Hucklebuck Scratch / Dig That Rock & Roll
1044 - Buddy Skipper - The Clock / No More Doggin'
1045 - The Starlites - Ain't Cha' Ever Coming Home / Silver Lining
1046 - Ike Nesbit - I Want You / I'm Lonely
1047 - Wilbert Harrison - Happy In Love / Calypso Dance

Soulful Kinda Music – The Rare Soul Bible Volume Two

1048 - Pearl & The Deltars - Teenage Dream / Dance Dance Dance
1049 - Charles Baker - Love Will Make You / Darling Here You Are
1050 - Gladys Knight & The Pips - Every Beat Of My Heart / Room In Your Heart
1051 - Buddy Skipper - Make Believe Baby / Back On The Beach Again
1052 - Gladys Knight & The Pips - Guess Who / Stop Running Around
1053 - Lee Dorsy - Ya Ya / Give Me You
1054 - Gladys Knight & The Pips - Letter Full Of Tears / You Broke Your Promise
1055 - Wilbert Harrison - Drafted / My Heart Is Yours
1056 - Lee Dorsey - Do-Re-Mi / People Gonna Talk
1057 - Jackie & The Starlites - I Found Out Too Late / I'm Coming Home
1058 - Barry & The Tots - Christmas Each Day Of The Year / I'm A Happy Little Christmas Tree
1059 - Wilbert Harrison - Let's Stick Together / Kansa City Twist
1060 - Little Joe Cook - This I Know / These Lonely Tears
1061 - Lee Dorsey - Eenie Meenie Miny Moe / Behind The 8 Ball
1062 - Buddy Skipper - Don't Be A Shame / Baby Please
1063 - Wilbert Harrison - Let's Stick Together / My Heart Is Yours
1064 - Gladys Knight & The Pips - Operator / I'll Trust In You
1065 - ?
1066 - Lee Dorsey - You Are My Sunshine / Give Me Your Love
1067 - The Pips - Darling / Linda
1068 - Slim & Little Ann - Send Me The Pillow You Dream On / I Love You Because
1069 - Tyron Rowe - Mama Don't Allow / I'm A Go'fer
1070 - Jimmy Ricks - I Wonder / Let Me Down Easy
1071 - The Channels - My Love Will Never Die / Bye Bye Baby
1072 - ?
1073 - Gladys Knight - Come See About / I Want That Kind Of Love
1074 - Lee Dorsey - Hoodlum Joe / When I Met My Baby
5000 - Billy Habric - Human / Talk To Me Baby
5001 - ?
5002 - Willie Hightower - If I Had A Hammer / So Tired
5003 - ?
5004 - Willie Hightower - Let's Walk Together / I Love You
5005 - Billy Hambrick - You're A Sweetheart / Flaming Mamie
5006 - Billy Hambre - This Is My Prayer / Everybody Needs Love
5050 - Johnny Jones - Tennessee Waltz / I Find No Fault
5051 - Ricky Lewis - Cupis / Somebody's Gonna Want Me
5052 - Joe Haywood - Ghost Of A Love / Debt Of Love

Kenny Gamble

Kenny Gamble (Born August 11, 1943 In Philadelphia, Pennsylvania)

The Romeos (Formed 1959, Philadelphia, U.S.A.. Members: Kenny Gamble, Thom Bell, Roland Chambers , Karl Chambers, And Winnie Walford)

Kenny Gamble And Tommy Bell

Heritage 108 - Someday You'll Be My Love / I'll Get By Without You - 1962

Kenny Gamble

Epic 9636 - Standing In The Shadows / No Mail On Monday - 1963
Columbia ? - You Don't Know What You Got Until You Lose It / ? - 1963

Kenny Gamble And The Floaters

Arctic 107 - Down By The Seashore Part 1/ Part 2 - 1965

Kenny Gamble & The Romeos

Arctic 114 - Ain't It Baby Part 1 / Ain't It Baby Part 2 - 1965

Kenny Gamble

Arctic 123 - Don't Stop Loving Me / The Joke's On You - 1966
Arctic 127 - Chains Of Love / (I'll Just) Keep On Smilin' - 1967

Kenny Gamble And The Romeos

Atco 6470 - (I'll Work) Eight Days A Week / Hard To Find The Right Girl - 1967

Unreleased - What Am I Gonna Say To My Baby - ?

Don Gardner

Donald Garner

Gotham 200 - Dearest Darlin / September Song - 1949
Gotham 244 - Heart Throb / September Song - 1950

Don Gardner & The Julian Dash Septet

Soulful Kinda Music – The Rare Soul Bible Volume Two

Sittin' In With 598 - Seems Like We Met Before / Why Was I Born - 1951

Dickie Smith with Don Gardner & His Sonotones (members Dickie Smith, Don Gardner, ...)

Bruce 103 - New Kind Of Love / When You're Gone - 1954 (Dickie Smith was a member of The Five Keys, having some time before entering the services, Willie Winfield, Dickie's cousin sets him up a recording session with BRUCE records)

Don Gardner Trio (members Don Gardner, Albert Cass (died 15-April-1969 at age 45) and Jimmy Smith)

Bruce 105 - How Do You Speak To An Angel / Sonotone Bounce - 1954

Don Gardner

Bruce 108 - I'll Walk Alone / Going Down To Big Mary's - 1954

Don Gardner & The Sonotones (members Don Gardner, ...)

Bruce 127 - It's A Sin To Tell A Lie / I Hear A Rhapsody - 1955

Don Gardner

Cameo 102 - Only Love Brings Happiness / Sneakin' In - 1957
Junior 393 - High School Baby / Crying All Alone - 1957
Junior 394 - Dark Alley / Up The Street - 1957
Deluxe 6133 - This Nearly Was Mine / A Dagger In My Chest - 1957
Deluxe 6155 - There! I've Said It Again / I Don't Want To Go Home - 1958
Kaiser 399 - Ask Anything / Humility - 1959
Val-Ue 214 - Glory Of Love / 'Deed I Do - 1960

Don Gardner & Dee Dee Ford

Fire 508 - I Need Your Lovin' / Tell Me - 1962 (Red Label)
Fire 508 - I Need Your Lovin' / Tell Me - 1962 (Multicoloured Label)
Fire 513 - Don't You Worry / I'm Coming Home To Stay - 1962
Barry 3130 - Don't You Worry / I'm Coming Home To Stay - 1962 (Canadian release)
Fire 517 - Lead Me On / T. C. B. (Taking Care Of Business) - 1963
Kc 106 - Glory Of Love / Deed I Do - 1962

Don Gardner And Dee Dee Ford

Red Top 6501 - People Sho' Act Funny / Shake A Leg Baby – 1963
Ludix 104 - Son, Oh Son / You Upset My Soul – 1963

Don Gardner

Jubilee 5482 - Talkin' About You / I Really Love You – 1963
Jubilee 5484 - I Don't Know What I'm Gonna Do / The Bitter With The Sweet – 1963

Soulful Kinda Music – The Rare Soul Bible Volume Two

Jubilee 5493 - I'm In Such Misery / Little Girl Blue – 1964

Don Gardner With The Alteers (Members Don Gardner,..)

G-Clef 704 - Let's Get A Thing Goin' / Let's Get A Thing Goin' – 1964

The Alteers (Members Don Gardner, ...)

G-Clef 705 - This Lovely Night / No End – 1964

Don & Dee Ford

M. O. C. 654 - I Love You / Why Don't You Love Me – 1964

Don Gardner & Dee Dee Ford

Sonet 45 - Shotgun / Heatwave - 1965 (Don Gardner and Dee Dee Ford lived in Sweden for a while, this is a Swedish release)
Flashback 10 - I Need Your Lovin' / Tell Me – 1965

Don Gardner

Tifton 201 - Dog Eat Dog / Maybe I'm Not What You Want Me To Be – 1965

The Don Gardner Orchestra (Members Don Gardner, ...)

Tifton 282 - Fool To Fool / I'm Sitting In - ?

Don Gardner Accomp. By Don Gardner's Orch. / Don Gardner Don Gardner's Orch.

T'n'T 500 -1039/1040 - Let's Party / There's Nothing I Want To Do (Unless It's With You) - 1965 ~ 1966

D G & The Checkmates (Members Don Gardner, ...)

Spectacular 1003 - I Can't Help Myself / Cooking – 1966
Spectacular 2002 - I Can't Help Myself / Cooking - ?

Don Gardner

Tru-Glo-Town 1002 - My Baby Likes To Boogaloo / I Wanta Know Where Did Our Love Go - 1966 (White Label)
Tru-Glo-Town 501 - My Baby Likes To Boogaloo / I Wanta Know Where Did Our Love Go - 1967 (Green Label)
Tru-Glo-Town 505 - Somebody's Gonna Get Hurt / Ain't Gonna Let You Get Me Down – 1967
Sack 4362 - Ain't Gonna Let You Get Me Down / Prove It – 1967
Verve 10582 - I'm A Practical Guy / You Babe – 1968
Mr. G. 824 - Your Love Is Driving Me Crazy / There Ain't Gonna Be No Loving –

Soulful Kinda Music – The Rare Soul Bible Volume Two

1969
Sedgrick 3001 - Cheatin' Kind / What Now My Love – 1969
Cedric 3003 - Is This Really Love / Tighten Up Your Love Bone - 1970

Baby Washington & Don Gardner

Master 5 901 - Baby Let Me Get Close To You / I Just Wanna Be Near To You - 1972
Master 5 9103 - Forever / Baby Let Me Get Close To You – 1973

Don Gardner

Master 5 91o8 - We're Gonna Make It Big / ? – 1973

Baby Washington And Don Gardner

Master 5 9110 - Lay A Little Lovin' On Me / Baby Let Me Get Close To You - 1974
People 101 - Forever / Baby Let Me Get Close To You - 1974

Don Gardner & Dee Dee Ford / The Orioles

Oldies 45 ? - I Need Your Loving / Happy Till The Letter* - ? *Flip By The Orioles.

Don Gardner & Dee Dee Ford / Buster Brown

Trip 25 - I Need Your Lovin' / Fannie Mae* - ? *Flip By Buster Brown.
Oldies 45 110/111 - I Need Your Loving / Is You Or Is You Ain't* - ? *Flip By Buster Brown.

Don Gardner & Dee Dee Ford

Goldies 2601 - I Need Your Lovin' / I'm Coming Home To Stay - ?
Lost Nite 384 - I Need Your Lovin' / Tell Me - ?
Arista 00010 - I Need Your Lovin' / Tell Me - ?

Barbara George

Barbara George (born 16-August-1942 in New Orleans)

A. F. O. 302 - I Know (You Don't Love Me No More)* / Love - 1961 (the "All For One" all orange label is scarcer than orange and black)
A. F. O. 304 - You Talk About Love / Whip-O-Will - 1962
Sue 763 - If You Think / If When You've Done The Best You Can - 1962
Sue 766 - Send For Me (If You Need Some Lovin') / Bless You - 1962
Sue 773 - Recipe (For Perfect Fools) / Try Again - 1962
Sue 796 - Something's Definitely Wrong / I Need Something Different - 1963
Lana 147 - I Know (You Don't Love Me No More) / Love - ?
Seven B 7019 - Something You Got / Satisfied With Your Love - 1967?

Soulful Kinda Music – The Rare Soul Bible Volume Two

Hep' Me 149 - Take Me Somewhere Tonight / I Got My Guard Up - 197?
Hep' Me 159 - This Is The Weekend / Leave Me Alone - 197?

Barbara George / Charles & Inez Foxx

United Artists Xw516 - I Know (You Don't Love Me No More) / Mockingbird* - 1974
*flip by Charles and Inez Foxx only.

Barbara George / Terry Stafford

?

Rosco Gordon

The Beale Streeters (members at one time or another of this loose knit group
were Johnny Ace (born John Marshall Alexander Jr.. on the 9-June-1929 in Memphis,
Tennessee --- died 25-December-1954 --- cause: playing Russian roulette), Earle
Lacy Forrest (born in Memphis - died 26-February-2003 at the Memphis Veterans
Medical Center - cause: cancer), Rosco Gordon, Tuff Green, B. B. King, Bobby "Blue"
Bland, Junior Parker (born 27-March-1932 in West Memphis, Arkansas --- died 18-
November-1971 --- cause: after surgery for brain tumor), Bill Duncan (saxophone),
Earl Forrest (drums),..................................)

Roscoe Gordon And His Orchestra

RPM 322 - Roscoe's Boogie / City Women - 1951

Roscoe Gordon

RPM 324 - Saddled The Cow (And Milked The Horse) / Ouch, Pretty Baby - 1951
RPM 336 - Dime A Dozen / A New Remedy For Love - 1951
RPM 344 - Booted / Cold, Cold Winter - 1952
Chess 1487 - Booted / Love You Till The Day I Die* - 1951 *with Bobby "Blue" Bland
(78 rpm format)
RPM 350 - No More Doggin' / Maria - 1952
RPM 358 - New Orleons Wimmen / I Remember Your Kisses* - 1952 *also recorded
as "I'll Remember All Your Kisses" in 1952 but unreleased until the 1970's by The G-
Clefs on Ditto 503.
RPM 365 - What You Got On Your Mind / Two Kinds Of Women - 1952
RPM 369 - Trying / Dream Baby - 1952
RPM 373 - Lucille (Looking For My Baby) / Blues For My Baby - 1953
RPM 379 - I'm In Love / Just In From Texas - 1953
RPM 384 - We're All Loaded / Tomorrow May Be Too Late - 1953
Duke101 - Tell Daddy / Hey Fat Girl - 1953

Rosco Gordon (born 10-April-1934 in Memphis, Tennessee --- died 11-July-2002
in Queens, New York --- cause: heart attack)

Duke 106 - T-Model Boogie / New Orleons Woman - 1953

Soulful Kinda Music – The Rare Soul Bible Volume Two

Duke 109 - Too Many Women / Wise To You Baby – 1953
Duke 114 - Ain't No Use / Roscoe's Mambo – 1953
Duke 129 - Three Can't Love / You Figure It Out – 1954
Sun 227 - Weeping Blues / Just Love Me Baby – 1955
Flip 227 - Weeping Blues / Just Love Me Baby – 1955
Sun 237 - The Chicken (Dance With You) / Love For You Baby – 1955
Flip 237 - The Chicken (Dance With You) / Love For You Baby – 1955
Sun 257 - Shoobie Oobie / Cheeese And Crackers – 1956
Duke 165 - Keep On Doggin' / Bad Dream – 1957
Duke 173 - I've Loved And Lost / Tummer Tee – 1957
Sun 305 - Sally Jo / Torro – 1958
Vee-Jay 316 - A Fool In Love / No More Doggin' – 1959
Vee-Jay 332 - Just A Little Bit* / Goin' Home - 1959 *covered in 1965 by Roy Head (&
The Traits) on Scepter 12116.
Vee-Jay 348 - Surely I Love You / What You Do To Me – 1960
Duke 320 - Dilly Bop / You'll Never Know – 1960
Vee-Jay 385 - What I Wouldn't Do / Let 'Em Try – 1961
ABC-Paramount 10351 - A Girl To Love / As You Walk Away – 1962
ABC Paramount 10407 - A Little Bit Of Magic / I Want Revenge – 1963
Modern 31 - Looking For My Baby / No More Doggin' - ?
ABC-Paramount 10501 - I Don't Stand A Chance / That's What You Did - 1963
(Barbara & Rosco Gordon)
Old Town 1167 - Gotta Keep Rollin' / Just A Little At A Time – 1964
Oldies 45   34 - Goin' Home / Just A Little Bit - 1964
Oldies 45   74 - A Fool In Love / No More Doggin' - 1964

Rosco & Barbara (Roscoe Gordon and Barbara Kerr - Rosco's wife (died 1984))

Old Town 1175 - It Ain't Right / Could This Be Love – 1965

Rosco Gordon / The Vows

Hollywood 1018 - T-Model Boogie / I Wanna Chance* - ? *Flip By The Vows.

Rosco Gordon

Jomada 602 - Jesse James* / You Got My Bait - 1966 *backing vocals by Dee Dee
Warwick.
Rae Cox 1002 - Goin' To A Party / I Really Love You - 1967
Calla 145 - Just A Little Bit / I Really Love You - 1968
Calla 145 - Just A Little Bit / I Really Love You – 1968

Rosco And Marc Gordon / Rosco Gordon-Barbara Kerr

Bab-Roc 004 - Don't Mess With My Stuff / Ain't Nobody's Business - 1970
Bab-Roc 004 - Little Bit Of Magic / Ain't Nobody's Business (Instrumental) – 1970

Rosco Gordon / Rosco Gordon & Barbara Kerr

Bab-Roc 005 - Find Yourself Another Fool / It Ain't Nobody's Business (What We

Soulful Kinda Music – The Rare Soul Bible Volume Two

Do)* - ? *flip by Rosco Gordon and Barbara Kerr.
Bab-Roc 008 - Find Yourself Another Fool / It Ain't Nobody's Business (What We Do)* - 1970 *flip by Rosco Gordon and Barbara Kerr.

Rosco Gordon

Bab-Roc 008 - Who's Been Doing It (Since I Been Gone) / Just A Little Bit - ?
Bab-Roc 009 - Who's Been Doing It (Since I Been Gone) / Just A Little Bit - ?
Bab-Roc 012 - Revenge / I Got Love - ?
Collectables Col 013417 - What You Do To Me / Surely I Love You - 1981

Rosco Gordon & Jane Powell

Ripete 2007 - Last Call For Alcohol / Makin' Whoopee - 1989

Roscoe Gordon

Ripete 217 - Let's Get High / No More Doggin' - 1990

Rosco Gordon / Martha Reeves

Ripete 270 - Just A Little Bit / It's The Same Old Song - 1990

Rosco Gordon

Ripete 271 - No More Doggin' Let's Get High - 1990

Updates by Jennings Falcon, Daniel Günther, and Jules Hardstone

Label Listings
Gama

45-296 - 'Doc' & The Interns – Baby I Know / We Can Work It Out
45-666 - Leroy Charlton – Why Can't You Love Me / Why Can't You Love Me (Instrumental)
45-674 - The Maskman And The Agents – Never Would Have Made It / There'll Be Some Changes - 1968
45-675 - Richie Kay – It's All Over / And One Forever

Gamble

201 - The Intruders - United / Up And Down The Ladder
202 - King Arthur & The Knights - Do You / So Sweet So Fine
203 - The Intruders - A Book For The Broken Hearted / Devil With An Angel's Smille

Soulful Kinda Music – The Rare Soul Bible Volume Two

204 - The Intruders - It Must Be Love / Check Yourself
205 - The Intruders - Together / Up And Down The Ladder
206 - Gail Anderson - Let's Fall In Love All Over / ?
207 - The Cruisers - I Need You So / Take A Chance
208 - ?
209 - The Intruders - A Love That's Real / Baby I'm Lonely
210 - The Music Makers - United Part 1 / Part 2
211 - The Bee Kays - Eric The Viking / It's Better
212 - The Mad Men - Do The African Twist Part 1 / Part 2
213 - The Baby Dolls - Please Don't Rush Me / There You Are
214 - The Intruders - Cowboys To Girls / Turn The Hands Of Time
215 - The Music Makers - Spring Fever Part 1 / Part 2
216 - Bobby Marchan - For Girls To Be Lonely (Ain't No Reason) Part 1 / Part 2
217 - The Intruders - Love Is Like A Baseball Game / Friends No More
218 - Jaggerz - (That's Why) Baby I Love You / Bring It Back
219 - Dee Dee Sharp - What Kind Of Lady / You're Gonna Miss Me
220 - Frankie Beverley - If That's What You Wanted / Your Pain Goes Deep
221 - The Intruders - Slow Drag / So Glad I'm Yours
222 - The Boss Man - When I Had Money / You're Taking Too Long
223 - The Intruders - Give Her A Transplant / Girls Girls Girls
224 - The Brothers Of Hope - I'm Gonna Make You Love Me / Nickol Nickol
225 - The Intruders - Me Tarzan You Jane / Favorite Candidate
226 - Jaggerz - Gotta Find My Way Back Home / Forever Together Together Forever
227 - Scorpio Ascendants - Billy B Moanin / ?
228 - Bob Crewe - Heartaches / More Than The Eye Can See
229 - The Space Walkers - Apollo No. 9 / ?
230 - The Panic Buttons - O Wow / Lisa
231 - The Intruders - Lollipop (I Like You) / Don't Give It Away
232 - Billy Paul - Somewhere / Bluesette
233 - The Butlers - She's Gone / Love Is Good
234 - Oliver Bush - I'll Make It Up To You / Soul In Motion
235 - The Intruders - Let's Go Downtown / Sad Girl
236 - The Panic Buttons - Come Out Smokin' / Bad Karma
237 - ?
238 - Jaggerz - Let Me Be Your Man / Together
239 - ?
240 - The Intruders - Old Love / Everyday Is A Holiday
241 - Donnie Van - Hold Back The Night / A Hundred Pounds Of Him
4000 - The Cruisers - Picture Us / Mink & Sable Mable
4001 - The Intruders - Tenderly As The Love We Knew / By The Time I Get To Phoenix
4002 - Dawn - Ba Ba Ba De Ba / In Love Again
4003 - The Brothers Of Hope - Spring Fever Part 1 / Part 2
4004 - The Intruders - Doctor Doctor / When We Get Married
4005 - Dee Dee Sharp - You're Gonna Miss Me (When I'm Gone) The Bottle Or Me
4006 - Faustus - Baby Please / Gotta See My Baby
4007 - The Intruders - This Is My Love / Let Me In Your Mind
4008 - Jaggerz - Higher And Higher / Ain't No Sun
4009 - The Intruders - I'm Girl Scoutin' / Wonder What Kind Of Bag She's In
4010 - Moses - Take This Load Off My Back / ?

Soulful Kinda Music – The Rare Soul Bible Volume Two

4011 - Joe Cook - America Don't Turn Your Back / Funky Hump
4012 - Jaggerz - Here's A Heart / Need Your Love
4013 - B K Marcus - Does She Care About Me / Hippie Of The City
4014 - The Intruders - Best Days Of My Life / Pray For Me
4015 - Bobby Wilburn - I'm A Lonely Man / I'm In A Daydream
4016 - The Intruders - I Bet He Don't Love You / Do You Remember Yesterday
4017 - Spring - Fever Part 1 / Part 2
4018 - Jimmy Jewels - I Should Have Listened / Women Gonna Rule The World
4019 - The Intruders - Memories Are Here To Stay / She's A Winner
2501 - The Intruders - She's A Winner / Memories Are Here To Stay
2502 - The Futures - Love Is Here / Stay With Me
2503 - Ruth McFadden - Ghetto Woman Part 1 / Part 2
2504 - Pat & The Blenders - Don't Say You Love Me / Candy Man
2505 - Ruby & The Party Gang - Ruby's Surprise Party / Too Much Pride
2506 - The Intruders - I Always Love My Mama Part 1 / Part 2
2507 - John & Gene - Super Groover All Night Mover / Don't Be So Mean
2508 - The Intruders - I Wanna Know Your Name / Hang On In There
2509 - Dandridge Choral Ensemble - Everybody Wants To Go To Heaven / If
2510 - Frankie & The Spindles - Makin' Up Time Part 1 / Part 2
2512 - Mello Moods - Stop Taking My Love For Granted / Inspirational Pleasure

Goldwax

101 - Lyrics - Darling / How A Woman Does Her Man
102 - Oboe - Day The World Cried (Pt. 1) / Day The World Cried (Pt. 2)
103 - Bobby Mcdowel - Our Last Quarrel / These Ain't Raindrops
104 - Oboe Mcclinton & The Keys - She's Better Than You / Too Slow
105 - Lyrics - The Side Wind / So Hard To Get Along
106 - O. V. Wright - That's How Strong My Love Is / There Goes My Used To Be
107 - Eddie Boyd - I Can't Fight This Much Longer / Now And Then
108 - James Carr - You Don't Want Me / Only Fools Run Away
109 - Phillip And The Faithfuls - Love Me / Rhythm Marie
110 - Ovations Featuring Louis Williams - Won't You Call / Pretty Little Angel
111 - Gene "Bowlegs" Miller - Bowlegged /Toddlin'
112 - James Carr - I Can't Make It / Lover's Competition
113 - Ovations Featuring Louis Williams - Dance Party / It's Wonderful To Be In Love
114 - Ovations Featuring Louis Williams - They Say / Me And My Imagination
115 - Dorothy Williams - The Well's Gone Dry / Country Style
116 - Al Vance - Every Woman I Know / Have You Seen Jean
117 - Ovations Featuring Louis Williams - Recipe For Love / I'm Living Good
118 - Spencer Wiggins - Love Works That Way / I'll Be True To You
119 - James Carr - She's Better Than You / Talk Talk
120 - Lamars - My Motor Byke Balked / Patsy
300 - Ovations - Don't Cry / I Need A Lot Of Loving
301 - Vel-Tones - Darling / I Do
302 - James Carr - You've Got My Mind Messed Up / That's What I Want To Know
303 - Yo Yo's - Leaning On You / I Can't Forget It
304 - Oboe - Trying To Make It / I'm Just That Kind Of Fool
305 - Gene "Bowlegs" Miller - Here It Is Now / What Time Ye Got

Soulful Kinda Music – The Rare Soul Bible Volume Two

306 - Ovations - I Believe I'll Go Back Home / Qualifications
307 - Ivory Joe Hunter / Every Little Bit Helped Me / I Can Make You Happy
308 - Spencer Wiggins - The Kind Of Woman That's Got No Heart / Take Me Just As I Am
309 - James Carr - Love Attack / Coming Back To You Baby - Goldwax
310 - Yo Yo's - Gotta Find A New Love
311 - James Carr - Pouring Water On A Drowning Man / Forgetting You
312 - Spencer Wiggins - Old Friend / Walking Out On You
313 - George & Greer - You Didn't Know It But You Had Me / Good Times
314 - Ovations - Me And My Imagination / They Say
315 - Percy Milem - Crying Baby Baby Baby / Call On Me
316 - Eddie Jefferson - Some Other Time / When You Look In The Mirror
317 - James Carr - Dark End Of The Street / Lovable Girl
318 - Barbara Perry - Say You Need Me / Inlovable
319 - Terry's - Cry Me A Handful / Stormy Love Affair
320 - Timmy Thomas - Have Some Boogaloo / Liquid Mood
321 - Spencer Wiggins - Uptight Good Woman / Anything You Do Is Alright
322 - Ovations - I've Gotta Go / Ride My Trouble And Blues Away
323 - James Carr - Let It Happen / A Losing Game
324 - Carmel Taylor - Here Comes The Fool / Did She Ask About Me
325 - Terry's - Stay Away From Brenda / I Don't Feel Guilty
326 - Percy Milem - I Don't Know What You Got / She's About A Mover
327 - Timmy Thomas - It's My Life / Whole Lotta Shakin' Going On
328 - James Carr - I'm A Fool For You / Gonna Send You Back To Georgia
329 - Wee Willie Walker - Ticket To Ride / There Goes My Used To Be
330 - Spencer Wiggins - The Power Of A Woman / Lonely Man
331 - Jeanne Newman - He Called Me Baby / Good Apples Fall
332 - James Carr - A Man Needs A Woman / Stranger Than Love
333 - Spencer Wiggins - That's How Much I Love You / A Poor Man's Son
334 - Five C's - Love Is A Tricky Thing / If You're Looking For A Man
335 - James Carr - Life Turned Her That Way / Message To Young Lovers
336 - Ben Atkins And The Nomads - Love Is Beautiful Thing / Love Is Beautiful Thing (Inst)
337 - Spencer Wiggins - Once In A While / He's Too Old
338 - James Carr - Freedom Train / That's The Way Love Turned For Me
339 - Spencer Wiggins - I Never Loved A Woman / Soul City USA
340 - James Carr - To Love Somebody / These Ain't Raindrops
341 - Ovations - Rocking Chair / Happiness - Goldwax
342 - Ovations - You Had Your Choice / I'm Living Good - Goldwax
343 - James Carr - Row Your Boat / Everybody Needs Somebody – Goldwax

Groove City

101 – The Professionals – That's Why I Love You / Did My Baby Call
201 – Robert Ward – My Love Is Strictly Reserved For You / I Will Fear No Evil
202 – Fred Bridges – Sound Off / I'm So Sorry
203 – Robbie D And The Robbettes / The Detroit Land Apples – Precious Memories /

Soulful Kinda Music – The Rare Soul Bible Volume Two

I Need Help
204 – Steve Mancha – Hate Yourself In The Morning / A Love Like Yours
205 – Sam Ward – Stone Broke / Sister Lee
206 – New Holidays – Easy Living / I've Lost You
960 – Cody Black – Because You First Loved Me / The Night A Star Was Born

Groovesville

1001 - Steve Mancha - You're Still In My Heart / She's So Good
1002 - Steve Mancha - I Don't Want To Lose You / I Need To Be Needed
1003 - Melvin Davis - I Must Love You / Still In My Heart
1004 - Steve Mancha - Friday Night / Monday Thru Thursday
1005 - Steve Mancha - Don't Make Me A Story Teller / I Won't Love And Leave You
1006 - J.J. Barnes - Baby Please Come Back Home / Chains Of Love
1007 - Steve Mancha - Sweet Baby (Don't Ever Be Untrue) / Just Keep On Loving Me
1008 - J.J. Barnes - Now That I Got You Back / Forgive Me
777 - Al Gardner - I'm Moving On / I'll Get Along

Groovy

3001 - Darrow Fletcher - The Pain Gets A Little Deeper / My Judgement Day
3002 - Danny Boy Thomas - Have No Fear / My Love Is Over
3003 - Towanda Barnes - Oh Darling / If I'm Guilty
3004 - Darrow Fletcher - My Young Misery / I've Gotta Know Why
3005 - Johnny Seville - You Lied / Make Up Your Mind
3006 - Jackye Owens - Tenderly Tenderly / You're Doing Something Awfully Good
3007 - Darrow Fletcher - Gotta Draw The Line / I've Gotta Know Why
3008 - Jackye Owens - Love That Guy / A Million To One
3009 - Darrow Fletcher - That Certain Little Something / My Judgement Day

H

Z Z Hill

Z. Z. Hill (born Arzel Hill on 30-September-1935 in Naples, Texas - died 27-April-1984 in Dallas, Texas cause: two months after a traffic accident he died in hospital from complications arising from a related blood clot)

MH 200 - You Were Wrong / Tumble Weed - 1963 (Mh Records Were Founded In Los Angeles By Z. Z. Hills Older Brother Matt)
MH 202 - Come On Home / One Way Love Affair - 1964
Mesa 200 - Five Will Get You Ten / The Right To Love - 1964
Kent 404 - You Don't Love Me / If I Could Do It All Over - 1964
Kent 416 - Have Mercy Someone / Someone To Love Me - 1965
Kent 427 - Hey Little Girl / Oh Darlin' - 1965
Kent 432 - What More / That's It - 1965
Kent 439 - Happiness Is All I Need / Everybody Has To Cry - 1965
Kent 444 - No More Doggin' / The Kind Of Love I Want - 1966
Kent 449 - I Found Love / Set Your Sights Higher - 1966
Kent 453 - Gimme Gimme / You Can't Hide A Heartache - 1966
Kent 460 - Greatest Love / Oh Darling - 1967
Kent 464 - Where She At / Baby I'm Sorry - 1967
Kent 469 - Everybody Needs Somebody / You Just Lie And Cheat - 1967
Kent 478 - What Am I Living For / You Gonna Need My Lovin' - 1967
Kent 481 - Nothing Can Change This Love I Have For You / Steal Away - 1968
Kent 494 - You Got What I Need / Have Mercy Someone - 1968
Kent 502 - Don't Make Promises (You Can't Keep) / Set Your Sights Higher - 1968
Atlantic 2659 - It's A Hang Up Baby / (Home Just Ain't Home) At Suppertime - 1969
Atlantic 2711 - Faithful And True / I Think I'll Do It Early In The Morning - 1970 (This Record Number Was Also Assigned To The 1970 Release By Mighty Sam "Your Love Is Amazing / Evil Woman")
Quinvy 7003 - Faithful And True / I Think I'd Do It - 1970
Hill 222 - Don't Make Me Pay For His Mistakes / Think People - 1971
Kent 4547 - I Need Someone (To Love Me) / Oh Darling - 1971
Mankind 12003 - Faithful And True / I Think I'd Do It - 1971
Kent 4550 - You Don't Love Me / Have Mercy Someone - 1971
Audrey 223 - You Better Take Time / It Can Be Fixed - 1971
Mankind 12007 - Chokin' Kind / Hold Back (One Man At A Time) - 1971
Kent 4560 - If I Could Do It All Over / You Won't Hurt No More - 1972
Audrey 224 - Sweet Woman By Your Side / Ain't To Proud To Beg - 1972
United Artists 50908 - Dream Don't Let Me Down / Your Love - 1972
Mankind 12012 - Second Chance / I Think I'd Do It - 1972
Mankind 12015 - It Ain't No Use / Ha Ha (Laughing Song) - 1972
United Artists 50977 - I've Got To Get You Back / Your Love Makes Me Feel So Good - 1972
Mankind 12017 - A Man Needs A Woman / Chokin' Kind - 1972
Hill / United Artists Xw225 - Ain't Nothing You Can Do / Love In The Street - 1973
Hill / United Artists Xw307 - I Don't Need Half A Love / Friendship Only Goes So Far - 1973
Hill / United Artists Xw365 - Let Them Talk / The Red Rooster - 1973

Soulful Kinda Music – The Rare Soul Bible Volume Two

Hill / United Artists Xw412 - Am I Groovin' You / Bad Mouth And Gossip - 1974
Hill / United Artists Xw536 - I Keep On Lovin' You / Who Ever's Thrilling You (Is Killing Me) - 1974
Hill / United Artists Xw631 - I Created A Monster / Steppin' In The Shoes Of A Fool - 1975
MHR 221 - Mr. Nobody, Somebody / Think People - 1975
MHR 224 - You Better Take Time / It Can Be Fixed - 1975
MHR 228 - My Girl / Don't Make Me Pay - 1976
Columbia 3-10552 - Love Is So Good When You Are Stealing It / Need You By My Side - 1977
Columbia 3-10680 - This Time They Told The Truth / Near But Yet So Far - 1978
Columbia 3-10748 - Universal Love / That's All That's Left - 1978
Columbia 1-11089 - Whip It On Me Baby / Just Because We're No Longer Lovers - 1979
Columbia 1-11156 - I Don't Want Our Love To Be No Secret / I Want To Be Your Every Need - 1979
Malaco 2069 - Please Don't Make Me (Do Something Bad To You) / Blue Monday - 1980
Malaco 2074 - Seperate Way / Chained To Your Love - 1981
Malaco 2076 - Bump And Grind / Something Good Going On - 1981
Malaco 2079 - Cheating In The Next Room / Right Arm For Your Love - 1982
Malibu 05820 - Touch 'Em With Love / Faithful And True - 1982
Malaco 2082 - When Can We Do This Again / When It Rains It Pours - 1982
Malaco 2085 - What Am I Going To Tell Her / Get You Some Business - 1983
Malaco 2090 - Open House At My House / Who You Been Givin' It To - 1983
Malaco 2094 - Get A Little, Give A Little / Blind Side - 1983
Malaco 2097 - Three Into Two Won't Go / Steal Away - 1984
Rare Bullet 4241 - Hold Back (One Man At A Time) / Put A Little Love In Your Heart - 1984
Malaco 2103 - Shade Tree Mechanic / Steppin' In Steppin' Out - 1984
Malaco 2109 - Personally / I'm Gonna Stop You From Giving Me The Blues – 1985

George Hobson

Sound City 1001 - Let It Be Real / A Place In My Heart - 1968

Cissy Houston

The Gospelaires (members **Dionne Warwick**, Delia Warwick and Cissy Houston)

The Drinkard Singers (members Lee Drinkard (who is Dionne and **Dee Dee Warwick**'s mother) and her sister Emily Drinkard (aka Cissy Houston -- Whitney Houston's mother) and later **Judy Clay** (who was "adopted" by Lee Drinkard, Ann Moss, Marie Epps, Nicholas Drinkard and Larry Drinkard)

Soulful Kinda Music – The Rare Soul Bible Volume Two

The Drinkard Singers (members Emily Drinkard,, Judy Clay, Marie Epps, Ann Moss, Sylvia Shemwell and Nicholas Drinkard)

Choice 24 - Out Of The Depths / You Can't Make Me Doubt Him - 1962
Choice 30 - Do You Love Him / Holding The Saviours Hand - 1962
Choice 36 - Joy Unspeakable / Out Of The Depths - 1962

Susie Houston

Congress 268 - Bring Him Back / World Of Broken Hearts - 1966

Sissie Houston

Kapp 814 - Don't Come Running To Me / One Broken Heart For Sale - 1967

The Sweet Inspirations (members Emily (Cissy) Houston, Estelle Brown (former member of The Gospel Wonders), Sylvia Shemwell and Myrna Smith (one time member of The Gospelaires)) This group sang backing vocals behind numerous artists including Nina Simone, Garnet Mimms, Aretha Franklin, **Chuck Jackson**, **Maxine Brown** and Dionne Warwick.

Atlantic 2410 - Why (Am I Treated So Bad) / I Don't Want To Go On Without You - 1967
Atlantic 2418 - Let It Be Me / When Something Is Wrong With My Baby - 1967
Atlantic 2436 - I've Been Loving You Too Long / That's How Strong My Love Is - 1967
Atlantic 2449 - Don't Fight It / Oh What A Fool I've Been - 1967
Atlantic 2465 - Do Right Woman - Do Right Man / Reach Out For Me - 1967
Atlantic 2476 - Sweet Inspiration / I'm Blue - 1968
Atlantic 2529 - To Love Somebody / Where Did It Go - 1968
Atlantic 2551 - Unchained Melody / Am I Ever Gonna See My Baby Again - 1968
Atlantic 2571 - What The World Needs Now Is Love / You Really Didn't Mean It - 1968
Atlantic 2620 - Crying In The Rain / Every Day Will Be Like A Holiday - 1969
Atlantic 2638 - Sweets For My Sweet / Get A Little Older - 1969
Atlantic 2653 - Don't Go / Chained - 1969
Atlantic 2686 - (Gotta Find) A Brand New Lover (Part 1) / (Gotta Find) A Brand New Lover (Part 2) - 1969 (after this release Cissy Houston leaves group to start solo career, she was temporarily replaced by Ann Williams)

Cissy Houston (born Emily Drinkard in 1933 in Newark, New Jersey)

Commonwealth United 3010 - I'll Be There / So I Believe - 1970
Janus 131 - I Just Don't Know What To Do With Myself / This Empty Place - 1970
Janus 145 - Be My Baby / I'll Be There - 1971
Janus 159 - Hang On To A Dream / Darling Take Me Back - 1971
Janus 177 - I Love You* / Making Love - 1971 *Written By Ed Townsend.
Janus 190 - Didn't We / It's Not Easy - 1972
Janus 206 - Midnight Train To Georgia* / Will You Still Love Me Tomorrow - 1972
*Song Was Originally Titled "Midnight Plane To Houston".

Soulful Kinda Music – The Rare Soul Bible Volume Two

Janus 230 - I'm So Glad I Can Love Again / The Only Time You Say You Love Me (Is When We're Making Love)* - 1973 Janus 255 - He - I Believe / Nothing Can Stop Me* - 1975 *Written By Tony Hestor.

Herbie Mann & Cissy Houston / Herbie Mann

Atlantic 3343 - Cajun Moon / So Get It While You Can* - 1976 *Flip By Herbie Mann.

Cissy Houston

Private Stock 45,137 - Love Is Something That Leads You / It Never Really Ended - 1977
Private Stock 45,137 - Love Is Something That Leads You / If I Ever Lose This Heaven - 1977
Private Stock 45,153 - Tomorrow / Love Is Holding On - 1977
Private Stock 45,171 - Things To Do / It Never Really Ended - 1977
Private Stock 45,204 - Think It Over / The Umbrella Song - 1978
Columbia 11058 - Warning - Danger (This Love Affair May Be Hazardous To You) / An Umbrella Song - 1979
Columbia 11208 - Break It To Me Gently / Gonna Take The Easy Way Out – 1980

Thelma Houston

The Art Reynolds Singers (members Thelma Houston, ...)

Capitol 5656 - Glory Glory Hallelujah* / I Won't Be Back - 1966 *lead Thelma Houston.

Thelma Houston

Capitol 5767 - Baby Mine / Woman Behind Her Man - 1966
Capitol 5882 - Don't Cry, My Soldier Boy / Let's Try To Make It (Just Once More) - 1967
ABC Dunhill 11 - Everybody Gets To Go To The Moon / Everybody Gets To Go To The Moon - 1969 (a special Apollo 11 promotional item - some copies issued with picture sleeve)
ABC Dunhill 4197 - Sunshower / If This Was The Last Song - 1969
ABC Dunhill 4212 - Jumpin' Jack Flash / This Is Your Life - 1969
ABC Dunhill 4222 - Save The Country / I Just Can't Stay Away - 1970
ABC Dunhill 4260 - The Good Earth / Ride, Louie, Ride - 1970
Mowest 5008 - I Want To Go Back There Again / Pick Of The Week - 1972 (promo issues came in blue vinyl) Mowest 5013 - Me And Bobby McGee / No One's Gonna Be A Fool Forever - 1972
Mowest 5023 - Piano Man / Me And Bobby McGee - 1972
Mowest 5027 - What If / There Is A God - 1972
Mowest 5046 - If It's The Last Thing I Do / And I Never Did - 1973 (Unreleased)
Mowest 5050 - I'm Just A Part Of Yesterday / Piano Man - 1973
Motown 1245 - I'm Just A Part Of Yesterday / Piano Man - 1973
Motown 1260 - No One's Gonna Be A Fool Forever / Together - 1973 (Promo Issue Only)

Soulful Kinda Music – The Rare Soul Bible Volume Two

Motown 1260 - Do You Know Where You're Going / Together - 1973 (Have Reference To This Release With This "A" Side Also)
Motown 1316 - You've Been Doing Wrong For So Long / Pick Of The Week - 1974

Thelma Houston / William Goldstein

Motown 1385 - The Bingo Long Song (Steal On Home) / Razzle Dazzle (Instrumental)* - 1976 *flip by William Goldstein (some copies issued with picture sleeve)

Thelma Houston

Tamla 54275 - One Out Of Every Six (Censored Version) / One Out Of Every Six (Uncensored Version) - 1976 (Promo Issues Only)
Tamla 54275 - One Out Of Every Six (Censored Version) / Pick Of The Week - 1976

Jerry Butler & Thelma Houston

Motown 1422 - It's A Lifetime Thing / Kiss Me Now - 1977

Diana Ross / Thelma Houston

Motown M 00010 - Your Love Is So Good For Me (6:32) / I Can't Go On Living Without Your Love (4:32) - 1978 (12" Release "A" Side Diana Ross Only - Flip Thelma Houston Only)

Thelma Houston

Tamla 54278 - Don't Leave Me This Way (Short Version)* / Today Will Soon Be Yesterday - 1977 *Originally Recorded In 1975 By Harold Melvin & The Blue Notes On Philadelphia International 3712.
Tamla 54278 - Don't Leave Me This Way (Short Version) / Don't Leave Me This Way (Long Version) - 1977 (Promo Issue Only)
Tamla 54283 - If It's The Last Thing I Do / If You Won't Let Me Walk On The Water - 1977
Tamla 54287 - I'm Here Again / Between Ourselves - 1977
Tamla 54287 - I'm Here Again / Sharin' Something Perfect - 1977
Tamla 54292 - I Can't Go On Living Without Your Love / Any Way You Like It - 1978
Tamla 54295 - I'm Not Strong Enough To Love You / Triflin' - 1978
Tamla 54297 - Saturday Night, Sunday Morning / Come To Me - 1979
Motown 00053 - Ride To The Rainbow / Love Machine - 1979 (12" Release)
RCA PB-11913 - Suspicious Minds / Gone - 1980
RCA PB-12215 - If You Feel It / Hollywood - 1981
RCA PD-12293 - 96 Tears / There's No Runnin' Away From Love - 1981 (12" release)
RCA PB-12285 - 96 Tears / There's No Runnin' Away From Love - 1981
MCA L33-1795 - Working Girl (3:45) / Working Girl (5:00) - 1983 (12" promo issue only)
MCA 13963 - Working Girl / Running In Circles - 1983 (12" release)
MCA 52196 - Working Girl / Running In Circles - 1983
MCA 52239 - Make It Last / Just Like All The Rest - 1983

Soulful Kinda Music – The Rare Soul Bible Volume Two

MCA L33-1253 - I'd Rather Spend The Bad Times With You (Three Versions) - 1983
(12" promo issue only)
MCA 52489 - (I Guess) It Must Be Love / Running In Circles - 1984
MCA 52491 - You Used To Hold Me So Tight / Love Is A Dangerous Game - 1984
MCA 23520 - You Used To Hold Me So Tight (12" Version) / You Used To Hold Me
So Tight (Dub) (Lp Version) - 1985 (12" release)

B. B. King / Thelma Houston

MCA 52574 - My Lucille / Keep It Light* - 1985 *flip by Thelma Houston. (some
copies issued with picture sleeve)

Thelma Houston

MCA 52582 - What A Woman Feels Inside / Fantasy And Heartbreak - 1985
Reprise Pro-A-4475 - High (Four Versions) - 1990 (12" Promo Issue Only)
Reprise 21765 - High (Five Versions) - 1990 (12" Release)
Reprise Pro-A-4487 - Out Of My Hands (Remix) / Out Of My Hands (Remix) - 1990
(12" Promo Issue Only)
Reprise 21769 - Out Of My Hands (Five Versions) - 1990 (12" Release)
Reprise 40080 - Throw You Down (Four Versions) - What He Has (Two Versions) -
1990 (12" Release)
Century 2000   1001 - Hold On (Four Versions) / Athens Grooves / Olympus Thunder
- 1990 (12" release)

Tommy Hunt

The Five Echoes with the Fats Coles Band (group had a fluctuating line-
up amongst group members were Tommy Hunt, Constant "Count" Sims, Earl Lewis,
Herbert Lewis, Jimmy Marshall, Johnnie Taylor (who replaced a drafted Tommy
Hunt), Walter Spriggs and Andre Williams)

Sabre 102 – Lonely Mood / Baby Come Back To Me – 1953 (Black Vinyl)
Sabre 102 – Lonely Mood / Baby Come Back To Me – 1953 (Red Vinyl)

The Five Echoes

Sabre 107 - Why Oh Why / That's My Baby - 1954 (Can anyone confirm that this 45
was released on this number ?)

The Flamingos (members Tommy Hunt, Nate Nelson, Jake Carey and Paul Wilson)
1957 line-up

Decca 30335 - The Ladder Of Love / Let's Make Up - 1957
Decca 30454 - Helpless / My Faith In You - 1957
Decca 30687 - Where Mary Go / The Rock And Roll March - 1958
End 1035 - Lovers Never Say Goodbye / That Love Is You – 1958
End 1040 - But Not For Me / I Shed A Tear At Your Wedding - 1959

Soulful Kinda Music – The Rare Soul Bible Volume Two

End 1044 - At The Prom / Love Walked In – 1959
End 1045 - I Only Have Eyes For You / At The Prom - 1959
End 1046 - I Only Have Eyes For You / Goodnight Sweetheart – 1959
Decca 30880 - Ever Since I Met Lucky / Kiss-A-Me - 1959
End 1055 - Love Walked In / Yours - 1959
Decca 30948 - Jerri-Lee / Hey Now! - 1959
End 1062 - I Was Such A Fool / Heavenly Angel - 1959
End 1065 - Mi Amore / You, Me And The Sea - 1960
End 1068 - Nobody Loves Me Like You / You, Me And The Sea – 1960
End 1070 - Besame Mucha / You, Me And The Sea – 1960
End 1073 - Mi Amore / At Night – 1960
End 1079 – When I Fall In Love / Beside You – 1960
End 1085 – That's Why I Love You / Ko Ko Mo – 1960
End 1092 – Time Was / Dream Girl – 1960
End 1099 – My Memories Of You / I Want To Love You - 1960

Tommy Hunt (born Charles Hunt on 18-June-1933 in Pittsburgh, Pennsylvania)

Scepter 1219 - Human / Parade Of Broken Hearts -1961
Scepter 1226 - The Door Is Open / I'm Wondering - 1962
Scepter 1231 - So Lonely / The Work Song – 1962
Scepter 1235 - Didn't I Tell You She'll Hurt You / Poor Millionaire You're So Fine – 1962
Scepter 1236 - And I Never Knew / I Just Don't Know What To Do With Myself* - 1962 *also recorded in 1965 by Dusty Springfield on Philips 40319
Scepter 1252 - Do You Really Love Me / Son, My Son - 1963
Scepter 1261 - I Am A Witness* / I'm With You - 1963 *written by Ed Townsend. Background vocalists include The Shirelles, Dee Dee Warwick and The Sweet Inspirations. The song was also recorded in 1964 by The Diplomats on Arock 1004.
Scepter 1275 - It's All A Bad Dream / You Made A Man Out Of Me – 1964
Atlantic 2278 - I Don't Want To Lose You / Hold On – 1965
Capitol 5621 - I'll Make You Happy / The Clown - 1966
Dynamo 101 - The Biggest Man / Never Love A Robin – 1967
Dynamo 105 - Words Can Never Tell It / How Can I Be Anything – 1967
Dynamo 110 - Complete Man / Searchin' For My Love – 1967
Dynamo 113 - I Need A Woman Of My Own / Searchin' For My Baby (Lookin' Everywhere) - 1967
Dynamo 124 - Born Free / Just A Little Taste (Of Your Sweet Lovin') - 1968
Private Stock 45,115 - Loving On The Losing Side / Sunshine Girl - 1976

Maxine Brown / Tommy Hunt

Collectables Col 030077 - Oh No Not My Baby / Human* - 1981 *Flip By Tommy Hunt.

Label Listings

Soulful Kinda Music – The Rare Soul Bible Volume Two

Harvey

―┼――――――――――――――――――――――――――――――――――

111 - Eddie Burns - Orange Driver / Hard Hearted Woman
112 - Loe & Joe - Little Ole Boy, Little Ole Girl / That's How I Am Without You
113 - Jr Walker & The All Stars - Twist Lackawanna / Willie's Blues - 1962
114 - Five Quails - Get To School On Time / Been A Long Time - 1962
115 - Eddie Burns - The Thing To Do / Mean And Evil (Baby) - 1962
116 – Quails - Never Felt Like This Before / My Love - 1962
117 - Jr Walker & The Allstars - Cleo's Mood / Brain Washer - 1962
118 - Eddie Burns - (Don't Be) Messing With My Bread / Orange Driver
119 - Jr Walker & The Allstars - Good Rockin' / Brain Washer Part 2 - 1963
120 – Quails - Over The Hump / I Thought
121 - Harvey & Ann - What Can You Do Now / Will I Do

Hi

―┼――――――――――――――――――――――――――――――――――

2001 - Carl McVoy - Tootsie / You Are My Sunshine -1957
2002 - Carl McVoy - Daydreamin' / Little John's Gone -1958
2003 - The Charmettes - My Love With All My Heart / Skating In Blue Light -1958
2004 - Buddy Holiday - Gloria (You're Only A Dream) / Walkin' Shoes - 1958
2005 - Joe Fuller - You Made A Hit / A Summer Love -1958
2006 - Mark Taylor - Linda Lou / My Greatest Dream -1958
2007 - Fern Fisher - Tommy / He's The Most -1958
2008 - Kaye Golden - Lover Boy / I'm Surrending -1958
2009 - Joe Fuller - Back To School / Nothing But You -1958
2010 - Kimball Coburn - Please, Please / Teenage Love -1958
2011 - Will Mercer - Call Of The Wild / Teenage Love -1958
2012 - Bobby Chandler - Voice Of A Fool / By-O -1958
2013 - Joe Fuller - Raining / ? - 1958
2014 - Tommy Tucker - Loving-Lil / A Man In Love - 1959
2015 - Charles Cockrell - Little Girl / I Want Somebody - 1959
2016 - Kimball Coburn - Darlin' / If I Were A King - 1959
2017 - Jay B. Lloyd With Bill Black's Combo - I'm So Lonely / I'll Be All Right - 1959
2018 - Bill Black's Combo - Smokie (Part 1) / Smokie (Part 2) - 1959
2019 - Moe Maharry - Just For A Moment / I Cry For You - 1960
2020 - Tommy Tucker - Miller's Cave / The Strangers - 1960
2021 - Bill Black's Combo - White Silver Sands / The Wheel - 1960
2022 - Bill Black's Combo - Josephine / Dry Bones - 1960
2023 - Jimmy McCracklin - Things I Meant To Say / Here Today And Gone Tomorrow -1960
2024 - Teddy Redell - Pipeliner / I Want To Hold You - 1960
2025 - Bill Black's Combo - Tuxedo Junction / Crankcase - 1960
2026 - Bill Black's Combo - Don't Be Cruel / Rollin' - 1960
2027 - Bill Black's Combo - Blue Tango / Willie - 1960
2028 - Bill Black's Combo - Hearts Of Stone / Royal Blue - 1961
2029 - Bill Black's Combo - Old Time Religion / He's Got The Whole World In His Hands - 1961 (stereo single plays at 33-1/3 rpm)

Soulful Kinda Music – The Rare Soul Bible Volume Two

2030 - Bill Black's Combo- Do Lord / When The Roll Is Called Up Yonder - 1961 (stereo single plays at 33-1/3 rpm)
2031 - Bill Black's Combo - Down By The Riverside / It Is No Secret (What God Can Do) - 1961 (stereo single plays at 33-1/3 rpm)
2032 - Bill Black's Combo - When The Saints Go Marching In / ? - 1961 (stereo single plays at 33-1/3 rpm)
2033 - Bill Black's Combo - Just A Closer Walk With Thee / This Old House - 1961 (stereo single plays at 33-1/3 rpm)
2034 - Gene Simmons - Teddy Bear / Your True Love - 1961
2035 - The Ramonos - Le Bistro / Gina, Gina - 1961
2036 - Bill Black's Combo - Ole Buttermilk Sky / Yogi - 1961
2037 - Bill Reeder - Till I Waltz Again With You / There Was A Time - 1961
2038 - Bill Black's Combo - Movin' / Honky Train - 1961
2039 - Gene Simmons - No Other Guy / The Shape You Left Me In -1961
2040 - Ace Cannon - Tuff / Sittin' Tight - 1961
2041 - Bill Reeder - Secret Love / Judy - 1961
2042 - Bill Black's Combo - Twist-Her / My Girl Josephine - 1961
2043 - Don Hines - Baby, Tell It Like It Is / I'm So Glad - 1962
2044 - Willie Mitchell - The Crawl (Part1) / The Crawl (Part 2) - 1962
2045 - Bill Black's Combo - Twist-Her / Night Train -1962 (stereo single plays at 33-1/3 rpm)
2046 - Bill Black's Combo - The Hucklebuck / Corrina, Corrina -1962 (stereo single plays at 33-1/3 rpm)
2047 - Bill Black's Combo - Johnny B. Goode / ? -1962 (stereo single plays at 33-1/3 rpm)
2048 - Bill Black's Combo - Josephine / My Girl Josephine - 1962 (stereo single plays at 33-1/3 rpm)
2049 - Bill Black's Combo - Slippin' And Slidin' / Twist With Me, Baby - 1962 (stereo single plays at 33-1/3 rpm)
2050 - Gene Simmons - "Twist" Caldonia / Be Her #1 - 1962
2051 - Ace Cannon - Blues (Stay Away From Me) / Blues In My Heart - 1962
2052 - Bill Black's Combo - Twistin' - White Silver Sands / My Babe - 1962
2053 - Willie Mitchell - Buddy Bear / Drippin' - 1962
2054 - Carl Mcvoy - It's A Crime / What Am I Living For - 1962
2055 - Bill Black's Combo - So What / Blues For The Red Boy - 1962
2056 - Don Hines - Stormy Monday Blues / Please Accept My Love - 1962
2057 - Ace Cannon - Volare / Looking Back - 1962
2058 - Willie Mitchell - Easy Now / Sunrise Serenade - 1962
2059 - Bill Black's Combo - Joey's Song / Hot Taco - 1962
2060 - Kenny Cain - Practice Makes Perfect / Words Can Never Say - 1962
2061 - The Apaches - Skippin' (Part 1) / Skippin' (Part2) - 1963
2062 - Benny Martin - My Lifetime Lovin' You / Love You Too Much - 1963
2063 - Ace Cannon - Love Letters / Since I Met You, Baby - 1963
2064 - Bill Black's Combo - Do It - Rat Now / Little Jasper - 1963
2065 - Ace Cannon - Cotton Fields / Mildew - 1963
2066 - Willie Mitchell - Empty Rooms / Percolatin' - 1963
2067 - Troy Williams - Anna Baby / Street Of Love - 1963
2068 - Don Hines - You Had To Pay / Trouble Is My Name - 1963
2069 - Bill Black's Combo - Monkey-Shine / Love Gone - 1963
2070 - Ace Cannon - Moanin' The Blues / Swanee River - 1963

Soulful Kinda Music – The Rare Soul Bible Volume Two

2071 - The Ringos - Ain't No Big Thing / I Still Love You - 1964
2072 - Bill Black's Combo - Comin' On / Soft Winds - 1964
2073 - Norm West - Daydreamin' / Angel Of My Dreams - 1964
2074 - Ace Cannon - Love Letters In The Sand / Searchin' - 1964
2075 - Willie Mitchell - Twenty - Seventy-Five / Secret Home - 1964
2076 - Gene Simmons - Haunted House / Hey, Hey Little Girl - 1964
2076 - Jumpin' Gene Simmons - Haunted House / Hey, Hey Little Girl - 1964
2077 - Bill Black's Combo - Tequila / Raunchy - 1964
2078 - Ace Cannon - Great Pretender / Gone - 1964
2079 - Bill Black's Combo - Little Queenie / Boo Ray - 1964
2080 - Jumpin' Gene Simmons - The Dodo / The Jump - 1964
2081 - Ace Cannon - Sunday Blues / Empty Arms - 1964
2082 - Norm West - Burning Bridges / Five Pages Of Heartache - 1964
2083 - Willie Mitchell - Empty Rooms / Check Me - 1964
2084 - Ace Cannon - Blue Christmas / Here Comes Santa Claus - 1964
2085 - Bill Black's Combo - Come On Home / He'll Have To Go - 1964
2086 - Gene Simmons - Skinnie Minnie / I'm A Ramblin' Man - 1965
2087 - Don Bryant - I Like It Like That / My Baby - 1965
2088 - Tommy Jay - Tender Love / Tomorrow - 1965
2089 - Ace Cannon - Sea Cruise / Gold Coins - 1965
2090 - Bobby Emmons - Blue Organ / Mack The Knife - 1965
2091 - Willie Mitchell - Buster Browne / Woodchopper's Ball - 1965
2092 - Jumpin' Gene Simmons - Mattie Rea / Folsom Prison Blues - 1965
2093 - Veniece Stalks - What More Do You Want From Me / You Gotta Take The Bitter With The Sweet - 1965
2094 - Bill Black's Combo - Spootin' / Crazy Feeling - 1965
2095 - Don Bryant - Don't Turn Your Back On Me / Star Of Love - 1965
2096 - Ace Cannon - Up Shore / Ishapan - 1965
2097 - Willie Mitchell - That Driving Beat / Everything Is Gonna Be Alright - 1965
2098 - Maurice Bower - Give Over To Me, Baby / You Got To Give A Little - 1966
2099 - Veniece - Let's-Stop / Yesterday Man - 1966
2100 - ?
2101 - Ace Cannon - Saxy Lullaby / Funny How Time Slips Away - 1966
2102 - Gene Simmons - The Batman / Bossy Boss - 1966
2103 - Willie Mitchell - Bad Eye / Sugar T - 1966
2104 - Don Bryant - Bound By Love / I'll Do The Rest - 1966
2104 - Don Bryant - Glory Of Love / I'll Do The Rest - 1966
2105 - The Antiques - Oh, So Many Ways / By My Side - 1966
2106 - Bill Black's Combo - Hey, Good Lookin' / Mountain Of Love - 1966
2107 - Ace Cannon - Mockin' Bird Hill / Dedicated To The One I Love - 1966
2108 - Big Amos - He Won't Bite Me Twice / Move With You Baby - 1966
2108 - Big Amos - He Won't Bite Me Twice / Don't Pass Me By - 1966
2109 - Janit And The Jays - Without A Reason / Hurtin' Over You, Boy - 1966
2110 - Narvel Felts - The Greatest Gift / I'd Trade All Of My Tomorrows (For Just One Yesterday) - 1966
2111 - Ace Cannon - More / Spanish Eyes - 1966
2112 - Willie Mitchell - Mercy / Sticks & Stones - 1966
2113 - Jumpin' Gene Simmons - Go On, Shoes / Keep That Meat In The Pan - 1966
2114 - Don Bryant - Coming On Strong / The Lonely Soldier - 1966
2115 - Bill Black's Combo - Rambler / You Call Everybody Darling - 1966

Soulful Kinda Music – The Rare Soul Bible Volume Two

2116 - Charlie Rich - Love Is After Me / Pass On By - 1966
2117 - Ace Cannon - Wonderland By Night / As Time Goes By - 1966
2118 - Narvel Felts - Bells / Eighty-Six Miles -1967
2119 - Willie Mitchell - Misty / Barefootin' -1967
2120 - Jerry Jaye - My Girl Josephine / Five Miles From Home -1967
2121 - Gene Miller - Goodest Man / She Is Good -1967
2122 - Don Bryant - The Call Of Distress / Doing The Mustang -1967
2123 - Charlie Rich - My Heart Would Know / Nobody's Lonesome For Me - 1967
2124 - Bill Black's Combo - Son Of Smokie / Peg Leg - 1967
2125 - Willie Mitchell - Slippin' & Slidin' / Aw Shucks - 1967
2126 - Narvel Felts - Don't Let Me Cross Over / Like Magic - 1967
2127 - Ace Cannon - Memory / I Walk The Line - 1967
2128 - Jerry Jaye - Let The Four Winds Blow / Singing The Blues - 1967
2129 - Janet & The Jays - Pleading For You / Love Watcha Doing To Me - 1967
2130 - George Jackson - I'm Gonna Wait / So Good To Me - 1967
2131 - Don Bryant - Don't Hide The Hurt / Is That Asking Too Much - 1967
2132 - Willie Mitchell - Lucky / Ooh Baby, You Turn Me On - 1967
2133 - Us Too - The Girl With The Golden Hair / I'll Leave You Crying - 1967
2134 - Charlie Rich - Hurry Up, Freight Train / Only Me - 1967
2135 - Don Bryant - There's Something On Your Mind (Part 1) / There's Something On Your Mind (Part 2) - 1967
2136 - Ace Cannon - San Antonio Rose / White Silver Sands - 1967
2137 - Narvel Felts - Starry Eyes / Dee-Dee - 1968
2138 - Life - One O'Clock Noontime / Snake Pit - 1968
2139 - Jerry Jaye - Brown Eyed Handsome Man / In The Middle Of Nowhere - 1968
2140 - Willie Mitchell - Soul Serenade / Mercy Mercy Mercy - 1968
2140 - Willie Mitchell - Soul Serenade / That's Just My Luck - 1968
2141 - Narvel Felts - Since I Met You, Baby / I Had To Cry Again - 1968
2142 - James Fry - Still Around / Tumbling Down - 1968
2143 - Don Bryant - Shop Around / I'll Go Crazy - 1968
2144 - Ace Cannon - Sleep Walk / By The Time I Get To Phoenix - 1968
2145 - Bill Black's Combo - Turn On Your Love Light / Ribbon Of Darkness - 1968
2146 - Billy Davis - It's All Over / Once In A Lifetime - 1968
2147 - Willie Mitchell - Prayer Meetin' / Bum Daddy - 1968
2148 - Ace Cannon - Alley Cat / Cannonball - 1968
2149 - Jim Robey - I Can Feel Every Step That You Take / Hurt - 1968
2150 - Jerry Jaye - Long Black Veil / I Started Loving You Again - 1968
2151 - Willie Mitchell - Up Hard / Red Light - 1968
2151 - Willie Mitchell - Up Hard / Beale Street Mood - 1968
2152 - Gene Miller - I Was Wrong / What Do You Mean - 1968
2153 - Bill Black's Combo - Red Light / Bright Lights, Big City - 1968
2154 - Willie Mitchell - 30-60-90 / Take Five - 1968
2155 - Ace Cannon - If I Had A Hammer / Soul For Sale - 1969
2156 - Don Bryant - That Ain't Right, Woman / You Cause Me To Wonder - 1969
2157 - Ann Peebles - Walk Away / I Can't Let You Go - 1969
2158 - Willie Mitchell - Young People / Kitten Korner - 1969
2159 - Al Green - I Want To Hold Your Hand / What Am I Gonna Do With Myself - 1969
2160 - Kim Melvin - Doin' The Popcorn / Keep The Faith - 1969
2161 - Gene Miller - Everybody Got Soul / Frankenstein Walk - 1969

Soulful Kinda Music – The Rare Soul Bible Volume Two

2162 - Lyndon - Very First Time / I Love My Baby - 1969
2163 - Crip Guerney - Understanding Each Other / Messing With The Man - 1969
2164 - Al Green - One Woman / Tomorrow's Dream - 1969
2165 - Ann Peebles - Give Me Some Credit / Solid Foundation - 1969
2166 - Ace Cannon - Down By The Riverside / Amen - 1969
2167 - Willie Mitchell - My Babe / Teenie's Dream - 1969
2168 - Bill Black's Combo - Creepin' Around / The Son Of Hickory Holler's Tramp - 1969
2169 - Don Bryant - It's So Lonely Being Me / What Are You Doing To My World - 1969
2170 - Nelson Diamond - Funny How Time Slips Away / You're The Reason I'm Living - 1969
2171 - Jerry Jaye - Never Going Back / You've Got To Go - 1969
2172 - Al Green - Gotta Find A New World / You Say It - 1969
2173 - Ann Peebles - Generation Gap (Between Us) / I'll Get Along - 1970
2174 - Ace Cannon - Ruby, Don't Take Your Love To Town / I Can't Stop Loving You - 1970
2175 - Willie Mitchell - Six To Go / Robbin's Nest - 1970
2176 - Ebony Web - Think About It / Mister Man - 1970
2177 - Al Green - All Because (I'm The Foolish One) / Right Now, Right Now - 1970
2178 - Ann Peebles - Part Time Love / I Still Love You - 1970
2179 - Imported Moods - What Have You Done To My Heart / I'm A Scorpio - 1970
2180 - Ace Cannon - Lodi / Rainy Night In Georgia - 1970
2181 - Willie Mitchell - Wade In The Water / Tails Out - 1970
2182 - Al Green - I Can't Get Next To You / Ride, Sally, Ride - 1970
2183 - Ebony Web - Time Of Me / Get Back, Baby - 1971
2184 - David Duke - Gimmie Some Lovin' / Is It Over - 1970
2185 - Bill Black's Combo - No More / Closin' Time - 1971
2186 - Ann Peebles - I Pity The Fool / Heartaches, Heartaches -1971
2187 - Ace Cannon - Chunck / Chicken Fried Soul - 1971
2188 - Al Green - True Love / Drivin' Wheel - 1971
2189 - Eddie Mcgee - What Made You Change / Be Yourself - 1971
2190 - Willie Mitchell - Too Sweet / Restless - 1971
2191 - Mike Ciccarelli - Sun Rises Here / Here - 1971
2192 - Ace Cannon - Me And Bobby McGee / Sweet Caroline - 1971
2193 - Eric Tig - Treat Her Right / Peace, Brother, Peace - 1971
2194 - Al Green - Tired Of Being Alone / Get Back, Baby - 1971
2195 - Joe L. - Please Mr. Foreman / As The Years Go Passing - 1971
2196 - Willie Mitchell - Breaking Point / Roadhouse - 1971
2197 - Ebony Web - This Morning / Find Yourself - 1971
2198 - Ann Peebles - Slipped, Tripped And Fell In Love / 99 Lbs - 1971
2199 - Ace Cannon - Misty Blue / Easy Loving - 1971
2200 - Iota - Within These Precincts / Love Come Wicked - 1971
2201 - Syl Johnson - Love You Left Behind / Anyone But You - 1971
2202 - Al Green - Let's Stay Together / Tomorrow's Dream - 1971
2203 - Joe L. - Let Me Know / I Can't Stand It - 1972
2204 - Veneice - 18 Days / Stepchild - 1972
2205 - Ann Peebles - Breaking Up Somebody's Home / Trouble, Heartaches And Sadness - 1972
2206 - Otis Clay - Home Is Where The Heart Is / Brand New Thing - 1972

Soulful Kinda Music – The Rare Soul Bible Volume Two

2207 - Al Perkins - I Don't Want To Lose / I Don't Want To Lose - 1972
2208 - Bill Black's Combo - Daylight / Four A.M. - 1972
2209 - Kim Melvin - One Monkey / Give It Up - 1972
2210 - Ace Cannon - Lovesick Blues / Cold, Cold Heart - 1972
2211 - Al Green - Look What You've Done For Me / La La For You - 1972
2212 - George Jackson - Aretha, Sing One For Me / I'm Gonna Wait - 1972
2213 - T-99 - Sweetness Ain't Sweet No More / We've Got Everything - 1972
2214 - Otis Clay - Precious, Precious / Too Many Hands - 1972
2215 - Syl Johnson - I Wanna Satisfy Your Every Need / Age Ain't Nothing But A Number - 1972
2216 - Al Green - I'm Still In Love With You / Old Time Lovin' - 1972
2217 - Ebony Web - This Morning / Way You Do The Things You Do - 1972
2218 - Al Perkins - I'm So Thankful / Moody - 1972
2219 - Ann Peebles - Somebody's On Your Case / I've Been There Before - 1972
2220 - Ace Cannon - To Get To You / Wabash Cannonball - 1972
2221 - Philip Mitchell - Little Things / That's What A Man Is For - 1972
2222 - Gene Anderson - Mixed Emotions / Congratulations - 1972
2223 - Quiet Elegance - Do You Love Me / I'm Afraid Of Losing You - 1972
2224 - Teacher's Edition - I Wanna Share Everything / Sleepy People (1972)
2225 - Bobo Mr. Soul - Hitch-Hike To Heartbreak Road / She's My Woman - 1972
2226 - Otis Clay - Let Me Be The One / Trying To Live My Life Without You - 1972
2227 - Al Green - You Ought To Be With Me / What Is This Feeling - 1972
2228 - The Box Tops - It's All Over / Sugar Creek Woman - 1972
2229 - Syl Johnson - Any Way The Wind Blows / We Did It - 1972
2230 - Joint Venture - When The Battle Is Over / I'd Rather Hurt You Now - 1973
2231 - Ace Cannon - Green Door / Tuffer Than Tuff - 1973
2232 - Ann Peebles - I'm Gonna Tear Your Playhouse Down / One Way Street - 1973
2233 - Quiet Elegance - I Need Love / Mama Said - 1973
2234 - Bill Black's Combo - Smokey Bourbon Street / Mighty Fine - 1973
2235 - Al Green - Call Me / What A Wonderful Thing Love Is - 1973
2236 - George Jackson - Let Them Know You Care / Patricia - 1973
2237 - Willie Mitchell - Last Tango In Paris / Six To Go - 1973
2238 - Ace Cannon - Ruff / Baby, Don't Get Hooked On Me - 1973
2239 - Otis Clay - I Can't Make It Alone / I Didn't Know The Meaning Of Pain - 1973
2240 - Philip Mitchell - Oh, How I Love You / The Same Folks That Put You There - 1973
2241 - Gene Anderson - Forgive This Foolish Man / I'm Your Lover, Not Your Brother - 1973
2242 - The Box Tops - Hold On, Girl / Angel - 1973
2243 - Ebony Web - Think About It / I'll Still Be Loving You - 1973
2244 - Darryl Carter - Looking Straight Ahead / Sunshine - 1973
2245 - Quiet Elegance - You've Got My Mind Messed Up / I Need Love - 1973
2246 - Ben Branch - Soul In De Hole / How Could I Let You Get Away - 1973
2247 - Al Green - Here I Am / I'm Glad You're Mine - 1973
2248 - Ann Peebles - I Can't Stand The Rain / I've Been There Before - 1973
2249 - Teacher's Edition - It Helps To Make You Strong / I Wanna Be Loved - 1973
2250 - Syl Johnson -Back For A Taste Of Your Love / Wind, Blow Her Back My Way - 1973
2251 - The Masqueraders - Let The Love Bells Ring / Now That I Found You - 1973
2252 - Otis Clay - If I Could Reach Out / I Die A Little Bit Each Day - 1973

Soulful Kinda Music – The Rare Soul Bible Volume Two

2253 - Erma Coffee - Any Way The Wind Blows / You Made Me What I Am - 1973
2254 - Donna Rhodes - I Just Can't Love You Enough / Where's Your Love Been - 1973
2255 - Africano - Satisfactorize Your Mind / I'm Willing, If You're Willing - 1973
2256 - Ace Cannon - Country Comfort / Closin' Time's A Downer - 1973
2257 - Al Green - Livin' For You / It Ain't No Fun To Me - 1973
2258 - Philip Mitchell - Ain't No Love In My Life / Turning Over The Ground - 1973
2259 - Odyssey - No One Else / No One Else - 1974
2260 - Syl Johnson - I'm Yours / Anyone But You - 1974
2261 - Ace Cannon - Last Date / Mathilda - 1974
2262 - Al Green - Let's Get Married / So Good To Be Here - 1974
2263 - Quiet Elegance - Love Will Make You Feel Better / Will You Be My Man - 1974
2264 - The Masqueraders - Wake Up Fool / Now That I've Found You - 1974
2265 - Ann Peebles - (You Keep Me) Hangin' On / Heartaches, Heartaches - 1974
2266 - Otis Clay - Woman Don't Live Here No More / You Can't Escape The Hands Of Love - 1974
2267 - Ben Branch - I Wish You Were Here / Mama - 1974
2268 - Africano - Open Your Hearts (Part 1) / Open Your Hearts (Part 2) - 1974
2269 - Syl Johnson - Let Yourself Go / Please Don't Give Up On Me - 1974
2270 - Otis Clay - You Did Something To Me / It Was Jealousy - 1974
2271 - Ann Peebles - Do I Need You / A Love Vibration - 1974
2272 - Gene Andersnon - Congratulations / Baby Love - 1974
2273 - Ace Cannon - Tennessee Saturday Night / There Goes My Everything - 1974
2274 - Al Green - Sha-La-La (Make Me Happy) / School Days - 1974
2275 - Syl Johnson - I Want To Take You Home (To See Mama) / I Hear The Love Chimes - 1974
2276 - Veniece - Every Now & Then / 18 Days - 1974
2277 - Bill Black's Combo - Soul Serenade / Pickin' - 1974
2278 - Ann Peebles - Until You Came Into My Life / Put Yourself In My Place - 1974
2279 - Hi Rhythm - Black Rock / Save All My Lovin' - 1975
2280 - Quiet Elegance - Have You Been Making Out O.K? / Do You Love Me - 1975
2281 - Known Facts - How Can I Believe You / He's Got It - 1975
2282 - Al Green - L-O-V-E (Love) / I Wish You Were Here - 1975
2283 - Bill Black's Combo - Truck Stop / Boilin' Cabbage / Truck Stop - 1975
2284 - Ann Peebles - Beware / You Got To Feed The Fire - 1975
2285 - Syl Johnson - Take Me To The River / Could I Be Falling In Love - 1975
2286 - Ace Cannon - Peace In The Valley / Raunchy - 1975
2287 - Gene Anderson - Your Love Must Be Voodoo / Your Love Must Be Voodoo - 1975
2288 - Al Green - Oh Me, Oh My (Dreams In My Arms) / Strong As Death (Sweet As Love) - 1975
2289 - Veniece - Trying To Live My Life Without You / I Still Love You - 1975
2290 - Quiet Elegance - Your Love Is Strange / Love Will Make You Feeel Better - 1975
2291 - Bill Black's Combo - Almost Persuaded / Back Up And Push - 1975
2292 - ?
2293 - Eric Tig - Treat Her Right / ? - 1975
2294 - Ann Peebles - Come To Mama / I'm Leaving You - 1975
2295 - Syl Johnson - Come On Home / I Only Have Love - 1975
2296 - Tuxedo - If You Can't Please Your Woman / Please Don't Leave - 1975

Soulful Kinda Music – The Rare Soul Bible Volume Two

2297 - Jean Plum - Look At The Boy / Back To You - 1975
2298 - Hindsight - Harlem Shuffle / Disco Hustle - 1975
2299 - Ace Cannon - Malt Liquor / Walk On By - 1975
5N-2300 - Al Green - Full Of Fire (Special Disco Version) (5:12) - 1975 (10" One-Sided 45 rpm Promo Issue Only)
2300 - Al Green - Full Of Fire / Could I Be The One - 1975
2301 - Bill Black's Combo - Fire On The Bayou / Memphis Soul - 1976
2302 - Ann Peebles - Dr. Love Power / I Still Love You - 1976
2303 - The Duncan Sisters - It's You That I Need (Part 1) / It's You That I Need (Part 2) - 1976
2304 - Syl Johnson - Starbright, Starlight / That's Just My Luck - 1976
2305 - Narvel Felts - This Time / I Had To Cry Again - 1976
2306 - Al Green - Let It Shine / There's No Way - 1976
2307 - Bobby McClure - Love Trap / Was It Something I Said - 1976
2308 - Syl Johnson - 'Bout To Make Me Leave Home / It Ain't Easy - 1976
2309 - Ann Peebles - I Don't Lend My Man / I Need Somebody - 1976
2310 - Jerry Jaye - Honky Tonk Women Love Redneck Men / What's Left - 1976
2311 - Bill Black's Combo - I Can Help / Jump Back Joe - 1976
2312 - Quiet Elegance - After You / Something That You Got - 1976
2313 - Ace Cannon - Blue Eyes Crying In The Rain / I'll Fly Away - 1976
2314 - Jean Plum - Here I Go Again / I Love Him - 1976
2315 - O.V. Wright - Rhymes / Without You - 1976
2316 - Hi Rhythm - Superstar / Since You've Been Gone - 1976
2317 - Bill Black's Combo - Redneck Rock / Yakety Sax - 1976
2318 - Jerry Jaye - Hot And Still Heatin' / Crazy - 1976
2319 - Al Green - Keep Me Cryin' / There Is Love - 1976
2320 - Ann Peebles - Fill This World With Love / It Was Jealousy - 1977
2321 - Bobby McClure - Doing It Right On Time / She's Miss Wonderful - 1977
2322 - Al Green - I Tried To Tell Myself / Something - 1977
2323 - Jerry Jaye - When Morning Comes To Memphis / ? - 1977
2324 - Al Green - Love & Happiness / Glory, Glory - 1977

59033 - Al Green - Tired Of Being Alone / Look What You've Done For Me - ?

77501 - O.V. Wright - Into Something (Can't Shake Loose) / Time We Have - 1977
77501 - O.V. Wright - Into Something (Can't Shake Loose) / Time We Have - 1977
77502 - Ann Peebles - If This Is Heaven / When I'm In Your Arms - 1977
77503 - Quiet Elegance - Roots Of Love / How's Your Lovelife? - 1977
77504 - Bobby McClure - I Ain't Gonna Turn You Loose / Hard Luck - 1977
77505 - Al Green - Belle / Chariots Of Fire - 1977
77506 - O.V. Wright - Precious, Precious / You Gotta Have Love - 1977
77507 - Syl Johnson - Fonk You / That Wiggle - 1977

77517 - Syl Johnson - Stand By Me / Main Squeeze - 1978

77680 - Al Green - White Christmas / Winter Wonderland - 2001 (Issued In Clear Vinyl)
78508 - Bill Black's Combo - Cashin' In (A Tribute To Luther Perkins) / L. A. Blues - 1978
78509 - Ann Peebles - Old Man With Young Ideas / A Good Day For Lovin' - 1978

Soulful Kinda Music – The Rare Soul Bible Volume Two

78510 - Al Green - I Feel Good (7:30) / I Feel Good (3:17) - 1978 (12" Release)
78511 - Al Green - Feels Like Summer / I Feel Good - 1978
78512 - Bobby McClure - To Get What You Got / High Heel Shoes - 1978
78513 - Willie Walker - Love Makes The World Go 'Round / Reaching For The Real Thing - 1978
78514 - O.V. Wright - I Don't Do Windows / I Feel Love Growin' - 1978
78515 - Jean Plum - Pour On The Loving / You Ask Me - 1978
78516 - Ace Cannon - It Was Almost Like A Song / ? - 1978
78517 - Syl Johnson - Stand By Me / Main Squeeze - 1978
78518 - Ann Peebles - I Didn't Take Your Man / Being Here With You - 1978
78519 - Ann Peebles - I Didn't Take Your Man (Disco Mix) (6:30) / Being Here With You (2:30) - 1978 (12" Release)
78520 - Rufus Thomas - Fried Chicken / I Ain't Got Time - 1978
78521 - O.V. Wright - No Easy Way To Say Goodbye / Bottom Line - 1978
78522 - Al Green - To Sir With Love / Wait Here - 1978
78523 - Al Green - To Sir With Love (4:05) / Wait Here (6:07) - 1978 (12" Release)
79527 - Majik - Back Into Your Heart / Dance, Dance, Dance – 1979
79528 - Ann Peebles - If You Got The Time (I've Got The Love) / Let Your Lovelight Shine - 1979
79529 - Syl Johnson - Mystery Lady / Let's Dance For Love - 1979
79530 - Larry T-Bird Gordon - Contact Of Funk / Laid Back - 1979
79531 - O.V. Wright - We're Still Together / I Don't Know Why - 1979
79532 - ?

80533 - Ann Peebles - Heartaches / I'd Rather Leave While I'm In Love - 1980

81534 - Ann Peebles - Mon Belle Amour / Waiting - 1981

LPs

HL-12001 - Bill Black's Combo - Smokie - 1959
Tracks: Smokie, Part 2 / Frankie And Johnny / Tuxedo Junction / Cyclone Bop / Dee J. Special / Anytime // Smokie, Part 1 / Crankcase / Deep Elm Blues / Before Dawn / Special Duty / Accentuate The Positive (Ac-Cent-Tchu-Ate)

SHL-32001 - Bill Black's Combo - Smokie - 1959
Tracks: Smokie, Part 2 / Frankie And Johnny / Tuxedo Junction / Cyclone Bop / Dee J. Special / Anytime // Smokie, Part 1 / Crankcase / Deep Elm Blues / Before Dawn / Special Duty / Accentuate The Positive (Ac-Cent-Tchu-Ate)

HL-12002 - Bill Black & His Combo - Saxy Jazz - 1960
Tracks: Smokie, Part 2 / Frankie And Johnny / Tuxedo Junction / Cyclone Bop / Dee J. Special / Anytime // White Silver Sands / The Wheel / Crankcase / Deep Elm Blues / Before Dawn / Accentuate The Positive (Ac-Cent-Tchu-Ate)

SHL-32002 - Bill Black & His Combo - Saxy Jazz - 1960
Tracks: Smokie, Part 2 / Frankie And Johnny / Tuxedo Junction / Cyclone Bop / Dee J. Special / Anytime // White Silver Sands / The Wheel / Crankcase / Deep Elm Blues / Before Dawn / Accentuate The Positive (Ac-Cent-Tchu-Ate)

Soulful Kinda Music – The Rare Soul Bible Volume Two

HL-12003 - Bill Black's Combo - Solid and Raunchy - 1960
Tracks: Don't Be Cruel / Singin' The Blues / Blueberry Hill / I Almost Lost My Mind /
Cherry Pink / Mona Lisa // Honky Tonk / Tequila / Raunchy / You Win Again / Bo
Diddley / Mack The Knife

SHL-32003 - Bill Black's Combo - Solid and Raunchy - 1960
Tracks: Don't Be Cruel / Singin' The Blues / Blueberry Hill / I Almost Lost My Mind /
Cherry Pink / Mona Lisa // Honky Tonk / Tequila / Raunchy / You Win Again / Bo
Diddley / Mack The Knife

HL-12004 - Bill Black's Combo - That Wonderful Feeling - 1961
Tracks: Nobody Knows (The Trouble I've Seen) / This Old House / When The Saints
Go Marching In / It's No Secret / Swing Low Sweet Chariot / Just A Closer Walk (With
Thee) // When The Roll Is Called Up Yonder / He's Got The Whole World In His
Hands / Do Lord (Remember Me) / Down By The Riverside / Old Time Religion / Dry
Bones

SHL-32004 - Bill Black's Combo - That Wonderful Feeling - 1961
Tracks: Nobody Knows (The Trouble I've Seen) / This Old House / When The Saints
Go Marching In / It's No Secret / Swing Low Sweet Chariot / Just A Closer Walk (With
Thee) // When The Roll Is Called Up Yonder / He's Got The Whole World In His
Hands / Do Lord (Remember Me) / Down By The Riverside / Old Time Religion / Dry
Bones

HL-12005 - Bill Black's Combo - Movin' - 1962
Tracks: Movin' / Hey Bo Diddley / Witchcraft / Work With Me Annie / Be Bop A-Lula /
What'd I Say // My Babe / 40 Miles Of Bad Road / Ain't That Loving You Baby /
Honky Train / The Walk / Torquay

SHL-32005 - Bill Black's Combo - Movin' - 1962
Tracks: Movin' / Hey Bo Diddley / Witchcraft / Work With Me Annie / Be Bop A-Lula /
What'd I Say // My Babe / 40 Miles Of Bad Road / Ain't That Loving You Baby /
Honky Train / The Walk / Torquay

HL-12006 - Bill Black's Combo - Bill Black's Record Hop - 1962
Tracks: Night Train / Corrina, Corrina / My Girl Josephine / Hucklebuck // Royal Twist
/ Slippin' And Slidin' / Twisteroo / Smokie, Part 2 / Twist Her / Yogi / Twist With Me
Baby / Johnny B. Goode

SHL-32006 - Bill Black's Combo - Bill Black's Record Hop - 1962
Tracks: Night Train / Corrina, Corrina / My Girl Josephine / Hucklebuck // Royal Twist
/ Slippin' And Slidin' / Twisteroo / Smokie, Part 2 / Twist Her / Yogi / Twist With Me
Baby / Johnny B. Goode

HL-12006 / SHL-32006 - Bill Black's Combo - Let's Twist Her - 1963
Tracks: Twist Her / Night Train / Corrina, Corrina / Huckle Buck (Twist) / Royal Twist /
Yogi (Twist) // My Girl Josephine / Twisteroo / Johnny B. Goode / Slippin' And Slidin'
(Twist) / Twist With Me Baby / Smokie, Part 2

SHL-32006 - Bill Black's Combo - Let's Twist Her - 1963

Soulful Kinda Music – The Rare Soul Bible Volume Two

Tracks: Twist Her / Night Train / Corrina, Corrina / Huckle Buck (Twist) / Royal Twist / Yogi (Twist) // My Girl Josephine / Twisteroo / Johnny B. Goode / Slippin' And Slidin' (Twist) / Twist With Me Baby / Smokie, Part 2

HL-12007 - Ace Cannon - "Tuff" Sax - 1962
Tracks: Tuff / Trouble in Mind / St. Louis Blues / Wabash Blues / Basin Street Blues / Cannonball // Blues In My Heart / Blues (Stay Away From Me) / The Lonesome Road / Careless Love / Kansas City / I've Got a Woman

SHL-32007 - Ace Cannon - "Tuff" Sax - 1962
Tracks: Tuff / Trouble in Mind / St. Louis Blues / Wabash Blues / Basin Street Blues / Cannonball // Blues In My Heart / Blues (Stay Away From Me) / The Lonesome Road / Careless Love / Kansas City / I've Got a Woman

HL-12008 - Ace Cannon - Looking Back - 1962
Tracks: Looking Back / Harlem Nocturne / Someday / My Blue Heaven / Jealous Heart / Blue Prelude // I Love You, Yes I Do / Volare / Lazy River / September Song / Night Life / Foggy River

SHL-32008 - Ace Cannon - Looking Back - 1962
Tracks: Looking Back / Harlem Nocturne / Someday / My Blue Heaven / Jealous Heart / Blue Prelude // I Love You, Yes I Do / Volare / Lazy River / September Song / Night Life / Foggy River

HL-12009 - Bill Black's Combo - The Untouchable Sound of the Bill Black Combo - 1962
Tracks: Joey's Song / Castle Rock / Red Top / Tippin' Inn / Skokiaan / Woodchopper's Ball // So What / Night Train / Your Cheatin' Heart / Ain't That A Shame / Little Brown Jug / I Can't Stop Loving You

SHL-32009 - Bill Black's Combo - The Untouchable Sound of the Bill Black Combo - 1962
Tracks: Joey's Song / Castle Rock / Red Top / Tippin' Inn / Skokiaan / Woodchopper's Ball // So What / Night Train / Your Cheatin' Heart / Ain't That A Shame / Little Brown Jug / I Can't Stop Loving You

HL-12010 - Willie Mitchell - It's Sunrise Serenade - 1963
Tracks: Sunrise Serenade / P.S. I Love You / Stardust / Cimarron / Twilight Time / Soft Summer Breeze // Moonlight And Roses / The Wayward Wind / Tumblin' Tumbleweeds / South Of The Border / Moonlight Cocktails / Now And Always

SHL-32010 - Willie Mitchell - It's Sunrise Serenade - 1963
Tracks: Sunrise Serenade / P.S. I Love You / Stardust / Cimarron / Twilight Time / Soft Summer Breeze // Moonlight And Roses / The Wayward Wind / Tumblin' Tumbleweeds / South Of The Border / Moonlight Cocktails / Now And Always

HL-12011 - Hi Tones - Raunchy Sounds - 1963
Tracks: Stormy Monday Blues / Coastin' / Cotton Sack / Honeysuckle / Lazy Walkin' / Peepin' In // Raunchy / Brown Gravy / Smokie, Part 2 / Green Onions / Tuff / Hello There

Soulful Kinda Music – The Rare Soul Bible Volume Two

SHL-32011 - Hi Tones - Raunchy Sounds - 1963
Tracks: Stormy Monday Blues / Coastin' / Cotton Sack / Honeysuckle / Lazy Walkin' /
Peepin' In // Raunchy / Brown Gravy / Smokie, Part 2 / Green Onions / Tuff / Hello
There

HL-12012 - Bill Black's Combo - Bill Black's Greatest Hits - `1963
Tracks: Do It-Rat Now / Josephine / Rollin' / Hearts Of Stone / Yogi / White Silver
Sands // Blue Tango / Willie / Ole Buttermilk Sky / Royal Blue / Don't Be Cruel /
Smokie, Part 2

SHL-32012 - Bill Black's Combo - Bill Black's Greatest Hits - `1963
Tracks: Do It-Rat Now / Josephine / Rollin' / Hearts Of Stone / Yogi / White Silver
Sands // Blue Tango / Willie / Ole Buttermilk Sky / Royal Blue / Don't Be Cruel /
Smokie, Part 2

HL-12013 - Bill Black's Combo - Bill Black Combo Goes West - 1963
Tracks: San Antonio Rose / Tumblin' Tumbleweeds / Deep In The Heart Of Texas /
There's A Gold Mine In The Sky / The Yellow Rose Of Texas / El Rancho Grande //
Home On The Range / Red River Valley / Down In The Valley / Cool Water / Ridin'
Down The Canyon / Cattle Call

SHL-32013 - Bill Black's Combo - Bill Black Combo Goes West - 1963
Tracks: San Antonio Rose / Tumblin' Tumbleweeds / Deep In The Heart Of Texas /
There's A Gold Mine In The Sky / The Yellow Rose Of Texas / El Rancho Grande //
Home On The Range / Red River Valley / Down In The Valley / Cool Water / Ridin'
Down The Canyon / Cattle Call

HL-12014 - Ace Cannon - The Moanin' Sax of Ace Cannon - 1963
Tracks: Moanin' The Blues / Trouble In Mind / Prisoner's Song / I Love You Because /
Last Date / Singing The Blues // It's All In The Game / No Letter Today / I Left My
Heart In San Francisco / I Can't Get Started With You / Prisoner Of Love / Moanin'

SHL-32014 - Ace Cannon - The Moanin' Sax of Ace Cannon - 1963
Tracks: Moanin' The Blues / Trouble In Mind / Prisoner's Song / I Love You Because /
Last Date / Singing The Blues // It's All In The Game / No Letter Today / I Left My
Heart In San Francisco / I Can't Get Started With You / Prisoner Of Love / Moanin'

HL-12015 - Bill Black's Combo - Bill Black's Combo Plays the Blues - 1964
Tracks: I'll Never Be Free / Birth Of The Blues / Midnight / Blues In My Heart / Blues
In The Night / Basin Street Blues // Comin' On / St. Louis Blues / Got You On My
Mind / Wabash Blues / Peter Gunn / Weary Blues

SHL-32015 - Bill Black's Combo - Bill Black's Combo Plays the Blues - 1964
Tracks: I'll Never Be Free / Birth Of The Blues / Midnight / Blues In My Heart / Blues
In The Night / Basin Street Blues // Comin' On / St. Louis Blues / Got You On My
Mind / Wabash Blues / Peter Gunn / Weary Blues

Soulful Kinda Music – The Rare Soul Bible Volume Two

HL-12016 - Ace Cannon - Aces Hi - 1964
Tracks: You Don't Know Me / Heartbreak Hotel / Because Of You / Willow Weep For Me / Searchin' / Shangri La // Cotton Fields / Lonely Street / Swanee River / Gone / So Fine / Honky Tonk Song

SHL-32016 - Ace Cannon - Aces Hi - 1964
Tracks: You Don't Know Me / Heartbreak Hotel / Because Of You / Willow Weep For Me / Searchin' / Shangri La // Cotton Fields / Lonely Street / Swanee River / Gone / So Fine / Honky Tonk Song

HL-12017 - Bill Black's Combo - Bill Black's Combo Plays Tunes By Chuck Berry - 1964
Tracks: School Days / Sweet Little Sixteen / Roll Over Beethoven / Maybellene / Carol / Little Queenie // Brown Eyed Handsome Man / Nadine / Thirty Days / Johnny B. Goode / Reelin' And Rockin' / Memphis Tennessee

SHL-32017 - Bill Black's Combo - Bill Black's Combo Plays Tunes By Chuck Berry - 1964
Tracks: School Days / Sweet Little Sixteen / Roll Over Beethoven / Maybellene / Carol / Little Queenie // Brown Eyed Handsome Man / Nadine / Thirty Days / Johnny B. Goode / Reelin' And Rockin' / Memphis Tennessee

HL-12018 - Gene Simmons - Jumpin' Gene Simmons - 1964
Tracks: Haunted House / You Can Have Her / Bony Maronie / The Green Door / Rock Around the Clock / Hotel Happiness // Teen-Age Letter / Don't Let Go / Slippin' And Sliddin' / (I'm) Comin' Down With Love / Just A Little Bit / No Help Wanted

SHL-32018 - Gene Simmons - Jumpin' Gene Simmons - 1964
Tracks: Haunted House / You Can Have Her / Bony Maronie / The Green Door / Rock Around the Clock / Hotel Happiness // Teen-Age Letter / Don't Let Go / Slippin' And Sliddin' / (I'm) Comin' Down With Love / Just A Little Bit / No Help Wanted

HL-12019 - Ace Cannon - Ace Cannon Plays the Great Show Tunes - 1964
Tracks: Hello Dolly / Stranger In Paradise / Moonglow And Theme From Picnic / Song From Moulin Rouge / Around The World / The High And The Mighty // Never On Sunday / Moon River / Some Enchanted Evening / A Summer Place / Love Is A Many Splendored Thing / Fascination

SHL-32019 - Ace Cannon - Ace Cannon Plays the Great Show Tunes - 1964
Tracks: Hello Dolly / Stranger In Paradise / Moonglow And Theme From Picnic / Song From Moulin Rouge / Around The World / The High And The Mighty // Never On Sunday / Moon River / Some Enchanted Evening / A Summer Place / Love Is A Many Splendored Thing / Fascination

HL-12020 - Bill Black's Combo - Bill Black's Combo Goes Big Band - 1964 Tracks: T.D.'s Boogie Woogie / Near You / Sentimental Journey / Tuxedo Junction / Canadian Sunset / Leap Frog // In The Mood / Java / Two O'clock Jump / So Rare /

Soulful Kinda Music – The Rare Soul Bible Volume Two

O (Oh!) / Stranger On The Shore

SHL-32020 - Bill Black's Combo - Bill Black's Combo Goes Big Band - 1964 Tracks: T.D.'s Boogie Woogie / Near You / Sentimental Journey / Tuxedo Junction / Canadian Sunset / Leap Frog // In The Mood / Java / Two O'clock Jump / So Rare / O (Oh!) / Stranger On The Shore

HL-12021 - Willie Mitchell - Hold It!!! Here's Willie Mitchell - 1964
Tracks: Hold It / Percolatin' / Night Train / You Can't Sit Down / The Dog / The Crawl // "20-75" / Rinky Dink / Last Night / Mashed Potatoes / Last Date / Watermelon Man

SHL-32021 - Willie Mitchell - Hold It!!! Here's Willie Mitchell - 1964
Tracks: Hold It / Percolatin' / Night Train / You Can't Sit Down / The Dog / The Crawl // "20-75" / Rinky Dink / Last Night / Mashed Potatoes / Last Date / Watermelon Man

HL-12022 - Ace Cannon - Christmas Cheer from Ace Cannon, His Alto Sax and Chorus - 1964
Tracks: White Christmas / Winter Wonderland / Santa Claus Is Coming To Town / Rudolph The Red Nosed Reindeer / Here Comes Santa Claus / Frosty The Snowman // Blue Christmas / Jingle Bells / I Saw Mommy Kissing Santa Claus / Let It Snow, Let It Snow, Let it Snow / Jingle Bell Rock / Rock Around The Christmas Tree

SHL-32022 - Ace Cannon - Christmas Cheer from Ace Cannon, His Alto Sax and Chorus - 1964
Tracks: White Christmas / Winter Wonderland / Santa Claus Is Coming To Town / Rudolph The Red Nosed Reindeer / Here Comes Santa Claus / Frosty The Snowman // Blue Christmas / Jingle Bells / I Saw Mommy Kissing Santa Claus / Let It Snow, Let It Snow, Let it Snow / Jingle Bell Rock / Rock Around The Christmas Tree

HL-12023 - Bill Black's Combo - More Solid & Raunchy - 1965
Tracks: Kansas City / You Better Move On / Hard Day's Night / Tea For Two Cha Cha / Good Rocking Tonight / Fannie Mae // Come On Home / Red River Rock / A White Sport Coat / Sunrise Serenade / Oh, Lonesome Me / He'll Have to Go

SHL-32023 - Bill Black's Combo - More Solid & Raunchy - 1965
Tracks: Kansas City / You Better Move On / Hard Day's Night / Tea For Two Cha Cha / Good Rocking Tonight / Fannie Mae // Come On Home / Red River Rock / A White Sport Coat / Sunrise Serenade / Oh, Lonesome Me / He'll Have to Go

HL-12024 - Bobby Emmons - Blues with a Beat with an Organ - 1965
Tracks: What'd I Say / Corrine, Corrina / Sittin' Home / I Got A Woman / Mack The Knife / Peg O' My Heart // Sentimental Journey / C C Rider / Strange Things Happening Every Day / Blue Organ / Cottonfields / Cherry Blue

SHL-32024 - Bobby Emmons - Blues with a Beat with an Organ - 1965
Tracks: What'd I Say / Corrine, Corrina / Sittin' Home / I Got A Woman / Mack The

Soulful Kinda Music – The Rare Soul Bible Volume Two

Knife / Peg O' My Heart // Sentimental Journey / C C Rider / Strange Things Happening Every Day / Blue Organ / Cottonfields / Cherry Blue

HL-12025 - Ace Cannon - Ace Cannon Live: The World's Tuffest Sax - 1965
Tracks: Memphis / You're The Reason I'm Living / Night Train / Girl From Ipanema / Yakety Sax / Stranger On The Shore // Honky Tonk / Moody River / Everybody Loves Somebody / When The Saints Go Marching In / Night Wagon / You Can't Sit Down

SHL-32025 - Ace Cannon - Ace Cannon Live: The World's Tuffest Sax - 1965
Tracks: Memphis / You're The Reason I'm Living / Night Train / Girl From Ipanema / Yakety Sax / Stranger On The Shore // Honky Tonk / Moody River / Everybody Loves Somebody / When The Saints Go Marching In / Night Wagon / You Can't Sit Down

HL-12026 - Willie Mitchell - It's Dance Time with Willie Mitchell - 1965
Tracks: Introduction / Buster Browne / Ram-Bunk-Shush / Poinciana / Morning After / Since I Met You Baby / When My Dreamboat Come Home // Twine Time / In The Mood / Wiggle Rock / Woodchopper's Ball / Fever / Apple Jack

SHL-32026 - Willie Mitchell - It's Dance Time with Willie Mitchell - 1965
Tracks: Introduction / Buster Browne / Ram-Bunk-Shush / Poinciana / Morning After / Since I Met You Baby / When My Dreamboat Come Home // Twine Time / In The Mood / Wiggle Rock / Woodchopper's Ball / Fever / Apple Jack

HL-12027 - Bill Black's Combo - Mr. Beat - 1965
Tracks: Spootin' / It's All In The Game / North To Alaska / Mr. Beat / Side By Side / Black Beat // Talk Back Trembling Lips / Oh Lonesome Me / From Here To Eternity / Make Love To Me / Swinging On A Star / Till I Waltz Again With You

SHL-32027 - Bill Black's Combo - Mr. Beat - 1965
Tracks: Spootin' / It's All In The Game / North To Alaska / Mr. Beat / Side By Side / Black Beat // Talk Back Trembling Lips / Oh Lonesome Me / From Here To Eternity / Make Love To Me / Swinging On A Star / Till I Waltz Again With You

HL-12028 - Ace Cannon - Nashville Hits - 1965
Tracks: Four Walls / Slipping Around / Any Time / Tomorrow Never Comes / Sweet Dreams / Empty Arms // She Thinks I Still Care / I'm So Lonesome I Could Cry / I've Got A Tiger By The Tail / Nashville Groove / Please Help Me I'm Falling / Hey Good Looking

SHL-32028 - Ace Cannon - Nashville Hits - 1965
Tracks: Four Walls / Slipping Around / Any Time / Tomorrow Never Comes / Sweet Dreams / Empty Arms // She Thinks I Still Care / I'm So Lonesome I Could Cry / I've Got A Tiger By The Tail / Nashville Groove / Please Help Me I'm Falling / Hey Good Looking

Soulful Kinda Music – The Rare Soul Bible Volume Two

HL-12029 - Willie Mitchell - Willie Mitchell's Driving Beat - 1966
Tracks: Everything Is Gonna Be All Right / Nick-O-Demus / Time Ain't Long /
Champion / I'm Moving On / Stone Face // That Driving Beat / Doing The Stroll / Pep
Talk / Fat Cat / Smiley

SHL-32029 - Willie Mitchell - Willie Mitchell's Driving Beat - 1966
Tracks: Everything Is Gonna Be All Right / Nick-O-Demus / Time Ain't Long /
Champion / I'm Moving On / Stone Face // That Driving Beat / Doing The Stroll / Pep
Talk / Fat Cat / Smiley

HL-12030 - Ace Cannon - Sweet & Tuff - 1966
Tracks: Funny How Time Slips Away / One Has My Name (The Other Has My Heart)
/ Spanish Eyes / Al Di La / More / Goldfinger // These Boots Are Made For Walkin' /
Ram-Bunk-Shush / Louie Louie / Hang On Sloopy / Mocking Bird Rock / Two For One

SHL-32030 - Ace Cannon - Sweet & Tuff - 1966
Tracks: Funny How Time Slips Away / One Has My Name (The Other Has My Heart)
/ Spanish Eyes / Al Di La / More / Goldfinger // These Boots Are Made For Walkin' /
Ram-Bunk-Shush / Louie Louie / Hang On Sloopy / Mocking Bird Rock / Two For One

HL-12031 - Willie Mitchell - It's What's Happenin' - 1966
Tracks: What Now My Love / The "In" Crowd / Hot Cha / Taste of Honey / Secret
Agent Man / Blueberry Hill // Bad Eye / 634-5789 / Honky Tonk / Wooly Bully / Java /
Shadow of Your Smile

SHL-32031 - Willie Mitchell - It's What's Happenin' - 1966
Tracks: What Now My Love / The "In" Crowd / Hot Cha / Taste of Honey / Secret
Agent Man / Blueberry Hill // Bad Eye / 634-5789 / Honky Tonk / Wooly Bully / Java /
Shadow of Your Smile

HL-12032 - Bill Black's Combo - Bill Black's Combo Plays All-Timers - 1966
Tracks: Hey, Good Lookin' / Bouquet Of Roses / Together Again / Anytime / Mountain
of Love / Your Cheatin' Heart // I Walk The Line / Half As Much / I'm So Lonesome I
Could Cry / Act Naturally / Under Your Spell Again / Love's Gonna Live Here

SHL-32032 - Bill Black's Combo - Bill Black's Combo Plays All-Timers - 1966
Tracks: Hey, Good Lookin' / Bouquet Of Roses / Together Again / Anytime / Mountain
of Love / Your Cheatin' Heart // I Walk The Line / Half As Much / I'm So Lonesome I
Could Cry / Act Naturally / Under Your Spell Again / Love's Gonna Live Here

HL-12033 - Bill Black's Combo - Black Lace - 1967
Tracks: You Call Everybody Darling / Jersey Bounce / Stardust / Stomping At The
Savoy / Bunny Hop / Rambler // Begin The Beguine / Moonlight Serenade / Sugar
Blues / Beer Barrel Polka / T.D.'s Boogie Woogie / South

SHL-32033 - Bill Black's Combo - Black Lace - 1967
Tracks: You Call Everybody Darling / Jersey Bounce / Stardust / Stomping At The

Soulful Kinda Music – The Rare Soul Bible Volume Two

Savoy / Bunny Hop / Rambler // Begin The Beguine / Moonlight Serenade / Sugar Blues / Beer Barrel Polka / T.D.'s Boogie Woogie / South

HL-12034 - Willie Mitchell - The Hit Sound of Willie Mitchell - 1967
Tracks: Mercy / Treat Her Right / When A Man Loves A Woman / Land Of 1000 Dances / So Rare / Cherry Pink And Apple Blossom White // Searching For My Love / Barefootin' / Winchester Cathedral / Shotgun / Misty / Sticks & Stones

SHL-32034 - Willie Mitchell - The Hit Sound of Willie Mitchell - 1967
Tracks: Mercy / Treat Her Right / When A Man Loves A Woman / Land Of 1000 Dances / So Rare / Cherry Pink And Apple Blossom White // Searching For My Love / Barefootin' / Winchester Cathedral / Shotgun / Misty / Sticks & Stones

HL-12035 - Ace Cannon - The Misty Sax of Ace Cannon - 1967
Tracks: Wonderland By Night / Almost Persuaded / Somewhere My Love / Blowin' In The Wind / As Time Goes By / Yesterday // When A Man Loves A Woman / Strangers In The Night / You'll Never Walk Alone / That's My Desire / Summertime / Michelle

SHL-32035 - Ace Cannon - The Misty Sax of Ace Cannon - 1967
Tracks: Wonderland By Night / Almost Persuaded / Somewhere My Love / Blowin' In The Wind / As Time Goes By / Yesterday // When A Man Loves A Woman / Strangers In The Night / You'll Never Walk Alone / That's My Desire / Summertime / Michelle

HL-12036 - Bill Black's Combo - King of the Road - 1967
Tracks: King Of The Road / Detroit City / I Left My Heart In San Francisco / Blue Hawaii / Mexico / Sidewalks Of New York // Sioux City Sue / Chicago / Pennsylvania Polka / Memphis, Tennessee / Tennessee Waltz / Washington Square

SHL-32036 - Bill Black's Combo - King of the Road - 1967
Tracks: King Of The Road / Detroit City / I Left My Heart In San Francisco / Blue Hawaii / Mexico / Sidewalks Of New York // Sioux City Sue / Chicago / Pennsylvania Polka / Memphis, Tennessee / Tennessee Waltz / Washington Square

HL-12037 - Charlie Rich - Charlie Rich Sings Country & Western - 1967
Tracks: My Heart Would Know / Take These Chains From My Heart / Half As Much / You Win Again / I Can't Help It / Hey Good Lookin' // Your Cheatin' Heart / Cold, Cold Heart / Nobody's Lonesome For Me / I'm So Lonesome I Could Cry / Wedding Bells / They'll Never Take Her Love From Me

SHL-32037 - Charlie Rich - Charlie Rich Sings Country & Western - 1967
Tracks: My Heart Would Know / Take These Chains From My Heart / Half As Much / You Win Again / I Can't Help It / Hey Good Lookin' // Your Cheatin' Heart / Cold, Cold Heart / Nobody's Lonesome For Me / I'm So Lonesome I Could Cry / Wedding Bells / They'll Never Take Her Love From Me

Soulful Kinda Music – The Rare Soul Bible Volume Two

HL-12038 - Jerry Jaye - My Girl Josephine - 1967
Tracks: My Girl Josephine / When My Dreamboat Comes Home / Don't Be Cruel /
Singing the Blues / Kansas City / I'm Gonna Be a Wheel Someday // White Silver
Sands / Ain't Got No Home / Ain't That A Shame / Let the Four Winds Blow / Whole
Lot Of Shakin' Going On / What Am I Living For

SHL-32038 - Jerry Jaye - My Girl Josephine - 1967
Tracks: My Girl Josephine / When My Dreamboat Comes Home / Don't Be Cruel /
Singing the Blues / Kansas City / I'm Gonna Be a Wheel Someday // White Silver
Sands / Ain't Got No Home / Ain't That A Shame / Let the Four Winds Blow / Whole
Lot Of Shakin' Going On / What Am I Living For

HL-12039 - Willie Mitchell - Soul Serenade - 1967
Tracks: Ooh Baby, You Turn Me On / Soul Finger / Cleo's Mood / Slippin' And Sliddin'
/ Soul Serenade / Willie's Mood // Sunny / Pearl Time / Papa's Got A Brand New Bag
/ Respect / Have You Ever Had The Blues / Toddlin'

SHL-32039 - Willie Mitchell - Soul Serenade - 1967
Tracks: Ooh Baby, You Turn Me On / Soul Finger / Cleo's Mood / Slippin' And Sliddin'
/ Soul Serenade / Willie's Mood // Sunny / Pearl Time / Papa's Got A Brand New Bag
/ Respect / Have You Ever Had The Blues / Toddlin'

HL-12040 - Ace Cannon - Memphis Golden Hits - Ace Cannon - 1967
Tracks: Last Night / Wooly Bully / Haunted House / Raunchy / "20-75" / Green Onions
// Tuff / Walking The Dog / In the Midnight Hour / Baby, Let's Play House / White
Silver Sands / I Walk The Line

SHL-32040 - Ace Cannon - Memphis Golden Hits - Ace Cannon - 1967
Tracks: Last Night / Wooly Bully / Haunted House / Raunchy / "20-75" / Green Onions
// Tuff / Walking The Dog / In the Midnight Hour / Baby, Let's Play House / White
Silver Sands / I Walk The Line

HL-12041 - Bill Black's Combo - Bill Black's Beat Goes On - 1967
Tracks: Funky Broadway / Ode To Billy Joe / Let The Good Times Roll / The Stripper
/ Soul Man / The Beat Goes On // A Whiter Shade of Pale / River Of Darkness /
Never My Love / Wipe It Out / Gotta Travel On / The Letter

SHL-32041 - Bill Black's Combo - Bill Black's Beat Goes On - 1967
Tracks: Funky Broadway / Ode To Billy Joe / Let The Good Times Roll / The Stripper
/ Soul Man / The Beat Goes On // A Whiter Shade of Pale / River Of Darkness /
Never My Love / Wipe It Out / Gotta Travel On / The Letter

HL-12042 - Willie Mitchell - Willie Mitchell Live - 1967
Tracks: 20-75 / My Girl / Mustang Sally / Mercy Mercy / Smokie / Late Date // Tequila
/ Bum Daddy / Boot-Leg / Honky Tonk / I'll Be In Trouble / Pin Head

SHL-32042 - Willie Mitchell - Willie Mitchell Live - 1967

Soulful Kinda Music – The Rare Soul Bible Volume Two

Tracks: 20-75 / My Girl / Mustang Sally / Mercy Mercy / Smokie / Late Date // Tequila / Bum Daddy / Boot-Leg / Honky Tonk / I'll Be In Trouble / Pin Head

HL-12043 - Ace Cannon - The Incomparable Sax of Ace Cannon - 1967
Tracks: Sleepwalk / Woman, Woman / Laura (What's He Got That I Ain't Got) / Mathilda / You Send Me / Come Back To Sorrento // By The Time I Get To Phoenix / Green Green Grass Of Home / Since I Fell For You / Unchain My Heart / Turn On Your Love Light / Young Love

SHL-32043 - Ace Cannon - The Incomparable Sax of Ace Cannon - 1967
Tracks: Sleepwalk / Woman, Woman / Laura (What's He Got That I Ain't Got) / Mathilda / You Send Me / Come Back To Sorrento // By The Time I Get To Phoenix / Green Green Grass Of Home / Since I Fell For You / Unchain My Heart / Turn On Your Love Light / Young Love

HL-12044 - Bill Black's Combo - Turn on Your Love Light - 1967
Tracks: Turn On Your Love Light / Simon Says / Bright Lights Big City / Red Light / Big Boss Man // In the Midnight Hour / Feel So Bad / Shoo- Bee-Doo-Be-Doo-Da-Day / Phily Dog / Soul Serenade / The Horse

SHL-32044 - Bill Black's Combo - Turn on Your Love Light - 1967
Tracks: Turn On Your Love Light / Simon Says / Bright Lights Big City / Red Light / Big Boss Man // In the Midnight Hour / Feel So Bad / Shoo- Bee-Doo-Be-Doo-Da-Day / Phily Dog / Soul Serenade / The Horse

HL-12045 - Willie Mitchell - Solid Soul - 1967
Tracks: Prayer Meetin' / Grazing In the Grass / Windy / Sunrise Serenade / The Horse / Groovin' // San-Ho-Zay / Up-Hard / Monkey Jump / Strawberry Solo / Hideaway / Willie-Wam

SHL-32045 - Willie Mitchell - Solid Soul - 1967
Tracks: Prayer Meetin' / Grazing In the Grass / Windy / Sunrise Serenade / The Horse / Groovin' // San-Ho-Zay / Up-Hard / Monkey Jump / Strawberry Solo / Hideaway / Willie-Wam

HL-12046 - Ace Cannon - Ace Cannon in the Spotlight - 1968
Tracks: You've Got Your Troubles / Goin'Away / Honey / Son Of Hickory Holler's Tramp / Words // Light My Fire / I Wanna Live / Release Me / Little Green Apples / Love Is Blue / Harper Valley P.T.A.

SHL-32046 - Ace Cannon - Ace Cannon in the Spotlight - 1968
Tracks: You've Got Your Troubles / Goin'Away / Honey / Son Of Hickory Holler's Tramp / Words // Light My Fire / I Wanna Live / Release Me / Little Green Apples / Love Is Blue / Harper Valley P.T.A.

HL-12047 - Bill Black's Combo - Soulin' the Blues - 1968
Tracks: Hoochie Coochie / Everyday I Have The Blues / Dust My Broom / Blue

Soulful Kinda Music – The Rare Soul Bible Volume Two

Shadows / Prowlin' / No Time // The Birds And The Bees / Things I Used To Do / Spoonful / Imperial Tempo / Mrs. Nelly B / Last Train

SHL-32047 - Bill Black's Combo - Soulin' the Blues - 1968
Tracks: Hoochie Coochie / Everyday I Have The Blues / Dust My Broom / Blue Shadows / Prowlin' / No Time // The Birds And The Bees / Things I Used To Do / Spoonful / Imperial Tempo / Mrs. Nelly B / Last Train

HL-12048 - Willie Mitchell - On Top - 1968
Tracks: Take Five / Poppin' / Canadian Sunset / Ain't Too Proud To Beg / Louie, Louie / Big Power House // 30-60-90 / Who's Making Love / I Say A Little Prayer / Come See About Me / I Wish It Would Rain / Sunshine Of Your Love

SHL-32048 - Willie Mitchell - On Top - 1968
Tracks: Take Five / Poppin' / Canadian Sunset / Ain't Too Proud To Beg / Louie, Louie / Big Power House // 30-60-90 / Who's Making Love / I Say A Little Prayer / Come See About Me / I Wish It Would Rain / Sunshine Of Your Love

HL-12049 - Various Artists - Hi Presents the Greatest Hits from Memphis - 1968
Tracks: White Silver Sands - Bill Black's Combo / Haunted House - Gene Simmons / 20-75 - Willie Mitchell / Tuff - Ace Cannon / My Girl Josephine - Jerry Jaye // Soul Serenade - Willie Mitchell / Cottonfields - Ace Cannon / Let The Four Winds Blow - Jerry Jaye / Don't Be Cruel - Bill Black's Combo / Long Tall Texan - Murry Kellum / Smokie, Part 2 - Bill Black's Combo

SHL-32049 - Various Artists - Hi Presents the Greatest Hits from Memphis - 1968
Tracks: White Silver Sands - Bill Black's Combo / Haunted House - Gene Simmons / 20-75 - Willie Mitchell / Tuff - Ace Cannon / My Girl Josephine - Jerry Jaye // Soul Serenade - Willie Mitchell / Cottonfields - Ace Cannon / Let The Four Winds Blow - Jerry Jaye / Don't Be Cruel - Bill Black's Combo / Long Tall Texan - Murry Kellum / Smokie, Part 2 - Bill Black's Combo

HL-12050 - Willie Mitchell - Soul Bag - 1968
Tracks: Apollo X / One Mint Julep / I'm A Midnight Mover / Cherry Tree / Young People / Blue Blue Light // Everyday People / Knock On Wood / Grand Slam / Honey Pot / Hawaii Five-O / Set Free

SHL-32050 - Willie Mitchell - Soul Bag - 1968
Tracks: Apollo X / One Mint Julep / I'm A Midnight Mover / Cherry Tree / Young People / Blue Blue Light // Everyday People / Knock On Wood / Grand Slam / Honey Pot / Hawaii Five-O / Set Free

HL-12051 - Ace Cannon - Ace of Sax - 1968
Tracks: Down By The Riverside / I've Been Loving You Too Long / Amen / Bad Moon Rising / Alley Cat // Who's Making Love / You Showed Me / Proud Mary / Groovin' / You Gave Me A Mountain / Soul For Sale

Soulful Kinda Music – The Rare Soul Bible Volume Two

SHL-32051 - Ace Cannon - Ace of Sax - 1968
Tracks: Down By The Riverside / I've Been Loving You Too Long / Amen / Bad Moon
Rising / Alley Cat // Who's Making Love / You Showed Me / Proud Mary / Groovin' /
You Gave Me A Mountain / Soul For Sale

HL-12052 - Bill Black's Combo - Solid and Raunchy the 3rd - 1968
tracks: Creepin' Around / Groovin' Easy / Watch Your Step / Hold It Down / Coco
Brown // Come See About Me / Son Of Hickory Holler's Tramp / Cab Driver / If I Had
A Hammer / Leavin' Town / Love Is Here And Now You're Gone

SHL-32052 - Bill Black's Combo - Solid and Raunchy the 3rd - 1968
tracks: Creepin' Around / Groovin' Easy / Watch Your Step / Hold It Down / Coco
Brown // Come See About Me / Son Of Hickory Holler's Tramp / Cab Driver / If I Had
A Hammer / Leavin' Town / Love Is Here And Now You're Gone

HL-12053 - Ann Peebles - This is Ann Peebles - 1969
Tracks: Give Me Some Credit / Crazy About You Baby / Make Me Yours / My Man
He's A Lovin' Man / Solid Foundation / Chain Of Fools // It's Your Thing / Walk Away
/ Rescue Me / Won't You Try Me / Steal Away / Respect

SHL-12053 - Ann Peebles - This is Ann Peebles - 1969
Tracks: Give Me Some Credit / Crazy About You Baby / Make Me Yours / My Man
He's A Lovin' Man / Solid Foundation / Chain Of Fools // It's Your Thing / Walk Away
/ Rescue Me / Won't You Try Me / Steal Away / Respect

HL-12054 - Don Bryant - Precious Soul - 1969 (The last Mono release)
Tracks: She's Looking Good / (You're A) Wonderful One / Funky Broadway / Can I
Change My Mind / Soul Man / Land Of 1,000 Dances // Slip Away / For Your
Precious Love / Expressway To Your Heart / Try Me / When Something Is Wrong
With My Baby / Cry Baby

SHL-32054 - Don Bryant - Precious Soul - 1969
Tracks: She's Looking Good / (You're A) Wonderful One / Funky Broadway / Can I
Change My Mind / Soul Man / Land Of 1,000 Dances // Slip Away / For Your
Precious Love / Expressway To Your Heart / Try Me / When Something Is Wrong
With My Baby / Cry Baby

SHL-32055 - Al Green - Green Is Blues - 1969
Tracks: One Woman / Talk To Me / My Girl / The Letter / I Stand Accused // Gotta
Find A New World / What Am I Gonna Do With Myself / Tomorrow's Dream / Get
Back Baby / Get Back / Summertime

SHL-32056 - Willie Mitchell - The Many Moods of Willie Mitchell - 1969
Tracks: Breaking Point / Sometimes I Wonder / Black Fox / Road House / Sack of
Woe // Too Sweet / White Silver Sands / Midnight Sun / Cuddlin' Up / Something
Nice

Soulful Kinda Music – The Rare Soul Bible Volume Two

SHL-32057 - Ace Cannon - The Happy and Mello Sax of Ace Cannon - 1969
Tracks: Ruby, Don't Take Your Love To Town / Are You From Dixie / Games People Play / Going Up The Country / Get Back / Mama Tried // I Can't Stop Loving You / You Win Again / He Called Me Baby / Your Cheatin' Heart / Crying Time / Suspicious Minds

SHL-32058 - Willie Mitchell - Robbin's Nest - 1969
Tracks: Robbin's Nest / On The Other Side / Last Date / This Guy's In Love With You / Tails Out / Raindrops Keep Fallin' On My Head // Wade In The Water / Turn Back The Hands Of Time / Greasy Spoon / Chilly, Chilly / Sing A Simple Song / Sleepy Lagoon

SHL-32059 - Ann Peebles - Part Time Love - 1970
Tracks: Part Time Love / I'll Get Along / I Still Love You / Make Me Yours / It's Your Thing // Generation Gap Between Us / Crazy About You Baby / Give Me Some Credit / Steal Away / Solid Foundation

SHL-32060 - Ace Cannon - Cool 'N Saxy - 1970
Tracks: Rainy Night In Georgia / My Elusive Dream / Let It Be / Don't It Make You Want To Go Home / Everybody's Talking / Sugar Sugar // Lodi / Am I That Easy To Forget / For The Love Of Him / Sunny / The House Of The Rising Sun / Chicken Fried Soul

SHL-32061 - Bill Black's Combo - More Bill Black Magic - 1970
Tracks: Ramblin' Rose / Careless Love / He'll Have To Go / I Got A Woman / We'll Sing In The Sunshine / Everybody Loves Somebody // Closin' Time / Tuff / Hey Ba Ba Re Bop / That Funky Feelin' / Kinda Lonesome / Tippin'

SHL-32062 - Al Green - Al Green Gets Next To You - 1971
Tracks: I Can't Get Next To You / Are You Lonely For Me Baby / God Is Standing By / Tired Of Being Alone / I'm A Ram // Driving Wheel / Light My Fire / You Say It / Right Now Right Now / All Because

SHL-32063 - Big Lucky, Big Amos and Don Hines - River Town Blues - 1970
Tracks: Please Don't Leave / Going To Vietnam / Goofer Dust / Stop Arguing / I've Been Hurt / Miss Betty Green // Stormy Monday Blues / You Better Mind / I'm Gone / Dog Man / You're Too Young / Please Accept My Love

SHL-32064 - Swift Rain - Coming Down - 1971
Tracks: You're Gonna Come Down / United / Everybird / Broken Love / Nancy's Song / Yo Sol Tuyo // Everywhere (In My Town) / If You Feel / Silver Paper / For La Hudala / The Laplander

SHL-32065 - Ann Peebles - Straight from the Heart - 1971
Tracks: Slipped, Tripped And Fell In Love / Trouble, Heartaches And Sadness / What

Soulful Kinda Music – The Rare Soul Bible Volume Two

You Laid On Me / How Strong Is A Woman / Somebody's On Your Case // I Feel Like Breaking Up Somebody's Home Tonight / I've Been There Before / I Pity The Fool / 99 Pounds / I Take What I Want

SHL-32066 - ?

SHL-32067 - Ace Cannon - Blowing Wild - 1971
Tracks: Montego Bay / For The Good Times / Dream Baby / Me And Bobby McGee / Drunk // I Hear You Knocking / Help Me Make It Through The Night / Sweet Caroline / Danny Boy / You Can Bet Your Life

SHL-32068 / 69 - Willie Mitchell - The Best of Willie Mitchell - 1972 (Double LP)
Tracks: Soul Serenade / Papa's Got a Brand New Bag / Mercy, Mercy, Mercy / Bum Daddy / Barefootin' // Have You Ever Had the Blues / Grazing In the Grass / Strawberry Solo / Misty / Buster Browne // Slippin' & Sliddin' / Bad Eye / Everything Is Gonna Be Alright / That Driving Beat / Crawl / 20-75 / Sunrise Serenade / Searching / The Horse / Woodchopper's Ball

SHL-32070 - Al Green - Let's Stay Together - 1972
Tracks: Let's Stay Together / La La For You / So You're Leaving / What Is This Feeling / Old Time Lovin' // I've Never Found A Girl / How Can You Mend A Broken Heart / Judy / It Ain't No Fun To Me

SHLX-32071 - Ace Cannon - Cannon Country: Ace, That Is - 1972
Tracks: Easy Loving / Ramblin' Rose / Crazy Arms / Red Red Wine / With Pen In Hand // Misty Blue / Love Sick Blues / Don't Touch Me / Hello Darlin' / Gentle On My Mind / Cold, Cold Heart

SHL-32072 / 73 - Ace Cannon - Ace's Back To Back - 1972 (Double LP)
Tracks: Tuff / Cannonball / Looking Back / Volare / It's All In The Game // So Fine / Never On Sunday / Memphis / Stranger On The Shore // Cottonfields / Four Walls / Slipping Around / I've Got A Tiger By The Tail / Funny (How Time Slips Away) // Almost Persuaded / Wooly Bully / Strangers In The Night / I Walk The Line / Searchin'

SHLX-32074 - Al Green - I'm Still in Love with You - 1972
Tracks: I'm Still In Love With You / I'm Glad You're Mine / Love And Happiness / What A Wonderful Thing Love Is / Simply Beautiful // Oh, Pretty Woman / For The Good Times / Look What You Done For Me / One Of These Good Old Days

SHL-32075 - Otis Clay - Trying to Live My Life Without You - 1972
Tracks: Trying To Live My Life Without You / I Die A Little Each Day / Holding On To A Dying Love / I Can't Make It Alone / That's How It Is // I Love You, I Need You / You Can't Keep Running From My Love / Precious Precious / Home Is Where The Heart Is / Too Many Hands

Soulful Kinda Music – The Rare Soul Bible Volume Two

SHL-32076 - Ace Cannon - Baby, Don't Get Hooked On Me - 1972
Tracks: Baby, Don't Get Hooked on Me / Tuffer Than Tuff / A Thing Called Sadness /
Put Your Hand In the Hand / Saxxy Waltz // Daddy Don't You Walk So Fast / To Get
To You / Tiny Bubbles / Green Door / Today I Started Loving You Again

SHLX-32077 - Al Green - Call Me - 1973
Tracks: Call Me (Come Back Home) / Have You Been Making Out O.K. / Stand Up /
I'm So Lonesome I Could Cry / Your Love Is Like The Morning Sun // Here I Am
(Come And Take Me) / Funny How Time Slips Away / You Ought To Be With Me /
Jesus Is Waiting

XSHL-32078 - - Bill Black's Combo Bill Black's Greatest Hits, Volume 2 - 1973
Tracks: Silver foil cover. Raunchy / Dry Bones / Cherry Pink And Apple Blossom
White / I Walk The Line / Movin' // Memphis Tennessee / The Stripper / Turn On
Your Love Light / Be-Bop A-Lula / So What

SHL-32079 - Ann Peebles - I Can't Stand The Rain - 1974
Tracks: I Can't Stand The Rain / Do I Need You / Until You Came Into My Life / (You
Keep Me) Hangin' On / Run, Run, Run // If We Can't Trust Each Other / A Love
Vibration / You Got To Feed The Fire / I'm Gonna Tear Your Playhouse Down / One
Way Street

SHLX-32080 - Ace Cannon - Country Comfort - 1973
Tracks: Country Comfort / Faded Love / Closin' Time's A Downer / The Easy Part's
Over / Wabash Cannon Ball // It's Not Love / Missing You / Rocky Top / Goodtime
Charlie / I Can't Help It

SHL-32081 - Syl Johnson - Back for a Taste of Your Love - 1973
Tracks: Back For A Taste Of Your Love / I'm Yours / I Let A Good Girl Go / Anyway
The Wind Blows / You Don't Know Me // Feelin' Frisky / We Did It / Wind, Blow Her
Back My Way / I Hate I Walked Away / The Love You Left Behind

SHLX-32082 - Al Green - Livin' for You - 1973
Tracks: Livin' For You / Home Again / Free At Last / Let's Get Married / So Good To
Be Here // Sweet Sixteen / Unchained Melody / My God Is Real / Beware

SHLX-32083 - ?

SHL-32084 - Charlie Rich - Charlie Rich Sings the Songs of Hank Williams & Others -
1974
Tracks: Reissue of Hi SHL-32037. My Heart Would Know / Take These Chains From
My Heart / Half As Much / You Win Again / I Can't Help It / Hey Good Lookin' // Your
Cheatin' Heart / Cold, Cold Heart / Nobody's Lonesome For Me / I'm So Lonesome I
Could Cry / Wedding Bells / They'll Never Take Her Love From Me

Soulful Kinda Music – The Rare Soul Bible Volume Two

SHL-32085 - Syl Johnson - Diamond In The Rough - 1974
Tracks: Let Yourself Go / Don't Do It / I Want To Take You Home (To See Mama) /
Could I Be Falling In Love / Stuck In Chicago // Diamond In The Rough / Keeping
Down Confusion / Please, Don't Give Up On Me / Music To My Ears / I Hear The
Love Chimes

SHL-32086 - Ace Cannon - That Music City Feeling - 1974
Tracks: Last Date / Born To Lose / Mathilda / Behind Closed Doors / Tuff // There
Goes My Everything / Stand By Your Man / Me And Jesus / Here Comes My Baby /
Tennessee Saturday Night

SHL-32087 - Al Green - Al Green Explores Your Mind - 1974 Tracks: Sha-La-La /
Take Me To The River / God Blessed Our Love / The City / One Nite Stand // I'm
Hooked On You / Stay With Me Forever / Hangin' On / School Days

SHL-32088 - Bill Black's Combo featuring Bob Tucker - Solid and Country - 1974
Tracks: Soul Serenade / Memphis Pickin' / Rub It In / Black's Boogie / Truck Stop //
Cottonfields / Boilin' Cabbage / Chelsea Blues / Faded Love / Hello Josephine

SHL-32089 - Al Green - Greatest Hits - 1975
Tracks: Tired Of Being Alone / Call Me (Come Back Home) / I'm Still In Love With
You / Here I Am (Come and Take Me) / How Can You Mend A Broken Heart //
Let's Stay Together / I Can't Get Next To You / You Ought To Be With Me / Look
What You Done For Me / Let's Get Married

SHL-32090 - Ace Cannon - Super Sax Country Style - 1975
Tracks: Love Me Tender / Welcome To My World / Heartaches By The Number /
Delta Dawn / A Legend In My Time // Raunchy / Malt Liquor / Green Green Grass Of
Home / You've Still Got A Place In My Heart / Satin Sheets

SHL-32091 - Ann Peebles - Tellin' It - 1975
Tracks: Come To Mama / I Don't Lend My Man / I Needed Somebody / Stand By
Woman / It Was Jealousy // Doctor Love Power / You Can't Hold A Man / Beware /
Put Yourself In My Place / Love Played A Game

SHL-32092 - Al Green - Al Green Is Love - 1975
Tracks: L-O-V-E (Love) / Rhymes / The Love Sermon / There Is Love / Could I Be
The One // Love Ritual / I Didn't Know / Oh Me, Oh My (Dreams In My Arms) / I
Gotta Be More (Take Me Higher) / I Wish You Were Here

SHL-32093 - Bill Black's Combo featuring Bob Tucker - World's Greatest Honky Tonk
Band - 1975
Tracks: Orange Blossom Special / I Can Help / Jump Back Joe Joe / Rangers Waltz /
Fire On The Bayou // Back Up And Push / Memphis Stroll / Almost Persuaded / Beer
Barrel Polka / Carroll County Blues

Soulful Kinda Music – The Rare Soul Bible Volume Two

SHL-32094 - ?

SHL-32095 - Herb Jubirt - Laff Me into the Big Time - 1975
Tracks: Prices And Inflation / Horse Meat / Streaking / My Wife / Hair Style / Soap
Operas / Hard Times // Democrats And Republicans / Hijacking / Rationing /
Cadillacs And Brothers / Religions / Women / Laff Me Into The Big Time

SHL-32096 - Syl Johnson - Total Explosion - 1975
Tracks: I Only Have Love / Bustin' Up Or Bustin' Out / Star Bright Star Lite / Watch
What You Do To Me / Steppin' Out // Take Me To The River / It Ain't Easy / 'Bout To
Make Me Leave Home / That's Just My Luck

SHL-32097 - Al Green - Full of Fire - 1975
Tracks: Glory, Glory / That's The Way It Is / Always / There's No Way / I'd Fly Away //
Full of Fire / Together Again / Soon As I Get Home / Let It Shine

SHL-32098 - Narvel Felts - This Time - 1975
This Time / Since I Met You Baby / Butterfly / You're Out Of My Reach / Chased By
The Dawn // No One Will Ever Know / Endless Love / A Little Bit Of Soap / Sound Of
The Wind / It's All In The Game

SHL-32099 - Hi Rhythm - On the Loose - 1975
Tracks: On The Loose / Superstar / Since You've Been Gone / Purple Rain Drops // I
Remember, Do Yo / Save All My Lovin' / You Got Me Comin' / Skinny Dippin'

SHL-32100 ?

SHL-32101 - Ace Cannon - Peace in the Valley - 1976
Tracks: Peace In The Valley / One Day At A Time / Just A Closer Walk With Thee /
You Can't Be A Beacon / It Is No Secret // Blue Eyes Crying In The Rain / I'll Fly
Away / Amazing Grace / Why Me / Everything Is Beautiful

SHL-32102 - Jerry Jaye - Honky Tonk Women Love Red Neck Men - 1976
Tracks: Honky Tonk Women Love Redneck Men / When Morning Comes to
Memphis / Drinkin' My Way Back Home / Standing Room Only / Ain't Got No Home
// Hot and Still Heatin' / Crazy / Forty Days / What's Left Never Will Be Right / Let
Your Love Flow

SHL-32103 - Al Green - Have a Good Time - 1976
Tracks: Keep Me Cryin' / Smile A Little Bit More / I Tried To Tell Myself / Something /
The Truth Marches On // Have A Good Time / Nothing Takes The Place Of You /
Happy / Hold On Forever

Soulful Kinda Music – The Rare Soul Bible Volume Two

SHL-32104 - Bill Black's Combo - It's Honky Tonk Time - 1977
Tracks: Rollin' In My Sweet Baby's Arms / Yakety Sax / Salty Dog Blues / Boilin'
Cabbage / Redneck Rock // Cotton Eyed Joe / Easy Pickin' / Lover Please / My Blue
Heaven / Cycoon (Southern Cyclone)

SHL-32105 - Al Green - Al Green's Greatest Hits, Volume II - 1977
Tracks: Love And Happiness / Sha La La (Make Me Happy) / Take Me To The River
/ L-O-V-E (Love) / Rhymes // For The Good Times / Keep Me Cryin' / Livin' For You /
Full Of Fire

HLP-6001 - O.V. Wright - Into Something-Can't Shake Loose - 1977
Tracks: Into Something (I Can't Shake Loose) / I Feel Love Growin' / Precious
Precious / The Time We Have / You Gotta Have Love // Trying To Live My Life /
Medley: God Blessed Our Love-When A Man Loves A Woman-That's How Strong My
Love Is

HLP-6002 - Ann Peebles - If This Is Heaven - 1977
Tracks: If This Is Heaven / A Good Day For Lovin' / I'm So Thankful / Being Here With
You / Boy I Gotta Have You // When I'm In Your Arms / You Gonna Make Me Cry /
Games / Lovin' You Without Love / It Must Be Love

HLP-6003 - Otis Clay - I Can't Take It - 1977
Tracks: Pussy Footing Around / Too Much Mystery / I Can't Take It / Home Is Where
The Heart Is / I've Got To Find A Way (To Get You Back) // Slow And Easy / House
Ain't A Home (Without A Woman) / Keep On Loving Me / Born To Be With You

HLP-6004 - Al Green - The Belle Album - 1977
Tracks: Belle / Loving You / Feels Like Summer / Georgia Boy // I Feel Good / All 'N
All / Chariots Of Fire / Dream

HLP-6005 - Bill Black's Combo - Award Winners - 1977
Tracks: Cashin' In (A Tribute To Luther Perkins) / Luckenbach Texas / Honky Tonk
Boogie / Blue Eyes Crying In The Rain / Rebel Rouser // Wipe Out / Lucille / Rocky
Top / L.A. Blues / Rock 'N' Roll Redneck Honky Tonk Cowboy Band

HLP-6006 - Ace Cannon - After Hours - 1977
Tracks: Soca After Hours / Don't It Make My Brown Eyes Blue / Blanket On The
Ground / Lonely Street / The Loveless Motel // Heaven's Just A Sin Away / It Was
Almost Like A Song / (Just Enough To Keep Me) Hangin' On / Twilight Over Texas /
Easy

HLP-6007 - Ann Peebles - The Handwriting Is on the Wall - 1977
Tracks: Old Man With Young Ideas / Bip Bam Thank You Mam / The Handwriting Is
On The Wall / I Didn't Take Your Man / You've Got The Papers (I've Got The Man) //

Soulful Kinda Music – The Rare Soul Bible Volume Two

Lookin' For A Lovin' / You're More Than I Can Stand / Livin' In, Livin' Out / If I Can't See You / Let Your Love Light Shine

HLP-6008 - O.V. Wright - The Bottom Line - 1977
Tracks: The Bottom Line / I Don't Do Windows / That's The Way I Feel About Cha / Your Good Thing Is About To End / Let's Straighten It Out // I Don't Know Why / No Easy Way To Say Goodbye / A Little More Time / Since You Left These Arms Of Mine / A Long Road

HLP-6009 - Al Green - Truth N' Time - 1978
Tracks: Blow Me Down / Lo And Behold / Wait Here / To Sir With Love // Truth N' Time / King Of All / Say A Little Prayer / Happy Days

HLP-6010 - Syl Johnson - Uptown Shakedown - 1979
Tracks: Mystery Lady / Let's Dance For Love / Gimme Little Sign / You're The Star Of The Show // Blue Water / Who's Gonna Love You / Otis Redding Medley: Respect-Wholesale Love-Snatch A Little Piece-I Can't Turn You Loose-Fa Fa Fa Fa Fa Fa (Sad Song)-(Sittin' On) The Dock Of The Bay

HLP-6011 - O.V. Wright - We're Still Together - 1978
Tracks: We're Still Together / I Found Peace / It's Cold Without Your Love / Baby Baby Baby / I'm Gonna Stay // The Hurt Is On / Today I Sing The Blues / Mirrors Of My Soul / Sacrifice

HLP-6012 - Al Green - Tokyo Live - 1978 (Double LP)
Tracks: L-O-V-E (Love) / Tired Of Being Alone / Let's Stay Together / How Can You Mend A Broken Heart? / All 'N All // Belle / Sha-La-La / Let's Get Married // God Blessed Our Love / You Ought To Be With Me / For The Good Times // Dream I Feel Good / Love And Happiness

HLP-8000 - Al Green - Tired of Being Alone - 1977
Tracks: One Woman / Talk To Me / My Girl / Tired Of Being Alone / I Stand Accused // Gotta Find A New World / What Am I Gonna Do With Myself / Tomorrow's Dream / Get Back Baby / Get Back / Summertime

HLP-8001 - Al Green - Can't Get Next to You - 1977
Tracks: I Can't Get Next To You / Are You Lonely For Me Baby / God Is Standing By / The Letter / I'm A Ram // Driving Wheel / Light My Fire / You Say It / Right Now, Right Now / All Because

HLP-8002 - Willie Mitchell - Willie Mitchell Live - 1978
Tracks: 20 - 75 / My Girl / Mustang Sally / Mercy Mercy Mercy / Smokie / Late Date // Soul Serenade / Bum Daddy / Boot-leg / Honky Tonk / I'll Be In Trouble / Pin Head

Soulful Kinda Music – The Rare Soul Bible Volume Two

HLP-8003 - Ace Cannon - Ace Cannon / Sax Man - 1978
Tracks: Tuff / Proud Mary / Alley Cat / Crying Time / Almost Persuaded //
Cottonfields / I Can't Stop Loving You / Games People Play / Rainy Night In Georgia /
Me & Bobby McGee

HLP-8004 -- Bill Black's Combo Memphis, Tennessee - 1978
Tracks: Smokie, Part 2 / Memphis, Tennessee / Leavin' Town / Turn On Your Love
Light / Creepin' Around // White Silver Sands / Don't Be Cruel / Ramblin' Rose / He'll
Have To Go / Wipe It Out

HLP-8005 - Ann Peebles - Part Time Love - 1978 Reissue of Hi SHL-32059.
Tracks: Part Time Love / I'll Get Along / I Still Love You / Make Me Yours / It's Your
Thing // Generation Gap Between Us / Crazy About You Baby / Give Me Some
Credit / Steal Away / Solid Foundation

HLP-8006 - Charlie Rich - So Lonesome I Could Cry - 1978 Reissue of Hi SHL-
32084.
Tracks: My Heart Would Know / Take These Chains From My Heart / Half As Much /
You Win Again / I Can't Help It / Hey Good Looking // Your Cheating Heart / Cold,
Cold Heart / Nobody's Lonesome For Me / I'm So Lonesome I Could Cry / Wedding
Bells / They'll Never Take Her Love From Me

HLP-8007 - Al Green - Let's Stay Together - 1978 Reissue of Hi HL-32070.
Tracks: Let's Stay Together / La-La For You / So You're Leaving / What Is This
Feeling / Old Time Lovin // I've Never Found A Girl / How Can You Mend A Broken
Heart / Judy / It Ain't No Fun To Me

HLP-8008 - Ace Cannon - Cannon Country - 1978 Reissue of Hi-32071.
Tracks: Easy Loving / Ramblin' Rose / Crazy Arms / Red Red Wine / With Pen In
Hand // Misty Blue / Love Sick Blues / Don't Touch Me / Hello Darlin' / Gentle On My
Mind / Cold, Cold Heart

HLP-8009 - Ann Peebles - Straight From The Heart - 1978 Reissue of Hi SHL-32065.
Tracks: Slipped, Tripped, Fell In Love / Trouble, Heartaches And Sadness / What You
Laid On Me / How Strong Is A Woman / Somebody's On Your Case // Breaking Up
Somebody's Home / I've Been There Before / I Pity The Fool / 99 Pounds / I Take
What I Want

Hi-Lite

101 – Jim Edwards – Burning My Bridges Behind Me / I'm So All Alone
102 – Jimmy Key – Super Market Day / Purple Sky
103 – Merle Everts – If I Had To Do It Over / Little White House
104 – George Garish – I Only Know / Please Close The Door Behind You

Soulful Kinda Music – The Rare Soul Bible Volume Two

105 – Tommy Frontera – Shy Boy / Dry Your Eyes
106 – The Elites – You Mean So Much To Me / Tell Him Again
107 – Tommy Frontera – (You're My) Leading Lady / I Heard Every Word
108 – The Elites – Have You Got A Love / Trouble In Mind
109 – The Seminoles (Featuring Joey Finazo) – Meant To Be / Cheating Heart
110 – The Seminoles – Drifting / You Meant Everything To Me
111 – Chris Peterson – I'll Get Even With You / I Love You
80443 - The Seminoles - I Can't Stand It / It Takes A Lot
84950 - Tommy Frontera – Mary Mary / To Be With You
84952 - Tommy Frontera – Be Mine / That's All I Want From You
87568 - The Seminoles - Trouble In Mind / Have You Got A Love

House Of Orange

2400 - Kitty Clark - Big Wheel / Funny You Should Ask - 1970
2401 - Geater (Jeater) Davis - Sweet Womans Love / Don't Marry A Fool - 1970
2402 - Geater Davis - My Love Is So Strong For You / I Can Hold My Own - 1971
2403 - Reuben Bell - I Can't Feel This Way At Home / What's Happening To The World – 1971
2404 - Don Varner - I Can If You Can / That's All Right - 1971
2405 - Geater Davis - For Your Precious Love / Wrapped Up In You - 1971
2406 - Reuben Bell - What's Happening To The World / Don't Give No More – 1971
2407 - Geater Davis - Best Of Luck To You / I Know (My Baby Loves Me) - 1971
2405e - Geater Davis - For Your Precious Love / Wrapped Up In You - 1975
2408 - ?
2409 - ?
2410 - Geater Davis - Cold Love / Cold Love (Long Version) - 1977
2411 - ?
2412 - ?
2413 - ?
2414 - ?
2615 - Geater Davis - Booty Music (Let's Go Dancin') / Breath Taking Girl - 1977
79-100 - Geater Davis - I'll Play The Blues For You / Disco Music - 1979
130 - Geater Davis - Your Heart Is So Cold / You Made Your Bed - ?

Lp's

House Of Orange Lps-6000 - Geater Davis - Sweet Woman's Love - 1971
Tracks: My Love Is So Strong For You / For Your Precious Love / I Love You / I Can Hold My Own /// Cry, Cry, Cry / Don't Marry A Fool / St. James Infirmary / Wrapped Up In You / Sweet Woman's Love.

Soulful Kinda Music – The Rare Soul Bible Volume Two

The Icemen

The Poindexter Brothers (members Robert Poindexter and Richard Poindexter)

Tuff 404 - Booga Man / Ride, Ride, Ride - 1965
Verve 10447 - Backfield In Motion / Give That Girl Some Slack - 1966

The Icemen (members Robert Poindexter and Richard Poindexter)

Samar 111 - (My Girl) She's A Fox / (I Wonder) What It Takes - 1966
Samar 117 - Sugar Baby / Only Time Will Tell - 1966
ABC-Paramount 45-11038 - How Can I Get Over A Fox Like You / Loogaboo (The Choice Is Yours) - 1968
Ole-9 1007/8 - It's Gonna Take A Lot To Bring Me Back Baby / It's Time You Knew - 196?

The Intruders

The Intruders (members

Gowen 1401 - I'm Sold On You / Come Home Soon – 1961

The Four Intruders (members

Gowen 1404 - This Is My Song / My Baby – 1962

The Intruders (members

Lost Nite 195 - I'm Sold On You / Come Home Soon - 1963

The Intruders (members Sam "Little Sonny" Brown (died ?-April-1995 --- cause: commited suicide by jumping off of the Strawberry Mansion bridge. When his body was found he had several Intruders cassettes and photos tied to him), Eugene "Bird" Daughtry (born 29-October-1939 in Kinston, North Carolina --- died 25-December-1994 --- cause: cancer), "Big" Sonny Edwards (born 22-February-1942 in Philadelphia, Pennsylvania) and Phil Terry (born 1-November-1943 in Philadelphia, Pennsylvania))

Music Voice 504 - But You Belong To Me / Jack Be Nimble - 1964
Excel 101 - Gonna Be Strong / All The Time – 1966
Gamble 201 - (We'll Be) United / Up And Down The Ladder - 1966
Gamble 203 - A Book For The Broken Hearted / Devil With An Angel's Smile - 1966 (some copies issued with picture sleeve)
Gamble 204 - It Must Be Love / (You Better) Check Yourself* - 1966 *also recorded in 1970 by I. A. P. CO. The Italian Asphalt & Pavement Company on Colossus 110.
Gamble 205 - Together / Up And Down The Ladder – 1967
Gamble 209 - A Love That's Real* / Baby I'm Lonely - 1967 *also recorded in 19 by

Soulful Kinda Music – The Rare Soul Bible Volume Two

The Eptones on Jox 070.
Gamble 214 - Cowboys To Girls / Turn The Hands Of Time - 1968
Gamble 217 - (Love Is Like A) Baseball Game / Friends No More - 1968
Gamble 221 - Slow Drag / So Glad I'm Yours – 1968
Gamble 223 - Give Her A Transplant / Girls, Girls, Girls – 1969
Gamble 225 - Me Tarzan, You Jane / Favorite Candidate – 1969
Gamble 231 - Lollipop (I Like You) / Don't Give It Away – 1969
Gamble 235 - Let's Go Downtown / Sad Girl* - 1969 *also released in 1963 by Jay
Wiggins on I. P.G. 1008 and in 1969 by Joe Bataan on Fania 492 plus by The
Emperors Soul 69 on Futura 1505 and yet again in 1982 by C. Q. on Arista 0659
Gamble 240 - Old Love / Everyday Is A Holiday – 1969
Gamble 4001 - Tender (Was The Love We Knew) / By The Time I Get To Phoenix -
1970

The Intruders (members Bobby Starr (born Robert Ferguson on 19-January-1937 in
Baltimore, Maryland), Eugene Daughtry, Sonny Edwards and Phil Terry)

Gamble 4004 - Doctor Doctor / When We Get Married* - 1970 *also recorded in 1961
by The Dreamlovers on Heritage 102
Gamble 4007 - This Is My Love Song / Let Me In Your Mind - 1970
Gamble 4009 - I'm Girl Scoutin' / Wonder What Kind Of Bag She's In – 1971
Gamble 4014 - Best Days Of My Life / Pray For Me – 1971
Gamble 4016 - I Bet He Don't Love You (Like I Love You) / Do You Remember
Yesterday - 1971
Gamble 4019 - (Win, Place Or Show) She's A Winner / Memories Are Here To Stay –
1972
Gamble 2501 - (Win, Place Or Show) She's A Winner / Memories Are Here To Stay –
1972

The Intruders (members Sam Brown, Eugene Daughtry, Sonny Edwards and Phil
Terry)

Gamble 2506 - I'll Always Love My Mama (Part 1) / I'll Always Love My Mama (Part 2)
– 1973
Gamble 2508 - I Wanna Know Your Name / Hang On In There – 1973
Gamble 2571 - I Wanna Know Your Name / I'll Always Love My Mama - 1974
T. S. O. P. 4758 - A Nice Girl Like You / To Be Happy Is The Real Thing - 1974
T. S. O. P. 4766 - Rainy Days And Mondays / Be On Time – 1975
T. S. O. P. 4771 - Energy Of Love / Plain Ol' Fashioned Girl   - 1975
Philadelphia International 3624 - I'll Always Love My Mama / I'll Always Love My
Mama (Long Version) – 1977
Philadelphia International 3689 - I'll Always Love My Mama / Save The Children –
1979

The Intruders (Members

King Tut 179 - Goodnight / Sweet Girl – 1979 (A previously unreleased Gowen
recording by The Four Intruders)
El Cee 708 - Who Do You Love / (Instrumental) - 1984
Kahn 34 - Who Do You Love / Track - 1984

Soulful Kinda Music – The Rare Soul Bible Volume Two

The Intruders (members Sam Brown, Eugene Daughtry, Sonny Edwards and Phil Terry)

Ripete 102 - I'll Always Love My Mama / (Love Is Like A) Baseball Game - 1985
Collectables Col 013287 - Come Home Soon / I'm Sold (On You) - ?
Collectables Col 046427 - I'll Always Love My Mama (Part 1) / I'll Always Love My Mama (Part 2) - ?
Collectables Col 046787 - (Love Is Like A) Baseball Game / Friends No More - ?

Luther Ingram

The Midwest Crusaders (members Luther Ingram, ...) 1947

The Gardenias (members Luther Ingram, ...)

Federal 12284 - My Baby's Tops / Flaming Love - 1957 (session: Ike Turner on guitar)

Luther Ingram (born Luther Thomas Ingram on 30-November-1937 in Jackson, Tennessee --- died 19-March-2007 in Belleville, Illinois --- cause: ?)

Decca - Oh Baby Don't You Weep - 1964 (unissued track from his first recording session in November-1964 this was released in 2008 in the U. K. on a Kent Cd "New Breed R&B With Added Popcorn" CDKEND 291 --- song was also recorded in 1962 by Fred Bridges on Versatile 111, and by Wilson Pickett as a Double L album track)
Decca 31794 - You Never Miss Your Water / Ain't That Nice - 1965

Luther Ingram & The G-Men (members Luther Ingram with his brothers Jesse Ingram, Frank Ingram and Tommy Ingram)

Smash 2019 - I Spy (For The F. B. I.)* / Foxy Devil - 1965 *also recorded in 1966 by Jamo Thomas & His Party Brothers Orchestra on Thomas 303.

Luther Ingram / Luther Ingram Orchestra

Hib 698 - If It's All The Same To You Babe / Exus Trek* - 1966 *flip by Luther Ingram Orchestra.

Luther Ingram

Ko Ko 101 - I Can't Stop / You Got To Give Love To Get Love - 1967
Ko Ko 103 - Missing You / Since You Don't Want Me - 1968
Ko Ko 2101 - You Can Depend On Me / Looking For A New Love - 1969
Ko Ko 2101 - Oh Baby, You Can Depend On Me / Looking For A New Love - 1969
Ko Ko 2102 - Pity For The Lonely* / Looking For A New Love - 1969 *also recorded in 1967 by Little Dooley on Koko 102.
Ko Ko 2103 - Puttin' Game Down / Since You Don't Want Me - 1969
Ko Ko 2104 - My Honey And Me* / I Can't Stop - 1969 *also recorded in 1972 by The Emotions on Volt 4077.

Soulful Kinda Music – The Rare Soul Bible Volume Two

Ko Ko 2105 - Ain't That Loving You (For More Reasons Than One)* / Home Don't Seem Like Home - 1970 *also recorded in 1967 by Johnnie Taylor on Stax 209 and in 1975 by The Skull Snaps on Grill 301 plus in 1980 by Lou Rawls on Philadelphia International 3102
Ko Ko 2106 - To The Other Man / I'll Just Call You Honey - 1970
Hurdy-Gurdy 102 - I Need You Now / Run For Your Life - 1971 (Recorded In 1966)
Ko Ko 2107 - Be Good To Me Baby / Since You Don't Want Me - 1971
Ko Ko 2108 - I'll Love You Until The End / Ghetto Train - 1971
Ko Ko 2110 - You Were Made For Me / Missing You - 1972
Ko Ko 2111 - (If Loving You Is Wrong) I Don't Want To Be Right* / Puttin' Game Down - 1972 *also recorded in 1974 by Hugh Boynton on Soul-Po-Tion 144 and in 1975 by Millie Jackson on Spring 155.
Ko Ko 2113 - I'll Be Your Shelter (In Time Of Storm) / I Can't Stop - 1972
Ko Ko 2115 - Always* / Help Me Love - 1973 *also recorded in 1976 by Tommy Tate on Ko Ko 722.
Ko Ko 2116 - Love Ain't Gonna Run Me Away / To The Other Man - 1973
Eric 284 - If Loving You Is Wrong I Don't Want To Be Right / Ain't That Loving You - 197?
Ko Ko 721 - Ain't Good For Nothing / These Are The Things - 1976
Ko Ko 724 - Let's Steal Away To The Hideaway / I've Got Your Love In My Life - 1977
Ko Ko 725 - I Like The Feeling / I'm Gonna Be The Best Thing - 1977
Ko Ko 726 - I Like The Feeling / I'm Gonna Be The Best Thing - 1977 (12" Release)
Ko Ko 728 - Do You Love Somebody / How I Miss My Baby - 1978
Ko Ko 729 - Do You Love Somebody / How I Miss My Baby - 1978 (12" Release)
Ko Ko 731 - Get To Me / Trying To Find My Love - 1978
Platinum Plus 1984 - Seeing You Again / I Am Wild About You - 1984
Profile 5125 - Baby Don't Go Too Far / How Sweet It Would Be - 1986
Profile 5132 - Don't Turn Around* / All In The Name Of Love - 1987 *also recorded and released as a 12" single in 1988 by Aswad on Mango MLPS 7823.
Profile 5143 - Gotta Serve Somebody* / All In The Name Of Love - 1987 *also recorded in 1979 by Bob Dylan on Columbia 11072.

Luther Ingram / Hot Butter

Collectables Col 031707 - (If Loving You Is Wrong) I Don't Want To Be Right / Popcorn* - ? *flip by Hot Butter.

Luther Ingram

Urgent / Ichiban 4119 - I Like The Feeling - 1991 (Cd Single)

The Gardenias (Members Luther Ingram, ...)

Federal ? - Miserable / You Found The Time - 1991 (recorded in 1956)

Lp's

Ko Ko Kds-2201 – I've Been Here All The Time – 1972
Tracks: Ain't That Lovin' You (For More Reasons than One) (4:07) / You Were Made For Me (3:57) / Oh Baby, You Can Depend On Me (2:08) / My Honey And Me (3:15) /

Soulful Kinda Music – The Rare Soul Bible Volume Two

I'll Just Call You Honey (2:51) / Since You Don't Want Me (4:18) /// Missing You (3:24) / I'll Love You Until The End (3:43) / Be Good To Me Baby (4:11) / Pity For The Lonely (2:46) / To The Other Man (4:00) / Ghetto Train (3:46).

Ko Ko   Kds-2202 – If Loving You Is Wrong I Don't Want To Be Right – 1972
Tracks: (If Loving You Is Wrong) I Don't Want To Be Right (3:32) / I'll Be Your Shelter (In Time Of Storm) (3:20) / Always (4:25) / Dying & Crying (3:48) / Help Me Love (3:47) /// I'm Trying To Sing A Message To You (4:20) / I Remember (3:20) / Love Ain't Gonna Run Me Away (5:06) / I Can't Stop (3:16).

Ko Ko   Koa 1300 – Let's Steal Away To The Hideaway – 1976
Tracks: Let's Steal Away To The Hideaway (4:20) / That's The Way Love Is (3:45) / Sweet Inspiration (3:15) / I'm Gonna Be The Best Thing (3:15) / I Like The Feeling (2:55) /// All That Shines (3:30) / What Goes Around Comes Around (2:55) / It's Too Much (3:05) / Your Love Is Something Special (3:25) / I've Got Your Love In My Life (2:30)

Ko Ko   Koa-1302 – Do You Love Somebody – 1977
Tracks: Do You Love Somebody (3:20) / How I Miss My Baby (4:23) / Get To Me (4:20) / Sorry (4:07) / Time Machine (4:05) /// Do You Think There's A Chance (2:56) / Trying To Find My Love (3:30) / Ain't Good For Nothing (3:06) / Funny People (3:23) / Faces (3:45).

Cd's

Kent CDKEND 279 – Luther Ingram Pity For The Lonely The Ko Ko Singles Vol 1 – 2007
Tracks: You've Got To Give Love To Get Love (2:09) / I Can't Stop (Version 1) (2:52) / Missing You (Version 1) (2:40) / Since You Don't Want Me (Version 1) (2:12) / Oh, Baby You Can Depend On Me (2:07) / Looking For A New Love (2:34) / Pity For The Lonely (2:53) / Puttin' Game Down (3:19) / Since You Don't Want Me (Version 2) (4:16) / My Honey And Me (3:21) / I Can't Stop (Version 2) (3:03) / Ain't That Lovin' You (For More Reasons Than One) (4:08) / Home Don't Seem Like Home (4:29) / To The Other Man (3:58) / I'll Just Call You Honey (2:48) / Be Good To Me Baby (4:11) / I'll Love You Until The End (3:43) / Ghetto Train (3:46) / My Honey And Me (Radio Promo) (0:40).

Kent CDKEND 292 – Luther Ingram I Don't Want To Be Right The Ko Ko Singles Vol 2 – 2008
Tracks: Missing You (Version 2) (3:23) / You Were Made For Me (3:53) / (If Loving You Is Wrong) I Don't Want To Be Right (3:33) / Puttin' Game Down (2:45) / I'll Be Your Shelter (In Time Of Storm) (3:17) / I Can't Stop (Version 3) (3:09) / Always (4:24) / Help Me Love (3:43) / Love Ain't Gonna Run Me Away (4:44) / Ain't Good For Nothing (3:35) / These Are The Things (3:30) / Let's Steal Away To The Hideaway (4:18) / I've Got Your Love In My Life (2:28) / I Like The Feeling (2:53) / I'm Gonna Be The Best Thing (3:13) / Do You Love Somebody (3:20) / How I Miss My Baby (4:15) / Trying To Find My Love (3:29) / Get To Me (4:18).

Kent CDKEND 315 – Luther Ingram I've Been Here All The Time / If Loving You Is Wrong I Don't Want To Be Right – 2009

Soulful Kinda Music – The Rare Soul Bible Volume Two

Tracks: Ain't That Lovin' You (For More Reasons than One) (4:08) / You Were Made For Me (3:56) / Oh Baby, You Can Depend On Me (2:08) / My Honey And Me (3:22) / I'll Just Call You Honey (2:48) / Since You Don't Want Me (4:17) / Missing You (3:23) / I'll Love You Until The End (3:44) / Be Good To Me Baby (4:11) / Pity For The Lonely (2:53) / To The Other Man (3:58) / Ghetto Train (3:46) / (If Loving You Is Wrong) I Don't Want To Be Right (3:32) / I'll Be Your Shelter (In Time Of Storm) (3:16) / Always (4:23) / Dying And Crying (3:45) / Help Me Love (3:42) / I'm Trying To Sing A Message To You (4:16) / I Remember (3:18) / Love Ain't Gonna Run Me Away (4:44) / I Can't Stop (3:11).

Kent CDKEND 328 – Luther Ingram Let's Steal Away To The Hideaway / Do You Love Somebody – 2009
Tracks: Let's Steal Away To The Hideaway (4:20) / That's The Way Love Is (3:44) / Sweet Inspiration (3:17) / I'm Gonna Be The Best Thing (3:13) / I Like The Feeling (2:54) / All That Shines (3:31) / What Goes Around Comes Around (2:55) / It's Too Much (3:06) / Your Love Is Something Special (3:26) / I've Got Your Love In My Life (2:28) / I'll Love You Until The End (Version 2) (5:16) / Do You Love Somebody (3:20) / How I Miss My Baby (4:15) / Get To Me (4:17) / Sorry (4:14) / Time Machine (4:47) / Do You Think There's A Chance (3:00) / Trying To Find My Love (3:30) / Ain't Good For Nothing (3:34) / Funny People (3:47) / Faces (3:42).

Label Listings

Impact

1001 – The Human Beings – An Inside Look / I Can't Tell – 1965
1002 – Mickey Denton – Mi Amore / Ain't Love Grand – 1966
1003 – The Boss Five – Please Mr President / You Cheat Too Much – 1966
1004 – Jock Mitchell – Work With Me Annie / You May Lose The One You Love – 1966
1005 – Kado Strings – Cryin' Over You / Nothing But Love – 1966
1006 – Human Beings – You're Bad News / Ling Ting Tong – 1966
1007 – The Shades Of Blue – Oh How Happy / Little Orphan Boy – 1966
1008 – Duke Browner – Crying Over You / Inst – 1966
1009 – Anthony Raye – Give Me One More Chance / On The Edge – 1966
1010 – The Tartans – I Need You / Nothing But Love – 1966
1011 – Mickey Denton – King Lonely The Blue / Heartache Is My Name – 1966
1012 – The Classmen – Susie Jones / Everything Is Alright – 1966
1013 – Not Released
1014 – The Shades Of Blue – Lonely Summer / With This Ring – 1966
1015 – The Shades Of Blue – Happiness / The Night – 1966
1016 – Nick & Dino – Wish I Was A Kid Again / Boy – 1966
1017 – The Volumes – The Trouble I've Seen / It's That Same Old Feeling – 1967
1018 – The Sheppards – Poor Man's Thing / When Johnny Comes Marching Home – 1967
1019 – Inner Circle – Sally Go Round The Roses / Sugar – 1967
1020 – Sincerely Yours – Shady Lane / Little Girl – 1967

Soulful Kinda Music – The Rare Soul Bible Volume Two

1021 – The Lollipops – Lovin' Good Feelin' / Step Aside Baby – 1967
1022 – The Human Beings – Yes Sir That's My Baby / Can't Tell – 1967
1023 – Jock Mitchell – Not A Chance In A Million / I Got To Know – 1967
1024 – John Rhys – Boy Watcher's Theme / Nothing But Love – 1967
1025 – Sixpence What To Do / You're The Love – 1967
1026 – The Shades Of Blue – How Do You Save A Dying Love / All I Want Is Love – 1967
1027 – Patti & Mickey – My Buy My Girl / You Can't Buy Back Yesterday – 1967
1028 – The Shades Of Blue – Penny Arcade / Funny Kind Of Love – 1967
1029 – The Wheels – Dancing In The Streets / A Taste Of Money – 1967
1030 – Anthony Raye – Give Me One More Chance / Hold Onto What You've Got – 1967
1031 – Rod Riquez – I'll Slip Away / You'd Like To Admit It – 1967
1032 – Narbay – Believe It Or Not Part 1 / Part 2 – 1968

Instant

3229 - Chris Kenner - I Like It Like That Part 1 / Part 2 - 1961
3230 – Gonzales Bonaparte – Fee Del / Wonderful Precious Me – 1961
3231 – Al Reed – Magic Carpet / Toying With Love – 1961
3232 – James Rivers – Closer Walk / Take Your Choice – 1961
3233 – Raymond Lewis – Miss Sticks / Miss Sticks Again – 1961
3234 – Chris Kenner – A Very True Story / Packin' Up – 1961
3235 – Shirkee & Zarnoff – Don't Worry / Shirley – 1961
3236 – Art Neville – That Rock 'N' Roll Beat / Too Much – 1961
3237 – Chris Kenner – Come See About Me / Something You Got – 1961
3238 – Al Reed – One Eyed Monster / Ring The Ding Dong Bells – 1962
3239 – Joe 'Mr Goggle Eyes' August – Everything Happens At Night / Tell Me – 1962
3240 – Errol Dee – I Love You / Love Or Money – 1962
3241 – Allen Collay – Bye Bye Blackbird / Four Days Four Nights – 1962
3242 – Raymond Lewis – I'm Gonna Put Some Hurt On You / Nine Cents Worth Of Chances – 1962
3243 – Johnny Meyers – Lonely Fool / Wonderful Girl – 1962
3244 – Chris Kenner – How Far / Time – 1962
3245 – Chick Carbo – In The Night / Run Henry – 1962
3246 – Art Neville – All These Things / Come Back Love – 1962
3247 – Chris Kenner – Johnny Little / Let Me Show You How (To Twist) – 1962
3248 – Allan Collay – Not Old Enough / Take Your Time – 1962
3249 – Johnny Meyers – Pillow Killer / Waiter – 1962
3250 – Raymond Lewis – Miss Lolly / Ruthless Lover – 1962
3251 – Chuck Dilday – You Never Looked Better / Losing You Would Hurt Me More – 1962
3252 – Chris Kenner – Land Of 1000 Dances / That's My Girl – 1962
3253 – Wayman Dixon – It's No Fun / You Put Love On My Mind – 1962
3254 – Chick Carbo – Two Tables Away / What Does It Take – 1962
3255 – The Neptunes – House Of Heartaches / Make A Memory – 1963
3256 – Art Neville – Skeet Skat / You Won't Do Right – 1963
3257 – Chris Kenner – Come Back And See / Go Thru Life – 1963

3258 – Eskew Reeder Jr – The Flu / Undivided Love – 1963
3259 – The Samfords – Another Like The Other / Chopin Was Nice – 1963
3260 – Ernie K-Doe – Baby Since I Met You / Sufferin' So – 1963
3261 – Al Michaels – Half A Crown / Jump And Shout - 1964
3262 – Clint West & The Bohings – I Need Your Loving / I Won't Cry – 1964
3263 – Chris Kenner – What's Wrong With Life / Never Reach Perfection – 1964
3264 – Ernie K-Doe – Reaping What I Sow / Talking Out Of My Head – 1964
3265 – Chris Kenner – Anybody Here See My Baby / She Can Dance – 1964
3266 – The Samfords – Ben's Creek / 40 Room Shack – 1964
3267 – ?
3268 – Eskew Reeder Jr – I Woke Up (With My Mind On My Baby) Part 1 / Part 2 – 1965
3269 – Polka Dot Slim – Ain't Broke Ain't Hungry / It's A Thing You Gotta Face – 1965
3270 – Sax Kari – All These Things / Something You Got – 1965
3271 – Diamond Joe – Too Many Pots / If I Say Goodbye – 1965
3272 – Norman John – Valley Of Love / ? – 1965
3273 – Cathy Savoy – Let This Love Of Ours Begin / Tough Guy – 1965
3274 – Nettie Marsh – No Tears Have I / String Of Lies – 1965
3275 – Big Wolfe – The Place (New Orleans) / A Good Foundation – 1965
3276 – Art Neville – Buy Me A Rainbow / Hook Line And Sinker – 1966
3277 – Chris Kenner – I'm Lonely Take Me / Cinderella – 1966
3278 – Traci – The Loser / Little Evil – 1966
3279 – Pitter Pats – It Do Me Good Part 1 / Part 2 – 1966
3280 – Chris Kenner – All Night Rambler Part 1 / Part 2 – 1966
3281 – ?
3282 – Aaron Neville – For Every Boy There's A Girl / I've Done It Again – 1967
3283 – Chris Kenner – Shoo Rah / Stretch My Hands To You – 1967
3284 – The Pitter Pats – Baby You Hurt Me / Whatcha Bet – 1967
3285 – The Pitter Pats – I've Got Everything / Naturally – 1967
3286 – Chris Kenner – Fumigate Funky Broadway / Wind The Clock – 1967
3287 – Huey Smith & The Pitter Pats – Bury Me Dead / I'll Never Forget You – 1967
3288 – The Tunics – Sandman / Moonlight Lover – 1968
3289 – The Hueys – You Ain't No Hippie / Coo Coo Over You – 1968
3290 – Chris Kenner – Memories Of A King (Let Freedom Ring) Part 1 / Part 2 – 1968
3291 – The Rainbows – Good Thing Going / Key To My Heart – 1968
3292 – The Hueys – Feeling Kinda Coo Coo Too / Smile For Me – 1968
3293 – Chris Kenner – Mini Skirts And Soul / Sad Mistake – 1968
3294 – The Sam Alcorn Orchestra – Bump Bump / Fat Cat – 1968
3295 – Curley Moore – Sophisticated Sissy Part 1 / Part 2 – 1968
3296 – Larry Darnell – Son Of A Son Of A Slave / Stomp Down Soul – 1968
3297 – Huey Smith – Two Way Pockaway Part 1 / Part 2 – 1969
3298 – The Hueys – Coo Coo Over You / You Ain't No Hippie – 1969
3299 – ?
3300 – ?
3301 – Huey Piano Smith – Eight Bars Of Amen / Epitaph Of Uncle Tom – 1969
3302 – Sam Alcorn – Midnight Green / My Love Ran Wild – 1969
3303 – Huey Smith & The Clowns – You Got Too Part 1 / Part 2 – 1969
3304 – Lee Bates – Simon Says / Bad Bad Understanding – 1970

Soulful Kinda Music – The Rare Soul Bible Volume Two

3305 – Huey Piano Smith – Ballad Of A Black Man / The Whatcha Call 'Em – 1970
3306 – Dolores Riley – About My Past / Hey ! Boy ! – 1970
3307 – Lee Bates – Look What They Done To My Song Ma / International Playboy – 1970
3308 – David Batiste & The Gladiators – Funky Soul Part 1 / Part 2 – 1970
3309 – Skip Easterling – Ooh Pooh Par Do / I'm Your Hoochie Koochie Man – 1970
3310 – Lee Bates – Why Don't You Write / Gonna Make You Mine – 1971
3311 – Skip Easterling – Too Weak To Break The Curtain / I'm Your Man – 1971
3312 – Skip Easterling – If I Ever Get Back / I Don't Know – 1971
3313 – Lee Bates – Mean Mistreater / Things Come Naturally – 1971
3314 – Boogie Jake – Early Morning Blues / Bad Luck And Trouble – 1971
3315 – Skip Easterling – Coo Coo Over You / Travellin' Mood – 1971
3316 – Lee Bates – You Won't Do Right / Three Trips Around The World – 1971
3317 – Brothers 2 – Come And Make Me / How To Make Love – 1972
3318 – Lee Bates – Project Queen / Give A Listen To Me – 1972
3319 – Steve Dixon – Sunday Afternoon In Memphis / A Good Time Is Hard To Find – 1972
3320 – Skip Easterling – Walking On Edges / Odeo Odeo Odeo – 1972
3321 – Lee Bates – Sittin' On The Dock Of The Bay / Key To My Heart – 1972
3322 – Point Of View – I Could Be A Fool For You / Mama I Want To Be Your Boy Again – 1972
3323 – ?
3324 – Tony Love – Just A Juvenile / Crying Time Is Over – 1972
3325 – Huey Piano Smith – The Watchcha Call 'Em / Ballad Of A Black Man – 1972
3326 – Alias Ducie – Singing La Dee Dah / Then You'll Be There – 1972
3327 – ?
3328 – ?
3329 – Lee Bates - What Am I Gonna Do / Love Is Slipping Away - 1972
3330 – Clemmon Smith - Are You Sleeping Brotherman / ? - 1972
3331 – Scooter Lee – About My Past / ?
3332 – Freddy Fender – Some People Say / Today's Your Wedding Day – 1972
3333 – ?
3334 – Scooter Lee - It Don't Matter Anymore / Looking For Me - 1972
3335 – ?
3336 – Hummingbird – Hot Dog You Must Be Santa Claus / ? - 1972

Invictus

9071 - Glass House - Crumbs Off The Table / Bad Bill Of Goods - 1969
9072 - New Play starring: Ruth Copeland - The Music Box / A Gift Of Me - 1969
9073 - Freda Payne - The Unhooked Generation / The Easiest Way To Fall - 1969
9074 - Chairmen Of The Board - Give Me Just A Little More Time / Since The Days Of Pigtails (And Fairy Tales) - 1970
9075 - Freda Payne - Band Of Gold / The Easiest Way To Fall - 1970
9076 - Glass House - I Can't Be You (You Can't Be Me) / He's In My Life - 1970
9077 - A Parliament Thang - Little Ole Country Boy / I Call My Baby Pussycat - 1970
9078 - Chairmen Of The Board - You've Got Me Dangling On A String / I'll Come Crawling - 1970
9079 - Chairmen Of The Board - Everything's Tuesday / Patches - 1970

Soulful Kinda Music – The Rare Soul Bible Volume Two

9080 - Freda Payne - Deeper And Deeper / The Unhooked Generation - 1970
9081 - Chairmen Of The Board - Pay To The Piper / Bless You - 1970
9082 - Glass House - Stealing Moments From Another Woman's Life / If It Ain't Love (It Don't Matter) - 1970
9083 - Barrino Brothers - Trapped In A Love / When Love Was A Child - 1971
9084 - Barrino Brothers - I Shall Not Be Moved / When Love Was A Child - 1972
9085 - Freda Payne - Cherish What Is Dear To You / The World Don't Owe You A Thing - 1971
9086 - Chairmen Of The Board - Chairman Of The Board / When Will She Tell Me She Needs Me - 1971
9087 - 8th Day - She's Not Just Another Woman / I Can't Fool Myself - 1971
9088 - Ruth Copeland - Haré Krishna / No Commitment - 1971
9089 - Chairmen Of The Board - Hanging On To A Memory / Tricked & Trapped - 1971
9090 - Glass House - Touch Me Jesus / If It Ain't Love (It Don't Matter) - 1971
9091 - Parliament - Red Hot Mama / Little Ole Country Boy - 1971
9092 - Freda Payne - Bring The Boys Home / I Shall Not Be Moved - 1971
9093 - General Johnson - I'm In Love Darling / Savannah Lady - 1971
9094 - Lucifer - Old Mother Nature / What I Am - 1971
9095 - Parliament - Breakdown / Little Ole Country Boy - 1971
9096 - Ruth Copeland - Gimme Shelter / No Commitment - 1971
9097 - Glass House - Look What We've Done To Love / Heaven Is There To Guide Us - 1971
9098 - 8th Day - You've Got To Crawl (Before You Walk) / It's Instrumental To Be Free - 1971
9099 - Chairmen Of The Board - Try On My Love For Size / Working On A Building Of Love - 1971
9100 - Freda Payne - You Brought The Joy / Suddenly It's Yesterday - 1971
9101 - Johnn Billy West - Nothing But The Devil / Yeah, I'm The Devil - 1971
9102 - Billie Sans - Solo / I Don't Want To Lose A Good Thing - 1971
9103 - Chairmen Of The Board - Men Are Getting Scarce / Bravo Hooray - 1971
9104 - Barrino Brothers - I Had It All / I Shall Not Be Moved - 1971
9105 - Chairmen Of The Board - Bittersweet / Elmo James - 1972
9106 - General Johnson   - All We Need Is Understanding / Savannah Lady - 1971
9107 - 8th Day - If I Could See The Light / Inst - 1971
9108 - Lucifer - We Gotta Go / Don't You (Think The Times A-Comin') - 1971
9109 - Freda Payne - The Road We Didn't Take / I'm Not Getting Any Better - 1971
9110 - Holland-Dozier - Don't Leave Me / Inst - 1972
9111 - Glass House - Playing Games / Let It Flow - 1972
9112 - Harrison Kennedy - Sunday Morning People / Up - The Organization (Instrumental) - 1972
9113 - Lucifer - Bloodshot Eyes / Old Mother Nature - 1972
9114 - Scherrie Payne -   V.I.P. / It Ain't The World (It's The People In It) - 1972
9115 - Melvin Davis - I'm Worried / Just As Longy - 1972
9116 - Danny Woods - Let Me Ride / It Didn't Take Long - 1972
9117 - 8th Day - Eeny-Meeny-Miny-Mo (There's A Crowd) / Rocks In My Head - 1972
9118 - Glass House - Giving Up The Ring / Let It Flow   - 1972
9119 - Harrison Kennedy - Come Together / Sunday Morning People - 1972
9120 - Ty Hunter - I Don't See Me In Your Eyes Anymore / Hey There Lonely Girl - 1972

Soulful Kinda Music – The Rare Soul Bible Volume Two

9121 - Barrino Brothers - Try It You'll Like It / I Had It All   - 1972
9122 - Chairmen Of The Board - Everybody's Got A Song To Sing / Working On A Building Of Love - 1972
9123 - Parliament - Come On In Out Of The Rain / Little Ole Country Boy - 1972
9124 - 8th Day - I Gotta Get Home (Can't Let My Baby Get Lone) / Good Book - 1972
9125 - Holland-Dozier - Why Can't We Be Lovers / Don't Leave Me (Instrumental) - 1972
9126 - Chairmen Of The Board - Let Me Down Easy / I Can't Find Myself - 1972
9127 - Unreleased
9128 - Freda Payne - Through The Memory Of My Mind / Thanks I needed That - 1972
9128 - Freda Payne - He's In My Life / Thanks I Needed That - 1972
9129 - Glass House - Glass House / I Don't See Me In Your Eyes Anymore - 1972
9130 - Barrino Brothers - Livin' High Off The Goodness Of Your Love / Instrumental - 1972
9131 - Unreleased
9132 - Danny Woods - Everybody's Tippin' / Roller Coaster - 1972
9133 - Holland-Dozier - Don't Leave Me Starving For Your Love (Part 1) / Part 2 - 1972
1251 - Chairmen Of The Board - Finder's Keepers (Vocal) / Inst - 1973
1252 - General Johnson - Only Time Will Tell (Vocal) / Inst - 1973
1253 - Holland-Dozier - Slipping Away / Can't Get Enough (Instrumental) - 1973
1254 - Holland-Dozier - New Breed Kinda Woman / If You Don't Want To Be In My Life - 1973
1255 - Freda Payne - Two Wrongs Don't Make A Right / We've Gotta Find A Way Back To Love - 1973
1256 - Barrino Brothers-Born On The Wild (Vocal) / Inst -1973
1257 - Freda Payne - For No Reason / Mother Misery's Favorite Child - 1973
1258 - Holland-Dozier - You Took Me From A World Outside / I'm Gonna Hijack Ya, Kidnap Ya, Take What I Want - 1973
1259 - Melvin Davis - You Made Me Over / I'm Worried - 1973
1260 - Lee Charles - Sittin' On A Time Bomb (Waiting For The Hurt To Come) / Get Your House In Order (Instrumental) - 1974
1261 - Unreleased
1262 - Unreleased
1263 - Chairmen Of The Board - Life & Death / Live With Me, Love With Me - 1974
1264 - Laura Lee - I Need It Just As Bad As You / If I'm Good Enough To Love (I'm Good Enough To Marry) - 1974
1265 - Brian Holland - I'm So Glad (Part I) / Part 2 - 1974
1266 - Unreleased
1267 - Natural High - Bump Your Lady (Part I) / Part 2 - 1974
1268 - Chairmen Of The Board - Everybody Party All Night / Morning Glory (Instrumental) - 1974
1269 - Tyrone Edwards - Can't Get Enough Of You / You Took Me from A World Outside - 1974
1270 - Unreleased
1271 - Chairmen Of The Board - Let's Have Some Fun / Love At First Sight - 1974
1272 - Brian Holland - Let's Get Together / Superwoman (You Ain't No Ordinary Woman) - 1974

Soulful Kinda Music – The Rare Soul Bible Volume Two

1273 - Laura Lee - Don't Leave Me Starving For Your Love / (If You Want To Try Love Again) Remember Me - 1974

1274 - Hi-Lites - That's Love (Vocal) / Inst - 1974

1275 - Earl English - Wanting You (Vocal) / Instrumental - 1974

1276 - Chairmen Of The Board - Skin I'm In / Love At First Sight - 1974

1277 - Eloise Laws - Stay With Me / Touch Me - 1974

1278 - Chairmen Of The Board - You've Got Extra Added Power In Your Love / Someone Just Like You - 1976

1279 - New York Port Authority - I Got It (Part 1) / Part 2 - 1976

1280 - Eloise Laws - Love Goes Deeper Than That / Put A Little Love Into It - 1977

1281 - New York Port Authority - I Use To Hate It (Till I Ate It) / I Got It - 1977

1282 - Eloise Laws - Put A Little Love Into It / Camouflage - 1977

1283 - New York Port Authority - I Don't Want To Work Today / Guess I'm Gonna Cry – 1977

J

Walter Jackson

The Velvetones (members Walter Jackson (lead), Ronald Head, Neil Magby, Bobby Jones and Marion ?) Detroit group.

Deb 1008 - Who Took My Girl / Stars Of Wonder - 1959

Walter Jackson (born 19-March-1938 in Pensacola, Florida -- died 19-June-1983 at his home in Chicago, Illinois -- cause: cerebral haemorrhage)

Columbia 42528 - I Don't Want To Suffer / This World Of Mine - 1962
Columbia 42659 - Then Only Then / Starting Tomorrow - 1963
Columbia 42823 - It Will Be The Last Time / Opportunity - 1963
Okeh 7189 - That's What Mama Said / What Would You Do - 1964
Okeh 7204 - It's All Over / Lee Cross - 1964
Okeh 7215 - Suddenly I'm All Alone / Special Love - 1965
Okeh 7219 - Welcome Home / Blowing In The Wind - 1965
Okeh 7229 - Where Have All The Flowers Gone / I'll Keep Trying - 1965
Okeh 7236 - Funny (Not Much) / One Heart Lonely - 1966
Okeh 7247 - It's An Uphill Climb To The Bottom / Tear For Tear - 1966 (some copies issued with picture sleeve)
Okeh 7256 - After You There Can Be Nothing / My Funny Valentine - 1966
Okeh 7260 - A Corner In The Sun / Not You - 1966
Okeh 7272 - Speak Her Name / They Don't Give Medals (To Yesterday's Heroes) - 1967 (some copies issued with picture sleeve)
Okeh 7285 - Deep In The Heart Of Harlem / My One Chance To Make It - 1967
Okeh 7295 - My Ship Is Comin' In / A Cold Cold Winter - 1967
Okeh 7305 - Everything Under The Sun / Road To Ruin - 1968
Epic 10337 - The Bed / The Look Of Love - 1968
Epic 10408 - No Butterflies / Ad Lib - 1968
Cotillion 44053 - Anyway That You Want Me / Life Has It's Ups And Downs - 1969
Cotillion 44077 - Bless You / Coldest Days Of My Life - 1970
U. S. A. 104 - The Walls That Seperate / A Fool For You - 1971
Wand 11247 - No Easy Way Down / I'm All Cried Out - 1972
Brunswick 55498 - I Never Had It So Good / Easy Evil - 1973
Brunswick 55502 - It Doesn't Take Much / Let Me Come Back - 1973
Chi-Sound / U. A. 908 - Feelings / Words (Are Impossible) - 1976
Chi-Sound / U. A. 964 - Baby I Love Your Way / What Would You Do - 1977
Chi-Sound / U. A. 1044 - It's All Over* / Gonna Find Me An Angel - 1977 *new version of 1964 track on Okeh 7204.
Chi-Sound / U. A. 1140 - If I Had My Way / We Could Fly - 1978
Chi-Sound / U. A. 1216 - I Won't Remember Ever Loving You / Manhattan Skyline - 1978
20th Century Fox 2426 - Magic Man / Golden Rays - 1979
Columbia 02037 - Tell Me Where It Hurts / When I See You - 1981
Columbia 02294 - Come To Me / What If I Walked Out On You - 1981

Soulful Kinda Music – The Rare Soul Bible Volume Two

Kelli-Arts 1006 - Touching In The Dark / If I Had A Chance - 1982
Chi Sound 110 - It's Cool / When The Loving (Goes Out Of The Loving) - 1983 (this 45 was released three days before Walter Jackson's death)

JESSICA RECORDS

As some people will be aware, my fiancé is called Jessica, so it came as no surprise to discover that she was collecting the Jessica label, and that she had also made the connection with the Essica label. There were however, several gaps in the numbering system used by the label, and we were never sure whether that was because we just didn't know what the missing releases were, or whether they even existed.

After a considerable amount of digging to try and find out what the missing numbers were, we finally made contact with Curtis Smith, and interviewed him by phone last weekend.

Here's what we found out:

The label is definitely from St Louis, and was owned by a gentleman called Matt McKinney, whose wife was called, you guessed it, Jessica.

Curtis doesn't really remember too much about Matt McKinney, other than the fact that he was a big friend of Harvey Fuqua, and had ambitions to get into Motown with his recordings. That didn't happen of course, so I'm still searching for a contact with Matt McKinney. The only possible thing I've turned up so far is this recording:

Danright DR115 - Matt McKinney - Ballad of My Lai / Hungry Road - 1970

And as this is a Nashville label, I'm not convinced it's even the same Matt McKinney.

Unfortunately Curtis was unable to explain why the label name changed from Jessica to Essica either.

So, onto the individual releases:

Jessica 401 - Willie Small - How High Can You Fly / Say You Will - 1965

Firstly, this is Curtis Smith. He wasn't under contract to Jessica at the time this record was released, so it was put out with the fictitious name of Willie Small. The catalogue number is also interesting as well. At the time this was released Curtis was working at the '401' club in Powderly,

Soulful Kinda Music – The Rare Soul Bible Volume Two

Birmingham, Alabama. (I believe the club was owned at the time by John Hayden, an Alabama resident, but unfortunately he passed away in 2012, and his brother Danny Hayden.) That's how the record came to be released as Jessica 401.

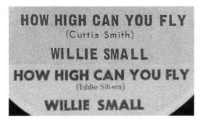

There are actually two different design labels for this release: The first shows Eddie Silvers as the writer, presumably because Curtis couldn't be associated with it, the second shows, correctly, Curtis Smith.

There is also, somewhat surprisingly a Dutch release of this record, although I do have certain doubts regarding its legitimacy.

Curtis Smith is the second from the left in this photo.

Soulful Kinda Music – The Rare Soul Bible Volume Two

Jessica 402 - Rozetta Johnson - That Hurts / It's Nice To Know – 1965 *(Also released on Atlantic 2297)*

At the same time that Curtis was working at the 401 Club, so was Rozetta Johnson (The correct spelling of her name is Roszetta Johnson), and her single was issued with catalogue number 402 because just up the road from the 401 Club was the 402 Diner !

She was born in Tuscaloosa, Alabama, and grew up singing in her local church choir. She joined a gospel vocal group, the Violet Harmonettes, and after her parents separated moved to Birmingham, Alabama, (and later McIntosh, Alabama). She started her singing career at the 401 Club, and the release on Jessica was her first recording. Following her stint at the 401 club she was then hired as a featured singer at the A G Gaston Lounge & Supper Club, subsequently toured as part of the Bill Doggett Revue, and then recorded several singles for the Clinton Moon's ClinTone label

CT-001 - A Woman's Way / Mine Was Real - 1970
CT-003 - Who Are You Gonna Love / I Can Feel My Love Comin' Down - 1971
CT-006 - Holding The Losing Hand / Chained And Bound - 1971
CT-007 - Can't You Just See Me / To Love Somebody - 1972
CT-008 - How Can You Love Something You Never Had / Personal Woman - 1972

Curtis has no knowledge of how the Jessica release also came to be released on Atlantic, however, as the ClinTone singles are all distributed by either Atco or Atlantic, and have Atlantic Master numbers, there must be some connection there.

– The Rare Soul Bible Volume Two

By the late Seventies Roszetta had left the music scene and followed a career in education.

Later in life, she returned to singing, primarily as a Gospel singer, and went onto international success using her married name Roszetta Johnson Scovil.

Sadly Roszetta passed away on the 24th March, 2011.

Jessica 403 - ?

Curtis doesn't think there was an actual release on this number, or if there was, he has no knowledge of it.

Jessica 404 - *Almost certainly released as Essica 404*

Curtis doesn't know of a Jessica 404 release, so would lean towards agreeing that it was actually released as Essica 404.

Jessica 405 - Little Edith - I Couldn't Take It / I Believe In You - 1965

Again, Curtis doesn't know anything about this release, or Little Edith.

There appear to be two different labels on this release as well. The first one is numbered Jessica 405 whereas the second is clearly numbered 1603 as well as 405, the flip side is number 1602, although the records are the same on each version.

Essica 404 - Curtis Smith - The Living End / Blank - 1965 *(DJ Copy only)*
Essica 404 - Curtis Smith - The Living End / Say You Will* - 1965 *(*Also released on Doma 101)*
Essica 404 - Curtis Smith - The Living End / How High Can You Fly - 1965 *(To complicate matters more, the two labels actually read the same, i.e. 'The Living End / Say You Will' . It's only from listening to the records or checking the matrix numbers that you know that 'Say You Will' plays*

'How High Can You Fly' which is identical to 'How High Can You Fly' by Willie Small)

To start with,

Curtis has no explanation as to why the miss-press of the single appeared. The Doma release is also something of a puzzle because it was released after the Essica single, on a label owned by Eddie Silvers

Doma 101 - Curtis Smith - Say You Will / I Like Everything - 1965

He was born, raised, and lived all his life in Atlanta, but was involved in the music

business as a guitarist from a very young age, and this led to him working all over the States, particularly involved with Chicago area bands and singers though.

He also worked as a session musician at various times, in particular playing guitar on Gladys Knight and the Pips original Vee Jay recording of 'Every Beat Of My Heart', although he wasn't on the re-recorded version that was later released on Fury.

Vee Jay 386 - Every Beat of My Heart / Room in Your Heart - 1961

Between the years 1961 to 1964 he led the band that supported Piano Red, also known as Dr Feelgood and The Interns. A local Atlanta band they were extremely successful, releasing several singles on Okeh. During this period Roy Lee Johnson, another guitarist in Dr Feelgood, & The Interns recorded a song 'Mr. Moonlight', that would in 1964 be covered by The Beatles on their fourth album. It was originally released as the flip side to a Dr Feelgood & The Interns single:

Okeh 7144 - Dr Feelgood & The Interns - Dr Feelgood / Mr Moonlight - 1961

Curtis also played guitar on Roy Lee Johnson's other Okeh and Columbia recordings:

Okeh 7160 - Roy Lee Johnson - Too Many Tears / Black Pepper Will Make You Sneeze - 1962
Okeh 7182 - Roy Lee Johnson - Nobody Does Something For Nothing / Busybody - 1962
Columbia 43286 - Roy Lee Johnson - My Best Just Ain't Good Enough / When A Guitar Plays The Blues - 1965

There were also four other tracks recorded by Curtis Smith during this period, but they remained unreleased until 2009 when the Bear Family label released them on their 'Roy Lee Johnson, featuring guest Curtis Smith' CD 'When A Guitar Plays The Blues'. The titles were:

Don't Do This To Me

Soulful Kinda Music – The Rare Soul Bible Volume Two

Two Wrongs (Won't Make It Right)
Come Here Baby
I've Got A Feeling

Around 1965 Curtis returned to Atlanta and formed his own band Count Curtis & The Counts, and they worked successfully for several years supporting visiting acts and playing their own local gigs. Curtis has also worked as a guitarist for Joe Tex and Aretha Franklin at various stages during his career.

Essica 002 - Ruff Francis And The Illusions - Give Me Mercy / Misery Loves Company - 1966

Ruff Francis & The Illusions were a typical 1960's showband, they played lots of local gigs, and a variety of music, Rock & Roll, R & B and Soul, and covered pop hits of the day. They were also used as backing bands for several big name acts who visited New York. The group appeared with Wilson Pickett; The Duprees; Mitch Ryder and the Detroit Wheels; The Orlons; Johnny Thunder; The Flamingos; The Dave Clark Five; Gary Lewis and the Playboys; The Isley Brothers; Jimi Hendrix

In 1966 Ruff Francis & The Illusions consisted of Eugene Boiani (Guitar); Jack (NewPort) Pender (Tenor & Alto Sax); Ruff

Francis (Leader, Vocal & Fender Jazz Bass); Phil "T McNasty" Bazicki (Tenor & Alto Sax) and Mike "Mickey" Caruso (Drums).

Essica 002 was their first ever recording. Despite there being a website for Ruff Francis, the contact email address doesn't work, so I've been unable to find out why a New York band had their first release on a St Louis label.

In November of 1977 Ruff Francis and some members from the original group and the 1967 group re-recorded "Give Me Mercy" as an up-tempo party sound at Cathedral Sound in Rensselaer New York. Musicians included Ruff Francis (Vocals); Lyman "Butch" Strong (Organ); Nick Brignola (Baritone Sax); Tony Sano (Guitar); Mark Galleo (Drums); Jack Pender (Tenor Sax); Larry "Mad Dog" Jackson (Percussion & Vocal) and Phil Bazicki (Tenor Sax).

Francis with Mitch Ryder, and below, Ruff Francis & The Illusions backing The Orlons, and finally Ruff Francis with The Flamingos.

Essica 004 - C-Quents - It's You And Me / Dearest One - 1966 *(Also released as Captown CTN4028)*

Captown is a Washington DC label, and I believe that the C-Quents were also from that area, so this is another strange release to end up on Essica. Unfortunately Curtis Smith doesn't remember the single, so can provide no explanation as to why there was an Essica release.

There was also a release on the Quest label, another Washington DC based label:

Quest 262 - C-Quents - I've Got To Love You Baby / Easy For You Baby

Essica 005 - The Sharpees - Just To Please You* /

Soulful Kinda Music – The Rare Soul Bible Volume Two

Hug Me Tight - 1966 *(*Also released as One-derful 4839)*

Although I've never seen a copy of this single on Essica, without prompting Curtis said that he played guitar on both this recording by the Sharpees, and on 'Do The 45', another One-deful recording, and respected Chicago collector Bob Abrahamian says he knows someone with a copy of it, so I have no doubt that it actually exists – if anybody has a copy for sale, please let us know.

The Sharpees were originally a St Louis group, and were originally known as The New Breed, members at this time were Benny Sharp, Stacy Johnson, Vernon Guy and Horise O'Toole. Vernon Guy and Stacy Johnson then left the group for a while and released a couple of solo singles each

By the time the group reached Chicago, and recorded their first single for One-Derful Records, Vernon Guy had already re-joined, and Stacy Johnson re-joined when Horise O'Toole had to leave the group for medical reasons.

One-Derful! 4835 - Do The 45 / Make Up Your Mind - 1965
One-Derful! 4839 - Tired Of Being Lonely / Just To Please You - 1965

The group went on to record two more singles for One-derful, although Curtis Smith wasn't involved in them.

One-Derful! 4842/4843 - I've Got A Secret / Make Up Your Mind - 1965
One-Derful! 4845 - The Sock / My Girl Jean - 1966

Stacy Johnson also recorded one solo single for M-Pac!

M-Pac! 7230 - I Stand Alone / Don't Try To Fool Me - 1966

Jessica 001 - Reuven Kall & Margaret Hines - Main Man / Misty - 1982

I know nothing about this single, but there is also a slight possibility that this is the same label because of the St Louis connection

That's about all that is known about the artists who recorded for Jessica and Essica. However, there is one thing that runs through most of the releases and would explain the Chicago connection to Jessica and Essica.

The name of Eddie Silvers or Angie Music Productions appears on all of the above releases, with the exception of the Ruff Francis release. (The Doma release by Curtis Smith is also an Angie Music Production)

Eddie Silvers, was originally a saxophonist from Chicago, working for Bobby Bland at one point, who started his own Production / Arranging / Publishing company, and called it Angie Music (After his wife). He worked as an independent producer and arranger for a multitude of small labels across Chicago (and obviously St Louis) until he became the Music Director for **George and Ernie Leaner's** One-Derful Records, in around 1966. This would certainly explain why the Curtis Smith release on Essica is distributed by One-Derful, and also confirm the Sharpees connection to Essica, because Eddie Silvers was involved with all the Sharpees's releases on One-Derful.

Further proof of the St Louis and Eddie Silvers connection is the fact that he wrote and produced several of Alvin Cash and The Crawlers singles for Mar-v-Lus Records, and of course Alvin Cash is originally from St Louis.

THE SOUL MERCHANTS

Recording Exclusively for:
Weis Productions, Inc.
Chicago, Illinois

By the late Sixties, Eddie Silvers was also working as saxophonist with his group The

Soulful Kinda Music – The Rare Soul Bible Volume Two

Soul Merchants, and they recorded at least three singles which were released on the Weis label. (He's the guy in the middle in the photo)

Weis 3001 - For: "Wes" / Light My Fire - 1968
Weis 3436 - For: "Wes" / Light My Fire - 1968
Weis 3439 - For: "Wes" / Little Green Apples - 1968

The 'For: "Wes"' track was arranged By The Soul Merchants, written by Eddie Silvers, Dawson & Hill, and produced by Eddie Silvers, The 'Light My Fire' track was conducted by him.

There was also a release on Unisfere that he appeared on (and wrote the flip side to)

UniSFERE 700 - Robert, Ron, & Eddie - Love Potion #9 / Robert & Ron - I Ain't Finish yet - 1969.

So that's it, the story of a little label in St Louis that released seven singles, recorded by artists from as far afield as St Louis, Atlanta, Washington, Birmingham, and New York.

As always, if anyone can add further information relevant to this article please get in touch with me through the email address **dave@soulfulkindamusic.net**

Sources:

Label scans - Jessica Wecker

Photos: Curtis Smith, Ruff Francis & The Illusions website: www.**rufffrancis**.com

Liner Notes: Roy Lee Johnson featuring guest Curtis Smith CD (Written by Martin Goggin)

Label Listings

Jacklyn

1001 - Paul Smith - I'll Run / Ain't That Something
1002 - Darrow Fletcher - Sitting There That Night / What Have I Got Now
1003 - Darrow Fletcher - Infatuation / Little Girl
1004 - Paul Smith - Ain't That Something / Only One In A Lifetime
1005 - Bobbie Brown - Love Won't Give Us A Chance / I Gotta Have You
1006 - Darrow Fletcher - Little Girl / What Good Am I Without You
1008 - Joe Young - I Don't Want To Lose You / Guitar Star
1009 - Lovemasters - Pushin' & Pullin' / Love Train
1010 - Joe Savage - All Power To The People / Same
1011 - Pam Colquitt - I Done Got Over Loving You / It's Gotta Be Love

Jamie

1033 - Marian Caruso - It's Great To Fall In Love / Truly
1034 - Inspirations - Good Bye / Dry Your Eyes
1035 - Tritones - Blues In The Closet / Sweet & Lovely
1036 - Rita Raines - Someone Else / Silence Is Golden
1037 - Waldron Sisters - Each Time / Rickety Tickety Melody
1038 - Don Blyer & The Tuesdayniters - Hey Big Man / Morning Light
1039 - Robert Byrd - Strawberry Stomp / Bippin' And Boppin'
1040 - The Sharps - Sweet Sweetheart / Come On
1041 - Rita Raines - I Told A Stranger / Sleepy Sunday Afternoon
1042 - Norman Brooks - Two Lovely Blue Eyes / I'm Never Satisfied
1043 - Chuck Crayne - It's A Cryin' Shame / Suppressed Desire
1101 - Duane Eddy - Movin' N' Groovin / Up And Down - 1958
1102 - Ernie Fields Orchestra - Strolling After School / Annie's Rock - 1958
1103 - Mark Robinson - Want Me / Pretty Jane - 1958
1104 - Duane Eddy - Stalkin' / Rebel Rouser - 1958
1107 - Sanford Clark - Sing 'Em Some Blues / Still As The Night - 1958
1108 - The Sharps - Have Love, Will Travel / Look At Me - 1958
1109 - Duane Eddy - The Walker / Ramrod - 1958
1110 - The Five Chords - Don't Just Stand There / Love Is Like Music - 1958
1111 - Duane Eddy - Cannonball / Mason Dixon Line - 1958
1112 - Jordan Brothers - Oh Lollie / Send Me Your Picture - 1958
1113 - Connie Conway - Can It Be? / Nothing Is Forever
1114 - The Sharps - Gig-A-Lene / Here's My Heart
1115 - Scamps - Noomi / Petite Fleur
1116 - Pierre Cavalli Orch - Come Prima / When
1117 - Duane Eddy - Detour / The Lonely One - 1959
1118 - Bob Please & The Pleases - The Monster / The Switch - 1959
1119 - Tony Allen & The Wonders - Looking For My Baby / Loving You - 1959
1120 - Sanford Clark - Bad Luck / My Jealousy - 1959
1121 - Curly Hamner & The Cooper Brothers - Tennessee Waltz / Smoochin' - 1959
1122 - Duane Eddy - Yep / Three Thirty Blues - 1959
1123 - Don Costa - I'm In Heaven / The Main One - 1959
1124 - Connie Conway - Beyond The Blue Horizon / Call It A Stormy Monday - 1959
1125 - Jordan Brothers - Never, Never / Don't Tell Me Now - 1959
1126 - Duane Eddy - Forty Miles Of Bad Road / The Quiet Three - 1959
1127 - Jacky Noguez & His Orchestra - Ciao, Ciao, Bambina / Serait Dommage - 1959
1128 - Ray Sharpe - Linda Lu / Red Sails In The Sunset - 1959
1129 - Clark, Sanford-Run Boy Run / New Kind Of Love - 1959
1130 - Eddy, Duane-Some Kind A Earthquake / First Love, First Tears - 1959
1131 - Ray, Anita-Someday I'm Comin' Home / You Always Hurt The One - 1959
1132 - Shieks, The-Tres Chic (Vocal) / Tres Chic (Instr.) - 1959
1133 - Jordan Bros.-Be Mine / Dream Romance - 1959
1134 - Angel, Johnny & The Creations-Where's My Love / We're Old Enough - 1959
1135 - Frazier, Dallas-Can't Go On / When You Got Love - 1959
1136 - Howe, Darrell-Gonna Go Round / I Make A Wish - 1959

Soulful Kinda Music – The Rare Soul Bible Volume Two

1137 - Noguez, Jacky-Marina / Adonis - 1959
1138 - Ray Sharpe -T. A. Blues / Long John - 1959
1139 - Sanford Clark - I Can't Help It / Son-Of-A-Gun - 1959
1140 - Johnny Dorelli - Love In Portofino / The World Outside - 1959
1141 - The Blackwells - You Are Free, I'm Alone / Depot - 1959
1142 - Wayne Rooks - Stop / Will You Stay In Love - 1959
1143 - Tony Allen - Train Of Love / God Gave Me You - 1959
1144 - Duane Eddy - Bonnie Come Back / Lost Island - 1959
1145 - Jesse Belvin - Goodnight My Love / My Desire - 1959
1146 - The Blackwells - Little Match Girl / The Christmas Holiday
1147 - The Sheiks - Candlelight Cafe / The Song Of Old Paree
1148 - Jacky Noguez & His Orchestra - Ampola / Mahzel - 1960
1149 - Ray Sharpe - Gonna Let It Go This Time / Bermuda - 1960
1150 - The Blackwells - Honey, Honey / Always It's You - 1960
1151 - Duane Eddy - Shazam / The Secret Seven - 1960
1152 - Pierre Cavalli & His Orchestra - Little Serenade / Smoke Gets In Your Eyes - 1960
1153 - Sanford Clark - Go On Home / Pledging My Love - 1960
1154 - Anita Carter - Mama Don't Cry At My Wedding / Moon Girl - 1960
1155 - Ray Sharpe - For You My Love / Red Sails In The Sunset - 1960
1156 - Duane Eddy - Because They're Young / Rebel Walk - 1960
1157 - The Blackwells - Unchained Melody / Mansion On The Wall - 1960
1158 - Duane Eddy - The Girl On Death Row / Words Mean Nothing - 1960
1159 - Umberto Bindi - Our Concerto / Let Me Dream - 1960
1160 - Darrell Howe - Gonna Go Round / Hucklebuck - 1960
1161 - Raymond Lefevre & His Orchestra . -Never On Sunday / Sleepy Time - 1960
1162 - Jack Dailey - Little Charmer / Please Understand - 1960
1163 - Duane Eddy - Kommotion / Theme From Moon Children - 1960
1164 - Ray Sharpe - Give 'N Up / Kewpie Doll - 1960
1165 - Gerald Calvi & His Orchestra - Our First Dance / Coral Flower - 1960
1166 - Craig Alden - Crazy Little Horn / Goggle-Eye'd - 1960
1167 - Anita Carter - Tryin' To Forget About You / That's All I Want From You - 1960
1168 - Duane Eddy - Peter Gunn / Along The Navajo Trail - 1960
1169 - Jordan Brothers-Things I Didn't Say / Polly Plays Her Kettle Drum
1170 - The Blackwells - Moulin Rouge / You're A Habit With Me
1171 - Raymond Lefevre & His Orchestra - Rendezvous / The Right Girl On The Left Bank
1172 - Savannah Churchill - Time Out For Tears / I Want To Be Loved
1173 - The Blackwells - Little Match Girl / The Christmas Holiday
1174 - Titus Turner - Sounds Off / Me & My Lovely Telephone
1175 - Duane Eddy - Pepe / Lost Friend - 1961
1176 - Jordan Brothers - No Wings On My Angel / Living For The Day - 1961
1177 - Titus Turner (With The Mort Grayson Orchestra) - Pony Train / Bla, Bla Bla, Cha Cha Cha - 1961
1178 - Dick Van Dyke - Three Wheels On My Wagon / One Part Dog, Nine Part - 1961
1179 - The Blackwells - Love Or Money / Big Daddy And The Cat - 1961
1180 - Arthur K Adams. -Willin To Die / If It Ain't One Thing, It's Another - 1961
1181 - Mirriam Johnson - Lonesome Road / Young And Innocent - 1961
1182 - Tommy And The Ding Dongs - Hossin' Around / Schubert's Rock - 1961

Soulful Kinda Music – The Rare Soul Bible Volume Two

1183 - Duane Eddy - Gidget Goes Hawaiian / Theme From Dixie - 1961
1184 - Titus Turner - Hey Doll Baby / I Want A Steady Girl - 1961
1185 - Bobby Bond - Livin' Doll / Sweet Love - 1961
1186 - Floyd Robinson - Mother Nature / Is There Something I Ought To Know - 1961
1187 - Duane Eddy - Ring Of Fire / Bobbie - 1961
1188 - Marvin & Johnny - Once Upon A Time / Tick Tock - 1961
1189 - Titus Turner - Horsin' Around / Chances Go Around - 1961
1190 - Pee Wee Crayton - Tain't Nobody's Business If I Do / Little Bitty Thing - 1961
1191 - Jim Dale - If You Come Back / Somewhere There's A Someone - 1961
1192 - Rosalie Mann - I Know A Boy / Mr. So And So - 1961
1193 - Mirriam Johnson - I Cried Long Enough / Making Believe - 1961
1194 - Chuck Reed - That Lucky Old Sun / So Long - 1961
1195 - Duane Eddy - Drivin' Home / Tammy - 1961
1196 - The Ragin' Storms - Mule Rock / Knock Out - 1961
1197 - The Creations - The Bells / Shang Shang - 1961
1198 - The Velaires - Roll Over Beethoven / Brazil - 1961
1198 - The Velaires - Frankie And Johnny / Brazil - 1961
1199 - The Blackwells - You Took Advantage Of Me / "I" - 1961
1200 - Duane Eddy - My Blue Heaven / Along Came Linda - 1961
1201 - The Pentagons - I Wonder / She's Mine - 1961
1202 - Titus Turner - Shake The Hand Of A Fool / Beautiful Stranger - 1961
1203 - The Velaires - Sticks And Stones / Dream - 1961
1204 - Timmy Shaw - Throw It Out Of Your Mind / A Letter From My Baby - 1961
1205 - Jordan Brothers - Whispering Wind / Love's Made A Fool Of You - 1961
1206 - Duane Eddy - The Avenger / Londonderry Air - 1961
1207 - Sue Winford - Love By The Jukebox Light / A Boy I Can Love
1208 - Johnny Mendell - Jingle Bell Twist U.S.A. / A Real Old-Fashioned
1209 - Duane Eddy - The Battle / Trambone - 1962
1210 - The Pentagons - Until Then / I'm In Love - 1962
1211 - The Velaires - It's Almost Tomorrow / Ubangi Stomp - 1962
1212 - The Inspirations - Dry Your Eyes / Good-Bye - 1962
1213 - Titus Turner - Walk On The Wild Twist / Twistin' Train - 1962
1214 - Johnny Mendell - Pretty Little Rita / Please Be My Love - 1962
1215 - Timmy Shaw - This I Know / Mine All Mine - 1962
1216 - Neil Brian - Lucky Coin / Fool Was I - 1962
1217 - Ben Higgins - A Whole Lot Of Lovin' / Really Paradise - 1962
1218 - Dick Jordan - Some Of These Days / I Want Her Back - 1962
1219 - Rick & The Keens -Y our Turn To Cry / Tender Years - 1962
1220 - Barbara Lynn - You'll Lose A Good Thing / Lonely Heartache - 1962
1221 - Roosevelt Jones - I Say! That's All Right / Any Old Time - 1962
1222 - The Key Brothers - Last Stand / Candle Of Fate - 1962
1223 - The Velaires - Candle Of Fate / Memory Tree - 1962
1224 - Duane Eddy - Runaway Pony / Just Because- 1962
1225 - Girard Gregory - On The Street Where You Live / Das Hab' Ich In Paris
1226 - The Matadors - Listen / So Near
1227 - Mac Davis - I'm A Poor Loser / Let Him Try
1228 - The Legends - Tell The Truth / You'll Never See The Forest
1229 - Billy & The Essentials - The Dance Is Over / Steady Girl
1230 - The Statesmen - A Matter Of Who / Two Days Out Of Delaware
1231 - Billy Jean Horton - Come Back To Witchita / I Should Have Been The Bride

Soulful Kinda Music – The Rare Soul Bible Volume Two

1232 - Al Jones - Lonely This Summer / You're Faithful Anna
1233 - Barbara Lynn - Second Fiddle Girl / Letter To Mommy And Daddy
1234 - The Wil-Ettes - Summertime Is Gone / One Love Is Lost
1235 - The Sonics - Beautiful Brown Eyes / Sugaree
1236 - The Timberland Four - Bring The Water, Sylvia / Hummingbird
1237 - Jennie Jordan - Tongue Twistin / Baby, We're Through
1238 - Don Forbes - She Who Would Love Me / The Shadow
1239 - Billy & The Essentials - Maybe You'll Be There / Over The Weekend
1240 - Barbara Lynn - I'm Sorry I Met You / You're Gonna Need Me
1241 - Denny Randall & The Orchestra - Limbow Low / Lonely Melody
1242 - Emily Evans - A Cake And A Candle / Just Another Fool
1243 - Al Jones - Chalk One Up For Bobby / What'cha Want To Do That
1244 - Barbara Lynn - Don't Be Cruel / You Can't Be Satisfied
1245 - Jon Sisco - Merri-Anne / Conquest
1246 - Burt Jackson - Mr. Everything / Just For Your Love
1247 - The Four Evers - Everybody South Street / One More Time
1248 - Aubrey Twins - Hip-Ity Hop / Take Me Home With You
1249 - Bobby Peterson - Love Or Misery / One Day
1250 - Arthur Thomas - Hey Mabel / Poker Game Of Life
1251 - Barbara Lynn - To Love Or Not To Love / Promises
1252 - Tony Panassi - Bye Bye Baby / My Cindy
1253 - The Intentions - Mr. Misery / Summertime Angel
1254 - Pervis Herder - Soul City (Vocal) / Soul City (Instr.)
1255 - Dean Scott - Don't You Know Right From Wrong / Congratulations
1256 - Dick Van Dyke - Three Wheels On My Wagon / Underwater Wonderland
1257 - Roland Dice - Everybody Loves Somebody / Velman
1258 - Emily Evans - Just Before Dawn / One Night Of Your Love
1259 - Lyn Earlington - Don't Make My Heart Bleed / I Really Go For You
1260 - Barbara Lynn - (I Cried At) Laura's Wedding / You Better Stop
1261 - Mark James Trio - Running Back / Free My Darling
1262 - Burt Jackson - What A Love / ?
1263 - Donna Prima - Dion My Dion/Bobby Come Home
1264 - Glenn Darell Orchestra & Chorus - Fountainbleu / Gaucho Guitar
1265 - Barbara Lynn - Dedicate The Blues To Me / Everybody Loves Somebod
1266 - The Chell-Mars - Romain' Heart / Feel Alright
1267 - The Four J's - Here Am I Broken-Hearted / Said That She Loved Me~
1268 - Lyn Earlington - Goodnight My Love / Midnight Heart
1269 - Barbara Lynn - Money / Jealous Love
1270 - The Beatlettes - Dance Beatle Dance / We Were Meant To Be Married
1271 - The Sundowners - Come On In / A Shot Of Rhythm & Blues
1272 - Lee Maye - Who Made You What You Are / Loving Fool
1273 - Gene Summers - Big Blue Diamond / You Said You Loved Me - 1964
1274 - The Four J's - By Love Posessed / My Love My Love - 1964
1275 - Lincoln Starr - Minus Your Highness / Just Friends - 1964
1276 - Lee Maye - How's The World Treating You / Loving Fool - 1964
1277 - Barbara Lynn - Ohoo Baby (We Got A Good Thing) / Unfair - 1964
1278 - Vic Vickers - These / Action Speaks Louder Than Words - 1964
1279 - Claudine Clark - (The Strength) To Be Strong / Moon Madness
1280 - Jimmy Hughes - I'm Qualified / My Loving Time
1281 - Barry & The Vikings - I Love You, Yes I Do / Last Night

Soulful Kinda Music – The Rare Soul Bible Volume Two

1282 - Marty Wilde & The Wild Cats - Kiss Me / My, What A Woman
1283 - The Lolly-Pops - The Happiest Birthday Party / Tough
1284 - Lee Maye - Only A Dream / The Breaks Of Life
1285 - Ricky Livid & The Tone Deafs - Tomorrow / Nuts And Bolts
1286 - Barbara Lynn - Don't Spread It Around / Let Her Knock Herself Out
1287 - Lee Maye - Even A Nobody / Who Made You What You Are
1288 - Allan Dean & His Problems - The Time It Takes / Dizzy Heights
1289 - Jimmy Briggs - Hideout / Like A Child
1290 - Yvonne Baker - What A Difference Love Makes / Funny What Time Can - 1965
1291 - Claudine Clark - A Sometimes Thing / Buttered Popcorn
1292 - Barbara Lynn - It's Better To Have It / People Gonna Talk
1293 - Mae Maria & The Maybees - Where's My Somebody / Try My Love
1294 - Carolyn Carter - (Don't You Know) It Hurts / I'm Thru
1295 - Barbara Lynn - (Don't Pretend) Just Lay It On The Line / Careless
1296 - The Riffs - Tell Her / I Been Thinkin'
1297 - Barbara Lynn - I've Taken All I'm Gonna Take / Keep On Pushing You
1298 - Joe Brown & His Bruvvers - Teardrops In The Rain / Lonely Circus
1299 - Jamie Power - Love's Gonna Go / She Don't Know
1300 - Pepe Lattanzi - Morning On The Mersey / The Mighty Amazon
1301 - Barbara Lynn - Can't Buy My Love / That's What A Friend Will Do
1302 - Crispian St. Peters - At This Moment / You'll Forget Me, Goodbye
1303 - Duane Eddy & The Rebels - Rebel Rouser / Moovin' N' Groovin
1304 - Barbara Lynn - All I Need Is Your Love / You're Gonna Be Sorry
1305 - The Mechanics - Co-Co Mo-Mo / It's What's Happening (Inst.)
1306 - Tony Liss - Need You / I Hope He Breaks Your Heart
1307 - Jamie Power - There's No Living Without Your Lovin' / Love's Gone
1308 - Jerry Stevens - Gettysburg Address (Battle Hymn Of The Republic) / ?
1309 - Crispian St. Peters - No No No / At This Moment
1310 - Crispian St. Peters - You Were On My Mind / What I'm Gonna Be
1311 - ?
1312 - Combo Kings - Do The Slow Fizz / Batman A Go Go
1313 - Marlena - I Don't Want To Go On Without You / He Don't Know
1314 - The Dantes - Can't Get Enough Of Your Love / 80-96 - 1966
1315 - Shorty Long & The Santa Fe Rangers - Greetings (Uncle Wants You) / Slippery Ground - 1966
1317 - Johnny Colmus - Failure Hasn't Changed Me / Nobody Cares For You - 1966
1318 - The Revels - Everybody Can Do The New Dog But Me / True Love - 1966
1319 - Pookie Hudson - All The Places I've Been / This Gets To Me - 1966
1320 - Crispian St. Peters - The Pied Piper / Sweet Dawn My True Love - 1966
1321 - Kit Kats - That's The Way / Won't Find Better Than Me
1322 - Johnny Pearson & His Orchestra - First One Asleep Whistle / Love Is In The Air
1323 - ?
1324 - Crispian St. Peters - Changes / My Little Brown Eyes
1325 - Ann D'andrea - Take Me For A Little While / Don't Send Him Away
1326 - Kit Kats - Let's Get Lost On A Country Road / Find Someone
1327 - Joe Brown - Sea Of Heartbreak / Mrs. O's Theme
1328 - Crispian St. Peters - Your Ever Changin' Mind / But She's Untrue
1329 - Bill Wright Sr. - Scarlet Ribbons / Anchorage A-Go-Go

Soulful Kinda Music – The Rare Soul Bible Volume Two

1330 - Anthony & Sophmores - Serenade (From Student Prince) / Work Out - 1967
1331 - Kit Kats - You Got To Know / Cold Walls - 1967
1332 - Steve Clayton - My Name Is On Your Heart / Are You Willing To Take - 1967
1333 - The New Silhouettes - Climb Every Mountain / We Belong Together - 1967
1334 - Crispian St. Peters - Almost Persuaded / You Have Gone - 1967
1335 - Steve Clayton - (Girls Are Imitating) Twiggy / The Boy Catchers Theme - 1967
1336 - Johnny Colmus - Curtain In The Window / Shenandoah - 1967
1337 - Kit Kats - Won't Find Better Than Me / Breezy - 1967
1338 - Peter Hamilton - Hey Girl / Hey Girl (Inst.) - 1967
1339 - The Rainbows - Balla Balla / Ju Ju Hand - 1967
1340 - Anthony & Sophmores - One Summer Night / Work Out (Inst.) - 1967
1341 - The New Breed - Sunny / P. M. Or Later - 1967
1342 - Steve Clayton - Give Love / The Feminine Heart - 1967
1343 - Kit Kats - Sea Of Love / Cold Walls - 1967
1344 - Crispian St. Peters - Free Spirit / I'm Always Crying - 1967
1345 - Kit Kats - Distance / Find Someone - 1967
1346 - Kit Kats - I Got The Feeling / That's The Way - 1967
1347 - Pat Leahy - Come On A Running / On Parting
1348 - Cole Brothers - I Can't See Nobody / I Got To Get You Into My Life
1349 - The Groop - Woman You're Breaking Me / Mad Over You
1350 - The Intros - Stop Look And Listen / Crystal
1351 - The Looters - Loot / Leapfrog
1352 - Ann D'andrea - Mister Good Time Friday / Don't Stop Looking
1353 - Kit Kats - I Want To Be / Need You
1354 - Kit Kats - You're So Good To Me / Need You
1355 - The Lords Of T.O.N.K. - Miniver Cheevy / White Knight
1356 - The Emotional Upsets - Maintain Your Cool / Baby Baby
1357 - Marke Jackson - Since You've Been My Girl / I'll Never Forget You
1358 - Dorothy & The Hesitations - Trying To Work A Plan / Don't Set Me Up For The Kill
1359 - Crispian St. Peters - Please Take Me Back / Look Into My Teardrops
1360 - Wheel Of Fortune - All The World / Funny Looks
1361 - The Ballistics - Please Come Home / A Woman Makes Or Breaks A Man
1362 - Kit Kats - Hey Saturday Noon / That's The Way
1363 - The Edge Of Darkness - So Many Years / Mean Town
1364 - The Magic Reign - Pop Goes The Weasel / Mirrors - 1968
1365 - Rumplestilskin Kartoon - Come To The Carnival / Last Night - 1968
1366 - Bobby Bradshaw - Make Someone Happy / It's A Miracle - 1968
1367 - The Teenmakers - Mo'reen / Dream World - 1968
1368 - Joey Kay - You Didn't Have To Be So Nice / 1300 Heartbreak Avenue
1369 - The Dovells - Our Winter Love / Blue
1370 - Carol Murray - The Arrangement / This Side
1371 - The Groop - Such A Lovely Way / We Can Talk
1372 - Alexandrow Karazov - Casatschok / Jacobuska
1373 - The Cole Brothers - Make Yourself Ready / Without Love
1374 - The Magic Reign - Jefferson Street / Charcoal Sketch - 1969
1375 - Microbe - Groovy Baby / Your Turn Now - 1969
1376 - Pal Crawford - The Bed / Show A Little Appreciation
1377 - Denny Ezba's Gold - Queen Mary / It's A Cryin' Shame
1378 - The Tygers - Sing It Altogether / Resurrection

Soulful Kinda Music – The Rare Soul Bible Volume Two

1379 - Spilt Milk - Save Me / Love Is Gone
1380 - Steve Lee - Country Fair / Does It Have To Be
1381 - The New Hope - Won't Find Better Than Me / (They Call It) Love
1382 - Pal & The Profits - Peace Pipe / Tea-Pee
1383 - Johnny & The High Key - The Christmas Game / Do You Believe
1384 - Sylvia De Leon - Simple Pleasures / On A Carousel
1385 - The New Hope - Rain / Let's Get Lost On A Country Road
1386 - Heroes Of Cranberry Farm - Big City Miss Ruth Ann / Fellow John (Has A Vision) - 1970
1387 - Bullring - Birmingham Brass Band / Lady Of The Morning Sun
1388 - The New Hope - Look Away / The Money Game
1389 - Los Vivos - You / Good Day
1390 - The Jordan Brothers - It's You Girl / Dream Romance
1391 - Toast - Flowers Never Bend With The Rainfall / Summer Of M
1392 - Stephen Monahan - The Flying Machine / A Little Bit
1393 - Stevie Howie - If You Knew How Long I've Been So Good For Christmas
1394 - Houston - Nightlight / Won't Be Comin' Home
1395 - Warren Bloom - Natural Sinner / Rollin' On My Own
1396 - Howard Boggess - Hollywood / 20th Generation Sad
1397 - Captain Freak & Lunacycle Band - 20th Generation Sad / What Ever Happen To Superman
1398 - C L Weldon & The Pictures - You Really Slipped One By Me / The Same People
1399 - The Sherry Sisters - I've Got A Whole Lot Of Music In My Soul / ?
1400 - Shira - Krishna / Sing Him A Song
1401 - Gary Grande - You're Still His Woman / We've Got The Vote Now
1402 - Michael Holm - I Will Return / You Left One Rainy Evening, Caroline
1403 - Sunday People - Stay Together / I've Found My Freedom
1404 - Stephen Monahan - Gonna' Dream Me A World / You Didn't Mean To Make
1405 - Johnny's Dance Band - I'm Walkin' / Porcelain Convenience
1406 - Cliff Nobles & Co. - The Horse / If You Don't
1407 - Lou Monte - She's Got To Be A Saint / An Old Fashioned Girl
1408 - The Sherry Sisters - If You Have The Love / And Then I Think Of You
1409 - Fat Back - Take Your Time / What Do You Want From Me
1410 - Chris Montez - Let's Dance / Somebody Loves You
1411 - Dick Roman - God The Giver / Don't Thank Me, I'll Thank You
1412 - Bruce Chanel - Going Back To Louisiana / The Times
1413 - Shira - Liar / Frank's Ant Farm
1414 - April & Ian Douglas - People's People / I Can Count On You
1415 - David Morris - Come Watch My Trains Go By / Carry That Weight
1416 - Juan Carlos Calderon - You're The One (Eres Tu) / April Song (Cancion De
1417 - Bill Stith - Big Bruce / Leap N' Lunge
1418 - Mashmakhan - Dance A Little Step / One Night Stand
1419 - Tommy Sears - When You Have Rock 'N Roll / Higher, Higher
1420 - Dialogue - Think Father Think / Alson, The Lion
1421 - Fady El Koury / Hovaness Hagop - Harlem Song (Vocal) / Harlem Song (Inst.)
1422 - New Hope - Find Someone / Breezy
1423 - Unit One - I Still Want To Make It With You / Theme For Dana
1424 - Clarel Betsy - In The Name Of The Lord / Highway Sister
1425 - Mark Middleton - Screw The People / Screw The People

Soulful Kinda Music – The Rare Soul Bible Volume Two

1426 - ?
1427 - Byron McNaughton & All News Orchestra - Right From The Shark's Jaws (The Jaws Interview) / Jaws Jam
1428 - Uncle Sam - Bicentennial Ball / Bicentennial Ball
1430 - Salix Alba - Italia / Ciao, Ciao
1431 - Rainbow Society Orchestra - All Of Me / All Of Me (Disco)
1432 - Loveland Orchestra-Love Song / Love Song
1433 - Monte Brothers - Starry Nights / Golden Glitter
1434 - Barbara Soehner - Dark Moon / I Found A Picture Of My Man
1435 - Flavor - Soul Saver / Take A Ride
1436 - Rex Allen - United (The Bald Eagle Song)
1437 - Barbara Soehner - I'm Not A Shoulder For Your Tears / You Never Bought Me Flowers
1438 - J Frank Wilson - He'll Only Hurt You / Red Satin Lady
1439 - White Fire - Tell Michelle / Don't Lock Away Your Love
1440 - Flavor - Albatross / Stardust In My Eyes
1441 - Small Change - I'm Still In Love With You / Hearts Will Break Tonight
1442 - Exodus II - 4 Seasons Medley

Jay-Walking

001 - Ray Gant & The Arabian Knights - Chattanooga Walk / A Night In Arabia
002 - The Little Scott Whites - There Is A God Somewhere / Joshua
003 - The Little Scott Whites - This Modern World / Save Me Jesus
004 - Melverine Thomas - A Letter From My Son Part 1 / A Letter From My Son Part 2
005 - The Mastermen - Why Do You Treat Me So Bad / Brighter Day
006 - Hank Sample - So In Love With You / You're Being Unfair To Me
007 - ?
008 - ?
009 - The Continental 4 - The Way I Love You / I Don't Have You
010 - Wee Willie Mason / Wee Willie & B Clark - Funky Funky (Hot Pants) / There She Blows
011 - The Continental 4 - Day By Day (Every Minute Of The Hour) / What You Gave Up
012 - The Continental 4 - Take A Little Time / Escape
013 - The Continental 4 - The Love You Gave To Me / How Can I Pretend
014 - Ray Gant & The Arabian Knights - Don't Leave Me Baby / I Need A True Love
015 - The Continental Four - Heaven Must Have Sent You / Running Away
016 - Gloria Spencer - I Got It / Stay Jesus Stay
017 - The Continental 4 - Escape From Planet The Earth / Take A Little Time To Know Me
018 - Eddie Parker - Can't You See(What You're Doing To Me) / Do The Choo Choo
019 - The Continental 4 - (You're Living) In A Dream World / Nite Moods

Jessica / Essica

Soulful Kinda Music – The Rare Soul Bible Volume Two

Jessica 401 - Willie Small - How High Can You Fly / Say You Will - 1965
Jessica 402 - Rozetta Johnson - That Hurts / It's Nice To Know – 1965 *(Also released on Atlantic 2297)*
Jessica 403 - ?
Jessica 404 - *Almost certainly released as Essica 404*
Jessica 405 - Little Edith - I Couldn't Take It / I Believe In You - 1965

Essica 404 - Curtis Smith - The Living End / Blank - 1965 *(DJ Copy only)*
Essica 404 - Curtis Smith - The Living End / Say You Will* - 1965 *(*Also released on Doma 101)*
Essica 404 - Curtis Smith - The Living End / How High Can You Fly - 1965 *(To complicate matters more, the two labels actually read the same, ie 'The Living End / Say You Will' . It's only from listening to the records or checking the matrix numbers that you know that 'Say You Will' plays 'How High Can You Fly' which is identical to 'How High Can You Fly' by Willie Small)*
Essica 002 - Francis, Ruff And The Illusions - Give Me Mercy / Misery Loves Company - 1966
Essica 004 - C-Quents - It's You And Me / Dearest One - 1966
Essica 005 - The Sharpees - Just To Please You* / Hug Me Tight - 1966 *(*Also released as One-derful 4839)*

Jessica 001 - Reuven Kall & Margaret Hines - Main Man / Misty - 1982 *(There is also a slight possibility that this is the same label because of the St Louis connection)*

Jetset

735 – Arthur Lee Maye – Have Love Will Travel / Loving Fool
765 - Eldridge Holmes - Gone, Gone, Gone / Worried Over You - 1965
766 - Suzy Cope - And Now I Don't Want You / You Can't Say I Never Told You
767 - Clarence Mobley - I'm Falling / I Knew You When
768 - Jimmy Armstrong - I Won't Believe It Till I See It / I'm About To Say Goodbye - 1966
45-5 – Don Robertson – California / Yesterday's Rain
1001 - Jimmy Castor - It's Ok / A Dream
1002 - Jimmy Castor - It's What You've Got / Block Party
1003 - Bill St.John - I Can't Hold Back The Tears / One More Mile
1004 - The Creations - Letters Of Love / Stop Your Sobbin'
1005 - Barbara Long - We Called It Love / Take It From Me
1006 - Eldridge Holmes - Humpback / I Like What You Do
1007 - Strings & Things - Charge / Fabulous New York
1008 - The Demon & June Conquest - The Only Way To Correct A Mistake / In My Dreams
1009 - Jimmy Castor - Why / Fabulous New York

Junior

Soulful Kinda Music – The Rare Soul Bible Volume Two

987 - Yvonne Baker - Foolishly Yours / There's No You - 1962

988 - The Sensations Feat. Yvonne Baker - That's What You Gotta Do / You Made A Fool Of Me - 1963

989 - Herb Goody - Getting Together Part 1 / Part 2 - 1963

990 - The Rivals - Come With Me / I Must See You Again - 1963

991 - Hollis Floyd - Southern Fried (Inst) / Be Happy (Inst) - 1963

992 - ?

993 - The Silhouettes - Rent Man / Your Love (Is All I Need) - 1963

994 - Ernestine Eady - Deep Down In Me / He's So Good - 1963

1000 - Joe Burrell - Teardrops Will Be Falling / The Horse - 1963

1001 - Yvonne Baker - What A Difference A Day Makes / Funny What Time Can Do - 1963

1002 - The Sensations Feat. Yvonne Baker - It's Good Enough For Me / We Were Meant To Me -1963

1003 - Jon Thomas - Feeling Good / Tizzy

1005 - Bobby Guitar Bennett - Goin Home / Lawdy Miss

1006 - The Sensations Feat. Yvonne Baker - Baby / Love, Love, Love

1007 - Ernestine Eady - The Change / That's The Way It Goes - 1966

1008 - Delores Lynn - The Big Search Is On / Just Tell It Like It Is - 1966

1009 - Bobby Guitar Bennett - You Did It Again / Evol - 1966

1010 - The Sensations Feat. Yvonne Baker - I Can't Change / Mend The Torn Pieces - 1966

1011 - Bobby Martin - It's Not Unusual / Taking It Easy - 1966

1012 - ?

1013 - ?

1014 - ?

1015 - Red Prysock - I Heard It Through The Grapevine / Groovy Sax - 1967

1071 - Yvonne Baker & The Sensations - I Can't Change / Mend The Torn Pieces - 1967

1097 - Rollie McGill & TheWhipoorwills - People Are Talking Part 1 / Part 2 - ?

5000 - The Big Five - Baby I Need You So / Wop-Ding-a-Ling - ?

5001 - Linda & Roberta - Grown Up / I'm In Love With You - ?

Soulful Kinda Music – The Rare Soul Bible Volume Two

Anna King

Anna King (Born 29-December-1937 In Philadelphia, Died 21-October-2002 At Her Home In Philadelphia - Cause: ? (Many years ago she was diagnosed with having sickle cell anaemia)

Malibu 1020 - In Between Tears / So In Love With You - 1961 (Philly Label)
End 1126 - Mama's Got A Bag Of Her Own / Sally - 1963
Ludix 103 - The Big Change / You Don't Love Me Anymore - 1963

Anna King

Smash 1858 - If Somebody Told You / Come And Get These Memories - 1963

Anna King - Bobby Byrd / Sammy Lowe

Smash 1884 - Baby, Baby, Baby / Baby, Baby, Baby (Instrumental)* - 1964
*Instrumental Version By Sammy Lowe. (Written By Carolyn Franklin)

Ann King

Rust 5090 - Tears On My Pillow / Ooba Dooba Doo - 1964 Is This Anna King?????????????????

Anna King

Smash 1904 - If You Don't Think / Make Up Your Mind - 1964
Smash 1942 - Come On Home / Sittin' In The Dark - 1964
Smash 1970 - That's When I Cry / Tennessee Waltz - 1965

Anna King / Anna King And Bobby Byrd

Smash 1410 - Make Up Your Mind / Baby, Baby, Baby* - ? *Flip Is A Duet With Anna King And Bobby Byrd. (Smash Reissue Series)

Eddie Kirkland

Eddie Kirkland (Born August 16, 1923, In Jamaica, Died February 27, 2011 I N A Car Crash In Crystal River, Florida)

Toured As A Member Of John Lee Hooker's Band From 1949 Through To 1962 Playing As Second Guitarist.

Soulful Kinda Music – The Rare Soul Bible Volume Two

Little Eddie Kirkland

RPM 367 - It's Time For Lovin' To Be Done / That's All Right - 1952

John Lee Hooker And "Little" Eddie Kirkland

Modern 876 - It Hurts Me So / I Got My Eye On You - 1952

Eddie Kirkland

King 4659 - Time For My Lovin' To Be Done / No Shoes – 1953
King 4680 - I Mistreated A Woman / Please Don't Think I'm Nosey 1953

Eddie Kirkland

Fortune 848 - I Miss You Baby / I Must Have Done Something Wrong – 1959

Eddie Kirk

Lu Pine 801 - Train Done Gone / I Tried - 1961

Eddie Kirkland With The King Curtis Band

Tru-Sound 409 - Something's Gone Wrong With My Life / Train Done Gone - 1962

Eddie Kirk

Volt 106 - The Hawg Pt. I / The Hawg Pt. II - 1963
Volt 111 - Them Bones / I Found A Brand New Love – 1963

Eddie 'Bluesman' Kirkland

Prestige 45-316 - Have Mercy On Me / Chill Me Baby - 1964

Eddie Kirk

Hi Q 5041 - Every Hour, Every Minute / Grunt – 1964
King 5895 - Let Me Walk With You / Monkey Tonight - 1964
King 5959 - Hog - Killin' Time / Treat Me The Way You Want Me – 1964

At This Point Eddie Kirk Became The Guitarist And Band Leader For Otis Redding Through To 1967.

Eddie Kirk

Fortune 5041 - Every Hour Every Day / The Grunt - 1968

Eddie Kirkland

Trix 4501 - Eddie's Boogie Chillum / Lonesome Talkin' Blues - 1970

Soulful Kinda Music – The Rare Soul Bible Volume Two

Eddie 'Bluesman' Kirkland

Sunland 101 - Disco Mary / Pickin' Up The Pieces 1983

Frederick Knight

Frederick Knight (Born August 15, 1944, Birmingham, Alabama)

Maxine 212 - Steppin' Down / Heart Complications - 1969
1-2-3 1724 - Have A Little Mercy / Saurkraut - 1970
Dial 1006 – Frederick Knight – Throw The Switch / I Know Where I've Been - 1971
Stax 0117 – I've Been Lonely For So Long / Lean On Me – 1972
Stax 0139 – Trouble / Friend – 1972
Stax 0167 – This Is My Song Of Love To You / Take Me On Home Witchita – 1973
Stax 0180 – Suzy / I Let My Chance Go By – 1973
Stax 0201 – Suzy / I Let My Chance Go By – 1974
Truth 3202 - Passing Thru / Sometimes Storm - 1974
Truth 3216 - I Betcha Didn't Know That / Let's Make A Deal - 1975
Truth 3228 - I Wanna Play With You / I Miss You - 1975
Castle 1232 - Claim To Fame / Uphill Peace Of Mind - 1976
Juana 3402 - I'm Falling In Love Again / Done Got Over Love - 1976
Juana 3404 - Sugar / I'm Falling In Love Again - 1976
Juana 3408 - High Society / High Society (Instrumental) - 1976
Stax 1013 - I've Been Lonely For So Long / I Betcha Didn't Know That - 1977

Frederick Knight And Fern Kinney

Chimneyville 10227 - Tonight's The Night / Sweet Life - 1977

Frederick Knight

Juana 3411 - Staying Power / Wrapped In Your Love - 1977
Juana 3415 - Sit Down On Your Love / Staying Power - 1978
Juana 3418 - You And Me / When It Ain't Right With My Baby - 1978
Juana 3420 - My Music Makes Me Feel Good / When It Ain't Right Way My Baby - 1978
Juana 3423 - If You Love Your Baby / You Can't Deny Me - 1978
Juana JU-1948 - Let Me Ring Your Bell Again / When It Ain't Right With My Baby - 1980
Juana JU-202 - Let Me Ring Your Bell Again / When It Ain't Right With My Baby (12" Single) - 1980
Juana JU-1984 - If Tomorrow Never Comes / Bundle Of Love - 1981
Juana JU-3700 - The Old Songs / Bundle Of Love - 1981
Juana JU-3702 - You're The Best Thing In My Life / When Will Love Need Me - 1981
Juana JU-1300 - You're The Best Thing In My Life / When Will Love Need Me - 1982

LPs

Soulful Kinda Music – The Rare Soul Bible Volume Two

Stax STS-3011 - Frederick Knight - I've Been Lonely So Long - 1973
Tracks: I've Been Lonely For So Long / This Is My Song Of Love To You / Take Me
On Home Witcha / Friend / I Let My Chance Go By / Your Love's All Over Me // Pick
'Um Up Put 'Um Down / Now That I've Found You / Lean On Me / Trouble / Someday
We'll Be Together

Juana 200,000 - Knight Kap - 1977
Tracks: I Betcha Didn't Know That / River Flowing / Wrapped Up In Your Love /
Staying Power / I Love The Way You Love / You Make My Life Complete / When It
Ain't Right With My Baby / Uphill Peace Of Mind

Juana 200,003 - Let The Sunshine In - 1978
Tracks: If You Love Your Baby / Bundle Of Love / Let The Sunshine In / Another
Knight For Love / My Music Makes Me Feel Good / You Can't Deny Me / / Raise
Your Hand / You And Me

Juana JU-4000AE - Knight Time - 1981
Tracks: The Old Songs / I'll Come Back To You / You´Re The Best Thing In My Life /
When Will Love Need Me / Shining Star / Even A Fool Would Let Go / Bundle Of
Love / If Tomorrow Never Comes

Label Listings

Karen

16 – The Capitols – Dog And Cat / The Kick
100 – Jimmy 'Soul' Clark – Soul / I Blew A Good Thing
113 – Billy Wells Outer Realm – Lotsa Papa Part 1 / Part 2
313 – Barbara Lewis My Heart Went Do Dat Da / The Longest Night Of The Year
314 – The Classics – Elmo / Twisting '62
315 – El Baron – Haunting Eyes / You Done Me Wrong
316 – The Classics – Noah's Ark / The Wheel Of Love
317 - The Quickest Way Out - Tick Tock / Baby (It's A Quarter To Love)
318 – The Antoinettes – Ronny Boy / Double Timing Lover
319 – Sharon McMahan – Love Is Wonderful / Here Comes That Boy I Love
320 – Grant Higgins – Shame Shame / The Way I Feel
321 – Mat Lucas – The M C Twine (Motor City) Part 1 / Part 2
322 – Rod Jordan – Don't Judge Me On The Outside / I Live In A Castle
1524 – The Capitols – Cool Jerk / Hello Stranger
1525 – The Capitols – I Got To Handle It / Zig Zagging
1525 – Sharon McMahon – Hello Stranger / Got To Find Another Guy
1525 - Sharon McMann - Hello Stranger / Got To Find Another Guy – 1966
1526 – The Capitols – We Got A Thing That's In The Groove / Tired Running From
You
1527 – The Ad Libs – Every Boy And Girl / Think Of Me
1528 - ?
1529 - ?
1530 - ?

Soulful Kinda Music – The Rare Soul Bible Volume Two

1531 – The Soul Twins – Mr Pitiful / Searching For My Baby
1532 - ?
1533 – The Soul Twins – Give The Man A Chance / Quick Change Artist
1534 – The Capitols – Patty Cake / Take A Chance On Me Baby
1535 – The Soul Twins – Just One Look / It's Not What You Do It's The Way You Do It
1536 – The Capitols – Cool Pearl / Don't Say Maybe Baby
1537 – The Capitols – Afro Twist / Cool Jerk '68
1537 – The Simms Twins – Mr Pitiful / Searching For My Baby
1538 – Jimmy Delphs – Don't Sign The Papers / Almost
1539 – Jimmy Clark – Do It Right Now / If I Only Knew Then
1540 – Bettye Levatte – Almost / Love Makes The World Go Round
1541 – Jimmy Delphs – Feels Like Summer's Coming On / Mrs Percy Please Have Mercy
1542 – Richard 'Popcorn' Wylie – Rosemary What Happened Part 1 / Part 2
1543 – The Capitols – Soul Brother Soul Sister / Ain't That Terrible
1544 – Bettye Lavette – Get Away / What Condition My Condition Is In
1545 – Bettye Lavette – Hey Love / With A Little Help From My Friends
1546 – The Capitols – When You're In Trouble / Soul Song
1547 – Marvin Simms – Sweet Thang / Your Love Is So Wonderful
1548 – Bettye Lavette - Ticket To The Moon / Let Me Down Easy
1549 – The Capitols - I Thought She Loved Me / When You're In Trouble
1550 – Jimmy Delphs – Am I Losing You / Love I Want You Back
1551 – The Volumes – Am I Losing You / Ain't Gonna Give You Up
2625 - Matt Lucas - Baby You Better Go Go / My Tune
714 – Billy Slayback – Here Comes Henry / Inst
715 – Richard 'Popcorn' Wylie – Move Over Babe (Here Comes Henry) / Inst
716 – Percy And Them – Sing A Sad Song Part 1 / Part 2
717 – The Quickest Way Out – Hello Stranger / Tick Tock Baby
718 – The Compacts – That's How My World Began / Why Can't It Be Me

Kellmac

1001 - Ruby Stackhouse - Wishing / Please Tell Me - 1965
1002 - Roger Pasll - The Shovel / Take The Stand
1003 - The C.O.D.'S - Michael / Cry No More
1004 - Paul Bascomb - Paul's Back / Michael (The Lover)
1005 - The C.O.D.'S - I'm A Good Guy / Pretty Baby
1006 - The Dreams - Young Man / Silent Gossip
1007 - The Combinations - Why / Come Back
1008 - The C.O.D.'S - I'm Looking Out For Me / I'll Come Running Back To You
1009 - Paul "Guitar Red" Johnson With Kenneth Wells Band - Red Rock / That I Love You
1010 - The C.O.D.S - She's Fire / It Must Be Love
1011 - The Combinations - Like I Never Did Before / What You Gonna Do
1012 - The C.O.D.'S - Coming Back, Girl / It Must Be Love

Soulful Kinda Music – The Rare Soul Bible Volume Two

Hoagie Lands

The Dynaflows (Members Victor I.Hoagland Sr., Billy Terrell, Major Williams, Leroy Pitman And Robert Grant) - High School Group.

The New Brunswick Heart Throbs (Members Victor I. Hoagland Sr., Bobby Thomas, Harvey Drayton, Charles Gregory, Mayola Gregory, George Gregory And Lorenzo Howell)

Hoagy Lands (Born Victor I. Hoagland Sr.,On The 4-May-1936 In New Brunswick, New Jersey. Died Saturday 12-January-2002 In Orange, New Jersey - Cause: Fall At Home)

Ivory ? - Oo-Be-Do / You're Only Young Once - 195?
Abc-Paramount 10171 - (I'm Gonna) Cry Some Tears / Lighted Windows - 1960
Judi 054 - (I'm Gonna) Cry Some Tears / Lighted Windows - 1960
Mgm K-13041 - My Tears Are Dry / It's Gonna Be Morning - 1961
Mgm K-13062 - Goodnight Irene / It Ain't Easy As That - 1962
ABC Paramount 10392 - Tender Years / I'm Yours - 1963
Atlantic 2217 - Baby Come On Home / Baby Let Me Hold Your Hand - 1964
Laurie 3349 - Theme From The Other Side / Friends And Lovers Don't Go Together - 1966
Laurie 3361 - Theme From The Other Side / September - 1967
Laurie 3372 - Yesterday / Forever In My Heart- 1967
Laurie 3381 - The Next In Line / Please Don't Talk About Me When I'm Gone - 1967 (Backing Vocals The Chiffons)
Laurie 3463 - Two Years And A Thousand Tears (Since I Left Augusta) / White Gardenia - 1968

Lily Field & Hoagy Lands

Spectrum 116 - Beautiful Music / Crying Candle - 1969
Spectrum 118 - Sweet Soul (Brother) / A Boy In A Man's World - 1970

Hoagy Lands

Spectrum 122 - Do You Know What Life Is All About / Why Didn't You Let Me Know - 1971
Spectrum 129 - Reminisce / Why Didn't You Let Me Know - 1971
Spectrum 130 - A Man Ain't No Stronger Than His Heart / Do It Twice - 1972
Spectrum 140 - The Bell Ringer / (Instrumental) - 1972
Paramount 0232 - Mary Ann / Pledging My Love - 1973
Stardust 028 - I'm Yours / The Tender Years - ?

Shorty Long

Shorty Long (born Frederick Earl Long on 20-May-1940 in Birmingham, Alabama - he died 29-June-1969 in a boating accident on the Detroit River in Michigan)

Soulful Kinda Music – The Rare Soul Bible Volume Two

Tri-Phi 1006 - Bad Willie / I'll Be There - 1962
Tri-Phi 1015 - Too Smart / I'll Be There - 1962
Tri-Phi 1021 - Going Away / What's The Matter - 1963
Soul 35001 - Devil With The Blue Dress / Wind It Up - 1964
Soul 35005 - It's A Crying Shame / Out To Get You - 1964
Soul 35021 - Function At The Junction / Call On Me - 1966
Soul 35031 - Chantilly Lace / Your Love Is Amazing - 1967
Soul 35040 - Night Fo' Last / Night Fo' Last - 1968
Soul 35044 - Here Comes The Judge / Sing What You Wanna - 1968
Soul 35054 - I Had A Dream / Ain't No Justice - 1969

Shorty Long on Vocal and Trumpets / Shorty Long

Soul 35064 - A Whiter Shade Of Pale / When You Are Available - 1969 (above title copies are promo issues only)

Shorty Long

Soul 35064 - A Whiter Shade Of Pale / When You Are Available - 1969

Jackie Lee

The Voices (members Robert Byrd, Earl Nelson and on / off member Jules Castron)

Cash 1011 - Two Things I Love* / Why** - 1955 *leads Robert Byrd and Earl Nelson. **lead Robert Byrd.

Ravon Darnell and The Voices (members Ravon Darnell, Robert Byrd, Earl Nelson and on / off member Jules Castron)

Million $ 2015 - One Of These Mornings* / I'll Be Back* - 1955 *Lead Ravon Darnell.

The Voices (members Robert Byrd, Earl Nelson and on / off member Jules Castron)

Cash 1014 - Hey Now* / My Love Grows Stronger* - 1955 *Lead Robert Byrd.
Cash 1015 - It Takes Two To Make A Home* / I Want To Be Ready** - 1955 *Lead Earl Nelson. **Lead Robert Byrd.
Cash 1016 - Santa Claus Boogie* / Santa Claus Baby** - 1955 *Lead Robert Byrd. **Group singing in unison.

Bobby "Baby Face" Byrd and The Birds (members Robert Byrd, Earl Nelson and on / off member Jules Castron)

Cash 1031 - Let's Live Together* As One / The Truth Hurts* - 1956 *Lead Robert Byrd.

Bobby Day & The Satellites (Robert Byrd, David Ford, Curly Dinkins and Earl

Nelson)

Class 207 - Come Seven* / So Long Baby* - 1957 *Lead Robert Byrd.

Earl Nelson and The Pelicans (members Robert Byrd, David Ford, Curtis Williams and Earl Nelson)

Class 209 - I Bow To You* / Oh Gee, Oh Golly** - 1957 *Lead Earl Nelson. **Leads Earl Nelson and Curtis Williams.

Robert Byrd and His Birdies (members Robert Byrd, David Ford, Curtis Williams and Earl Nelson)

Spark 501 - Bippin' And Boppin' (Over You) / Strawberry Stomp (Instrumental) – 1957

Bobby Day and the Satellites (Robert Byrd (Bobby Day), David Ford, Curtis Williams and Earl Nelson)

Class 211 - Little Bitty Pretty One* / When The Swallows Come Back To Capistrano - 1957 *this was written by Bobby Day but the version by Thurston Harris & The Sharps on Aladdin 3398 became the hit.

Bob & Earl (Robert Byrd (born 1-July-1932 in Fort Worth, Texas --- died 15-July-1990 --cause: cancer) and Earl Nelson)

Class 213 - That's My Desire / You Made A Boo-Boo - 1957

The Hollywood Flames (members Robert Byrd, Earl Nelson, David Ford, Curley Dinkins)

Ebb 119 - Buzz-Buzz-Buzz* / Crazy* - 1957 *Lead Earl Nelson.

Bobby Day & The Satellites (members Robert Byrd, David Ford, Don Wyatt and Earl Nelson)

Class 215 - Beep-Beep-Beep* / Darling, If I Had You** - 1957 *Lead Robert Byrd. **Bobby Day solo.
Class 220 - Sweet Little Thing / Honeysuckle Baby – 1957

Robert Byrd and His Birdies (members Robert Byrd, David Ford, Curtis Williams and Earl Nelson)

Jamie 1039 - Bippin' And Boppin' (Over You) / Strawberry Stomp (Instrumental) – 1957

The Hollywood Flames (members Robert Byrd, Earl Nelson, David Ford, Curtis Williams and Clyde Tillis)

Ebb 131 - Give Me Back My Heart* / A Little Bird** - 1958 *Lead David Ford. **Lead Earl Nelson.

Soulful Kinda Music – The Rare Soul Bible Volume Two

The Hollywood Flames (members Robert Byrd, Earl Nelson, David Ford, Curley Dinkins)

Mona-Lee 135 - Buzz-Buzz-Buzz* / Crazy* - 1958 *Lead Earl Nelson.

The Hollywood Flames (members David Ford, Earl Nelson, Clyde Tillis, Prentice Moreland and Don Wyatt (later member of Creative Source))

Ebb 144 - Strollin' On The Beach* / Frankenstein's Den** - 1958 *Lead Earl Nelson. **leads Don Wyatt and Clyde Tillis.

The Tangiers (members Joe Jefferson, David Ford, Earl Nelson, Clyde Tillis, Prentice Moreland and Don Wyatt)

Class 224 - Don't Try* / Schooldays Will Be Over* - 1958 *Lead Joe Jefferson.

Bobby Day & The Satellites (members Robert Byrd, Earl Nelson, David Ford and ?)

Class 225 - Saving My Love For You* / Little Turtle Dove* - 1958 *Lead Robert Byrd.

Bobby Day (although a Bobby Day solo recording the group was Robert Byrd, Earl Nelson, David Ford and Curtis Williams)

Class 229 - Rock-In Robin / Over And Over* - 1958 (lead on both tracks Robert Byrd) *also recorded in 1965 by The Dave Clark Five on Epic 9863.

The Hollywood Flames (members Robert Byrd, David Ford, Earl Nelson and Curtis Williams)

Ebb 146 - Chains Of Love* / Let's Talk It Over** - 1958 *lead Robert Byrd and Earl Nelson. **lead David Ford.

Bob & Earl (Robert Byrd and Earl Nelson)

Class 231 - Gee Whiz* / When She Walks - 1958 *also recorded in 1960 by The Innocents on Indigo 111.
Class 232 - Sweet Pea / Chains Of Love – 1958

The Satellites (members David Ford, Earl Nelson, Curtis Williams and ?)#

Class 234 - Heavenly Angel* / You Ain't Sayin' Nothin'** - 1958 *Lead Curtis Williams. **lead Earl Nelson.

The Hollywood Flames (members David Ford, Earl Nelson, Curtis Williams and ?)

Ebb 149 - A Star Fell* / I'll Get By* - 1958 *Lead Earl Nelson.

The Hollywood Flames (members David Ford, Earl Nelson, Curtis Williams and Jesse Belvin)

Soulful Kinda Music – The Rare Soul Bible Volume Two

Ebb 153 - I'll Be Seeing You* / Just For You* - 1958 *Lead Earl Nelson.

Bobby Day (Robert Byrd plus The Satellites - members David Ford, Earl Nelson, Curtis Williams and ?)

Class 241 - The Bluebird, The Buzzard & The Oriole* / Alone Too Long* - 1958 *Lead Robert Byrd.

The Hollywood Flames (members David Ford, Earl Nelson, Curtis Williams and ?)

Ebb 158 - So Good* / There Is Something On Your Mind* - 1959 *Lead Earl Nelson.

Bobby Day (Robert Byrd plus The Satellites - members David Ford, Earl Nelson, ...)

Class 245 - Say Yes / That's All I Want – 1959

Bob & Earl (Robert Byrd and Earl Nelson)

Class 247 - That's My Desire / You Made A Boo Boo – 1959

Bobby Day (Robert Byrd plus The Satellites - members David Ford, Earl Nelson, ...)

Class 252 - Got A New Girl / Mr. & Mrs. Rock "N" Roll – 1959

Bobby Day (Robert Byrd plus The Satellites - members David Ford, Earl Nelson, ...)

Class 255 - Ain't Gonna Cry No More / Love Is A One Time Affair – 1959
Class 257 - Three Young Rebs From Georgia / Unchained Melody – 1959

Bob & Earl (Robert Byrd and Earl Nelson)

Malynn 232 - That's My Desire / You Made A Boo Boo – 1959

The Satellites (members David Ford, Earl Nelson, Curtis Williams and ?)

Malynn 234 - Heavenly Angel* / You Ain't Sayin' Nothin'** - 1959 *Lead Curtis Williams. **lead Earl Nelson.

The Hollywood Flames (members David Ford, Earl Nelson, Eddie Williams and Ray Brewster (later member of The Cadillacs on Capitol))

Atco 6155 - Every Day, Every Way* / If I Thought I Needed You** - 1959 *Lead Earl Nelson. **lead Eddie Williams.
Atco 6164 - Ball And Chain* / I Found A Boy* - 1960 *Lead Earl Nelson.
Atco 6171 - Devil Or Angel / Do You Ever Think Of Me - 1960 (an early to mid sixties photo shows the group line-up to be David Ford, Earl Nelson, Ray Brewster and Eddie Williams (of The Aladdins on Aladdin)

Soulful Kinda Music – The Rare Soul Bible Volume Two

Bob & Earl (Bob Relf (born Robert Nelson Relf on 10-January-1937 in Los Angeles --- died 21-November-2007 at home in Bakersfield, California --- cause: ? (a former member of The Laurels) and Earl Lee Nelson)

Tempe 101/2 - Don't Ever Leave Me / Fancy And Free - 1962
Tempe 104 - Deep Down Inside / Oh, Baby Doll – 1962

Bob & Earl (Bob Relf and Earl Lee Nelson)

Marc 104 - Harlem Shuffle / I'll Keep Running Back - 1963 *also recorded in 1965 by Wayne Cochran on Mercury 72507.
Marc 105 - My Woman / Puppet On A String – 1964
Marc 106 - Your Lovin' Goes A Long, Long Way / Your Time Is My Time – 1964

Charles and Walter (Robert Byrd and Earl Lee Nelson)

Chene 102 - Kissin' And Huggin' / Night – 1964

Bob & Earl (Bob Relf and Earl Lee Nelson)

Chene 103 - Baby I'm Satisfied / Sissy – 1964
Tip 1013 - As We Dance / Oh Yea (Have You Ever Been Lonely) - 1964
Loma 2004 - Everybody Jerk / Just One Look In Your Eyes – 1964

Bobby Day / Wade Flemons

Oldies 45 38 - Rockin' Robin / Keep On Lovin Me* - 1964 *Flip By Wade Flemons.

The Dells / Bob & Earl

Oldies 45 57 - Zing Zing Zing / Gee Whiz* - 1964 *Flip By Bob & Earl

The Hollywood Flames (members Robert Byrd, Earl Nelson, David Ford, Curley Dinkins)

Lute 119 - Buzz-Buzz-Buzz / Crazy - ?

Earl Cosby (Earl Lee Nelson)

Mira 204 - Ooh Honey Baby / I'll Be There - 1965

Jackie Lee (born Earl Lee Nelson on 8-September-1928, Lake Charles, Los Angeles --- died 12-July-2008 --- cause: ?)

Mirwood 5502 - The Duck / Let Your Conscience Be Your Guide - 1965
Mirwood - The Duck (Stereo) - 1965 (this was released in 1990 in the U. K. on a Goldmine CD "C'mon & Dance Volume 1" GSCD 8Z)

Soulful Kinda Music – The Rare Soul Bible Volume Two

Bob & Earl (Bob Relf and Earl Lee Nelson)

? - Harlem Shuffle '65 - 1965   (can be found on the 1997 U. K. Goldmine/Life On Mars triple CD release "The Cream Of ... Vintage Soul Volume 1" MARSCD2)
Mirwood 5507 - Dancin' Everywhere / Baby It's Over - 1966

Jackie Lee

Mirwood 5509 - Try My Method / Your P-E-R-S-O-N-L-I-T-Y - 1966
Mirwood 5510 - Do The Temptation Walk / The Shotgun And The Duck - 1966
Mirwood - Temptation Walk (Stereo) - 1966 (This Was Released In 1990 In The U. K. On A Goldmine CD "C'mon & Dance Volume 1" GSCD 8Z)
Mirwood - Temptation Walk (Backing Track) - 1966 (although unissued on vinyl at the time this was released 1991 in the U. K. on a Goldmine CD "Jackie Lee Dance Favourites" GSCD 11)

Earl Cosby (Earl Lee Nelson)

Mirwood 5515 - Land Of A 1000 Dances / Ooh Honey Baby - 1966

Bob & Earl (Bob Relf and Earl Lee Nelson)

Mirwood 5517 - Baby It's Over / Dancin' Everywhere – 1966

Jackie Lee

Mirwood 5519 - You're Everything / Would You Believe - 1966
Mirwood - Would You Believe - 1966 (although unissued on vinyl at the time this alternate mix was released in the U. K. on a 2006 Kent CD "The Mirwood Soul Story Volume 2" CDKEND 264)

Bob & Earl (Bob Relf and Earl Lee Nelson)

Mirwood 5526 - I'll Keep Running Back / Baby Your Time Is My Time - 1966

Jackie Lee

Mirwood 5527 - Don't Be Ashamed / Oh, My Darlin' - 1966

Jackie Lee & Delores Hall

Mirwood 5528 - Baby I'm Satisfied / Whether It's Right Or Wrong - 1966

Jackie Lee

Mirwood - Anything You Want A. K. A. Any Way You Want* - (slated to be released as by Earl Nelson but unissued on vinyl this was released in the U. K. on a 2005 Kent CD "The Mirwood Soul Story" CDKEND 237.)
Mirwood - Trust Me - (unissued at the time this was released in the U. K. on a 2006 Kent CD "The Mirwood Soul Story Volume 2" CDKEND 264 track was also

Soulful Kinda Music – The Rare Soul Bible Volume Two

recorded in 1967 by Bobby Womack on Minit 32024)
Keymen 109 - Glory Of Love / Bring It Home - 1967
Keymen 114 - African Boo-Ga-Loo / Bring It Home – 1968
ABC-Paramount 11146 - Darkest Days / One For The Road - 1968

Bob & Earl (Bob Relf and Earl Lee Nelson)

White Whale 310 - Harlem Shuffle / I'll Come Running – 1969
Crestview 9011 - Send For Me, I'll Be There / Dancing Everywhere – 1969
Uni 55196 - (Pickin' Up) Love's Vibrations / Uh Uh Naw, Naw Naw – 1970

Jackie Lee

Uni 55206 - I Love You / The Chicken - 1970

Bob & Earl (Bob Relf and Earl Lee Nelson)

Uni 55248 - Get Ready For The New Day / Honey Sugar, My Sweet Thing – 1970

Jackie Lee

Uni 55259 - Your Sweetness Is My Weakness / You Were Searching For A Love – 1971
Capitol 3145 - Pershing Square / Twenty-Five Miles To Louisiana – 1971

Smoke (Jackie Lee and Tracey Andrews)

Mo Soul 1971 - Oh Love (We Finally Made It / Love Let's Be Happy Now – 1971

Jay Dee (Jackie Lee)

Warner Bros. 7798 - Strange Funky Games And Things (Part 1) / Strange Funky Games And Things (Part 2) - 1974 (written, arranged and produced by Barry White)

Bobby Day (Robert Byrd)

Trip 29 - Rockin' Robin / Over And Over – 1975

Bob & Earl / Gene Allison

Trip 75 - Harlem Shuffle / You Can Make It If You Try* - 1975 *Flip By Gene Allison.

The Hollywood Flames / Dale Ward

Underground 1190 - Buzz, Buzz, Buzz / Letter To Sherry* - ? *Flip By Dale Ward.

Sammy Turner / Bobby Day

Collectables Col 031467 - Lavender Blue / Over And Over* - ? *Flip By Sammy Turner.

Soulful Kinda Music – The Rare Soul Bible Volume Two

Bobby Day / The Willows

Collectables Col 3897 - Rockin Robin / Church Bells May Ring* - ? *flip by The Willows.

Label Listings

Lamp

?
‾‾‾

? – The Vanguards - Somebody Please / I Can't Use You Girl
6510-11 – The Ebony Rhythm Band - Soul Heart Transplant / Drugs Ain't Cool
157 – Allison And Calvin Turner - Shake What Your Mamma Gave You / Yeah, Memories
651 – The Diplomatics - (Aka Diplomats Show Band) - Humbug Pt.1 / Humbug Part 2
652 – The Vanguards - The Thought Of Losing Your Love / It's To Late For Love
653 – The Pearls - Can I Call You Baby / Shooting High
653 – The Moonlighters - Lonely Baby / Right On Brother
80 – The Vanguards - The Thought Of Losing Your Love / It's Too Late For Love
81 – The Vanguards - Girl Go Away (It's Wrong To Love) / Man Without Knowledge
82 – The Moonlighters - More Than I Can Stand / Just Like She Said She Would
83 – The Montiques - Fool Am I / Take Another Look
84 – Squidd - Mystic Illusion / High On A Hill
85 – Orange Wedge (David Capps) - Prejudice And Discrimination / Reject Me Not
86 – The Vanguards - The Thought Of Losing Your Love / Before You Take Another Step Girl
87 – The P.H.D.'s - It Swells My Desire / The Way It Use To Be
88 – Amnesty - Everybody Wants To Be Free Part 1 / Part 2
89 – Tony Black & The Revolution Compared To What - Huh / Go To Work
90 – ?
91 – Indy's - Come See About Her / Another Weekend
92 – The Vanguards - Falling Out Of Love / Gotta Have Love
93 – Funder Cooper - I've Got To Get Around / I Didn't Know (Don't Shoot Me)
94 – The Vanguards - Good Times Bad Times / Man Without Knowledge
95 – Words Of Wisdom - You Made Me Everything / Do You Understand Me Now ?

Landa

‾‾‾

666 - Mort Garson - Cry For Happy / Yes, We Have No Bananas
667 - Ronnie & The Rainbows - Loose Ends / Sombrero
668 - Pee Wee King - Slow Poke / Looking Back To See
669 - Ronnie Master - I Don't Know (If You Really Love Me) / I Love You
670 - Elmore Morris & The Spinner - Paradise Hill / She's A Wonderful One
671 - Beverly Ann Gibson - Love's Burning Fire / Without Love
672 - Lane Sisters - Birmingham Rag / Peek-A-Boo-Moon

Soulful Kinda Music – The Rare Soul Bible Volume Two

673 - Pee Wee King Orchestra - Bumming Around / When, When, When
674 - Joe Reisman Orchestra & Chorus - The Guns Of Navarone / Yassu
675 - Peter Elliott - Three Little Piggies / The Devil's Workshop
676 - The Tronics - Cantina / Pickin' And A Stompin'
677 - Sue Landers & The Cliff Parman Orch - It Hurts Too Much To Laugh / Lonely Sunday Night
678 - Rocky Cole - Heaven And Earth / Huey's Song
679 - Terry Tyler - A Thousand Feet Below / Answer Me
680 - The Tronics - The Big Scroungy / South American Sunset
681 - Robie Lester With The Don Ralke Orch - The Miracle Of Life / Ballad Of Cheating John
682 - Johnny Macrae - Parade Of The Fools / Such A Fool
683 - Rickie Page - Why Did You Lie / Je Vous Aime
684 - The Stompers - Quarter To 4 Stomp / Foolish One
685 - Maureen Gray - People Are Talking / Remember Me
686 - The Payments - Brand New Automobile / Cantina
687 - Johnny Madara - Heavenly / Save It
688 - Lena Anna - Iwan Iwanowitsch / Sentimental Baby
689 - Maureen Gray - Dancin' The Strand / Oh My
690 - Robert Maxwell - Dolce / Lost Patrol
691 - Little Billy And The Essentials - The Dance Is Over / Steady Girl
692 - Maureen Gray - Oh My / People Are Talkin
693 - ?
694 - ?
695 - ?
696 - ?
697 - ?
698 - ?
699 - ?
700 - Larry France - Last Kiss / Germ City
701 - Buddy And The Hearts - Thirty Days / Let It Rock
702 - Rollee McGill - Come Home / You Can Keep It
703 - Melvin, Harold & The Blue Notes - Get Out (And Let Me Cry) / You May Not Love Me
704 - Covay, Don-You're Good For Me / Truth Of The Light
705 - Carol Robinson - Wild Man / How Many Tears Must Fall
706 - Sheila Ferguson - How Did That Happen / Little Red Riding Hood
707 - The Jolly Jacks - There's Something On Your Mind / Rock The House
708 - The Flares - Forever / I Found Out
709 - Arthur & The Knights - Lovin' You Baby / I Shall Not Move
710 - Unreleased
711 - Jose Mendoza - The Puerto Ricans / You Gotta Come A Little Closer

Loma

701 – The Ermines – True Love / Peek Peek A Boo – 1955
702 – Gene & Billy Zerlene / Billy & The Billy Goats – The Whip / Zerlone – 1955
703 – The Ermines – Keep Me Alive / Muchacha Muchacha – 1955

Soulful Kinda Music – The Rare Soul Bible Volume Two

704 – The Ermines – I'm Sad / One Thing – 1955
705 – The Ermines – I'm Sad / One Thing - 1955
706 – Chuck Higgins – Betwixt And Between / Double Dip – 1956
301 – Randy Stevens – Sweet Shop / All My Love – 1958
2001 – Billy Storm – Baby Don't Look Down / I Never Want To Dream Again – 1964
2002 – The Singers – Midnight Prowl / (I Was) Born To Lose – 1964
2003 – Clyde & The Blue Jays – The Big Herk Part 1 / Part 2 – 1964
2004 – Bob & Earl – Everybody Jerk / Just One Look In Your Eyes – 1964
2005 – Little Jerry Williams – I'm The Lover Man / The Push Push Push – 1964
2006 – Lucky Carmichael – Hey Girl / Blues With A Feelin' – 1964
2007 – Sugar 'N' Spice – Come Go With Me / Playboy – 1964
2008 – Reb Foster – Something You Got / Quetzal And Jude – 1965
2009 – Billy Storm – Goldfinger Theme / Debbie And Mitch – 1965
2010 – The Olympics – I'm Comin' Home / Rainin' In My Heart – 1965
2011 – Ike & Tina Turner – I'm Thru With Love / Tell Her I'm Not Home – 1965
2012 – The Enchanters – I Paid For The Party / I Want To Be Loved – 1965
2013 – The Olympics – Good Lovin' / Olympic Shuffle – 1965
2014 – Baby Lloyd – There's Something On Your Mind Part 1 / Part 2 – 1965
2015 – Ike & Tina Turner – Somebody Needs You / Just To Be With You – 1965
2016 – Bobby Bennet – Soul Jerk Part 1 / Part 2 – 1965
2017 – The Olympics – No More Will I Cry / Baby I'm Yours – 1965
2018 – Walter Foster – Waitin' / Your Search Is Over – 1965
2019 – The Apollas – Lock Me In Your Heart / You're Absolutely Right – 1965
2020 – Brenda Hall – Soldier Baby Of Mine / Oh Eddy My Baby – 1965
2021 – Dick Jenson – Tom Dooley / Since I Fell For You – 1965
2022 – The Young Lions – Live And Learn / We Better Get Along – 1965
2023 – Kell Osborne & The Chicks – That's What's Happening / You Can't Outsmart A Woman – 1965
2024 – The Shirley Lewis Band – Bells Are Ringing / Walkin' The Girl – 1965
2025 – The Apollas – Just Can't Get Enough Of You / Nobody's Baby – 1966
2026 – Little Joe Cook – Hold Onto Your Money / Don't Have Feelings – 1966
2027 – The Soul Shakers – Cold Letter / Get Hip To Yourself – 1966
2028 – The Romeos – Mucho Soul / Are You Ready For That – 1966
2029 – Dick Jenson – Back In Circulation / Uncle John's Good Time Band – 1966
2030 – Ray Johnson – Girl Talk / Sherry's Party – 1966
2031 – Charles Thomas – Looking For A Love / Man With A Golden Touch – 1966
2032 – The Invincibles – So Much In Love / Can't Win – 1966
2033 – Kell Osborne – You Can't Outsmart A Woman / That's What's Happening – 1966
2034 – The G-Clefs – Little Lonely Boy / Party 66 – 1966
2035 – The Enchanters – God Bless The Girl And Me / You Were Meant To Be My Baby – 1966
2036 – The Dolls – And That Reminds Me / The Reason Why – 1966
2037 – Paul Davis – Juvenile Jungle / Wake Me Up Baby – 1966
2038 – Alton Joseph & The Jokers – Where's The Place / The Other Place – 1966
2039 – The Apollas – Pretty Red Ballons – You'll Always Have Me- 1966
2040 – The Autographs – Sad Sad Feeling Part 1 / Part 2 – 1966
2041 – The Romeos – Calypso Chilli / Mon Petite Chow – 1966
2042 – James Cotton – Laying In The Weeds / Complete This Order – 1966
2043 – Larry Laster – Help Yourself / Go For Yourself – 1966

Soulful Kinda Music – The Rare Soul Bible Volume Two

2044 – Mart Lee Whitney – Don't Coma A Knockin' / This Could Have Been Mine – 1966
2045 – The Marvellous – Something's Burning / We Go Together – 1966
2046 – Charlie Underwood & The Glide Band – It Will Stand / Doggin' Around – 1966
2047 – The Soul Shakesr – I'm Getting Weaker / It's Love ('Cause I Feel It) – 1966
2048 – The G-Clefs – I Can't Stand It / Whirlwind – 1966
2049 – Delilah Kennelbrew – Bright Lights / We'll Be Together – 1966
2050 – Charles Underwood & The Glide Band – Let's Go Get Stoned / It Will Stand – 1966
2051 – The Belfast Gypsies – Secret Police / Gloria's Dream – 1966
2052 – Sandy Layne – Push My Love Button / How Many Times – 1966
2053 – The Apollas – My Soul Concerto / Sorry Mama – 1966
2054 – The Enchanters – I've Lost All Communication / We Got Love – 1966
2055 – Dick Jenson & The Imports – Mr Pitiful / You Don't Love Me Anymore – 1966
2056 – Bobby Freeman – Shadow Of Your Love / Soulful Sound Of Music – 1966
2057 – The Invincibles – I Couldn't Stand It / How Many Times – 1966
2058 – Barry 'Barefoot Beefus – Barefoot Beefus / Go Ahead On – 1966
2059 – Limey & The Tanks – Gather My Things And Go / Out Of Sight Out Of Mind – 1966
2060 – The Belfast Gypsies – Portland Town / People Let's Freak Out – 1966
2061 – The Marvellous – You're Such A Sweet Thing / Why Do You Want To Hurt The One You Love – 1966
2062 – The Poor – Once Again / How Many Tears – 1966
2063 – Don Crawford – Along Came Rose / If You Need Me – 1966
2064 – Kim Fowley – Lights / Something New And Different – 1966
2065 – Butch Engle & The Styx – Going Home / I Like Her – 1966
2066 – The Teen Turbans – Didn't He Run We Need To Be Loved – 1966
2067 – Lukas Lollipop – Hoochi Coochi Coo / Don't Hold On To Someone – 1967
2068 – Tony Amaro & The Chariots – Runnin' Around / Hey Baby – 1967
2069 – Ben Aiken – If I Told You Once (I Told You A Million Times / You Were Meant To Be My Baby – 1967
2070 – Linda Jones – I Can't Stop Lovin' My Baby / Hypnotized – 1967
2071 – Roy Redmond – Ain't That Terrible / A Change Is Gonna Come – 1967
2072 – The Jammers – Where Can She Run To / What Happened To The Good Times – 1967
2073 – Artie Lewis – Ain't No Good – Falling (In Love With You) / Ain't No Good – 1967
2074 – Lorraine Ellison / Cry Me A River / Heart Be Still – 1967
2075 – Roy Redmond – Good Day Sunshine / That Old Time Feeling – 1967
2076 – Ben Aiken – God Bless The Girl And Me / Callin' – 1967
2077 – Linda Jones – What Have I Done (To Make You Mad) / Make Me Surrender (Baby Baby Please) – 1967
2078 – Vicky Baines – Sweeter Than Sweet Things / We Can Find That Love – 1967
2079 – The Realistics – What 'Cha Gonna Do / If This Ain't Love – 1967
2080 – Bobby Freeman – I Got A Good Thing / Lies – 1967
2081 – Lonny Youngblood – African Twist Part 1 / Part 2 – 1967
2082 – J J Jackson – Try Me / Sho Nuff (Gotta Good Thing Going – 1967
2083 – Lorraine Ellison – I Want To Be Loved / When Love Flies Away – 1967
2084 – Ben Aiken – Life Of A Clown / Satisfied – 1967
2085 – Linda Jones – I Can't Stand It / Give My Love A Try – 1967

Soulful Kinda Music – The Rare Soul Bible Volume Two

2086 – Carl Hall – You Don't Know Nothing About Love / Mean It Baby – 1967
2087 – The Implements – Old Man Soul Part 1 / Part 2 – 1968
2088 – The Realistics – Brenda Brenda / How Did I Live Without You – 1968
2089 – Bobby Reed – I Wanna Love You So Bad / I'll Find A Way – 1968
2090 – J J Jackson – Down But Not Out / Why Does It Take So Long – 1968
2091 – Linda Jones – My Heart Needs A Break / The Things I've Been Through (Loving You) – 1968
2092 – Roy Redmond – Good Day Sunshine / That Old Time Feeling – 1968
2093 – Mighty Hannibal – Somebody In The World For You / Get In The Groove – 1968
2094 – Lorraine Ellison – In My Tomorrow / Try (Just A Little Bit Harder) – 1968
2095 – Tommy Starr – Better Think Of What You're Losing / Love Wheel – 1968
2096 – J J Jackson – Come See Me (I'm Your Man) / I Don't Want To Live My Life Alone – 1968
2097 – Lonnie Youngblood – Roll With The Punches / Tomorrow – 1968
2098 – Carl Hall – The Dam Busted / I Don't Wanna Be (Your Used To Be) – 1968
2099 – Linda Jones – What Can I Do Without You / Yesterday – 1968
2100 – Ben Aiken – Baby You Move Me / Thanks To You – 1968
2101 – The Voice Box – Baby Baby Don't You Know / I Want It Back (Your Love) – 1968
2102 – J J Jackson – Too Late / You Do It Cause You Wanna – 1968
2103 – Mighty Hannibal – I Just Want Some Love / Good Time – 1968
2104 – J J Jackson – Courage Ain't Strength / That Ain't Right – 1968
2105 – Linda Jones – I Who Have Nothing / It Won't Take Much – 1968
2106 – John Wonderling – Midway Down / Man Of Straw - 1968

Lu Pine

Lu Pine 0001 - The Just Brothers - Things Will Be Better Tomorrow / Sliced Tomatoes -?
Lu Pine 100 - ?
Lu Pine 101 - ?
Lu Pine 102 - ?
Lu Pine 103 - The Falcons And Band Ohio Untouchables - I Found A Love / Swim - 1962
Lu Pine 104 - The Corvells - Baby Sitting / He's So Fine - 1962
Lu Pine 105 - The Fourmost - Why Can't I Have You / Twist-A-Taste - 1962
Lu Pine 106 - Gene Martin - I Got The Blues / Lonely Nights - 1962
Lu Pine 107 - The Sax Kari Orchestra Featuring Ella Reed - Sweet Man / I'll Never Forsake You - 1962
Lu Pine 108 - The Conquerors - Bill Is My Boyfriend / Dutchess Conquers Duke - 1962
Lu Pine 109 - Benny McCain & The Ohio Untouchables - What To Do / She's My Heart's Desire - 1962
Lu Pine 110 - The Ohio Untouchables - Love Is Amazing / Forgive Me Darling - 1962
Lu Pine 111 - Bobby Williams - I'm Depending On You / Tell It To My Face - 1962
Lu Pine 112 - The Minor Chords - Let Her Go Now / Many A Day - 1962
Lu Pine 113 - ?

Soulful Kinda Music – The Rare Soul Bible Volume Two

Lu Pine 114 - ?
Lu Pine 115 - Eddie Floyd - Will I Be The One / Set My Soul On Fire - 1962
Lu Pine 116/117 - The Ohio Untouchables - I'm Tired / Uptown - 1962
Lu Pine 118 - The Rivals With T. J. Fowler's Band - It's Gonna Work Out / Love Me - 1962
Lu Pine 119 - Mack Rice - Baby I'm Coming Home / My Baby - 1962
Lu-Pine 120 - Joe Stubbs - Keep On Loving Me / What's My Destiny - 1962
Lupine 120 - The Primettes - Tears Of Sorrow / Pretty Baby - 1962
Lupine 121 - Al Garner - I'll Get Along / All I Need Is You - 1962
Lu-Pine 121 - Tina Marvel & Group - Promises You Made To Me / I Can't Love No One But You - 1962
Lu Pine 122 - Phil Waddel Rocket Specials - Rocket Walk / Arkansas Special - 1962
Lu Pine 122 - Eddie Floyd - A Deed To Your Heart / I'll Be Home - 1962
Lu-Pine 123 - Betty Lavett - Witch Craft In The Air / You Killed The Love - 1962
Lu Pine 124 - The Falcons - Has It Happened To You Yet / Lonely Nights - 1962
Lu Pine 125 - Mack Rice - The Whip / Feels Fine - 1962
Lu Pine 126 - Benny McCain -You're On My Mind / I Don't Want No Part Time Love - 1962
Lu Pine 136 - The Falcons - I Found A Love / Swim - 1962
Lu Pine 711 - Richard T. And The Trans Ams - I Found You / Bus Stop - ?
Lu Pine 712 - Sons Of The 7 Sisters Featuring Silk And Satin - You're So Fine / You're On My Mind - ?
Lu Pine 713 - ?
Lu Pine 801 - Eddie Kirkland - Train Done Gone / I Tried - ?
Lu Pine 1003 - The Falcons & Band (Ohio Untouchables) - I Found A Love / Swing - ?
Lu Pine 1004 - The Corvells - Baby Sitting / He's So Fine - ?
Lu Pine 1005 - ?
Lu Pine 1006 - Gene Martin - I Got The Blues / Lonely Nights - ?
Lu Pine 1007 - ?
Lu Pine 1008 - ?
Lu Pine 1009 - Benny Mccain & The Ohio Untouchables - She's My Heart's Desire / What To Do - ?
Lu Pine 1010 - The Ohio Untouchables - Love Is Amazing / Forgive Me Darling - ?
Lu Pine 1011 - The Ohio Untouchables - I'm Tired / Uptown - ?
Lu Pine 1012 - ?
Lu Pine 1013 - ?
Lu Pine 1014 - ?
Lu Pine 1015 - ?
Lu Pine 1016 - ?
Lu Pine 1017/1018 - The Ohio Untouchables - I'm Tired / Uptown - ?
Lu Pine 1019 - Mack Rice - My Baby / Baby I'm Coming Home - ?
Lu Pine 1020 - The Falcons - Lonely Nights / Has It Happened To You Yet - ?
Lu Pine 1021 - ?
Lu Pine 1022 - Eddie Floyd - I'll Be Home / A Deed To Your Heart - ?
Lu Pine 1023 - ?
Lu Pine 1024 - The Falcons - Lonely Nights / Has It Happened To You - ?
Lu Pine 1025 - Mack Rice - The Whip / It Feels Good - ?
Lu Pine 1026 - Benny McCain - I Don't Want No More Part Time Love / ? - ?
Lu Pine 1027 - ?

Soulful Kinda Music – The Rare Soul Bible Volume Two

Lu Pine 1028 - The Minor Chords - Many A Day / Let Her Go Man - ?
Lu Pine 001 - McKinley & Delores And The Minor Chords - She's So Fine / I Fell In Love - ?
Lu Pine 002 - Eddie Floyd - Set My Soul On Fire / Will I Be The One - ?
Lu Pine 003 - The Falcons - You're On My Mind / Anna - ? .
Lu Pine 004 - ?
Lu Pine 005 - Joe S. Maxey Little 14 Yr. Old And His 15 Piece Orchestra The City Flames - May The Best Man Win / Right
On! (The Cream) - ?
Lu Pine 5896 - The Falcons - I Found A Love / ? - ?

Like

1000 - Rex Garvin & The Mighty Cravers - Soul Street / Evening Mist - 1963
45-301 - Rex Garvin (And The Might Cravers) - Sock It To 'Em J. B. (Part 1) / Sock It To 'Em J. B. (Part 2) - 1966
45-302 - Rex Garvin - I Gotta Go Now (Up On The Floor) / Believe It Or Not - 1967

Lo Lo

2101 - Big Ella - It Takes A Lot Of Loving (To Satisfy My Man) / I Need A Good Man
2102 - Tony Lawrence & The Cultural Festivals - Harlem Cultural Festival / Me And You
2103 - Sam Dees - It's All Wrong (It's All Right) / Don't Keep Me Hangin' On
2304 - Top Shelf - No Second Thoughts (About Who You Really Love) / Give It Up
2305 - Bobby Hill - I Wanna Be With You / The Children
2306 - Sam Dees - Easier Said Than Done / Soul Sister
2307 - Bobby Hill - To The Bitter End / Tell Me You Love Me

The Main Ingredient

The Poets (members Donald McPherson (born 9-July-1941 in Indianapolis, Indiana - died 4-July-1971 cause: Leukemia), Enrique Antonio Silvester (born 7-October-1941 in Colon, Panama), Luther Simmons Jr. (born 9-September-1942 in New York City))

Red Bird 10-046 - Merry Christmas Baby / I'm Stuck On You - 1965

The Insiders (members Donald McPherson, Enrique Antonio Silvester and Luther Simmons Jr.)

Red Bird 10-055 - I'm Stuck On You / Chapel Bells Are Calling - 1966
RCA 47-9225 - I'm Better Off Without You / I'm Just A Man - 1967
RCA 47-9325 - If You Had A Heart / Movin' On - 1967

The Main Ingredient (members Donald McPherson , Enrique Antonio Silvester and Luther Simmons Jr.) It is said that the group got their unique name after reading the writing on a Coca~Cola bottle!

RCA 47-9748 - I Was Born To Lose You / Psychedelic Ride - 1969
RCA 74-0252 - Brotherly Love / Get Back - 1969
RCA 74-0313 - The Girl I Left Behind / Can't Stand Your Love - 1970
RCA 74-0340 - You've Been My Inspiration / Life Won't Be The Same - 1970
RCA 74-0382 - I'm Better Off Without You* / Need Her Love - 1970 *a re-recording of their 1967 release as The Insiders on RCA 9225.
RCA 74-0401 - I'm So Proud / Brotherly Love - 1970
RCA 74-0456 - Spinning Around (I Must Be Falling In Love) / Magic Shoes - 1971 (after this release Donald McPherson dies of leukemia)

The Main Ingredient (members Cuba Gooding (born 27-April-1944 in New York City), Enrique Antonio Silvester and Luther Simmons Jr.)

RCA 74-0517 - Black Seeds Keep On Growing / Baby Change Your Mind - 1971 (some copies issued with picture sleeve)
RCA 74-0603 - I'm Leaving This Time / Another Day Has Come - 1971
RCA 74-0731 - Everybody Plays The Fool / Who Can I Turn To (When Nobody Needs Me) - 1972
RCA 74-0856 - You've Got To Take It (If You Want It) / Traveling - 1972
RCA 74-0939 - I'm Better Off Without You / You Can Call Me Rover - 1973
RCA 0046 - Girl Blue / Movin' On - 1973
RCA 0205 - Just Don't Want To Be Lonely / Goodbye My Love - 1973
RCA 0305 - Happiness Is Just Around The Bend / Why Can't We All Unite - 1974
RCA 10095 - California My Way / Looks Like Rain - 1974
RCA 10224 - Rolling Down A Mountainside / Family Man - 1975 RCA 10334 - The Good Old Days / I Want To Make You Glad - 1975
RCA 10431 - Shame On The World (Short Version) / Shame On The World (Extended Version) - 1975
RCA 10431 - Shame On The World / Lillian - 1975
RCA 10606 - Instant Love / Let Me Prove My Love To You - 1976

Tony Sylvester & The New Ingredient (members Enrique Antonio "Tony" Silvester, ...)

Mercury 73831 - Magic Touch / Very White - 1976

Cuba Gooding

Motown 1440 - Mind Pleaser / Where Would I Be Without You - 1978

The Main Ingredient featuring Cuba Gooding (members Cuba Gooding, Enrique Antonio Silvester and Luther Simmons Jr.)

RCA 12060 - Think Positive / Spoiled - 1980

The Main Ingredient (members Cuba Gooding, Enrique Antonio Silvester and Luther Simmons Jr.)

RCA 12107 - Makes No Difference To Me / What Can A Miracle Do - 1980
RCA 12320 - Evening Of Love / Evening Of Love - 1981
RCA 12340 - I Only Have Eyes For You / Only - 1981
RCA 13045 - Party People / Save Me - 1982

Cuba Gooding

Streetwise 1114 - Happiness Is Just Around The Bend (6:59) / ? - 1983 (12"Release)

The Main Ingredient (members Cuba Gooding, Enrique Antonio Silvester and Luther Simmons Jr.)

Zakia 015 - Do Me Right / ? - 1986
Collectables Col 045407 - Spinning Around / Happiness Is Just Around The Bend - 1988
Collectables Col 045557 - Just Don't Want To Be Lonely / You've Been My Inspiration - 1988

The Main Ingredient (members Cuba Gooding, Enrique Antonio Silvester and Jerome Jackson)

Polygram ? - I Just Wanna Love You / ? - 1990

Cuba Gooding

Ichiban 635 - My One And Only Love / I'd Rather Leave While I'm In Love - ?

The Main Ingredient (members Enrique Antonio Silvester, Luther Simmons Jr. and Carlton Blount) 2001 line-up.

Hugh McCracken

Congress 257 - You Blow My Mind / Buzz In My Head - 1965
Congress 261 - What I Gotta Do To Satisfy You / Runnin', Runnin' - 1966

Soulful Kinda Music – The Rare Soul Bible Volume Two

The Powers Of Blue

MTA 113 - Good Lovin' / (I Can't Get No) Satisfaction - 1966 (Hugh Mccracken Member Of Group)
MTA 118 - Cool Jerk / You Blow My Mind - 1967

Barbara Mason

Barbara Mason & The Larks

Crusader 111 - Trouble Child / Dedicated To You - 1964

Barbara Mason (Born Barbara Juanita Mason, 9-August-1947 In Philadelphia, Pennsylvania)

Arctic 102 - Girls Have Feelings Too / Come To Me – 1964
Arctic 105 - Yes, I'm Ready / Keep Him - 1965
Arctic 108 - Sad, Sad Girl / Come To Me – 1965
Arctic 112 - You Got What It Takes / If You Don't (Love Me, Tell Me So) – 1965
Arctic 116 - Don't Ever Want To Lose Your Love / Is It Me - 1965
Arctic 120 - I Need Love / Bobby Is My Baby – 1966
Arctic 126 - Hello Baby / Poor Girl In Trouble – 1966
Arctic 134 - You Can Depend On Me / Game Of Love – 1967
Arctic 137 - Oh, How It Hurts / Ain't Got Nobody – 1967
Arctic 140 - Dedicated To The One I Love / I Don't Want To Lose You - 1968
Arctic 140 - Dedicated To The One I Love / Half A Love – 1968
Arctic 142 - Half A Love / (I Can Feel Your Love) Slipping Away – 1968
Arctic 146 - Don't Ever Go Away / I'm No Good For You – 1968
Arctic 148 - Take It Easy (With My Heart) / You Never Loved Me (At All) – 1969
Arctic 154 - You Better Stop It / Happy Girl – 1969
National General 005 - Raindrops Keep Fallin' On My Head / If You Knew Him Like I Do - 1970
Buddah 249 - The Pow Pow Song (Sorry Sorry Baby) / Your Old Flame – 1971
Buddah 296 - Bed And Board / Yes It's You – 1972
Buddah 319 - Woman And Man / Who Will You Hurt Next – 1972
Buddah 331 - Give Me Your Love / You Can Be With The One You Don't Love - 1972
Buddah 355 - Yes I'm Ready / Who Will You Hurt Next – 1973
Buddah 375 - Child Of Tomorrow / Out Of This World – 1973
Buddah 395 - Caught In The Middle (Of A One Sided Love Affair) / Give Him Up – 1973
Buddah 405 - World War Iii / I Miss You Gordon – 1974
Buddah 409 - The Devil Is Busy / All In Love Is Fair* - 1974 *Written By Stevie Wonder.
Buddah 424 - Our Day Will Come / Half Sister, Half Brother – 1974
Buddah 441 - From His Woman To You* / When You Wake Up In Georgia - 1974 *An "Answer" Record To The 1974 Release "Woman To Woman" By Shirley Brown On

Soulful Kinda Music – The Rare Soul Bible Volume Two

Truth 3206
Buddah 459 - Shackin' Up / One Man Between Us – 1975

Barbara Mason & The Futures (Members Barbara Mason, ...)

Buddah 481 - Make It Last / We Got Each Other - 1975 (Some Copies Issued With Picture Sleeve)

Barbara Mason & Bunny Sigler

Curtom Pro 689 - Love Song (Disco Mix) (6:14) / Locked In This Position (Disco Mix) (10:05) - 1977 (12" Promo Issue Only)

Barbara Mason

Prelude 71103 - I Am Your Woman, She Is Your Wife / Take Me Tonight – 1977
Prelude 71111 - Darling Come Back Home Soon / It Was You Boy – 1978
WMOT 5352 - I'll Never Love The Same Way Twice / ? – 1980
WMOT 02506 - She's Got The Papers (But I've Got The Man) / (Instrumental) – 1981
WMOT 70077 - On And Off / You're All Inside Of Me – 1981
West End 1264 - Another Man (Vocal) (Short) / Another Man (Instrumental) – 1984
Phonorama ? – 1984

Barbara Mason With M. C. Boulevard

I. T. P. ? - Give Me Your Love / ? – 1996

Joe Matthews

Joe Matthews (born in Juliet, Illinois)

Thelma 104 - She's My Beauty Queen* / Is It Worth It All - 1966 *the backing track on this song was also used on the 1966 release "I'll Never Forget" by The Tempos on Diamond Jim 8792.
Thelma 107 - Sorry Ain't Good Enough / You Better Mend Your Ways - 1966

The Fabulous Apollos / The Valtone Band

Valtone 107 - What's So Good To You* / (Instrumental)** - 1968 *lead Joe Matthews. **flip by The Valtone Band.

Joe Matthews

Kool Kat 1001 - Ain't Nothing You Can Do / Check Your Self - 1968
Westbound 146/147 – What Every Little Girl Needs / Third World – 1969 (possibly unissued)
New Moon 0001 - Little Angel (That's What You Are) / I Had To Moan - ?
New Moon 0002 - I Got Chose / Cause I Love You - ?

Soulful Kinda Music – The Rare Soul Bible Volume Two

Label Listings

Magnum

+————————————————————————————————————

700 – Quinn Miller – Sea Witch / Things Are Bound To Happen
701 – The Cobra Brothers – Lu Lu's Party / My Baby Doll
702 - ?
703 – Dee Dee Dorety – Daddy / Tommy Green
714 - Uptones - Wear My Ring / Dreamin' - 1963
715 - Ron Barrett & The Buckskins - Louie Louie / Lilli - 1964
716 – Don Julian & The Meadowlarks – Lie / The Booglay
717 - Sir Stan & The Counts - Soulin' / The Nitty Gritty's In Town
718 - Elliot Shavers - A Swingin' Party / Fool, Fool, Fool
719 - Jimmy Johnson - Don't Answer The Door Part 1 / Part 2
720 - King Solomon - I Want To Know / Yodelling This Morning
721 - King Solomon - Scratch My Back / Separation
722 - The Paramounts - Under Your Spell / Time Will Bring About A Change
723 - Joe Houston - Hog Maws Part 1 / Part 2
724 - Jimmy Johnson - Black Cat Bone Part 1 / Part 2
725 - Joy Holden - Teenage Rage / Blowing Out The Candles
726 - Johnny Guitar Watson - Big Bad Wolf / You Can Stay
727 - Jimmy Johnson - The Hunch / Forgive Me
728 - Charles Perry - How Can I (Keep From Crying) / Move On Love - 1965
729 - Joe Houston - Chicken Gravy Part 1 / Part 2
730 - Maxine Womack – Hello Lover / When You're Through
731 - Lee Harvey - Only True Love / Prove It
732 - Jimmy Johnson - Special Built Part 1 / Part 2
733 - Johnny Wyatt – The Bottom Of The Top / Once Upon A Time
734 - Hank Alexander - Our Secret Love Part 1 / Part 2
735 - Jimmy Johnson - Now Looking Back Part 1 / Part 2
736 - Johnny Wyatt - Once Upon A Time / The Bottom Of The Top
737 - Ollie Jackson -Wipe Away The Teardrops / The Day My Heart Stood Still
738 - Elliot Shavers - Soulin' Back / Ugly In-Laws
739 - Model "T" Slim (Elmon Mickle) - Shake Your Boogie / Good Morning Little Schoolgirl 1966
740 - ?
741 - Bennie Conn - I'm So Glad To Be Back Home / Forgive Me

Mar-V-Lus

+————————————————————————————————————

6000 - Johnny Sayles - Don't Turn Your Back On Me / You Told A Lie - 1965
6001 - Johnny Sayles - Got You Off My Mind / You Did Me Wrong - 1965
6002 - Alvin Cash & The Crawlers - Twine Time / The Bump - 1965

Soulful Kinda Music – The Rare Soul Bible Volume Two

6003 - Du-Ettes - Sugar Daddy / Every Beat Of My Heart - 1965
6004 - Cicero Blake - Sad Feeling / You're Gonna Be Sorry - 1965
6005 - Alvin Cash - The Barracuda / Do It One More Time - 1965
6006 - Alvin Cash - The Penguin / Unwind The Twine - 1965
6007 - Vicky Clay - It's Alright / Gee Whiz - 1966
6008 - Joseph Moore - I'm Lost Without You / I Still Can't Get You - 1966
6009 - Alvin Cash & The Registers - Unwind The Twine / Boston Monkey - 1966
6010 - Blenders - Love Is A Good Thing Going / Your Love Has Got Me Down - 1966
6011 - Josephine Taylor - You're The Sweetest Thing / Good Lovin' - 1966
6012 - Alvin Cash & The Registers - The Philly Freeze / No Deposit No Return - 1966
6013 - Josephine Taylor - What Is Love / I Wanna Know Do You Care - 1966
6014 - Alvin Cash - Alvin's Boogaloo / Let's Do Some Good Thing - 1966
6015/6016 - Alvin Cash - Doin' The Ali Shuffle / Feel So Good - 1967
6017 - Josephine Taylor - Ordinary Guy / Ain't Gonna Cry No More - 1967
6018 - Young Folk - Joey / Lonely Girl - 1967
6019 - Alvin Cash - Different Strokes For Different Folks / The Charge - 1967
6019 - Miss Madelinne - Lonely Girl / Behave Yourself – 1967
6020 - The Ultimations - Would I Do It Over / With Out You – 1967

Midas

300 - Irene Scott - Everyday Worries / You're No Good
301 - No No Starr - Swing Your Love My Way / Pull Yourself Together
304 - The Compliments - Borrow Til Morning / Beware Beware
9001 - Al Tamms - Come Here, You / I Like The Way You Are
9002 - Lonnie Brooks - Popeye / Mister Hotshot
9003 - The Inspirations - Your Wish Is My Command / Take A Chance On You
9004 - The Danderliers - All The Way / Walk On With Your Nose Up
9005 - Reginald Day - My Girl, Jean / Lost Love
9006 - Big Daddy Rogers - I'm A Big Man / Be My Lawyer
9011 - Brothers & Sisters - For Brothers Only / Make Me Sad (Also On Toddlin' Town)

Minit (First Series)

601/2 – Matthew Jacob (Boogie Jake) - Bad Luck And Trouble / Early Morning Blues
603 - Nolan Pitts - What Is Life / Middle Of The Night
604 - Ernie K-Doe - Make You Love Me / There's A Will There's A Way
605 - Doyle Templet - Betty Jane / Is It Really Love
606 - Benny Spellman - Life Is Too Short / Ammerette
607 - Jessie Hill - Ooh-Poo-Pah-Doo (part 1) / Ooh-Poo-Pah-Doo (part 2)
608 - Mathew Jacobs - Chance For Your Love / Loaded Down
609 - Allen & Allen - Heavenly Baby / Tiddle Winks
610 - Del-Royals - She's Gone / Who Will Be The One
611 - Jessie Hill - Whip It On Me / I Need Your Love
612 - Aaron Neville - Over You / Everyday

Soulful Kinda Music – The Rare Soul Bible Volume Two

613 - Benny Spellman - Darling No Matter Where / I Didn't Know
614 - Ernie K-Doe - Hello My Lover / 'Tain't It The Truth
615 - Allen Orange - Forever / Just A Little Love
615 - Allen Orange - Forever / Lighted Windows
616 - Jessie Hill - Scoop Scoobie Doobie / Highhead Blues
617 - Lee Diamond - It Won't Be Me / Please Don't Leave
618 - Aaron Neville - Show Me The Way / Get Out Of My Life
619 - Roy Montrell - The Montrell / Mudd
620 - Del Royals - Close To You / Got You On My Mind
621 - Awood Magic - It's Better To Dream / Pretty Pretty Waitress
622 - Jessie Hill - I Got Mine / Oh Me, Oh My
623 - Ernie K-Doe - Mother In Law / Wanted $10000 Reward
624 - Aaron Neville - Don't Cry / Reality
625 - Irma Thomas- Cry On / Girl Needs Boy
626 - Lonnie Heard & Five Knights - Times Are Getting Harder / Let Me In
627 - Ernie K-Doe - Real Man / Te-Ta-Te-Ta-Ta
628 - Jessie Hill - Oogsey Moo / My Love
629 - Diamond Joe - Moanin' And Screamin' (part 1) / Moanin' And Screamin' (part 2)
630 - Allen Orange - When You're Lonely / True Love Never Dies
631 - Aaron Neville - Let's Live / I Found Another Love
632 - Showmen - It Will Stand / Country Fool
633 - Irma Thomas - It's Too Soon To Know / That's All I Ask
634 - Ernie K-Doe - Certain Girl / I Cried My Last Tear
635 - Lee Diamond - I Need Money / Let Me Know
636 - Tony Taylor & Five Knights - I Want Somebody / Polly Want A Cracker
637 - Del-Royals - Always Naggin' / I Fell In Love With You
638 - Jessie Hill - Sweet Jelly Roll / It's My Fault
639 - Aaron Neville - I'm Waiting At The Station / How Many Times
640 - Allen Orange - Miss Nosey / The Letter
641 - Ernie K-Doe - Popeye Joe / Come On Home
642 - Irma Thomas - I Done Got Over It / Gone
643 - Showmen - Fate Planned It This Way / The Wrong Girl
644 - Benny Spellman - Fortune Teller / Lipstick Traces (On A Cigarette)
645 - Ernie K-Doe - Hey Hey Hey / Love You The Best
646 - Jessie Hill - Can't Get Enough Of That Ooh-Poo-Pah-Doo / The Pots On Strike
647 - Showmen - Comin' Home / I Love You Can't See
648 - Eskew Reeder - Green Door / I Waited Too Long
649 - Diamond Joe - Help Yourself / Fair Play
650 - Aaron Neville - Humdinger / Sweet Little Mama
651 - Ernie K-Doe - Beating Like A Tom Tom / I Got To Find Somebody
652 - Benny Spellman - I'm In Love / Every Now And Then
653 - Irma Thomas - It's Raining / I Did My Part
654 - Showmen - The Owl Sees You / True Fine Mama
655 - Calvin Lee - I'll Be Home (Wait And See) / Valley Of Tears
656 - Ernie K-Doe - Get Out Of My House / Lovin' You
657 - Aaron Neville - Wrong Number (I'm Sorry Goodbye) / How Could I Help But Love You
658 - Eskew Reeder - Never Again / We Had Love
659 - Benny Spellman - You Got To Get It / Stickin' Which A' Baby
660 - Irma Thomas - Two Winters Long / Somebody Told You

Soulful Kinda Music – The Rare Soul Bible Volume Two

661 - Ernie K-Doe - Easier Said Than Done / Be Sweet
662 - Showmen - 39-21-46 / (You) Swish Fish
663 - Calvin Lee - You / Ammerette
664 - Benny Spellman - Ammerette / Talk About Love
665 - Ernie K-Doe - I'm The Boss / Pennies Worth Happiness
666 - Irma Thomas - Ruler Of My Heart / Hittin' On Nothing

Miracle

1 - Jimmy Ruffin - Don't Feel Sorry For Me / Heart
2 - Little Iva & Her Band - When I Needed You / Continental Strut
3 - Gino Parks - Blibber Blabber / Don't Say Bye Bye
4 - Andre Williams - Rosa Lee / Shoo Ooo
5 - The Temptations - Oh,Mother Of Mine / Romance Without Finance
6 - The Valadiers - Greetings (This Is Uncle Sam) / Take A Chance
7 - The Equadors - Someone To Call My Own / You're My Desire
8 - Pete Hartfield - Love Me / Darling Tonight
9 - Joel Sebastian - Angel In Blue / Blue Cinderella
10 - Don McKenzie - Whose Heart (Are You Gonna Break Now) / I'll Call You
11 - Freddie Gorman - The Day Will Come / Just For You
12 - The Temptations - Check Yourself / Your Wonderful Love

Mirwood

5501 - Gas Company - Blow Your Mind / Your Time's Up
5502 - Jackie Lee - The Duck / Let Your Conscience Be Your Guide
5503 - Bees - She's An Artist / Leave Me Be
5504 - Olympics - Secret Agents / We Go Together (Pretty Baby)
5505 - Belles - Don't Pretend / Words Can't Explain
5506 - Josh White - Jelly, Jelly Blues / Strange Fruit
5507 - Bob & Earl - Dancin' Everywhere / It's Over
5508 - Bobby Garrett - I Can't Get Away Part 1 / Part 2
5509 - Jackie Lee - Try My Method / Your P-E-R-S-O-N-A-L-I-T-Y
5510 - Jackie Lee - Do The Temptation Walk / The Shotgun And The Duck
5511 - Bobby Garrett - Big Brother / My Little Girl

5512 - Music Company - I've Just Seen A Face / I've Just Seen A Face
5513 - Olympics - Mine Exclusively / Secret Agents
5514 - Mirettes - He's Alright With Me / Your Kind Ain't no Good
5515 - Earl Cosby - Land Of A Thousand Dances / Ooh Honey Baby
5516 - Hideaways - Hide Out / Jolly Joe
5517 - Bob & Earl - Baby, It's Over / Dancin' Everywhere
5518 - J. W. Alexander - Baby, It's Real / Keep A Light In The Window
5519 - Jackie Lee - You're Everything / Would You Believe
5520 - Bobby Lee Timberlake - You Hurt Me / Another Girl's Boyfriend

Soulful Kinda Music – The Rare Soul Bible Volume Two

5522 - Jimmy Thomas - Just Tryin' To Please You / Where There's A Will
5523 - Olympics - Western Movies / Baby Do The Philly Dog
5524 - James Bond - Man With A Golden Gun / Casino Royale
5525 - Olympics - Bounce / Th Duck
5526 - Bob & Earl - I'll Keep Running Back / Baby Your Time Is My Time
5527 - Jackie Lee -Don't Be Ashamed / Oh My Darlin'
5528 - Jackie Lee - Baby, I'm Satisfied / Whether It's Right Or Wrong
5529 - Olympics - Same Old Thing / I'll Do A Little Bit More
5530 - Jimmy Conwell - Second Hand Happiness / Cigarette Ashes
5531 - Mirettes - He's Alright With Me / Now That I've Found You baby
5532 - Richard Temple - That Beatin' Rhythm / Could It Be
5533 - Olympics - Big Boy Pete / Hully Gully
5534 - Sheppards - How Do You Like It / Stubborn Heart
5535 - Performers - I Can't Stop You / L A Stomp
5536 - Performers Day - When She Wanted Me / Set Me Free

Moira

101 - Jimmy (Soul) Clark - If I Only Know Then (What I Know Now) / Do It Right Now (Instrumental)
102 - Firestones - I Just Can't Wait / Buy Now Pay Later Plan
103 - Fabulous Counts - Jan Jan (Instrumental) / Girl From Kenya (Instrumental)
104 - Jimmy (Soul) Clark - Tell Her / Hold Your Horses
105 - Fabulous Counts - Scrambled Eggs (Instrumental) / Dirty Red (Instrumental)
106 - Belita Woods - Magic Corner / Grounded
107 - Belita Woods - You Do Your Thing And I'll Do Mine / That's When I'll Stop Loving You
108 - Fabulous Counts - Get Down People / Lunar Funk (Instrumental)

M-Pac!

7200 - Bobby Davin - A Human's Prayer / Damper Down - 1963
7201 - Harold Burrage - The Master Key / Faith And Understanding - 1963
7202 - Dorothy Prince - Why Not Tonight / Lost A Love - 1963
7203 - Du-Ettes - Mister Steel / I'm Yours - 1963
7204 - Harold Burrage - Long Ways Together - 1963
7205 - Rainbows - Come Rain Come Shine / No Greater Thing Than Love - 1963
7206 - Dorothy Prince - Seek And You'll Find / If I Could Live My Life Over –1963
7207 - Billy "The Kid" Emerson - The Whip Pt. 1 / The Whip Pt. 2 - 1963
7208 - Dorothy Prince - Hey Mister / Every Night - 1964
7208 - Dorothy Prince - Hey Mister / I Lost The Love - 1964
7209 - Du-Ettes - Move On Down The Line / Have You Seen My Baby - 1964
7210 - Harold Burrage - That's A Friend / Everybody's Dancing - 1964
7211 - Harold Burrage - Baby I'm Alright / Fifty Fifty - 1964
7212 - Maurice Dollison - Earth Worm Part 1 / Earth Worm Part 2 - 1964
7213 - Salem Travelers - Joy / Save Me - 1964
7214 - Du-Ettes - I'm Gonna Love You / The Cool Bird - 1964

Soulful Kinda Music – The Rare Soul Bible Volume Two

7215 - Benny Turner - Love Me / You Gonna Miss Me - 1964
7216 - Accents - New Girl / Do You Need A Good Man - 1964
7216 - Accents - New Girl / ? - 1964
7217 - Lucky Cordell - Good Morning Lord / If Jesus Came To Your House - 1965
7219 - Benny Turner - I Don't Know / Good To Me – 1965
7220 - Salem Travelers - Before This Time Another Year / Thing I Used To Do – 1965
7221 - Leroy Dulley - The Army Of The Lord / Halleluja – 1965
7222 - Harold Burrage - Your Friends / Take Me Now – 1965
7223/7224 - Big Daddy Melvin Simpson - You Won't Believe A Word I Say / What Can I Do - 1965
7225 - Harold Burrage - Got To Find A Way / How You Fix You Mouth - 1965
7226 - Big Daddy Simpson - Give Me Back My Ring / Let Your Hair Down Baby - 1965
7227 - Mike Miller & The Reflections - Shake A Tail Feather / He Never Came Back – 1965
7227 - Harrold Burrage – You Made Me So Happy / Things Ain't What They Used To Be (Since You've Been Gone) – 1965
7228 - Andrew Tibbs - I Made A Mistake / Stone Hearted Woman - 1966
7229 - Harold Burrage - More Power To You / A Long Way Together – 1966
7230 - Stacey Johnson - Stand Alone / Don't Try To Fool Me – 1966
7231 - Elmore James - Cry For Me / Take Me Where You Go – 1966
7232 - Ringleaders – Baby, Baby What's Happened To Our Love / Let's Start Over – 1966
7233 - Willie Parker - I've Got To Fight It / Let's Start A Thing Now – 1966
7234 - Harold Burrage - Take Me Now / You Made Me So Happy - 1966
7235 - Willie Parker - Salute To Lovers / Don't Hurt The One You Love - 1967
7236 - Willie Parker - I Live The Life I Love / You Got Your Finger In My Eye – 1967
7237 - Willie Parker - Don't Hurt The One You Love / The Town I Live In – 1967

Music Merchant

1001 - Brenda Holloway - Let Love Grow / Some Quiet Place - 1972
1002 - Just Brothers - Tears Ago / Sliced Tomatoes - 1972
1003 - Jones Girls - Come Back / You're The Only Bargain I've Got - 1972
1004 - Brotherly Love - Mama's Little Baby / Bingo - 1972
1005 – Warlock - You've Been My Rock / The Judgement Day - 1972
1006 - Sweet Rock - Big Train / 1984 - 1972
1007 - Brotherly Love - Growing Pains / I Don't See Me In Your Eyes Anymore - 1972
1008 - Just Brothers - You've Got The Love To Make Me Over / Sliced Tomatoes - 1972
1009 - Jones Girls - Your Love Controls Me / You're The Only Bargain I've Got - 1972
1010 - Just Brothers - You've Got The Love To Make Me Over / Sliced Tomatoes - 1972
1011 - Eloise Laws - Tighten Him Up / You Made Me An Offer I Can't Refuse - 1972
1012 - Smith Connection - I've Been In Love / I Can't Hold On Much Longer - 1973
1013 - Eloise Laws - Love Factory / Stay With Me - 1973
1014 - Smith Connection - The Day You Leave / I've Come To Stay - 1973

Soulful Kinda Music – The Rare Soul Bible Volume Two

1015 - Smith Connection - I'm Bugging Your Phone / I'm Bugging Your Phone (Part 2) - 1973
1016 - Raynel Wynglass - Bar B Q Ribs / Bar B Q Ribs (Inst) – 1973

Johnny Nash

Johnny Nash (born 9-August-1940 in Houston, Texas)

ABC-Paramount 9743 - Out Of Town / A Teenager Sings The Blues – 1956
ABC-Paramount 9844 - The Ladder Of Love / I'll Walk Alone – 1957
ABC-Paramount 9874 - A Very Special Love / Won't You Let Me Share My Love With You - 1957
ABC-Paramount 9894 - My Pledge To You / It's So Easy To Say – 1958
ABC-Paramount 9927 - Please Don't Go / I Lost My Love Last Night – 1958
ABC-Paramount 9942 - Truly Love / You're Looking At Me – 1958

Johnny Nash with Sid Feller's Orchestra

ABC-Paramount 9960 - Almost In Your Arms (Love Song From Houseboat) / Midnight Moonlight – 1958

Paul Anka, George Hamilton IV, Johnny Nash / Don Costa's Orchestra and Chorus

ABC-Paramount 9974 - The Teen Commandments / If You Learn To Pray* - 1958
*flip by Don Costa's Orchestra and Chorus.

Johnny Nash

ABC-Paramount 9989 - Roots Of Heaven / Walk With Faith In Your Heart – 1958
ABC-Paramount 9996 - As Time Goes By / The Voice Of Love - 1959 (some copies issued with picture sleeve)
ABC-Paramount 10026 - And The Angels Sing / Baby, Baby, Baby – 1959
ABC-Paramount 10046 - Take A Giant Step / But Not For Me – 1959
ABC-Paramount 10060 - The Wish / Too Proud – 1959
ABC-Paramount 10076 - A Place In The Sun / Goodbye – 1960
ABC-Paramount 10095 - Never My Love / (You've Got The) Love I Love – 1960
ABC-Paramount 10112 - Let The Rest Of The World Go By / Music Of Love – 1960
ABC-Paramount 10137 - (Looks Like) The End Of The World / We Kissed – 1960
ABC-Paramount 10160 - Kisses / Somebody – 1960
ABC-Paramount 10181 - World Of Tears / Some Of Your Lovin' – 1961
ABC-Paramount 10205 - I Need Someone To Stand By / A House On The Hill – 1961
ABC-Paramount 10212 - A Thousand Miles Away / I Need Someone To Stand By Me – 1961
ABC-Paramount 10230 - I'm Counting On You / I Lost My Baby* - 1961 *also recorded in 1962 by Joey Dee & The Starliters on Roulette 4456.
ABC-Paramount 10251 - Too Much Love / Love's Young Dream – 1961
Warner Bros. 5270 - Don't Take Your Love Away / Moment Of Weakness – 1962
Warner Bros. 5301 - Ol' Man River / My Dear Little Sweetheart – 1962
Warner Bros. 5336 - Cigarettes, Whiskey And Wild, Wild Women / I'm Movin On –

1963
Groove 58-0018 - Helpless / I've Got A Lot To Offer, Darling - 1963 (some copies issued with picture sleeve)
Groove 58-0021 - Deep In The Heart Of Harlem / What Kind Of Love Is This* - 1963 (some copies issued with picture sleeve) *also recorded in 1962 by Joey Dee & The Starliters on Roulette 4438.
Groove 58-0026 - It's No Good For Me / Town Of Lonely Hearts – 1963
Groove 58-0030 - I'm Leaving / Oh Mary Don't You Weep – 1964
Argo 5471 - Talk To Me / Love Ain't Nothin' – 1964
Argo 5479 - Then You Can Tell Me Goodbye / Always – 1964
Argo 5492 - Spring Is Here / Strange Feeling – 1965
Argo 5501 - Teardrops In The Rain / I Know What I Want – 1965
JoDa 102 - Let's Move & Groove (Together) / Understanding – 1965
JoDa 105 - One More Time / Got To Find Her – 1965
JoDa 106 - Somewhere / Big City – 1966
Cadet 5528 - Teardrops In The Rain / Get Myself Together – 1966
Atlantic 2344 - Big City / Somewhere – 1966
MGM 13637 - Amen / Perfumed Flower – 1966
MGM 13683 - Good Goodness / You Never Know - 1967
MGM 13805 - Stormy / (I'm So) Glad You're My Baby - 1967
Jad 207 - Hold Me Tight / Cupid* - 1968 *also recorded in 1961 by Sam Cooke on RCA-Victor 47-883.
Jad 209 - You Got Soul / Don't Cry – 1968

Kim Weston & Johnny Nash

Banyan Tree 1001 - We Try Harder / My Time - 1969

Johnny Nash

Jad 214 - Lovey Dovey / You Got Soul – 1969
Jad 215 - Sweet Charity / People In Love – 1969
Jad 218 - Love And Peace / People In Love – 1969
Jad 220 - Cupid / Hold Me Tight – 1969
Jad 223 - What A Groovey Feeling / You Got Soul (Part 1) – 1970
Janus 136 - Falling In And Out Of Love / You've Got To Change Your Ways – 1970
Epic 10873 - Stir It Up / Cream Puff – 1972
Epic 10902 - I Can See Clearly Now* / How Good It Is - 1972 *also recorded in 1977 by Ray Charles on Atlantic 3443.
Epic 10949 - Stir It Up / Ooh Baby You've Been Good To Me – 1973
Epic 11003 - My Merry-Go-Round / (Oh Jesus) We're Trying To Get Back To You – 1973
Epic 11034 - Ooh What A Feeling / Yellow House – 1973
Epic 11070 - Loving You / Open Up My Heart Again – 1973
Epic 50021 - You Can't Go Halfway / The Very First Time – 1974
Epic 50051 - Beautiful Baby / Celebrate Life – 1974
Epic 50091 - Good Vibrations / The Very First Time – 1975
Epic 50138 - Tears On My Pillow (I Can't Take It) / Beautiful Baby – 1975
Epic 50219 - (What A) Wonderful World / Rock It Baby (We've Got A Date) – 1976
Epic 50386 - Back In Time / That Woman – 1977

Soulful Kinda Music – The Rare Soul Bible Volume Two

Epic 50737 - Closer / Mr. Sea – 1979
Epic 50821 - You're The One / Don't Forget - 1980

Vikki Nelson

Brunswick 84011 - I've Got To Keep Movin' / My Poor Life Blues – 1952
Brunswick 84021 - Toys / I Belong To You – 1952
Premium 402/403 - Bright And Early / By My Side – 1955

Vikki Nelson & Sounds (Members Vikki Nelson, ...)

Vik 0273 - Like A Baby* / I Was A Fool For Leaving - 1957 *also recorded on 3-April-1960 by Elvis Presley and released on his 1960 Lp "Elvis Is Back!" on RCA-Victor LSP-2231.

Vikki Nelson

Vik 0292 - You Can't Get Away From Me / Just One More Smile – 1957
Dauntless 042 - Every Day / I Will Love No One But You - ?
Mala 434 - Baby, I'm Yours / Playboy – 1961

Vicki Nelson / The Starfires

Discovery 41541 - Stoney Face* / Stoney Face (Instrumental)** - ? *also recorded in 1966 by Barbara and The Castles on Ruby-Doo 12. **flip by The Starfires. (The original 45 is vinyl with moulded over label. Bootleg is styrene with stick-on label. L.A. booted with a Delta # 97749)

Label Listings

Neptune

12 - The O'Jays - One Night Affair / There's Someone (Waiting Back Home)
13 - The Corner Boys - Gang War (Don't Make No Sense) / Take It Easy Soul Brother
14 - Bunny Sigler - Great Big Liar / Where Do The Lonely Go
15 - Bunny & Cindy - We're Only Human / Sure Didn't Take Long
16 - The Indigos - Taboo / I Love You (Je Vous Aime Oui Je Fais)
17 - Linda Jones - I'll Be Sweeter Tomorrow / That's When I'll Stop Loving You
18 - The O'Jays - Branded Bad / You're The Best Thing Since Candy
19 - The Vibrations - Expressway To Your Heart / Who's Gonna Help Me Now
20 - The O'Jays - Christmas Ain't Christmas, New Year's Ain't New Year's Without The One You Love / There's Someone Waiting (Back Home)
21 - The Vibrations - Smoke Signals / Who's Gonna Help Me Now
22 - The O'Jays - Deeper (In Love With You) / I've Got The Groove
23 - The Three Degrees - What I See / Reflections of Yesterday
24 - Bunny Sigler and Cindy Scott - Conquer The World Together / We're Only

Soulful Kinda Music – The Rare Soul Bible Volume Two

Human
25 - Bunny Sigler - Don't Stop What You're Doing / Where Do The Lonely Go
26 - Linda Jones - Oh Baby You Move Me / Can You Blame Me
27 - Cupit - Trainman (Akiwawa) / Squeeze Your Knees
28 - The Vibrating Vibrations - Surprise Party For Baby / Right On Brother - Right On
29 - The New Direction - Ride My Carousel / Didn't We
30 - Billy Paul - Mrs. Robinson / Let's Fall In Love All Over
31 - The O'Jays - Looky Looky (Look At Me Girl) / Let Me In Your World
32 - The Indigos - Keep Our Love In Sunshine / Keep It In
33 - The O'Jays - Christmas Ain't Christmas, New Year's Ain't New Year's Without The One You Love / Just Can't Get Enough
34 - ?
35 - New Direction - Feelin' Good / ?

Nola

701 - The Medallions - You Are Irresistible / Why Do You Look At Me
702 - Charles Brown - Standing On The Outside / I'll Love You
703 - Warren Lee - Anna / Rev Unk
704 - Eddie Bo - Everybody's Somebody's Fool / Heap See
705 - Betty Taylor - I'm Going Home / You're A Winner
706 - Smokey Johnson - It Ain't My Fault / Part 2
707 - Curley Moore - Soul Train / Please Do Something For Me
708 - Willie Tee - Teasin' You / Walkin' Up A One Way Street
709 - Jimmie J. - The Jet / No More
710 - ?
711 - Warren Lee Taylor - Every Day, Every Hour / Key To Your Door
717 - Smokey Johnson – Dirty Red / ?
718 - ?
719 - ?
720 - Smokey Johnson - I Can't Help It / Part 2
721 - Robert Parker - Barefootin' / Let's Go, Baby (Where The Action Is)
722 - Smokey Johnson - Whip It / ?
723 - ?
724 - Raymond Parker - Ring Around The Roses / She's Coming Home
725 - Frankie Cherval - To Make A Big Man Cry / A Girl Has A Right
726 - Robert Parker - Scratch / Happy Feet
727 - Smokey Johnson - It Ain't My Fault / Dirty Red
728 - Jerry Foucha - Music Time / Come On, Baby
729 - Robert Parker - Tip Toe / Soul Kind Of Loving
730 - Robert Parker - C.C. Rider / Letter To Santa
731 - Marie Boubarere - I Know / I'm Going Home
732 - Smokey & Matt - Did You Hear What I Saw / Did You Hear What I Saw
733 - Robert Parker - Yak, Yak, Yak / Secret Service (Makes Me Nervous)
734 - ?
735 - Robert Parker - Foxy Mama / Everybody's Hip-Hugging
736 - Bates Sisters - Symphony For The Broken Hearted / So Broken Hearted
737 - Willie Tee - My Heart Remembers / Please Don't Go

Soulful Kinda Music – The Rare Soul Bible Volume Two

738 - Robert Parker - I Caught You In A Lie / Holdin' Out
739 - Robert Parker - Soul Sister / Barefootin' Boogaloo
740 - Robert Parker - Bow Legs / Boss Lovin'
741 - Marlyn Barbarin - Just A Teenager / One Little Word
742 - Robert Parker / The Wardell Quezerque Band - Funky Soul Train / Robert &
WQ's Train (Instrumental)

Nosnibor

1001 - Cleveland Robinson - A Man Goes Out / Inspiration
1002 - Cleveland Robinson, Jr. - Love Is A Trap / A Loaf Of Bread
1003 - Cleveland Robinson - Woman In Motion / My Place In The World
1003 - Cleveland Robinson - Boy / Woman In Motion
1004 - Cleveland Robinson - Work Song / A Man Gets Tired
1005 - Cleveland Robinson - This Is America / If I Had A Hammer
1006 - Cleveland Robinson - Boy / Let It Be Me
1007 - Cleveland Robinson - Take A Fools Advice / Mr. Wishing Well
1008 - Cleveland Robinson - Loch Lomond / A Loaf Of Bread
1009 - Cleveland Robinson - Jungle Dollar / Understanding
1010 - Cleveland Robinson - Loving Time / Let It Be Me
1011 - Cleveland Robinson - Boy / Let Somebody To Love
1012 - Cleveland Robinson - Boy / Let Somebody To Love
1723 - Cleveland Robinson - Jungle Dollar / No One's Gonna Take Your Place

The following singles are possibly also Nosnibor releases, can anyone confirm this
with catalogue numbers ?

? - Cleveland Robinson - My Inspiration / A Man Goes Out
? - Cleveland Robinson - X-mas Time / An Artist's Hand
? - Cleveland Robinson - Gonna Go Back Home / You

O'Kaysions

The Kays (members Wayne Pittman, Steve Watson, Donne Weaver, Gerald Toler, and Jimmy Hinnant)

JCP 1007 - Hey Girl / Shout - 1964

The O'Kaysions (members Donnie Weaver, Steve Watson, Jimmy Hinnant, Eddie Dement, Wayne Pittman and Gerald Toler)

North State 1001 - Girl Watcher / Deal Me In - 1968 (one thousand copies were issued with a picture sleeve)
ABC 11094 - Girl Watcher / Deal Me In - 1968
Sparton 1676 - Girl Watcher / Deal Me In - 1968 (Canadian release)
ABC 11153 - Love Machine / Dedicated To The One I Love - 1968
ABC 11207 - Colors / Twenty Four Hours From Tulsa - 1969
Cotillion 44089 - Watch Out Girl / Happiness - 1970
Cotillion 44134 - Life And Things / Travelin' Life - 1971
Roulette 130 - Girl Watcher / Deal Me In - 1973
I-Katcher 821 - Girl Watcher / Boy Watcher /// Freedom Lady - 1982

The O'Kaysions / The Esquires

Collectables Col 031297 - Girl Watcher / Get On Up* - ? *flip by The Esquires

Ep's

ABC 664 - Girl Watcher - 1968 Tracks: How Are You Fixed For Love? / Dedicated To The One I Love / The Soul Clap /// Little Miss Flirt / Sunday Will Never Be The Same / My Baby's Love.

The Olympics

The Ward Brothers (family group comprising of Walter Ward, His Father and three uncles) early 1950's gospel group.

The West Coast Gospel Singers (members Walter Ward, Eddie Lewis, James Lloyd and Jimmy Ward)

The Challengers (members Walter Ward, Eddie Lewis, Marcus Banks, Freddie Lewis and Nathan ?) 1954 group line-up.

The Challengers (members Walter Ward, Eddie Lewis, Marcus Banks, Charles Fizer and Walter Hammond)

Melatone 1002 - I Can Tell / The Mambo Beat - 1958

Soulful Kinda Music – The Rare Soul Bible Volume Two

The Olympics (members Walter Ward, Eddie Lewis, Charles Fizer, and Walter Hammond (younger brother of Clay Hammond). Melvin King replaced Charles Fizer in 1958 and remained in group as a replacement Walter Hammond when Charles Fizer returned in 1959. Charles Fizer (born 3-June-1940, died ?-August-1965 - cause: was killed during the Watts rioting) replaced by Julius "Mack Starr" McMichael, former member of The Paragons. Melvin King left in 1966. Kenny Sinclair former member of The Six Teens joined in 1970)

Demon 1508 - Western Movies / Well! - 1958
Demon 1512 - (I Wanna) Dance With The Teacher / Ev'rybody Needs Love – 1958
Demon 1514 - Chicken / Your Love – 1959
Arvee 562 - Private Eye / (Baby) Hully Gully – 1959
Arvee 595 - Big Boy Pete* / The Slop -1960 *originally recorded in 1959 by Don & Dewey on Speciality 659.
Arvee 5006 - Shimmy Like Kate / Workin' Hard – 1960
Arvee 5020 - Dance By The Light Of The Moon / Dodge City – 1960

The Olympics / Cappy Lewis

Arvee 5023 - Little Pedro / Bull Fight* - 1961 *Flip By Cappy Lewis.

The Olympics

Arvee 5031 - Stay Where You Are / Dooley – 1961
Titan 1718 - Cool Short / The Chicken – 1961

Jody Reynolds / The Olympics

Titan 1801 - Endless Sleep / Western Movies* - 1961 *flip by The Olympics. (some copies issued with picture sleeve)

The Olympics

Arvee 5044 - The Stomp / Mash Them Taters – 1961
Arvee 5051 - Everybody Likes To Cha Cha Cha / Twist – 1962
Arvee 5056 - Baby, Its Hot / The Scotch – 1962
Arvee 5073 - What'd I Say Part 1 / What'd I Say Part 2 – 1963

Jody Reynolds / The Olympics

Liberty 54514 - Endless Sleep / Western Movies* - 1963 *Flip By The Olympics.

The Olympics

Zee 103 - Western Movies / ? - 196? (does anyone know if this was a legal reissue?)
Tri Disc 105 - Return Of Big Boy Pete / Return Of The Watusi – 1962
Tri Disc 106 - The Bounce / Fireworks - 1963
Tri Disc 107 - Dancin' Holiday / Do The Slauson Shuffle – 1963
Tri Disc 110 - Bounce Again / A New Dancin' Partner – 1963
Tri Disc 112 - Broken Hip / So Goodbye – 1963

Soulful Kinda Music – The Rare Soul Bible Volume Two

Duo Disc 104 - The Boogler (Part 1) / The Boogler (Part 2) -1964
Duo Disc 105 - Return Of Big Boy Pete / Return Of The Watusi – 1964
Arvee 6501 - Stay Where You Are / Big Boy Pete '65 – 1965
Loma 2010 - Rainin' In My Heart / I'm Comin' Home – 1965
Loma 2013 - Good Lovin' / Olympic Shuffle (Instrumental) - 1965 (the instrumental tracks to The Blossoms' "Latin Boy Shuffle").
Loma 2017 - Baby I'm Yours / No More Will I Cry – 1965
Mirwood 5504 - Secret Agents / We Go Together (Pretty Baby) – 1966
Mirwood 5513 - Secret Agents / Mine Exclusively – 1966
Mirwood 5523 - Baby Do The Philly Dog / Western Movies – 1966
Mirwood 5525 - The Duck / The Bounce – 1966
Mirwood 5529 - The Same Old Thing / I'll Do A Little Bit More – 1966
Mirwood 5533 - (Baby) Hully Gully / Big Boy Pete – 1967

The Olympics / The Olmpics

Parkway 6003 - Good Things / Lookin' For Love - 1967 (D. J. copies have been found with the group name mis-spelled on flip side)

The Olympics

Parkway 6003 - Good Things / Lookin' For Love – 1967
Jubilee 5674 - The Cartoon Song / Things That Made Me Laugh – 1969

The Olympics (members Walter Ward, Kenny Sinclair (former member of The Bagdads), Mack Starr,)

Warner Brothers 7369 - Please, Please, Please / Girl, You're My Kind Of People – 1970

The Olympics

Songsmith 1 - There Ain't No Way / Three Billion People – 1971
Eric 135 - Big Boy Pete / Dance By The Light Of The Moon – 1973

The Olympics (members Walter Ward, Kenny Sinclair, Mack Starr, ...)

Pride 1024 - The Apartment / Worm In Your Wheatgerm – 1973
MGM 14505 - The Apartment / Worm In Your Wheatgerm – 1973

The Olympics

Mac Winn 102 - I Feel Your Love (Coming On) / Papa Will - ?
Crestview 20010 - The Duck / The Bounce - ?
Lost-Nite 311 - Big Boy Pete / Mine Exclusively - ?
Collectables Col 030407 - Western Movies / Endless Sleep - ?

Soulful Kinda Music – The Rare Soul Bible Volume Two

The Olympics / Jody Reynolds

Era 026 - The Bounce / Endless Sleep* - ? *flip by Jody Reynolds.

Label Listings

Okeh (from 1962 to 1970)

7168 - Major Lance - Delilah / Everytime
7169 - Sherry Sisters - Stay Away From Bobby / Dancing With Tears In My Eyes
7170 - Jerry McCain - Hop Stroll / Turn The Lights On Popeye
7171 - Ted Taylor - Be Ever Wonderful / That's Life I Guess
7172 - Belgianettes - The Train / My Blue Heaven
7173 - Sheppards - Walkin' / Pretend You're Still Mine
7174 - Rex Garvin & Mighty Cravers - Emulsified / Go little Willie
7175 - Major Lance - The Monkey Time / Mama Didn't Know
7176 - Ted Taylor - Him Instead Of Me / You Have Me Nothing To Go On
7177 - Artists - I Need Your love / What'll I Do
7178 - Billy Butler & Enchanters - Found True Love / Lady Love
7179 - Ted Taylor - Ill Make It Up To You / It Ain't Like That No More
7180 - Unreleased
7181 - Major Lance - Hey Little Girl / Crying In The Rain
7182 - Roy Lee Johnson - Busybody / Nobody Does Something For Nothing
7183 - Gerald Sims - Cool Breeze / There Must Be An Answer
7184 - Clifford Davis - Finders Keepers Losers Weepers / Take it light
7185 - Dr Feelgood - The Doctors Boogie / Blang Dong
7186 - Jimmy Church - The Hurt / Only You
7187 - Major Lance - Um Um Um Um Um Um / Sweet Music
7188 - Opals - Does It Matter / Tender Love
7189 - Walter Jackson - Thats What Mama Say / What Would You Do
7190 - Ted Taylor - So Hard / Need You Home
7191 - Major Lance - The Matador / Gonna Get Married
7192 - Billy Butler & Enchanters - Gotta Get Away / I'm Just A Man
7193 - Ted Taylor - Get My Hands On Some Lovin' / I'll Leave It Up To You
7194 - Kayvettes - Im Not Sorry For You / You Broke Your Promise
7195 - Charades - Can't Make It Without You / Love Of My Life
7196 - Ernie Harris - Hold on / Betty
7197 - Major Lance - Girls / It Ain't No Use
7198 - Ted Taylor - Somebody's Always Trying / Top Of The World
7199 - ?
7200 - Major Lance - Think Nothing About It / Its Alright (Allocated a number, but was it ever issued ?)
7201 - Billy Butler & Enchanters - Can't Live Without Her / My Heart Is Hurtin'
7202 - Opals - You Can't Hurt Me No More / Youre Gonna Be Sorry
7203 - Major Lance - Rhythm / Please Don't Say No More
7204 - Walter Jackson - It's All Over / Lee Cross
7205 - Vibrations - Watusi Time / Sloop Dance

Soulful Kinda Music – The Rare Soul Bible Volume Two

7206 - Ted Taylor - If It Wasn't For You / Don't Deceive me
7207 - Billy Butler & Chanters - Nevertheless / My Sweet Woman
7208 - Dave "Baby" Cortez - Popping Popcorn / The Question (do you love me)
7209 - Major Lance - I'm So Lost / Sometimes I Wonder
7210 - Keystoners - After I Propose / Magic Kiss
7211 - Little Joe Cook - Meet Me Down In Soulsville / You Make Me Want To Cry
7212 - Vibrations - Keep On Keeping On / Hello Happiness
7213 - Marlina Mars - Is It Love That Really Counts In The Long Run / Just Another Dance
7214 - Ted Taylor - So Long Bye Bye / I Love You Yes I Do
7215 - Walter Jackson - Special Love / Suddenly I'm All Alone
7216 - Major Lance - Come See / You Belong To Me My Love
7217 - Artistics - Patty Cake / In Another Mans Arms
7218 - Marie Knight - Nothing / Come Tomorrow
7219 - Walter Jackson - Blowing In The Wind / Welcome Home
7220 - Vibrations - Ain't Love That Way / End Up Crying
7521 - Billy Bultler & Chanters - I Can't Work No Longer / Tomorrow Is Another Day
7222 - Ted Taylor - Ramblin' Rose / I'm So Satisfied
7223 - Major Lance - Ain't It A Shame / Gotta Get Away
7224 – Opals - I'm so afraid / Restless Days
7225 - Otis Williams & Charms - Baby You Turn Me On / Love Don't Grow On Trees
7226 - Major Lance - Too Hot To Hold / Dark & Lonely
7227 - Billy Butler - You Ain't Ready (You Make Me Think) / You're Gonna Be Sorry
7228 - Vibrations - Talkin' Bout Love / It You Only Knew
7229 - Walter Jackson - I'll Keep On Trying / Where Have All The Flowers Gone
7230 - Vibrations - Misty / Finding Out The Hard May
7231 - Ted Taylor - Walking Out Of Her Life/Stay Away From My Baby
7232 - Artistics - This Heart Of Mine / I'll Come Running
7233 - Major Lance - Everybody Loves A Good Time / I Just Can't Help it
7234 - Teacho & Students - Chills And Fever / Same Old Beat
7235 - Otis Williams - I Fall To Pieces / Gotta Get Myself Together
7236 - Walter Jackson - One Heart Lonely / Funny
7237 - Joyce Davis - Hello Heartaches Goodbye Love / Along Came You
7238 - ?
7239 - S.O. Reeder - I Want To Know / Just In Time
7240 - Ted Taylor - Daddy's Baby / Mercy Have Pity
7241 - Vibrations - Canadian Sunset / The Story Of A Starry Night
7242 - Tommy Tate - Are You From Heaven / I'm Taking on Pain
7243 - Artistics - Loveland / So Much Love In My Heart
7244 - Titus Turner - Eye To Eye / What Kinda Deal Is This
7245 - Billy Butler & Chanters - Right Track / Boston Monkey
7246 - Chymes - I Got Loving / Let's Try It Aqain
7247 - Walter Jackson - It's An Uphill Climb To The Bottom / Tear For Tear
7248 - Otis Williams - I Got Loving / Welcome Home
7249 - Vibrations - Forgive & Forget / Gonna Get Along Without You Now
7250 - Major Lance - Investigate / Little Young Lover
7251 - Little Richard - Well / Poor Dog (who cant wag his own tail)
7252 - Ted Taylor - Big Wheel / No One But You
7253 - Tommyy Tate - Big Blue Diamonds / Lover's Reward
7254 - S.Q. Reeder - Tell All The World About You / Two Ton Tessie

Soulful Kinda Music – The Rare Soul Bible Volume Two

7255 - Major Lance - It's The Beat / You'll Want Me Back
7256 - Walter Jackson - After You There Can Be Nothing / Mv Funny Valentine
7257 - Vibrations - Soul A Go-Go / And I Love Her
7258 - Sam Scott - A Change Is Gonna Come / Down Hearted Blues
7259 - Larry Williams - I'd Rather Fight Than Switch / This Old Heart Is Lonely
7260 - Walter Jackson - Not You / Corner In The Sun
7261 - Otis Williams - Ain't Gonna Walk Your Dog No More / Your Sweet Love
7262 - Little Richard - I Need Love / The Commandments Of Love
7263 - Johnny Guitar Watson - Keep 0n Lovin' You / South Like West
7264 - Hank & Rover - Lot To Be Done / Rock Down On My Shoe
7265 - Herbie's People - Semi Detached Surburban Mr Jones / Residential Area
7266 - Major Lance - Ain't No Soul (in these old shoes) / I Wait Till I Get you In My Arms
7267 - Roy Thompson - Sookie Sookie / Love You Say
7268 - Carl Douglas - Crazy Feeling / Keep It To Myself
7269 - The Wolf Man - Stranqe / Back Side
7270 - Johnny Guitar Watson - Wolfman / Hold On I'm Coming
7271 - Little Richard - I Don't Want To Discuss It / Hurry Sundown
7272 - Walter Jackson - Speak Her Name / They Don't Give Medals
7273 - Triumphs - Workin' / Memories
7274 - Larry Williams & Johnny Watson - Quitter Never Wins / Mercy Mercy
7275 - Washington Smith - Fat Cat / Don't Take Your Love
7276 - Vibrations - Pick Me / You Better Beware
7277 - Sandi Sheldon - You're Gonna Make Me Love You / Baby You're Mine
7278 - Little Richard - Never Gonna Let You Go / Don't Deceive Me
7279 - Cookie Jackson - Your Good Girl's Gonna Go Bad / Things Go Better With Love
7280 - Larry Williams - You Ask For One Good Reason / I Am The One
7281 - Larry Williams & Johnny Watson - Two For The Price Of One / Too Late
7282 - Link Wray & Wraymen - Hambone / Rumble Mambo
7283 - Roy Thompson - Keep On Dancing / Something Greater Than Love
7284 - Major Lance - Wait Till I Get You In My Arms / You Don't Want Me No More
7285 - Walter Jackson - My One Chance To Make It / Deep In Heart 0f Harlem
7286 - Little Richard - A Litte Bit Of Somethinq / Money
7287 - Carl Douglas & Big Stampede - Let The Birds Sing / Somethinq For Nothing
7288 - Dottie Jean - Sweet Daddy Wouldn't Do That / Let Me Go Lover
7289 - Seven Souls - I Still Love You / I'm No Stranger
7290 - Johnny Watson - I'd Rather Be Your Baby / Soul Fool
7291 - Triumphs - I'm Coming To Your Rescue / The World Owes Me A Lovin'
7292 - Cookie Jackson - Fresh Out Of Texas / Suffer
7293 - Autoqraphs - I Can Do It / I'm Gonna Show You How To Love Me
7294 - Larry Williams - Boss Lovin' / Just Because
7295 - Walter Jackson - My Ship Is Comin' In / A Cold Cold Winter
7296 - Franky Coe - Game Of Love / Game Of Love Part 2
7297 - Vibrations - Come To Yourself / Toqether
7298 - Major Lance - Forever / Without A Doubt
7299 - Malcolm Hayes - Baby Please Don't Leave Me / I Can Make It Without You Baby
7300 - Larry Williams & Johnny Watson - Find Yourself Someone To Love / Nobody

Soulful Kinda Music – The Rare Soul Bible Volume Two

7301 – Fundamentals - I Wouldn't Blame You / Let Me Show It To You
7302 - Johnny Watson - She'll Blow Your Mind
7303 - Ken Williams - Come Back / Baby If You Were Gone
7304 - Margie Joseph - See Me / Why Does A Man Have To Lie
7305 - Walter Jackson - Evervthing / Road To Ruin
7306 - ?
7307 - Johnny Robinson - Gone But Not Forgotten / I Need Your Love So Bad
7308 - Detroit City Limits - Honey Chile / Ninety Eight Cents Plus Tax
7309 - ?
7310 - Sandra Phillips - I Wish I Had Known / Hoping You'll Come Back
7311 - Vibrations   Love In Them There Hills / Remember The Rain
7312 - Little Foxes - Love Made To Order / So Glad Your Love Don't Change
7313 - Margie Joseph - Matter 0f Life Or Death / Show Me
7314 - Major Harris - Just Love Me / Loving You More
7315 - Ernie Lucas - What Would I Do Without You / Love Thief
7316 - Leah Dawson - Good Man / You Got To Change (your evil ways)
7317 - Johnny Robinson - Poor Man / When A Man Cries
7318 - Cane Black - Hold On To What You Got / Sometimes
7319 - Tangeers - Let Mv Heart And Soul Be Free / What's The Use Of Me Trying
7320 - Watson T Brown - Some Lovin' / Home Is Where Your Heart Lies
7321 - Ernie Lucas - What We Pay For Love / Nothing Can Separate Me From Your Love
7322 - The Brothers Soul - I Shall Be Released / Look Ahead
7323 - ?
7324 - Variations - Empty Words / Yesterday Is Gone
7325 - Little Richard - Lucille / Whole Lotta Shakin' Goin' On
7326 - Different Strokes - Everyday People / Sing A Simple Song
7327 - Major Harris - Like A Rolling Stone / Call Me Tomorrow
7328 - Johnny Robinson - You've Been With Me / Green Green Grass Of Home
7329 - Carstairs - He Who Picks A Rose / Yesterday
7330 - Black Velvet - Just Came Back / Come On Heart
7331 - Cheers - Take Me To Paradise / I Made Up My Mind
7332 - Johnny Otis Show - You Can Depend On Me / The Watts Breakaway
7333 - George Freeman - All Right Now / You lied I Cried Love Died
7334 - ?
7335 - Bernice Willis - Breakfast In Bed / Confidence
7336 - Azie Mortimer - One Way Love (is a wrong way love) / You Can't Take It Away
7337 - Azie Mortimer - I Don't Care / Prove It
7338 – Cheers - Can't Let You Do It / I'm Glad I Waited

One-Derful

4803 - Mckinley Mitchell - I Found An Angel / ? - 1962
4804 - Mckinley Mitchell - The Town I Live In / No Love (Like My Love) - 1962
4806 - Betty Everett - I Got A Claim On You / Your Love Is Important To Me - 1962
4807 - Benny Turner - Come Back Home / When I'm Gone - 1962
4808 - Mckinley Mitchell - All Of A Sudden / I Found An Angel - 1963
4809 - Mark Fours - Washington And Lee Swing / Robert E. Lee - 1963
4810 - Mckinley Mitchell - I'm So Glad / All Of A Sudden - 1963

Soulful Kinda Music – The Rare Soul Bible Volume Two

4811 - Five Du-Tones - Please Change Your Mind / The Flea - 1963
4812 - Mckinley Mitchell - Darling That's What You Said / Never Gonna Break My Heart - 1963
4814 - Five Du-Tones - Come Back Baby / Dry Your Eyes – 1963
4815 - Five Du-Tones - Shake A Tail Feather / Divorce Court – 1963
4816 - Mary Silvers - I / Power Of Love - 1963
4817 - Mckinley Mitchell - Handful Of Sorrows / A Bit Of Soul - 1963
4818 - Five Du-Tones - The Gouster / Monkey See - Monkey Do - 1964
4819 - Jay Jordan - Man Of The Town / Highest Quality - 1964
4820 - Rockmasters - My Lonely One (Where Are You) / Wonderful Thing (Love) - 1964
4821 - Five Du-Tones - Nobody But (My Baby) / That's How I Love You - 1964
4822 - Mckinley Mitchell - Tell It Like It Is / Uncle Willie - 1964
4823 - Betty Everett - I'll Be There / Please Love Me - 1964
4824 - Five Du-Tones - The Cool Bird / The Chicken Astronaut - 1964
4825 - Lucky Laws - Broken Heart / Who Is She - 1964
4826 - Mckinley Mitchell - You Know I've Tried / It's Spring - 1965
4827 - Du-Ettes - Lonely Days / Please Forgive Me - 1965
4828 - Five Du-Tones - Sweet Lips / Let Me Love You - 1965
4829 - Bobby Star - Hey Bobby / Hey Cinderella - 1965
4830 - Joe & Mack - Prettiest Girl / Don't You Worry - 1965
4831 - Five Du-Tones - We Want More / The Woodbine Twine - 1965
4832 - Mckinley Mitchell - I'm Ready / Watch Over Me - 1965
4833 - Accents - Who You Gonna Love / You Better Think Again - 1965
4834 - Otis Clay - There Is A Crowd / Flame In Your Heart - 1966
4835 - Sharpees - Do The 45 / Make Up Your Mind - 1966
4836 - Five Du-Tones - Mountain Of Love / Outside The Record Hop - 1966
4837 - Otis Clay - I Paid The Price / Tired Of Falling In (& Out Of Love) - 1966
4838 - Beverly Shaffer - Even The Score / Where Will You Be Boy - 1966
4839 - Sharpees - Tired Of Being Lonely / Just To Please You – 1966
4840 - Beverly Shaffer - I Simply Love Him / When I Think About You - 1966
4841 - Otis Clay - I Testify / I'm Satisfied - 1966
4842/4843 - Sharpees - I've Got A Secret / Make Up Your Mind - 1967
4844 - Gordon Keith - I'll Try To Please You / This Is How I Feel - 1967
4845 - Sharpees - My Girl Jean / The Sock - 1967
4846 - Otis Clay - It's Easier Said Than Done / Flame In Your Heart – 1967
4846 - Otis Clay - It's Easier Said Than Done / Must I Keep On Waiting – 1967
4847 - Liz Lands - One Man's Poison / Don't Shut Me Out - 1967
4848 - Otis Clay - That's How It Is / Show Place - 1967
4849 - Admirations - Wait Till I Get To Know You / (Instrumental) - 1967
4850 - Otis Clay - A Lasting Love / Got To Find A Way – 1967
4851 - Admirations - Don't Leave Me / All For You - 1967
4852 - Otis Clay - Don't Pass Me By - That'll Get You What You Want - 1967
4853 - Redemption Singers - Black Is Beautiful / Hone In The Bee-O - 1968

Ovide

222 - Archie Bell & The Drells - She's My Woman, She's My Girl / Yankee Dance
223 - The T.S.U. Tornadoes - The Toronado / A Thousand Wonders

Soulful Kinda Music – The Rare Soul Bible Volume Two

224 - The Soul Meditations - The Bird / ?
225 - ?
226 - Archie Bell - A Soldier's Prayer / One In One
227 - The T. S. U. Toronadoes - You're Mine / Back After The News
228 - Archie Bell & The Drells - Tighten Up / Dog Eat Dog
229 - The 4 Avalons - (I Dont Wanna Be A) Playboy / The Congar
230 - The T. S. U. Toronadoes - Song For A Princess / Work On It
231 - The Americans Of '68 - Baby Baby Baby / Come On Mama
232 - The Masters Of Houston - Please Wait For Me / Love Loves Love
233 - The T. S. U. Toronadoes - What Good Am I / Getting The Corners
234 - The African Echoes - Zulu Lunchbag / Big Time
235 - ?
236 - The Ambassadors Of Soul - Cool Sticks Beat Pt 1 / Pt 2
237 - Mark Putney - Todays Man / Don't Come Around Here Anymore
238 - The Entertainers - Po Boy / Why?
238 - The Ambassadors Of Soul - Gotta Find Her / Cool Sticks Beat
239 - ?
240 - Calvin Owens & The Fascinators - The Cat / Saw Dust Alley
241 - The Masters Of Soul - Do You Really Love Me / By The Time I Get To Phoenix
242 - James Taylor - Love With Hope / Everything About You
243 - The T.S.U. Tornadoes - My Thing Is A Moving Thing / I Still Love You (also on Volt 4030)
244 - Charles Berry And The Cherries - Isn't That Something / Father Of The Land
245 - Pete Mayes - A Crazy Woman / Moving Out
246 - ?
247 - The Masters Of Soul - Count The Times / I Need You
248 - Acres Of Grass - Football / Sondra
248 - Acres Of Grass - Football / Football (Promo without vocals)
249 - Sebastian Williams - Get Your Point Over / I Don't Care What Mama Said
250 - The T. S. U. Toronadoes - Only Inside / Nothing Can Stop Me
251 - The Masters Of Soul - The Vow / Right On
252 - Bobo Mr. Soul - H.L.I.C. / Answer To The Want Ads
253 - The Masters Of Soul - Sad Face / Lord Bless My Woman
254 - ?
255 - ?
256 - Bad Albert (Coleman) - No Money Down / Claba Daba
257 - Pete Mayes - Peace / Lowdown Feeling
258 - Bobo Mr. Soul - Hitchhike To Heartbreak Road / She's My Wonder Woman
301 - Ja' Nai - Thinking Of You / Me And My Man
002 - Pete Mays - Crazy Woman / My Life

Soulful Kinda Music – The Rare Soul Bible Volume Two

Bobby Paris

The Golden Keys (Members Bobby Paris, ...) Quintet Circa 1956 ~ 1957

Bobby Paris (Born New York City, New York)

Indigo 13007 - Rockin' Concerto / How Did Your Vacation Go – 1960
International Guild 13007 - Rockin' Concerto / How Did Your Vacation Go - 1960
Magenta 03 - Dark Continent (Part 1) / Dark Continent (Part 2) - 1961 (All Instruments Played By Bobby Paris)
Jolar 1001 - Is It You / Wishing Well - 1962
Jairick 204 - Are You The One / Torch Is Out - 1963
Chattahoochee 631 - Little Miss Dreamer / Who Needs You - 1963
Chattahoochee 672 - Love Passed Me By / Fight - 1965
Cameo 396 - Night Owl / Tears On My Pillow - 1966
Capitol 5929 - I Walked Away / Kansas City - 1967
Tetragrammaton 1504 - Per-So-Nal-Ly / Tragedy - 1968
Tetragrammaton 1509 - Bye, Bye Blackbird / Let Me Show You The Way - 1968
Tetragrammaton 1517 - Let The Sunshine In / You - 1969
Capitol P-3592/Pro 6659 - Baby, Spread Your Love On Me (Mono) / Baby, Spread Your Love On Me (Stereo) - 1973 (Promo Issue Only)
Capitol 3592 - Baby, Spread Your Love On Me / You're A Friend - 1973
Capitol 3664 - Baby, Spread Your Love On Me / You're A Friend - 1973
Capitol 3727 - Love Looks So Good On You / Day Dreamer - 1973

Robert Parker

Robert Parker (born 14-October-1930 in New Orleans. Saxophonist / vocalist / bandleader. In Professor Longhair's (Henry Roeland Byrd) band from 1949)

Ron 327 - All Nite Long (Part 1) / All Nite Long (Part 2) - 1959
Ron 331 - Walkin' / Across The Track - 1960
Imperial 5842 - Mash Potatoes All Night Long / Twistin' Out Of Space - 1962
Imperial 5889 - You're Looking Good / Little Things Mean A Lot - 1962
Imperial 5916 - Please Forgive Me / You Got It - 1963

Robert Parker & Band

Booker 506 - The Laughing Monkey / Let's Do The Thing - ?

Robert Parker

Nola 721 - Barefootin' */ Let's Go Baby (Where The Action Is) - 1966 *covered in 1986 by Pete Townshend on ATCO 7-99499.
Nola 724 - Ring Around The Roses / She's Coming Home - 1966
Nola 726 - Happy Feet / The Scratch - 1966

Soulful Kinda Music – The Rare Soul Bible Volume Two

Nola 729 - Tip Toe / Soul Kind Of Loving - 1966
Nola 730 - A Letter To Santa / C. C. Rider - 1966
Nola 733 - Yak Yak Yak / Secret Agents - 1967
Nola 735 - Everybody's Hip-Hugging / Foxy Mama - 1967
Nola 738 - I Caught You In A Lie / Holdin' Out - 1967
Silver Fox 12 - You Shakin' Things Up / You See Me - 1969
SSS International 819 - Hiccup / Rockin' Pneumonia - 1970

Robert Parker / Jesse Gresham Plus 3

Head 1050 - Barefootin' / Shootin' The Grease* - 1972 *flip by Jesse Gresham Plus 3.

Robert Parker

Island 015 - Get Ta Steppin' / Get Right On Down - 1974
Island 044 - Give Me The Country Side Of Life / It's Hard But It's Fair - 1975
Island 074 - A Little Bit Of Something / Better Luck In The Summer - 1976

Harold Dorman / Robert Parker

Collectables Col 3031 - Mountain Of Love / Barefootin'* - ? *Flip By Robert Parker.

Aaron Neville / Robert Parker

Good Old Gold 003 - Tell It Like It Is / Barefootin'* - ? *Flip By Robert Parker

Winfield Parker

Winfield Parker (The Skydells Band)

Atco 6474 - What Do You Say / Sweet Little Girl - 1967

Little Winfield Parker

Ru-Jac 07 - One Of These Mornings / My Love For You - ?

Wynfield Parker

Ru-Jac 0017 - I Love You Just The Same / My Love - ?
Ru-Jac 0019 - Go Away Playgirl / Wandering - ?
Ru-Jac 0020 - Sweet Little Girl / What Do You Say? - 1968 (With The Shyndells Band)
(Please Note That Ru-Jac 0020 Is Also A Release By The Caressors Titled "I Can't Stay Away / Who Can It Be").
Ru-Jac 0022 - She's So Pretty / Oh My Love - 1968 (Label Is From Baltimore)
Ru-Jac 0024 - Fallen Star / I Love You Just The Same - 1968
Ru-Jac 0024 - I Love You Just The Same / Oh My Love - 1968
Ru-Jac 200 - Funkey Party / Oh My Love - 1968 Nov.
Ru-Jac 45007 - Rockin' In The Barnyard / ? - ?

Soulful Kinda Music – The Rare Soul Bible Volume Two

Arctic 151 - Shake That Thing / Brand New Start - 1969
Wand 11218 - I'm Wondering / Will There Ever Be Another Love For Me - 1970
Spring 116 - S. O. S. (Stop Her On Sight) / I'm On My Way - 1971
Spring 126 - Starvin' */ 28 Ways (She Loves Me) - 1972 *Co-Written By Bunny Sigler
G. S. F. 6883 - Baby, Don't Get Hooked On Me / Trust Me - 1972
P & L 62142 - My Love For You / I Wanna Be With You - ?

Best Of Both Worlds (Members Winfield Parker, ...)

Calla 5002 - I Want The World To Know / Momma Bakes Biscuits - 1975 (Winfield
Parker Lead Vocals)

George Pepp

Coleman 8 - The Feeling Is Real / ? - ?
Coleman 79 - Say It Once In A While / You Gotta Get A Wig - ?
Masque 2936 - For You / He Created Woman - ?

The Fabulous Peps

Tom Storm & The Peps

Ge Ge 501 - That's The Way Love Is / I Love You - 1965

The Peps

Ge Ge 503 - This Love I Have For You / She's Going To Leave You - 1965
The Peps

D - Town 1049 - You Never Had It So Good / Detroit, Michigan - 1965
D - Town 1060 - Thinking About You / This I Pray - 1965

The Fabulous Peps

D - Town 1065 - My Love Looks Good On You / Speak Your Peace - 1966
Premium Stuff 1 - Why Are You Blowing My Mind / I Can't Get Right - 1967
Premium Stuff 3 - So Fine / I'll Never Be The Same Again - 1967
Premium Stuff 7 - Gypsy Woman / Why Are You Blowing My Mind - 1967
Wee-3 233 - With These Eyes / I've Been Trying - 1967
Wheelsville 109 - With These Eyes / Light Of My Life – 1968

Pic & Bill

Pic & Bill (Charles Edward Pickens and Billy Mills (b. North Carolina, U.S.A.).

Soulful Kinda Music – The Rare Soul Bible Volume Two

Charay 60 - What Would I Do / What Does It Take (To Keep A Girl Like You Satisfied)
Charay 60 - What Would You Do / Patsy
Charay 60 - Together Till The End Of Time / Patsy - 1967
Charay 67 - It's Not You / All I Want Is You - 1967
Charay 60 - Soul Of A Man / Patsy
Charay 60 - Patsy / Over The Mountain - 1970
Charay 73 - This Is It / Nobody But My Baby

Fiery Spartans

Charay 74 - Cool / Talk About Love* - ? * The 'Talk About Love' track is the same recording as the Pic & Bill credited version.

Pic & Bill

Charay 99 - Talk About Love / A Man Without A Woman
Charay 99-A/99-B - Talk About Love / For The Good Times

Willie Hobbs

Soft 1030 - Action* / A Woman Like Her - 1968 *Backing Vocals By Pic & Bill.

Pic & Bill

Le Cam 92975 - All I Want Is You / Just A Tear – 1967
Smash 2109 – Yesterday / Don't Put Me Down - 1967
Smash 2132 - Just A Tear / Sad World Without You - 1967
Smash 2177 - Moments Like These / Love Is A Many Splendored Thing - 1968
Blue Rock 4073 - Gonna Give It To You / The Soul Of A Man - 1969
Charay 60 - How Many Times / Patsy - 1969
Charay 60-A - Funny How Time Slips Away / How Many Times - 1969
Charay 60 - I Love You, Baby / How Many Times - 1969
Bandit 10 A - Hang On In There Baby / Wait A Minute (I Don't Wanna Lose You) - 1987 (12" Single)
Bandit 10 B - Hang On In There Baby / Wait A Minute (I Don't Wanna Lose You) - 1987 (7" Single)
Bandit 12 - You Can Never Go Back Part 1 / You Can Never Go Back Part 2 - 1987

Ray Pollard

The Singing Wanderers (members Bob Yarborough, Ray Pollard, Frank Joyner and Sheppard Grant) this was the 1953 group line-up.

The Wanderers (members Bob Yarborough, Ray Pollard, Frank Joyner and Sheppard Grant)

Savoy 1109 - We Could Find Happiness/ Hey Mae Ethel - 1953 .

Soulful Kinda Music – The Rare Soul Bible Volume Two

Dolly Cooper

Savoy 1121 - You Gotta Be Good To Yourself / Love Can't Be Blind - 1954 (The Wanderers sing back-up vocals)

The Singing Wanderers (members Bob Yarborough, Ray Pollard, Frank Joyner and Sheppard Grant)

Decca 29230 - Say Hey, Willie Mays / Don't Drop It - 1954
Decca 29298 - Three Roses / The Wrong Party Again - 1954

The Wanderers (members Bob Yarborough, Ray Pollard, Frank Joyner and Sheppard Grant)

Onyx 518 - Thinking Of You / Great Jumpin' Catfish - 1957
Orbit 9003 - A Teenage Quarrel / My Shining Hour - 1958 (Green Label 45 Is Scarcer Than Red Label 45)
Cub 9003 - A Teenage Quarrel / My Shining Hour - 1958
Cub 9019 - Two Hearts On A Window Pane / Collecting Hearts - 1958
Cub 9023 - Please / Shadrach, Meshack And Abednego - 1959
Cub 9035 - I'm Not Ashamed / Only When You're Lonely - 1959
Cub 9054 - I Walked Through A Forest / I'm Waiting In Green Pastures - 1959
Cub 9075 - I Could Make You Mine / I Need You More - 1960
Cub 9089 - For Your Love / Sally Goodheart - 1961
Cub 9094 - I'll Never Smile Again / A Little Too Long - 1961
Cub 9099 - Somebody Else's Sweetheart / She Wears My Ring - 1961
Cub 9109 - As Time Goes By / There Is No Greater Love - 1962
MGM13082 - As Time Goes By / There Is No Greater Love - 1962
United Artists 570 - After He Breaks Your Heart / Run Run Senorita - 1963
United Artists 648 - I'll Know / You Can't Run Away From Me - 1963

Ray Pollard

Shrine 103 - No More Like Me / This Time (I'm Gonna Be True) - 1965
United Artists 856 - Darling Take Me Back / My Girl And I - 1965
United Artists 916 - The Drifter / Let Him Go (And Let Me Love You) - 1965
United Artists 50012 - All The Things You Are / It's A Sad Thing - 1966
Decca 32111 - Lie, Lips, Lie / This Is My Song - 1966
Decca 32189 - This Is No Laughing Matter / Wanderlust – 1966

Joe Cuba Sextet (members Joe Cuba, Ray Pollard (joined group 1972), ...)

Don Robey And Peacock Records

Peacock Records was the first record label owned by Don Robey, but to understand the history of the label you have to look back a little further.

Born on the 1st of November, 1903, in Houston's Fifth Ward, Don D Robey had a pretty unremarkable childhood until he dropped out of school aged just 16, to become a professional gambler. He was obviously quite successful because within five years he could be found owning/managing his own taxi business. It's never been clear whether he owned the business, or just managed it on behalf of someone else, but that sort of cloudy distinction was to be a feature of Don's business dealings throughout his career. He also got married and had a son during the time he worked in the taxi business.

One of his passions was music and although it's not known when Don became involved in promoting dances, but by 1939 he had moved to Los Angeles where he gained employment as the manager of The Harlem Grill, a well known night club that featured live acts. Sometime in 1942, don returned to Houston and worked on the fringes of the entertainment industry for a couple of years until he opened his own club called The Bronze Peacock Dinner Club, at 2809 Erastus Street in 1945. 'The Peacock' as it became known locally, soon began featuring some of the biggest live acts of the day, and became a great success amongst the better off black residents of Houston. Although a complete list of artists that appeared at the club is not known, there are details that Ruth Brown, Louis Jordan, Lionel Hampton, and T-Bone Walker were among the club's featured guests.

Sometime between 1945 and 1947, it's also believed that Don Robey opened a record shop as well, but details are, again, a little hazy. What is known, is in 1947, Don Robey became involved in artist management for the first time when he agreed to represent a local Houston Blues singer called Clarence 'Gatemouth' Brown.

Allegedly, Brown, who was able to play a variety of instruments, jumped onto the stage at the Bronze Peacock during a T-Bone Walker set, and stole the show. Never one to dismiss an opportunity, Don Robey spoke to him after the show and as a result took over his management through a new company that he formed; The Buffalo Booking Agency. Having installed Evelyn Johnson to run the booking agency he concentrated on The Bronze Peacock.

The arrangement was obviously profitable for both Robey and Brown though, because two years later Don Robey decided that he wanted to record Clarence 'Gatemouth' Brown. Being the entrepreneurial type, rather than go to an established label, where he might lose some control, Don Robey just decided to set up his own record label. So, in late 1949, Peacock Records was formed.

In early 1950, Brown recorded six tracks in one session, and four of these formed the

Soulful Kinda Music – The Rare Soul Bible Volume Two

first three singles for the label. Confusingly, the first two releases were both number 1500, and two tracks were used twice.

However, it set the stage for one of the biggest, and best, Rhythm & Blues, Gospel, and Soul labels ever to have existed, and lasted until Don Robey's death in 1975.

The next three years saw a steady succession of releases for the label, although none were huge hits, they all sold well enough to establish the label and give it a good financial footing. So much so that Don Robey eventually closed The Bronze Peacock as a nightclub and made it the headquarters, and recording studio for Peacock Records.
In 1952 Duke Records was formed by David J. Mattis (Who was the the program director at Memphis radio station WDIA) and Bill Fitzgerald in Memphis, Tennessee. A similar type of set up to Peacock, Duke had already had hits with Johnny Ace and Roscoe Gordon by the summer of the 1952. The two labels, Duke and Peacock were combined in a partnership in August 1952. By April 1953, Don Robey had managed to obtain full control of both labels, and their base became 2809 Erastus Street in Houston.

It really started to come together though in 1953.

One artist, and one song, made more money for the fledgling company than any other. Willie Mae 'Big Mama' Thornton had a number one R & B record that took the whole nation by storm. So many copies were sold of this one record that Peacock managed to keep three record pressing plants going on this one track alone. Of course three years later, it was covered by Elvis Presley, and became an even bigger hit all over the world.

It wasn't just a one artist company though, the Duke label was racking up hit after hit from Johnny Ace, and it is this that was to cause the first really major problem for the label, and led in some ways to a change in direction.

On Christmas Eve 1954 Johnny Ace was found dead backstage at the City Auditorium in Houston. During a break between sets, Ace allegedly decided to play a game of Russian Roulette. He aimed a .45 caliber revolver at his girlfriend, Olivia Gibbs, and pulled the trigger. He then attempted to shoot her friend, Mary Carter. Both times, the hammer fell on an empty chamber. He then swiftly turned the gun on himself and lost the gamble. Not only did it end the life of the label's biggest star, but accusations later surfaced that Don Robey was in some way responsible for the death of Johnny Ace because of the way he conducted the renegotiation of Johnny Ace's contract. Mind you, it's also claimed that these allegations originated from Huey P Meaux, who just happened to be a competitor of Don Robey's !

There were only nine releases on Peacock in 1955, but they did include the wonderfully titlled 'Tarzan And The Dignified Monkey' by Big Mama Thornton. Duke though, was going from strength to strength with Bobby Bland and Little Junior Parker becoming the stars of the label.

The next five years saw the consolidation of the Duke and Peacock labels and in 1957, the formation of the Back Beat label. I guess what happened over the next couple of years would be what we now call a re-structuring, or re-alignment of the business.

By the beginning of the next decade, Duke and Back Beat released almost exclusively R & B and Soul music, and Peacock became a label that released purely Gospel.

Right from the start of the label, Gospel had been a big part of the output, but it was mixed in with the Rhythm & Blues, and by the mid Fifties Peacock had most of the really big name acts under contract. The Dixie Hummingbirds, The Mighty Clouds Of Joy, The Five Blind Boys Of Mississippi, Reverend Cleophus Robinson, The Sensational Nightingales, The Gospelaires of Dayton, Ohio, The Pilgrim Jubilee Singers, The Loving Sisters, all recorded for Peacock. In fact Peacock released 99 Gospel albums in total.

This accounts for some of the confusion over the numbering of the records. Starting in 1950 with number 1500, the Gospel releases started in 1952, with number 1700, and ran concurrent to the 1500 series. In fact by 1960 there were only five releases on the R & B side compared to sixteen on the Gospel side of Peacock.

Of course, by then Duke was becoming a major force, and in 1957, Back Beat had been formed as A subsidiary label for R & B. By the early Sixties though, Back Beat was issuing records that were clearly recognised as Soul music. A further Gospel label, Song Bird, was opened in 1963 and Sure-Shot was to join the group later in the Sixties.

Don Robey's reputation as a hard bargaining business man was growing in line with the success of the label's records. It's also claimed that his reputation as a gangster ! It's often acknowledged that he conducted negotiations with artists with a .45 revolver on his desk, and had a tendancy to brandish it in the air at sticky points in the negotiations. It's also rumoured that he was well connected with the local mobsters. Certainly, back in the late Fifties / early Sixties, it would have been impossible for anyone in the entertainment business to not be aware of, and deal with organised crime, and don't forget Don Robey had been in this business for nearly fifteen years by now

 It wasn't just in his dealings with artists that the reputation for sharp business practices was deserved either. At the beginnings of the label Don realised that there was as much money top be made from song publishing as there was from record sales. Consequently you will find his name on a huge proportion of the Peacock and Duke releases as writer, but using the pseudonym Deadric Malone. Deadric was Don's middle name and Malone was his first wife's maiden name. The four label scans below show clear examples of this.

It was estimated that at the time of his death in 1975, Don Robey held the copyright title on 2,500 songs, in all probability, he didn't write any of them ! It wasn't illegal though.

In almost every case, the writer of the song would have not only sold the song, but also his rights to it at the same time, simply because he needed the $20 right then ! In cash ! On other occasions, writers would be under contract to another label, thus to earn some cash on the side by writing they would sell songs to Don Robey. Obviously their own name couldn't go down as the writer, so it became D. Malone on the label. Oscar Perry in particular has admitted to doing this.

There is also a story about Don Robey's continued dabbling in gambling. He owned a racehorse called Sunrise County. Entered into a race in which the horse was viewed as an also ran by the bookies, it romped home by twenty lengths. It's claimed Robey's winnings had to be carried out in sacks. Clearly the horse was doped up to the eyeballs, so the Stewards called for an enquiry. It didn't last long though, because when they went to test the horse, Don Robey claimed it had bolted from it's horse box and couldn't be found. It was never seen again !

Then there are the legal cases. Don Robey sued Checker records in 1963 over their interference in the contract of The Five Blind Boys. The case was essentially won by Don Robey because he had a contract signed by the group in 1960. He was awarded $250,000 in damages, plus $10,000 costs. That was a hell of a lot of money in 1963 ! Checker appealed against the decision some months later, and won. Why ? Because it turned out that the contract The Five Blind Boys had signed in 1960 had actually been signed in 1961, and backdated by Don Robey.

Quinton Claunch of Goldwax records also tells a story about Don Robey demanding royaties from a song jointly written by O V Wright ('There Goes My Used To Be') who happened to be under contract to Peacock as a member of the Sunset Travellers. I gather he got them as well

Despite all this, and whilst some artists hated him, most of the people who dealt with Don Robey have fond memories of him. Certainly his biggest artist, Bobby Bland, acknowledges that without Don Robey he might never have become the star he is.

This brings us to the early Sixties, where the label had finally achieved it's aims in becoming a national force in Black music. R & B was gradually fading as Soul music took centre stage, and although many of Peacock's releases are aimed at the new market they always retained the rawer edge of Texas R & B. I'm not going to delve into the release and artists of the Sixties in any great detail, that's for another day, and another article.

In 1973, with his health failing, Don Robey sold the Peacock / Duke / Back Beat / Song Bird and Sure-Shot labels to ABC-Dunhill.

Even this deal was shrouded in controversy, because it's alleged that Don Robey sold the labels to settle a rather pressing gambling debt. He stayed on as a consultant, to co-ordinate the reissue programme that ABC Dunhill put together on the newly created ABC Peacock label in 1974

Sadly on June 16, 1975, Don Robey died in his native Houston.

What also has to be remembered is that although his mother was white, Don Robey was regarded as a Black man through his whole life. He created an independent business empire in the record business a full ten years before Berry Gordy Jr named his first label, and as Don Robey himself said "I had two strikes against me before I started, I was Black, and I was in the Record Business". No mean achievement by any standard, and a wonderful legacy to leave..

Label Listings

Palmer

5000 - Tobi Lark - I'll Steal Your Heart / Talk To An Angel - 1965
5001 - The Girls From Syracuse - Love Is Happening To Me / Now We Could Have Danced - 1965
5002 - Tim Tam and The Turn-Ons - Wait A Minute / Ophelia - 1965
5003 - Tam and The Turn-Ons - Cheryl Ann / Sealed With A Kiss - 1966
5004 - The New Arrivals - Big Time Girl / Somebody Else - 1966
5005 - The Shy Guys - Lay It On The Line / You Gotta Go - 1966
5006 - Tim Tam and The Turn-Ons - Kimberly / I Leave You In Tears - 1966
5007 - Black Cloud - Me And Dem Guys / Come On Little Sweetheart - 1966
5008 - The Shy Guys - Where You Belong / A Love So True - 1966
5009 - People's Choice - Hot Wire / Ease The Pain - 1966
5010 - The Shaggs - The Way I Care / Ring Around The Rosie - 1966
5011 - Al Williams - I Am Nothing / Brand New Love - 1967
5012 - The Inside-Outs - Gundred Goon / My Love - 1967
5013 - ?
5014 - Tim Tam The Turn-Ons - Don't Say Hi (Vocal) / Don't Say Hi (Instrumental) - 1967
5015 - Tommy Frontera - Street Of Shame / Merry-Go-Round - 1967
5016 - Donna Lynn - Don't You Dare / It Was Raining - 1967
5017 - The Canadian Rogues - Keep In Touch / Ooh-Poo-Pa-Do - 1967
5018 - The Trade Marks - I Need You / If I Was Gone - 1967
5019 - Jimmy Mack - Go On / My World Is On Fire - 1967
5020 - People's Choice - Easy To Be True / Savin' My Lovin' For You - 1967
5021 - J.T. Rhythm - My Sweet Baby / All I Want Is You - 1967
5022 - G. Gaylord and B. Holiday - Place To Hide Away / Love (Where Have You Gone) - 1967
5023 - Joey Welz - Maybe, You're A Girl / Rhapsody For A Summer Night - 1967
5024 - Tommy Nash - Goin' To A Happenin' / Tomboy - 1968
5025 - The Grifs - Northbound / Keep Dreamin' - 1968
5026 - The Belaires - I Got That Feelin' / The Rabbit - 1968
5026 - The Belaires - I Got That Feelin' / Why Did You Call - 1968
5027 - The Morticians - It's Gonna Take Awhile / Another Guy - 1968
5028 - ?
5029 - ?
5030 - Joey Welz and The New Century Singers   - (I'll Remember) Our Summer Love / What Did She Wear - 1968
5031 - People's Choice   - Savin' My Lovin' For You / Easy To Br True - 1968
5032 - Joey Welz and The Bluze Revival - Mini Rock 'N Roll / A Rose And A Baby Ruth - 1968
5033 - ?

Soulful Kinda Music – The Rare Soul Bible Volume Two

5034 - Joey Welz - Pretty Is The Word / For Love Return To Me - 1968
5035 -
5036 - Joey Welz - Come Go With Me / Runaway - 1968
5037 -
5038 - Joey Welz - Touch Them With Love / Flamingo Love - 1968

Parkway

801 - Jerry Fields - The Trial / Easy Steppin' - 1958
802 - Denny Mela - Forget My Past / Blondie - 1958
803 - The Temptations - Birds N' Bees / Temptations - 1958
804 - Chubby Checker - The Class / Schooldays Oh Schooldays - 1958
805 - Johnny Stevens - Apple Taffy / Mm Baby Mm - 1958
806 - Scott McKay - Rollin' Dynamite / Evenin' Time - 1958
807 - The Premiers - Tonight / I Think I Love You - 1958
808 - Chubby Checker - Whole Lotta Laughin' / Samson & Delilah - 1959
809 - Georgie Young - Gold Rush / That's Tough - 1959
810 - Chubby Checker - Dancing Dinosaur / Those Private Eyes 1959
811 - Chubby Checker - The Twist / Toot - 1959
811 - Chubby Checker - The Twist / Twistin' U S A - 1959
812 - Wayne Handy - So Much To Remember / You'll Never Be Mine - 1959
813 - Chubby Checker - The Hucklebuck / Whole Lotta Shakin' Goin' On - 1959
814 - Timmie Rogers - I Love Ya I Love Ya I Love Ya / Tee Hee - 1959
815 - Little Sis - The Twist / The Pony - 1960
816 - Philadelphia Strummers - I Ain't Down Yet / Every Moment You Live - 1960
817 - ?
818 - Chubby Checker - Pony Time / Oh Susannah - 1960
819 - The Dovells - No No No / Letters Of Love - 1960
820 - The Turbans - When You Dance / Golden Rings - 1960
821 - ?
822 - Chubby Checker - Good Good Lovin' / Dance The Mess Around - 1960
823 - The Cousins - St Louis Blues / No One Knows - 1960
824 - Chubby Checker - Let's Twist Again / Everything's Gonna Be Alright - 1960
825 - Eddie Curtis - Let It Live / How Long Will It Last - 1960
826 - Billy Barnette - Two Brothers / Marlene - 1960
827 - The Dovells - Bristol Stomp / Out In The Cold Again - 1960
827 - The Dovells - Bristol Stomp / Out In The Cold Again - 1960
828 - Joe Van Loan - Hurricane / Broken Shoes - 1960
829 - Reggie Van Dyke - Sweetness / Happy Music - 1960
830 - Chubby Checker - The Fly / That's The Way It Goes - 1960
831 - Ronnie Lavelle - Cartoons / The Crazy Ways Of Love - 1960
832 - Freddy Furure - Don't Forget Me / Like Soiree - 1961
833 - The Dovells - Do The New Continental / Mope Itty Mope Stomp - 1961
834 - George Tindlay - Fairy Tales / Just For You - 1961
835 - Chubby Checker - Slow Twistin' / La Paloma Twist - 1961
836 - Rocky Fellers - Long Tall Sally / South Pacific Twist - 1961
837 - Ronnie Lavelle - A Dog's Life / Let Her Go - 1961
838 - The Dovells - Bristol Twistin Annie' / The Actor - 1961

Soulful Kinda Music – The Rare Soul Bible Volume Two

839 - Pookie Hudson & The Spaniels - Turn Out The Lights / John Brown - 1961
840 - Sandy Trapp - Love Sickness / I Don't Know - 1961
841 - The Scott Brothers - Memories / Beggin' For Your Love - 1961
842 - Chubby Checker - Dancin' Party / Gotta Get Myself Together - 1961
843 - Leon & The Dreamers - Haircut / If It Hadn't Been For You - 1961
844 - Donnie Elbert - Baby Cakes / Set My Heart At Ease - 1961
845 - The Dovells - Hully Gully Baby / Your Last Chance - 1961
846 - Ray Rush - So What / Can This Be Love - 1961
847 - Tina Powers - Making Up Is Fun To Do / Back To School - 1961
848 - The Cousins - Some Of These Days / When My Baby Smiles At Me - 1961
849 - Chubby Checker - Limbo Rock / Popeye - 1961
850 - Diablito - The Jungle / Meringue Potatoes - 1961
851 - The Chavis Brothers - Slippin' And Slidin' / Good Old Mountain Dew - 1961
852 - Ruth Bachelor / Mr Principal / Lemon Drops Lolly Pops - 1961
853 - John Zacherle- Dinner With Drac / Hurry Bury Baby - 1961
854 - The Swagmen - By The Yonder Tree / East Virginia - 1961
855 - The Dovells - Jitterbug / Kissin' In The Kitchen - 1961
856 - John Linde Combo - Bossa Nova Bill / Round Sound - 1961
857 - Buddy Savitt - Smoke Gets In Your Eyes / Come Blow Your Horn - 1961
858 - Patricia May - What Christmas Means To Me / Angel Of Love - 1961
859 - Rune Overman - Madison Piano / Big Bass Boogie - 1961
860 - Lee Andrews - I'm Sorry Pillow / Gee But I'm Lonesome - 1962
861 - The Dovells - You Can't Run Away From Yourself / Save Me Baby - 1962
862 - Chubby Checker - Let's Limbo Some More / 20 Miles - 1962
863 - The Tams - Memory Lane / A Lonely Piano - 1962
864 - Merle Kilgore - I Am / When It Rains The Blues On You - 1962
865 - The Impacs - I'm Gonna Make You Cry / Tears In My Heart - 1962
866 - Lee Andrews - Looking Back / Operator - 1962
867 - The Dovells - You Can't Sit Down / Stompin' Everywhere - 1962
867 - The Dovells - You Can't Sit Down / Wildwood Days - 1962
868 - The Tip Tops - Oo Kook A Boo / He's A Braggin' - 1962
869 - Frank Taylor - Snow White Cloud / Send Her Back To Me - 1962
870 - The Cousins - Sweet Georgia Brown / Outside The Wall - 1962
871 - The Tymes - So Much In Love / Roscoe James McLain - 1962
872 - The Taffys - Everybody South Street / Can't We Just Be Friends - 1962
873 - Chubby Checker - Birdland / Black Cloud - 1962
874 - Billy Abbott And The Jewels - Groovy Baby / Come On And Dance With Me - 1962
875 - Bobby Freeman - She's A Hippy / Whip It Up Baby - 1962
876 - Freddy Bender - Miss Daisy De Lite / Let's Twist Again - 1962
877 - Little Joe Vespe - Caravn / Conservative Twist - 1962
878 - Marshall West - This House Is Gonna Live / I Hurt Myself - 1962
879 - Chubby Checker - Twist It Up / Surf Party - 1962
880 - The Valrays - Get A Board / Pee Wee - 1962
881 - The Swans - Daydreamin' Of You / The Promise - 1962
882 - The Dovells - Betty In Bermuda / Dance The Frog - 1962
883 - George McCannon - I I I Lana / What Am I Gonna Do - 1962
884 - The Tymes - Wonderful Wonderful / Come With Me To The Sea - 1962
885 - Zacherley - Surfboard 109 / Clementine - 1962
886 - Neil Brian - Three Rows Over / My Haunted Heart - 1962

Soulful Kinda Music – The Rare Soul Bible Volume Two

887 - Tootie & Bouquets - The Conqueror / You Done Me Wrong - 1962
888 - Zacherey - Scary Tales From Mother Goose / Monster Monkey - 1962
889 - The Dovells - Stop Monkeyin' Around / No No No - 1962
890 - Chubby Checker - Loddy Lo / Hooka Tooka - 1962
891 - The Tymes - Somewhere / View From My Window - 1962
892 - The Expressions - On The Corner / To Cry - 1963
893 - The Cleems - Sandra Baby / You Are The One - 1963
894 - Don Covay - Ain't That Illy / Turn It On - 1963
895 - Neil Brian - Lilac And Spanish Moss / I Made Her Forget - 1963
896 - Patti Labelle & The Bluebelles - You'll Never Walk Alone / Decauter Street - 1963
897 - The Lydells - There Goes The Boy / Talking To Myself - 1963
898 - ?
899 - The Haircuts - She Loves You / Love Me Do - 1963
900 - Carl Holmes & The Commanders - I'm At My Best (When I'm Down) / I Want My Ya Ya - 1963
901 - The Dovells - Be My Girl / Dragster On The Prowl - 1963
902 - ?
903 - Larry Halloway - Beatle Teen Beat / Going Up - 1963
904 - The Valrays - Yo Me Pregunto / Tonky - 1963
905 - Billy Abbott - It Isn't Fair / Hey Good Lookin' - 1963
906 - Buzz Kirby - Speedo / She's My Girl - 1963
907 - Chubby Checker - Spread Joy / Hey Bobba Needle - 1963
908 - The Tymes - To Each His Own / Wonderland Of Love - 1963
909 - The Undertakers - Just A Little Bit / Stupidity - 1963
910 - Don Covay - The Froog / One Little Boy Had Money - 1963
911 - The Dovells - One Potatoe / Happy Birthday Just The Same - 1963
912 - The Ribbons - Melody D'amour / They Played A Sad Song - 1963
913 - Pattie Labelle & The Bluebelles - One Phone Call / You Will Fill My Eyes No More - 1963
914 - Plato - Copy Cat / Claudia's Theme - 1963
915 - John Paul Jones - Baja / A Foggy Day In Vietnam - 1963
916 - The Thin Men - Indian Love Call / Guitar Blues - 1963
917 - The Prizes - Summer's Here At Last / I Found Someone New - 1963
918 - Rod & Carolyn - Young Love / Talk To Me - 1963
919 - The Tymes - Magic Of Our Summer Love / With All My Heart - 1963
920 - Chubby Checker - Rosie - Lazy Elsie Molly - 1963
921 - The Rag Dolls - Society Girl / Ragen (Society Girl Bossa Nova) - 1963
922 - Chubby Checker - She Wants T'swim / You Better Believe It Baby - 1963
923 - Alaine Williams - When Are We Getting Married / So This Is Goodbye - 1963
924 - The Tymes - Malibu / Here She Comes - 1963
925 - The Dovells - What In The World's Come Over You / Watusi With Lucy - 1963
926 - The Defenders - Island Of Love / I Laughed So Hard - 1963
927 - Jerome Powell - Home To Stay / Live And Let Live - 1963
928 - Hattie Wilson - Pictures Don't Lie / Please Write Back To Me - 1963
929 - The Bronzettes - Hot Spot / Run Run You Little Fool - 1963
930 - The Possessions - No More Live / You And Your Lies - 1963
931 - Nikki Blu - (Whoa Whoa) I Love Him So / Inst - 1963
932 - Antoinette - There He Goes / Little Things Mean A Lot - 1963
933 - Tymes - The Twelth Of Never / Here She Comes - 1963

Soulful Kinda Music – The Rare Soul Bible Volume Two

934 - Rod & Carolyn - Love Is Where You Are / I've Got You On My Mind - 1963
935 - Patti Labelle & The Bluebelles - Danny Boy / I Believe - 1963
936 - Chubby Checker - Lovely Lovely / The Weekend's Here - 1963
937 - The Blue Rondos - Little Baby / Baby I Go For You - 1964
938 - The Jack Dorsey Big Band - Ringo's Dog / March Of The Gonks - 1964
939 - The Greenbeats - You Must Be The One / If This World Were Mine - 1964
940 - The Primitives - Help Me / Let Them Fall - 1964
941 - Jackie Trent - How Soon / Don't Stand In My Way - 1964
942 - Sounds Orchestral - Cast Your Fate To The Wind / To Wendy With Love - 1964
943 - Sandra Barry - We Were Lovers / The End Of The Line - 1964
944 – Billy Harner – All Through The Night / Toot - 1964
945 - The Jordan Brothers - What's Wrong With You Baby / The Jordan Theme - 1964
946 - John L Watson & The Hummelfugs - Lookin' For Love / I Only Came To Dance With You - 1964
847 - Tina Powers - Making Up Is Fun To Do / Back To School - 1964
848 - The Cousins - Some Of These Days / When My Baby Smiles At Me - 1964
949 - Chubby Checker - Let's Do The Freddie / At The Discotheque - 1964
950 - Billy Harner - Let's Get In Line / All Through The Night - 1964
951 - Ray Brown & The Whispers - 20 Miles / Devoted To You - 1964
952 - Eddie King - Always At A Distance / If You Wish - 1964
953 - Sandra Barry - We Were Lovers / End Of The Line - 1964
954 - Sandra Barry - Question / You Can Take It From Me - 1964
955 - Jackie Trent - Where Are You Now / On The Other Side Of The Tracks - 1964
956 - Hattie Winston - Pass Me By / Pictures Don't Lie - 1964
957 - Vickie Baines - Got To Run / Losing You - 1964
958 - Sounds Orchestral - Canadian Sunset / Have Faith In Your Love - 1964
959 - Chubby Checker - Everything's Wrong / Cum Ma La Be Stay - 1964
960 - Eddie Holman - This Can't Be True / A Free Country - 1965
961 - Hariette Blake - Dansero / Why Did Our Love Go Wrong - 1965
962 - Marcello - Zorba's Dance / L'isola Del Dole - 1965
963 - Jackie Trent - When Summertime Is Over / To Show I Love Him - 1965
964 - Joe Graves - See Saw / Beautiful Girl - 1965
965 - Chubby Checker - You Just Don't Know / Two Hearts Make One Love - 1965
966 - Vickie Baines - Are You Kidding / Country Girl - 1965
967 - Bobby Sherman - Goody Galumshush / Anything Your Little Heart Desires - 1965
968 - Sounds Orchestral - A Boy And A Girl / Go Home Girl - 1965
969 - Len Barry - Hearts Are Trump / Little White House - 1965
970 - Toni Stante - It's My Life / Donde Esta Santa Claus - 1965
971 - Christine Cooper - S O S / Say What You Feel - 1965
972 - ?
973 - Sounds Orchestral - Thunderball / Mr Kiss Kiss - 1965
974 - The Campers - Ballad Of Batman / Batmobile - 1965
975 - ?
976 - The De Vonns - Freddie / Put Me Down - 1965
977 - ?
978 - Richard Rome - Happiness Is / Back In Sixty Seconds - 1965
979 - ?
980 - ?

Soulful Kinda Music – The Rare Soul Bible Volume Two

981 - Eddie Holman - Don't Stop Now / Eddie's My Name - 1965
982 - Janie Grant - And That Reminds Me Of You / My Heart Your Heart - 1965
983 - Christine Cooper - Heartaches Away My Boy / (They Call Him) A Bad Boy - 1965
984 - ?
985 - The Warmest Spring - Younger Girl / It Doesn't Matter Now - 1965
986 - The Four Exceptions - You Got The Power / A Sad Goodbye - 1965
987 - Johnny Maestro & The Crests - Heartburn / Try Me - 1965
988 - Jimmy Jones - Don't You Just Know It / Dynamite - 1965
989 - Chubby Checker - Hey You Little Boo Ga Loo / Pussy C - 1965t
990 - The Warmest Spring - Suddenly (You'll Find Love) / Hard Hard Girl - 1965
991 - Roddie Joy - A Boy Is Just A Toy / Stop - 1965
992 - The Bronzettes - Hot Spot Part 1 / Part 2 - 1965
993 - The Hollywood Producers - White Silk Glove / You're Not Welcome - 1965
994 - Eddie Holman - Return To Me / Stay Mine For Heaven's Sake - 1965
995 - The Hi Hopes / The Trends - Now That Love Has Come My Way / Inst - 1965
996 - Ben Zine - What The Heck's The Hanky Panky / Village Of Tears - 1965
997 - The Street Corners - My Generation / I Don't Care - 1965
998 - T J K / P S 13 Blues Band - Boo Ga Loo Baby / Shades Of Blue (Something Blue) - 1965
999 - Johnny Maestro & The Crests - Come See Me (I'm Your Man) / I Care About You - 1965
100 - Jerry Jackson - It's Rough Out There / I'm Gonna Paint A Picture - 1966
101 - Roddie Joy - Something Strange Is Coming On / Stop - 1966
102 - Chuck Day - Memphis / It Hursts So Bad - 1966
103 - Joe Graves - Debbie / A Boy & A Girl Fall In Love - 1966
104 - Mr. Wiggles - Fat Back Pt 1 / Fat Back Pt 2 - 1966
105 - Chubby Checker - Looking At Tomorrow / You Got The Power - 1966
106 - Eddie Holman - Am I A Loser / You Know That I Will - 1966
107 - The Revlons - Ya Ya / It Could Happen To You - 1966
108 - The GTO's - Missing Out On The Fun / Girl From New York City - 1966
109 - The Rites Of Spring - Why / Coming On To Me - 1966
111 - The Palace Guard - Saturday's Child / Party Lights - 1966
112 - Chubby Checker - Karate Monkey / Her Heart - 1966
113 - Mike Finnegan - Bread And Water / Help Me Somebody - 1966
114 - Lou Barrington - The Kwella / Swella Stroll - 1966
115 - Action Unlimited - Thinking To Myself / My Heart Cries Out - 1966
116 - ?
117 - ?
118 - Johnny Maestro - My Times / Is It You - 1966
119 - Johnny Daye - A Lot Of Progress / You're On Top - 1966
120 - Sounds Orchestral - Pretty Flamingo / Sounds Like Jacques - 1966
121 - Me & You - Let The World In / I've Got My Time Baby - 1966
122 - Christine Cooper - I Must Have You (Or No One) / Good Looks (They Don't Count) - 1966
123 - Bunny Sigler - Girl Don't Make Me Wait / Always In The Wrong Place At The Wrong Time - 1966
124 - The Palace Guard - Calliope / Greed - 1966
125 - Leather Boy - Jersey Thursday / Black Friday - 1966
126 - Doug Billare & Soul Patrol - Genuine Jade / Emily - 1966

Soulful Kinda Music – The Rare Soul Bible Volume Two

127 - Senator Bobby & Senator Mckinley - Wild Thing Pt 1 / Wild Thing Pt 2 - 1967
128 - TheTwilights - Shipwreck / For The First Time - 1967
129 - Jaxon Reese - Hurry Sundown / How Do You Speak To An Angel - 1967
130 - John D'andrea & Young Gyants - Sunny / Uptight - 1967
131 - Daniel E. Skidmore - Little Old Groovemaker / Listen To The Wind - 1967
132 - Chuck Day & Young Gyants - We Gotta Get Out Of This Place / Tom Dooley - 1967
133 - Eddie Holman - Somewhere Waits A Lonely Girl / Stay Mine For Heaven's Sake - 1967
134 - Roddie Joy - Every Breath I Take / Walkin' Back - 1967
135 - Sir Cedric Smith - Until It's Time For You To Go / Gonna Sing For You - 1967
136 - The Vandals - You Captivate Me / Fifth Avenue New York City - 1967
137 - Senator Bobby & Senator McKinley - Mellow Yellow / White Christmas - 1967
138 - The Unluv'd - Ain't Gonna Do You No Harm / An Exception To The Rule - 1967
139 - ?
140 - Yvonne Baker - You Didn't Say A Word / To Prove My Love Is True - 1967
141 - The Ventrills - Alone In The Night / Confusion - 1967
142 - Jackson Reese - Cry Me A River / Pretty Girl - 1967
143 - Ronnie Dio - Prophets / Waking In Different Circles - 1967
144 - ?
145 - Sure Cure - Anything You Want / I Wanna Do It - 1967
146 - The Renaissance - Mary Jane (Get Off The Devil's Merry-Go Round) / Daytime Lovers - 1967
147 - The Zoo - Good Day Sunshine / Where Have All The Good Times Gone - 1967
148 - The Butlers - Shop Around / It's A Fine Time - 1967
149 - The Volcanics - Your Kind Of Loving / But I Love Her - 1967
150 - Hardly Wothit Players - The Congressional Record / The Hardly Worthit Melody - 1967
151 - Roddie Joy - I Want You Back / Let's Start All Over - 1967
152 - Little Caesar - The Empire / Everybody Dance Now - 1967
153 - Bunny Sigler - Let The Good Times Roll / No Love Left (In This Old Heart Of Mine) - 1967
154 - Googy & Joe's Workshop - To Fernanda With Luv Pt 1 / To Fernanda With Luv Pt 2 - 1967
155 - Sounds Orchestral - A Man And A Woman / West Of Carnaby - 1967
156 - The Vandals - Don't Fight It / Fifth Avenue New York City - 1967
157 - Eddie Holman - Never Let Me Go / Why Do Fools Fall In Love - 1967
158 - The Casual Association - Georgy Girl / Nickles And Dimes - 1967
6000 – Bunny Sigler & Lovey – You're So Fine / Sunny Sunday - 1967
6001 - Bunny Sigler - Follow Your Heart / Can You Dig It - 1967
6002 - The Simms Twins - Baby It's Real / Together - 1967
6003 - The Olympics - Lookin' For A Love / Good Things - 1968

Peachtree

101 - Jimmy Church - Thinking About the Good Times / Shadow of Another Man's Love - 1968
102 - Johnny Jones & the King Casuals - Soul Poppin / Blues for the Brothers
103 - Peg Leg Moffett - Teeny Weeny Bit / The Shocker

Soulful Kinda Music – The Rare Soul Bible Volume Two

104 - Eddie Billups - Ask my Heart / Soldier's Prayer
105 - Gorgeous George Love's Not A Hurtin' Thing / Get Up Off It
106 - Sue Rainey - I've Had Enough / You Hurt So Good
107 - Emory and the Dynamics - It Sure Would Be Nice / Let's Take A Look At Our Life
120 - Emory and the Dynamics - Love That's Real / Pretty Little Schoolgirl - 1970
121 - Mitty Collier - You Hurt So Good / I Can't Lose - 1970
122 - Mitty Collier - I'd Like To Change Places / Share What You've Got - 1970
123 - Mitty Collier - True Love Never Comes Easy / Fly Me To the Moon - 1970
124 - James Fountain - Burning Up For Your Love / My Hair Is Nappy - 1970
125 - Mitty Collier - One Heck of a Lover / Lovin' on Borrowed Time
126 - Johnny Jones - Mighty Low / Mighty Low Part 2
127 - James Fountain - Seven Day Lover / Malnutrition
128 - Mitty Collier - Your Sign Is A Good Sign / Mama He Treats Your Daughter Mean
129 - Four Dynamics - That's What Girls Are Made For / Things That A Lady Ain't Supposed To Do
130 - Velvetones - Funky Sweat / Funky Sweat Part 2
131 - Johnny Jones – Do Unto Others / Hong Cong Harlem
132 - Johnny Jones - Do Unto Others / Hong Kong Harlem
134 - Clyde Terrell - Danny Boy / This Guy's in Love with You

Penny

101 - Cheers - (I'm Not Ready To) Settle Down / Mighty, Mighty Lover - 1967
102 - ?
103 - The Voices - Fall In Love Again / Fall In Love Again (Inst) - 1967
104 - Stanley Anderson - My Little Angel / Politics - 1967
105 - The Voices - Forever Is a Long Long Time / Forever Is A Long Long Tine (Inst) - 1968
106 - Little Ben & The Cheers - Never More / I'm Gonna Get Even With You - 1968
107 - Norvells - Why Do You Want To Make Me Sad / Without You
108 - Jerry Townes - Never More / You Are My Sunshine - 1969
109 - Little Ben & The Cheers - (I'm Not Ready To) Settle Down / Mighty, Mighty Lover -
9021 - The Joy Rockers - The Gauster Bop / ? - ?
9022 - The Creations - We're In Love / Lady Luck - ?
2016 - The Matta Baby – Do The Pearl Girl Part 1 / Do The Pearl Girl Part 2 - 1967
(The catalogue number is from the Chess catalogue, although no copies have ever been found on the Chess label.)

Phil La Of Soul

300 - Helene Smith - Like A Baby / A Woman Will Do Wrong
301 - The New Clarence Reid - Cadillac Annie / Tired Blood
302 - The Kayettes - Moonlight In Vermont / Let's Talk It Over
303 - Dee Irwin - Better To Have Loved And Lost / Linda

Soulful Kinda Music – The Rare Soul Bible Volume Two

304 - Frank Williams & Rocketeers - The Spanish Flyer / You Got To Be A Man
305 - Fantastic Johnny C - Boogaloo Down Broadway / Look What Love Can Make You Do
306 - Frank Williams, & Rocketeers - Soul Stuff - Part 1 / Soul Stuff - Part 2
307 - Little John Bowie - Go Go Annie / My Love, My Love
308 - The Imperial C's - I'll Live On / Someone Tell Her
309 - Fantastic Johnny C - Got What You Need / New Love
310 - Cliff Nobles - The More I Do For You Baby / This Love Will Last
311 - The Emanons - One Heart / Reap What You Sow
312 - Herb Ward - Wrong Place At The Wrong Time / You Can Cry
313 - Cliff Nobles - The Horse / Love Is All Right
314 - Benny Sigler - Who You Gonna Turn To / I Can Give You Love
315 - Fantastic Johnny C - Hitch To The Horse / Cool Broadway
316 - James Boys - The Horse / The Mule
317 - Neil Brown - My Soul Is Running Over With Love / Tallahatchie B
318 - Cliff Nobles - Judge Baby, I'm Back / The More I Do For You Baby
319 - Wonda Maria - I Feel Complete / Open Arms, Close Heart
320 - Fantastic Johnny C - Some Kind Of Wonderful / Baby I Need You
321 - Benny Harper - Don't Let It Happen To You / In The Middle Of The Night
322 - Sandra Lopez - I'm So Lonely / Look What You've Done
323 - African Echoes - Zulu Lunchbag / Big Time
324 - Cliff Nobles & Co. - Switch It On/ Burning Desire
325 - Helene Smith - You Got To Be A Man / Without Some Kind Of A Man
326 - Bobby Bennett - Big New York / Baby, Try Me
327 - Fantastic Johnny C - Is There Anything Better Than Making Love / New Love
328 - Pal & The Prophets - Lotta Good Lovin' / I Keep Foolin' Myself
329 - Nobles, Cliff-Gettin' Away / The Camel
330 - Helene Smith - And Away We Go / You Got To Be A Man
331 - Buster Jones - Down Silent Streets / A Good Thing
332 - Pal & The Prophets - he Whip / I Keep Foolin' Myself
333 - Les Tres Femmes - What's A Matter Baby / Listen To Your Mama
334 - Alfreda Brockington - Your Love Has Got Me Chained And Bound / I'll Wait
335 - Helene Smith - Let's Wait Until Dark / Too Good To Be True
336 - The Fabulettes - Because Of Love / If The Morning Ever Comes
337 - John Ellison - Giving Up On Love / You've Got To Have Rythm
338 - Alfreda Brockington - You Made Me A Woman / Crushing Me
339 - Marla Debrick - I've Got To Find A Place / Um Um Darling
340 - The Willy Cole - Right On / A Pretty Good "B" Side
341 - John Ellison - All I Want Is Your Love / Doggone Good Feeling
342 - Tyrone Ashley & Funky Music - Let Me Be Your Man / I Want My Baby Back
343 - Ernie Andrews - Bridge Over Troubled Water/ Something
344 - Jo Ann King - (Let's Leave It) This Lovin' Way / Hey Lancelot
345 - Joey Gilmore - Somebody Done Took My Baby And Gone/ Do It To Me O
346 - Ernie Andrews - Say Hello To Yesterday
347 - Ernie Andrews - Fire And Rain / It Was A Good Time
348 - Tyrone Ashley & Funky Music - Love Sweet Love / Sing Your Song Sister
349 - The People's Choice - I Likes To Do It / Big Ladies Man
350 - Thunder, Lightning & Rain - Super Funky - Part I / Super Funky - Part Ii
351 - Benny Gordon - Give A Damn - Part I / Give A Damn - Part Ii
352 - The People's Choice - The Wootie-T-Woo / Cause That's The Way I Know

Soulful Kinda Music – The Rare Soul Bible Volume Two

353 - Carolyn Veal - Don't The Good Book Say We're Brothers / Your Love
354 - Jackie Lavant & The Fashions - What Goes Up / I Don't Mind Doin' It
355 - John Ellison & Soul Brothers Six - Funky Funky Way Of Makin' Love / Let Me Be The One
356 - The People's Choice - Magic / Oh How I Love It
357 - Alphie & The Explosions - Safire / True Love
358 - The People's Choice - Let Me Do My Thing / On A Cloudy Day
359 - Sunshine - Goin' Home To An Empty House / Leave Me (And See W
360 - Soul Brothers Six - You Gotta Come A Little Closer / You're My World
361 - Fantastic Johnny C - Don't Depend On Me / Waitin' For The Rain
362 - Witch Way - Clapping Song / Hold On To Love
363 - Fantastic Johnny C - Just Say The Word / I'm A Man
364 - Great Expectations - Welcome To The World (Part I) / Welcome To The Wor
365 - Soul Brothers Six - Lost The Will To Live / Let Me Do What We Ain't Do
366 - Captain Freak & Lunacycle Band - What Ever Happened To Superman / I Wouldn't Pull Y
367 - The Coalitions - Instead...How Are You / I Don't Mind Doin' It
368 - Cynthia Sheeler - Nobody Wins / One Minute Of Your Time
369 - The Philly Sound - Waitin' For The Rain / Don't Depend On Me
370 - Mody-Vation - Ghetto Kung Fu - Part I / Ghetto Kung Fu - Part Ii
371 - The Coalitions - Later Than You Think / Instead...How Are You
372 - Harold Melvin & Blue Notes - Get Out (And Let Me Cry) / You May Not Love Me
373 - Raw Image - Black Bourgeoise / Go For Broke
374 - The Delites - It's As Simple As That / I've Got Enough Sense
375 - L J Waiters / Electrifiers - If You Ain't Getting' Your Thing, Parts 1 And 2
376 - Sharon Ridley - Stay A While With Me / When A Woman Falls In Love
377 - L J Waiters & The Electrifiers - Can You Deal With It? / Instrumental
378 - Bob Green - Sweet Sweet Memories / Running And Hiding
379 - The Delights - Face The Music / Things Ain't What They Used To Be
380 - Oscar Perry - Gimme Some / Come On Home To Me
381 - Raw Image - Just A Little Taste / Sound Freak
382 - Titus Turner - Bla Bla Bla, Cha Cha Cha / Pony Train
383 - Flick Wilson - Keep The Troubles Down / Troubled
384 - Brutal Force - Dreams For Sale / The Number For Groove
385 - Paradise - We Belong Together / Tell Her
386 - Superior Elevation - (It Was) September / Computer Woman

Planetary

101 – Dorothy Berry – Ain't That Love / You Better Watch Out
102 – Margaret Mandolph – If You Ever Need Me / Silly Little Girl
103 – Del Ashley – Brighter Side / Little Miss Stuck Up
104 – Grady & Brady – Just A Lot Of Talk / Love Or Money
105 – Dorothy Berry – Shindig City / Standing On The Corner
106 – Margaret Mandolph – I Wanna Make You Happy / Something Beautiful
107 – Grady & Brady – Sad September / Star Of The Show
108 – David Gates – Let You Go / Once Upon A Time

Soulful Kinda Music – The Rare Soul Bible Volume Two

Port

5000 – The Five Chancellors – Tell Me You Love Me / There Goes My Girl
5001 – The Five Dreamers – Beverly / You Don't Know
5002 - Fay Simmons – I Can See Through You / Hangin' Around
70001 – Casanova Jr – Sally Mae / They Call Me Casandra
70002 – Chuck Howard – Can't You Tell / Crazy Crazy Baby
70003 – Sunny & The Gang – Babette / I'm A Rollin'
70004 – The Ssedates – Please Love Me Forever / I Found
70005 – Birdie Castle & The Sungazers – Crazy Beat / Rockin' With The DJs
70006 – The Gofers – The Headhunter / Scotch On The Rocks
70007 – Al & Jet – C'mon Baby / Come Please Dance With Me
70008 – Tony Reese – Lesson In Love / Just About This Time Tomorrow
70009 - ?
70010 – The Fascinates – Pizza Train / Southern Flashback
70011 – The Suburbans – Alphabet Of Love / Sweet Diane Cha Cha
70012 – Tony Alamo – Fabulous / For All We Know
70013 - The Eboniers – Hand In Hand / Shut Your Mouth
70014 – The Channels – The Closer You Are / Now You Know (I Love You So)
70015 – The Bean Brothers – Honey Babe / Tuh Too Duh Doo
70016 – Jimmy Oliver & The Rockers – Slim Jim Part 1 / Part 2
70017 – The Channels – The Gleam In Your Eye / Stars In The Sky
70018 – The Continentals – Dear Lord / Fine Fine Frame
70019 – The Teardrops – The Stars Are Out Tonight / Oh Stop It
70020 – Little Woo Woo – My One And Only / This Wonderful Girl Of Mine
70021 – The Bluenotes – If You Love Me / There's Something In Your Eyes Eloise
70022 – The Channels – Flames In My Heart / My Lovin' Baby
70023 – The Channels – I Really Love You / What Do You Do
70024 – The Continentals – Picture Of Your Love / Soft And Sweet
70026 – The Ebb Tons – Ram Induction / Rockin' On The Range
70027 – Bobby Holiday – Come Home / My Letter
70028 - ?
70029 – The Beaumarks – Little Miss Twist / Lovely Little Lady
70030 – The Latons – Love Me / So In Love
70031 – The Impressions – Listen – Shorty's Got To Go
70032 – The RPMs – Love Me / Street Scene
70033 – The Laurie Sisters – Somethingold Something New / Stand A Littklle Closer
70034 – Hal Hearn – Turkey In The Straw / King Kemo
70035 – Curtis Blandon – Mr Imagination / Soul
70036 – Lafayette & Le Sabres – Free Way / Cure For Love
70037 – The Royaltones – See Saw / Poor Boy
70038 – The Caterpillars – Happy Happy Happy Goodbye / The Caterpillar Song
70039 – Charlie Russo – Goofin' / Party
70040 – Jimmy Jones & The Pretenders – Close Your Eyes (Sleep And Dream / Part Time Sweetheart
70041 – The Soothers – The Little White Cloud That Cried / I Believe In You
70042 – The Jades – He's My Guy / There Will Come A Day
70043 – Doug Clark – Chestnuts / Peanuts

Soulful Kinda Music – The Rare Soul Bible Volume Two

3000 - Carol Fran - Crying In The Chapel / I'm Gonna Try
3001 - Tarheel Slim & Li'l Ann - Close To You / I Submit To You
3002 - Big Maybelle - Let Me Go / No Better For You
3003 - Wilbert Harrison - Baby Move On / You're Still My Baby
3004 – The Clovers - Poor Baby / He Sure Could Hypnotise
3005 - Carol Fran - It's My Turn Now / You Can't Stop Me
3006 - Carol Fran - I Know / World Without You
3007 - Daisy Burris - I've Learned My Lesson / Take The Same Thing
3008 - Johnny Newbag - Sweet Thing / Little Samson
3009 - Wilbert Harrison - Don't Take It So Hard / Sugar Lump
3010 – The El Dorados - Knock Knee / New Breed
3011 – The Gee's - It's All Over / Love's A Beautiful Thing
3012 - Carol Fran - Any Day Love Walks In / Just A Letter
3013 - Baby Jane & Rockabyes - Heartbreak Stomp / Dance Till My Feet Get Tired
3014 - Jimmy Mayes & Soul Breed - Drums For Sale / Pluckin'
3015 - King Coleman - Do The Booga Lou Part 1 / Part 2
3016 - The Jets - I Was Born With It / Everything I Do
3017 - King Coleman - When The Fighting's Over / Get On Board
3018 – The Intrigues - Don't Refuse My Love / Girl Let's Stay Together
3019 – The Jury – Please Forget Her / Who Dat
3020 - Robert Neal - Goodbye Now / I'm So Glad /
3021 - Chris Towns Unit - Turn To Me / You Don't Know What You're Getting
3022 - Bobby Lee - Cut You Loose / I'm Just A Man
3023 - Kathy & Calendars - Back In Your Arms Again / Please Don't Go
3024 - I, She & Me – Look / McDougal Street
3025 - Kathy Young - A Thousand Stars / Eddie My Darling
3026 - The Innocents - Gee Whiz / Please Mr Sun
3027 – Conroy Wilson - Canadian Sunset / Secret Love

Premium Stuff

1 - Fabulous Peps - Why Are You Blowing My Mind/I Can't Get Right
2 - ?
3 - Fabulous Peps - I'll Never Be The Same Again / So Fine
4 - Lee Rogers - Sweet Baby Talk / Jack The Playboy
5 - Dee Edwards - I'll Shed No Tears / Inst
6 - Lee Rogers - Sock Some Love Power To Me / The Same Things That Make You Laugh
7 - Fabulous Peps - Why Are You Blowing My Mind / Gypsy Woman
8 - Timmy Shaw - Get To Steppin' / Can't We Make This Love Last
9 - Dee Edwards - A Girl Can't Go By What She Hears / Inst
10 - Sanders Sect - A Girl Can't Go By What She Hears Part 1 / Part 2
11 - Lee Rogers - I Need Your Love / Jack The Playboy

Prix

Soulful Kinda Music – The Rare Soul Bible Volume Two

6901 - Royal Esquires - Ain't Gonna Run / Our Love Used To Be - 1969
6902 - Soul Ensemble - Melon Jelly / Move Out – 1969
6903 - ?
6904 - Orchestra Kin Bantou - Soyez Reconnainenoir / Naleli Eve Elvire - 1969
7001 - Eddie Ray - You Got Me / Glad I Found You - 1970
7001 - Eddie Ray - You Got Me / Glad I Found You - 1970   (no address on label,
alternate mix)
7002 - Joe King - Speak On Up / What's Wrong - 1970
7101 - Eddie Ray - I Stand Accused / Part.2 - 1971
7102 - Marion Black - I'm Gonna Get Loaded / You're Not Alone - 1971
7201 - Marion Black - Listen Black Brother / Part 2 - 1972
7202 - Chip Willis & the Double Exposure - I'm Gonna Gitcha / Part 2 - 1972
7301 - OFS Unlimited - Mister Kidneys / Mystic - 1973
7302 - Marion Black - (More Love) Is All We Need / Inst. - 1973
7303 - Mitch Mitchell & Gene King -Never Walk Out On You / Inst. – 1973

Pzazz Records

001 - Lorez Alexandria - I'm Wishin' / Endless - 1968
002 - Fortson & Scott - Better Than Anyone / Just A Little Step - 1968
003 - Lorez Alexandria - The One You Love Is You / Didn't We - 1968
004 - Louis Jordan - Amen Corner / Watch The World - 1968
005 - T. V. Slim - My Heart's Full Of Pain / Don't Knock The Blues - 1968
006 - Lynn Brown - Here In This Room / The Ballad Of Gail And Tom - 1968
007 - The Sinceres - Don't Waste My Time / Girl, I Love You - 1968
008 - Anne Bartee - 24th Day Of July / Living For Someone - 1968
009 - Johnnie Ruth King - Still I Love You / Don't Tell Me About My Man - 1968
010 - Misty Moore - Can't Believe You're Gone / Little Things - 1968
011 - Louis Jordan - Wild Is The Night / New Orleons And A Rusty Old Horn - 1968
012 - Fortson & Scott - Sweet Lover / My Dreams Of You - 1968
013 - Misty Moore - Magnifico / More Than The Eye Can See - 1968
014 - Ray Smith - My Mama Didn't Raise No Fool / Rather You Or The Bottle - 1968
015 - Louis Jordan - Sakatumi / Santa Claus, Santa Claus - 1968
016 - Ronnell Bright Here It Is Again / To Be Alone With You - 1968
017 - Lorez Alexandria - Nonchalantly / Santa Is Here - 1968
018 - Misty Moore - Children Listen / Just Another Piece Of Paper - 1968
019 - Ray Smith - Papa And Santa Claus / Hitch Hiking Hippie - 1968
020 - ?
021 - The Soul Machine - Twitchie Feet / Bag Of Goodies - 1968
022 - Bongo Bean - Some Girl's Gonna Get Me / We Come From The Dirt Of The
Ground - 1969
023 - Louis Jordan - Bullitt / What's On Your Mind - 1969
024 - Little Janice - Not 'Til Him / Mirror Mind - 1969
025 - Lorez Alexandria - Hey Jude / I Don't Want To Hear It Anymore - 1969
026 - Walter Scott - Soul Stew Recipe / Feelin' Something New Inside - 1969
027 - Robby Fortson - Are You For Real / Ain't It Lonely - 1969
028 - Shuggy Ray Smith - My Momma Didn't Raise No Fool / Hitch Hikin' Hippie -
1969
029 - Good Time Charlie - I Remember Mini Ginny / Rover Or Me - 1969

030 - T. V. Slim Love Bounce / You Can't Buy Love - 1969
031 - Little Janice - Texas Woman / Goodbye Baby - 1969
032 - Misty Moore - Don't Mail The Letter / Windy Curtains - 1969
033 - Anne Bartee - Come Into My Arms Again / I'll Be Yours - 1969
034 - Little Janice - I Am A Soul / Since You've Been Gone - 1969
035 - Kevin & Air Keith - Michael's Theme / Euphoria - 1969
036 - Misty Moore - Wherefore And Why / Hello Hello Hello - 1969
037 - ?
038 - Charlie Taylor - Stop Callin' The Police On Me / Law And Order - 1969
039 - Warm Excursion (Terrible Three) - Hang Up (Part 1) / Hang Up (Part 2) - 1969
040 - Ronnell Bright - Cocoa / Nobody Seems To Care - 1969
041 - Janice Tyrone - I'm Gonna Make It / Meet Me Baby - 1969
042 - Kijana - Did You Really Choose Me / A Man And A Woman - 1969
043 - Dave Dixon - Hitch Hiking Hippie / Sock It To Me On The Highway - 1969
044 - Lynn Brown - And I'm In Love / Home Where Love's In Vain - 1969
045 - Alice & The Soul Sensations - Funky Judge / I Found A Love - 1969
046 - Lorez Alexandria - My Way / Hello There Girl - 1969
047 - The Fourth Coming - We Got Love / Take Time - 1969
048 - Misty Moore - Chicago Over The Rise / It Ain't Me Babe - 1969
049 - Pimbrock Skiggs - That Was Yesterday / Wake Up - 1969
050 - Len Jewell - All My Good Lovin' (Is Going To Waste) / The Elevator Song - 1969
051 - ?
052 - Peaches Daniels - Feeling Something New Inside / I Hate To Forget When I Try To Remember - ?
053 - ?

The Radiants

┼───

The Golden Gospeltones (members Maurice McAlister, Leonard Caston Jr., Barbara Gaston and Richard Dickerson)

The Greater Harvest Baptist Church Choir (members Maurice McAlister, Leonard Caston Jr (whose father was a member of The Five Breezes with Willie Dixon), ...)

The Troubadors (members Maurice McAlister, Wallace Sampson, Jerome Brooks, Elzie Butler and Charles Washington)

The Troubadors (members Maurice McAlister, Wallace Sampson, Jerome Brooks, Elzie Butler and Green "Mac" McLauren)

The Radiants (members Maurice McAlister, Wallace Sampson, Jerome Brooks, Elzie Butler and Green "Mac" McLauren) - this version of the group submitted a demo to Chess of their original songs titled "Hit It", "Joyce", "Please Don't Leave Me" and "Father Knows Best".

The Radiants (members Maurice McAlister, Wallace Sampson, Jerome Brooks, Elzie Butler and Green "Mac" McLauren)

Chess 1832 - Father Knows Best / One Day I'll Show You - 1962

The Greater Harvest Baptist Church Choir

Sharp 632 - What A Difference In My Life* / Without God - 1962 *lead Green "Mac" McLauren.

The Radiants (Maurice McAlister, Wallace Sampson, Jerome Brooks, Elzie Butler and Green "Mac" McLauren)

Chess 1849 - Heartbreak Society / Please Don't Leave Me - 1963
Chess 1865 - I Got A Girl / I'm In Love - 1963 (Withdrawn)

Maurice McAlister and The Radiants (members Maurice McAlister, Wallace Sampson, Jerome Brooks, Elzie Butler and Frank McCollum)

Chess 1872 - Shy Guy / I'm In Love* - 1963 *on flip side Green "Mac" McLauren is with the group and Frank McCollum is not.

Maurice and The Radiants (members Maurice McAlister, Wallace Sampson, Jerome Brooks, Elzie Butler and Frank McCollum)

Chess 1887 - I Gotta Dance To Keep My Baby / Noble The Bargain Man - 1964

The Radiants (members: A varying combination of Maurice McAlister, Wallace Sampson and Leonard Caston Jr., Jerome Brooks, Elzie Butler, Green 'Mac' Mclauren)

Chess 1904 - Voice Your Choice / If I Only Had You - 1964
Chess 1925 - It Ain't No Big Thing / I Got A Girl - 1965 (some copies issued with picture sleeve)
Chess 1939 - Whole Lot Of Woman / Tomorrow - 1965

Maurice and The Radiants (members Maurice McAlister, Wallace Sampson and James Jameson)

Chess 1954 - Baby You've Got It / I Want To Thank You Baby - 1966 (Minnie Riperton on backing vocals)

The Radiants (The Confessions (members Mitchell Bullock, ...))

Chess 1986 - (Don't It Make You) Feel Kinda Bad / Anything You Do Is Alright - 1966

Maurice McAlister

Chess 1988 - Baby Hang On / I'd Rather Do It Myself - 1966

The Radiants (members Mitchell Bullock, Wallace Sampson, James Jameson and Victor Caston)

Chess 2021 - The Clown Is Clever / Don't Take Your Love - 1967

Maurice & Mac (members Maurice McAlister and Green "Mac" McClauren)

Checker 1179 - So Much Love / Try Me - 1967

Checker 1197 - You Left The Water Running / You're The One - 1968

The Radiants (members Mitchell Bullock, Wallace Sampson, James Jameson and Victor Caston)

Chess 2037 - Hold On / I'm Glad I'm The Loser - 1968
Chess 2057 - Tears Of A Clown / I'm Just A Man - 1968

Maurice & Mac (Maurice McAlister and Green "Mac" McClauren)

Checker 1206 - Lean On Me / Why Don't You Try Me - 1968
Checker 1218 - Lay It On Me / What Am I Gonna Do - 1969

The Radiants (members Mitchell Bullock, Wallace Sampson, James Jameson and Victor Caston)

Chess 2066 - Choo Choo / Ida Mae Foster - 1969

Maurice & Mac (Maurice McAlister and Green "Mac" McClauren)

Soulful Kinda Music – The Rare Soul Bible Volume Two

Checker 1224 - Oh What A Time / Baby You're The One - 1969

The Radiants (members Mitchell Bullock, Wallace Sampson, James Jameson and Victor Caston)

Chess 2078 - Book Of Love / Another Mule Kicking In Your Stall - 1969
Chess 2083 - Shadow Of A Doubt / I'm So Glad I'm A Loser - 1969

Maurice & Mac (Maurice McAlister and Green "Mac" McClauren)

Checker 1232 - Kick My Dog And I'll Kick Your Cat / But You Know I Love You - 1970
Chess 2102 - You Can't Say I Didn't Try / Lay It On Me - 1971

The Radiants (members Mitchell Bullock, Wallace Sampson, James Jameson and Maurice McAlister)

Twinight 153 - My Sunshine Girl / Don't Wanna Face The Truth - 1971

Maurice & Mac (Maurice McAlister and Green "Mac" McClauren)

Brown Sugar 0103 - Use That Good Thing / Ain't No Harm To Moan - 1972

The Radiants (members Maurice McAlister, Wallace Sampson and Leonard Caston Jr.,)

Eric 231 - It Ain't No Big Thing / Voice Your Choice - 1973

The Radiants (members

Chess 15967 - Don't Take Your Love / ? - ?

The Ravens / The Radiants (members Maurice McAlister, Wallace Sampson and Leonard Caston Jr.,)

Chess 138 - Dear One / Voice Your Choice* - ? *flip by The Radiants

Bobby Moore & The Rhythm Aces / The Radiants (members Maurice McAlister, Wallace Sampson and Leonard Caston Jr.,)

Collectables 03423 - Searchin' For My Love / It Ain't No Big Thing* - ? *flip by The Radiants.

The Nu-Radiants (members Wallace Sampson, James Jameson, Shalaby Karim and Nora Ellis)

 Trivia

Maurice White of Earth, Wind and Fire played drums on all The Radiants sessions. Maurice McAlister, Wallace Sampson and Leonard Caston provided backing vocals on Tony Clarke's 1965 release "The Entertainer" on Chess 1924.

Soulful Kinda Music – The Rare Soul Bible Volume Two

The Rumblers

The Rumblers (members Mike Kelishes, Johnny Kirkland, Wayne Matteson and Eddie Braracco) 1961 line-up.

The Rumblers (members Adrian Lloyd, Mike Kelishes, Johnny Kirkland, Wayne Matteson and Bob Jones)

Highland 1026 - Intersection / Stomping Time - 1962
Downey 103 - Boss / I Don't Need You No More - 1962
Dot 16421 - Boss / I Don't Need You No More - 1962
Downey 106 - Boss Strikes Back / Sorry - 1963
Dot 16455 - Boss Strikes Back / Sorry - 1963

The Rumblers (members Greg Crowner, Mike Kelishes, Johnny Kirkland, Wayne Matteson and Bob Jones)

Downey 107 - Angry Sea (Walmea) / Bugged - 1963
Dot 16480 - Angry Sea (Walmea) / Bugged - 1963

The Nylons (members Greg Crowner, Mike Kelishes, Rex Delong (former member of The Fig Leaf five), Wayne Matteson and Bob Jones)

Downey 109 - Maid'n Japan / Gospel Truth - 1963

The Rumblers (members Greg Crowner, Mike Kelishes, Johnny Kirkland, Wayne Matteson, Bob Jones and Rex Delong)

Downey 111 - It's A Gas / Tootananny - 1963
Dot 16521 - It's A Gas / Tootananny - 1963

Adrian & The Sunsets (members Adrian Lloyd, Bobby Forest, Ron Eglit, Clyde Brown, Dick Lambert and Bruce Riddar)

Sunset 602 - Breakthrough / Cherry Pie - 1963 (Some Copies Issued With Picture Sleeve)
Sunset 603 - Justine / Donna - 1964
Sunset 603 - Justine / She Treats Me Better Than You - 1964

The Rumblers (members Greg Crowner, Mike Kelishes, Johnny Kirkland, Wayne Matteson, Bob Jones and Rex Delong)

Downey 114 - High Octane / Night Scene - 1964

Little Johnny & The Rumblers (members Greg Crowner, Mike Kelishes, Johnny Kirkland, Wayne Matteson, Dave Allen and Rex Delong)

Downey 119 - The Hustler / Riot In Cell Block # 9 - 1964

The Rumblers (members Greg Crowner, Mike Kelishes, Johnny Kirkland, Wayne Matteson, Dave Allen and Rex Delong)

Downey 127 - Soulful Jerk / Hey Did-A-Da-Do - 1964 (also released in the U. K. on KING 1021)

The Bel-Cantos (members Barry White (vocals), Greg Crowner, Mike Kelishes, Johnny Kirkland, Wayne Matteson, Dave Allen and Rex Delong)

Downey 128 - Feel Awright (Part 1) / Feel Awright (Part 2) - 1965

The Rumblers (members Greg Crowner, Mike Kelishes, Johnny Kirkland, Wayne Matteson, Dave Allen and Rex Delong)

Downey 133 - Boss Soul / Till Always - 1965 (group disbands after Johnny Kirkland is drafted)

Adrian LLoyd (was born in England then moved to L.A.)

Charger 112 - Lorna / Got A Little Woman – 1966

Label Listings

Rampart

611 - Phil & Harv – Darling (Please Bring Your Love) / Friendship – 1964
612 - Phil & Harv – Sweeter Than Candy / The Facts Of Love - 1964
641 - Blendells - La La La La La / Huggies Bunnies - 1964
642 - Cannibal & The Headhunters - Land Of 1000 Dances / I'll Show You How To Love Me - 1965
643 - Atlantics – Beaver Shot / Fine Fine Fine – 1965
644 - Cannibal & The Headhunters – Here Comes Love / Nau Ninny Nau – 1965
645 - Ron Holden - Girl I Love You / Nothing I Wouldn't Do – 1965
646 - Cannibal & The Headhunters – Follow The Music / I Need Your Loving – 1965
647 - Atlantics - Sloop Dance / Sonny And Cher - 1966
648 - Soul-Jers – Chinese Checkers / Poochum - 1965
649 - Soul-Jers - Gonna Be A Big Man / Crazy Little Things
650 - Unused number
651 - Sammy Lee & The Summits - Hey Joe, Where You Gonna Go? / Walkin' – 1966
652 - Pvt Randy Thomas - The Great Crusade / The Great Crusade - 1966
653 - Sammy Lee - It Hurts Me / Nursery Rhymes – 1966
654 - Cannibal & The Headhunters – Please Baby Please / Out Of Sight - 1966
655 - Four Tempos – Showdown (At The Union Hall / Memories - 1967
656 - Phil & Del – These Feelings / It Hurts Me - 1967
657 - Four Tempos - Got To Have You (Can't Live Without You) / Come On Home – 1967
658 - Four Tempos - I Had A Strange Dream / This Is The Way I Feel - 1967

Soulful Kinda Music – The Rare Soul Bible Volume Two

659 - Village Callers – Hector / I'm Leaving – 1968

660 - Village Callers – Mississippi Delta / Hector Part 2 - 1968

661 - East Bay Soul Brass - The Panther / Let's Go Let's Go Let's Go - 1968

662 - David & Ruben – (I Love Her So Much) It Hurts Me / The Girl In My Dreams - 1969

663 - Village Callers - Evil Ways / When You're Gone – 1969

664 - Four Tempos - Lonely Prisoner / Strange Dream - 1969

665 - Invincibles - Crystal Blue Persuasion / If I Should Win Your Love - 1970

721 - Eastside Connection - A Cho Cho San Part 1 / A Cho Cho San Part 2 - 1970

761 - Eastside Connection - La Cucaracha / La Cucaracha (Long Version) – 1976 (7" Single)

762 - Eastside Connection – La Cucaracha / Quizas Quizas Quizas – 1976 (12" Single)

771 - Eastside Connection – You're So Right For Me (Vocal) / You're So Right For Me (Inst) – 1977 (12" Marbled, Coloured Vinyl, Single)

772 - Eastside Connection – You're So Right For Me / Over Please - 1977 (7" Single)

003 - East Side Connection – You're So Right For Me / Frisco Disco – 1978 (7" Single)

781 - Eastside Connection – Frisco Disco / Birthday Medley – 1978

791 - Skylite – Boogie Butt / Smile (You Make Me Want To Smile) -1979

004 - Skylite – Boogie Butt / Boogie Butt (Long Version) – 1979 (7" Single)

811 - Slylite – The Na Na Song (Land Of A 1000 Dances) / Dance And Be Healthy – 1981 (12" Single)

006 - Topazz – Vision Love / Vision De Amor – 1988 (7" Single

881 - Topaz – Vision Love (Club Mix) / Vision Love (Inst) – 1988 (12" Single)

882 - Gary Brock – Stuck Between A Rock And A Hard Place (Club Mix) / Stuck Between A Rock And A Hard Place (Radio Edit) / Stuck Between A Rock And A Hard Place (House Dub) – 1988 (12" Single)

891 - Tapazz – Vision Love (Super Dance Remix) / Vision Love (Spanish Radio Edit / Spanish Language Dub) // Vision Love (American Radio 7") / Vision Love (Special Vision Dub Mix) – 1989 (12" Single)

892 - Yuarr & Metoo – Robo Love (The Story) / Robo Love (Epilog) // Robo Love (Extended Club Mix) / Robo Love (Special Radio Mix) – 1989 (12" Single)

893 - Alexio / Didi – Coqueto / Just So Sorry – 1989 (12" Single)

894 - Topaz - Seduction (Dance Mix) / Seduction (Radio Edit) / Seduction (Instrumental Dub) / Seduction (Bass Dub) – 1989 (12" Single)

901 - Latin Force Featuring Nengue – La Charanga / Latin Hottie / La Charanga (Radio Edit) – 1990 (12" Single)

902 - Latin Force Featuring Nengue – Leyla (Extended Dance Mix) / Leyla (Deep Underground Dub) / Leyla (Drumapella) / Leyla (Club House Mix) / Leyla (Club Pop Mix) / Leyla (Radio Mix) – 1990 (12" Single)

921 - Javier – Rave It Up (7" Version) / Rave It Up (Extendo-Matic) / Rave It Up (Technosis: Rave) // Rave It Up (Club Dub) / Lucky Pierre's Proclamation / Rave It Up (Rave En Español) – 1992 (12" Single)

Red Coach

_____

Soulful Kinda Music – The Rare Soul Bible Volume Two

801 – Every Day People – The Bump Part 1 / Part 2 - 1973
802 – The Carstairs – It Really Hurts Me Girl / Story Of Our Love - 1973
803 – Shalong – I'm In Love With You / Lady - 1973
804 – Hot Line – I Like What I Like / Get Down - 1973
805 – Richmond International – Maybe, If I Leave You / Back On The Road Again - 1973
806 – Shalong – How I'm Gonna Love You / Lady - 1974
807 – Universal Mind – Something Fishy Going On / For You Girl - 1974
808 – Hot Line – Juice It Up Part 1 / Part 2 - 1974
809 – Chicago Gangsters – I Choose You / My Ship - 1974
810 – Richmond International – If You Should Ever / The Way You Do The Things You Do - 1974
811 – Universal Mind – Reach Out For Me / I'll Never Let You Get Away - 1975
812 – Music Machine – By The Hair Of My Chinny Chin Chin / (Instrumental) - 1975
813 – Hot Line – How Funky Do You Do Part 1 / Part 2 - 1975
814 – The Exceptionals – Gotta Let Some Sunshine Into My Life / What Is Living - 1975
900 - The Galations - There's A Place / Steal Away - ?

Renfro

112 - Sequins - Case Of Love / You're All I Need
113 - Carl Henderson - That Girl / Sharing You
113 - Sequins - That Boy / He's A Flirt
114 - John Westly - Just Believe / Don't Give It Away
115 - Carl Henderson - That Girl / You're All I Need
116 - Carl Henderson - I Love You So / Sadness
117 - Attractions - Find Me / Destination You
118 - Ron Saunders Soul Group - The Skate Part1 / Part 2
120 - Stunners - Nobody But Me / Without You
122 - Anthony Renfro - At The Dance / This Is Our Moment Of Love
125 - Buddy McKnight - Everytime Part 1 / Everytime Part 2
126 - Sequins - Hes A Flirt / Case Of Love
127 - Renfro Orch - Case Of Love (Single Sided White Demo's)
1118 - Carl Henderson - I'm Scheming / Gotta Keep On Moving
314 - Little Tony & Hawks - The Tears / Sweet Little Girl
338 - Carl Henderson - Sharing You / Please Stop Laughing At Me
817 - Little Tony & Hawks - Don't Try To Fight It / My Little Girl
843 - Carl Henderson - See What You Have Done / You're All I Need
1917 - Sam Cox - Life Is Love / Destination
61627 - Helen Moore - The Run Around / Get Away Blues
37 - Viola Edwards - Love Me Baby / Gotta Get Over
38 - Rare Gems Odyssey - Touchdown / It Don't Take Much
40 - Luke Day/Anthony C.Renfro & Friends - Love Line / A Whole Lot Of Nothin'
43 - Anthony C.Renfros's Orchestra/& Friends - Gloria's Theme / A Whole Lot Of Nothin'
44 - Renfro Orch - He's A Flirt / A Whole Lot Of Nothin'
45a - Anthony C.Renfro's Group. - Feel Like Dancing Funky / Gloria's Theme

Soulful Kinda Music – The Rare Soul Bible Volume Two

A1 - Tender Loving Care - My World Is Falling / Two Fools Are We

Revilot

201 - Darrell Banks - Our Love Is (In The Pocket) / Open The Door To Your Heart
202 -
203 - Darrell Banks - Somebody (Somewhere) Needs You / Baby What 'Cha Got (For Me)
204 - Rose Batiste - I Miss My Baby / Hit And Run
205 – Holidays - Love's Creeping Up On Me / Never Alone
206 - Rose Batiste - I Will Wait For You / Come Back In A Hurry
207 – Parliaments - (I Wanna) Testify / I Can Feel The Ice Melting
208 - Jackey Beavers - A Love That Never Grows Old / I Need My Baby
209 - Little Sonny - The Creeper / Latin Soul
210 – Holidays - I Know She Cares / I Keep Holding On
211 – Parliaments - All Your Goodies Are Gone / Don't Be Sore At Me
212 - Ronnie Taylor - Without Love / I Can't Take It
213 -
214 – Parliaments - Little Man / The Goose (That Laid The Golden Egg)
215 - Little Sonny - Don't Ask Me No Questions / Stretchin' Out
216 - J.J. Barnes - Now She's Gone / Hold On To It
217 – Parliaments - Look What I Almost Missed / What You Been Growing
218 - J.J. Barnes - Sad Day A Coming / I'll Keep Coming Back
219 -
220 -
221 -
222 - J.J. Barnes - Our Love Is In The Pocket / All Your Goodies Are Gone (Inst.)
223 – Parliaments - Good Old Music / Time
224 - Terry Felton - You're Welcome Back / I Don't Want To Have To Wait
225 - J.J. Barnes / Lebaron Strings - So Called Friends / Now She's Gone (Inst)
226 – Holidays - All That Is Required (Is You) / I'll Keep Coming Back (Inst)
227 - Little Sonny - We Got A Groove / Sonny's Bag
228 – Parliaments - A New Day Begins / I'll Wait

Revue Records, a review !

Revue records was a subsidiary of MCA Records, and was nominally based at 8255 Sunset Boulevard, Hollywood, California. Set up to serve the Black music market, the label itself tended to lease recordings in rather than actually record the artists themselves. Consequently there are recordings from Detroit, Chicago, the West coast, and several points in between on the label.

In existence for four years, 1966 to 1969, there were a total of 71 singles released, and 12 albums. In some ways though the Revue label acted as a feeder label for Uni,

Soulful Kinda Music – The Rare Soul Bible Volume Two

in the sense that the artists who were successful on Revue, tended to be transferred to the Uni label for future releases, especially for albums.

So, who were the artists that recorded for the label:

Garland Green -

Garland Green was born on June 23, 1942, in Dunleath, Mississippi. He soon found his way to Chicago though, and his first recordings were done on the Giant label under the guidance of Jo Armstead and Mike Terry. This Giant release was then leased to Revue for national distribution. Several more singles were recorded, and then Garland was transferred to the Uni label for his classic 'Jealous Kinda Fella album.

The Mirettes -

When the 1964-1966 edition of the Ikettes, Robbie Montgomery, Vanetta Fields, and Jessie Smith, decided to leave Ike Turner's organization to record on their own, they used the name The Mirettes to record for Revue. The trio's cover of In The Midnight Hour just missed the Top 40 in 1968, and Revue released a similarly titled LP later that year.

Jack Montgomery -

Only four records exist by Jack Montgomery, and he was the mystery man of Northern Soul for a long while until I discovered his real identity was Marvin Jones during an interview with Don Mancha. From Detroit, Jack recorded the Revue release in New York at Scepter's studio at the same session as 'My Dearly Beloved' and leased to Revue by Johnny Terry, somewhat illegally by all accounts. The track of course turned out to be 'Baby Baby Take A Chance On Me' on Revue 11009. Which also has a rather strange configuration of releases: Demos with the vocal on both sides, the rarer demo with vocal and instrumental, and issues with vocal and instrumental.

The Chi-Lites -

The Chi-Lites were formed in Chicago in 1959. Originally called the Hi-Lites, they consisted of Marshall Thompson, Creadel "Red" Jones, Eugene Record, Robert Lester, and Clarence Johnson. Originally called the Chanteurs, the released one single on Renee Records. Between 1960 and 1964 they recorded as The Hi-Lites, and then Marshall & The Hi-Lites and finally changing their name to the Chi-Lites at the end of 1964. Several local releases followed until they found themselves with a couple releases on Revue. They must have done the job, because straight after the Revue releases they were signed by Brunswick, and the rest is history

Marvin L Sims -

Marvin L Sims was born on December 11th 1944, in Sedalia, Missouri. After he graduated from high school, he joined the Air Force in 1961 and finished his term of service in 1965. Almost immediately he joined a group called The Gaypoppers, although no records were released.

Soulful Kinda Music – The Rare Soul Bible Volume Two

By 1966 he was recording as a solo artist, releasing three singles over a two year period on the Mellow label, then in 1968 the first of his two releases on Revue came out. Several singles followed on Mercury, and then after a break of twenty five years in his recording career, Marvin released a CD in 1998.

Darrow Fletcher -

Darrow Fletcher was only 15 years old when he made his first recording for the Groovy label, two more followed, and then a move to the Jacklyn label. Although he was getting localized success, even appearing on television several times in Chicago, he just couldn't make it to the big time. A move to Revue in 1968 was supposed to get him the national distribution, but in all honesty the songs were not quite up to the standard of the Groovy and Jacklyn releases, so in 1969 he moved to Congress for one release, and then found himself recording for Uni. Several other releases followed until 1979 when his recording career ended. He made a triumphant return to live singing though at the Cleethorpes weekender a couple of years ago.

Alder Ray -

Other than the photograph on the next page, there is surprisingly little known about Alder Ray. It's almost certain that she is the same artist who recorded as Alder Ray Black, and Alder Ray Mathis in the early 1970's, and has some involvement with Phil Spector in the early Sixties, but that's about all I know.

The Sunlovers -

The Sunlovers are originally from Los Angeles, and are the same group that recorded on Mutt & Jeff. They also recorded as Charles Pennywell And The Inspirations on Breakthrough, and a series of labels as The Fairlanes. Charles 'Diamond' Pennywell was the constant member between both The Sunlovers, The Inspirations and The Fairlanes, and sang lead on all the group's releases. He is still working today a s a live act with the Fairlanes Band, and has performed in a variety of tribute groups as well.

The picture of the group below is from their Mutt & Jeff days so actually preceeds the Revue release (As does the individual photo of Charles Pennywell.

Lee Charles -

Lee Charles was an artist that legendary arranger / producer Carl Davis took under his wing. Hios first recordings were for the Dakar label in 1966. Further recordings were cut at Dakar, but for some reason they were leased out to Revue through 1967 and 1968. Altogether there were two releases on Revue, and then Lee went onto record on Brunswick and Bamboo.

Tony Borders –

Tony Borders is one of the legendary names of Southern Soul, recording far too few sides over the years. Little is known of him as an artist though. His early recordings were patchy, to say the least, but once he hooked him with Quin Ivy, and started

Soulful Kinda Music – The Rare Soul Bible Volume Two

recording in Muscle Shoals the true sound emerged. The two Revue releases were, like most releases leased in by the label, and are probably the best examples of Southern Soul put out by Revue.

Marvin Holmes & The Uptights –

A strange release for the label this time. The exact same recording had already been released as 'Funky Mule' on Boola Boola.by Marvin Holmes. So why, and how, it ended up on Revue is a complete mystery. It obviously did some sales though because Marvin Holmes and the Uptights went on to record an album for the Uni label. He also went on to form Marvin Holmes' Justice, who recorded some heavy Funk tracks in the '70s.

Third Avenue Blues Band –

All I know about the Third Avenue Blues Band is that they were a white group fronted by a black singer called Harold Jones. They were originally from Texas, and all their tracks were cut at IRI Studios, Dallas, Texas

Mike & The Censations -

Mike Kirkland's brother Robert bet some friends at a party that he and his brother could release a record every bit as good as the Motown tracks that were storming up the charts at the time. Unbelievably, the group they formed, Mike & The Censations released their first record within a couple of months of the bet being made. Released on their own label, Bryan, it went onto gather radio play and led to not only a second release, but a two record deal with Revue.

David T Walker –

Recognised for many years as one of the top Jazz guitar session musicians in the States, david T Walker also released quite a large number of tracks in his own name. Certainly there were several singles on Revue, and two albums.

Eddie & Ernie –

Eddie Campbell and Ernie Johnson Jnr recorded some of the most blistering Deep Soul you are ever likely to hear. Their two voices blend perfectly, with that raw edge that is so necessary for true Soul Music. Often compared to Sam & Dave, they never really received any recognition internationally until Dave Godin started championing their cause. Although they had long been know to Soul aficionados via their uptempo records, Dave Godin worked with Kent records to make sure that the Eddie & Ernie compilation CD was released. That, plus the inclusion of their recordings in the Dave Godin Deep Soul series of releases ensured that their legacy will live on forever. How they came to have a record released on Revue though is a complete mystery to me.
The following artists all had at least one release for the label, but I have no more information than that to be honest.

Joyce Hopson –

Soulful Kinda Music – The Rare Soul Bible Volume Two

Joyce Hopson is an artist that I can find no information on at all, so other than the fact she cut this wonderful mid tempo Crossover track for the label in 1968. I don't even know what area of the States it was recorded in, but it does sound Chicago, and the production credits do hint that way.

Charles Lamont

I can only assume that this is the same Charles lamont that recorded for Challenge.

Discography

11001 – Garland Green – Girl I Love You / It Rained Forty Days And Nights - 1966
11002 – Jimmy Coleman – Cloudy Days / Don't Seem Like You Love Me - 1966
11003 – Lonnie B & Viki G – Pops / High On The Mountain - 1966
11004 – The Mirettes – In The Midnight Hour / To Love Somebody - 1966
11005 – The Chi-Lites – Love Is Gone / Love Me - 1967
11006 – The Johannesburg Street Band – Capetown / Wimbube (Wim-O-Way) - 1967
11007 – Lee Charles – If That Ain't Lovin' You / Standing On The Outside - 1967
11008 – Darrow Fletcher – I Like The Way I Feel / Way Of A Man - 1967
11009 – Jack Montgomery – Baby Baby Take A Chance On Me / Inst - 1967
11010 – Stu Gardner – I Can't Make It By Myself / Never Gonna Hurt Again - 1967
11011 – Deacon Lee & The Prophets – Buckaroo / Bad - 1967
11012 – Patti-Cakes – Peas Porridbe / Viva La Venezuela - 1967
11013 – The Living Souls – Drop It On Me / Soul Searchin' - 1967
11014 – Alder Ray – Love Will Let You Down / Run Baby Run - 1967
11015 – ?
11016 – Lonnie B & Viki G – Lovin' Feeling / Oops - 1968
11017 – The Mirettes – Real Thing / Take Me For A Little While - 1968
11018 – The Chi-Lites – (Um Um) My Baby Loves Me / That's My Baby For You - 1968
11019 – Chic Carbo – Biggest Fool In Town / Touch Me - 1968
11020 – Garland Green – Mr Misery / You Played On A Player - 1968
11021 – June Gatlin – Baby Cakes / Good Girl Gone Bad - 1968
11022 – Lee Charles – Someone Somewhere / Wrong Number - 1968
11023 – Darrow Fletcher – Gonna Keep Loving You / We Can't Go On This Way - 1968
11024 – Marvin L Simms – Old Man Time / Talkin' 'Bout Soul - 1968
11025 – Tony Borders – Cheaters Never Win / Love And A Friend - 1968
11026 – Marvin Holmes & The Uptights – Ride Your Mule Part 1 / Part 2 - 1968
11027 – Stu Gardner – I Got You / 634-5789 - 1968
11028 – Third Avenue Blues Band – If You Don't Love Me / It's Got To Be Love - 1968
11029 – The Mirettes – First Love / I'm A Whole New Thing - 1968
11030 – Garland Green – Ain't That Good Enough / Love Now Pay Later - 1968
11031 – Chic Carbo - The Story Of My Life / Ordinarily - 1968
11032 – David T Walker – Reach Out For Me / Sidewalk - 1968
11033 – Two People – Love Dust / Stop Leave My Heart Alone - 1968
11034 – Joyce Hopson – I Surrender To You / This Time - 1968
11035 – Darrow Fletcher – Sitting There That Night / Those Hanging Heartaches -

Soulful Kinda Music – The Rare Soul Bible Volume Two

1968
11036 – Harold Johnson Sextet – Sorry About That / Think - 1968
11037 – Goody Colbert – Baby I Like It / I Wanna Thank You - 1968
11038 – Marvin L Simms – Danger / Get Off My Back - 1968
11039 – Lonnie B & Viki G – High On The Mountain / We're Gonna Stay In Love -
1968
11040 – Tony Borders – I Met Her In Church / What Kind Of Spell - 1968
11041 – Mike & The Censations – Split Personality / You're Living A Lie - 1968
11042 – Micki Lynn – In The Meantime / Sure Is Something - 1968
11043 – Skyline Drive – Make It To Spain / Tonight Could Be The Night Little Darling
- 1968
11044 – Jimmy Graham – Soul Walk / Soul Walk In - 1968
11045 – Sun Lovers – Main Street / Main Street Shuffle - 1968
11046 – Party Brothers – Do The Grounding / Nassau Daddy - 1968
11047 – Charles Lamont – Before It's Over / Hog Blues - 1968
11048 – Frankie Vance – Can't Break The Habit Of Your Love / Do You Hear Me
Baby - 1968
11049 – Eddie & Ernie – Thanks For Yesterday / Woman What Do You Be Doing -
1968
11050 – Harold Johnson – Right On / Soul Perception - 1968
11051 – 3rd Avenue Blues Band – Pipedream / Don't Make Me Laugh - 1968
11052 – Mark Eric – Don't Cry Over Me / Night Of The Lions - 1968
11053 – Chris Bernard – Mother / Good Hearted Woman - 1968
11054 – Tony Borders – Polly Wally / Gentle On My Mind - 1968
11055 – Johnny & Mark V – Down The Pike / Sands Of Malibu - 1968
11056 – Mike & The Censations – Shopping For Love / The Straw (That Broke The
Camel's Back) - 1968
11057 – Pleasure – Born A Girl / It Ain't Right - 1968
11058 – Roy Gene Crimpton – Beautiful Lady At 8 / She Was Good To Me - 1968
11059 – Abraham & His Sons – I Can't Do Without You / Your Mother Understood -
1968
11060 – David T Walker – Can I Change My Mind / My Baby Loves You - 1969
11061 – Charles Lamont – Lefty / Two Thousand Years Ago - 1969
11062 – Frankie Vance – Somewhere In Your Life (You've Been Hurt) / You Are My
Solution - 1969
11063 – Eddie & Ernie – Tell It Like It Is / You Give Me Love To Go On - 1969
11064 – Mark Eric – California Home / Where Do The Girls Of Summer Go - 1969
11065 – Jimmy Graham – Love Can't Be Modernized / We Shall Overcome - 1969
11066 – King Biscuit Entertainers – Rollin' Free Man / Sunset Blues - 1969
11067 – 3rd Avenue Blues Band – Come On And Get It / Rose Garden - 1969
11068 – Mike & The Censations – Gonna Try To Get You Back / A Man Ain't Nothing'
But A Man - 1969
11069 – The Saints – Mirror Mirror On The Wall /Come On Let's Dance - 1969
11070 – David T Walker – Watch Out Dynamite / Baby I Need Your Loving - 1969
11071 - Len Woods - I'm In Love / Do It Funky - 1969

Ric-Tic

Soulful Kinda Music – The Rare Soul Bible Volume Two

100 - Gino Washington - Gino Is A Coward / Puppet On A String - 1965
101 - Freddie Gorman - In A Bad Way / There Can Be Too Much - 1965
102 - Freddie Groman - Can't Get It Out Of My Mind / Take Me Back - 1965
103 - Edwin Starr - Agent Double-O-Soul / Instrumental - 1965
104 - San Remo Golden Strings - Hungry For Love /All Turned On - 1965
105 - Rose Batiste - That's What He Told Me / Holding Hands - 1965
106 - J.J Barnes - Please Let Me In / I Think I Found A Love – 1965
107 - Edwin Starr - Backstreet / Instrumental - 1966
108 - San Remo Golden Strings - I'm Satisfied / Blueberry Hill - 1966
109 - Edwin Starr - I Have Faith In You / Stop Her On Sight - 1966
109x - Edwin Starr - Scott's On Swingers - 1966
110 - J.J Barnes - Real Humdinger / I Ain't Gonna Do It - 1966
111 - Laura Lee - To Win Your Heart / So Will I - 1966
112 - San Remo Golden Strings - Festival Time / Joy Road - 1966
113 - Unreleased
114 - Edwin Starr - Headline News / Harlem - 1966
115 - J.J Barnes- Day Tripper / Don't Bring Me Bad News- 1966
116 - San Remo Golden Strings - International Love Theme / Quanto Sei Bella - 1966
117 - J.J Barnes - Say It / Deeper In Love - 1966
118 - Edwin Starr - Girls Are Getting Prettier / It's My Turn Now - 1966
119 - Fantastic Four - Girl Have Pity / Live Up To What She Thinks - 1966
120 - Edwin Starr - My Kind Of Woman / You're My Mellow – 1966
121 - Fantastic Four - Can't Stop Looking For My Baby / Just The Lonely - 1967
122 - Fantastic Four - The World Is A Stage / Ain't Love Wonderful - 1967
123 - Al Kent - The Way You Been Acting Lately / Instrumental -1967
124 - Andre Williams - You Got It And I Want It / I Can't Stop Cryin - 1967
125 - Willie "G" - Money In The Bank / Meet Me Halfway - 1967
126 - Unreleased
127 - Al Kent - You've Got To Pay The Price / Where Do I Go From Here - 1967
128 - Fantastic Four - Romeo And Juliet / You Gave Me Something - 1967
129 - Flaming Embers - Let's Have A Love In / Instrumental - 1967
130 - Fantastic Four - As Long As I Live / To Share Your Love - 1967
131 - Flaming Embers - She's A Real Live Wire / Let's Have A Love-In - 1967
132 - Flaming Embers - Hey Mama / Let's Have A Love In - 1967
133 - Al Kent - Finders Keepers / Ooh! Pretty Lady - 1967
134 - Fantastic Four - As Long As The Feeling Is There / Goddess Of Love – 1967
135 - Detroit Emeralds - Show Time / Instrumental - 1968
136 - Fantastic Four - Love Is A Many-Splendored Thing / Goddess Of Love - 1968
137 - Fantastic Four - No Love Like Your Love / Man In Love - 1968
138 - Detroit Emeralds - Shades Down / Ode To Billy Joe - 1968
139 - Fantastic Four - Win Or Lose / I've Got To Have You - 1968
140 - Flaming Embers / Al Kent - Bless You / Bless You - 1968
141 - Detroit Emeralds - I'll Keep On Coming Back / Take Me The Way I Am- 1968
142 - Little Ann - Going Down A One Way Street / I'd Like To Know You Better - 1968
143 - Flaming Embers - Children / Instrumental - 1968
144 - Fantastic Four - I Love You Madly / Instrumental - 1968
145 - Flaming Embers - Just Like Children / Tell It Like It Is – 1968

Soulful Kinda Music – The Rare Soul Bible Volume Two

Ru-Jac

925 - Jessie Crawford - Please Don't Go / I Love You So - 1963
45001 - Jessie Crawford & Kay Keys Band - Please Don't Go / I Love You So - 1963
45002 - Sonny Daye & The Shyndel's Band - I'm Through With You / A Woman Like You - 1963
45006 - Little Winfield Parker - My Love For You / One Of Those Mornings - 1963
45007 - Winfield Parker - When I'm Alone / Rockin' In The Barnyard - 1963
45009 - The Fruitland Harmonizers - Take Care Of Me / My Father Watches Over Me - 1963
45010 - ?
45011 - Shirley (Of The Soul Sisters & Brothers) - What More (Can Anyone Want) / You Don't Really Care - 1963
07 - Little Winfield Parker - One Of These Mornings / My Love For You - 1963
08 - Brenda Jones - Let's Go Back To School / Can't You See - 1963
09 - Jolly Jax - Meadow Of Love / Monkey Cha Cha - 1963
009 - Butch Cornell's Trio - Goose Pimples / Here 'Tis Now - 1963
0011 - Shirley Of The Soul Sisters & Brothers - What More (Can Anyone Want)/ You Don't Really Care - 1963
0012 - Brenda Jones - It Must Be Love / I'm So Afraid - 1963
0013 - The Reekers - Don't Call Me Flyface / Grindin' - 1963
0014 - Arthur Conley - Where You Lead Me / I'm A Lonely Stranger - 1964
0014 - Harold Holt & Band - Where You Lead Me / I'm A Lonely Stranger – 1964
0015 - Bobby Sax & The Housekeepers - Get Right / Soul At Last
0017 - Winfield Parker - I Love You Just The Same / My Love (Blue label)
0017 - Rita Doryse & The Bob Craig Combo - Please Let Me Love You / Goodie Goodie
0018 - The Henchmen - She Still Loves You / Think Of Me
0018 - Kitty Lane - It's Love I Need / Sweetheart
0019 - Winfield Parker - Go Away Playgirl / Wandering
0020 - Winfield Parker (With The Shydells Band) - Sweet Little Girl / What Do You Say - 1968
0020 - The Caressors - I Can't Stay Away / Who Can It Be - 1968
0022 - Winfield Parker - Oh My Love / She's So Pretty - 1968
0023 - Gene And Eddie - I Would Cry / I Tell You - 1968
0024 - Winfield Parker - Fallen Star / I Love You Just The Same - 1968 (Yellow Label)
0024 - Winfield Parker - I Love You Just The Same / Oh My Love - 1968
025 - The Fred Martin Review - I'm The One Who Loves You / Contagious - 1968
102668 - Fred Martin Jr & The Exciters - Hot Dog / Love Don't Leave Me Now - 1968
2413 - Leon Gibson - Working Hard / Do The Roller - 1968
101-1 - Winfield Parker - Mr Clean Part 1/ Part 2 - 1968
200 - Winfield Parker - Funkey Party / Oh My Love - 1968
201 - Gene & Eddie - It's So Hard / Sweet Little Girl* - 1969 *(Same as #0020)
202 - Gene & Eddie - Let Me Go Easy / She's True Enough
218 - The Neltones - Come On Over / C'est La Vie
220 - Maskman & The Cap-Tans - Love Can Do Wonders / Chicken Wings (Harmon Bethea)

Soulful Kinda Music – The Rare Soul Bible Volume Two

302 - Wilson Conroy - Canadian Sunset / Secret Love
980 - Jimmy Dotson Rhythm By Inner Light Band - Think Of Me As Your Soldier / To Be Your Lover
9170 - The Fred Martin Review - Take Me Back Again / I Know It's Going To Happen - 1970
41070 - Sir Joe - Baby I'd Drop Everything / Every Day (I'll Be Needing You - 1970 (Joe Quarterman)
52670 - Gene & Eddie - It's No Sin / You've Got To Love Sometime (Also released on Mon'ca 52670)
1613 - Tiny Tim (Mr. T) Harris - Saving All My Loving / It's Everything To Me
1671 - Gene & Eddie - Why Do You Hurt Me / Darling I Love You - 1971
1771 - The Dynamic Corvettes - Keep Off The Grass / It's A Trap - 1971
2-1771- Fred Martin Revue - Sugar / When I Am Alone - 1971
5771 - Utopian Concept / Francine Long - Days May Come, Days May Go / Same - 1971
81171 - Saturday - The Drums & Bells Of Christmas / The Love Of A Child - 1971
1871 - Saturday - Changes Part 1 / Part 2 - 1971
1971 - Saturday - Changes Part 1 / Part 2 - 1971
32272 - The Fred Martin Review - I Loved You Once / Go On Back - 1972

? - Rita Dorsey - Wait Till Then / When I'm Alone
? - Lance Hill - Angel In The Sky / Through

This must be the most dis-organised catalogue that I have ever come across. Thanks to the combined efforts of several people, not least the Soul Source Forum and the Rare Soul forum, and Joe Vaccarino, this is probably the most accurate listing ever compiled.

Soulful Kinda Music – The Rare Soul Bible Volume Two

The SOUL Master - Edwin Starr
January 21st, 1942 - April 2nd, 2003

As far as I'm concerned, there was no man who was more deserving of the title 'The Soul Master'. Charles Edwin Hatcher was one of the greatest exponents of Soul music the world has ever seen, and now, like so many before him, he's gone.

I was originally going to do a full biography, but realised that other people will also do that, so I'm just going to recount some of my own memories and experiences of, and with, Edwin Starr.

He's the artist I have seen do a live show more than any other, right back to the Seventies I must have seen him live on at least one occasion a year, and it was at one of these live back in the Eighties shows that I actually got to meet him, and chat with him on a one to one basis for the first time. Funnily enough, it was the same night that I met Bill Randle for the first time as well. Edwin had always been approachable for autographs and a quick chat after a show, but on this occasion I probably spent almost an hour chatting to him, and walked away with an invitation to his home to get all my albums, singles, and photographs autographed.

I subsequently went round to Pooley Hall in Tamworth where Edwin lived and you couldn't have been greeted in a more friendly way. How many other singers who have had world wide hits can you imagine inviting you into their home and making you a cup of tea as though they had known you for years ?

That's what Edwin was like though, he was friendly to everyone, and always had time to speak to you once he knew you. Another example: At one of the Great Yarmouth Weekenders at the end of the Eighties I introduced Edwin to my wife Margie. It was only a brief few minutes whilst we chatted. However, Edwin not only remembered the introduction, he remembered Margie's name as well, because the following night I was off looking at records leaving Margie in charge of my sales stall. I returned about half an hour later to find Edwin sitting behind my stall chatting away to Margie as though they had been friends for years. As I say, amongst all the people who were there, he not only remembered who she was, but her name as well . That in itself is some achievement when you consider how many people must have spoken to him over the course of the previous two days.

On another occasion I went to watch The Temptations do a live show at Wolverhampton Civic Hall, they did a fabulous show, but guess who was their surprise guest ? That's right Edwin. He not only received a standing ovation as he walked onto the stage, he stole the show with three songs ! From a personal point of view though the night just got better. After the show I went round to the staircase which led up to the dressing rooms to try and get some autographs from the Temptations. The nice gorilla in a suit wouldn't let anyone through, that is until Edwin noticed Margie and me standing there. He immediately told the gorilla that we were his guests and he had to let us through. So there we were, at the Temptations backstage party, courtesy of Edwin Starr.

My mate Wilko put Tommy Hunt on to do a P.A. at Ritzy's in Nottingham. It turns out that Edwin and Tommy had been good friends back in the Sixties but hadn't seen each other for nearly twenty years, so Edwin came along to see the show. Towards the end of Tommy's set we were treated to what must have been a unique duet. Tommy Hunt and Edwin Starr on stage together, and from Edwin's point of view, he enjoyed it as much as everyone else.

How many people can claim that they have had a Soul superstar from Detroit (Yes, I know he was born in Cleveland) come and stand on the stairs in their house and sing for them. I can. Edwin had asked me to do some design work for him and came round to the house one evening. Whilst posing for a photograph with my kids on the stairs he decided to sing to us. Talk about an exclusive show !

The one show that I missed that I would have killed to attend was in the mid Nineties. Bill Randle was doing a lot of driving for Edwin back then and one evening when he was round at my house putting the Soul world to rights, as we still do, he mentioned that Edwin had a gig in the Wembley area of London but he didn't know where. So there I was Saturday afternoon, settling down at home to watch the mighty Wigan Rugby League Club demolish their opponents in the Rugby League Challenge Cup Final at Wembley when they announced who the special guest for the pre match entertainment was (It was Diana Ross one year as well). You guessed it..........Edwin Starr, the gig in the Wembley area of London was actually at Wembley Stadium !!!

In the late Nineties Edwin approached Bill Randle, Micky Nold, and me with a view to running a weekly Soul night at a club in Wolverhampton on a Sunday night. At the time it was a very ambitious project, there were three rooms, and it was a big place. The idea was to have the night on weekly, advertised as 'Hosted By Edwin Starr' and when Edwin wasn't working he would come along, and would also bring along any of the live acts that were in the Midlands on tour as his guests. A lot of planning went into the promotion, including a visit to the Club owner's head office in Romford, and several meetings at Edwin's house in Tamworth. Unfortunately the club owners' went bankrupt before we could get it up and running. A real shame because I think it would have been a considerable success.

I have actually DJ'ed on two occasions where Edwin has performed live. The first one was an alldayer somewhere near Bristol. Again it was down to a club owner. This guy had booked Edwin to do a Soul Alldayer, and then realised at the last minute that he didn't have a DJ. He rang Edwin, and Edwin rang me. What I didn't realise at the first conversation was that I was the ONLY DJ booked for the alldayer, all ten hours of it ! I hurriedly arranged for Micky Nold to share the job with me and off we set on Edwin's band bus (And it really was a bus, well an old coach to be honest), a lack of local promotion meant that the place only had the local hardcore Soul scene people in, but Edwin and the Band still gave a fantastic show.

My final story concerning Edwin is about the ill fated allnighters in Birmingham. Bill Randle promoted these, and over the three events we had live shows from Edwin Starr, J J Barnes, Steve Mancha, Carolyn Crawford, Bobby Taylor, and The

Contours. Edwin was at the same time as the nighters doing a national tour with Martha Reeves and Mary Wilson of The Supremes, so he brought them along for a night out. Needless to say, neither of them could resist getting on the stage and doing a couple of numbers as well. The story I have though is that I was set up in the back bar selling when Edwin arrived with Mary Wilson. He called me over, introduced me to Mary Wilson, and then said Dave will look after you. So after a thirty second conversation, there I am sitting next to Mary Wilson, who was once a member of the biggest Girl Group the world has ever seen. Other people soon realised who she was, and the queue of autograph hunters soon meant that I had to actually shut the sales stall and clear some space for Mary to sit and sign autographs. It was just the way that Edwin did it though, at the end of the day, although I DJ regularly, I produce the mag you are reading right now, I've had a book published, and run a very large and busy web site, I an essentially still a fan of Soul music, as much as the next man. So for Edwin Starr to introduce me to Mary Wilson of The Supremes was a big thing to me.

For that, and all the other personal memories, I'm grateful that I knew Edwin Starr as a friend rather than just a wonderful performer. His music will live on forever, as will your own memories of him as a performer, but let's just reflect for a minute on the enjoyment he must have brought to so many people during his life. If I could go knowing that I had brought that much enjoyment into that many lives, I think I'd be quite happy.

Rest In Peace Edwin, you'll be missed, but never forgotten.

The Sapphires

The Sapphires (Members Carol Jackson, Joe Livingston And George Garner)

Swan 4143 - Where Is Johnny Now / Your True Love - 1963
Swan 4162 - Who Do You Love* / Oh, So Soon - 1964 *Written By Kenny Gamble.
Itzy 5 - Who Do You Love / Oh, So Soon - 1964
Swan 4177 - I Found Out Too Late / I've Got Mine, You Better Get Yours - 1964 (Backing Vocals By The Swans)
Swan 4184 - Gotta Be More Than Friends / Moulin Rouge (Where Is Your Heart) - 1964
ABC-Paramount 10559 - Let's Break Up For A While / Hearts Are Made To Be Broken - 1964 (Backing Vocals By Nick Ashford, Valerie Simpson And Melba Moore)
ABC-Paramount 10590 - Thank You For Loving Me / Our Love Is Everywhere - 1964
ABC-Paramount 10639 - Gotta Have Your Love / Gee I'm Sorry Baby - 1965
ABC-Paramount 10693 - Evil One / How Could I Say Goodbye - 1965
ABC-Paramount 10753 - Gonna Be A Big Thing / You'll Never Stop Me From Loving You - 1965
ABC-Paramount 10778 - Slow Fizz / Our Love Is Everywhere - 1966
Eric 0122 - Who Do You Love / Where Is Johnny Now - 197?
Collectables Col 010827 - Who Do You Love / Oh So Soon - 198?
Collectables Col 010837 - Gotta Have Your Love / Gee I'm Sorry - 198?
Collectables Col 010847 - Thank You For Loving Me / Our Love Is Everywhere - 198?

Soulful Kinda Music – The Rare Soul Bible Volume Two

The Sheppards

The Sheppards (Members John Pruitt, Albert Bell, Nat Tucker, and James Issac)

Theron 112 – Love / Cool Mambo – 1955
United 198 – Sherry / Mozelle – 1956

The Sheppards (Members Murrie Eskridge, O C Perkins, Mill Edwards, Jimmy Allen, James Isaac, Kermit Chandler)

Apex 7750 – Island Of Love / Never Felt Like This Before – 1959
Apex 7752 – Just Like You / Feel Like Lovin' - 1960
Apex 7755 – Meant To Be / It's Crazy - 1960
Apex 7759 – Society Gal / Just When I needed You Most - 1960
Apex 7762 – Tragic / Come Home Come Home - 1961

Murrie Eskridge (Released as a solo artist because the rest of the group had already left Apex)

Apex 7764 – So In Need For Love / Never Felt This Way Before - 1961

The Sheppards

Pam 1001 - Never Let Me Go / Give A Hug To Me - 1961
Wes 7750 - Glitter In Your Eyes / Every Now And Then - 1961
Vee Jay 406 - Every Now And Then / Glitter In Your Eyes - 1961
Vee Jay 441 - Come To Me / Tragic - 1962
Abner 7006 - Loving You / Elevator Operator - 1962
Okeh 7173 - Pretend You're Still Mine / Walkin' - 1962

The Sheppards (Members Murrie Eskridge, O C Perkins, Jimmy Allen, James Isaac, Kermit Chandler)

Constellation 123 – Island Of Love / Give A Little Hug To Me – 1964
Owl 330 – Queen Of Hearts / Forgotten - ?

The Shepards (Members Murrie Eskridge, O C Perkins, Kermit Chandler)

ABC Paramount 10758 – Let Yourself Go / Little Girl Lost – 1966

The Sheppards

Mirwood 5534 – Stubborn Heart / How Do You Like It – 1967

The Sheppards (Members Murrie Eskridge, O C Perkins, Jimmy Allen, James Isaac, Kermit Chandler)

Sharp 6039 – Glitter In Your Eyes / What's The Name Of The Game – 1969
Bunky 7764 – Island Of Love / Steal Away – 1969
Bunky 7766 – Your Love (Has A Hole In It) / I'm Not Wanted – 1969

Soulful Kinda Music – The Rare Soul Bible Volume Two

Sandi Sheldon

Kenni Woods (Kendra Spotswood)

Philips 40112 - That Guy Is Mine / Can't He Take A Hint - 1963 (backing vocals Dee Dee Warwick, Cissy Houston and Doris Troy)

The Four Buddies (members

Philips 40122 - Lonely Summer / Slow Locomotion - 1963 (backing vocals Kendra Spotswood and Van McCoy)

Kenni Woods (Kendra Spotswood)

Philips 40156 - Do You Really Love Me / Back With My Baby - 1963 (backing vocals Dee Dee Warwick, Cissy Houston and Doris Troy)

The Shirelles In 1964, Kendra Spotswood joined The Shirelles but didn't record with the group because she was still under contract to Philips but performed live with them for a year or two. The Shirelles were in litigation over royalties with Scepter records at the time and, for some reason, Beverly Lee wasn't able to work live with the others. So Kendra Spotswood took her place on the road with Shirley Owens, Doris Coley and Addie "Miki" Harris.

The Pacettes (members Kendra Spotswood, Van McCoy,

Regina 306 - You Don't Know Baby / Don't Read The Letter - 1964

Jack & Jill (members Van McCoy and Kendra Spotswood)

Maxx 330 - Two Of A Kind / Just As You Are - 1964

The Fantastic Vantastics (members Kendra Spotswood, Van McCoy,

Tuff 406 - Gee What A Boy / Oh Happy Day (Tra La La) - 1965

Kenrda Spotswood (from Englewood, New Jersey)

Tuff 407 - Stickin' With My Baby / Jive Guy - 1965

Sandi Sheldon (Kendra Spotswood)

Okeh 7277 - You're Gonna Make Me Love You / Baby You're Mine - 1967

The Vonettes (members Kendra Spotswood, Lillian Dore (ex - Correctone singer), Van McCoy ....)

Cobblestone 703 - Touch My Heart / You Don't Know Me - ?

Soulful Kinda Music – The Rare Soul Bible Volume Two

The Sherrys

The Sherrys (members Delthine Cook and Dinell Cook (daughters of Little Joe Cook), Charlotte Butler and Delores "Honey" Wylie)

<u>Guyden</u> 2068 - Pop Pop Pop-Eye / Your Hand In Mine – 1962
Guyden 2077 - Slop Time / Let's Stomp Again – 1963
Guyden 2084 - Saturday Night / I've Got No One – 1963
Guyden 2094 - Monk, Monk, Monkey / That Boy Of Mine - 1963 (after this release Delthine Cook and Charlotte Butler leave group to get married. Group manager Little Joe Cook forms a new group using the same name)

The Sherrys (members

Mercury 72256 - No No Baby / That Guy Of Mine – 1964
Roberts 701 - Slow Jerk / Confusion – 1965
JJ 1002 - Put Your Arms Around Me* / Happy Girl - 1966 (*first track played at the first all-nighter starting at 2 a.m. on 23-September-1973 at Wigan Casino with 634 people in attendance)

Joe Simon

The Golden Tones (Members Joe Simon, ...)

Hush 101 - Little Island Girl / Doreetha - 1959
Hush 102 - You Left Me Here To Cry Alone / Ocean Of Tears - 1959

Joe Simon (Born 2-September-1943 In Simmesport, Louisiana)

Hush 103 - It's A Miracle / Land Of Love - 1960
Hush 104 - Call My Name / Everybody Needs Somebody - 1961
Hush 106 - Pledge Of Love / It's All Over - 1961
Hush 107 - I See Your Face / Troubles - 1961
Hush 108 - Land Of Love / I Keep Remembering - 1962
Irral 778 - Only A Dream / Just Like Yesterday - 1963
Dot 16570 - Only A Dream / Just Like Yesterday - 1964
Gee Gee 077 - My Adorable One / Say - 1964 (Some Copies Issued With Picture Sleeve)
Vee-Jay 609 - My Adorable One / Say (That My Love Is True) - 1964
Vee-Jay 663 - When You're Near / When I'm Gone - 1965
Vee-Jay 694 - Let's Do It Over / The Whoo Pee - 1965
Mell-O-Soun 8001 - Stay Love / ? - ?
Sound Stage 7 2564 - A Teenager's Prayer / Long Hot Summer - 1966
Sound Stage 7 2569 - Too Many Teardrops / What Makes A Man Feel Good - 1966
Sound Stage 7 2577 - My Special Prayer / Travelin' Man - 1966
Sound Stage 7 2583 - Put Your Trust In Me (Depend On Me) / Just A Dream - 1967
Sound Stage 7 2589 - Nine Pound Steel / The Girl's Alright With Me - 1967
Sound Stage 7 2602 - No Sad Songs / Come On And Get It - 1967

Soulful Kinda Music – The Rare Soul Bible Volume Two

Sound Stage 7 2608 - (You Keep Me) Hangin' On / Long Hot Summer - 1968
Sound Stage 7 2617 - Message From Maria / I Worry About You - 1968
Sound Stage 7 2622 - Looking Back / Standing In The Safety Zone - 1968
Sound Stage 7 2628 - The Chokin' Kind / Come On And Get It - 1969
Sound Stage 7 2634 - Baby, Don't Be Looking In My Mind / Don't Let Me Lose The Feeling - 1969
Sound Stage 7 2637 - Oon-Guela (Part 1) / Oon-Guela (Part 2) - 1969
Sound Stage 7 2641 - It's Hard To Get Along / San Francisco Is A Lonely Town - 1969
Sound Stage 7 2651 - Moon Walk (Part 1) / Moon Walk (Part 2) - 1969
Sound Stage 7 2656 - Farther On Down The Road / Wounded Man - 1970
Sound Stage 7 2664 - Yours Love / I Got A Whole Lotta Lovin' - 1970
Sound Stage 7 2667 - That's The Way I Want Our Love / When - 1970
Spring 108 - Your Time To Cry / I Love You More (Than Anything) - 1970
Spring 113 - Help Me Make It Through The Night / To Lay Down Beside You - 1971 (Some Copies Issued With Picture Sleeve)
Spring 115 - You're The One For Me / I Ain't Givin' Up - 1971
Spring 118 - Georgia Blues / All My Hard Times - 1971
Spring 120 - Drowning In The Sea Of Love / Let Me Be The One - 1971
Sound Stage 7 1508 - Misty Blue / That's The Way I Want Our Love - 1972
Spring 124 - Pool Of Bad Luck / Glad To Be Your Lover - 1972
Spring 128 - Power Of Love / The Mirror Don't Lie - 1972
Spring 130 - Trouble In My Home / I Found My Dad - 1972
Spring 130 - Step By Step / Talk Don't Bother Me - 1973
Sound Stage 7 1512 - Who's Julie / The Girl's Alright With Me - 1973
Spring 138 - Theme From "Cleopatra Jones" / Who Is That Lady - 1973 (Some Copies Issued With Picture Sleeve)
Spring 141 - River / Love Never Hurt Nobody - 1973
Sound Stage 7 1514 - Someone To Lean On / I Got A Whole Lotta Lovin' - 1974
Spring 145 - Carry Me / Do You Know What It's Like To Be Lonesome - 1974
Spring 149 - The Best Time Of My Life / What We Gonna Do Now - 1974
Spring 156 - Get Down, Get Down (Get On The Floor) / In My Baby's Arms - 1975
Spring 159 - Music In My Bones / Fire Burning - 1975
Spring 163 - I Need You, You Need Me / I'll Take Care (Of You) - 1975
Spring 166 - Come Get To This / Let The Good Times Roll - 1976
Spring 169 - Easy To Love / Can't Stand The Pain - 1976
Sound Stage 7 1521 - Funny How Time Slips Away / Message From Maria - 1976
Spring 172 - You Didn't Have To Play No Games / What's Left To Do - 1977
Spring 025 - One Step At A Time (5:33) / One Step At A Time (3:39) - 1977 (12" Promo Issue Only)
Spring 176 - One Step At A Time / Track Of Your Love - 1977
Spring 178 - For Your Love, Love, Love / I've Got A Jones On You Baby - 1977
Spring 184 - I. O. U. / It Must Be Love - 1978
Spring 057 - Love Vibration / Love Vibration - 1978 (12" Promo Issue Only)
Spring 190 - Love Vibration / (Instrumental) - 1978
Spring 194 - Going Through These Changes / I Can't Stand A Liar - 1979
Spring 3003 - I Wanna Taste Your Love / Make Every Moment Count - 1979
Spring 3006 - Hooked On Disco Music / I Still Love You - 1980
Posse 5001 - Baby, When Love Is In Your Heart (It's In Your Eyes) / Are We Breaking Up - 1980

Soulful Kinda Music – The Rare Soul Bible Volume Two

Posse 5005 - Glad You Came My Way / I Don't Wanna Make Love - 1980
Posse 5010 - Are We Breaking Up / We're Together - 1981
Posse 5014 - Fallin' In Love With You / Magnolia - 1981

Joe Simon & Clare Bathe

Posse 5018 - You Give Life To Me / (Instrumental) - 1982

Joe Simon

Posse 5019 - Go Sam / (Instrumental) - 1982
Posse 5021 - Get Down, Get Down "82" / It Be's That Way Sometimes - 1982
Posse 5038 - Deeper Than Love / Step By Step - 1983
Compleat 140 - It Turns Me Inside Out / Morning, Noon And Night - 1985
Compleat 146 - Mr. Right Or Mr. Right Now / Let Me Have My Way With You - 1985
Monument 03465 - (You Keep Me) Hangin' On / The Chokin' Kind - ?
Monument 03466 - My Special Prayer / Nine Pound Steel - ?
Sound Plus 2178 - Nine Pound Steel / Put Your Trust In Me (Depend On Me) - ?
Collectables Col 033097 - Get Down, Get Down (Get On The Floor) / Theme From "Cleopatra Jones"
Collectables Col 033107 - The Chokin' Kind / Nine Pounds Steel - ?

Marvin L Simms

The Valentinos (members Marvin L. Sims, Leroy Rowe, Larry Allen, William Evans and Grant Ray) 1961 group.

The Gaypoppers (members Marvin L. Sims, Edward Lane, Bobby Lane, John Green and Sidney C. Coleman) 1965 group.

Marvin L. Sims (born 11-December-1944 in Sedalia, Missouri)

Mellow 1002 - Now I'm In Love With You / What Can I Do? - 1966
Mellow 1004 - (Nina) Have You Seen My Baby (Part 1) / (Part 2) - 1967
Mellow 1005 - Disillusioned / Hurting Inside - ?
Revue 11024 - Talkin' Bout Soul / Old Man Time - 1968

Marvin Sims

Karen 1547 - Sweet Thang / Your Love Is Wonderful - 1969

Marvin L. Sims

Revue 11038 - Get Off My Back / Danger - 1969
Uni 55217 - It's Your Love / I Can't Understand It - 1970

Marvin Sims

Mercury 73288 - Dream A Dream / I Can't Turn You Loose - 1972

Soulful Kinda Music – The Rare Soul Bible Volume Two

Mercury 73340 - Love Is No Sin / You Gotta Go - 1972
Mercury 73364 - It's Too Late / ? - 1973
Rivertown 498 - Love Is On The Way / Blow Away Breezes - 1980

The Soul Sisters

The Canjoes (Members Joe Louis Johnson (Later A.K.A Lou Johnson), Theresa Cleveland And Ann Gissendanner)

Dapt 208 - Speaking Of Love / Dance The Boomerang - 1962

The Soul Sisters With The Sweet Pea King Band (Members.....?)

Guyden 2066 - The Warm-Up / Because I Love You - 1962 (Unsure if this is the same group)

The Soul Sisters (Members.......?)

Kayo 5101 - I Can't Let Him Go / You Can't Be My Boyfriend - 1963 (Unsure if this is the same group)

The Soul Sisters (Members Theresa Cleveland And Ann Gissendanner)

Sue 799 - I Can't Stand It / Blueberry Hill - 1963

The Kolettes (Members Rumoured To Be Theresa Cleveland And Ann Gissendanner)

Barbara 1094 - Who's That Guy / Just How Much (Can One Heart Take) - 1964
Checker 1094 - Who's That Guy / Just How Much (Can One Heart Take) - 1964

The Soul Sisters (Members Theresa Cleveland And Ann Gissendanner)

Sue 10-005 - Good Time Tonight / Some Soul Food - 1964
Sue 107 - Foolish Dreamer / ? - 1964
Sue 107 - Loop De Loop / Long Gone - 1964
Sue 111 - Just A Moment Ago / I Won't Be Your Fool Anymore - 1964
Sue 130 - The Right Time / Think About The Good Times - 1965
Sue 140 - Give Me Some Satisfaction / Flashback - 1966
Sue 148 - So Much Love / Big Boy - 1967
Sue 5 - Good Time Tonight / Foolish Dreamer - 1968
Veep 1291 - You Got 'Em Beat / A Thousand Mountains - 1968

The Soul Sisters / Baby Washington

Collectables Col 031497 - I Can't Stand It / Only Those In Love* - ? (Flip By Baby Washington)

Soulful Kinda Music – The Rare Soul Bible Volume Two

The Soul Twins

The Soul Twins (Hal Bergrattenreid And Harold Bergrattenreid ..... Real Life Twins)

Karen 1531 - Mr. Pitiful / Searching For My Baby -1967
Karen 1533 - Quick Change Artist / Give The Man A Chance - 1967
Karen 1535 - Just One Look / It's Not What You Do, It's The Way You Do It - 1967
Karen 1537 - Mr. Pitiful / Searching For My Baby - 1968 (There were two Karen 1537 releases. The other being by The Capitols "Afro Twist / Cool Jerk '68")
Back Beat 599 - She's The One / Mr. Independent - 1969
Atlantic 1535 - It's Not What You Do / Just One Look - ?

The Gas & Funk Factory (Members Hal Bergrattenreid, Harold Bergrattenreid,.................)

Brunswick 55434 - The Goodnight Song / Everybody Gets Some (Love) - 1970

Candi Staten

The Four Golden Echos (members of gospel group, Canzetta Staton (when she was eight years old), Maggie Staton, Leatha Mae Malcolm and Betty Jean Byers)

The Jewel Gospel Trio (members Canzetta Staton, Maggie Staton and Naomi Harrison)

Aladdin ? - 1953
Aladdin ? - 1953
Nashboro 550 - Take My Hand, Precious Lord / Many Little Angels In The Band - 1955
Nashboro ?- I Looked Down The Line (And I Wondered)/ Somebody's Knocking At Your Door - 1955
Nashboro 588 - Jesus Is Listening / The Gospel Ship - 1956
Nashboro 599 - Praying Time / Sin Is To Blame - 1957
Nashboro 617 - Too Late / Ease My Troublin' - 1958

Candi Staton (born Canzetta Maria Staton on 13-March-1943, in Hanceville, Alabama)

Unity 7-11 - Now You've Got The Upper Hand / You Can't Stop Me - 1967

Candy Staton & Billy Walker

Minaret 137 - The Judgement / XYZ - 1967 (Candi Staton has stated that she knows nothing about this 45)

Candi Staton

Soulful Kinda Music – The Rare Soul Bible Volume Two

Fame 1456 - I'd Rather Be An Old Man's Sweetheart (Than A Young Man's Fool) / For You - 1969
Fame 1459 - Never In Public / You Don't Love Me No More - 1969
Fame 1460 - I'm Just A Prisoner (Of Your Good Lovin') / Heart On A String - 1970
Fame 1466 - Sweet Feeling / Evidence - 1970
Fame 1472 - Stand By Your Man / How Can I Put Out The Flame (When You Keep The Fire Burning) - 1970

Fame 1476 - He Called Me Baby / What Would Become Of Me - 1971
Fame 1478 - Mr. And Mrs. Untrue / Too Hurt To Cry - 1971
Fame 91000 - In The Ghetto / Sure As Sin - 1972

Candi Staton with Clarence Carter

Atlantic 2875 - If You Can't Beat 'Em / Lonesomest Lonesome - 1972

Candi Staton

Fame 91005 - Lovin' You, Lovin' Me / You Don't Love Me No More - 1972
Fame 91009 - Do It In The Name Of Love / The Thanks I Get For Loving You - 1973
Fame 256 - Something's Burning / It's Not Love (But It's Not Bad) - 1973
United Artists Xw-256 - Something's Burning / It's Not Love - 1973
United Artists Xw-328 - Love Chain / I'm Gonna Hold On - 1973
Fame 328 - Love Chain / I'm Gonna Hold On (To What I Got This Time) - 1973
Warner Bros. 8032 - As Long As He Takes Care Of Home / A Little Taste Of Love - 1974
Warner Bros. 8038 - Little Taste Of Love / As Long As He Takes Care Of Home - 1974
Warner Bros. 8078 - Here I Am Again / Your Opening Night - 1975
Warner Bros. 8112 - Six Nights And A Day / We Can Work It Out - 1975
Warner Bros. 8181 - Young Hearts Run Free / I Know - 1976
Warner Bros. Pro 643 - Run To Me / Run To Me - 1976 (12" Promo Issue Only)
Warner Bros. 8249 - Run To Me / What A Feeling - 1976
Warner Bros. Pro 670 - A Dreamer Of A Dream / A Dreamer Of A Dream - 1977 (12" Promo Issue Only)
Warner Bros. 8320 - A Dreamer Of A Dream / When You Want Love - 1977
Warner Bros. 8387 - Nights On Broadway / You Are - 1977
Warner Bros. 8461 - Cotton Candi / Music Speaks Louder Than Words - 1977
Warner Bros. 8477 - Listen To The Music / Music Speaks Louder Than Words - 1977
Warner Bros. Pro-A-749 - Victim / Victim - 1978 (12" Promo Issue Only)
Warner Bros. 8582 - Victim / So Blue - 1978
Warner Bros. Pro-A-772 - Honest I Do Love You (6:31) / Honest I Do Love You (6:31) - 1978 (12" Promo Issue Only)
Warner Bros. 8691 - Honest I Do Love You / I'm Gonna Make You Love Me - 1978
Warner Bros. Wbsd 8820 - When You Wake Up Tomorrow / Rough Times - 1979 (12" Release)
Warner Bros. 8821 - When You Wake Up Tomorrow / Rough Times - 1979
Warner Bros. Pro-A-827 - Chance (5:34) / Rock (7:16) - 1979 (12" Promo Issue Only)

Soulful Kinda Music – The Rare Soul Bible Volume Two

Warner Bros. 49061 - Chance / Rock - 1979
Warner Bros. 49061 - Chance / I Live - 1979
Warner Bros. 49091 - I Ain't Got Nowhere To Go / I Live - 1979
Warner Bros. Pro-A-867 - Looking For Love / Looking For Love - 1980 (12" Promo Issue Only)
Warner Bros. 49240 - Looking For Love / It's Real - 1980Warner Bros. 49536 - The Hunter Gets Captured By The Game / If You Feel The Need - 1980
L.A. 0080 - Without You I Cry / (Instrumental) - 1981
L.A. 12-8012 - Without You I Cry / ? - 1981 (12"Release)
Sugarhill 770 - Count On Me / Hurry Sundown - 1981
Sugarhill 12-568 - Count On Me / (Instrumental) - 1981 (12"Release)
Sugarhill 776 - Suspicious Minds / In The Still Of The Night - 1982
Sugarhill 784 - Hurry Sundown / Count On Me - 1982

The Source featuring Candi Staton

Source 9001 - You Got The Love / Version - 1986

Candi Staton

Berica 229-227 - Have You Tried God / ? - ?

The Steelers

Glow Star 815 - Crying Bitter Tears / Walk Alone - 1966
Crash 428 - The Flame Remains / Heavens Gift - 1966
Crash 430 - Crying Bitter Tears / Just Beginning To Love You - 1967
Date 1642 - Get It From The Bottom / I'm Sorry - 1969
Epic 10587 - Can't Take The Pain / a Thousand Tomorrow's - 1970
Epic 10773 - You're What's Missing From My Life / You Got Me Calling - 1970

Wes Wells & The Steelers

Torrid 100 - From The Top of My Heart / it Must Be Love - 1974

The Steelers

Torrid 101 - From The Bottom of My Heart / It Must Be Love - 1974
AMG 607317 - Disturbing Thoughts / Love Love Love For Me - 1976
Triple T 002 - It Must Be Love / Dancing Girl - 1984
Tre 83183 - Pretty Lady / Instrumental - 1985
Triple T 004 - Feed Your Own / same - 1985

Label Listings

Sansu

450 Betty Harris: I'm Evil Tonight / What A Sad Feeling
451 Willie Harper: You, You / Soda Pop
452 Betty Harris: I Don't Wanna Hear It / Sometime
453 ?
454 Diamond Joe: Wait A Minute Baby / How To Pick A Winner
455 Betty Harris: Twelve Red Roses / What'd I Do Wrong
456 Rubaiyats: Omar Khayyam / Tomorrow
457 Curly Moore: Get Low Down / Part 2
458 Jimmy London: Untrue / Come On Back
459 John Williams & The Tick Tocks - A Little Tighter / Operation Heartbreak
460 Diamond Joe: Hurry Back To Me / Don't Set Me back
461 Betty Harris: Lonely Hearts / Bad Luck
462 Benny Spellman: Sinner Girl / If You Love Her
463 Lee Calvin: Easy, Easy / You Got Me
464 Willie & Allen: I Don't Need No One / Baby Do Little
465 Prime Mates: Hot Tamales / Pt 2
466 Betty Harris: I'm Evil Tonight / Nearer To You
467 Wallace Johnson: Something To Remember You By / If You Leave Me
468 Curly Moore: Goodbye / We Remember
469 Eldridge Holmes: Until The End / Without A Word
470 Raymond Lewis: Goodbye My Love / Smooth Operator
471 Betty Harris: Can't Last Much Longer / I'm Gonna Git Ya
472 John Williams & The Tick Tocks: Do Me Like You Do Me / Blues Tears And Sorrows
473 Curly Moore: You Don't Mean / Don't Pity Me
474 Lee Dorsey & Betty Harris - Love Lots Of Lovin' / Take Care Of Our Love
475 Diamond Joe: It Doesn't Matter Anymore / Gossip Gossip
476 Wallace Johnson - Baby Go Ahead / I'm Grown
477 Eldridge Holmes: Beverly / Wait For Me baby
478 Betty Harris: Mean Man / What'd I Do Wrong
479 Betty Harris: Show It / Hook Line'n Sinker
480 Betty Harris: Ride Your Pony / Trouble With My Lover
481 Art Neville: Bo Diddley / Bo Diddley Part 2
482 Art Neville: Heartaches / I'm Gonna Put Some Hurt On You
483 ?
1000 Sam (Ironing Board) Moore: This Is A New Day / ?
1001 Tommy Ridgley: Sometimes You Get It / ?
1002 Lee Bates: Shake Baby Shake / Shake Baby Shake [Disco Version]
1003 ?
1004 Tony Owens: Confessin' A Feeling / ?
1005 ?
1006 Ernie K-Doe: You Got To Love Me / Stoop Down
1007 ?
1008 ?
1009 Lee Bates: Watching, Wishing, Hoping / Easy Easy
1010 ?
1011 Bobby Marchan: Shake It, Don't Break It / ?
1012 Lee Dorsey: Hey Babe / Say It Again
1013 The Specials: I Can't Find Another
1014 Meters: They All Ask For You / Hey Pocky A-Way

Soulful Kinda Music – The Rare Soul Bible Volume Two

1015 Meters: Mardi Gras Mambo / ?
1016 Ernie K-Doe: Hotcha Mama / She Gave It All To Me
1017 Lee Dorsey Soul Mining / Draining
1018 Atg: Dancin' Lady

Soul Clock

101 - The Fuller Brothers - Let Me Love You / Don't Knock Me '69
103 - Vernon Garrett - Just Ain't My Day / same
104 - The Whispers - Great Day / I Can't See Myself Leaving You
105 - The Fuller Brothers - Time's A-Wasting* / Moaning, Groaning & Crying
106 - Sugar Pie DeSanto - Be Happy / Feeling's Too Strong
107 - The Whispers - Time Will Come / Flying High
108 - The Ebonys - Don't Knock Me / Can't Get Enough
109 - The Whispers - What Will I Do / Remember Me
109 - The Whispers - What Will I Do / Remember
1001 - The Whispers - I Can Remember / Planets Of Life '70
1002 - The Fuller Brothers - I Want Her By My Side / Stranger At My Door
1003 - Sugar Pie DeSanto - My Illusions / Maybe I'm A Fool
1004 - The Whispers - Seems Like I Gotta Do Wrong / Needle In A Haystack
1005 - The Whispers - I'm The One / You Must Be Doing All Right

St Lawrence

701 - The Inspirationals - Jesus, Take Me Through / God's Ever Near - ?
702 - The Mighty Messiahs - I'm So Tired / I'll See You On The Other Side - ?
703 - The Taylor Singers - Don't Leave Me / Somebody Bigger Than You And I - ?
704 - (Singing) (Rev) Sammy Lewis - Hold Out / Trouble In The World - ?
705 - Lucy Rodgers - My Soul Needs Resting / (The) Day Is Passed And Gone - ?
706 - The Faithful Wonders - Jesus Is Coming / I'll Never Forget - ?
1001 - The Ideals - Go Get A Wig / Cathy's Clown – 1965
1002 - Baby Huey & The Babysitters - Beg Me / Monkey Man – 1965
1003 - The Vectors - What In The World / It's Been A Day Or Two - 1965
1004 - Mamie Galore - I Wanna Be Your Radio / Special Agent 34-24-38 – 1965
1005 - Billy Bland - My Divorce / She's Already Married – 1965
1006 - Oscar Lindsay - I'm Joining The Crowd / It Could Happen To You – 1966
1007 - The Vontastics - Peace Of Mind / No Love For Me – 1966
1008 - Mamie Galore - Have Faith In Me / Too Many Memories – 1966
1009 - The Vontastics - Keep On Rolling / I Need You – 1966
1010 - Butch Baker - Robin At The Go-Go / Batman At The Go-Go – 1966
1011 - Butch Baker - Fat Man / Working At The Go-Go – 1966
1012 - Mamie Galore - Don't Think I Could Stand It / It Ain't Necessary – 1966
1013 - Monk Higgins - These Days Are Filled With You / Who Dun It – 1966
1014 - The Vontastics - My Baby / Day Tripper – 1966
1015 - Sister Soul & Lucy Rodgers Singers - I'm Fighting For My Rights / I Have One More River – 1966
1016 - Monk Higgins - Now That's Sayin' Sumpin' / Easy Does It – 1966

Soulful Kinda Music – The Rare Soul Bible Volume Two

1017 - The Faithful Wonders - I Found Out For Myself / When I'm Gone – 1966
1018 - McKinley Mitchell - Boogaloo And Chili Dog / I'm Sorry About That – 1967
1019 - The Inspirationals - Meet Me At The River / God's Ever Never – 1967
1020 - The Ideals - Tell Her I Apologize / I Got Lucky (When I Found You) – 1967
1021 - The Messiahs Of Glory - Peace Of Mind / Help Me Carry On, Jesus – 1967
1022 - Monk Higgins - Creatrix Did It / What Fah (Instrumental) – 1967
1022 - Monk Higgins - What Fah (Instrumental) - 1967 (One Sided Disc)
1023 - The Vontastics - You Can Work It Out / Never Let Your Love Grow Cold – 1967
1024 - Johnny Sayles - I Can't Get (Enough Of Your Love) / Hold My Own Baby – 1967
1025 - Chuck Bernard - Send For Me / I Can't Fight It - 1967

Sue

700 – The Matadors – Vengeance (Will Be Mine) / Pennies From Heaven
701 – The Matadors – Be Good To Me / Have Mercy Baby
702 – Mamie Bradley – I Feel Like A Million / The Patty Cake
703 – The Four Jokers – Written In The Stars / The Run Around
704 – Sleepy King & His Orcehestra – One Leg Woman / Come Back Darling
705 – Marie Taylor – Uncle Sam / Great Big Daddy
706 – Bobby Hendricks – Itchy Twitchy Feeling / A Thousand Dreams
707 – Jimmy Oliver – The Sneak / One Love
708 – Bobby Hendricks – Molly B Good / Dreamy Eyes
709 – Don Covay – Believe It Or Not / Betty Jean
710 – Bobby Hendricks- It's Misery / Cast Your Vote
711 – Billy & Ricky – Mama Papa Please / Baby Doll
712 – Bobby Hendricks – Good Things Will Come / I'm A Big Boy Now
713 – The Nite Riders – Pretty Plaid Skirt / I'll Never Change
714 – The Aristocrats – Lawdy (When She Kissed Me) / So In Love With You
715 – Mary Lou Williams Trio – Chunk A Lunk Jug Part 1 / Part 2
716 – Billy & Ricky – How You Sound / Buttercup
717 – Bobby Hendricks – Little John Green / Sincerely Your Lover
718 – Mamie Bradley – In Love Again / Bye Bye I'm Gone
719 – The Nite Riders – Looking For My Baby / St. Loo
720 – Tony Taylor – Come What May / Candy Kisses
721 – Johnny Pancake – Wonderful Baby / Shock
722 – Ike Turner's Kings Of Rhythm – That's All I Need / My Love
723 – The Dudes – Rudolph The Red Nosed Reindeer / Jingle Bells
724 – May Lou Williams – Night And Day / I Got Rhythm
725 – The Dudes Mack The Knife / Organ Grinder's Swing
726 – Johnny Darrow – Hand In Hand / Why Do You Treat Me This Way
727 – Bobby Hendricks – If I Just Had Your Love / Cry Of Angels
728 – Johnny Darrow – Don't Start Me Talking / Jo Ann Delilah
729 - Bobby Hendricks – Busy Flirtin' / I Want That
730 – Ike & Tina Turner – A Fool In Love / The Way You Love Me
731 – The Night Riders – Night Ridin' / Talk To Me Baby
732 – Bobby Hendricks – Psycho / Too Good To Be True

Soulful Kinda Music – The Rare Soul Bible Volume Two

733 – Johnny Darrow – That's Good / Hold Hands Break Hearts
734 – Ike & Tina Turner – A Fool Too Long / You're My Baby
735 - Ike & Tina Turner – I Idolise You / Letter From Tina
736 – Jackie Brenston – Trouble Up The Road / You Ain't The One
737 – Chip Young – Great Day-A-Coming / Just As You Are
738 – Johnny Darrow – Love Is A Nightmare / Poor Boy Needs A Preacher
739 - ?
740 – Ike & Tina Turner – I'm Jealous / You're My Baby
741 – Johnny Darrow – Love Is A Nightmare / Poor Boy Needs A Preacher
742 – Eloise Hester – My Man Rockhead / I Need You
743 – Jimmy & Jean – I Can't Believe / I Want To marry You
744 – Sonny Jackson – St Louis Blues / My Babe
745 The Duals – Stick Shift / Crusing
746 – The Honey Dews – Honey Dew / Someone
747 – Tommy Williams – I'll Follow You / It Must Be Love
748 - ?
749 – Ike & Tina Turner – It's Gonna Work Out Fine / Won't You Forgive Me
750 – Pearl Woods – Keep Your Business To Yourself / I Loved Too Much
751 – Hannibal – I Need A Woman / The Biggest Cry
752 – Sammy Lynn – Blue Butterfly / You Should Know I'm Still Your Baby
753 – Ike & Tina Turner – Poor Fool / You Can't Blame Me
754 – ?
755 - Johnnie Mae Matthews – My Little Angel / The Headshrinker
756 – The Senors – May I Have This Dance / Searching For Olive Oil
757 – Ike & Tina Turner – Tra La La La / Puppy Love
758 – The Duals – Cha Cha Guitars / Travelin' Guitars
759 – Jo Perry – The King Of Kings (The Song Of All Faith) / There Is A Moon Tonight
760 – Ike Turner's Kings Of Rhythm – Prancing / It's Gonna Work Out Fine
761 – The Chandeliers – She's A Heartbreaker / Give Me Your Love
762 - ?
763 – Barbara George – If You Think / If When You've Done The Best
764 – Baby Washington – No Tears / Go On
765 – Ike & Tina Turner – You Should A Treated Me Right / Sleepless
766 – Barbara George – Send For Me (If You Need Some Lovin') / Bless You
767 – Baby Washington – Hush Heart / I've Got A Feeling
768 – Ike & Tina Turner – I Idolise You / Tina's Dilemma
769 – Baby Washington – Hush Heart / I've Got A Feeling
770 – Jimmy McGriff – I've Got A Woman Part 1 / Part 2
771 – Jimmy Barnes – Maybe Never / If By Any Chance
772 – Ike & Tina Turner – Mind In A Whirl / The Argument
773 – Barbara George – The Recipe / Try Again
774 – Ike & Tina Turner – Please Don't Hurt Me / Worried & Hurtin' Inside
775 – Freddy Cole – It's Christmas Time / Right Now
776 – Jackie Shane – Any Other Way / Sticks And Stones
777 - Jimmy McGriff – M.G. Blues / All About My Girl
778 – Jimmy Thomas – You Can Go / Hurry And Come Home
779 – Joey Vincent – Drip Drop / Trudy
780 – The Dough Boys – Pricilla's Walk / Copy Cat
781 - ?

Soulful Kinda Music – The Rare Soul Bible Volume Two

782 - ?
783 – Baby Washington – That's How Heartaches Are Made / There He Is
784 – Ike & Tina Turner – Don't Play Me Cheap / Wake Up
785 – The Camptown Singers – Toni / Troubles With A Woman
786 – Jimmy McGriff – The Last Minute Part 1 / Part 2
787 – Ray Steele – Sugar Coated Lies / The Silent Sea
788 – Jackie Shane – In My Tenement / Comin' Down
789 – The Escardrilles / Ferde & The Fifers – Monsieur Lafayette / Monsieur Lafayette
790 – Baby Washington – Leave Me Alone / You And The Night And The Music
791 – Jimmy McGriff – Broadway / One Of Mine
792 – Robert & Johnny – A Perfect Wife / Pretty Brown Eyes
793 – Earnestine Anderson – Out Of My Continental Mind / Keep An Eye On Love
794 – Baby Washington – Hey Lonely One / Doodlin'
795 – Hank Jacobs – So Far Away / Monkey Hips And Rice
796 – Barbara George – Something's Definitely Wrong / I Need Something Different
797 – Justine Washington – I Can't Wait Until I See My Baby's Face / Who's Gonna Take Care Of Me
798 - The Superbs - The Dawning Of Love / So Glad You're Home
799 – The Soul Sisters – I Can't Stand It / Blueberry Hill
800 – Bobbi Bolden – Chiles Chie-O-La Man / Need Me Tonight
801 – Ray Bryant – Joey / Glissamba
802 – Jimmy McGriff – Lonely Avenue Part 1 / Part 2
803 – Ernestine Anderson – The Best Is Yet To Come / Will I Find My Love Today
804 – Jimmy McGriff – Christmas With McGriff Part 1 / Part 2
805 – Sylvia Robins – Don't Let Your Eyes Get Bigger Than Your Heart / From The Beginning
806 - ?
807 – Joe Thomas & Orch.With Bill Elliot – I Don't Want Nobody To Have My Love But You Pt 1 / Pt 2
100 – Percy Dixon And His Merry Boys – Balimbo / Bloodshot Eyes
101 – Harry 'Sweets' Edison – I Wish You Love / Hello Dolly
102 – Hank Jacobs – Bacon Fat / Out Of Sight
103 – Debra Dion – Don't Bug Me Baby / I Want To Know (If Your Love Is Real)
104 – Baby Washington – The Clock / Standing On The Peir
105 – Jimmy McGriff – Hello Betty / Close Your Eyes
106 – Sylvia Robbins – Our Love / I Can't Tell
107 – The Soul Sisters – Loop De Loop / I Can't Tell You
108 – Ray Bryant – Shake A Lady / Blues March
109 – Tyree Glenn Jr & The Fabulous Imperials – Yesterday / Hold My Hand
110 – Jimmy McGriff – All Day Long / When You're Smiling
111 – The Soul Sisters – Just A Moment Ago / I Won't Be Your Fool
112 - Jimmy McGriff – Tokapi / The Man With The Golden Arm
113 – Hank Jacobs – Heidi / Playboy's Penthouse
114 – Baby Washington – I'll Never Be Over For Me / Move On Drifter
115 – Ernestine Anderson – I Pity The Fool / You're Not The Guy For Me
116 – Joan Shaw – Through A Long And Sleepless Night / Make Someone Happy
117 – Harry 'Sweets' Edison – Blues For Christine / On Green Dolphin Street
118 – Derek Martin – Too Soon To Know / Cha Cha Skate
119 – Baby Washington – Run My Heart / Your Fool

Soulful Kinda Music – The Rare Soul Bible Volume Two

120 – Jimmy Mcgriff – Sho-Nuff / Bilbo
121 – The Birds – He's My Guy (And I Love Him) / I'd Love To
122 – Juggy Murray & His Orchestra – Birmingham Blues / March On Washington
123 – Jimmy McGriff – Discotheque USA / People
124 – Justine Washington – I Can't Wait Until I See My Baby / Who's Gonna Take Care Of Me
125 – Ray Bryant – Adalia / Goldfinger
126 – Beverley Wright – Only When You're Lonely / Life Must Still Go On
127 – Beverley McKay – He'll Never Change / No No I Can't Help You
128 – Jimmy McGriff – Turn Blue / Bump De Bump
129 – Baby Washington – Only Those In Love / The Ballad Of Bobby Dawn
130 – The Soul Sisters – Think About The Good Times / The Right Time
131 – Sandy Contella – Collecting Girls / Promise Her Everything
132 – Marjorie Black – One More Hurt / You Still Love Her
133 – Billy Prophet – What Can I Do / Sad Sam
134 – Margaret Ann Williams – Ten Commandments Of Soul / The Words (I Love You)
135 – Ike & Tina Turner – Two Is A Couple / Tin Top House
136 – Jeff Adams – From The Beginning / Oki
137 – Baby Washington – No Time For Pity / There He Is
138 – Ike Turner & His Kings Of Rhythm – The New Breed Part 1 / Part 2
139 – Ike & Tina Turner – Can't Chance A Break Up / Stagger Lee & Billy
140 – The Soul Sisters – Flashback / Give Me Some Satisfaction
141 - ?
142 – Juggy – Soul At Sunrise / Just A Minute
143 – Derek Martin – Count To Ten / If You Go
144 – Bobby Lee – I Was Born A Loser / My Luck Is Bound To Change
145 – Bobby Lee – I Missed It By That Much / I'm Not Afraid
146 – Ike & Tina Turner – Dear John – I Made A Promise
147 - ?
148 – The Soul Sisters – So Much Love / I'm A Big Boy Now
149 – Baby Washington – White Christmas / Silent Night
150 – Baby Washington – You Are What You Are / Either You're With Me (Or Either You're Not)
1 – Betty Brewton – Heavy Heavy Lovin' / Pershing Square
2 – Bill Dogget – Fatback / Ci Ci Cisco
3 – Lovelace Watkins – Who Am I / Dreams
4 – Baby Washington – I Know / It'll Change
5 – Soul Sisters – Good Time Tonight / Foolish Dreams
6 - ?
7 – Lord Superior – The Gun Control / I Wouldn't Go To Chicago
8 - Pat Lucky - You Sure Can Love / Earthquake
9 – Juggy – The Spoiler / Oily
10 – Billy Nicholls – Shake A Leg / You Can't Fool This Fool
11 – Wilbert Harrison One Man Band – Let's Work Together Part 1 / Part 2
12 – The Superiors – I'd Rather Die / Heavenly Angel
13 – Joe Ponds – Don't Let My Love Pass You By / When We Get On Cloud # 9
14 – Juggy – Thock It To Me Honi / Buttered Popcorn
15 – Rev. Erskine Faush – Let Him Fix It / Somewhere
16 – Shaine – Try My Love / Call Me Sweet Things

Soulful Kinda Music – The Rare Soul Bible Volume Two

17 – Gary Us Bonds – One Broken Heart / Can't Use You In My Dreams
10-001 Jimmy McGriff – Kiko / Jumpin' At The Woodside
10-002 – Bill Doggett – Fat Back / Si Si Cisco
10-003 – Lovelace Watkins – Dreams / Who Am I
10-004 – Ernestine Anderson – You Deserve The Best / You're Not The Guy For Me
10-005 – The Soul Sisters – Good Time Tonight / Some Soul Food

Sure-Shot

5000 - E. Lois Foreman - Two For Me To Love / Stop,Look And Listen - 1963
5001 - Verna Rae Clay - He Loves Me,He Loves Me Not / I've Got It Bad - 1963
5002 - Mr. Lee & The Cherokees - Party Time / Will My Baby Come Back - 1964
5003 - Bobby Williams - Play A Sad Song / Try Love - 1964
5004 - The Mustangs - First Love / A Change - 1964
5005 - Bobby Williams - Keep On Loving Me / You Waited Too Long - 1965
5006 - Mr. Lee & The Cherokees - Take Your Time / Come Closer - 1965
5007 - Lisa Richards - Mean Old World / Let's Take A Chance - 1965
5008 - The Malibus - A Chance For You And Me / Strong Love - 1965
5009 - Norma Rudd - He's Mine / Something Keeps Telling Me - 1965
5010 - The Mighty Mustangs - Believe I Do / Outside-Inside - 1965
5011 - Ruth McFadden - Do It Up Right / I'll Cry - 1965
5012 - The Bell Brothers - Don't You Know, She's Alright / Not Your Kind Of Love - 1965
5013 - Bobby Williams - When You Play (You Gotta Pay) / It's All Over - 1965
5014 - The Malibus - Two At A Time / I Had A Dream - 196?
5015 - Little Mr. Lee & The Cherokees - I Dont Want To Go / Young Lover - 196?
50016 - Bobby Williams - I'll Hate Myself Tomorrow / The Last Time - 196?
5017 - J. J. Daniels - Mr. Lonesome / Deep Down Inside - 1966
5018 - Al Haskins & The Mastertones - You Got Me / Take Me - 1966
5019 - Troy Marrs & The Dynamics - Rhythm Message (Part 1) / Rhythm Message (Part 2) - 1966
5020 - Kurtis Scott - No, No, Baby / No Place Like Home - 1966
5021 - Ricky Ricks - Chained And Bound / Why Did I - 1966
5022 - Buster Jones - Baby Boy / You've Got To Learn - 196?
5023 - The Bell Brothers - Look At Me / Pity Me - 196?
5024/5025 - Bobby Williams - Baby I Need Your Love / Try It Again - 196?
5026 - Rhonda Washington - Swing Town U. S. A. / What About Love - 196?
5027/5028 - The Malibus - Gee Baby I Love You / Whats This Coming - 1967
5029/5030 - Lee Mitchell - Where Does Love Go / Your Gonna Miss Me - 1967
5031 - Bobby Williams - I've Only Got Myself To Blame / I'll Hate Myself Tomorrow - 1967 .
5032 - The Tornadoes - Little Sally Walker / Road Man - 1967
5033 - Buster Jones - You Know What To Do / I'm Satisfied - 1967
5034 - Lavell Kamma - Try To Keep Yourself Uptight / Begging - 1967
5035 - Kim Tolliver - In Return For Your Love / Get A Little Soul - 1967
5036 - Bobby Day - Spicks And Specks / So Lonely (Since You've Been Gone) - 1967
5037 - The Malibus - Summertime / Ten Times A Day - 1968

Soulful Kinda Music – The Rare Soul Bible Volume Two

5038 - The Bell Brothers - Tell Him No / Throw Away The Key - 196?
5039/5040 - Quality Controls - Grapevine (Part 1) / Grapevine (Part 2) - 196?

Sylvia

400/1 – Henry Strogin – I Cried Like A Baby / Misery
122 – Joan Moody – Don't Do Me That Way / Big Time Operator
124 – Billy Washington – Later For Romance / I Wanna Come In
129 – Joan Moody – Lend A Helping Hand / Music To My Ears
5000 – King Coleman – Just A Little Bit Of Love / Salt & Pepper
5001 – Chet Poison Ivey – Something Else / Beautiful Life
5002 – Joan Moody – Big Time Operator / Anything Worth Having
5003 – Corvairs – Victim Of Her Charms / Love Is Such A Good Thing ~
5004 – The Crestmen – The Mouse / The Loop
5005 – Bobby Donaldson – Bash Dance / K-El-Dee
5006 – Jim Randolph – The Act / Donna's Been Kissed
5007 – Joan Moody – We Must Be Doin' Something Right / The Life Of The Party
5009 – Sterling Magee – Keep On / Get In My Arms Little Girlie
500 – Chet Poison Ivey & Fabulous Avengers – Funky Chicken Part 1 / Part 2
501 – Chet Poison Ivey & Fabulous Avengers – So Fine / bad on Bad
503 – Chet Ivey – When Love Comes Home / ?
504 – Chet Poison Ivey & Fabulous Avengers – Get With The Geeter / Dose Of Soul
505 – Chet Poison Ivey & Fabulous Avengers – Party People Part 1 / Part 2
506 – Chet Poison Ivey & Fabulous Avengers – Recipe To Get Down Part 1 / Part 2

Symbol

900 - Commandos - Chicken Scratch / June's Blues - 1959
901 - Jess Johnson - So In Love Am I / Cute Little Girl - 1959
902 - Bobby Grier Adams - Banjo Rock / This Feeling - 1959
903 - Lloyd Nelson - Blues After Midnight / Rose From My Garden - 1959
904 - Sleepy King - Begging / My Time Ain't Long - 1959
905 - Bobby Adams - Don't Leave / It Doesn't Matter - 1959
906 - Commandos - Pony Express / Groovey Feeling - 1959
907 - Four Hunks - Mashin' The Madison / Sweet Tooth - 1960
908 - Bobby Adams - I Suffered / Little Miss America - 1960
909 - King Coleman - Let's Shimmy / Shortnin' Bread - 1960
910 - Bob Nichols - Hambone / Part 2 - 1960
911 - Bobby Adams - Let Me Love You / What A Mess - 1961
912 - Art Lassiter - It's Alright/My Loneliness - 1961
913 - Dell & Escorts - You Don't Love Me / Skokiaan - 1961
914 - Shockettes - Hold Back The Tears / My Pen's Not Filled With Ink - 1961
915 - Russell Byrd - Hitch Hike / Part 2 - 1962
916 - Everglades - Shimmy, Shimmy, Shimmy Sherry / You Stole My Heart Away - 1962
917 - Parliaments - I'll Get You Yet / You're Cute - 1962
918 - Hockadays - Fairy Tales / Hold On, Baby - 1962

Soulful Kinda Music – The Rare Soul Bible Volume Two

919 - Inez Foxx - Mockingbird / Jaybirds - 1962
920 - Everglades - Limbo Lucy / Make A Bulldog Hug A Mule - 1962
921 - Chuck Johnson - Competition / Here We Go 'Round The Mulberry Bush - 1963
922 - Inez Foxx - Broken Hearted Fool / He's The One You Love - 1963
923 - Jimmy Helms - Suzie's Gone / You're Mine, You - 1963
924 - Inez Foxx - Hi Diddle Diddle / Talk With Me - 1963
925 - Jesse Crawford - I Love You So / Please Don't Go - 1963
926 - Inez Foxx - Ask Me / I See You, My Love - 1963
20001 - Inez Foxx - Hurt By Love / Confusion - 1964
200 - Joe Thomas - Speak Your Peace, Brother / I Hear Music - 1964
201 - Inez Foxx - La De Da, I Love You / Yankee Doodle Dandy - 1964
202 - Pancho Villa & Bandits - Ain't That Bad/ Progress - 1964
204 - Inez & Charlie Foxx - Don't Do It No More/ I Fancy You - 1964
205 - Tom Jones - Trying To Get To My Grits / Nothing But Fine - 1965
206 - Inez & Charlie Foxx - I Feel Alright / My Momma Told Me - 1965
207 - Jimmy Oliver - Bye, Bye, Baby, I'm Gone / Whirl A Girl - 1965
208 - Inez & Charlie Foxx - I've Come To One Conclusion / Down By The Seashore - 1965
209 - Floyd Barber - In The Morning / Part 2 - 1965
210 - ?
211 - Hollywood Flames - Dance Senorita / Annie Don't Love Me No More - 1965
212 - Entertainers - Love In My Heart / My Pad - 1965
213 - Inez & Charlie Foxx - Hummingbird / If I Need Anyone - 1966
214 - Poets - She Blew A Good Thing / Out To Lunch - 1966
215 - Hollywood Flames - I'm Coming Home / I'm Gonna Stand By You - 1966
216 - Poets - So Young / Sure Thing - 1966
217 - Quovans - Boogaloo / Part 2 - 1966
218 - Little Tony Talent - All That's Good, Baby / You're Too Young - 1966
219 - Poets - I'm Particular / I've Got Two Hearts - 1966
220 - Soundbreakers - Tryin' To Get Back To You / Jerk Is Catching – 1966
221 - Magnificents - Take Me On / Skokie Drive – 1966

Tommy Tate

Tommy Tate (born 29-September-1945 in Homestead, Florida)

ABC-Paramount 10626 - What's The Matter / Ordinarily - 1965

Tommy & The Derby's (members Tommy Tate, Dorothy Moore, Cliff Thomas, Ed Thomas, Patsy McKewn and Rosemary Taylor, backed by The Tim Whitsett Imperial Showband)

Swing 1001 - Handy Andy / Don't Play The Role - 1966 (both sides penned by Cliff Thomas)
Kool 1034 - Goin' Back To Houston / Standin' In My Way - ?

The Turrabull Brothers (Actually The Tim Whitset Imperial Showband, Tim Whitsett singing lead, Tommy Tate (backing vocals) and Jimmy Hodo (backing vocals and saxophone))

Temporaire 0000000 - Push Push / Don't Do It - 1966

Tommy Tate

Okeh 7242 - I'm Taking On Pain / Are You From Heaven - 1966

Tim Whittset and The Imperial Showband featuringTommy Tate (members Tommy Tate, Tim Whitsett (trumpet), Hank Martin (guitar), Buzz Arledge (guitar), Carson Whitsett (keyboards --- born 1-May-1945 in Jackson, Mississippi --- died 8-May-2007 in Nashville, Tennessee --- cause: brain cancer) ....)

Big Ten 1003 - Stand By Me* / Dee's Village (Instrumental) - 1966 *also recorded in 1961 by Ben E. King on Atco 6194 and recorded in 1964 by Cassius Clay on Columbia 43007.

Tommy Tate

Okeh 7253 - A Lover's Reward / Big Blue Diamonds - 1967 (issued in the UK on Columbia DB8046)

Tommy Yates

Verve 10556 - Darling, Something's Gotta Give / If You're Looking For A Fool - 1967

Andy Chapman

Atco 6558 - Happy Is The Man* / Double Your Satisfaction** - 1968 *confirmed by Tommy Tate as being him, apparently he remembers doing it as a demo only and was unaware of it's release. **rumoured to be Ben Atkins.

The Imperial Showband featuring Tommy Tate (members Tommy Tate (lead

Soulful Kinda Music – The Rare Soul Bible Volume Two

vocals and drums), Tim Whitsett, Carson Whitsett, ...)

Malaco - You're Not To Blame - 1968 (unissued at the time this was released in the
U. K. on the 2008 Soulscape Cd "Tommy Tate Hold On" SSCD 7010)

The Imperial Showband featuring Tommy Tate (members Tommy Tate, Tim
Whitsett, Bucky Barnett (guitar), Carson Whitsett (keyboards) and Jimmy Hodo)

Musicor 1340 - The Whole World Is The Same / Where Did I Go - 1968

Tommy Tate

Malaco - So Hard To Let A Good Thing Go - 1968 (unissued at the time this was
released in the U. K. on the 2008 Soulscape Cd "Tommy Tate Hold On" SSCD 7010)
Malaco - Get It Over Anyway - 1968 (this was released in the U. K. on the
2003 Grapevine Cd "Troubled Waters Deep Soul From The Deep South" GVCD 3010
and released in the U.K. on the 2008 Soulscape Cd "Tommy Tate Hold On" SSCD
7010)
Malaco - Hold On - 1969 (this was released in the U. K. on the 2003 Grapevine Cd
"Troubled Waters Deep Soul From The Deep South" GVCD 3010 --- also recorded in
1971 by James Carr on Atlantic 2803)
Jackson Sound 1005 - Peace Is All I Need / Let Us Be Heard (A Prayer For Peace) -
1970
Glenaire 1005 - Peace Is All I Need / Let Us Be Heard (A Prayer For Peace) - 1970

The Nightingales (members Tommy Tate, Quincy Billops, Rochester Neal and Bill
Davis)

Stax 0076 - You're Movin' Much Too Fast / Don't Let A Good Thing Go - 1970
Stax - You're Movin' Much Too Fast (Unedited Version) - 1970 (unissued until it
was released in the U. K. on the 2007 Kent Cd "Tommy Tate I'm So Satisfied The
Complete Ko Ko Recordings And More" CDKEND 289)
Stax 0091 - Just A Little Overcome / I Don't Want To Be Like My Daddy - 1971

Tommy Tate

Ko Ko 2109 - I Remember / Help Me Love - 1971
Ko Ko 2112 - I Remember / School Of Life - 1972
Ko Ko 2114 - I Ain't Gonna Worry / More Power To You - 1972

Southern Passion (members Tommy Tate, ...) Tommy Tate gigged locally on and
off with the band but didn't record anything with them.

Tommy Tate

Ko Ko 722 - Hardtimes S. O. S. / Always* - 1976*also recorded in 1973 by Luther
Ingram on Ko Ko 2115.
Ko Ko 723 - If You Ain't Man Enough / Revelations - 1976
Ko Ko 726 - If You Got To Love Somebody / Do You Think There's A Chance -
1977 (promo issue only - only two copies known to exist - it has been reported that

Soulful Kinda Music – The Rare Soul Bible Volume Two

this is a one-sided disc does anyone know for certain, or is it as rumoured the flip side being "Do You Think There's A Chance" - Officially Koko 726 is the 1977 twelve inch release by Luther Ingram "I Like The Feeling / I'm Gonna Be The Best Thing")
Ko Ko 727 - I'm So Satisfied / If You Ain't Man Enough - 1977
Sundance 5000 - The End Of The World / You Taught Me How To Love – 1979
Juana 1950 - For The Dollar Bill / We Don't – 1981
Juana 1955 - On The Real Side / This Train - 1981
Sundance 5001 - Crescent City U. S. A. / (Instrumental) – 1984
Sundance 5003 - If I Gave You My Heart / What Gives You The Right – 1984
Sundance (No Number) - I'm Wrapped Up / Linger A Little Longer - 1985 (only 500 copies pressed)
White Label 2 - If You Gotta Love Somebody / ? - ?

Bobby Taylor & The Vancouvers

The Columbus Pharoahs (members Morris Wade, Bobby Taylor, Ron Wilson and Bernard Wilson)

Esta 290 - Give Me Your Love / China Doll - 1958

The Four Pharaohs (members Morris Wade, Bobby Taylor, Ron Wilson, Bernard Wilson and Tommy Willis)

Ranson 100 - Pray For Me / Move Around - 1958
Ransom 101 - Give Me Your Love / China Doll - 1958

Morris Wade

Ransom 102 - It Was A Nite Like This / Is It Too Late - 1958

The Four Pharoahs

Paradise 109 - Give Me Your Love / China Doll - 1958

The Egyptian Kings (members Morris Wade, Leo Blakely, Pete Oden, Paul Moore and Sylvester Moore)

Nanc 1120 - Give Me Your Love / I Need Your Love - 1961 (has company address under label name - scarcer copies)
Nanc 1120 - Give Me Your Love / I Need Your Love - 1961 (has "Dist. By Swingin' Records" under name - common copies)

King Pharoah & The Egyptians (members Harold "King Pharoah" Smith, Morris Wade, Bernard Wilson and Pee Wee Lowrey)

Federal 12413 - By The Candlelight / Shimmy Sham - 1961

The Shades (members Tommy Chong, ...) Canadian multi racial group (hence the name)

Soulful Kinda Music – The Rare Soul Bible Volume Two

Little Daddy & The Bachelors (members Bobby Taylor, Wes Henderson, Ted Lewis, Eddie Patterson, Robbie King and Tommy Chong)

? - Too Much Monkey Business / Come On Home - ? Canadian released 45 (the group was known to have recorded at least two tracks - unsure but suspect that they are on the same 45 - does anyone know?)

Four Niggers and a Chink (members Bobby Taylor, Wes Henderson, Ted Lewis, Eddie Patterson, Robbie King and Tommy Chong)

Bobby Taylor & The Vancouvers (members Bobby Taylor, Wes Henderson, Ted Lewis, Eddie Patterson, Robbie King and Tommy Chong (later to have fame as one half of the well documented comedy / recording duo Cheech & Chong)) an interracial sextet based in Vancouver, Canada. Jimi Hendrix working as an R & B sideman joined the group in December-1962 until he met up with and left with Little Richard. Bobby Taylor "discovered" The Jackson Five.

Gordy 7069 - Does Your Mama Know About Me* / Fading Away - 1968 (some copies released in red vinyl) Gordy 7073 - I Am Your Man / If You Love Her - 1968
Gordy 7079 - Malinda / It's Growing - 1968
Integra 103 - This Is My Woman / ? - 1968

Bobby Taylor

Gordy 7088 - Oh I've Been Bless'd / It Should Have Been Me Loving Her - 1969 (Unissued)
V. I. P. 25053 - Oh I've Been Bless'd / Blackmail - 1969
V. I. P. 25053 - Blackmail / Blackmail - 1969 (Promo Issue Only)
Gordy 7092 - My Girl Has Gone / It Should Have Been Me Loving Her - 1969

Wes Henderson

Rare Earth 5007 - In Bed / Reality - 1969

Bobby Taylor

Mowest 5006 - Hey Lordy / Just A Little Bit Closer - 1971
Sunflower 126 - There Are Roses Somewhere In The World / It Was A Good Time - 1972
Tommy - 1973
Hour - ?
Playboy 6046 - Why Play Games / Don't Wonder Why - 1975

Evil Twang (members Robbie King , Chris Houston, Brian Goble, Adam Drake, Luke Doucet, Jerry Doucette and Steven Drake) - unsure of any group recordings.

Johnnie Taylor

Soulful Kinda Music – The Rare Soul Bible Volume Two

The Melody Masters (members Johnnie Taylor, ...)

The Five Echoes (group had a fluctuating line-up Johnnie Taylor was not on
their 1953 release "Lonely Mood / Baby Come Back To Me" on SABRE 102 amongst
group members were Tommy Hunt, Constant "Count" Sims, Earl Lewis, Herbert
Lewis, Jimmy Marshall, Johnnie Taylor (who replaced a drafted Tommy Hunt), Walter
Spriggs and Andre Williams)

Sabre 105 - So Lone-Some / Broke - 1954
Sabre ? - Why Oh Why / That's My Baby - 1954 (with Tommy Hunt back with group
after going AWOL, after this recording he was back in the Armed Services)
Vee-Jay 129 - I Really Do / Tell Me Baby - 1954
Vee-Jay 156 - Fool's Prayer / Tastee Freeze* - 1955 *penned by Johnnie Taylor.
Vee-Jay 190 - Soldier Boy / Pledging To You - 1956

The Highway QC's (members Johnnie Taylor, ...)

?

The Soul Stirrers (members Johnnie Taylor, ...) replaced Sam Cooke
and was in turn later replaced by Jimmy Otler.

?

Johnnie Taylor (born Johnnie Harrison Taylor 5-May-1938 in Crawfordsville,
Arkansas - died 31-May-2000 at hospital in Duncanville, Dallas. Cause: heart attack)

Sar 114 - A Whole Lotta Woman / Why Why Why - 1961
Sar 131 - Rome (Wasn't Built In A Day)* / Never Never - 1962 *Lou Rawls, J. W.
Alexander and Sam Cooke on background vocals.
Sar 156 - Oh, How I Love You / You Can Run (But You Can't Hide) - 1963

Johnnie Taylor

Acetate (No #) - Love On A Lease Plan / Me And My Baby - 1963? (found on an
acetate by a collector this was released on the bootleg label JOANNE 3001 as being
by Johnny Burke)
Derby 1001 - Dance What You Wanna / Shine Shine Shine - 1963
Derby 1006 - Baby We've Got Love / (I'll Always Be) In Love With You - 1963
Derby 1010 - I Need Lots Of Love / Getting Married Soon - 1964
Stax 186 - I Had A Dream / Changes - 1965
Stax 193 - I Got To Love Somebody's Baby / Just The One I've Been Looking For -
1966
Stax 202 - Little Bluebird / Toe Hold - 1966
Stax 209 - Ain't That Loving You (For More Reasons Than One) / Outside Love -
1966
Stax 226 - You Can't Get Away From It / If I Had To Do It All Over - 1967
Stax 235 - Somebody's Been Sleeping In My Bed / Strange Things - 1967
Stax 247 - Next Time / Hello Sundown - 1967
Stax 253 - I Ain't Particular / Where There's Smoke There's Fire - 1968

Soulful Kinda Music – The Rare Soul Bible Volume Two

Stax 0009 - Who's Making Love / I'm Trying - 1968
Stax 0023 - Take Care Of Your Homework / Hold On This Time - 1968
Stax 0033 - Testify (I Wonna) / I Had A Fight With Love - 1968

Johnnie Taylor / Johnnie Taylor, Eddie Floyd, William Bell, Pervis Staples, Carla Thomas, Mavis Staples, Cleotha Staples

Stax 0040 - Soul-A-Lujah (Part 1) / Soul-A-Lujah (Part 2)* - 1969 *flip by Johnnie Taylor, Eddie Floyd, William Bell, Pervis Staples, Carla Thomas, Mavis Staples, Cleotha Staples.

Johnnie Taylor & Mavis Staples

Stax 0041 - Never Let You Go / Ain't That Good - 1969

Johnnie Taylor & Carla Thomas

Stax 0042 - Just Keep On Loving Me / My Life - 1969

Johnnie Taylor

Stax 0046 - I Could Never Be President / It's Amazing - 1969
Stax 0055 - Love Bones / Mr. Nobody Is Somebody - 1969
Stax 0068 - Steal Away / Friday Night - 1969
Stax 0078 - I Am Somebody (Part 1) / I Am Somebody (Part 2) - 1970
Stax 0085 - Jody's Got Your Girl And Gone / A Fool Like Me - 1970
Stax 0089 - I Don't Wanna Lose You / Party Life - 1971
Stax 0096 - Hijackin' Love / Love In The Streets (Ain't Good As The Love At Home) - 1971
Stax 0114 - Standing In For Jody / Shackin' Up - 1971

Johnnie Taylor (The Soul Philosopher)

Stax 0122 - Doin' My Own Thing (Part 1) / Doin' My Own Thing (Part 2) - 1972

Johnnie Taylor

Stax 0142 - Stop Doggin' Me / Stop Teasin' Me - 1972
Stax 0155 - Don't You Fool With My Soul (Part 1) / Don't You Fool With My Soul (Part 2) - 1972
Stax 0161 - I Believe In You (You Believe In Me) / Love Depression - 1972 (with "A" side listed at 4:37)
Stax 0161 - I Believe In You (You Believe In Me) / Love Depression - 1972 (with "A" side listed at 3:58)
Stax 0176 - Cheaper To Keep Her / I Can Read Between The Lines - 1973
Stax 0193 - We're Getting Careless With Our Love / Poor Make Believer - 1973
Stax 0208 - I've Been Born Again / At Night Time - 1973
Citizens Alliance For VD Awareness - Something To Remember Her By / ? - 1974
Stax 0226 - It's September / Just One Moment - 1974
Stax 0241 - Try Me Tonight / Free - 1975

Soulful Kinda Music – The Rare Soul Bible Volume Two

Stax 0251 - I'm So Glad I Met You / I'm So Grateful - 1975
Stax 0253 - Just Keep On Loving Me / It Don't Pay To Get Up In The Morning - 1976
Stax 3201 - Just Keep On Loving Me / It Don't Pay To Get Up In The Morning - ?
Columbia 10281 - Disco Lady / You're The Best In The World - 1976 (this was the first single certified platinum by R. I. A. A.)
Columbia 10334 - Somebody's Gettin' It / Please Don't Stop (That Song From Playing) - 1976
Columbia 10478 - Love Is Better In The A. M. (Part 1) / Love Is Better In The A. M. (Part 2) - 1977
Stax 3201 - It Just Don't Pay To Get Up In The Morning / Just Keep On Loving Me - 1977
Columbia 10541 - Your Love Is Rated X / Here I Go (Through These Chains Again) - 1977
Columbia 10610 - Disco 9000 / Right Now - 1977
RCA 11137 - Heaven Bless This Home / I Want You Back Again - 1977

Johnnie Taylor / Deniece Williams

Columbia Ae7 1153 - God Is Standing By / God Is Amazing* - 1977 *flip by Deniece Williams only. (promo issue only with "Suggested Christmas Programming" on label)

Johnnie Taylor

Columbia 10709 - Keep On Dancing / I Love To Make Love When It's Raining - 1978
Columbia 10776 - Ever Ready / Give Me My Baby - 1978
Columbia 11084 - (Ooh-Wee) She's Killing Me / Play Something Pretty - 1979
Columbia 11315 - I Got This Thing For Your Love / Signing Off With Love - 1980
Columbia 11373 - I Wanna Get Into You / Babt Don't Hesitate - 1980
Beverly Glen BG2002 - What About My Love / Reagonomics - 1982 (12" single release)
Beverly Glen 2003 - What About My Love / Reagonomics - 1982
Beverly Glen 2004 - I'm So Proud / I Need A Freak - 1983
Beverly Glen 2007 - Just Ain't Good Enough / Don't Wait - 1983
Beverly Glen 2008 - Seconds Of Your Love / Shoot For The Stars - 1984
Malaco 2107 - Lady My Whole World Is You / L-O-V-E - 1984
Malaco 2111 - Good With My Hips / This Is Your Night - 1985
Malaco 2118 - Still Called The Blues / She's Cheating On Me - 1985
Malaco 2125 - Wall To Wall / ? - 1986
Malaco 2128 - Can I Love You / There's Nothing I Wouldn't Do - 1986
Malaco 2132 - Just Because / When She Stops Asking - 1987
Malaco 2135 - Don't Make Me Late / Happy Time - 1987
Malaco 2140 - If I Lose Your Love / Something Is Going Wrong - 1987
Malaco 2143 - Everything's Out In The Open / Got To Leave This Woman - 1988
Malaco 2149 - Now That You've Cheated / You Knocked My Heart Out Of Line - 1988
Malaco 2153 - In Control / I Found A Love - 1989
Malaco 2159 - Still Crazy For You / ? - 1989
Malaco 2343 - Big Head Hundreds / I'm From The Old School - 198?

The Tokays

Bonnie 102 - Lost And Found / Fatty-Boom Bi Laddy - 1962
Scorpio 403 - Ask Me No Questions / Now - 1966
Brute 001 - Baby Baby Baby / Hey Senorita - 1967 (Produced By Tony Clarke)
To-Kay 273 - Out Of Hand / ? - 196?

The Trammps

The Volcanos (members Gene Jones (vocals), Steve Kelly (vocals), John Hart (keyboards), Stanley Wade (guitar, vocals), Harold "Doc" Wade (bass, vocals) and Earl Young (drums))

Arctic 103 - Baby / Make Your Move - 1964
Harthon 138 - It's Gotta Be A False Alarm* / Movin' And Groovin' - 1964 *written by Del Shar (a pseudonym for Carl Fisher of The Vibrations)
Harthon 146/147 - Take Me Back Again / All Shucks - 1965
Arctic 106 - Storm Warning / Baby - 1965
Arctic 111 - Help Wanted / Make Your Move - 1965
Arctic 115 - (It's Against) The Laws Of Love / It's Against The Laws Of Love (Instrumental) - 1965
Arctic 115 - (It's Against) The Rules Of Love / It's Against The Rules Of Love (Instrumental) - 1965
Arctic 125 - A Lady's Man / Help Wanted - 1966
Arctic 128 - You're Number 1* / Make Your Move - 1966 *co-written by Eddie Holman and James Solomon.

Gene Faith (Gene Jones)

Virtue 2508 - Comin' Home / Love Of A Women-Soul Of A Man - ? (note, this is the correct spelling of WOMEN as it appeared on the 45)
Virtue 2510 - When My Ship Comes In / If You Don't Love Me (Why Don't You Leave Me) - ?
Virtue 2511 - Lady In The Harbor / Hung Up On A Feeling - ?
Virtue 2512 - My Baby's Missing / Family Man - ?

The Volcanos (members Gene Jones, Steve Kelly, John Hart, Stanley Wade, Harold Wade and Earl Young)

Virtue 2513 - No Trespassing / That's How Strong My Love Is - ?

Gene Faith

Virtue 2515 - You're Love Is Like A Merry Go Round / I Fell In Love With An Angel - ?
Virtue 111175 - Lowdown Melody / Le La-Dee Da Da - ?

The Moods (members

Wand 11224 - Rainmaker / Lady Rain - 1970
Scepter 12296 - With A Woman / King Hustler - 1970
Reddog ? - Hustlin' / King Hustler - ?

The Body Motions (members Gene Jones, Steve Kelly, John Hart, Stanley Wade, Harold Wade and Earl Young)

Harthon 103074 - False Alarm / Puttin' You On - ?

Tramps (members John Hart, Stanley Wade, Harold Wade, Earl Young, ...)

Buddah 306 - Zing Went The Strings Of My Heart / Penguin At The Big Apple - 1972 (scarcer issue)

The Trammps (members John Hart, Stanley Wade, Harold Wade, Earl Young,...)

Buddah 306 - Zing Went The Strings Of My Heart / Penguin At The Big Apple - 1972
Buddah 321 - Sixty Minute Man / Scrub Board - 1972
Buddah 339 - Rubber Band / Pray All You Sinners - 1973
Golden Fleece 3251 - Love Epidemic / I Know That Feeling - 1973
Golden Fleece 3253 - Where Do We Go From Here / Shout - 1974
Golden Fleece 3255 - Trusting Heart / Down These Dark Streets - 1974
Golden Fleece 3257 - Stop And Think / Trammps' Disco Theme - 1974
Buddah 507 - Hold Back The Night / Tom's Song - 1975
Atlantic 3286 - Hooked For Life / I'm Alright - 1975
Atlantic 3306 - That's Where The Happy People Go (Short Version) / That's Where The Happy People Go (Long Version) - 1975
Atlantic 3345 - Soul Searchin' Time / Love Is A Funky Thing - 1976
Atlantic 3365 - Ninety-Nine And A Half (Won't Do) / Can We Come Together - 1976
Atlantic 3389 - Disco Inferno / You Touch My Hot Line - 1977 (Some Copies Issued With Picture Sleeve)
Atlantic 3403 - I Feel Like I've Been Livin' (On The Dark Side Of The Moon) / Don't Burn Bridges - 1977
Atlantic 3442 - The Night The Lights Went Out / I'm So Glad You Came Along - 1977
Atlantic 3389 - Disco Inferno / You Touch My Hot Line - 1978 (Reissued Due To The Success Of "Saturday Night Fever")
Atlantic 3460 - Seasons For Girls / Love Ain't Been Easy - 1978
Atlantic 3460 - Seasons For Girls / Body Contact Contract - 1978
Atlantic 3537 - Soul Bones / Love Magnet - 1979
Atlantic 3573 - More Good Times To Remember / Teaser - 1979
Atlantic 3654 - Dance Contest / Hard Rock And Disco - 1980
Atlantic 3669 - Music Freak / V. I. P. - 1980
Atlantic 3777 - Mellow Out / Looking For You - 1980
Atlantic 3797 - I Don't Want To Ever Lose Your Love / Breathtaking View - 1981

The TSU Toronados

Soulful Kinda Music – The Rare Soul Bible Volume Two

Ovide 223 - The Toronado / A Thousand Wonders
Rampart Street 644 - Please Heart, Don't Break / Ain't Nothin' Nowhere
Ovide 227 - You're Mine / Back After The News
Ovide 230 - Song For A Princess / Work On It
Ovide 233 - What Good Am I / Getting The Corners
Atlantic 2579 - What Good Am I / Getting The Corners
Ovide 243 - My Thing Is A Moving Thing / I Still Love You
Atlantic 2614 - The Goose / Got To Get Through To You
Volt 4030 - My Thing Is A Moving Thing / I Still Love You
Volt 4038 - Play The Music Tornados / One Flight Too Many
Ovide 250 - Nothing Can Stop Me / Only Inside"

Spyder Turner

The Glee Club and Boys Ensemble (members Dwight Turner..........)

The Nonchalants (members Dwight Turner......................)

Chroma 1000 - Honky Tonk Joe / ? - ?

DeWight (Spider) Turner & The Stereophonics and The Bellhops Band (members

Chatok 1001 - You're Alone / Happy Story - 196?

The Monticellos

Red Cap 1-2 - I Can't Wait Until I See My Baby's Face / Don't Hold Back - ?
Is This The Monticellos Spyder Was A Member Of??????????????????I Am Unsure!!!!!!!!
Red Cap 102 - I Can't Wait Until I Love You / Don't Hold Back - 196?

Spider Turner / The Fortune Bravos

Fortune 225 - Ride In My 225 / One Stop (Instrumental)* - 1964 *flip by The Fortune Bravos.
Fortune 570 - Ride In My 225 / One Stop (Instrumental)* - 1964 *flip by The Fortune Bravos.

Spider Turner

Mastersound 65-1 - Calling Girls (Part 1) / Calling Girls (Part 2) - 1965

Spider Turner

Good Time 1019 - I've Got To Get Myself Together (Before I Lose My Mind) / When I See My Baby (My Troubles Are Over) -

Soulful Kinda Music – The Rare Soul Bible Volume Two

Spyder Turner (born Dwight D. Turner in 1947 in Beckley, West Virginia. Moved to Detroit, Michigan in the late 1950's)

MGM 13617 - Stand By Me / You're Good Enough For Me - 1966.
MGM 13692 - I Can't Make It Anymore / Don't Hold Back - 1967
MGM 13739 - For Your Precious Love / I Can't Wait 'Til I See My Baby's Face - 1967
MGM 14263 - I Can't Make It Anymore / I'm Alive With A Lovin' Feeling - 1971

Miki Stokes & Spyder Turner

Sounds Of Soul 1004 - My Troubles Are Over / Get Yourself Together - ?

Spyder Turner

Kwanza 7688 - Since I Don't Have You / Happy Days - 1973
Whitfield 8526 - I've Been Waiting / Tomorrow's Only Yesterday - 1978
Whitfield 8596 - Get Down / Is It Love You're After - 1978
Whitfield 49190 - You're So Fine / Only Love - 1980

Johnny Bristol / Spyder Turner

Polydor 813982-7 - Hang On In There Baby / Stand By Me* - 1983 *flip by Spyder Turner

Spyder Turner

Polydor ? - 1984
Web Brothers Productions ? - ? - 1998

Titus Turner

Mr. T & His Band

Aladdin 3053 - Where Are You / I'm Just A Lucky So-And-So - 1950

Titus Turner (born 1-May-1933 in Atlanta, died 13-September-1984 in Atlanta)

Regal 3322 - Stop Trying To Make A Fool Of Me / Let's Forget The Whole Thing - 1951
Okeh 6844 - The Same Old Feeling / Don't Take Everybody To Be Your Friend - 1952
Okeh 6883 - Got So Much Trouble / What'cha Gonna Do - 1952
Okeh 6907 - Jambalaya / Please Baby - 1952
Okeh 6929 - Be Sure You Know / Christmas Baby - 1952
Okeh 6938 - It's Too Late Now / My Plea - 1953
Okeh 6961 - Living In Misery / (Going Down To) Big Mary's -
Okeh 7027 - My Lonely Room / Over The Rainbow - 1954
Okeh 7038 - Devilish Woman / Hello Stranger - 1954

Soulful Kinda Music – The Rare Soul Bible Volume Two

Wing 90006 - All Around The World / Do You Know - 1955
Wing 90033 - Sweet And Slow / Big John - 1955
Wing 90058 - Get On The Right Track Baby / I'll Wait Forever - 1956
Atlantic 1127 - Hungry Man / A-Knockin' At My Baby's Door - 1957
King 5067 - Have Mercy Baby / You Turned The Lamps Down Low - 1957
King 5095 - Stop The Pain / Hold Your Loving - 1957
King 5129 - Way Down Yonder / Follow Me - 1958
King 5140 - Tears Of Joy Fill My Eye's / Coralee - 1958
King 5186 - Return Of Stagger Lee / Answer Me - 1959
King 5213 - Tarzan / Fall Guy - 1959
King 5243 - Miss Rubberneck Jones / Bonnie Baby - 1959
Dart 102 - Sodom And Gomorrah / Sodom And Gomorrah - 1959
King 5465 - Miss Rubberneck Jones / Way Down Yonder - 1960
Glover 200 - Run Home Little Girl / Together You And Me - 1960
Glover 201 - We Told You Not To Marry / Takin' Care Of Business - 1960
Glover 202 - When The Sergeant Comes Marching Home / Up Jumps The Devil - 1960
Glover 206 - Get Up Betty Jean / Cool Down - 1960
Carton 201 - We Told You Not To Marry / Takin' Care Of Business - 1960
Barrel 630 - We Told You Not To Marry / Takin' Care Of Business - 1960
Jamie 1174 - Sounds Off / Me And My Telephone - 1961

The Conductor (Titus Turner)

Jamie 1177 - Pony Train / Bla Bla Bla Cha Cha Cha - 1961

Titus Turner

Jamie 1184 - Hey Doll Baby / I Want A Little Girl - 1961
Jamie 1189 - Horsin' Around / Changes Go Around - 1961
Jamie 1202 - Beautiful Stranger / Shake The Hand Of A Fool - 1961
Jamie 1213 - Walk On The Wild Side Twist / Twistin' Train - 1961
Enjoy 1005 - People Sure Act Funny (When You Get A Little Money) / My Darkest Hour - 1962
Enjoy 1015 - Soulville / My Darkest Hour - 1962
Columbia 42873 - Goodbye Rose / Young Wings Can Fly - 1962
Columbia 42947 - Make Someone Love You / I'm A Fool About My Mama - 1963
Enjoy 2010 - Bow Wow / I Love You Baby - 1963
Atco 6310 - Baby Girl, Pt. 1 / Baby Girl, Pt. 2 - 1964
Blue-Tones 401 - Keep On Lovin' Me Baby / Still In The Dark - 1964
Bell 620 - I Am A Member Of The Club / Sportin' Tom - 1964
Murbo 1001 - Hoop Hoop Hoop A Hoopa Doo / Huckle Buckle Beanstalk - 1965
Okeh 7244 - Eye To Eye / What Kinda Deal Is This - 1966
Philips 40445 - (I'm Afraid) The Masquerade Is Over / Mary Mack - 1967
Josie 990 - People Sure Act Funny (When You Get A Little Money) / I Just Can't Keep It To Myself - 1968
Josie 1012 - His Funeral, My Trial / Do You Dig It - 1968
Glover 3006 - Last Of The Big Time Spenders / Help The Blind - 196?
Maggie 609 - Your Lovin' Is Killin' Me Baby / ? - 196?

Soulful Kinda Music – The Rare Soul Bible Volume Two

Phil-L. A. Of Soul 382 - Just A Little Taste / Sound Freak - 1976
Turbo 007 - Get Down Off Train / Saga Pete Latimore - ?

Trivia

Titus Turner also wrote Little Girl Lost by Maxine Brown on Wand 152 a 1964 release.

Northern Soul ? It's a UK thing isn't it?

Well it certainly used to be, and if you listen to Pete Waterman, it was all big hairy miners who worked down t'pit, who went out at weekends to dance. Of course that was rubbish then, and is still rubbish now.

In addition, the claim that Northern Soul is a UK thing is also rubbish as well, or it certainly been has for the last twenty years or so. My own personal experience of Northern Soul outside of mainland UK only goes back sixteen of those years, so whilst I know there were events outside the UK prior to 1998, I didn't attend them, so can't really talk about them.

However, I thought though it would be nice to do a bit of a look back at all the places I've DJ'ed outside of the UK (And at this point I'll explain that I'm referring to anywhere I had to fly or get a ferry to here, thus Belfast get's counted as out of the UK) I've also included some of the venue reports I wrote at the time.

I reckon I've now done over 50 DJ spots outside the UK, and have DJ'ed in eleven different countries ! I feel honoured that the promoters of these events have booked me to DJ, and hope that I did the job expected of me when I got there. So, rather than do the events chronologically, I'm going to group them by country.

So, where did I get my first 'foreign' booking ? It was of course the 'Turning My Heartbeat Up Weekender' in Nurnberg, run by two people who have become firm friends, Michael and Silke. I first went out there in December 1998, and it was a bit of a culture shock for me. At this point the German Northern scene was still very much based around scooter clubs, and as I've never owned one, I'd also never attended a scooter club event. So it was a little surprising to find nearly everybody was wearing their scooter club colours, and that the dancefloor etiquette we are used to in the UK, didn't apply.

Mind you, as very few German DJs used the microphone at this point I suppose it came as a bit of a culture shock to them finding me announcing records and things in my usual quiet intimate style ! John Mills, my sadly missed friend from Bolton, was the other guest DJ, and we had a great time, and were genuinely honoured to be asked back the next year. In addition Johnny Weston was added to the line up (And when John Mills stopped coming he was replaced by Chris Anderton, another good mate) the following year, so I had eleven years of riotous, drunken adventures in a beautiful Bavarian city, and one year of sightseeing and shopping when Margie came with me !.

Nuremburg Weekender - December 2009

Thursday saw Chris Anderton collecting me and meeting John Weston at home for the drive down to Stansted. It's the Nuremburg Weekender of course. This is the eleventh year I've done this weekender, and it's still getting better each year. We arrived on a snowy night at around 11.30 pm, to be met by the promoters, Osi and Dominic. Straight to the hotel where the hotel receptionist told us there were two rooms; a double and a single. Quick thinking by me led me to say straight away "I'm the single", and I grabbed the key, smirking. This left Chris and John with the double room. It got even funnier when they went to the room, because it was a double bed, rather than twin beds....Ohhh, did I laugh ? Yes I did. I've shared a caravan at Cleethorpes with John, and I'll tell you now, he snores ! Very loudly ! He also has problems with wind when he's been drinking !

Anyway, enough of that, we decided to attend to the more important things in life, and just dumped the bags in the room and set off to the pub. Finnegan's Irish pub was, again, to be our base for the weekend, and we managed a couple of beers before they closed at 1am. I have to admit, when we got back to the hotel, I slept like a log. Chris though, gave up trying to sleep around 3 am and packed his bag, went up to reception and booked a room for himself.

Now, I can't say I blame Chris for moving out, but the saga continued. The hotel was booked completely for the Friday and Saturday nights, so without Chris knowing, during the following morning they moved all of John's stuff into his new room, which at least had twin beds rather than a double. More of the hotel rooms later though.

By Midday, I'd had breakfast, wandered around the city for a while, bought a load of cheap tobacco, and was feeling thirsty. Finnegan's it was then. John and Chris came in within minutes of my arrival, and we settled down to have a few beers and await the arrival of some of our German friends. By 4.30pm, none of them had arrived, so I decided to go back to the hotel for a quick kip.

Chris and I met up back at Finnegan's around 9pm, no John though, he was still asleep. The venue was the same as it's always been, called K4, it's just across the road from the pub, so we wandered over just after 10pm to find it already quite busy. It's been a while now, so I can't remember what I played in any of my four spots, except the very first one was all R & B, which went down a storm. Suffice to say that the DJs had free beer all night, and you have no need to wonder why I can't remember what I played. John can't remember what he played either, mostly because he was still asleep and didn't turn up for his first spot ! He did arrive a little later though, and played a storming set in the Northern room.

By the time my second spot came around, at 3.30am, the place was heaving. Certainly as many as last year, and well in excess of 600 people, all willing to dance to almost everything that was played.

I stayed until just before the end, and then sneaked off to bed. Chris Anderton had already left, to try and get some sleep before John arrived back. So, somewhat to the annoyance of Chris (and the rest of the hotel) when John arrived back and couldn't get into the room he decided to bang and kick the door rather loudly.

Soulful Kinda Music – The Rare Soul Bible Volume Two

I can now reveal that Chris feigned sleep in the hope that John would go away. It didn't happen though, John did go away, only to return with the Night Porter and a master key, so that was a plan that went wrong !

Saturday afternoon was fairly predictable I'm afraid. Finnegan's again ! But at least it was livened up by Chris recounting the tale of the night before. Then back to the hotel for a quick wash and change and then off to meet Osi and Dominic to go for a meal. All told about twenty of us went for the meal and we had to travel a couple of stops on the Metro to get to the restaurant owned by Stefan (Who also provided the excellent dark beer for all the DJs from his own brewery). Remember I said it had been snowing when we arrived in Nuremburg, well John decided that snowballs would be a good idea. We didn't quite think so.

The meal is always a bit of an adventure, because I don't speak German, and even though some of the Germans speak excellent English, the translation of a menu presents it's own unique problems. However, the recommendation was for the Pork and Dumplings, so that's what I had, and it was very nice too. On the way back to the Metro John again threw a few snowballs, so Chris just grabbed him and dumped him face down in the snow. Shame that the snow was melting and it was a piece of muddy ground underneath. He looked like a down and out ! When we arrived back, John went to get changed, fell asleep and promptly missed his first spot again. Chris and I were pleased to see that the venue was if anything busier than the night before, and yet again, the dancefloor was heaving.

John arrived late, mumbling something about not realising he was on early, and promptly disappeared again, just in time to miss his second spot of the night. You've got to give him credit for being consistent !

So, just before 4am I played my last record and thanked the crowd for dancing, and said what a great time I'd had, again, in Nuremburg. I must admit I was slightly taken aback by the cheer that went up (Or perhaps they were cheering because I'd finished my set !!!). Great people, great venue. Love it.

Chris had again left before John to try and get some sleep. John arrived back and went through the banging and kicking of the door routine, only for Chris to open the door and say "It wasn't locked".

A quiet Sunday, spent in Finnegan's and then a lift to the airport from Dominic. The flight was on time, and the drive home went smoothly, so I was in bed by just gone 1am on the Monday. Another weekender survived.

Of all the European countries, Germany has always had the strongest scene, and I was invited to DJ in Berlin at the Downtown Soulsville allnighter a few years after I DJ'ed in Nurnberg for the first time. Of course I accepted, and even though it was only one night the promoter, Mario, kindly paid for accommodation for both Margie and me for the whole weekend. So we had a great time sightseeing, in glorious sunshine in October, in one of the most fascinating cities in Germany.

Soulful Kinda Music – The Rare Soul Bible Volume Two

I was then asked to DJ at the inaugural Baltic Soul Weekender by Dan Dombrowe in 2007. By far the most 'corporate' event I'd ever worked at because the whole thing was sponsored by Bacardi, and the emphasis was undoubtedly on the more Modern side, with a huge 'Dance Music' room, and a plethora of live acts. In fact the event has retained that Modern feel and I believe that the Northern Soul room has now been dropped. Full marks for the promoters though, the whole thing was expertly planned and organised and went without a hitch. The only downside was it was on a holiday camp site (although with smart apartments rather than chalets) which appeared to be miles from anywhere else, so in between being collected at the airport, and returned there, I never saw anything else of the countryside because I stayed on the site.

Onto Hamburg in 2007. Ralf and Jan invited me to DJ at the first weekender in Hamburg. At the time, it seemed a huge number of people had travelled over from the UK for the weekend. In reality I suppose it was only around 30, but that was a large contingent from the UK at any European event at the time.

We, Johnny Weston was the other UK guest DJ, had a great time at what is probably the highest attended Northern / Modern weekender in Germany. Of course when John and I get out on the town, alcohol is usually involved and this led to the usual escapades.

Lost In Hamburg With A Crocodile And A Snake
October 2007

Another adventure for the UK's Rare Soul warriors to sally forth onto the continent. And what a great adventure it was.

John Weston picked me up, on time, at 8 am on the Friday morning and we set off to drive to Manchester airport. Arriving a couple of hours later we set off to find the check in and everything went smoothly. A couple of pints in the bar, and then we bumped into the Greatstone crew. At the security checks they even let John and me though without having to open the records up. The guy asked what they were, and when we said "Records" he just waved us through. that's the difference between Manchester and Stansted though. In Manchester they understand what records are !

AirBerlin did us proud and we arrived at Hamburg International on time, a slight wait for the baggage and we were through to find Ralf and Jan (The co-promoters) waiting with Dave and Malayka Thorley, who had flown in an hour earlier from Birmingham, for us. Into the mini bus and off to the hotel.

We knew we were staying in the Kogge Rock and Roll hotel. John had the Tikki Room. Although he actually had black satin sheets with a dragon motif ! Oh yes, that's where the crocodile comes in, there was a stuffed one hanging from the ceiling !!

I had the Honneker Men's Room. Very strange because there wasn't even a wardrobe in the room.

As soon as we had dumped the bags it was downstairs to the bar to sample the local

Astra beer, and then next door to a restaurant where we had a tasty meal, but more of the restaurant later. Claire, Pete and Karen turned up just as we were finishing our meal, and were duly taken on a tour of the Hotel rooms.

John and I left to go and have a wander up and down the Reeperbahn. I knew of it's reputation as a centre of bars and sex shows, but in all honesty it wasn't as outrageous as I expected. A few beers in a bar and then Toby texted us to say he'd found an Irish bar, so off we went to meet up with the Letchworth Mobsters. On the way back to the hotel to meet up with Ralf we bumped into Mike Bolderson so it was looking to be a good English turnout. Ralf had asked us to meet him so that he could show us the way to the venue. and when we got there I began to wonder if it was the right place ? Surrounded by scaffolding and barbed wire it looked more like a stalag than a weekender venue !

How wrong can you be. Inside the main room was probably as big as Bidds with the Modern room not much smaller. The only down side to the whole weekend was that the dancefloor was concrete rather than wood, but it was lavishly covered in talc, before the niter started.

As we walked in Jan gave us all ten tickets for free drinks, and then told us that when we had used them not to worry because there was a fridge behind the stage that was full of beer for us anyway. It's like telling a kiddie to take whatever sweets they want in a sweetshop isn't it !! We indulged ourselves of this charming facility for the DJs, to say the least.

Musically, the Friday night seeemd to be a little up and down to start with. There was nothing wrong with the records played, they just aren't what I would have expected, particulalrly in the first couple of hours of an allnighter. So fuelled by Astra, Jevers, Kilkenny, and Becks, I set about playing a stomping Oldies set for my first spot. It seemed to do the job nicely and the dancefloor was rammed.

In fact, Mr Weston over indulged, there's a novelty, and left before his second DJ spot. Overall I don't think I heard a bad spot all night, and I would guess that the 600 or so people in the venue agreed.

Saturday morning I was off into the city centre on the Ubahn to do some shopping and buy Margie a present. It seems a nice city but very Modern compared to other cities I've visited in Germany. then again I suppose most of that was our fault back in the war ! Lunch at the train station, because if there is one thing you can guarantee in Germany it's that the main train station will have lots of different food outlets and at least one specialist tobacconist where they sell Old Holborn.

Back to St Pauli, and I met up with Toby at the Irish bar. Which was closed ! Fortunately I'd spotted an English pub earlier just round the corner, so eventually Dave and Pete turned up as well and we settled down to watch the football. Dave is a Man U fan, so was well pleased when they beat Wigan. We of course pointed out that he was a typical Man U fan because he lived near London !

Johnny Weston eventually surfaced and asked where we were by text. I gave him some simple directions. Twenty minutes later he was lost

Soulful Kinda Music – The Rare Soul Bible Volume Two

I eventually had to go out and find him. We discovered the Juke box had 'The Soul Survivors CD on it, which is where The Snake comes in because it was one of the records I picked. Don't know why they all complained, they all sang along to it. Following that it was the Rugby Union. Now it's fairly well known that I'm not keen on Union, but to see England beat Australia, when you are in an English pub in Germany creates a special atmosphere, and it was a terrific afternoon. Onto the alldayer for a couple of more beers and then John and I went back to the same restaurant for some food then, I ordered spaghetti bolognese, which arrived and tasted lovely. But I'm sure it was self reproducing itself on the plate as I ate it. I ate solidly for twenty minutes and there didn't seem to be any less on the plate than when I started !

Onto the Saturday niter. Three rooms tonight, with the introduction of an R & B / Crossover room. Good job there was a third room as well because the numbers were well up on Friday's attendance. The whole night went in a blur of Becks, but my last spot left Ralf and Jan with a fairly full floor as they were starting the last spot of the night.

Sunday morning we all met up at the English pub again before setting out on the boat trip. Great idea, and of course it was free beer for the DJs again. We'd been round a couple of times when I was asked to DJ, and that's when someone managed to fall into the decks and knock beer all over the place. Enough was enough and I ended my spot there and then. Dave Thorley played one of the best Sixties spots I've heard him play in a long time as well.

Stayed on board until 8pm and then decided to go for something to eat at the same restaurant. To our surprise we found Osi from Nuremburg already there with a group of friends, so we joined them.

Eventually we wandered off to the alldayer venue, only to find the three representatives of Scotland at the weekender holding court at the Irish pub next door. We joined them for a couple and then went into the Riverside Five bar. A couple of more drinks and it was gone 11pm. As I'm quite sensible the day before an early morning flight I left and went to bed. John stayed, and I'm told was later seen dancing with a partially dressed mannekin. But I wasn't there so have no photographic evidence.

Monday morning I was up at 7 am feeling fine. John looked like death. Oh happy days. Straight to the airport, and although there were long queues everywhere we made the flight in plenty of time and landed back in Manchester right on schedule.

A really great weekend, and it's only keft for me to thank Ralf and Jan for booking me, the sixty or so English (and Scottish) people who came over for the weekend, and all the other German DJs and punters who all contributed to making it such a fun time.

The most recent booking in Germany that I've had was at the 2013 Aachen weekender. Hosted by Lazy and Daniela the weekender is smaller in numbers than the others I've attended in Germany, but certainly made up for it in quality. A beautiful medieval town, with superb architecture, and delicious food, it was my new partner Jessica's first trip out of the UK to a Soul event, and she absolutely loved it.

Soulful Kinda Music – The Rare Soul Bible Volume Two

Aachen Weekender 2013

So, my weekender started on the Wednesday night when I left work, because I had to go down to Wales to collect Jessica because she was quite ill, and didn't think she was capable of the four hour train journey to my house on the Thursday on her own. However, she had never been to Germany, or a European Soul Weekender, so was desperate to come, and I thought the excitement of the weekend would see her through. When I arrived, she was in bed, where she'd spent the whole day with a temperature of 101.4 degrees. Hmmm, was she going to make it?

I fed her, with food and medicine, made arrangements for someone to light her fire on the Monday, and packed her case for her. Now when someone says:

"Four bra's, the black or beige ones." To me that doesn't mean two black ones and two beige ones, it means any combination of colours........So I packed four black ones. Of course I was wrong and should have correctly interpreted it correctly as two of each !

On the Thursday morning she wasn't much better, so I made her stand in the yard whilst I washed her down with a hosepipe and we caught the 10 am train successfully. As soon as we got on the train Jessica went to sleep, and stayed asleep until we arrived in Wolverhampton, which was quite an achievement as we changed trains in Shrewsbury !

Back at my house, she went to bed, and slept through until the alarm went off at 4.15 am on Friday morning. She took her temperature and it was back to 98.6 degrees, and she felt much better. Result !

We headed out for the airport, met Johnny Weston at the check in, and everything proceeded smoothly until we went through the departures barrier.

John and I both use the same type of record box to fly with, and we were in different queues. I was waved straight through, John was stopped and not only had to open his box, but also had to take every record out of it so the miserable sour faced customs woman could examine the box for a secret compartment that might have contained four illegal emigrants! It's a box of records! What did she expect to find under the records? Ah well, we had to have a beer to commiserate with John.

So that's when the weekend really started, at 7 am, with a pint of John Smiths!

The flight was fine and we arrived at Dusseldorf, and as we were waiting to collect the cases the exit door kept opening, and I could hear someone shouting abuse at us. I could have sworn it looked like Eddie Piller as well.

When we had collected our luggage we went through, and it was Eddie Piller! He was DJing that weekend in Dusseldorf with Henry Storch and had arrived at the airport half an hour before us, bumped into Lazy and The Jan, so decided to hang around to say hello. The Strange World Of Northern Soul!

Stefan, known to everyone by his DJ name of 'Lazy' introduced himself and

Soulful Kinda Music – The Rare Soul Bible Volume Two

performed the introductions to everyone else. The Jan was there, along with Andreas, and his wife Anne (better known as the DJ MS Dienel) Then we headed out to the van for the drive to Aachen.

The drive took an hour, and Jan Drews gently poked fun at Jessica all the way, explaining that in Germany they had autobahns, and bridges, and boats, and Jessica naively, said that they had them in the States as well.

We arrived at the hotel, booked in, and within minutes of getting to our room a guy delivered a goody bag from Lazy to our room. He also delivered a book. Now that in itself is quite a funny story.

Jessica's next door neighbour in Wales wanted to buy a book connected with his work. It was called something like 'The Architecture Of Welsh Cottages', and is out of print and quite expensive now, like £200 expensive!. However, he found a copy of German Ebay, at the equivalent of £25, but the seller would only sell to a German address. So the network of Northern Soul fans came into play, and the book was delivered to Lazy a couple of weeks before we arrived. The thing that really puzzled us though is why, and how, did a copy of the book end up in Germany? Still, that was a plan that came together.

Once we'd settled in to the hotel we were met by Lazy and taken on a tour of the city. Now the city is one of the oldest in Germany, and twelve hundred years ago was one of the most important, because the king at the time, Charlemagne, thought the Spa waters were beneficial to his health, so he ruled the kingdom from the city. He also built an amazing cathedral! It's hard to describe how amazing it is, but when you consider it was built in 800 BC, the workmanship and craftsmanship astound you.

Then we went to sit in the sun and have a coffee, and in Jessica's case, a Spaghetti Ice. She's a bit of a foody really, and has a rule that if she see's something on a menu that she's never tried before, orders it. It really does look like spaghetti, but it's really ice cream! (And was very nice too!)

Aachen is also famous as a Spa town, and Lazy took us to the point in the city centre where there are two outlets for 'Stinkendes Wasser' (I think that's right!). Which were water pumped up from the ground, rich in sulphur, and as you can guess, it really is stinking water!

A quick beer, to try the local brew; Bitburger, and then it was back to the hotel for a rest for a couple of hours.

Around 6 pm I used my finely tuned navigation skills to find our way round to Lazy's flat for a meal, and to meet up with all the other DJs. When we got there he wasn't in, (He was driving back from Cologne station with some of the other DJs), so his girlfriend Daniela was host. She gave us all a beer, and explained what food was available, and left us to chat with the others that were already there. You couldn't ask for more really. What a great start to the evening.

The Hamburg crew were the next to arrive, so it was great for me to meet up with Ralf, Lars, and Tolbert again after a couple of years. Then Henning from Switzerland

Soulful Kinda Music – The Rare Soul Bible Volume Two

arrived, and John Weston performed the introductions there because they knew each other.

The meal was a local speciality, and consisted of a stew with a special type of cabbage in it which is only available locally, and during the winter season. Jessica of course ripped me to pieces because I tend to have a preference for meals with meat in them, and she thinks I avoid healthy meals with vegetables in them! To my joy, I discovered there was a healthy quantity of good German sausage in the stew as well, so I wolfed my portion down with glee.

The beer was flowing nicely as more people arrived. I think Marc Forest was next, then MS Dienel, certainly at some point another old friend, Peter Werhand, had arrived.

As the time neared 9.15 pm, the mini bus arrived to ferry us all to the venue, and the weekender started promptly at 10.00 pm.

As usual, with all my reviews of weekenders, I couldn't tell you who played what, when, but I do have to say the music was of a standard, and variety that would have only been reached at a few of the current UK weekenders !

Jessica was having a ball though. As I've already said, it was her first time in Germany, and she was absolutely fascinated by the difference between here and the UK. In particular how much younger the crowd was than in the UK. Because of this, we played a game of spot the English people, and Jessica said one guy in particular had to be English because he was older than most other people. I said he wasn't English because of the way he danced.

She was also quite surprised by how many people spoke such good English. To my shame I've been DJing in Germany for over fifteen years now, and still speak almost no German (Although I can read a fair bit, and understand some conversations now), Jessica though, had made a valiant attempt to learn some useful phrases from her 1951 edition of the Collins 'Useful German Phrases' book. (More about that later though!)

I DJ'ed at 1.15 am, and am pleased to say managed to keep the dancefloor busy, and then we stayed for another hour or so, and then surrendered to the need for sleep. We'd been up for twenty two hours, and had to go back to the hotel.

Breakfast was served up until 11 am, so we made an appearance at about 10.30 am, and Jessica's spirits were immediately lifted to discover that they served 'Everything' Bagels as part of the help yourself buffet breakfast. Now I'm not a big fan of bagels, so I contented myself with the fresh rolls and ham and cheese. Jessica though, loves bagels, and regaled me with stories of having bagels for breakfast in New York (I did tell you she was a foody!).

We did the sensible thing after breakfast and went back to bed for a couple of hours because the alldayer didn't start until 3 pm.

Around 2 pm we met Johnny Weston in the foyer, and wandered off into the town to

Soulful Kinda Music – The Rare Soul Bible Volume Two

do a little exploring and shopping. Jessica bought a huge pile of Aachen Printen, which are a kind of gingerbread biscuit made in all sorts of different varieties, chocolate covered and so on (Do you see a theme developing here...Jessica and food!), I bought some tobacco, and Johnny boy bought a round of beers in the Irish pub! Good to see we took the healthy option.

Onto the alldayer, again at the Jacobshof, with Miss Twist from Utrecht DJing, record sales in the bar area, and a hot buffet provided for the DJs. I got the beers, whilst John started digging through the records, and then Jessica and I wandered through to the food area. It was a very tasty spicy pasta, with salad, or an extremely peppery mushroom soup. I was hungry, so I had both. Having eaten we wandered back into the bar area, only to find John had gone in search of food. He reappeared ten minutes later, with sweat on his brow, and his tongue hanging out. His face was also rather red:

"Have you tried that soup! They were all laughing at me in there, because it was burning my tongue."

I did wonder why he carried on eating it if he found it that hot, but this is Johnny Weston, so thought better of it.

Jessica meanwhile was practicing her German. Now I've mentioned her 1951 phrase book, that was full of useful phrases. I particularly like the one in the aeroplane section which asked "Do you mind if I open a window?" However, it was more about trying out her pronunciation than actually saying anything meaningful. Anyway, all her new German friends got collared and had to try and decipher what she was saying. I think Lazy got the most confusing one. He was asked something along the lines of "Can you strip and degrease the engine in the motor car.". The look on his face was classic!

Jan Drews had had to pay import duty on a record the day before, so Jessica tried him with "I will pay no tax". Several other people got trapped by her though, and I was helpless on occasions just watching the expression of confusion crossing people's faces.

Jessica actually spoke to the guy who she had said was English the night before. He was from Belgium! So that was one-nil to me!

Johnny Weston, having been in the venue for two hours by now, suddenly realised it was the same venue as the night before, but looked different because the lights were on! I ask you, what is he like?

Then there was the cake! Daniela apparently had spent the whole day previously baking. What a superb selection, not wishing to be greedy, Jessica and I only tried small portions of three different ones, and each one was delicious in it's own way.

Back to the hotel around five for a few hours sleep and then back to the venue for the Saturday allnighter. As is typical with all my reviews, I again have no idea who played what, I know I did two spots, both of which went well. I know we drank more Bitburger on the Saturday than we had on the Sunday, and we stayed to the end of the allnighter. I made Jessica practice her German by sending her to the bar everytime we ran out of beer, so at least she now knows at least one useful German phrase! The rest is just a blur, of laughs, conversations, and fun.

We just made it for breakfast on the Sunday morning, and to Jessica's disappointment there were just ordinary bagels, no 'Everything' bagels (It's something to do with the topping on the bagel I'm informed.) and then despite my protestations that nowhere would be open, we went for a walk round the town again.

Having walked past all the closed shops, we were back at the hotel in time to pack and be ready to leave the hotel at 3 pm back to Dusseldorf airport. Andreas and Anne were with us, as they now live in Sweden, so were catching a flight after ours. We said our goodbyes to Lazy in the car park at the airport, and went to check our baggage.

We then had a last cigarette with Andreas and Anne, and went airside. This time it was my turn to be stopped by the border control and be asked to open my record box. I tried pointing out Johnny Weston, in the hope rthat they would grab him as well and make him empty his record box again, but no such luck. They just made me open the box though, and swabbed it for drugs, but didn't ask me to take any of the records out, so that was ok. A quick beer and a sandwich, meant we were ready to fly, just as they announced boarding.

On the plane it was a female pilot, so Jessica was treated to all the jokes we used when travelling to Belfast last year….have trouble with the pedals because of her high heels, extra mirror for her makeup, and most upset that other people were wearing the same outfit etc, etc! I have to say though, it was obvious that a man was doing the actual flying and she was just there to make the announcements because we landed right on schedule in Birmingham.

UK Border control. The queues were horrendous, fortunately the queue for the automated chip reading control barrier was the shortest, so that's where we headed.

Now you may have noticed that this review doesn't contain any classic Johnny Weston moments.,…well here it comes: There are huge signs over all the kiosks, they say three things basically. 1. You have to have a chipped passport. 2. You have to be over 18 years of age, and 3. Your passport has to have the logo on the front of it to say it's a chipped passport. So John's behind me in the queue, and he's grumbling about people who can't use the self service passport scanner, and the number of people in the queue with children. Fair point I suppose!

I scan my passport, and the facial recognition software recognises me and lets me through. Jessica was in front of me, and waiting for me, so we wait for John.

And we wait, and we wait. Then we see the Border Control guard gesturing John towards the huge queue for people who can't get through.

We left him to it and went to collect the bags. We had time to collect both bags and sit down and wait for him. Eventually he turns up. The conversation went:

Soulful Kinda Music – The Rare Soul Bible Volume Two

"Show me your passport."

"No"

"Show me your passport, I want to see if it's got the logo on it."

"I just followed you, I didn't know my passport wasn't chipped."

When Jessica and I had stopped laughing we trundled out of the airport for a cigarette and said our goodbyes to John.

It had been a fabulous weekender. Everything was organised for the DJs, down to the last detail, the food was great, the beer was strong, and free! And it's like a breath of fresh air to DJ to a crowd that have no hangups about Oldies or Newies, or Funk, or R & B. If it's a good record, they will dance and enjoy it! It was also good to see so many of my German friends again, and people from Sweden, Italy, Switzerland, Holland, France, Belgium, and Luxembourg, and to make new friends, from all over Europe. And if you include Jessica from Wales, and John and myself from England, that means people travelled from ten different countries to be at the weekender.

Lazy and Daniela especially, what a great couple, the amount of work they both put in to make the weekender a success is phenomenal, and the whole weekend is a credit to them both.

I knew what to expect in Germany, and anticipated a good time, but Jessica was blown away by the whole weekend, and is now a sure convert to the European way of doing things. We'll be back to Aachen again, and probably several other European destinations over the next few years. Hopefully we'll see our friends again later this year in Manchester, when they come to visit the UK.

Onto Ireland, and I'm going to group Belfast and Dublin together, because I can't, and wouldn't want to separate the two in terms of the good times, and the great people.

I've DJ'ed three times in Belfast. Twice at the Belfast Soul Club weekenders that were run by Phil Shields and Liam Quinn. (Both of whom have now moved to England) On both occasions a whole crew from Rugby Soul Club travelled over, and we had a great laugh amongst good company. The second time we took over a complete hotel about 200 yards from the venue, and the hotel owner just let us carry on when the venue shut !

Belfast Soul Club 4th Anniversary
October 2007

Another weekender survived ! I've been through five different airports, done the equivalent of three allnighters and four alldayers in the last eleven days and it's all catching up with me now !

Belfast though was worth every minute though. Those Irish guys know how to party.

Margie and I set off Saturday morning and made it to Birmingham airport in good time

Soulful Kinda Music – The Rare Soul Bible Volume Two

to have a cooked breakfast, with the obligitory pint, for me not Margie, before the Rugby crew turned up and then we went through security no problems. The Rugby crew decided they needed to have something to eat and mobbed Burger King. Shame it was so close to boarding, Denise managed to get through the boarding gate still eating hash browns though ! The flight was on time and we landed at a sunny Belfast International airport. Chic and Dean Anderson had arrived before us, so we retired to the bar to wait for guy Hennigan. Denise and I decided we would have a quick cigarette outside. It was only when we got there that we discovered we weren't supposed to return to the arrivals hall. Well my records were still in there so we decided to walk back in though a very long corridor.

As we got about halfway down the PA system announced "STOP ! You cannot return to the arrivals hall once you have left". We ignored it. They repeated it, we ignored it. I had visions of ending up spreadeagled on the floor with a policeman aiming a machine gun at me. At this point someone else passed us. Denise decided it was him they were talking to, so we just carried on. I tell you, it was the longest corridor I have ever seen, especially as they repeated the warning again before we made it to the end !!!

After some protracted discussions with the biggest Policeman I have ever seen, he must have been nearly seven feet tall, Sian arranged a Taxi and a minibus (Why, and how, she arranged this with a Policeman I never actually worked out !). Tina, Fudge, Margie and me were in the Taxi, and Tina set the tone for the weekend by keeping the rest of us in stitches. Her first question was to ask the cabbie what his name was, because the last time she had been in Ireland the Taxi driver was called John, and she wanted a cabbie with a proper Irish name. Now I don't know whether it was his real name, or whether he was just humouring Tina, but this guy said his name was "Paddy", and Tina then quizzed him all the way to the hotel about various aspects of Belfast. I don't know how he kept a straight face because there were tears of laughter streaming down my face at one point when Tina asked him whether there were any prisons in Belfast. Why did she need to know that ?

We arrived at The Parador Hotel, and I'm sure that's the Gaelic way of spelling Fawlty Towers. No, to be fair, they couldn't have been more accommodating to us, mind you, we had booked every room in the hotel between us. We were on the top floor, which in a way was a blessing, but I'm not sure if the hot water ever reached that far up, or whether it was because the whole hotel was so hot that the boiler couldn't heat any more water up. I kid you not, the place was like a sauna all the time, yet the radiator in our room, and all the other rooms were turned off !

The Saturday alldayer started at 3pm, so once we'd all unpacked, we wandered up the road to the venue, The Errigle Inn. A nice bar downstairs which served fabulous meals, and the actual venue was upstairs. A low ceiling in a fairly large room with the decks opposite the bar and dancefloor in the middle, dark and atmospheric, all ready to go ! We retired back downstairs for a meal and I ordered the roast beef. I think I got half a cow with roast, and new potatoes. Delicious though.

Once we'd all eaten it was back upstairs to set up the base camp for the weekend, and the music started. As more and more people started to arrive it was great to renew friendships with the many people I've met from Ireland. If you include last year's Anniversary this was my fourth trip to Ireland (Dublin and Belfast) in the last twelve months. I know it's a cliche, but eveyone is so friendly you immediately feel welcome and at home. I struggle to associate any of the Irish people I've met with the troubles that beset Northern Ireland for so many years, but that's religion for you ! Fortunately we were here for a different religion though... Soul music.

There were so many good sets played throughout the day that the copious amounts of Smithwicks Irish Ales I consumed means they have all blurred into a mish mash of great music. I have no idea who played what, and have a very blurred recollection of what I played, but it seemed to go down ok because the dancefloor was full. I did the penultimate spot on the Friday and Guy Hennigan finshed the night off until 1am, then it was back to the hotel.

As I'd mentioned earlier, we had booked every room in the hotel between us (Chris and Carlos, as well as Budgie, Jo and Jeanette had the other rooms) so the decks were brought back to the hotel and set up in the bar. There were about thirty who came back in total, and along with about eight rather bemused locals, we set about having a party. Peter the hotel manager had arranged a late bar, opened the back door of the hotel for the smokers, and as it was a polished wooden floor anyway, we had a dancefloor. For the first time ever I saw Phil Shields with a drink in his hand, and apparently he carried on drinking through the night. I must admit to being a bit of a part timer here because I only lasted until about 3.30am before I had to go to bed. In my defense I did do two niters and two dayers the previous weekend !!! This is why being on the top floor was a blessing, the sound proofing in the hotel was superb and I couldn't hear the music from our bedroom.

I don't know what time they finished in the bar, but room 2 had been designated the party room, and it was still going on when I surfaced for breakfast about 7.30 am. Breakfast was termed 'Continental', which meant you made your own toast and coffee, but the real killer was the sign on the door. "Dinning Room". Now when you think about it, someone, 'designed' this sign, someone else made it, and someone from the hotel bought it, and probably someone else screwed it to the door, and not one of them noticed that it was spelt wrongly ! Did I mention Fawlty Towers, oh yes I did ! So, cereal, toast and coffee, with a healthy slug of Bushmills courtesy of Chris Morgan was breakfast. Margie came down slightly after me, so we just sat around chatting with everyone else who alternated between the Dinning Room and room 2.

As the alldayer on the Sunday didn't start until 4pm we decided to go into the City centre to look at the shops. Not knowing what Belfast was like on a Sunday I asked Phil whether the shops would be open. He said yes, but not until midday. Now I'll assume Phil doesn't do much shopping on a Sunday, rather than it was anything to do with the alcohol in his system, but the only shop open before 1pm was McDonalds ! So after a quick Strawberry shake (Which isn't really the best thing for you if you are diabetic, but it was my treat for the weekend) we hit the shops. I bought nothing, Margie bought four new tops (I don't know why she bothered packing any to bring with her to be honest !!!), but best of all, she paid for them herself !!

Across to the venue for something to eat, again superb, and then back to the hotel to discover the party was still going on in room 2 ! Margie decided on a couple of hours sleep, and I, because I didn't know what time I was DJing went back to the venue to *discover I was on at 10pm. Hmm, only another six hours drinking then before my spot !!.*

Guy and Dean were leaving around 8pm so they did a spot each early doors, and I actually paid attention this time. Great stuff from both of them. I spent a fair bit of time outside on the roof garden where you could smoke, and as people came and went it made it a really pleasant afternoon just chatting with different Irish Soulies.

By 8pm, all the UK crowd had turned up, and a fair few Irish as well, and although the numbers were down from Saturday, it was still quite a healthy crowd. Paul Grant played the standout spot of the day for me, great tunes, put together as a great set. Especially the one he dedicated to me (And I'm not saying what it was until I've got a copy). I suspect that Phil Shields had been indulging again because he was spotted Pole Dancing round one of the pillers in the room, I blame that Rugby crowd because he used to be such a shy and unassuming chap !! At this point I do really have to say thanks to Phil, he put the whole weekend together, and with assistance from Joe and Jo, organised everything on both days. It all ran like clockwork, even the non appearance of Liam (A flat tire meant he missed his plane) wasn't noticed.

A midnight finsh, with the last spot from Phil himself meant it was all back to the hotel again. A few less people this time, and we were in the Dinning Room as well. Joe and Jim appeared with crates of beer and bottles of wine as the decks were set up. No sound though, and Tina was directing operations. Fuses were changed, plugs were taken apart, cables were plugged in and taken out again. This went on for half an hour, so being nosey I decide to have a look. From where I was sitting I noticed a rather significant problem. "Try connecting the mixer to the amp". Lo and behold, twenty seconds later the music was on.

Again, I part timed it, and sloped off to bed around 2 am, only to be told I missed the funniest thing of the weekend. I bet you thought you'd got away with this one didn't you guys.

Apparently, as the alcohol flowed, Joe, Kev, and Jim decided to do their own version of the X Factor, and lined three chairs up in the middle of the room to stand on as a stage. I believe Marv Johnson was the record, with Kev doing lead vocals over the microphone, with Joe and Jim doing back up either side of him. Oh I wish I'd seen it !

I was again up early, mostly because our double bed only had two pillows and Margie had pinched both of them, again, so I didn't sleep very well and wandered down to the Dinning Room, to find Phil and Jo Brock just finishing tidying the room up. Jo was actually wearing the ice bucket on her head ! Not wanting to intrude on this bizarre spectacle I went out to find a coffee at Subway. Coming back a bit later I roused Margie (That means woke her up for those of you with a limited vocabulary and dirty minds) and we went back down to the Dinning room to find there was no milk left. Sian texted me and suggested that I go and knock on all the doors taking breakfast orders, I texted her back suggesting I didn't, or words to that effect.

The flight out was at 2.35pm, so with nothing else to do we decided to go out to City airport early. Checking out was the last dealings we had with the hotel, and what should have been a simple task turned into Fawlty Towers again. In the end, i paid

Soulful Kinda Music – The Rare Soul Bible Volume Two

using my card, for my room, Denise's room, and Sian and Dean's room (Because Sian had neglected to bring her cards with her). The young girl who dealt with it had no idea what she was doing and in the end we just said take £160 off this card. She said Ok, and put it through as £1.60. I was tempted, but then thought it would all come back on Phil in the end, which wasn't fair, so I told the truth and paid the full amount.

The flight back was fine, even watching the Rugby crowd using the self service check in was funny, and we landed on time in Birmingham. Our last sight of the Rugby crowd was of Denise licking the window of the bus stop as we waved goodbye. It says it all really.

Another fantastic weekend, with so many laughs, and such good company. If you have never been across to Ireland, you must go. You're made to feel so welcome, and everyone just wants to party. Brilliant time. I just need to recover now !

My third booking was earlier this year at the Cregagh Soul patrol night. Again, we had a wonderful, if brief stay (We flew in first thing Saturday and back out Sunday) although the Irish weather did it's best to dampen proceedings (It was torrential rain almost all the time we were there) the company, the craic, and the music was top notch.

Dublin, and Danny Dugan, Danny has recently retired the Soul night he used to run in Dublin for over a decade, but I was fortunate enough to DJ at Sleepless Nights on two occasions, and attend as a punter on a couple of others. What a great weekend each time though, hilarious times with great people, and of course some great music as well.

Sleepless Nights, Dublin
December 2009

The Friday following my return from Nuremburg I was off to the airport again, on the second leg of my European Tour 2008. This time, Margie and I met Woody and Lou at Birmingham airport for a flight to Dublin. It set the tone for the weekend when we discovered Scooby Doo was on the same flight..........

If you remember last year when we went to Dublin Lou was scared of flying and virtually assumed the crash position as soon as she got on the plane. She's got over it now, but still sat directly in front of me, so I went through the usual routine of shaking her seat quite violently as we took off. A few choice words later and we were off.

We were booked into The Belvedere Hotel, which is right above the venue used for Sleepless Nights, so pretty much just unpacked, had a quick wash and change, and then went down stairs to the bar. Now I remembered last time I was in Dublin I thought it was expensive, but this year, because of the exchange rate I discovered that it was horrendously expensive....4.60 Euros a pint ! That works out at almost £4.60 a pint. Ah what the hell, it's Christmas, hang the expense. Margie and I decided to have a meal called a 'Turkey Packet', and it was delicious, roast vegetables, covered in mashed potatoes, with a huge slice of ham, and one of turkey on the top, covered in gravy. Woody and Lou joined us, and a few of the Irish crowd had started arriving, so naturally a few more beers were consumed. Well, it would be rude not to, wouldn't it.

Downstairs for the advertised opening time (Because Lou was DJing first) and Danny Duggan was still setting the decks up. This is where the fun started because the decks are on quite a high stand, and Lou is, well, not to put too fine a point on it, short. We could just about see her head behind the decks. It didn't alter the fact that she did a great spot though, as did Woody a few hours later.

Pretty much the same as Nuremburg, I can't remember what I played, I've slept since then, and if I don't write the playlist down the next day I have no hope of remembering it. I do know that the floor seemed full enough of Irish Soulies to keep me happy, and that it was overall, another great night. We sneaked off to our room just before the end, and discovered that there was some after event entertainment arranged. Our room was on the front of the hotel, and we discovered we could lean out of the window and watch the drunks fighting in the street below. Great stuff !

As usual I was awake early, and bored, so I woke Margie up and told her it was time to get up. To her credit, she didn't tell me to bugger off, and actually got up, mind you, she knows I have the attention span of a small child if I'm bored, and would only have kept her awake fidgeting and moving around in the bedroom. So, we packed the case, left it at reception, and went round the corner to the nearest pub, where we knew from previous occasions we would get a really good breakfast.

I'd booked the flights for the four of us, and Lou had booked the hotel, so I was quite surprised to receive a call from Woody about an hour later asking if I could remember how much Lou had paid for the rooms. As it happens I could, so I said that she'd only paid an 8 Euro deposit. Which explained to Woody why the Hotel were insisting that both rooms still had to be paid for ! Profuse apologies from Lou, and we agreed to meet them in the pub for Lunch later.

A pleasant, liquid, lunch, then a flight back and then home to sleep. Another great weekend spent in Dublin, I can only say exactly the same as I did about Nuremburg; Great people, great venue. Love it.

Italy next. Rimini has now established itself as the premier weekender in Italy, but before it really got going the top allnighters were held in a little town about thirty miles from Venice called Vicenza ! I DJ'ed there twice, the first time I went out on my own in 2003, and then returned in 2007 with Margie. I realise that my write up is beginning to sound very 'samey' for each country, i.e. beer, music, people, so I'll just let the venue report from 2007 say the rest.

A Tale Of Three Margarets
February 2007

Well, got back last night from DJing at the Wildcats Soul Club allnighter in Vicenza, Italy.

Soulful Kinda Music – The Rare Soul Bible Volume Two

We travelled out on the Friday afternoon, and I tell you, I was a bit worried on the Thursady night before we left. There was a slight matter of some snow during the Thursday morning, which meant that when I went to bed on Thursday, Stansted Airport was closed, and Central trains were cancelling everything to Stansted !

Still, intrepid adventurers that we are, we set off Friday morning, and amazingly the train was running, the airport was open, and the flight was almost on time !

Arrived at Venice Treviso around 11.30 pm and Andrea & Renato were waiting to collect us. We went straight off to the local bar they all use in Vicenza where they had some decks set up. Arriving there about midnight I had to laugh. I'd expected a venue type of bar, but it wasn't, if you could get ten people in the bar it was rammed, but there were about sixty people standing outside as well ! I was asked if I'd do an hour's DJing, and of course I said yes, especially as I had heard the magic words 'Your money is no good in this bar'

Several beers later, we eventually arrived at our apartment, sixteen hours after having left home !

Saturday morning was spent exploring Vicenza with Margie, because although I'd been five years ago, she didn't come with me that time. Saturday afternoon was back at the bar. Vicenza were playing the mnighty Juventos that afternoon, so it ended up with me and Roccia having a few beers and discussing life in general (as you do) Margie had gone back to bed !

Saturday night it was back to the Nuovo Astra Bar to meet up and get a lift to the venue. As the niter was advertised to start at 11 pm I was a little surprised that we didn't set off for the venue until about 9.30 pm because there was a meal booked first. It was so Italian though, not only did 22 of us sit down for a four course meal an hour before the nighter started, it meant that the music didn't start until 12.15 am because all the DJs were still eating !

The venue itself was rather special as well, a restaurant, hotel, and night club, up the side of a mountain somewhere near Vicenza. Like a small version of Mr M's with the balconey, and it was still unchanged from the Seventies when it was turned into a club, well maintained, but not updated if you know what I mean.

A real mixture of music followed, from Fifties R & B, a little Ska, Latin Boogaloo, Oldies, Rarities, Uptempo, Midtempo, you name it, if it was Black American, one of the DJs probably played it. There were even two Seventies records played !

Back down the mountain, at twenty five miles an hour round the hairpin bends, in thick fog ! I was tempted by the idea of going for breakfast with Andrea and Renato, but Margie needed sleep again, so we declined and went to bed. The offer of meeting up for Sunday lunch was also there but we also politely declined that as well and decided to do the tourist bit and go to Venice on the train. A fabulous day out, enhanced by the fact it was 'Carnivale' in Venice, meant we arrived back at the apartment after 9pm, packed the case, and went to bed. An early start the next day saw us arriving back home, on time as well.

Soulful Kinda Music – The Rare Soul Bible Volume Two

The tale of three Margarets ? Well there were three English women in the venue Saturday night: Margie from Dudley. Maggie from Sunderland, and Margaret from Liverpool, how about that for a coincidence !

I've also DJ'ed in Amsterdan twice, at, funnily enough, The Amsterdam Soul Club. The first time I was looking to attend a few nights in Europe, not even DJ, and Jos contacted me about Amsterdam, and promptly offered me a spot. Of course I accepted, went and had a great time. That was in 2007. We'd been talking about a return vist for a couple of years and eventually got it sorted out for earlier this year when I returned, with Jessica this time, and had a superb weekend doing the tourist thing, in glorious weather. The Saturday night was spent at the club, which is well worth a visit.

No Tulips from Amsterdam, but a whole lot of soul.
November 2007

When I asked on Soul Source for the dates of European Soul nights, Jos from the Amsterdam Soul Club was the only person who replied. As I'd never been to Amsterdam before I soon arranged a date with Jos, and that date was the 19th November. So here's the lookback:

In the intervening weeks I had offered my services as a DJ for the night and Jos had offered to provide me with overnight accommodation, so I was all set for a weekend in Amsterdam.

Of course things never work out quite as planned, and without thinking of the date I accepted a booking at Sonic Soul at Lutterworth for the Friday night. I really enjoy Sonic Soul, and wanted to do the booking, but this meant I couldn't fly out to Amsterdam until the Saturday morning (and it meant very little sleep on the Friday night as well !)

Nevertheless, I caught the flight on time, landed early in Amsterdam (And a quick tip for anyone considering going to Amsterdam, all the Budget airlines that fly there are cheaper initially, but once you start to add on booking fees, card fees, baggage fees, it turned out that the scheduled KLM flight was about £20 cheaper), and contacted Jos by phone. He came out to the airport and collected me, and via a combination of train and tram we arrived back at his apartment, where I was introduced to his wife. Jos then took me upstairs to the other apartment where he showed me what his hobby in connection with Soul music was, but more of that later.

Jos then took me into Amsterdam for a quick tour of the tourist sites. I was amazed that there were loads of 'Coffee Shops', that you couldn't get a coffee in ! And there were some rather strange odours wafting out of the doors. We also did a tour of the red light district (Without stopping before you ask). It was strange to see what were often beautiful girls standing in windows wearing very little, and whilst I appreciate it's an accepted part of Amsterdam (and some of the girls were really fit) it did come across as a bit of a meat market.

The other thing that astounded me was the sheer number of people riding bicycles at breakneck speed on the Cycle roads. Each road had what we would call a cycle path on each side of it, and you literally do have to dodge the cyclists (It probably didn't help that I automatically looked the wrong way first though). So, all I needed for the full tourist set was to see some clogs, and yes there were tourist shops selling souvenir clogs.

To be honest Jos is a proud Amsterdamer though, and provided a running commentary all the way, on architecture, history, and events that had happened, so it really was an interesting tour Back to the apartment, and a lovely meal prepared by his wife for a group of people all of whom would be attending the Soul night later. I was introduced to Paul and Mandy, and as they were originally from Shrewsbury, we found we had lots of mutual friends.

By now it was approaching 9.00pm, so we set off for the venue in Jos's van.

De Badcuyp is a fairly small and intimate bar, which when the tables were moved was all dancefloor. There is an upstairs balcony, but very few people used it. A fairly good range of draft and bottled beer, and I was advised to try a Belgian beer called La Choofe as it was the closest beer to English bitter. Very nice as well, except it was almost twice as strong as the typical English beer !

Very quickly it seemed the room filled up, most of the early arrivals were all ex-pats, quickly followed by the core of the Dutch Soul fans who support the venue. I was introduced to almost everyone who arrived in the first half hour, and promptly forgot almost everyone's name (I'm blaming the strong beer !).

The first spot came from Jos himself, and this is where his hobby came in. For a living, Jos works for the Dutch Television News company, thus is well versed in video editing. For his hobby, he appears to have scoured the world for video clips of Soul artists. He then edits the clips, improves the picture quality, and in many cases removes poor quality sound tracks and replaces them with the original recording. This is where the editing skill comes to the fore, because not all live recordings are word perfect reproductions of the records, as we all know. Jos though has done a fabulous job, and I found it fascinating. Several venues in the UK have made use of screens to show clips of artists, but none have actually shown the clips of the artists performing the song that was being played at the time. Not only that, but Jos has some really, and I mean really, rare clips, that I had never seen before. I think my favourite was the one of Edwin Starr performing 'Agent OO Soul', but there were so many that I hadn't seen before that it was an absolute delight.

Next to the decks was Pete45, an ex-pat from Manchester, (also a Man U fan, but we won't go there !). A great set of Club Classics, Oldies and R & B, all on original labels as well. Then it was time for the first of my two sets.

Jos had explained that the club attracted people of all ages, with a huge range of knowledge of Soul music, from those who only knew the Motown hits, to out and out anoraks, so the first set was a bit of a jump into the unknown.

It must have gone ok because the dancefloor remained full (As it did all night

Soulful Kinda Music – The Rare Soul Bible Volume Two

actually), and nobody threw anything. The beer kept coming, and every time I tried to buy a round I was told I couldn't. In fact Jos gave me some drinks tokens to buy beer with, but I gave them back to him towards the end of the night because I hadn't had chance to spend them.

Jos and Pete both did a second set each, and then at 2.00am it was down to me to finish the night off. A few of the younger crowd had started to leave by this time, but the room still had healthy numbers, and the requests from the ex-pats were coming in thick and fast, so the second set was a bit more on the rare side than the first.

When my set finished I sort of helped load the van up (I actually stood around chatting making sure nothing was stolen). To my amazement, a considerable number of people got on their bicycles and rode off into the foggy night, including at least one ex pat.

By this time I was seriously the worse for wear. I'd had little sleep the night before, it had been a long day, and the beer was strong, and arrived with startling regularity, so I was pleased to get back to Jos's spare apartment and get some sleep.

I woke early the next morning of course, and spent a couple of hours reading before going upstairs to get Jos out of bed. After a breakfast of bacon and eggs (Which they had bought specially for me which I thought was a wonderful touch), we all set out for the city centre again. Jos's wife is a lawyer, and despite it being a Sunday, had to work, so Jos and I went on a tour of the Heineken Brewery. Great fun, and a lot better than the Guinness tour in Dublin I might add, which meant we got back to the apartment in good time for Jos to give me a lift to the airport.

The fog from the night before was still around, and although my flight was delayed for an hour I still managed to fly out at 5.30pm. which was a lot better then the people who were on the morning scheduled flight because it was cancelled.

I eventually arrived home around 7.15pm, tired but happy having spent a marvellous night in Amsterdam. I have only two regrets, firstly it appears that you cannot buy Old Holborn tobacco in Holland anymore, and I didn't see a single Tulip !

Seriously though, if you are looking for a great night out, in a wonderful city with lots of history, I would thoroughly recommend Amsterdam Soul Club. I had a great time, and I'm sure you would as well.

France: Loren and Tanguy invited me to DJ at their weekender in Brittany in 2009. I never really worked out where the holiday camp site was, but the nearest city was Concarneau. Again, I'll let the venue report do the talking for me.

Ken And His Plastic Sack Suitcase On Tour In France
October 2009

Margie and I set off for Rugby just after lunch on the Thursday to meet up with Sian and Dean, Phil, and Matt. We arrived in good time to find Sian issuing orders to all and sundry, I'm sure a complete stranger who just happened to walk past was instructed to put a case in the car ! Amazingly, we were ready to leave on schedule, so set off for London to collect Back Door Kenny in Tottenham. Ken being Ken, pops out of the door carrying his clothes in a plastic sack as his suitcase.

No problems getting into London, but of course the M25 was a virtual carpark on the way back out to get down to Portsmouth. A little bit of rally driving from Sian for the last hour got us to the Ferry just in time to board almost straight away (Because everyone else was already on board !

Find the cabin, dump the stuff, and do what all sensible people do, go and have a meal. (Ha, you thought I was going to say go to the bar didn't you !), then we went to the bar. It was about 8.30pm and the 'live entertainment' in the bar had already started. Dear God, a poor vocal duo, a very bad magician followed by a pub singer. It meant Margie went to bed almost immediately, and I of course went back to the bar. Despite the cabin having bunk beds, and you needed to be a dwarf to not bang your head if you are in the top bunk, I slept quite well. The Ferry docked on time and we left with no problem (In fact I didn't even notice where the Customs people were, we just appeared to drive straight out into France.).

I was going to try and write this part of the blog in French, but have had to admit defeat, so I'll just carry on in English. We drove for an hour or so with Sian leading the way because her satnav spoke French so it knew where we were going and eventually stopped for coffee in a charming little town called Pontivy. Having first visited a Patisserie so that Ken could indulge his passion for French bread, and Margie and Sian could get cakes, we wandered round the town looking for a cafÃƒ© to have a coffee. As the ladies of the group were making all the decisions we ended up an hour later at the first cafÃƒ© we saw, and discovered that the waitress was English !

Another hour's drive saw us arrive at the site. It was a very clean, modern campsite with chalets that have got Prestatyn, and even the new caravans at Cleethorpes, beaten hands down. Really good accommodation that we couldn't find any fault with at all. We even found our Weekender programs, the weekender CD, and a free bottle of the local cider waiting for us. (By the way, we had four CDs, so if anyone wants a copy just PM me)

By now it was almost 10 pm, when the first allnighter started, so off we set, to discover we are the first ones there, we were quickly followed through the door by Suzanne, her sister and brother in law, and Paddy and Liz. So the first people to arrive in the venue, and at the bar were the twelve English (I'm including Phil Shields as English to save having to write one Northern Irish every time) people on the site ! Mind you, it was free beer for the DJs, and the locally brewed beer was called Britt !

Tanguy and Loren, who were the promoters DJ'ed for the first two hours and to my immense delight showed that the R & B side of things was popular in France. Then Phil Shields did his first spot, followed by Lionel Girard from Paris. It was now midnight and the place had started to fill up. Matt Smart followed Lionel, to be followed by me. Then came Christophe Bidaud, a guy I'd never met or heard of before. But he played a fantastic set that was really unexpected. Phil, Lionel, me, then Loren and Tanguy finished the night off.

Soulful Kinda Music – The Rare Soul Bible Volume Two

Overall the music was top quality throughout the night. All of the French DJs played some big records, and could all DJ as well (But none of them used the mike). Sixties almost exclusively with a decent mixture of R & B to Oldies, rarities, and even quite a few unknowns. It did make me wonder whether most of the dancers actually knew any of the records they were dancing to, but hey, what the hell does that matter as long as they are dancing.

Talking of which, there was some highly imaginative dancing by the French. Certainly not what you would see over here. Talking to one of the French dancers on the Saturday, she explained that Northern Soul wasn't really part of their culture, it's part of English culture, so dancing to Northern Soul in an English way wasn't part of their culture either.

Guess who the last dozen people to leave the venue were when it finished at 6am !

Saturday morning arrived late, so we decided to all go out for the afternoon. In France, a country with a long history of culture, fashion, and food, guess where we went ? Wherever you thought of, you were wrong. We went to a record fair ! Kenny had been given his pink bucket and spade (He wanted to go to the beach as well), so wandered round the record fair with the spade, said he was crate diggin'. On the way back he came up with a really surreal comment...

Ken "It's weird where the wheels are on this van"

Margie "What one at each corner"

A quick stop at a patisserie so that Ken could stock up on fresh bread and we were back in time for the afternoon session.

DJs for the afternoon were Ken and Andrew 'Paddy' Hadfield, originally from Wigan. Ken played his usual eclectic mixture of things ranging from R & B to the odd bit of Seventies and Crossover, Paddy played a really well put together set of Crossover

Sian decided to do some display dancing, and show them how it was done, well actually she was just dancing until we encouraged her a little bit. Little did she know Margie was also filming. The results can be seen below. She couldn't understand why we were laughing hysterically until she sat down and was shown the video. I'm sure I'll pay for this at some stage in the future, but it was worth it.

We wandered off around 7pm to get something to eat, wash and change, and were back in the venue by 10.15pm. And yes, the first dozen people in the place were all English again.

It was the same DJ line up as Friday, but with the addition of Philippe Lezineaud for one spot, and again the music was top quality all night. I've been to allnighters in the UK that haven't come anywhere near the quality of things played both Friday and Saturday, and all off original vinyl as well, so all credit to Loren, Tanguy, Lionel, Christophe, and Philippe.

It was on the Saturday night that the only down note of the whole weekend crept in,

Soulful Kinda Music – The Rare Soul Bible Volume Two

and it was down to a half dozen French who were to say the least, pissed. It wasn't that they were deliberately causing trouble, but they were on the dancefloor all through the early part of the night, bumping into people, deliberately on occasion, and to the point where a couple of people were actually knocked over. OK, it wasn't an English dancefloor, so English dancefloor etiquette didn't apply, but it became a little annoying, both to us, and to the French who did want to dance properly. Fortunately by 2am, most of them had burnt out and left the floor to the proper dancers.

Margie wanted to leave at 5am, but I gather the last ones to leave the venue all had UK accents !

We weren't leaving the site until the Monday, so had the whole of the Sunday free to do some sight seeing. Off we went to the nearest city, Concarneau, and the 'Closed City'. It was a walled fort that stretched out into the sea from the rest of the city, full of quaint little tourist trap shops. One of these in particular sold every type of sweet and chocolate you could imagine, they even had sculptures made of chocolate in the most exacting detail. We were really shocked though when Sian suggested licking part of the anatomy of one to see if it tasted of sugar.......I thought she was a good Catholic girl who didn't do things like that !

Back to the site, via a patisserie for Ken, and then onto a local bar where we stocked up on beer for the evening. As we had to leave at 4.30am for the ferry it was quite a restrained evening with virtually everyone in bed by 10.30pm. The torrential rain started at about 2am and woke every one of us up. Now you wouldn't have thought that would be much of a problem, except the campsite had a barrier with a code to get on and off, and the power was turned off between 11pm and 7am, so the car and van were parked outside the barrier, which was about a quarter mile from the chalets !

Margie came up with the solution, we 'borrowed' the sun shade umbrellas from the chalets to get to the cars whilst we loaded the records and the last of our stuff up. So if the campsite owners are wondering where the sunshade left leaning against the venue door is from, it's out of G11 !

What must have been a quite stressful drive for Sian and Phil, pitch black, pouring rain, and the wrong side of the road, was successfully undertaken and we arrived at St Malo in plenty time for the ferry. We had Sian and Dean, and Margie and me in our van, which meant Phil, Kenny, and Matt were in the car. Now we sailed through the French customs no problem, but didn't see Phil come through and had visions of them being stopped and searched. Phil's car in bits on the side of the road, Kenny arrested for kicking off when they put the rubber gloves on for the body search, and Matt claiming that Phil and Kenny were gay and his parents ! As it turned out they had been stopped and asked a few questions, but they asked at Kenny's side of the car and his dulcet Barnsley tones just confused them. Apparently they asked where they had been, and the only answer Kenny could come up with was "campsite", so they let them through anyway.

Onto the Ferry, and it actually sailed ten minutes early, a quick breakfast and then do what all good non-driving people do, we retired to the bar. We were sitting outside in the smoking area when Kenny decided to brag that he would be home before *everyone else. It was as he leaned back with a smug expression on his face that the plastic chair he was sitting in decided to just collapse under him with a load bang. Cue helpless laughter from me and Matt made even worse when we realised that Kenny couldn't get back up again. It really was one of those moments where you laugh so much your face hurts, even the other people on the deck were howling with laughter.*

The live entertainment on the way back was even worse. There were so few people in the bar that the first group only did one song and cleared off, they didn't do the quiz, which just left the pub singer. He slaughtered a few songs then wandered over to us to "have a chat with the lads in the corner". I'm sure our mixture of accents confused him, after all there was Kenny with a strong Yorkshire accent, me from Lancashire, Phil from Belfast, and Matt from Rugby. He tried to get a laugh from the rest of the 'crowd' at our expense, and then said "If anyone wants to take the mike feel free". So I did. I took the mike and walked straight out of the bar (It was a good thirty yards) and left it on a window cill and walked back in without it. He wasn't quite sure what to do, but eventually realised I wasn't going to go back for it, so had to admit defeat and slunk off to fetch the mike. He didn't bother us again after that !

Straight through Customs again, and then an easy run back to Rugby where Margie and I swapped cars and drove home.

We had a brilliant weekend, with loads of laughs. The company was great, and although I had a distinct feeling that I had swapped John Weston for Kenny, it wouldn't have been half as much fun without him. My thanks to 'Mummy' Sian for doing all the organising, it made a really nice change for me to be able to just sit back and enjoy the trip, and of course my thanks to Loren and Tanguy for inviting me. I hope I was what you were expecting !

Finally, the one I, as a Northern Soul DJ, am most proud of doing. Last year I achieved a lifetime ambition to take the music home, and DJ in the States.

Over 40 years of listening to, collecting, buying, and DJing black American Soul music, and thanks to Matt Weingarden (And Jessica) I DJ'ed in New York last September at Botanica.

The reason I decided to write this article now, is because of a booking I have later this month in Paris, at the Magic City Soul Club. It got me thinking that I'd been really fortunate to have received invitations to DJ all over Europe, and how much I've enjoyed each and every one of those bookings, and I'm looking forward to my first booking in Spain in the near future as well !

I started DJing at my local youth club, and eventually worked my way up the hierarchy, getting better spots each year. Then an allnighter followed, then a weekender, then The 100 Club, then my first booking in Europe, so the only thing left for me to achieve was to DJ in the States. It took a few years to get from the youth club to New York, but what a journey to have undertaken. Great friends, great music, great times !

Label Listings

Soulful Kinda Music – The Rare Soul Bible Volume Two

Thelma

Roger Wade - Little Girl / I Can Only Hurt You
Richard Street & The Distants - Answer Me / Save Me For This Misery
Emanuel Lasky - I Need Somebody / Tomorrow
Alberta Adams - I Got Feeling / Without Your Love
Will Hatcher - This And That / It Takes Two
Magnificent Seven - The Groove / The Leap Frog
(The first six releases were not allocated catalogue numbers)
501 - Jimmy Gilford - Nobody Loves Me Like My Baby / Too Late To Cry
601 - Robert Ward & The Ohio Untouchables - Your Love Is Real / Nobody Does Something For Nothing
602 - Robert Ward & The Ohio Untouchables - Your Love Is Real / I'm Gonna Cry A River
100 - Emanuel Laskey - The Monkey / Welfare Cheese
101 - Emanuel Laskey - Crazy / Welfare Cheese
102 - Rose Batiste - I Can't Leave You / Somebody
103 - Emanuel Laskey - Lucky To Be Loved (By You) / Our World
104 - Joe Matthews - She's My Beauty Queen / Is It Worth It All
105 - Eddie Hill - You Got The Best Of Me / Baby I Cried
106 - Emanuel Laskey - Don't Lead Me On Baby / What Did I Do Wrong
107 - Joe Matthews - Sorry Ain't Good Enough / You Better Mend Your Ways
108 - Emanuel Laskey - I'm A Peace Loving Man / Sweet Lies
109 - Billy Kennedy - Sweet Thing / This Is A Groovy Generation
110 - Emanuel Laskey - (I've Got To) Run For My Love / You Better Be Sure
111 - Martha Starr - No Part Time Love For Me / It's Too Bad Baby
112 - Martha Starr - Love Is The Only Solution / I'm Lonely
113 - Martha Starr - Sweet Louie / I Wanna Be Your Girl

Top & Bottom

400 - Oscar Weathers - Bad Woman / Contract Of Love
401 - Brenda & The Tabulations - The Touch Of You / Stop Sneaking Around
402 - Oscar Weathers - Your Fool Still Loves You / Just To Prove I Love You
403 - Brenda & The Tabulations - And My Heart Sang (Tra La La) / Lies, Lies, Lies
404 - Brenda & The Tabulations - Don't Make Me Over / You've Changed
405 - Oscar Weathers - You Wants To Play / The Spoiler
406 - Brenda & The Tabulations - A Child No One Wanted / Scuze Uz Y"All
407 - Brenda & The Tabulations - Right On The Tip Of My Tongue / Always & Forever
408 - Brenda & The Tabulations - A Part Of You / Where There's A Will (There's A Way)
409 - Kevin Lassiter - It's My Love / It's My Love (Inst.)
410 - Oscar Weathers -When You Steal / I'm Scared

Soulful Kinda Music – The Rare Soul Bible Volume Two

411 - Brenda & The Tabulations - Why Didn't I Think Of That / A Love You Can Depend On
412 - Oscar Weathers - Pledging My Love / I'm Your Good Thing

Topper

1010 – Priscilla Page / Priscilla Page & Pepe The Poodle – I'm Pretending / Throw The Poor Dog A Bone
1010RM - 1010 – Priscilla Page / Priscilla Page & Pepe The Poodle – I'm Pretending / Throw The Poor Dog A Bone
1011 – Tobi Lark – Happiness Is Here / Talkin' About Love
1012 - Priscilla Page & Rony Darrell – You Did / Shoo Be Doo Bee (Now That You're Gone)
1013 – The Decisions – Tears Tears / Don't You Know It's Love
1014 – Dottie & Millie – Talkin' About My Baby / Nothing In This World (Dottie Haynes & Millie Weaver)
1015 – Tobi Lark – Challenge My Love / Sweep It Out In The Shed

Tragar

6801 - Tokay Lewis - What Can the Matter Be / ?
6802 - Tee Fletcher - Would You Do It For Me / Down In the Country
6803 - Franciene Thomas - I'll Be There / Too Beautiful To Be Good
6804 - Chuck Wilder - Why / The Clown
6805 - Frankie & Robert - Sweet Thing / Love (It's Been So Long)
6806 - The Knights - Hump / Tripping Strings
6808 - J.J. Jones - Summertime / Moody's Mood For Love
6809 - Eula Cooper - Shake Daddy Shake / Heavenly Father (also released on Atlantic)
6810 - Tee Fletcher - All Because of You / Instrumental
6811 - Richard Cook - Love Is So Mean / Somebody's Got'A Help Me
6812 - L Daniels - Nitecap / Aquarius
6813 - Langston and French - Let's Get Funky / Tumbling Down
6814 - Eula Cooper - Try / Love Makes Me Do Foolish Things
6815 - Sandy Gaye - Watch The Dog That Bring The Bone / Talk Is Cheap - ?
6816 - Eula Cooper - I Can't Help If I Love You / Since I Fell For You
6817 - Nathan Wilkes - Now That I'm Wise / Who Wants Me Now
7324 - Bill Wright - You're the Only Thing I've Got Going For Me / You're the Only Thing I've Got Going For Me
7325 - Bill Wright - You're the Only Thing I've Got Going For Me / You've Got A Spell On Me

Tri-Phi

1001 – Spinners - That's What Girls Are Made For / Heebie Jeebies

Soulful Kinda Music – The Rare Soul Bible Volume Two

1002 - Johnnie & Jackie - Carry Your Own Load / So Disappointing
1003 - Lorri Rudolph - Don't Let Them Tell Me (Tell Me Yourself) / Grieving About A Love
1004 – Spinners - I'm So Glad (Love I Found You) / Sud Duster
1005 - Johnny & Jackie - Someday We'll Be Together / Sho - Don't Play
1006 - Shorty Long - I'll Be Here / Bad Willie
1007 – Spinners - What Did She Use / Itchin' For My Baby (But I Don't Know What To Scratch
1008 - Davenport Sisters - You've Got Me Crying Again / Hoy Hoy
1009 - Jordan Harmonisers - Do You Know Him / I Won't Mind"
1010 – Harvey - Whistling About You / She Loves Me So
1011 - Merced Blue Notes - Midnite Session (Part 1) / Midnite Session (Part 2)
1012 – Challengers - Honey Honey Honey / Stay With Me
1013 – Spinners - I've Been Hurt / I Got Your Water Boiling Baby
1014 - Ervin Sisters - Changing Baby / Do It Right
1015 - Shorty Long - I'll Be Here / Too Smart
1016 - Johnny & Jackey - Do You See My Love For You Growing / Carry Your Own Load
1017 – Harvey - She Loves Me So / Any Way You Wanta
1018 - Bobby Smith & The Spinners - She Don't Love Me / Too Young, Too Much, Too Soon
1019 - Johnny & Jackie - Baby Don't Cha Worry / Stop What You're Saying
1020 - Challengers 3 Featuring Ann Bogan & Harvey Fuqua - Everday /I Hear An Echo
1021 - Shorty Long - What's The Matter / Going Away
1022 - Ervin Sisters - Why I Love Him / Every Day's A Holiday
1023 - Merced Blue Notes - Whole Lotta Nothing / Fragile
1024 – Harvey - Come On And Answer Me / Memories Of You

Tru-Glo-Town

1002 - Don Gardner – I Wanta Know Where Did Our Love Go / My Baby Likes To Boogaloo - 1966
501 – Don Gardner – I Wanta Know Where Did Our Love Go / My Baby Likes To Boogaloo - 1967
502 – Sandpipers – All Over But The Crying / Ballad To A Missing Lover
503 – Frankie Cole – I'd Have It Made / The Best Part Of My Life
504 – Ed Townsend – Don't Lead Me On / I Want To Be With You
505 – Don Gardner – Somebody's Gonna Get Hurt / Ain't Gonna Let You Get Me Down
506 – Royal Robins – Something About You Sends Me / Roller Coaster
507 – Susaye Greene – That's The Way Love Is / Please Send Him Back To Me
508 – Sylvia Robinson – Oo Wee Baby / Love Is The Only Thing
509 – Joe Moore – Hang Right In There / Nobody Loves Me

Was the Don Gardner single released twice ? I've been told it was, and it wasn't, by lots of different people ! It does appear that the 1002 catalogue number might be the

Soulful Kinda Music – The Rare Soul Bible Volume Two

Matrix number because the number ties in with the rest of the matrix numbers on the label, but I am assured that there are two different releases by quite knowledgeable people.

Tuff

1 - The Four Sounds – The Ring / Peter's Gun
102 - The Corsairs – It Won't Be A Sin / Time Waits
3027 - The Corsairs - Time Waits / It Won't Be A Sin
1808 - The Corsairs – Smokey Places / Thinkin' Maybe She's Changed Her Ways
1818 - The Corsairs – I'll Take You Home / Sitting On Your Doorstep
1830 - The Corsairs – Dancing Shadows / While
1840 - The Corsairs – (It's Almost) Sunday Morning / Stormy
369 - The Jaynetts - Sally Go 'Round The Roses / Inst.
370 - The Hearts - Dear Abby / Inst
371 - The Jaynetts - Keep An Eye On Her / Inst
372 - The Poppies - Johnny, Don't Cry / Inst
373 - The Clickettes - I Just Can't Help It / Inst
374 - The Jaynetts - Snowman, Snowman, Sweet Potatoe Pie / Snowman Snowman Sweet Potato Nose
375 - The Corsairs - Save A Little Monkey / Inst
376 - January Star - And So She Took A Ring / America The Beautiful
377 - The Jaynetts - No Love At All / Tonight You Belong To Me
378 - Patty Cakes - I Understand Them / Inst
379 - Johnnie & Joe - Here We Go, Baby / That's The Way You Go
380 - ?
381 - Vernell Hill - Long Haired Daddy / Sometimes Love
400 - Sue Wellington - Spoiled / Save A Little Monkey
401 - Jimmie Raye - Look At Me, Girl / I Tried
402 - Landy Mcneil & The Corsairs - On The Spanish Side / The Change In You
404 - The Poindexter Brothers - Booga Man / Ride Ride Ride
405 - Roscoe Robinson - What Makes A Man Do Wrong / Too Many Lies
406 - The Fantastic Vantastics - Oh, Happy Day / Oh Happy Day
407 - Kendra Sportswood - Stickin' With My Baby / Jive Guy
408 - Landy Mcneil - What Are You Trying To Prove / A Little Tear Fell
409 - Ray Raymond - It Breaks My Heart / She's Alright
411 - Jackie Day - Come On And Try Me / It's Over
413 - Landy Mcneil - Hang Your Soul On Me / Show Me
414 - Bobby Copney - Love Au-Go-Go / Ain't No Good
415 - Bobby Treetop - So Sweet, So Satisfying / R & B Time
416 - Ronnie Savoy - Pitfall / ?
417 - Bobby Treetop - Wait Till I Get To Know Ya / R & B Time
418 - E. Rodney Jones - R & B Time / Part 2
419 - Little Joe Roman - When You're Lonesome / We Got A Love
420 - Vicki Anderson - I Can't Stop Loving You / I Got A Good Man (And I Know It)
421 - E. Rodney Jones - Peace Of Mind / Do The Thang

Soulful Kinda Music – The Rare Soul Bible Volume Two

422 - Mickey & Larry - My One Chance To Make It/ Reaper Of Rain
1715 - The Corsairs – Time Waits / It Won't Be A Sin

1971
155 - Syl Johnson - That's Why / Everybody Needs Love - 1971
156 - Nate Evans - Pardon My Innocent Heart / Main Squeeze - 1971

U

Lesley Uggams

Lesley 'Uggams' Crayne

MGM 11437 - Easter Bunny Day / Percy The Pale Faced Polar Bear - 1953

Leslie 'Uggams' Crayne

MGM 11626 - My Stocking Is Empty / This Is Santa Claus - 1953

Lesley 'Uggams' Crayne

MGM 11676 - My Candy Apple / Kickin' Up A Storm - 1954

Leslie Uggams (born 25-May-1943 in New York City)

MGM 11755 - Ev'ry Little Piggy's Curley Tail / Palsy Walsy Land – 1954
MGM 11868 - Uncle Santa / The Fat, Fat Man – 1954
MGM 11965 - Meet My Friend, Mr. Sun / Did You Ever Dream - 1955

Leslie Uggams with Hugo Peretti & His Orch.

Roulette 4078 - I'm Old Enough / Ice Cream Man - 1958

Leslie Uggams

Columbia 4-41451 - One More Sunrise (Morgen) / The Eyes Of God – 1959
Columbia 4-41531 - My Favorite Things / Sixteen Going On Seventeen – 1959
Columbia 4-41564 - Carefree Years / Lullaby Of The Leaves – 1960
Columbia 4-41654 - I Grew Up Last Night / I'm Just A Little Sparrow – 1960
Columbia 4-41798 - Inherit The Wind / Love Is Like A Violin – 1960
Columbia 4-42055 - He Doesn't Know / I Love Him – 1961
Columbia 4-42255 - Get Happy / Birth Of The Blues – 1961
Columbia 4-42611 - Each And Ev'ry Day / Is He The Only Man In The World – 1962
Columbia 4-43012 - (I'd Be) A Legend In My Time / My Wish – 1964
Columbia 4-43064 - Little Bird / This Is My Prayer – 1964
Columbia 4-43121 - Who Do You Think / And I Love Her* (Him) - 1965 *Originally Released In 1964 By The Beatles On Capitol 5235.
Atlantic 2313 - Don't You Even Care / Who Killed Teddy Bear – 1965
Atlantic 2371 - If My Friends Could See Me Now / We Can Work It Out – 1967
Atlantic 2397 - Hallelujah Baby / My Own Morning – 1967
Atlantic 2469 - I (Who Have Nothing) / The House Built On Sand – 1967
Atlantic 2524 - River Deep, Mountain High / Land Of Make Believe – 1968
Atlantic 2675 - Just To Satisfy You / That Old Sweet Roll (Hi-De-Ho) – 1969
Atlantic 2698 - Home / Save The Country – 1969
Atlantic 2727 - He Can Do It / Walk Him Up The Stairs – 1970
Sonday 6006 - Love Is A Good Foundation / I Just Can't Help Believing – 1970
Sonday 701- Try To See It My Way / ? – 1971

Soulful Kinda Music – The Rare Soul Bible Volume Two

Motown 1391 - I Want To Make It Easy For You / Two Shoes - 1976 (unissued - also planned for release but unissued on this number was The Supremes "I'm Gonna Let My Heart Do The Walking / Early Morning Love") Gordy 7149 - I Want To Make It Easy On You / Two Shoes - 1976

The Undisputed Truth

The Undisputed Truth (Members: Joe Harris (Of The Fabulous Peps), Billie Rae Calvin, and Brenda Joyce Evans)

Gordy 7108 - Smiling Faces Sometimes / You Got The Love I Need - 1971
Gordy 7112 - You Make Your Own Heaven / Ball Of Confusion (That's What The) - 1971
Gordy 7114 - What It Is / California Soul - 1972
Gordy 7117 - Papa Was A Rollin' Stone / Friendship Train - 1972
Gordy 7122 - Girl You're Alright / With A Little Help From My Friends - 1972
Gordy 7124 - Mama I Got A Brand New Thing / Gonna Keep On Trying Till I Win - 1972
Gordy 7130 - Law Of The Land / Just My Imagination (Running Away) - 1973
Gordy 7134 - Help Yourself / What's Going On - 1974
7139 - Undisputed Truth - I'm A Fool For You / The Girl's Alright With Me - 1974
Gordy 7140 - Lil' Red Ridin' Hood / Big John Is My Name - 1974
Gordy 7143 - UFO's / Got To Get My Hands On Some Lovin' - 1975
Gordy 7145 - The Undisputed Truth – Glass House / The Prophet - 1975
Gordy 7147 - Boogie Bump Boogie / I Saw You When You Met Her - 1975

The Undisputed Truth (Members: Virginia McDonald, Tyrone 'Big Ty' Douglas, Tyrone 'Lil Ty' Barkley, and Calvin 'Doc' Stephenson, Taka Boom)

Whitfield 8231 - You + Me = Love / You + Me = Love (Inst) - 1976
Whitfield 8306 - Let's Go Down To The Disco / You + Me = Love - 1976
Whitfield 8362 - Sunshine / Sunshine - 1976
Whitfield 8783 - Show Time / Misunderstood - 1979
Whitfield 8873 - I Can't Get Enough Of Your Love / I Can't Get Enough Of Your Love - 1979

LPs

Gordy G-955L - The Undisputed Truth - 1971
Tracks: You Got The Love I Need / Save My Love For A Rainy Day / California Soul / Aquarius / Ball Of Confusion (That's What the World Is Today) // Smiling Faces Sometimes / We've Got A Way Out Love / Since I've Lost You / Ain't No Sun Since You've Been Gone / I Heard It Through The Grapevine / Like A Rolling Stone

Gordy G-959L - Face to Face with the Truth - 11972
Tracks: You Make Your Own Heaven And Hell Right Here On Earth / What Is It? / Ungena Za Ulimengu (Unite The World) Friendship Train // Superstar (Remember

Soulful Kinda Music – The Rare Soul Bible Volume Two

How You Got Where You Are) / Take Me In Your Arms And Love Me / Don't Let Him Take Your Love From Me / What's Going On

Gordy G-963L - Law of the Land - 1973
Tracks: Law Of The Land / Papa Was A Rollin' Stone / Girl You're Alright / Killing Me Softly With His Song / Just My Imagination (Running Away With Me) / This Child Needs It's Father // Mama I Gotta Brand New Thing (Don't Say No) / Feelin' Alright / Love And Happiness / With A Little Help From My Friends / If I Die / Walk On By

Gordy G6-968S1 - Down to Earth - 1974
Tracks: Help Yourself / Big John Is My Name / Brother Louie / I'm A Fool For You / Our Day Will Come // Just You 'N' Me / Love And Happiness / Law Of The Land / The Girl's Alright With Me / Save My Love For A Rainy Day

Gordy G6-970S1 - Cosmic Truth - 1975
Tracks: Earthquake Shake / Down By The River / UFO's / Lil' Red Ridin' Hood / Squeeze Me Tease Me // Spaced Out / Got To Get My Hands On Some Lovin' / 1990 / (I Know) I'm Losing You

Gordy G6-972S1 - Higher than High - 1975
Tracks:) Higher Than High / Poontang / Life Ain't So Easy / Boogie Bump Boogie // Help Yourself / I'm In The Red Zone / Overload / I Saw You When You Met Her / Ma

Whitfield 2967 - Method To The Madness - 1977
Tracks: Cosmic Contact / Method To The Madness / Sunshine / You + Me = Love / Hole In The Wall / Loose / Life Ain't So Easy / Take A Vacation From Life (And Visit Your Dreams) / Let's Go Down To The Disco

Whitfield 3202 - Smokin' - 1979
Tracks: Smokin' / Talkin' To The World / Atomic Funk / I Can't Get Enough Of Your Love / Misunderstood / Sandman / Tasmanian Monster / Space Machine

The Utopias

The Utopias (members David Lasley, Julie Lasley and Joan Hughes)

Fortune 568 - Welcome (Baby To My Heart) / Sally Bad – 1966
Hi-Q 100/101 - (We Gotta Be) Good Friends Forever / Maybe – 1967
Lasalle 0072 - Girls Are Against Me / I Want To Go Back To My Dream World - 1967
Lasalle ? - Look At The Clock / Back In The Woods - 1967 (Unreleased)

David Lasley (born David Eldon Lasley 1947 in Sault St. Marie, Michigan)

Philly Groove 178 - One Fine Day* / Merry-Go-Round** - 1973 *also recorded in 1963 by The Chiffons on Laurie 3179.

Rosie (members David Lasley, Lynn Pitney and Lana Marrano)

RCA 10610 - Roll Me Through The Bushes / Danny's Ditty - 1976

Soulful Kinda Music – The Rare Soul Bible Volume Two

RCA 11090 - The Words Don't Matter / Mississippi Baby – 1977

Roundtree (members Diva Gray, Luther Vandross, David Lasley, Bernard Edwards (bass --- member of Chic), ...)38 members

Omni 5000 - Get On Up (Get On Down) (6:47) / Ocho Rios (5:15) - 1978 (12" Release)
Island/Warner Bros. Isd 8654 - Get On Up (Get On Down) (6:47) / Manhattan (4:17) - 1978 (12" release)

Label Listings

Up Look

10869 - Charlie Mintz - Since I Found You Girl / Blues So Bad - 1969
51470 - Delegates Of Soul - What A Lucky Guy I Am / I'll Come Running Back - 1970
12270 - Gene Faith - Give A Man A Break / Finders Keepers - 1970
42671 - Carlie Mintz - Lucky Guy / Running Back - 1971
42671 - Charles Mintz Orchestra - Running Back / Running Back (Instrumental) - 1971

Uni

55001 - Daily Flash - French Girl / Green Rocky Road - 1967
55002 - The Rainy Daze - That Acapulco Gold / In My Mind Lives A Forest - 1967
55003 - Urral Thomas - Can You Dig It? / I'm A Whole New Thing - 1967
55004 - The Hippy Dippys - Thoroughly Modern Millie / Jimmy - 1967
55005 - The Factory - Smile, Let Your Life Begin / When I Was An Apple - 1967
55006 - Marcia Strassman - The Flower Children / Out Of The Picture - 1967
55007 - Johnny Booth - I Think I Can / Wishful Thinkin' - 1967
55008 - Big Game Hunters - Swingin' Shepherd Blues / See The Children - 1967
55009 - The Blues Scene - Close To You / Love - 1967
55010 - Hamilton Walker - Graveyard Shift / You Must Be The One - 1967
55011 - The Rainy Daze - Discount City / Good Morning, Mr. Smith - 1967
55012 - Boenzee Cryque - Sky Gone Gray / Still In Love With You Baby - 1967
55013 - ?
55014 - Julie Gregg - This Time / Sunshine - 1967
55015 - The Osmond Brothers - Flower Music / I Can't Stop - 1967
55016 - The Pleasure Fair - Morning Glory Days / Fade In, Fade Out - 1967
55017 - Urral Thomas - Pain Is The Name Of Your Game / Since You Went Away - 1967
55018 – Strawberry Alarm Clock - Incense And Peppermints / The Birdman Of Alcatrash - 1967
55019 - The Jades - The Glide / Flower Power - 1967
55020 - David Essex - She's Leaving Home / He's A Better Man Than Me - 1967
55021 - The Druids of Stonehenge - A Garden Where Nothing Grows / Painted

Soulful Kinda Music – The Rare Soul Bible Volume Two

Woman - 1967
55022 - Boenzee Cryque - Watch The Time / You Won't Believe It's True - 1967
55023 - Marcia Strassman - The Groovy World Of Jack And Jill / The Flower Shop - 1967
55024 - Hugh Masekela - Baby, Baby, Baby / Lily The Fox - 1967
55025 - Barry Richards - Two For The Road / We Ain't Makin' It Baby - 1967
55026 - The Rainy Daze - Stop Sign / Blood Of Oblivion - 1967
55027 - Emil Richards and Factory - No Place I'd Rather Be / Bo Diddley - 1967
55028 - Sandy Knox - Helpless / Toy Heart - 1967
55029 - Jan Davis - International Love Process Part 1 / International Love Process Part 2 - 1967
55030 - Patrick and Paul - Big City Blues / Love Country - 1967
55031 - The Visions - How Can I Be Down / Threshold Of Love - 1967
55032 - The Jades - Privilege / Privilege - 1967
55033 - The Goode - September In The Rain / Faded Picture - 1967
55034 - Looking Glass - Virginia Day's Ragtime / Cry Memories What Am I Doin' - 1967
55035 - The Shy Guys - Rockin' Pneumonia And Boogaloo Flu / You Are My Sunshine - 1967
55036 - Jimmy Luke - Billie Sue / Without A Love - 1967
55037 - Hugh Masekela - Up Up And Away / Son Of The Ice Bag - 1967
55038 - The Foundations - Baby, Now That I've Found You / Come On Back To Me - 1967
55039 - The Sonics - Anyway The Wind Blows / Lost Love - 1967
55040 - Rose Maddox - Bottom Of The Glass / Step Right In - 1967
55041 - Skeets McDonald - It's Genuine / Old Indians Never Die - 1967
55042 - The Visions - Keepin' Your Eyes On The Sun / Small Town Commotion - 1967
55043 - The Yellow Payges - Our Time Is Running Out / Sweet Sunrise - 1967
55044 - Alexander's Timeless Bloozband - Love So Strong / Horn Song - 1967
55045 - Tim Gilbert - Early October / If We Stick Together - 1967
55046 – Strawberry Alarm Clock - Tomorrow / Birds In My Tree - 1967
55047 - Hound Dog Clowns - Superfox / Wicked Witch - 1968
55048 - John Rosasco - Coffee And Tea / Love Comes In - 1968
55049 - Hugh Masekela - There Are Seeds To Sow / Ha Lese Le Di Khana - 1968
55050 - The Lollipop Shoppe - You Must Be A Witch / Don't Close The Door - 1968
55051 - Big Black - The Snakecharmer / Come On And Get It Baby - 1968
55052 - Paul and Paula - All These Things / Wedding - 1968
55053 - Candy Graham - The Room / Cry A Little Tear - 1968
55054 - Michael Procyszyn - Me And Little Mary-O / Me And Little Mary-O - 1968
55055 - Strawberry Alarm Clock - Pretty Song From Psych-Out / Sit With The Guru - 1968
55056 - Marcia Strassman - Star Gazer / Self   -   Analysis - 1968
55057 - The Hook - Son Of Fantasy / Plug Your Head In - 1968
55058 - The Foundations - I Can Take Or Leave Your Loving / Back On My Feet Again - 1968
55059 - Lori Hampton - I Feel Love Coming On / I'm Under The Influence Of Love - 1968
55060 - Fever Tree - San Francisco Girls (Return Of The Native) / San Francisco Girls (Return Of The Native) - 1968 (Promo only Cyan vinyl)

Soulful Kinda Music – The Rare Soul Bible Volume Two

55060 - Fever Tree - San Francisco Girls (Return Of The Native) / Come With Me (Rainsong) - 1968
55061 - Cliff Richard - All My Love / Our Story Book - 1968
55062 - ?
55063 - ?
55064 - Sunny and Phyllis Danes - I've Been Lost / Love Love Love - 1968
55065 - Neil Diamond - Brooklyn Roads / Holiday Inn Blues - 1968
55066 - Hugh Masekela - Bajabula Bonke / Grazing In The Grass - 1968
55067 - Roy Gaines - I Doubt It / Ella Speed - 1968
55068 - John Rowles - If I Only Had Time / Now Is The Hour - 1968
55069 - Cliff Richard - Congratulations / High 'N' Dry - 1968
55070 - ?
55071 - Bobby Skel - Sheila Ann / Three Candles - 1968
55072 - The Yellow Payges - Judge Carter / Childhood Friends - 1968
55073 - The Foundations - Any Old Time / We Are Happy People - 1968
55074 - Rabbitt MacKay - Candy / Big Sur Country - 1968
55075 - Neil Diamond - Two - Bit Manchild / Broad Old Woman - 1968
55076 - Strawberry Alarm Clock - Barefoot In Baltimore / Angry Young Man - 1968
55077 - The Hook - Love Theme In E Major / Homes - 1968
55078 - The Pleasure Fair - Today / I'm Gonna Hafta Let You Go - 1968
55079 - Michael Procyszyn - Charlie's Rainbow / The World Went Around And Around - 1968
55080 - Larry Carlton - Monday, Monday / The Odd Couple - 1968
55081 - ?
55082 - Future - 52% / The Shape Of Things To Come - 1968
55083 - ?
55084 - Neil Diamond - Sunday Sun / Honey - Drippin' Times - 1968
55085 - Hugh Masekela - Do Me So Lo, So So / Puffin' On Down The Track - 1968
55086 - Fun and Games - Elephant Candy / The Way She Smiles - 1968
55087 - Lori Hamilton - Runaway Boy / Fragile, Handle With Care - 1968
55088 - Orange Colored Sky - Orange Colored Sky / The Shadow Of Summer - 1968
55089 - The Yellow Payges - You're Just What I Was Looking For Today / Crowd Pleaser - 1968
55090 - Jimmy Stewart and The Sirs - Wow / Sixteen Candles - 1968
55091 - Sunny and Phyllis - If We Had To Do It All Over / When I Look Into Your Eyes - 1968
55092 - Bobby Skel - Soul Of A Man / Gentle Woman - 1968
55093 - Strawberry Alarm Clock - Paxton's Back Street Carnival / Sea Shell - 1968
55094 - Giant Crab - Hi Ho Silver Lining / Hot Line Conversation - 1968
55095 - Fever Tree - What Time Did You Say It Is In Salt Lake City / Where Do You Go? - 1968
55096 - Michael J. James - She Needs The Same Things I Need / Thinking Of Myself - 1968
55097 - Derry O'Leary - Hush a Bye Mountain / The Name Of The Game - 1968
55098 - Fun and Games - The Grooviest Girl In The World / It Must Have Been The Wind - 1968
55099 - Big Black - Come On Down To The Beach / Love, Sweet Like Sugarcane - 1968
55100 - Betty Everett - Take Me / There'll Come A Time - 1968
55101 - The Foundations - Build Me Up Buttercup / New Direction - 1968

Soulful Kinda Music – The Rare Soul Bible Volume Two

55102 - Hugh Masekela - Mace And Grenades / Riot - 1968
55103 - Giant Crab - Believe It Or Not / Lydia Purple - 1968
55104 - Paper Dolls - Someday / Any Old Time You're Lonely And Sad - 1969
55105 - East Side Kids - Is My Love Strong / Taking The Time - 1969
55106 - The Fields - Bide My Time / Take You Home - 1969
55107 - The Yellow Payges - The Two Of Us / Never Put Away My Love For You - 1969
55108 - ?
55109 - Neil Diamond - Brother Love's Travelling Salvation Show / A Modern - Day Version Of Love - 1969
55110 - The Mirettes - Stand By Your Man / If Everybody'd Help Somebody - 1969
55111 - Marvin Holmes - Ooh, Ooh, The Dragon Part 1 / Ooh, Ooh, The Dragon Part 2 - 1969
55112 - Rabbitt MacKay - Somebody Beat Me / Tendency To Be Free - 1969
55113 - Strawberry Alarm Clock - Stand By / Miss Attraction - 1969
55114 - Kim Vassy - Farewell / Hello L.A. Bye Bye Birmingham - 1969
55115 - Orange Colored Sky - Happiness Is / Another Sky - 1969
55116 - Hugh Masekela - A Long Ways From Home / Home Boy - 1969
55117 - The Foundations - Give Me Love / In The Bad, Bad Old Days (Before You Loved Me) - 1969
55118 - Bobby Skel - Banks Of The Ohio / Baby Come Back - 1969
55119 - Consortium - Spending My Life Saying Goodbye / All The Love In The World - 1969
55120 - Larry Carlton - Moon People / Son Of A Preacher Man - 1969
55121 - Derry O'Leary - How Can I Be Sure / Name Of The Game - 1969
55122 - Betty Everett - I Can't Say No To You / Better Tomorrow Than Today - 1969
55123 - Sandra Alexandra - Got To Get You Off My Mind / Ooh Baby I Love You - 1969
55125 - Strawberry Alarm Clock - Good Morning Starshine / Me And The Township - 1969
55126 - The Mirettes - Heart Full Of Gladness / Ain't You Trying To Cross Over - 1969
55127 - Dino, Desi and Billy - Thru Spray Colored Glasses / Someday - 1969
55128 - Fun and Games - Gotta Say Goodbye / We - 1969
55129 - Desmond Dekker and The Aces - Israelites / My Precious World - 1969
55130 - Hugh Maskela - Gettin' It On / 10,000 Miles To Memphis - 1969
55131 - Lovelace Watkins - A Man Without A Dream / Gone Away - 1969
55132 - The Blue Notes - Hot Chills And Cold Thrills / Never Gonna Leave You - 1969
55133 - Blue Bull - I'm A Loser / Shame, Shame, Shame - 1969
55134 - John Fred and his Playboy Band - Back In The U.S.S.R. / Silly Sarah Carter - 1969
55135 - Giant Crab - Cool It / Intensify My Soul - 1969
55136 - Neil Diamond - Sweet Caroline (Good Times Never Seemed So Good) / Dig In - 1969
55137 - The Foundations - My Little Chickadee / Solomon Grundy - 1969
55138 - Zodiac - "X" Rated / Then Goodbye - 1969
55139 - Kim Vassy - I Think I Just Found My Mind / That's The Big I'm In - 1969
55140 - Orange Colored Sky - Mr. Peacock / Knowing How I Love You - 1969
55141 - Betty Everett - 1900 Yesterday / Maybe - 1969

Soulful Kinda Music – The Rare Soul Bible Volume Two

55142 - Quincy Jones - The Lost Man / Main Squeeze - 1969
55143 - Garland Green - Jealous Kind Of Fella / I Can't Believe You Quit Me - 1969
55144 - Michael J. James - Get The Message / Love's Funny - 1969
55145 - Cliff Richard - The Day I Met Marie / Sweet Little Jesus Boy - 1969
55146 - Fever Tree - Love Makes The Sun Rise / Filigree and Shadow - 1969
55147 - The Mirettes - Whirlpool / You Ain't Trying To Cross Over - 1969
55148 - The Wasters - Don't Stop / Accept My Love - 1969
55149 - The Hook - In The Beginning / Show You The Way - 1969
55150 - Desmond Dekker and The Aces - It Mek / Problems - 1969
55151 - Matt and Robert - These Arms Of Mine / Soul Of A Man - 1969
55152 - The Cascades - Maybe The Rain Will Fall / Naggin' Cries - 1969
55153 - The Yellow Payges - Would You Mind If I Loved You / Vanilla On My Mind - 1969
55154 - Smoke - Choose It - Part 1 / Choose It - Part 2 - 1969
55155 - Giant Crab - ESP / Hot Line Conversation - 1969
55156 - Orange Colored Sky - The Sun And I / Sweet Potato - 1969
55157 - The Sunday Funnies - Baby, I Could Be So Good At Loving You / See Things My Way - 1969
55158 - Strawberry Alarm Clock - Desiree / Changes - 1969
55159 - Charity - Never Change Your Mind / I Still Love You - 1969
55160 - John Fred and his Playboy Band - Open Doors / Three Deep Is A Feeling - 1969
55161 - Nate Turner and The Mirettes / Venetta Fields and The Mirettes - Rap Run It On Down / Sweet Soul Sister - 1969
55162 - The Foundations - Why Did You Cry / Born To Live Born To Die - 1969
55163 - Great Love Trip - Why Can't We Be / Noah - 1969
55164 - War Babies - Together Forever / War Baby - 1969
55165 - Hugh Masekela - Where Has All The Grass Gone / I Haven't Slept - 1969
55166 - Robin Hood Brians - Goodbye So Long Honolulu / Webb Of Love - 1969
55167 - Bobby Skel - Red Light Green Light / Where Has All The Grass Gone? - 1969
55168 - ?
55169 - The Cascades - Indian River / Big City Country Boy - 1969
55170 - Thee Midniters - She Only Wants What She Can't Get / I've Come Alive - 1969
55171 - Jesse James - Ain't Much Of A Home / Don't Fight It - 1969
55172 - Fever Tree - Clancy / The Sun Also Rises - 1969
55173 - The Marketts - The Undefeated / They Call The Wind Maria - 1969
55174 - Betty Everett - Been A Long Time / Just A Man's Way - 1969
55175 - Neil Diamond - Holly Holy / Hurtin' You Don't Come Easy - 1969
55176 - The Yellow Payges - Slow Down / Fresco Annie - 1969
55177 - ?
55178 - Dewey Martin and Medicine Ball - Jambalaya (On The Bayou) / Ala-Bam - 1969
55179 - Johnny Garret and Rising Signs - Get Around Downtown Girl / People - 1969
55180 - Tony Borders - Lonely Weekend / You Better Believe It - 1969
55181 - The Lovelites - How Can I Tell My Mom And Dad / Hey! Stars Of Tomorrow - 1969
55182 - Rubber Bucket - We're All Living In One Place / Take Me Away - 1969
55183 - Davey Payne - Why Can't I Be Your Man / Bad Girls - 1969

Soulful Kinda Music – The Rare Soul Bible Volume Two

55184 - Bill Cosby and Bunions The Bradford Band - .Hikky Burr / Hikky Burr - 1969
55185 - Strawberry Alarm Clock - Small Package / Starting Out The Day - 1969
55186 - The Green Berets - Send Me Somebody / We Must Make Things Right - 1969
55187 - John Fred and his Playboy Band - Love My Soul / Julia Julia - 1969
55188 - Garland Green - All She Said (Was Goodbye To Me) / Don't Think That I Am A Violent Guy - 1969
55189 - Betty Everett - Sugar / Just A other Winter - 1969
55190 - Strawberry Alarm Clock - I Climbed The Mountain / Three - 1969
55191 - Pat Shannon - Back To Dreamin' Again / Moody - 1969
55192 - The Yellow Payges - Little Women / Follow The Bouncing Ball - 1970
55193 - Brian Hyland - You And Me / Could You Dig It - 1970
55194 - Banana Boys - Come Into My Life / What Will Your Mama Say - 1970
55195 - Kim Vassy - I Just Wanna Give My Love To You / Blue Bird - 1970
55196 - Bob and Earl - Uh Uh No No / (Pickin' Up) Love's Vibrations - 1970
55197 - Jan Davis - Flamenco Funk / Walk Don't Run - 1970
55198 - New World Soul Choir - Keep Talkin' / You Better Be Goin' - 1970
55199 - The Sister and Brothers - Jed Klampet Part 1 / Jed Klampet Part 2 - 1970
55200 - The Cascades - But For Love / Hazel Autumn Cocoa Brown - 1970
55201 - The Blue Notes - This Time Will Be Different / Lucky Me - 1970
55202 - Fever Tree - What Time Did You Say It Is In Salt Lake City / Catcher In The Rye - 1970
55203 - Sunshower - Hands Off My Man / Really Really - 1970
55204 - Neil Diamond - Until It's Time For You To Go / And The Singer Sings His Song - 1970
55205 - Scotty McKay - High On Life / If You Really Want Me To, I'll Go - 1970
55206 - Jackie Lee - The Chicken / I Love You - 1970
55207 - Jerry and Susan - Come Saturday Morning / The Hills Of Yesterday - 1970
55208 - The Aquarians - Bayu   -   Bayu / Excuses, Excuses - 1970
55209 - Buddy Randell - Be My Baby / Randi Randi - 1970
55210 - The Foundations - Take A Girl Like You / I'm Gonna Be A Rich Man - 1970
55211 - Lovelace Watkins - Fool On The Hill / Je Vous Aime Beaucoup - 1970
55212 - Gene Watson - Florence Jean / John's Back In Town - 1970
55213 - Garland Green - Angel Baby / You Played On A Player - 1970
55214 - Deni Lynn - Whatsa Matter Baby / Cross My Heart And Hope To Die - 1970
55215 - Donny Mann - This Love Is Real / The Girl Next Door - 1970
55216 - Atwood the Electric Iceman (Sir Douglas Quintet with Atwood Allen) - Bossier City / Michoacan - 1970
55217 - Marvin L. Sims - I Can't Understand It / It's Your Love - 1970
55218 - Strawberry Alarm Clock - California Day / Three - 1970
55219 - Betty Everett - Unlucky Girl / Better Tomorrow Than Today - 1970
55220 - John Fred and his Playboy Band - Come With Me / Where's Everybody Going - 1970
55221 - High and Mighty - Luckie / Come With Me - 1970
55222 - The Lovelites - Who You Gonna Hurt Now / Oh My Love - 1970
55223 - Bill Cosby - Grover Henderson Feels Forgotten (Vocal) / Grover Henderson Feels Forgotten (Instrumental) - 1970
55224 - Neil Diamond - Soolaimon (African Trilogy II) / And The Grass Won't Pay No Mind - 1970
55225 - The Yellow Payges - I'm A Man / Home Again - 1970

Soulful Kinda Music – The Rare Soul Bible Volume Two

55226 - Robin Hood Brians - Crazy 'Bout Your Sunshine / Miami - 1970
55227 - Karl Tarleton - Along Came You / Stay With Me - 1970
55228 - Fever Tree - I Am / Grand Candy Young Sweet - 1970
55229 - Pat Shannon - It's So Easy / 102 Times A Day - 1970
55229 - Pat Shannon - It's So Easy / The Story Of Your Life - 1970
55230 - The Passionettes - Stand By Your Man / Sister Watch Yourself - 1970
55231 - The Cascades - April, May, June And July / Big Ugly Sky - 1970
55232 - Durango - My Love Is Gonna Grow On You / Lubricated Love Affair - 1970
55233 - Marvin Holmes - Sweet Talk / Thang - 1970
55234 - Daybreak - I Could Have Heard The Crying / Good Morning Freedom - 1970
55235 - Sylvanus - I Want To Take You Higher / Tightrope - 1970
55236 - Artistry in Sound - Bridge Over Troubled Water / Jean - 1970
55237 - Duane Eddy - Something / The Five   -   Seventeen - 1970
55238 - The Sister and Brothers - Yeah, You Right / Dear Ike - 1970
55239 - The Green Berets - Give Me A Try / Just An Ugly Rumor - 1970
55240 - Brian Hyland - Gypsy Woman / You And Me - 1970
55241 - Strawberry Alarm Clock - Girl From The City / Three - 1970
55242 - The Lovelites - This Love Is Real / Oh My Love - 1970
55243 - Paris - Change Is Gonna Come / Gone Again - 1970
55244 - Darrow Fletcher - Changing By The Minute / When Love Calls - 1970
55245 - Dewey Martin and Medicine Ball - Indian Child / I Do Believe - 1970
55246 - Elton John - Border Song / Bad Side Of The Moon - 1970
55247 - Bill Cosby and Bad Foot Brown - Hybish Skybish / Martin's Funeral - 1970
55248 - Bob and Earl - Get Ready For The New Day / Honey, Sugar, My Sweet Thing - 1970
55249 - Ray Peterson - Love The Understanding Way / Oklahoma City Rimes - 1970
55250 - Neil Diamond - Cracklin' Rosie / Lordy - 1970
55251 - Happy Day - Heighty   -   Hi / Easy To Be Free - 1970
55252 - Mudd - Light Gonna Shine / Medicated Goo - 1970
55253 - Jiminy Crickett - Isabella / Love Is A See Saw - 1970
55254 - Society of Seven - Sweet Sad Clown / Ten Cents In My Pocket - 1970
55255 - Cash and Carry - Mary's In The Closet / Green Mountain Girl - 1970
55256 - Dyna-Mite - Borrache / Need You - 1970
55257 - Barry Mason - High Time / Monte Carlo - 1970
55258 - Rachael and The Strawberry Shephards - Follow The Lamb / Other Days - 1970
55259 - Jackie Lee - Your Sweetness Is My Weakness / You Were Searching For A Love - 1971
55260 - Barry Allen - Wednesday In Your Garden / If You Look Away - 1971
55261 - Desmond Dekker and The Aces - You Can Get It If You Really Want It / Perseverance - 1971
55262 - Kim Vassy - Revelation / After All (I Live My Life) - 1971
55263 - Happy Day - Retribution / Everybody, I Love You - 1971
55264 - Neil Diamond - He Ain't Heavy He's My Brother / Free Life - 1971
55265 - Elton John - Your Song / Take Me To The Pilot - 1971
55266 - God's Children - Lonely Lullabye / Hey, Does Somebody Care - 1971
55267 - Tom Northcott - I Think It's Gonna Rain Today / It's True - 1971
55268 - Ray Peterson - Tell Laura I Love Her / To Wait For Love - 1971
55269 - Georgy - As Easy As Singing / She's My Melody - 1971
55270 - Darrow Fletcher - What Is This / Dolly Baby - 1971

Soulful Kinda Music – The Rare Soul Bible Volume Two

55271 - Silver Fleet - C'mon Plane / Look Out World - 1971
55272 - Brian Hyland - Lonely Teardrops / Lorraine - 1971
55273 - The Green Berets - Too Young / I've Got To Be Loved - 1971
55274 - Bobby Skel - Help Me Make It Through The Night / Woman Has A Way - 1971
55275 - Ray Peterson - Fever / Changes - 1971
55276 - The Osmond Brothers - I Can't Stop / Flower Music - 1971
55277 - Elton John - Friends / Honey Roll - 1971
55278 - Neil Diamond - I Am...I Said / Done Too Soon - 1971
55279 - Society of 7 - Howzit Brah / We Can Make It Girl - 1971
55280 - Colorado - My Babe / Country Comfort - 1971
55281 - Olivia Newton -   John - If Not For You / The Biggest Clown - 1971
55282 - Poe - There's A River / Up Through The Spiral - 1971
55283 - D.C. Hawk - No, No, No / Since You've Been Gone - 1971
55284 - John Hetherington - Can't Nobody See My Face / North Western - 1971
55285 - Studd Pump - Floating / Spare The Children - 1971
55286 - Colin Young - You're No Good / Any Time At All - 1971
55287 - Brian Hyland - So Long, Marianne / No Place To Run - 1971
55288 - Tom Northcott - Spaceship Races / Suzanne - 1971
55289 - Michael and Choctaw Robin - California, Hollywood / Mary Miles - 1971
55290 - Happy Day - Give Me Some Love / Why Don't You Get To Know Yourself - 1971
55291 - Nigel Olsson's Drum Orchestra - Some Sweet Day / Weirdhouse - 1971
55292 - Dyna-Mite - Sunshine Goddess / Message To My Brother - 1971
55293 - Big Black - Long Hair / Diggin' What You're Doing - 1971
55294 - Bobby Skel - Next To Jesus / Atlanta Bound - 1971
55295 - God's Children - Put Your Head On My Shoulder / That's The Way God Planned It - 1971
55296 - Boondoggle and Balderdash - Any Road / Songs I'm Singing - 1971
55297 - Infinity - Sapphire / Shoes - 1971
55298 - Society of Seven - Frisco Bay / I Can't Seem To Explain - 1971
55299 - ?
55300 - Donna Theordore - What Am I Gonna Do / You Make Me Feel So Good - 1971
55301 - John Letherington - Hello / Home - 1971
55302 - Colorado - Dogwood / Moonshine - 1971
55303 - George Hamilton - Evel Knievel / Boy From The Country - 1971
55304 - Olivia Newton John - Banks Of The Ohio / It's So Hard To Say Goodbye - 1971
55305 - Rabon - Choctaw / Texas Sparrow - 1971
55306 - Brian Hyland - Out Of The Blue / If You Came Back - 1971
55307 - Saratoga Trunk - Party Song / Can't You Help Me Help Myself - 1971
55308 - Nigel Olsson - Sunshine Looks Like Rain / And I Know In My Heart - 1971
55309 - Mike Settle - Saturdays Only / The Nights Of Your Life - 1971
55310 - Neil Diamond - Stones / Crunchy Granola Suite - 1971
55311 - ?
55312 - Tony Hazzard - Hang Over Blue / Woman And The West - 1971
55313 - Smile - A Year Every Night / Southbound - 1972
55314 - Elton John - Goodbye / Levon - 1972
55315 - The Foundations - I'll Give You Love / Stoney Ground - 1972

Soulful Kinda Music – The Rare Soul Bible Volume Two

55316 - Tony Hazzard - Blue Movie Man / Abbot Of The Vale - 1972
55317 - Olivia Newton John - I'm A Small And Lonely Light / What Is Life - 1972
55318 - Elton John - Tiny Dancer / Razor Face - 1972
55319 - Love Unlimited - I Should Have Known / Walkin' In The Rain With The One I Love - 1972
55320 - Thomas and Richard Frost - Got To Find The Light / St. Petersburg - 1972
55321 - Mike Settle - Take It Easy On The Cryin' / Singing A Lonely Song - 1972
55322 - White Duck - Billy Goat / Really - 1972
55323 - Brian Hyland - I Love Every Little Thing About You / With My Eyes Wide Open - 1972
55324 - ?
55325 - Patti Dahlstrom - Wait Like A Lady / Comfortable - 1972
55326 - Neil Diamond - Song Sung Blue / Gitchy Goomy - 1972
55327 - Infinity - (What Happens) In The Darkness / Do Your Thing Like Jesus - 1972
55328 - Elton John - Rocket Man / Suzie (Dramas) - 1972
55329 - D. Brown - Carolina Sun / Highway Moon - 1972
55330 - Vigrass and Osborne - Men Of Learning / Forever Autumn - 1972
55331 - Donna Theodore - There's No Holding You / My Name Is Woman - 1972
55332 - Andy Kim - Who Has The Answers? / Shady Hollow Dreamers - 1972
55333 - Mike Settle - If You Really Love Me / Yestertime - 1972
55334 - Brian Hyland - Only Wanna Make You Happy / When You're Lovin' Me - 1972
55335 - Gove - Carry On / I've Been Thinking Of You Lately - 1972
55336 - Smile - Tonight / One Night Stand - 1972
55337 - Big Black - Mellow / Diggin' What You're Doin' - 1972
55338 - J.H. Burnett - Linda Lu / I Don't Want To Hear You Cry No More - 1972
55339 - Geronimo Black - Let Us Live / '59 Chevy - 1972
55340 - Richard Frost - Mona Lisa And Mad Hatters / Kentucky Moon - 1972
55341 - Balderdash - Crow Pie / Back To The Wilderness - 1972
55342 - Love Unlimited - Another Chance / Is It Really True Boy   -   Is It Really Me - 1972
55343 - Elton John - Honky Cat / Slave - 1972
55344 - Vigrass and Osborne - Ballerina / Virginia - 1972
55345 - White Duck - Baby / Again - 1972
55346 - Neil Diamond - Play Me / Porcupine Pie - 1972
55347 - Mike Settle - Funky Street Band / Sometimes Love Is Better When It's Gone - 1972
55348 - Olivia Newton John - Just A Little Too Much / My Old Man's Gotta Gun - 1972
55349 - Love Unlimited - Another Change / Are You Sure - 1972
55350 - White Duck - Carry Love / Honey You'll Be Alright - 1972
55351 - ?
55352 - Neil Diamond - Walk On Water / High Rolling Man - 1972
55353 - Andy Kim - Love Song / Love The Poor Boy - 1972
55354 - Gove Scrivenor - Mobile Blue / Goin' To The Country - 1972
55355 - Vigrass and Osborne - Mister Deadline / Remember Pearl Harbor - 1972
55356 - Andy Kim - Oh What A Day / Sunshine - 1972

Unart Records

2001 - The Rays - Souvenirs Of Summertime / Elevator Operator - 1958
2002 - The Demons - Tadpole / Doo Doo Dah - 1958
2003 - The Five Delights - There'll Be No Goodbye / Okey Dokey Mama - 1958
2004 - Willis Sanders and The Embers - Lovable You / Honey - Bun - 1958
2005 - Jackie Clark - Walkie Talkie / Pajama Party - 1958
2006 - The Acorns - Angel / I'm Gonna Stick To You - 1958
2007 - The Avalons - Hearts Desire / Ebbtide - 1958
2008 - The Del Knights - Compensation / Everything - 1959
2009 - Bobbie and / The Beans - Losing Game / Melvin - 1959
2010 - The Kittens - It's All Over Now / Letter To Donna - 1959
2011 - Billy Eldridge - Let's Go Baby / My Blue Tears - 1959
2012 - Bob Carroll - I Can't Get You Out Of My Heart / Since I'm Out Of Your Arms - 1959
2013 - The Falcons - You're So Fine / Goddess Of Angels - 1959
2014 - Danton Phillips - Deep Dream / Sweetwater Boy - 1959
2015 - The Acorns - Please Come Back / Your Name And Mine - 1959
2016 - Charlie Grant - If / Night And Day - 1959
2017 - The Delicates - Black And White Thunderbird / Ronnie Is My Lover - 1959
2018 - ?
2019 - Mary Swan - Dancin' / Cryin' In The Chapel - 1959
2020 - ?
2021 - Wendell Smith - Nashville, Tennessee / No Matter What You Do - 1959
2022 - The Falcons - You're Mine / Country Shack - 1959
2023 - Bobby Long - Did You Ever Dream Lucky / Calling (For The One I Love) - 1959
2024 - The Delicates - Ringa Ding / Meusurry - 1959
2025 - Kay Martin - Come By Sunday / No More Tears To Cry - 1959

Don Varner

Don Varner (born 25-June-1943 in Birmingham, Alabama died 7-October-2002 cause: heart attack)

Downbeat 102 - Here Come My Tears / I Finally Got Over - ?
Quinvy 8002 - Tear Stained Face / Mojo Mama - 1967 Track cut on the 23-September-1967.
Veep 1296 - Tear Stained Face / Meet Me In Church - 1967
Diamond 264 - More Power To Ya / Handshakin' - 196?
South Camp 7003 - Down In Texas / Masquerade - 1967
South Camp 7005 - Home For The Summer / The Sweetest Story - 1967
House Of Orange 2404 - I Can If You Can / That's All Right - 196?
Roaring 62543 - Keep On Doing What You're Doing / I'd Like To Be - ?

Label Listing

Vando

101 – Chris Bartley – The Sweetest Thing This Side Of Heaven / Love Me Baby - 1967
102 – Art Robins – I Can't Stand To See You Cry / Fountain Of Love – 1967
3000 – Chris Bartley – Baby It's Wonderful / I'll Be Loving You – 1967
3001 – Tony Talent – Gotta Tell Somebody (About My Baby) / Hooked On You - 1967
3002 – Chris Bartley – For You / You Get Next To My Heart – 1967
14000 – Chris Bartley – Truer Words Were Never Spoken / This Feeling You Give Me – 1968
14001 – Chris Bartley – I Found A Goodie / Be Mine Forever - 1968

Veep

1200 - The Feathers – The Dummy / Them Onions - 1964
1201 – Barry Lee - Make It / Things Gotta Change - 1964
1202 – Windsor Strings – Woman Of Straw / Babylon - 1964
1203 – Bobby Lee Smith – No Survivors / Forbidden Affair - 1964
1204 – Duffy Power – Where Am I / I Don't Care - 1964
1205 – Gerry Granahan – All The Live Long Day / Sophia - 1964
1206 – The D Men – Don't You Know / No Hope For Me - 1965
1207 – Bobby Gregg And Friends – Charly Ba-Ba / Hullabaloo - 1965
1208 – The Five Shades – I'll Give You Love / Vickie - 1965
1209 – The D Men – Just Don't Care / Mousin' Around - 1965
1210 – The Tammys – Gypsy / Hold Back The Light Of Dawn - 1965
1211 – The Galaxies IV – Let Me Hear You Say Yeah / Till Then You'll Cry - 1965

Soulful Kinda Music – The Rare Soul Bible Volume Two

1212 – The Marshmallows – When I Look At My Love / I Don't Even Know It's Name - 1965

1213 – Timothy Wilson – Come On Home / Hey Girl Do You Love Me - 1965

1214 – The Four Havens – Let's Have A Good Time Baby / What Time Is It - 1965

1215 – The Previews – Lovey Dove / Riders In The Sky - 1965

1216 – Bobby Byrd – My Type Of Dancin' / Where Were You - 1965

1217 – Don Caron – Road Runner / That's My Desire - 1965

1218 – The G-Clefs – I Have / On The Other Side Of Town - 1965

1219 – Not Released

1220 – The Tammys – Blues Sixteen / His Actions Speak Louder Than Words - 1965

1221 – The Viscayues – Pauline / Question - 1965

1222 – Zena Foster – Make It Me / Baby Let Me Teach You - 1965

1223 – Timothy Wilson – He Will Break Your Heart / Oh How I Wish She Were Mine - 1965

1224 – Little Romeo & The Casanovas – Remember Lori / That's How Girls Get Boys - 1966

1225 – Zena Foster – You're Biting Off More Than You Can Chew / You've Got A Lot In Your Favour - 1966

1226 – The G-Clefs – This Time / On The Other Side Of Town - 1966

1227 – Willie & The Hand Jives – Gotta Find A New Love / Runnin' Girl - 1966

1228 – Little Anthony & The Imperials – Better Use Your Head / The Wonder Of It All - 1966

1229 – Eugene Pitt – Another Rainy Day / Why Why Why - 1966

1230 – The Isley Brothers – Love Is A Wonderful Thing / Open Up Her Eyes - 1966

1231 – Rose St John & The Wonderettes – Fool Don't Laugh / I Know The Meaning - 1966

1232 – Garnett Mimms – It's Been Such A Long Way Home / Thinkin' - 1966

1233 – Little Anthony & The Imperials – You Better Take It Easy Baby / Gonna Fix You Good (Every Time You're Bad - 1966

1234 – Garnett Mimms – My Baby / Keep On Smiling - 1966

1235 – Chuck Corty & The Chances – Happy Go Lucky / Man Loves Too - 1966

1236 – Sleepy King – Hello Martha / Please Let A Fool In Out Of The Rain – 1966

1237 – Johnny Dunn – False Pride / You're Hangin' Me Up - 1966

1238 – The Group From Queens – Boss Man / Your Search Is Over - 1966

1239 – Little Anthony & The Imperials – Tears On My Pillow / Who's Sorry Now - 1966

1240 - Little Anthony & The Imperials – I'm On The Outside Lookin' In / Please Go - 1966

1241 - Little Anthony & The Imperials – Goin' Out Of My Head / Shing A Ling - 1966

1242 - Little Anthony & The Imperials – Huirt So Bad / Reputation - 1966

1243 - Little Anthony & The Imperials – Our Song / Take Me Back - 1966

1244 - Little Anthony & The Imperials – Get Out Of My Life / I Miss You So - 1966

1245 - Little Anthony & The Imperials – Hurt / Never Again - 1966

1246 – Elbie Parker – Lucky Guy / Please Keep Away From Me - 1966

1247 – Barbara Banks – Living In The Past / River Of Tears - 1966

1248 - Little Anthony & The Imperials – It's Not The Same / Down On Love - 1966

1249 – Johnny Noble – No Use Cryin' / You're So Smooth - 1966

1250 – Not Released

1251 – Larry & The Larks – The Girl I Love / Tell Me - 1966

1252 – Garnett Mimms – All About Love / Truth Hurts - 1967

Soulful Kinda Music – The Rare Soul Bible Volume Two

1253 – Cindy Scott – I Love You Baby / In Your Spare Time - 1967
1254 – The Star-Treks – Dreamin' / Gonna Need Magic - 1967
1255 - Little Anthony & The Imperials – Don't Tie Me Down / Where There's A Will There's A Way - 1967
1256 – The Remember Whens – A 1000 Miles Away / Lost In Love - 1967
1257 – Not Released
1258 – Ivory Joe Hunter – What's The Matter Baby / Don't You Believe Me - 1967
1259 – Wally & The Knights – I Need You / Uncle Sam - 1967
1260 – Jonathon Cartwright – I'm Walking Behind You / So Tired Of Being Alone - 1967
1261 – Tender Joe Richardson – The Choo Choo / Shing A Ling - 1967
1262 - Little Anthony & The Imperials – Hold Onto Someone / Lost In Love - 1967
1263 – Sharon Redd – Half As Much / I've Got A Feeling - 1967
1264 – Bill Pinkney & The Original – I Found Some Lovin' / The Masquerade Is Over - 1967
1265 – Jimmy Cliff – Aim & Ambition / Give And Take - 1967
1256 – Jackie Edwards – Come Back Girl / Tell Him You Lied - 1967
1267 – Charlotte Gilbert – Chances Go 'Round / Falling In Love With Him - 1967
1268 – Cindy Scott – I've Been Loving You Too Long / Time Can Change A Love - 1967
1269 - Little Anthony & The Imperials – You Only Live Twice / Hungry Heart - 1967
1270 – Ivory Joe Hunter – Did She Ask About Me / From The First Time We Met - 1967
1271 – George & Co. – Layers & Layers / When The Love Light Starts Shining Through Her Eyes - 1967
1272 – John Thomas – Lonely Man / Who Could Ever Love You (More Than I) - 1967
1273 - ?
1274 – Baby Washington – White Christmas / Silent Night - 1968
1275 - Little Anthony & The Imperials – Beautiful People / If I Remember To Forget - 1968
1276 – Jimmy Cliff – Thank You / That's The Way Life Goes - 1968
1277 – Truman Thomas – Funky Broadway / Respect- 1968
1278 - Little Anthony & The Imperials – I'm Hypnotised / Hungry Heart - 1968
1279 – Timmy Willis – I'm Wondering / Mr Soul Satisfaction - 1968
1280 – Tina Britt – I Found A New Love / Who Is That - 1968
1281 – Sari & The Shalimars – You Walked Out On Me Before / It's So Lonely - 1968
1282 – John Thomas- Come See Me / It Sure Is Groovy - 1968
1283 - Little Anthony & The Imperials – What Greater Love / In The Back Of My Heart - 1968
1284 – Samuel Douglas & The Continentals – Just Because Part 1 / Part 2 - 1968
1285 - Little Anthony & The Imperials – Yesterday Has Gone / My Love Is A Rainbow - 1968
1286 – The Poets – The Hustler / Soul Brothers Holiday - 1968
1287 – Smokey Brooks – Beat The Heat / 7 Grooves For 7 Moods - 1968
1288 – Timmy Willis – Don't Let Temptation (Come Between You And Me) / Gotta Get Back To Georgia - 1968
1289 – Ricky J Thomas – Little Miss Funky Soul / Why Did I Ever Let You Go - 1968
1290 – Sari & The Shalimars – No Reason To Doubt My Love / Too Anxious - 1968
1291 – The Soul Sisters – Thousand Mountains / You Got 'Em Beat - 1968
1292 – Ricky Thomas – Little Miss Funky Soul / Why Did I Ever Let You Go - 1969

Soulful Kinda Music – The Rare Soul Bible Volume Two

1293 - Little Anthony & The Imperials – Gentle Rain / The Flesh Failures - 1969
1294 – Maurice Williams & The Zodiacs – My Reason For Living / The Four Corners - 1969
1295 – Truman Thomas – After Loving You / My Soul - 1969
1296 – Don Varner – Meet Me In The Church / Tearstained Face (Was This Ever Released ?) - 1969
1297 – Baby Washington – Think About The Good Times / Hold Back The Dawn - 1969
1298 – Tina Britt – Key To The Highway / Sooki Sooki - 1969
1299 – Robi Patterson Singers – Give Him A Chance / Top Mountain - 1969
1300 – Mighty Gospel Giants – It's A Needed Time / Going Up To Heaven - 1969
1301 – The Swindell Bros. - Judge Not / Power - 1969
1302 – The Jubilators – The Knock At The Door / Togetherness - 1969
1303 – Little Anthony & The Imperials – Anthem / Goodbye Goodtimes - 1969
1304 – Johnny & Lilly – Cross My Heart / This Is My Story - 1969
1305 – Truman Thomas – It's Your Thing / The Weight (Withdrawn) - 1969
1306 – Truman Thomas – Twenty-Five Miles / The Weight – 1969

Vivid

100 - Shakey Jake - Roll Your Money Maker / Call Me If You Need Me
101 - Harold Burrage - She Knocks Me Out / A Heart Filled With Pain
102 - Harold Burrage - I Cry For You / Betty Jean
103 - The Veteran Singers - Give It Up / Old Account Was Settled
104 - Eddie Taylor - I'm Sitting Here / Do You Want Me To Cry
105 - Barbara Greene - I Should Have Treated You Right / Young Boy
106 - Joe Murphy - It's A Weakness / So Blue
107 - John Wesley - Girl With The Red Dress On / You're Gonna Miss Me
108 - John Sardo - Love Can Make You Cry / I Can Understand
109 - Billy Boy - Prisoner's Plea / I Wish You Would
110 - Barbara Greene - Our Love Is No Secret Now / A Lover's Plea

Soulful Kinda Music – The Rare Soul Bible Volume Two

W

Dee Dee Warwick

The Gospelaires (Members Dionne Warwick, Delia Warwick And Cissy Houston)

The Drinkard Singers (Members Lee Drinkard (Who Is Dionne And Dee Dee Warwick's Mother) And Her Sister Emily Drinkard (Aka Cissy Houston -- Whitney Houston's Mother) And Judy Clay (Who Was "Adopted" By Lee Drinkard)

Dee Dee Warwick (Born 1945 In New Jersey - Younger Sister Of Dionne Warwick - Sang Backup Vocals For Many Artists)

Jubilee 5459 - You're No Good / Don't Call Me - 1963
Tiger 103 - Don't Think My Baby's Coming Back / Standing By - 1964
Blue Rock 4008 - Do It With All Your Heart* / Happiness - 1965 *Written By Ed Townsend.
Blue Rock 4027 - We're Doing Fine / I Want To Be With You - 1965
Blue Rock 4032 - Gotta Get A Hold Of Yourself / Baby I'm Yours - 1965
Hurd 79 - I (Who Have Nothing) / I Can't Go Back - 1966
Mercury 72584 - I Want To Be With You / Lover's Chant - 1966 (From The Broadway Musical "Golden Boy")
Mercury 72638 - I'm Gonna Make You Love Me / Yours Until Tomorrow - 1966
Mercury Dj-83 - When Love Slips Away (Mono) / When Love Slips Away (Stereo) - 1967
Mercury 72667 - When Love Slips Away / House Of Gold - 1967
Mercury 72710 - Locked In Your Love / Alfie - 1967
Mercury 72738 - Don't You Ever Give Up On Me / We've Got Everything Going For Us - 1967
Mercury Dj-94 - Girls Need Love (Mono) / Girls Need Love (Stereo) - 1968 (Promo Issue Only)
Mercury 72788 - Girls Need Love / It's Not Fair - 1968
Mercury 72834 - I'll Be Better Off (Without You) / Monday, Monday - 1968
Mercury 72880 - Foolish Fool / Thank God* - 1969 *With The Teaneck Choir.
Mercury 72927 - That's Not Love / It's Not Fair - 1969
Mercury 72940 - Next Time (You Fall In Love) / Ring Of Bright Water - 1969
Mercury 72966 - I (Who Have Nothing) / Where Is That Rainbow - 1969
Atco 6754 - She Didn't Know (She Kept On Talkin') / Make Love To Me - 1970 (Backed By The Dixie Flyers)
Atco 6769 - I'm Only Human / If This Was The Last Song - 1970 (Backed By The Dixie Flyers)
Atco 6796 - Cold Night In Georgia / Searchin' - 1971
Atco 6810 - Suspicious Minds / I'm Glad I'm A Woman - 1971
Atco 6840 - Everybody's Got To Believe In Somebody / Signed, Dee Dee - 1971
Mercury 73397 - All That Love Went To Waste / I Haven't Got Anything Better To Do - 1973
Private Stock 45,011 - Get Out Of My Life / Funny How We Change Places - 1975
Private Stock 45,033 - This Time Maybe My Last / Funny How We Change Places -

1975
Sutra 134 - Move With The World / The Way We Used To Be - 1984 (Some Copies
Issued With Picture Sleeve)
Collectables Col 044977 - Foolish Fool / I Want To Be With You - ?

Justine 'Baby' Washington

One of the most underrated and neglected singers of the sixties and seventies, Justine 'Baby' Washington has finally achieved some of the recognition she deserves here in the UK. Her recordings for Sue Records in the mid sixties have become recognised as classics by the UK Rare Soul Scene, and I had hoped that we would have had the chance to see her live at this year's Weekender. Unfortunately, because of a clash in dates that's not going to happen this year, but I'd written the article before I heard she wasn't coming, and I thought the story was worth telling anyway.

So for a career that spans almost forty years now, let's go back and tell the story from the beginning.

Born on 13th October, 1940, Justine Washington spent her very early years in Bamberg, South Carolina. Although no actual date is known for the move to New York, she attended High School in Manhattan at the Charles Evans Hughes High School. In addition to her normal schooling Baby was also taking vocal lessons, and dancing lessons (tap and ballet) at the Zell Sanders School of Dancing. It was here in 1956 that she made her professional debut.

To give a little more background, Zell Sanders was one of the earliest black, female, record pioneers. She had been running her own label J&S for some years by 1956. She had also had some success as well, with a group called The Hearts who had scored a notional R&B hit in early 1955 with a Doo Wop track, composed by Sanders that had been leased to Baton Records, of New York. Zell Sanders though was a legendary hard task master and the roster of The Hearts changed with alarming regularity. In early 1956 she had fired two of the four members and was looking for a

new line up. What better place to start than your own School of Dancing. Justine Washington and Anna Barnhill were both successful at the audition and were accepted into the group. It's at this stage that the name 'Baby' is first used for two reasons; Justine is still only 15, and is the youngest member of the group. The new line up recorded one single, 'Going Home To Stay / Disappointed Bride' which was released on Baton 222 in March 1956. It wasn't a hit, but the group, The Hearts, were so Baby went out and performed live, singing the hits the group had previously recorded.

As was common in the fifties and sixties, label owners' always tried to optimise the earning potential of any acts that were signed to them, Zell Sanders was no different, so whilst Baby was out performing as a member of The Hearts who were signed to Baton Records, she was also out performing as a member of The Jaynetts, a girl group signed to J&S.

To complicate things even further Zell Sanders decided to promote Baby as a solo artist (and keep her working as a member of the two groups!) Accordingly her first solo single appeared on J&S 1656 in April 1957. Entitled 'Everyday' the flip was an instrumental by The Shytone Five Orchestra called 'Smitty's Rock', Again, it wasn't a hit

The live work though was still producing money (Hardly surprising really, as a soloist and part of two groups). Zell Sanders though, could see the potential in Baby Washington, and if nothing else was a trier. So the next single was released in December 1957 on J&S 1604. 'Congratulations Honey' / 'There Must Be A Reason' contains, on both sides, a surprisingly mature performance from a girl just turned 17.

The next single, in February 1958 employed the male group The Plants as backup to a Doo Wop single entitled simply 'Ah-Ha' which credited Justine Washington as joint writer with Zell Sanders. Apparently though (I haven't heard this single) the words were actually very few and the song relied almost totally on Baby's vocal talents manipulating the title thoughout. The B side 'Been A Long Time Baby' was a short but lively attempt at Rock and Roll. Faced with another nonhit, J&S tried once more whilst Baby was signed to the label. The last single was issued on J&S 1619, 'Hard Way To Go', and the title says it all. It was another flop, so Baby was released by J&S.

The end of her contract with J&S meant that Baby Washington now had to rely on live dates for her income. She had however, received a considerable amount of live work whist with J&S, and their house bandleader Cliff Drivers asked her to become the singer on his live dates. She promptly accepted, and within months both Baby Washington, and the Cliff Drivers Combo, had new recording contracts with Donald Shaw's Newark label, Neptune.

The first release was in November 1958, by January 1959 the single, 'The Time / You Never Could Be Mine' had entered the Billboard national R&B charts. It spent five weeks on the chart, peaking at #22. Both sides of the record, Neptune 101, were composed by Baby Washington.

Never one to miss a trick, Zell Sanders promptly put out a previously unissued track ' I Hate To See You Go' coupled with 'Knock Yourself Out' which was a retitling of 'Been A Long Time Baby'. The single was issued locally on J&S 1632, but was picked up for national distribution when Zell sold the track to Chess, who put it out as Checker 918. Despite having the backing of Leonard and Phil's mighty Chicago organization the record still wasn't a hit.

So it was back to Donald Shaw's tiny Neptune label in May '59 to put Baby Washington back where she deserved, back in the national charts. The single, Neptune 104, 'The Bells' entered the chart on 22nd June 1959, spent five weeks on the R&B chart, and peaked at #20. There is some evidence that Zell Sanders again approached Chess with another unreleased side at this time. In fact, the song 'The Last Word' was allocated a matrix number by Chess, but never released.

Soulful Kinda Music – The Rare Soul Bible Volume Two

Justine's next release for Neptune was a reunion of her old male backing group The Plants. The single though, 'Work Out' despite being written by Baby, failed to chart.

Three more Neptune singles #116 'Deep Down Love' / 'Your Mama Knows Right' (June 1960) , #120 'Medicine Man' / 'Tears fall' (Aug 1960) and #121 'Too Late' / 'Move On' (Dec 1960) all failed to chart. However, her last single for the label 'Nobody Cares(About Me)' / 'Moneys Funny' on Neptune #122, released in March 1961 hit the Billboard R&B chart on 5th June 1961. It spent only four weeks on the chart, peaked at #17 and significantly entered the pop 100, peaking there at #60.

Soulful Kinda Music – The Rare Soul Bible Volume Two

From all accounts the label itself folded on the heels of its biggest hit leaving Baby Washington without a recording contract. It did leave her with two things, a new name on her single, Jeanette Baby Washington which would appear periodically throughout her career, and a taste of success in the pop charts.

Looking to the future her experience with Neptune also got her a contract with one of the majors. She signed with ABC-Paramount in May 1961 and released the first of two singles on the label the same month. The two tracks 'Let Love Go By' / 'My Time To Cry' were both written by Baby and credited to Jeanette 'Baby' Washington on the label. Unfortunately neither this, nor the follow up in September 1961, 'There You Go Again' / 'Don't Cry, Foolish Hearts' made any impression on the charts.

Up until this point the majority of Baby's recordings had been either Doo Wop or Rock and Roll. It was in 1962 that things began to change.

Juggy Murry's Sue label picked up her contract in New York in the early part of 1962. The label itself had been founded in 1957 by Juggy Murry to record the wonderful R&B and Rock and Roll talent he found in New York himself. After a reasonably successful five years he could see the way forward in the new 'Soul Style'. It was not yet recognized as 'Soul', but Juggy knew what he wanted, and Justine 'Baby' Washington fitted the bill.

Juggy is quoted in an interview with Alan Warner as saying "I'd rather record Baby Washington than eat". And that's what he did.

The first single for Sue was 'Go On' / 'No Tears' on Sue 764 released in June 1962. Having said that Juggy was aiming for a new sound he took Baby Washington to her most bluesy on this first single. It wasn't a hit!

The second release though, Sue 767, 'Handful Of Memories' / 'Careless Hands' took her back into the charts with a superb dancer. Entering the Billboard R&B chart on 15th September 1962 it peaked at #16, her highest position yet, but only spent three weeks on the chart.

Her third single on Sue, 'Hush Heart' / 'I've Got A Feeling' had two self written songs on it. Whilst it almost made the Pop top 100 (it got to #102), this gospel based sound didn't make any impression on the R&B charts.

This brings us to March 1963 when Sue 783 was released. The record became Baby Washington's biggest hit, reaching #40 on the pop chart, and one of only two top ten hits on Billboards R&B chart reaching #10 in it's fourth week on the chart in June 1963. The title ? 'That's How Heartaches Are Made' of course. For both Juggy Murry and Baby Washington the future looked assured with the success of this mid-paced gem.

It also looked pretty good for Zell Sanders as well. She approached Chess again with two more unreleased masters, and whilst they accepted them, Chess didn't release them. Never one to see an opportunity wasted, Zell put the two tracks out herself on J&S 1001. 'Oh, Leave Me Alone' / 'It's Been A Long Time' was a throwback to the

Doo Wop sound of the late fifties though and didn't make any impression on the 1963 charts.

Sue Records, just to complicate matters released their official follow up in June 1963 entitled 'Leave Me Alone' / 'He's Been A Long Time', it was a totally unrelated song to the J&S release, but had a very similar title. That didn't harm it's chart potential though in August '63 it reached #21 R&B and #62 Pop.

In June of 1963 Baby Washington was considered enough of a success to have an album released entitled 'That's How Heartaches Are Made' it was really just a compilation of the four singles already released (A+B sides) and four tracks that were due to become singles. The next release, Sue 794, 'Hey Lonely' / 'Doodlin' just made the R&B chart at #100 on 10th December 1963.

1964 saw no real upturn in chart terms of the next three singles, Sue 797 was billed as Justine Washington rather than Baby Washington, but 'I Can't Wait Until I See My Baby's Face' only made #93. Sue 104, 'The Clock' / 'Standing On The Pier' only made #100 and Sue 114, 'It'll Never Be Over For Me' (Yes, the same as Timi Yuro) only made #98 on Billboard's R&B chart (but made #22 on the Cashbox version of the charts)

The last single of 1964, Sue 119, 'Run My Heart' / 'Your Fool', released in December, failed to make any impression on the charts at all.

In March 1965, Juggy Murry decided to try again with 'I Can't Wait Until I See My Baby's Face' re-issuing it with the new catalogue number of Sue 124. Unfortunately it failed to make the charts at all this time.

The next single though repaid all Juggy's faith, another mid-tempo beat ballad, 'Only Those In love' / 'The Ballad of Bobby Dawn', entered the chart on 10th July 1965 and spent nine weeks there eventually peaking at #10. It was Baby's eleventh chart entry, and arguably her most successful so far.

One further single followed in November 1965, Sue 137 'No Time For Pity' / 'There He Is' failed to chart though, and it was possibly this inconsistency that led Baby Washington to stay out of the studio for 12 months exactly.

No further releases were made until November 1966 when 'White Christmas' / 'Silent Night' was issued. It didn't chart (In fact it's a barely passable version which makes it's reissue on Veep later even more puzzling).

Juggy Murry though was eyeing the big prize by late '66. He released one further Baby Washington single in January 1967 'You Are What You Are' / 'Either You're With Me (or Either You're Not)' Which through a lack of promotion failed to even sniff at the charts. The big prize for Juggy though was to sell the whole Sue organization to United Artists, which he did in 1968.

Baby Washington was assigned to the subsidiary label Veep, where the first release in November 1967, was as already mentioned, the appalling 'White Christmas'. To try and make it a bit more palatable Veep remixed and overdubbed it, Baby

Washington's vocals are still the same though. It also had the same effect on the charts as well, none!

The story gets a little confusing here. As I understand it, U.A. released Baby Washington from her contract after the one single and failed album. She was signed up by Juggy Murry again to his new Sue label. One single was released on Sue 4, a remake of the Barbara George classic 'I Know' coupled with an instrumental called 'It'll Change'. It wasn't a hit, so Juggy in February 1969 took his next production on Baby back to Veep who leased the master. It was released as Veep 1297, 'Hold Back The Dawn' / 'Thinkin About The Good Times'. The 'B' side incidentally was composed by J.J.Jackson and Sidney Barnes. Again, the single failed to make the charts and Baby Washington and Juggy Murry parted company for the final time.

Juggy had been a major influence over Baby Washington for the last eight years, and although they had had two top ten hits during this time, it was almost the end of the decade in which Soul music came of age. It was time to move on.

For Baby Washington this meant a contract with Atlantic subsidiary Cotillion, and a trip to the Muscle Shoals Sound Studio on June 27th 1969 where she recorded eight tracks.

The first two coupled together were 'I Don't Know' / 'I Can't Afford To Lose Him', released on Cotillion 44047 in August 1969. It did the trick and returned Ms Washington to the charts, entering on 27th September and peaking at #35 R&B, but not making the Pop charts.

The next three Cotillion singles though didn't chart, although 44055 'Breakfast In Bed' / 'What Becomes Of The Broken Hearted' got a UK release on Atlantic. The other two were Cotillion 44065 'Let Them Talk' / 'I Love You Brother' (March 1970) and Cotillion 44086 'I'm Good Enough For You' / 'Don't Let Me Lose This Dream' which was released in November 1970.

It must be remembered though that these tracks were recorded almost 18 months earlier, and by the time of the last one being released, Baby Washington had already relocated to Chicago, to hook up with Chess records.

Only one single was released, Chess 2099 'Is It Worth It' / 'Happy Birthday' in December 1970 although four more tracks were recorded in early 1971, none of them have ever surfaced. Baby Washington then returned to New York and remained without a record deal for two years until 1973.

Clarence Lawton, owner of the Master Five label took her to Philadelphia to record some tracks at the Sigma Sound Studio. The first release, Master Five 9103 'Forever' / 'Baby Let Me Get Close To You' came out in May 1973 and was a duet with Don Gardner. It returned Baby to the charts for the thirteenth time spending seven weeks on the R+B chart peaking at #30 (#119 Pop).

The next two singles also charted Master Five 9104 'Just Can't Get You Out Of My Mind' / 'You (Just A Dream)' in August '73 (#76) and Master Five 9107 'I've Got To

Break Away' which being released in November 1973 finally peaked at #32 in early 1974 spending 12 weeks on the chart.

In April 1974 an album was released of duets between Baby and Don Gardner, although only five of the ten tracks were actually duets. To coincide with this a single was released, a duet, on Master Five 9110 called 'Lay A Little Lovin On Me' / 'Baby Let Me Get Closer To You'. Unfortunately it failed to chart so it was back to solo singles for Baby.

The next release on Master Five represents her last solo effort which made the charts entitled 'Can't Get Over Losing You' / 'Care Free', released in December 1974 it made the charts on 11th January 1975, spending four weeks there and peaking at #88. The single was a remake of the 1970 Donnie Elbert hit.

Clarence Lawton released one more single on his Master Five logo on Baby Washington, Master Five 3502 'Tell Me A Lie' / 'Just Can't Get You Out Of My Mind', in 1975. It wasn't a hit so Clarence Lawton folded the label.

It wasn't the end of his association with Baby Washington though. Her next single was produced by him and placed with the RCA Victor Subsidiary, Sixth Avenue. Again though, the single 'Either You Love Me' / 'Cup (Runneth Over)', failed to chart so the association was ended after the one single.

Two years later, in 1978 the Californian label AVI released an album and single by Jeanette Baby Washington. It was a straight reissue of her Master Five recordings plus the two Sixth Avenue tracks. One single was also issued.

Releases were now few and far between. We have to go onto 1979 for the next single, a terrible 12" disco thing on Lawtons 7L label entitled 'Turn Your Boogie Loose' / 'Turn Turn Turn (inst)'. This was followed by another disco outing in 1980 on Law-Ton 1660 called 'Come See About Me' / 'You Are Just A Dream'. Yes it is the old Supremes single!

By May 1980 Baby was guesting on a Parlet single called 'Wolf Tickets' which did make the charts (#67), then nothing until she guested on a Jive Five album track (a remake of 'Time') in 1982.

As far as I am aware Justine Baby Washington's last recorded output was for Clarence Lawton's revamped Master Five label in 1988 called 'Crying In The Midnight Hour' / 'Pedestal'!

Having said that, a recording career which spans 1956 to 1988 and includes 17 entries on the Billboard R&B chart is an achievement that any artist can be suitably proud. It's a shame that despite this record Baby Washington didn't become a major star. At least, and perhaps belatedly, she would have received some acknowledgment and been treated as a star at the forthcoming Cleethorpes Weekender.

Discography

Soulful Kinda Music – The Rare Soul Bible Volume Two

The Hearts Vocal Quartet Dave McRae Orch. (members Justine Washington, Anna Barnhill, Joyce Peterson and Theresa Chatman)

Baton 222 - Going Home To Stay / Disappointed Bride - 1956 (with Rex Garvin on piano)

The Jaynetts (Members Justine Washington, Anna Barnhill, Joyce Peterson And Theresa Chatman)

J&S 1765/1766 - I Wanted To Be Free / Where Are You Tonight - 1956

Baby Washington / The Shytone Five Orchestra

 J&S 1655/1656 - Everyday / Smitty's Rock (Instrumental)* - 1957 *Flip By The Shytone Five Orchestra.

The Hearts (Members Justine Washington, Anna Barnhill, Joyce Peterson And Theresa Chatman)

J&S 1660 - You Say You Love Me / So Long Baby - 1957
J&S 1657 - Dancing In A Dream World / You Needn't Tell Me, I Know - 1957

Baby Washington (Born Justine Washington On 13-October-1940 In Bamberg, South Carolina)

J&S 1604 - Congratulations Honey / There Must Be A Reason - 1957

Baby Washington With Orchestra

J&S 1607/1608 - Ah-Ha / Been A Long Time Baby - 1958

Baby Washington / The Jaynetts

J&S 1619/1620 - Hard Way To Go / Be My Boyfriend* - 1958 *Flip By The Jaynetts.

The Jaynetts

J&S 1765/1766 - I Wanted To Be Free / Where Are You Tonight - 1958 (this 45 is actually "Baby" Washington singing lead on two songs for The Hearts, that had been recorded in 1957. This set of The Jaynetts was Zell Sanders (the president of J &S records) way of keeping all The Hearts various members together and also of having enough members to form two groups. Zell Sanders would not use this name again for another five years)

Baby Washington with Orchestra

Neptune 101 - The Time* / You Never Could Be Mine - 1958 *covered in 1961 by The Del Pris on Varbee 2003 and in 1973 by Inez Foxx on Volt 4093.

Soulful Kinda Music – The Rare Soul Bible Volume Two

Baby Washington

J&S 1632/33 - I Hate To See You Go / Knock Yourself Out - 1959
Checker 918 - I Hate To See You Go / Knock Yourself Out – 1959
Neptune 104 - The Bells (On Our Wedding Day) / Why Did My Baby Put Me Down - 1959 (background vocals by The De Vaurs)
Neptune 107 - Workout / Let's Love In The Moonlight - 1959 (backing vocals The Plants and background vocals by The De Vaurs)
Neptune 116 - Deep Down Love / Your Mama Knows What's Right - circa 1960

Jeanette B. Washington

Neptune 120 - Medicine Man / Tears Fall - 1960 (background vocals by The De Vaurs)

Jeanette (Baby) Washington

Neptune 121 - Too Late / Move On – 1960
Neptune 122 - Nobody Cares (About Me) / Money's Funny - 1961 (background vocals by The De Vaurs)

Jeanette "Baby" Washington

ABC Paramount 10223 - Let Love Go By / My Time To Cry – 1961
ABC Paramount 10245 - There You Go Again / Don't Cry, Foolish Heart – 1961

Baby Washington

Sue 764 - Go On / No Tears – 1962
Sue 767 - A Handful Of Memories* / Careless Hands - 1962 *also recorded by Tutti Hill but unissued until released in the U. K. on a 2002 Kent CD "The Arock & Sylvia Story" CDKEND 212.
Sue 769 - Hush Heart / I've Got A Feeling – 1962
Sue 783 - That's How Heartaches Are Made* / There He Is** - 1963 *also recorded in 1968 by Bobby Hutton on Blue Rock 4055. **also recorded in 1964 as "There She Is" by Roy Hamilton on M-G-M 13217.
J&S 1001 - (Love Me) Or Leave Me Alone / It's Been A Long Time – 1963
Sue 790 - Leave Me Alone / You And The Night And The Music – 1963
Sue 794 - Hey Lonely / Doodlin' – 1963

Justine Washington

Sue 797 - I Can't Wait Until I See My Baby's Face* / Who's Going To Take Care Of Me - 1963 *also recorded in 1964 by Pat Thomas on Verve 10333 and in 1967 by The Monticellos on Red Cap 102 plus in 1969 by Sonji Clay on Songee 1002.

Baby Washington

Sue 104 - The Clock / Standing On The Pier - 1964
Sue 114 - It'll Never Be Over For Me* / Move On Drifter - 1964 *also released in the

Soulful Kinda Music – The Rare Soul Bible Volume Two

U. K. in 1968 by <u>Timi Yuro</u> on Liberty 15182
Sue 119 - Run My Heart / Your Fool – 1964

Justine Washington

Sue 124 - I Can't Wait Until I See My Baby's Face / Who's Going To Take Care Of Me – 1965

Baby Washington

Sue 129 - Only Those In Love / The Ballad Of Bobby Dawn – 1965
Sue 137 - No Time For Pity / There He Is – 1965
Sue 149 - White Christmas / Silent Night - 1966
Sue 150 - You Are What You Are / Either You're With Me (Or Either You're Not) – 1967
Veep 1274 - White Christmas / Silent Night- 1967
Sue 4 - I Know* / It'll Change (Instrumental) - 1968 *also recorded in 1961 by Barbara George on A. F. O. 302.
Veep 1297 - Think About The Good Times* / Hold Back The Dawn - 1969 *written by Sidney Barnes & J. J. Jackson.
Cotillion 44047 - I Don't Know / I Can't Afford To Lose Him* -1969 *also recorded in 1967 by Ella Washington on Sound Stage 7 2597.
Cotillion 44055 - Breakfast In Bed* / What Becomes Of A Broken Heart** - 1969 *also recorded in 1969 by Dusty Springfield on Atlantic 2606. **also recorded as "What Becomes Of The Brokenhearted" in 1966 by Jimmy Ruffin on Soul 35022
Trip 6 - That's How Heartaches Are Made / Only Those In Love - 1970
Cotillion 44065 - I Love You Brother / Let Them Talk – 1970
Cotillion 44086 - Don't Let Me Lose This Dream / I'm Good Enough For You – 1970
Chess 2099 - Is It Worth It / Happy Birthday – 1970
Master 5 901 - Baby Let Me Get Close To You / I Just Wanna Be Near To You - 1972
Master 5 9102 - Tell Me A Lie / Just Can't Get You Off My Mind - 1972
Trip 100 - The Time / Nobody Cares (About Me) - 1972
Trip 101 - The Bells (On Our Wedding Day) / Work Out - 1972

Baby Washington & Don Gardner

Master 5 9103 - Forever* / Baby Let Me Get Close To You - 1973 *originally recorded in 1957 as "Darling Forever" by The Four Chevelles on Delft 357

Baby Washington

Master 5 9104 - Just Can't Get You Out Of My Mind / You (Just A Dream) - 1973
Master 5 9107 - I've Got To Break Away From You / You (Just A Dream) - 1973
Master 5 9109 - Can't Get Over Losing You* / Just Can't Get You Out Of My Mind - 1974 *also recorded in 1972 by Donnie Elbert on All Platinum 2336.

Baby Washington & Don Gardner

Master 5 9110 - Lay A Little Lovin' On Me / Baby Let Me Get Closer To You - 1974

Soulful Kinda Music – The Rare Soul Bible Volume Two

People 101 - Forever* / Baby Let Me Get Close To You - 1974? *also recorded in 1963 by The Marvelettes on Tamla 54077.

Baby Washington

Master 5 3500 - Care Free / Can't Get Over Losing You* - 1975 *written by Donnie Elbert.
Master 5 3502 - Tell Me A Lie / Just Can't Get You Out Of My Mind – 1975

Jeanette (Baby) Washington

Sixth Avenue 10816 - Either You Love Me Or Leave Me (3:40) / Either You Love Me Or Leave Me (4:27) - 1976 (promo issue only)
Sixth Avenue 10816 - Either You Love Me Or Leave Me / Cup (Runneth Over) - 1976

Baby Washington

Master 5 545 - Tear After Tear / I've Got To Break Away – 1978

Jeanette "Baby" Washington

Avi 253 - I Wanna Dance / I Can't Get Over Losing You – 1978

Baby Washington

7I 3000 - Turn Your Boogie Loose / Turn, Turn, Turn – 1979
Law-Ton 1660 - Come See About Me / You Are Just A Dream – 1980

Baby Washington / Charles Brown

Liberty 1393 - Silent Night / Merry Christmas Baby* - 1980 *Flip By Charles Brown Only.

Baby Washington

Collectables Col 013097 - That's How Heartaches Are Made / There He Is - 1980's
Collectables Col 014107 - The Bells / Why Did My Baby Put Me Down - 1980's

The Soul Sisters / Baby Washington

Collectables Col 031497 - I Can't Stand It / Only Those In Love* - 1980's (flip by Baby Washington)

Baby Washington

Master Five 1001 - Crying In The Midnight Hour / Pedestal – 1988

LPs

Soulful Kinda Music – The Rare Soul Bible Volume Two

Sue 1014 - That's How Heartaches Are Made - 1963
Tracks: Ballad Of Bobby Dawn / Leave Me Alone / Doodlin' / You And The Night And The Music / That's How Heartaches Are Made / Standing On The Pier / I've Got A Feeling / Careless Hands / Hush Heart / Go On / A Handful Of Memories.

Sue 1042 - Only Those In Love - 1965
Tracks: Only Those In Love / I Can't Wait Until I See My Baby's Face / Who's Going To Take Care Of Me ? / It'll Never Be Over For Me / Your Fool / Hey Lonely / Careless Hands / Go On / Run My Heart / Money's Funny / White Christmas / Silent Night. ~

Veep ? - With You In Mind - 1968
Tracks: All Around The World / I Got It Bad And That Aint Good / It's All Over But The Crying / I'm On The Outside Looking In / I'm Calling You Baby / Take Me Like I Am // Get A Hold Of Yourself / This Old World / People Sure Act Funny / At Last / It's A Hang Up Baby / Hurt So Bad

Unart S21020/M20020 - The Soul Of Baby Washington - ?
Tracks: Only Those In Love / I Can't Wait Until I See My Baby's Face / There He Is / Who's Going To Take Care Of Me / The Clock // Careless Hands / It'll Never Be Over For Me / Move On Drifter / Your Fool / Go On

Trip 8009 - The One And Only - ?
Tracks: ?

CDs

Collectables COL 5040 – The Best Of Baby Washington – 1993
Tracks: Time / Only Those In Love / Move On Drifter / There He Is / You Could Never Be Mine / The Clock / That's How Heartaches Are Made / Nobody Cares / Leave Me Alone / Handful Of Memories / Lets Love In The Moonlight / Bells (On Our Wedding Day)

Collectables VCL5124 – That's How Heartaches Are Made – 1994
Tracks: Ballad Of Bobby Dawn / Leave Me Alone / Doodlin' / You And The Night And The Music / That's How Heartaches Are Made / Standing On The Pier / I've Got A Feeling / Careless Hands / Hush Heart / Go On / A Handful Of Memories

Collectables COL CD 5108 – Only Those In Love - 1994
Tracks: Only Those In Love / I Can't Wait Until I See My Baby's Face / Who's Going To Take Care Of Me ? / It'll Never Be Over For Me / Your Fool / Hey Lonely / Careless Hands / Go On / Run My Heart / Money's Funny / White Christmas / Silent Night

Collectables COL8828 – For Collectors Only – 1995 (Double CD)
Tracks: CD1 - Time / You Never Could Be Mine / Bells (On Our Wedding Day) / Why Did Baby Put Me Down / Work Out / Let's Love In The Moonlight / Tears Fell / Medicine Man / Your Mam Knows What's Right / Deep Down Love / Too Late / Move On / Nobody Cares (About Me) / Money's Funny / Go On / Handful Of Memories / Careless Hands / Hush Heart / I've Got A Feeling / There He Is CD2 – That's How

Soulful Kinda Music – The Rare Soul Bible Volume Two

Heartaches Are Made / Leave Me Alone / You And The Night And The Music / Hey Lonely One / Doodlin' / I Can't Wait Until I See My Baby's Face / Who's Going To Take Care Of Me / The Clock / Standing On The Pier / It'll Never Be Over For Me / Move On Drifter / Run My Heart / Your Fool / Only Those In Love / Ballad Of Bobby Dawn / No Time For Pity / White Christmas / Silent Night / You Are What You Are / Either You're With Me (Or Either You're Not) / I Know

Kent CDKEND 136 – The Sue Singles – 1996 (UK Release)
Tracks: No Tears / Go On / A Handful Of Memories / Careless Hands / I've Got A Feeling / Hush Heart / Standing On The Pier / The Clock / That's How Heartaches Are Made / There He Is / Leave Me Alone / Hey Lonely / I Can't Wait Until I See My Baby's Face / Who's Gonna Take Care Of Me / It'll Never Be Over For Me / Move On Drifter / Run My Heart / Your Fool / Only Those In Love / No Time For Pity / You And The Night And The Music / Doodling' / The Ballad Of Bobby Dawn / You Are What You Are / Either You're With Me (Or Either You're Not) / I Know / White Christmas / Silent Night

Ace CD CHD 1089 - Baby Washington And The Hearts - 2006 (Uk Release)
Tracks: You Needn't Tell Me, I Know (The Hearts) / I Want Your Love Tonight (The Hearts) / Congratulations Honey (Baby Washington) / If I Had Known (The Hearts) / You Weren't Home (The Hearts) / I Feel So Good (The Hearts) / Ah-Ha (Baby Washington) / There Is No Love At All (The Hearts) / There Must Be A Reason (Baby Washington) / Been A Long Time Baby (Baby Washington) / You Say You Love Me (The Hearts) / Dancing In A Dream World (The Hearts) / Every Day (Baby Washington) / I Hate To See You Go (Baby Washington) / A Thousand Years From Today (The Hearts) / Dear Abby (The Hearts) / I Couldn't Let You See Me Crying (The Hearts) / Goodbye, Baby (The Hearts) / Like, Later Baby (The Hearts) / There Are So Many Ways (The Hearts) / My Love Has Gone (The Hearts) / So Long Baby (The Hearts) / You Or Me Have Got To Go (The Hearts) / Do You Remember (The Hearts) / Don't Let Me Down (The Hearts).

Jay Wiggins

Jay Wiggins (Born Washington DC. Was jailed in the Sixties for refusing the draft following his conversion to Islam, and a change in name to Majeed)

IPG 45-1008 - Sad Girl* / No Not Me - 1963 * Also recorded by The Intruders on Gamble 235
JW 1015 - My Lonely Girl / Forgive Then Forget - 1964
IPG 1015V - My Lonely Girl / Forgive Then Forget - 1964
Solid Sound 3001 - You're On My Mind / Tears Of A Lover - 1964
Solid Sound 3001 - You're On My Mind / No One - 1964
Solid Sound 3002 - I Work So Hard / I Am The Man - 1964
Amy 955 - Sad Girl / No Not Me - 1966
Eric 154 - Sad Girl / No Not Me - 1966
Lost Nite 258 - Sad Girl / No Not Me - ?

LPs / CDs

Soulful Kinda Music – The Rare Soul Bible Volume Two

Leeric CDB5638059584.2 - Jay Wiggins AKA Majeed - 2012
Tracks: Movin' / Everything You Say / Sad Girl / Streetlights / It's Heaven / The Bridge / Voices / Turn This Thing Around / Where Eagles Fly / Everything You Say Dance Mix

Betty Wilson

The Four Bars featuring Betty Wilson (members Betty Wilson, Melvin Butler, Elsworth Grimes and Eddie Daye)

Falew! 108 - I've Got To Move / Waiting On The Right Guy* - 1964 *lead Betty Wilson.

Eddie Daye & 4 Bars (members Betty Wilson, Melvin Butler, Elsworth Grimes and Eddie Daye)

Shrine 112 - Guess Who Loves You / What Am I Gonna Do - 1966

The Four Bars (members Betty Wilson, Melvin Butler, Elsworth Grimes and Eddie Daye)

Dayco 104 - We Are Together / Speak Now - 1967
Dayco 4564 - Lean On Me When Heartaches Get Rough / Why I've Got To Know* - 1967

Betty Wilson and The 4 Bars (members Betty Wilson, Melvin Butler, Elsworth Grimes and Eddie Daye)

Dayco 1631 - I'm Yours / All Over Again* - 1967

Eddie "Jasper" Daye & The Four Bars (members Betty Wilson, Melvin Butler, Elsworth Grimes and Eddie Daye)

Flying Hawk 15101 - Speak Now (Or Forever Hold Your Peace) / We Are Together (No One Can Tear Us Apart - 1967

Betty Wilson

Dayco 2109 - Anything To Please My Man / Don't Give Up - 1969

The Four Bars (members Betty Wilson, Melvin Butler, Elsworth Grimes and Eddie Daye)

Dayco 2500 - Stay On The J-O-B / Poor Little Me - 1969

Soulful Kinda Music – The Rare Soul Bible Volume Two

Betty Wilson

Warren 109 - Let Me Groove You / Love Of My Man - 1971

Brenton Wood

The Dootones (members Alfred Smith, ...)

The Quotations (members Brenton Wood ....) group formed by Brenton Wood while at Compton College.

Little Freddy & The Rockets (members Brenton Wood, ...)

Chief 33 - All My Love / Too Fat - 1958

Brenton Wood (born Alfred Jesse Smith on 26-July-1941 in Shreveport, Louisiana - raised in San Pedro, California)

First President 428 - The Kangaroo / That's The Way It Is - 1960
Wand 154 - Mr. Schemer / Hide-A-Way - 1963

Breton Wood

Brent 7052 - Good Lovin' / I Want Love - 1966 (some copies have mis-spelled name)

Brenton Wood

Brent 7052 - Good Lovin' / I Want Love - 1966
Brent 7057 - Cross The Bridge / Sweet Molly Malone - 1966
Brent 7068 - I Want Love / Sweet Molly Malone - 1967
Double Shot 111 - The Oogum Boogum Song / I Like The Way You Love Me - 1967
Double Shot 116 - Gimme Little Sign / I Think You've Got Your Fools Mixed Up - 1967
Double Shot 121 - Baby You Got It / Catch You On The Rebound - 1967
Double Shot 126 - Lovey Dovey Kinda Lovin' / Two-Time Loser - 1968
Double Shot 130 - Some Got It, Some Don't / Me And You - 1968
Double Shot 135 - Trouble / It's Just A Game Love - 1968
Double Shot 137 - Where Are You / A Change Is Gonna Come - 1969
Philco-Ford Hp-38 - Gimme Little Sign / Oogum Boogum - 1969 (4" plastic "Hip Pocket Record" came with colour sleeve)
Double Shot 142 - Whoop It On Me / Take A Chance - 1969
Ode 116 - Gimme Little Sign / I Think You've Got Your Fools Mixed Up - 1969
Double Shot 147 - Can You Dig It / Great Big Bundle Of Love - 1970
Double Shot 150 - Bogaloosa, Louisian' / Need Your Love So Bad - 1970
Double Shot 156 - Sad Little Song / Who But A Fool - 1971
Mr. Wood 009 - Sticky Boom Boom Too Cold (Part 1) / Sticky Boom Boom Too Cold (Part 2) - 1972
Prophesy 3002 - Sticky Boom Boom Too Cold (Part 1) / Sticky Boom Boom Too Cold (Part 2) - 1973

Soulful Kinda Music – The Rare Soul Bible Volume Two

Prophesy 3003 - Another Saturday Night / ? - 1973
Midget 101 - All That Jazz / Rainin' Love (You Gotta Feel It) - 1975
Warner Bros. 8079 - All That Jazz / Rainin' Love (You Gotta Feel It) - 1975
Warner Bros. 8144 - Better Believe It / It Only Makes Me Want It More - 1975
Cream 7602 - All That Jazz / Bless Your Little Heart - 1976
Cream 7716 - Come Softly To Me / You're Everything I Need - 1977
Cream 7720 - Number One / ? - 1977
Cream 7833 - Let's Get Crazy Together / Love Is Free - 1978
Cream 7834 - Let's Get Crazy Together / Love Is Free - 1978 (12" Single Release)
Eric 0302 - The Oogum Boogum Song / Gimme Little Sign - ?

Label Listings

Wand

101 - Lynn Sisters - Which Way Did My Heart Go / You've Had Your Play
102 - The Leeds - Mr Cool / Heaven Only Knows
103 - Bette Watts - Sweet Carrie Masintie / Big Paul Bunyan
104 - Bette Watts - Let It Be Me / Do Me A Favor
105 - The Titones - My Movie Queen / Symbol Of Love
106 - Chuck Jackson - I Don't Want To Cry / Just Once
107 - Russell Byrd - You'd Better Come Home / Let's Tell Him All About It
108 - Chuck Jackson - In Real Life / The Same Old Story
109 - Del Marind - Cupid's Arrow / I'll Never Be The Same Again
110 - Chuck Jackson - I Wake Up Crying / Everybody Needs Love
111 - The Jokers - So Tight / Whisper
112 - Jocko - A Little Bit Of Everything / Blast Off To Love
113 - ?
114 - Renaults - Just Like Mine / Another Train Pulled Out
115 - Chuck Jackson - The Breaking Point / My Willow Tree
116 - ?
117 - Deep River Boys - Are You Certain / Vanishing American
118 - Isley Brothers - The Snake / Right Now
119 - Chuck Jackson - Band Of Angels / Watcha Gonna Say
120 - The Renaults - Only You / Hully Gully Lamb
121 - Russell Byrd - Little Bug / Nights Of Mexico
122 - Chuck Jackson - Any Day Now / The Prophet
123 - Tammy Montgomery - Voice Of Experience / I Want'cha To Be True
124 - Isley Brothers - Twist And Shout / Spanish Twist
125 - Soul Brothers - Notify Me / Parade Of Broken Hearts
126 - Chuck Jackson - I Keep Forgettin' / Whois Gonna Pick Up The Pieces
127 - Isley Brothers - Twistin' With Linda / You Better Come Home
128 - Chuck Jackson - Gettin' Ready For The Heartbreak / In Between Tears
129 - Eloise - You Shoulda Treated Me Right / Ooh Baby
130 - The Tabs – Footsteps / The Wallop
131 - Isley Brothers - Nobody But Me / 110th And Lenox Ave
131 - Isley Brothers – Nobody But Me / I'm Laughing To Keep From Crying
132 - Chuck Jackson - Tell Him I'm Not Home / Lonely Am I

133 - Billy Adams - Skip To My Lou / Billy Boy
134 - Pancho Villa Orch - Non Stop / Tanya
135 - Maxine Brown - Ask Me / Yesterdays Kisses
136 - Ed Bruce - It's Coming To Me / The Greatest Man
137 - Isley Brothers - I Say Love / Hold On Baby
138 - Chuck Jackson - I Will Never Turn My Back On You / Tears Of Joy
139 - The Tabs - Take My Love With You / I'm With You
140 - Ed Bruce - See The Big Man Cry / You Need A New Love
141 - Chuck Jackson - New York, Big New York / Any Other Way
142 - Maxine Brown - Coming Back To You / Since I Found You
143 - Kingsmen - Louie Louie / Haunted Castle /
144 - ?
145 - Brenton Wood – Hideaway / Mr. Schemer
146 - Timmy Shaw - Gonna Send You Back To Georgia / I'm A Lonely Guy
147 - Gino Washington - Out Of This World / Come Monkey With Me
148 - Ed Bruce - The Workingman's Prayer / Don't Let It Happen To Us
149 - Chuck Jackson - Hand It Over / Look Over Your Shoulder
150 - The Kingsmen - Money / Bent Scepter
151 - Timmy Shaw - If I Catch You / There Goes My Baby
152 - Maxine Brown - Little Girl Lost / You Upset My Soul
153 - Nornetts - Happy Boy / Papa Knew
154 - Chuck Jackson - Beg Me / This Broken Heart
154 - Chuck Jackson - Beg Me / For All Time
155 - Gino Washington - Baby Be Mine - I'm Comin' Home
156 - Ed Bruce - I'm Gonna Have A Party / Half A Love
157 - Kingsmen - Little Latin Lupe Lu / David's Mood
158 - Maxine Brown - I Cry Alone / Put Yourself In My Place
159 - Richard Walker - Sally's Party / Wedding Day
160 - The Mighty Sparrow - Village Ram / She's Been Gone Too Long
161 - Chuck Jackson - Somebody New / Stand By Me
162 - Maxine Brown - Oh No,Not My Baby / You Upset My Soul
163 - Bessie Banks - Do It Now / (You Should Have Been) A Doctor
164 - Kingsmen - Death Of An Angel / Searching For Love
165 - Don & The Goodtimes - Turn On / Make It
166 - Lois Lane - Turn Me Loose / My Only Prayer
167 - Nella Dodds - Come See About Me / You Don't Love Me Anymore
169 - Chuck Jackson - Since I Don't Have You / Hand It Over
170 - Gary Weston - Red Feather Basket / I Should Say Not
171 - Nella Dodds - Finders Keepers,Losers Weepers / A Girl's Life
172 - Kingsmen - Jolly Green Giant / Long Green
173 - Maxine Brown - It's Gonna Be Alright / You Do Something To Me
174 - Diplomats - There's Still A Tomorrow / So Far Away
175 - ?
176 - ?
177 - ?
178 - Nella Dodds - Your Love Back / P's And Q's
179 - Chuck Jackson - I Need You / Chuck's Soul Brother Twist
180 - Peter Jay & The Jaywalkers - Parchmen Farm / What's Easy
181 - Chuck Jackson & Maxine Brown - Something You Got / Babe,Take Me
182 - Inspirations - Let's Kiss And Make Up / Love Is Wonderful

Soulful Kinda Music – The Rare Soul Bible Volume Two

183 - Kingsmen - The Climb / The Waiting
184 - Don & The Goodtimes - Something On My Mind / Straight Scepter
185 - Maxine Brown - One Step At A Time / Anything For A Laugh
186 - ?
187 - Nella Dodds - Come Back Baby / Dream Boy
188 - Chuck Jackson - If I Didn't Love You / Just A Little Bit Of Your Soul
189 - Kingsmen - Annie Fannie / Give Her Lovin'
190 - ?
191 - Chuck Jackson & Maxine Brown - Can't Let You Out Of My Sight / Don't Go
192 - Smith Girls - The Way I Love My Baby(Milk Is Milk) / All You Gotta Do
193 - Princetons - Little Miss Sad / Bony Moronie
194 - John Steele & The Del-Mates - The Fat Man / You're Gonna Miss Me
195 - Diplomats - Love Ain't What It Used To Be / I've Got A Feeling
196 - Lu Ann Simms - If It's Gonna Happen / After The Party
197 - The Magi - Rockin' Crickets / Double Tough
198 - Chuck Jackson & Maxine Brown - I Need You So / 'Cause We're In Love
199 - Headlyters - You Better Come Home / I Need You
1100 - Diane & Annita - One By One / Why Do You Take So Long To Say Goodnight
1101 - ?
1102 - Bobby Bond - You've Got Time / Honey,You've Been On My Mind
1103 - Johnny Copeland - It's Me / The Invitation
1104 - Maxine Brown - If You Gotta Make A Fool Of Somebody / You're In Love
1105 - Chuck Jackson - Good Things Come To Those Who Wait / Yah
1106 - Clarence Reid - I Refuse To Give Up / Somebody Will
1107 - The Kingsmen - (You Got)The Gamma Goochee / It's Only The Dog
1108 - Billy Thompson - Kiss Tomorrow Good-Bye / Black-Eyed Girl
1109 - Chuck Jackson & Maxine Brown - I'm Satisfied / Please Don't Hurt Me
1111 - Nella Dodds - Gee Whiz / Maybe Baby
1112 - The Charts - Desiree / Fall In Love With You Baby
1113 - Mickey & Clean City - Soapy / Static Electricity
1114 - Johnny Copeland - Blowing In The Wind / I' m Gonna Make My Home Where I Hang My Hat
1114 - Johnny Copeland - Dedicated To The Greatest / I' m Gonna Make My Home Where I Hang My Hat
1115 - The Kingsmen - Killer Joe / Little Green Things
1116 - Shirley & Jessie - Ivory Tower / You Can't Fight Love
1117 - Maxine Brown - Anything You Do Is Alright / One In A Million
1118 - Kingsmen - The Climb / Krunch
1119 - Chuck Jackson - All In My Mind / And That's Saying A Lot
1120 - Monzas - Hey I Know You / Forever Walks A Drifter
1121 - Clarence Reid - I'm Your Yes Man / Your Love Is All The Help I Need
1122 - The Last Five - Kicking You / Weather Man
1123 - Diane & Annita - All Cried Out / I'm Ready If You Are
1124 - The Charts - Nobody Made You Love Me / Livin' The Nightlife
1125 - Roscoe Robinson - That's Enough / One More Time
1126 - Grant Nelson - My Heart Can't Understand It / Billy & Sue
1127 - Kingsmen - My Wife Can't Cook / Little Sally Tease
1128 - Maxine Brown - We Can Work It Out / Let Me Give You My Lovin'
1129 - Chuck Jackson - These Chains Of Love (Are Breaking Me Down) / Theme To The Blues

Soulful Kinda Music – The Rare Soul Bible Volume Two

1130 - Johnny Copeland - Wake Up Little Suzie / You're Gonna Reap Just What You Sow
1131 - Shirley & Jessie - Too Much Too Soon / Oh Baby (We Got A Good Thing Going)
1132 - Tiny Goldust & His Golden Trumpet - One Last Walk / Walking The Streets
1133 - ?
1134 - Earl Harrison - Humphrey Stomp / Can You Forgive Me
1135 - Al Wilson - Help Me / Help Me - Inst
1136 - Nella Dodds - Honey Boy / I Just Got To Have You
1137 - Kingsmen - If I Needed Someone / Grass Is Green
1138 - Alan Bruce - Where Do We Go From Here / I Feel Better
1139 - Shirley Mondaine - Ain't That Cold / Confused
1140 - Jessie Hill - Something Ought To Be Done / My Children My Children
1141 - The Honey Bees - Let's Get Back Together / Never In A Million Years
1142 - Chuck Jackson - I've Got To Be Strong / Where Did She Stay
1143 - Roscoe Robinson - How Much Pressure / Do It Right Now
1144 - Just Brothers - Carlena / She Broke His Heart
1145 - Maxine Brown - I Don't Need Anything / The Secret Of Livin'
1146 - The Rivals - Hollerin' For My Darlin' / It Won't Be Long Now
1147 - The Kingsmen - Trouble / Daytime Shadows
1148 - Chuck Jackson & Maxine Brown - Hold On I'm Coming / Never Had It So Good
1149 - Roscoe Robinson - What You're Doin' To Me / A Thousand Rivers
1150 - Ernie Hines - Party Rain / Rain
1151 - Chuck Jackson - Need You There / Every Man Needs A Down Home Girl
1152 - Ivories - Please Stay / I'm In The Groove
1153 - Walter Wilson - Not Now But Later / Love Keeps me Crying
1154 - The Kingsmen - The Wolf Of Manhattan / Children's Caretaker
1155 - Chuck Jackson & Maxine Brown - Daddy's Home / Don't Go
1156 - The Moving Sidewalks - 99th Floor / What Are You Going To Do
1157 - The Kingsmen - Don't Say No / (I Have Found) Another Girl
1158 - Sammy Jones - Don't Touch Me / Cinderella Jones
1159 - Chuck Jackson - Hound Dog / Love Me Tender
1160 - Lou Lawton - Knick Knack Patty Wack / It's That Time Of Day
1161 - Roscoe Robinson - I Gotta Keep Tryin' / Just A Little Bit
1162 - Chuck Jackson & Maxine Brown - Tennessee Waltz / C.C. Rider
1163 - The Groove - Love It's Getting Better / The Light Of Love
1164 - The Kingsmen - Bo Diddley Bach / Just Before The Break Of Day
1165 - Johnny Moore - Haven't I Been Good To You / A Dollar Ninety Eight
1166 - Chuck Jackson - Shame On Me / Candy
1167 - The Moving Sidewalks - Need Me / Every Night A New Surprise
1168 - The Masqueraders - I Don't Want Nobody To Lead Me On / Let's Face Facts
1169 - Sandy Waddy - Everything Is Everything / Secret Love
1170 - The Next Five - Mama Said / Talk To Me Girl
1171 - L.C.Cooke - Half A Man / Let's Do It Over
1172 - The Masqueraders - Sweet Lovin' Woman / Do You Love Me Baby
1173 - Marvin Preyer - What Can I Call My Own / It's Coming To Me
1174 - The Kingsmen - Get Out Of My Life Woman / Since You Been Gone
1175 - Joe Arnold - Share Your Love With Me / Soultrippin'
1176 - Billy Thornhill - The Key / What's Going On In The Barn

Soulful Kinda Music – The Rare Soul Bible Volume Two

1177 - Dee Clark - Nobody But You / Nobody But You
1178 - Chuck Jackson - My Child's Child / Theme To The Blues
1179 - Maxine Brown - Soul Serenade / He's The Only Guy I'll Ever Love
1180 - The Kingsmen - On Love / I Guess I Was Dreamin'
1181 - Marvin Preyer - Climbing Up To Love / Don't Stop Loving Me This Time
1182 - Freddie Hughes - Send My Baby Back / Where's My Baby
1183 - Diane Lewis - I Thank You Kindly / Please Let Me Help You
1184 - The Gentleman Four - You Can't Keep A Good Man Down / It Won't Hurt
1185 - The Joneses - Baby / Washington Square
1186 - Joe Arnold - Let It Be Me / Cooking Gear
1187 - The Peter Thomas Group - Scufflin' / Hittin' Hard
1188 - Benny Gordon - Gonna Give Her All The Love I Got / Turn On Your Love Light
1189 - Mel Wynn & The Rhythm Aces - Don't Want To Lose You / Emmy Lou
1190 - The Stone Cantaloupe - (Way Back) In 19 And 68 / The Unconventional Blues
1191 - Diane Lewis - Without Your Love / Giving Up Your Love
1192 - Freddie Hughes - Natural Man / I Gotta Keep My Bluff In
1193 - The Esquires - You've Got The Power / No Doubt About It
1194 - Warren Lee - Born In The Ghetto / Funky Belly
1195 - The Esquires - I Don't Know / Part Angel
1196 - Mel Wynn & The Rhythm Aces - Stop Sign / Give When You Take
1197 - Freddie Hughes - He's No Good / I Gotta Keep My Bluff In
1198 - Stemmons Express - Love Power / Woman, Love Thief
1199 - Glen Goza - The Box / Incredible Shrinking Man
11200 - Joe Jeffrey Group - My Pledge Of Love / Margie
11201 - The Esquires - Whip It On Me / It Was Yesterday
11202 - Betty Moorer - It's My Thing / Speed Up
11203 - Brenda J. Jones - Point Of No Return / Encore
11204 - Jackie Moore - Loser Again / Who Told You
11205 - George Tindley - It's All Over But The Shouting / Ain't That Peculiar
11206 - Lee Allen - Don't Wait Till Morning Comes / All Too Soon
11207 - Joe Jeffrey - Dreamin' Till Then / The Train
11208 - George Tindley - Honky Tonk Woman / So Help Me Woman
11209 - Darryl Stewart - Cross My Heart / Name It And Claim It
11210 - ?
11211 - Benny Conn - Satisfy My Hunger / I Just Wanna Come In Outta The Rain
11212 - Bobby Bradshaw - Show Me A Man / Loving You
11213 - Joe Jeffrey - Hey Hey Woman / The Chance Of Loving You
11214 - Paul Flagg - Tell The Truth / Georgia Pines
11215 - George Tindley - Wan Tu Wah Zuree / Pity The Poor Man
11216 - Wheatstraw - One Am / Face Outside My Window
11217 - Abraham - Kangaroo I / Kangaroo II
11218 - Winfield Parker - I'm Wondering / Will There Ever Be Another Love For Me
11219 - Joe Jeffrey - My Baby Loves Lovin' / The Chance Of Loving You
11220 - The Alliance - Pass The Pipe / Cupid's Holding
11221 - Mod Lads - Let's Have Some Fun Part I / Let's Have Some Fun Part 2
11222 - Jerry-0 - Funky Football / Wang Dang Do
11223 - Freedom Of Choice - Doctor Tom / Fat Man
11224 - The Moods - Rainmaker / Lady Rain
11225 - Something New - You Babe / What's This I See
11226 - Sylvia Jenkins - It's Gonna Be Alright / You Do Something To Me

Soulful Kinda Music – The Rare Soul Bible Volume Two

11227 - Frankie Newsome - Don't Mess With My Love Maker Part I / Don't Mess With My Love Maker Part 2
11228 - Triumphs - Houston Won't Call Me / Warner The Drummer
11229 - Soul Dynamics - Stay In The Groove Part I / Stay In The Groove Part 2
11230 - Earl King - Tic Tac Toe / A Part Of Me
11231 - Little Grady Lewis - Soul Smokin Part I / Soul Smokin Part 2
11232 - Earl King - Mama & Papa / This Is What I Call Living
11233 - Wally Cox - This Man / I've Had Enough
11234 - The Luv Bugs - Mama's Gonna Whip Yuh / Soul In The Ghetto
11235 - Joe Jeffrey - A Hundred Pounds Of Clay / Power Of Love
11236 - Ralfi Pagan - Make It With You / Stray Woman
11237 - Reflection - Just Realized / Someone To Love (Never Thought I'd Find)
11238 - Lee Charles - You Got To Get It For Yourself / I Get High On My Baby's Love
11239 - Kent Drake - Boss Thing Together / Without A Lady's Hand
11240 - Terri Crispino - This Is Your Life / Someone Is Standing Outside
11241 - Curtis Blandon - In The Long Run / Push Comes To Shove
11242 - Lee Charles - When The Deal Goes Down / Let's Play House
11243 - Kevin Lindsay - Sing Children Sing / Hang-Ups Of A Child
11245 - Independants - Just As Long As You Need Me Part I / Just As Long As You Need Me Part 2
11246 - Reflection - Living In A World Of Fantasy / Four Walls (And A Telephone)
11247 - Walter Jackson - No Easy Way Down / I'm All Cried Out
11248 - Silhouettes - You Cheated You Lied / Exodus
11249 - Independants - I Just Want To Be There / Can't You Understand It
11250 - Chuck Jones & Company - Boo On You / Booties
11251 - South Side Movement - I've Been Watching You / Have A Little Mercy
11252 - Independants - Leaving Me / I Love You, Yes I Do
11253 - The Rivingtons - Pa Pa Oom Mow-Mow / I Don't Want A New Baby
11254 - Jimmi Green - The Robot / The Robot(Inst)
11255 - Patti Jo - Make Me Believe In You / Keep Me Warm
11256 - JT - That's A No No / Grinder Man
11257 - Ultra High Frequency - Get On The Right Track / Get On The Right Track (Instr)
11258 - Independants - Baby I've Been Missing You / Couldn't Hear Nobody Say (I Love You Like I Do)
11259 - South Side Movement - Can You Get To That / Mud Wind
11260 - General Crook - The Best Years Of My Life / Testification
11261 - Clara Lewis - Needing You / Needing You (Inst)
11262 - Ultra High Frequency - Incompatible / Saddest Smile
11263 - Independants - It's All Over / Sara Lee
11264 - Southside Movement - Can You Get To That / Mud Wind
11265 - Ann Bailey - Sweeping Your Dirt Under My Rug / Fun City Woman
11266 - Ike Lovely - Fool's Hall Of Fame / Little Miss Sweet Thing
11267 - Independants - The First Time We Met / Show Me How
11268 - Brandy Lane - Share Your Love With Me / Need Somebody To Tell My Troubles To
11269 - LTG Exchange - Corazon / A Young Mother's Love
11270 - General Crook - Tell Me What'cha Gonna'do (When You Want To Be Loved) / Reality
11271 - ?

Soulful Kinda Music – The Rare Soul Bible Volume Two

11272 - Chuck Cornish - Ali Funky Thing Part 1 / Ali Funky Thing Part 2
11273 - Independents - Arise & Shine(Let's Get It On) / I Found Love On A Rainy Day
11274 - Sam Williams Singers - For My People (From Hob Records) / God Is Not Dead
11275 - LTG Exchange - Water Bed Part 1 / Water Bed Part 2
11276 - General Crook - Fever In The Funkhouse / Fever In The Funkhouse (Inst)
11277 - ?
11278 - LTG Exchange - Keep On Trying / Tsen Si Yen Yen
11279 - Independents - No Wind No Rain / Let This Be A Lesson To You
11280 - Philadelphia Story - You Are The Song (I've Been / Writing For All My Life) / If You Lived Here You'd Be Home Now
11281 - General Crook - I'm Satisfied / Thanks, But No Thanks
11282 - LTG Exchange - My Love(Does It Good To Me) Part I / My Love(Does It Good To Me) Part 2
11283 - Gene Toone - He Outdid Himself / Baby Boy
11284 - Smallwood Brothers - One Last Memory / ?
11285 - Five Blind Boys Of Alabama / Reach Out And Touch Somebody's Hand / Bridge Over Troubled Waters
11286 - Will Hatcher - Who Am I Without You Baby / What Is Best For Me Is Better For You
11287 - South Shore Commission - Free Man / Free Man (Disco Mix)
11288 - Secrets - Baby(Save Me) / Baby(Save Me(Disco Version)
11289 - ?
11290 - Smallwood Brothers - I Don't Want To Go Back / I Don't Want To Go Back (Instr)
11291 - South Shore Commission - We're On The Right Track / I'd Rather Switch Than Fight
11292 - Smokey Joe Gruff & His 1946 Hudson - The Breakdown / The Breakdown(Disco Version)
11293 - Gene Toone & The Chapter IV - Baby Boy Part 1 / Baby Boy Part 2
11294 - South Shore Commission - Train Called Freedom / Train Called Freedom(Disco Version)
11295 - Sweet Music - I Get Lifted / I Get Lifted(Inst)

Way Out

2605 - Lou Ragland & Bandmasters - Never Let Me Go / Party At Lesters - 1964
2699 - The Springers - I Know Why / I Know My Baby Loves Me - 1964
2699 - The Springers - I Know Why / Last Heartbreak - 1964
2799/80 - The Springers - Last Heartbreak / Why - 1964
3359/60 - The Gaylords - Never Go Back To GA / Loose Beat - 196?
5564 - Joan Bias - I Don't Know What's Right Any More / Crazy Over You - 196?
5696 - The Springers - You Can Laugh / It's Been A Long Time - 1965
1966 - Verna & Bob - More Soul / I'm In Love With You - 1965
W01 - Norman Scott - Baby Don't Go / Ain't That A Heartache - 1966
1047 - The Sensations - Get On Up Mama / I Won't Be Hurt - 1966
5945 - Laura Green - Don Deopo / Come Have A Drink With Me - 1966
2001 - Bobby Wade - Four Walls And One Window / Can't You Hear Me Calling -

Soulful Kinda Music – The Rare Soul Bible Volume Two

1966
2003 - The Harmonics - Which Way / Harmonics On The Warpath - 1966
2005 - The Sensations - Gonna Step Aside / Demanding Man - 1966
2006 - Volcanic Eruption - I've Got Something Going For Me / Red Robin - 1966
? - Ben Iverson & The Hornets - Love Me / Fool's Rush In - 1967
4957 - Lester Johnson & The Hornets - Wedding Day / Jamaica Farewell - 1967
5947 - The Sensations - Too Shy / Please Baby, Please - 1967
5696 - The Springers - It's Been A Long Time / You Can Laugh - 1967
2669 - The Springers - I Know My Baby Loves Me So / I Know Why - 1967
2699 - The Springers - I Know Why / Last Heartbreak - 1967
1000 - The Sensations - Gotta Find Myself Another Girl / Lonely World - 1968
1001 - The Soul Notes - Don't Make Me Beg / How Long Will It Last - 1968
1002 - Fred Towles - Too Much Monkey Business / Part 2 - 1968
1003 - The Sensations - Oh / I Guess That's Life - 1968
1004 - Fred Towles & The Jacksonians - Hook It To The Mule / Inst. - 1969
1005 - The Sensations - It's A New Day / Two Can Make It - 1969
1006 - The Soul Notes - How Long Will It Last / I Got Everything I Need - 1969
1051 - The Soul Notes - How Long Will It Last / Don't Make Me Bag - 1969
011 - The Boss Singers - My God On High / So Many Years - 1970
101 - Ruby Carter & The Exceptional Three - Unlucky Girl / What About Me - 1971
103 - Bobby Wade - I'm In Love With You / Down Here On The Ground - 1971
104 - Jesse Fisher - You're Not Loving A Beginner / Waiting - 1971
105 - Embryo Infinity Rebirth - Let Me Tell You A Story / Walls - 1971
106 - Jesse Fisher - Why / Little John - 1971
984 - Jesse Fuller - Super Funky / Part 2 - 1972
100 - Jesse Fuller - Mr.Super Nobody / Don't Cheat On Me - 1973

Wheelsville

101 - Jimmy Gilford - I Wanna Be Your Baby / Misery Street
102 - Steve Mancha - Did My Baby Call / Whirlpool
103 - Little Sonny - Let's Have A Good Time / Orange Pineapple Blossom Pink
104 - Debora Healey – Don't Do Nothing I Wouldn't Do / Can't Erase My Old Love's Face
105 - ?
106 - Magic Tones - Got To Get A Little Closer / Me And My Baby
107 - Cody Black - I Will Give You My Love / I Am Particular
108 - Hindal Butts Trio -Back Up Baby / Waltzing With The Parson
109 - Fabulous Peps -With These Eyes / Love Of My Life
110 - Lee Rogers -Love Of My Love / How Are You Fixed For Love
111 - Lil' Soul Brotilers - I've Got Heart Aches / What Can It Be
112 - Connie Van Dyke -These Words Wont Come / Dont Do Nothing I Wouldnt Do
113 - Buddy Lamp -You've Got The Loving Touch / I Wanna Go Home
114 - Magic Tones -How Can I Forget /Me And Mv Baby
115 - International Kansas City Playboys - Evervbody Going Wild / Quitting Time
116 - Silky Hargreaves -I'll Keep On Trying / Love Lets Try Again
117 - Don De Andre Trio –Sunny / Watermelon Man

Soulful Kinda Music – The Rare Soul Bible Volume Two

118 - Lee Rogers -How Are You Fixed For Love / Cracked Up Over You
119 - Lee Rogers -How Are Vou Fixed For Love / The Same Things That Make You Laugh
120 - Buddy Lamp -I Wanna Go Home / Confusion
121 - Lee Rogers - Love Can Really Hurt You Deep / Love For A Love
122 - Buddy Lamp -Save Your Love /I Wanna Go Home
10001 - Freddie Butler -Save Your Love / All Is Well
10002 - Rudi Robinson Trio -I Want To Have Everything / Funny
001 - Will Hatcher – You Haven't Seen Nothing / Ain't That Loving You (For More Reasons Than One)
01 - Deliance - Pieces Of Love / Instrumental (Is this the same Wheelesville label ?)

Whip

276 - The Famous Shades - People Talking About Me / The Monkey Funk
346 - Barbette & Mel / Doc Calhoun & Hitmen - Let's Get It Together / Swing It Together
347 - Carol Anderson - Taking My Mind Off Love / I'm Not Worried
347 - Little Mell / Jimmy Landers & All-Stars - Ain't That Funky Monkey / Ain't That Funky Monkey (Inst)

Wild Deuce

1000 - Reuben Williams - Piggy Wiggy / Half A Man - 1964
1001 - Sharon Soul - How Can I Get To You / Don't Say Goodbye My Love - 194
1002 - ?
1003 - Emanuel Lasky - Lucky To Be Loved (By You) / Our World - 1965
1004 - Deena Johnson - The Breaking Point / Mama's Boy - 1965

Windy C

601 – The Five Stairsteps - Don't Waste Your Time / You Waited Too Long
602 - The Five Stairsteps - World Of Fantasy / Playgirls Love
603 - The Five Stairsteps - Come Back / You Don't Love Me
604 - The Five Stairsteps - Danger She's A Stranger / Behind The Curtains
605 - The Five Stairsteps - I Ain't Gonna Rest(Til I Get You) / You Can't See
605 - The Five Stairsteps – Ain't Gonna Rest / You Can't See
606 - June Conquest - Take Care / All I Need
607 - The Five Stairsteps - Ooh Baby Baby / The Girl I Love

Wingate

001 - Ronnie Savoy - Memories Linger / Loving You - 1965

Soulful Kinda Music – The Rare Soul Bible Volume Two

002 - Sam Bowie & The Blue Feelings - (Think Of) The Times We Had Together / Swoop - 1965
003 - Dick Glass - The Golden Touch / Love Is Like A Baseball Game - 1965
004 - Al Kent - Country Boy / You Know I Love You - 1965
005 - Unreleased
006 - Sonny Stitt - The Double-O-Soul Of Sonny Stitt (Part One) / (Part Two) - 1965
007 - Pack - The Tears Come Rollin' / The Color Of Our Love - 1965
008 - Juanita Williams - Some Things You Never Get Used To / You Knew What You Was Gettin' - 1965
009 - Unreleased
010 - Sonny Stitt - Concerto For Jazz Lovers / Just Dust - 1965
011 - Sonny Stitt / Hank Marr - Stitt's Groove / Marr's Groove - 1966
012 - Hank Marr - White House Party / The "Out" Crowd - 1966
013 - Unreleased
014 - Andre Williams & His Orchestra - Loose Juice / Sweet Little Pussycat - 1966
015 - Mark III Trio   G'Wan (Go On) / Good Grease - 1966
016 - Unreleased
017 - Unreleased
018 - Dynamics - Bingo! / Somewhere - 1966
019 - Unreleased
020 - Royal Jokers -   Love Game (From A To Z) / From A To Z (Love Game) (Instrumental) - 1966
021 - Andre Williams & His Orchestra - Do It! (Part 1) / Do It! (Part 2) - 1966

022 - Dramatics - Inky Dinky Wang Dang Doo / Baby I Need You - 1967

Winner 7-11

101 - Geraldine Latham - Lazy Lover / Mr. Fix It - 1966
102 - Priscilla Thomas - Step Aside / Sympathy - 1966

Soulful Kinda Music – The Rare Soul Bible Volume Two

The X-Cellents

The Original Playboys (members Jerry ?, Moon ?, Ray ? and Roger Sayre)

Leisure Time 1206 - I'll Always Be On Your Side / Hey Little Willie - 1965

The X-Cellents (members Jerry ?, Moon ?, Ray ? and Roger Sayre)

Smash 1996 - I'll Always Be On Your Side / Hey Little Willie - 1965
Sure Play 0003 - And I'm Cryin' / The Slide - 1966
Sure Play 1206-45-0003 - Little Wooden House / Hang It Up! - 1966

The Vacant Lot (members Jerry ?, Moon ?, Ray ? and Roger Sayre)

Ltd 0004 - Don't You Just Know It / This Little Feelin' - 196? (some copies issued with picture sleeve)

The Xplosions

Funk City 2040 - Wait A Minute / Tell Me Face To Face - 1972

Johnny York

Johnny Jack (John A. Greco)

Great 101 - Smack Madam (Get It All) / Starving For Love - 1961
Dore 617 - The Wonderful World Of Love / Love Of My Own - 1961
Ricky 212 - Need You / Need You - 1962 (Back Up Vocals Lou Christie)
Gone 5132 - The Beggar That Became King / Touch Me - 1962
Lawn 226 - True Love At First Sight / Forever - 1964
Lawn 230 - Forever (And A Day) / Love Must Be - 1964
Lawn 233 - Let's Have A Party / ? - 1964
Fabor 142 - Magic Of Love / Gone Away Party - 1965
Masterdon 100 - Forever / Oh What A Way To Be Loved - ?

Johnny York (John A. Greco died 23-May-1997 in Presbyterian University Hospital, Pittsburgh, cause: cancer he was 57)

Bev Mar 605 - True Lovers / Got My Eyes On You / ? - ?

The Young Folk

The Baby Miracles (members Madeline Strickland and her brother Glenn Strickland, brothers Johnny and Arthur Methune, Patrice Skaggs and Jerry Starks) 1964 line-up.

The Young Folk (members Madeline Strickland, Glenn Strickland, Johnny Methune, Arthur Methune, Patrice Skaggs and Jerry Starks)

Mar-V-Lus 6018 - Joey / Lonely Girl - 1967

Miss Madeline (Madeline Strickland)

Mar-V-Lus 6019 - Lonely Girl / Behave Yourself - 1967 (this 45 has the same label number as the 1967 release by Alvin Cash "Different Strokes For Different Folks / The Charge")

Young - Holt Unlimited

The Cleffs (Members Wallace Burton, Ramsey Lewis, Eldee Young, Isaac "Red" Holt, ...)

The Gentlemen Of Swing (Members Ramsey Lewis, Eldee Young And Isaac Holt)

The Ramsey Lewis Trio (Members Ramsey Lewis (Piano - Born 27-May-1935 In Chicago, Illinois), Eldee Young (Bass - Born Eldee Devon Young On 7-January-1936 In Chicago, Illinois --- Died 13-February-2007 In Singapore, Thailand --- Cause:

Soulful Kinda Music – The Rare Soul Bible Volume Two

Cardiac Arrest) And Isaac Holt (Drums - Born 16-May-1932 In Rosedale, Mississippi))

Argo 5506 - The 'In' Crowd / Since I Fell For You - 1965
Cadet 5522 - Hang On Sloopy / Movin Easy - 1965

The Young-Holt Trio (Members Eldee Young, Isaac Holt And Hysear Don Walker)

Brunswick 55305 - Wack Wack / This Little Light Of Mine - 1966
Brunswick 55317 - Ain't There Something Money Can't Buy / Mellow Yellow - 1967
Brunswick 55338 - The Beat Goes On / Doin' The Thing - 1967

Young-Holt Unlimited (Members Eldee Young, Isaac Holt And Ken Chaney)

Brunswick 55356 - Dig Her Walk / You Gimmie Thum - 1967
Brunswick 55374 - Soul Sister / Give It Up - 1968
Brunswick 55391 - Soulful Strut* / Country Slicker Joe - 1968 *Backing track tTo hhe 1969 recording "Am I The Same Girl" by Barbara Acklin on Brunswick 55399 with Floyd Morris (Died 1988) on piano replacing the vocal. It has been stated that neither Eldee Young or Isaac Holt played on this track and that it was in fact the Brunswick Studio Band.
Brunswick 55400 - Who's Making Love / Just Ain't No Love - 1969
Brunswick 55410 - Just A Melody / Young And Holtful - 1969
Brunswick 55417 - Straight Ahead / California Montage - 1969
Brunswick 55420 - Soulful Samba = Segura Esse Samba / Horoscope - 1969
Cotillion 44092 - Mellow Dreaming / Got To Get My Baby Back Home - 1970
Cotillion 44111 - Luv-Bugg / Wah Wah Man - 1971
Cotillion 44120 - Hot Pants / I'll Be There - 1971
Paula 380 - Super Fly* / Give Me Your Love - 1973 *Also Recorded In 1972 By Curtis Mayfield on Curtom 1978.
Paula 382 - Could It Be I'm Falling In Love / Hey! Pancho - 1973

Isaac "Redd" Holt Unlimited

Paula 392 - Flo / Listen To The Drums - 1973

The Ramsey Lewis Trio (members Ramsey Lewis, Eldee Young and Isaac Holt)

Goldies 45 2640 - The 'In' Crowd / Since I Fell For You - 1974

Isaac "Redd" Holt Unlimited

Paula 412 - Do It Baby / I Shot The Sheriff - 1975

Redd Holt Unlimited

Paula 415 - Gimme Some Mo' / Nothing From Nothing - 1975

Barbara Acklin / Young-Holt-Unlimited

Eric 4503 - Love Makes A Woman / Soulful Strut* - 1983 *flip by Young-Holt-

Soulful Kinda Music – The Rare Soul Bible Volume Two

Unlimited.

The Lost Generation / Young-Holt Unlimited

Collectables Col 039287 - The Sly, Slick And The Wicked / Soulful Strut* - ? *Flip by Young-Holt Unlimited

Lp's

The Young-Holt Trio

Brunswick Bl-54121 - Wack-Wack - 1966 (Mono)
Tracks: You Know That I Love You / Yesterday / Wack Wack / This Little Light Of Mine / Sunny / Strangers In The Night / Song For My Father / Red Sails In The Sunset / Monday Monday / Girl Talk.

Brunswick Bl-754121 - Wack-Wack - 1966 (Stereo)
Tracks: You Know That I Love You / Yesterday / Wack Wack / This Little Light Of Mine / Sunny / Strangers In The Night / Song For My Father / Red Sails In The Sunset / Monday Monday / Girl Talk.

Young-Holt Unlimited

Brunswick Bl-54125 - On Stage - 1967 (Mono)
Tracks: Mellow Yellow / Medley: In Crowd, Wade In The Water, Ain't There Something / Wack Wack /// Lady Godiva / You Gimme Thum.

Brunswick Bl-754125 - On Stage - 1967 (Stereo)
Tracks: Mellow Yellow / Medley: In Crowd, Wade In The Water, Ain't There Something / Wack Wack / Lady Godiva / Yon Gimme Thum.

Eldee Young and Red Holt (of The Ramsey Lewis Trio)

Cadet Lp-791 - Feature Spot - 1967 (Mono)
Tracks:

Cadet Lps-791 - Feature Spot - 1967 (Stereo)
Tracks:

Young-Holt Unlimited

Brunswick Bl-54128 - The Beat Goes On - 1967 (Mono)
Tracks: The Beat Goes On / Yum Yum / Doin' The Thing / Ain't No Mountain High Enough / Good Vibrations / Dig Her Walk / You Gimme Them / How Insensitive (Insensatez) / Listen Here / Baby Your Lights Is Out.

Brunswick Bl-754128 - The Beat Goes On - 1967 (Stereo)
Tracks: The Beat Goes On / Yum Yum / Doin' The Thing / Ain't No Mountain High Enough / Good Vibrations / Dig Her Walk / You Gimme Them / How Insensitive (Insensatez) / Listen Here / Baby Your Lights Is Out.

Soulful Kinda Music – The Rare Soul Bible Volume Two

Brunswick Bl-754141 - Funky But! - 1968
Tracks: Funky Duck / Lady Madonna / Country Slicker Joe / Orient / Valley of the
Dolls Theme / Look of Love / Sombrero Sam / Eleanor Rigby / Honey / Secret Love.

Brunswick Bl-754144 - Soulful Strut - 1968
Tracks: Who's Making Love / Please Sunrise, Please / Be By My Side / What Now My
Love (Et Maintenant) / Baby Your Light Is Out / Soulful Strut /// Just Ain't No Love /
Little Green Apples / Funky Is As Funky Does / Love Makes A Woman / Ain't There
Something Money Can't Buy.

Brunswick Bl-754150 - Just A Melody - 1969
Tracks: Young And Holtful / When I'm Not Around / My Whole World Ended / Light
My Fire / Just A Melody / I Wish You Love / I Heard It Through The Grapevine / Give
It Away / By The Time I Get To Phoenix.

Cotillion Sd-18001 - Mellow Dreamin' - 1971
Tracks: The Devil Made Me Do Dat / Going in Circles / Wichita Lineman / Mellow
Dreamin' /Trippi' /// Raindrops Keep Falling on My Head / The Creeper / There'll Be a
Greater Day / Black and White / Midnight Cowboy.

Cotillion Sd-18004 - Born Again - 1972
Tracks: I'll Be There / Something / We've Only Just Begun / Hot Pants /// Make It With
You / Luv Bugg / Wah Wah Man / Queen Of The Nile / Blood In The Streets / Save
The Day.

Paula Lps-4002 - Young-Holt Unlimited Plays Super Fly - 1973
Tracks: Freddie's Dead / Give Me Your Love / Pusher Man / Superfly / Hey Pancho ///
Could It Be I'm Falling In Love / (They Long To Be) Close To You / People Make The
World Go Round / Mystical Man.

Atlantic Sd-1634 - Oh, Girl - 1973
Tracks: Yes We Can Can / Oh Girl / Can't Get Enough Of You / Hi-Fly / Where Is The
Love? / Rubber Lips / Such A Beautiful Feeling / Food Stamps / I'm Still Here
/ Bumpin' On Young Street.

Lonnie Youngblood

Lonnie Youngblood (Born: Lonnie Thomas in Augusta, GA, on August 3, 1941)

Lonnie Youngblood Combo

Earth ? – Heartbreak / ?
Earth 701 – Nitty Gritty / Riverside Rock -

Lonnie Youngblood

Cameo 374 - Come On Let's Strut / Youngblood Feeling – 1965
Fairmount 1002 - Gogo Shoes / Gogo Place - 1966
Fairmount 1016 - The Grass (Will Always Sing For You) / Wooly Bully - 1966
Fairmount 1022 - Soul Food / Goodbye Bessie Mae – 1967

Soulful Kinda Music – The Rare Soul Bible Volume Two

Loma 2081 - African Twist Part 1 / Part II – 1967
Loma 2097 - Roll With The Punches / Tomorrow – 1968

Jimi Hendrix & Lonnie Youngblood

Maple 1003 – Wipe The Sweat Off My Brow / ? – 1971

Lonnie Youngblood

Turbo 013 – Let's Party / theme - 1972
Turbo 026 - Sweet Sweet Tootie / In My Lonely Room – 1972

Lonnie Youngblood / Blood Brothers

Turbo 029 – Super Cool / Black Is So Black – 1972

Lonnie Youngblood

Turbo 031 – I Only Hurt Myself / My Wife, My Woman, and Me - 1973
Shakat 708 - Man To Woman / Man To Woman (Instrumental) – 1974
Shakat ? – Young Free And Single / ? - 1974
Vibration 568 – Reaching For A Dream / Reaching For A Dream (Inst) - 1976
Turbo 050 - Gonna Fly Now / Happiness Is music - 1976
Calla 109 - Let My Love Bring Out The Woman In You / Right Back Where We Started - 1976
Phillips 6164 454 – Push It In (As Far As You Can) / Happiness Is Music – 1977
Radio 3866 – Feelings / Expressions – 1981
Radio 272 – The Best Way To Break A Habit / The Best Way To Break A Habit – 1981 (12" Single)

Dave 'Baby' Cortez With Lonnie Youngblood & His Bloodhounds / Lonnie Youngblood & His Bloodhounds

Norton 9664 – Jumpin' Jack Flash / Monkey Man - 2011

Label Listings

Yan-G

Y-401 - Jimmy Ed Trio - Baby, Baby Oh Baby / Lips
4662/4663 - Lennie Lynn with the Jimmy Ed Trio - Exodus / Leave Me Alone
4664/4665 - The Classics - One Dance / So Glad That I Found You

Yew

Soulful Kinda Music – The Rare Soul Bible Volume Two

1000 - Florence De Vore - He Doesn't Love You / He's Got The Money Bags
1001 - The Intrigues - In A Moment / Scotchman Rock
1002 - The Intrigues - I Gotta Find Out For Myself / I'm Gonna Love You
1003 - Phyllis Smith - The Feeling Is Gone / I Need Somebody To Love
1004 - The Radars - Finger Lickin' Chicken / Soul Serenade
1005 - Tommy Mc Cook and The Supersonics - Liquidator / Tribute To Don
1006 - Ed Woods and Afro '70 - Mockingbird Hill / Cuguzza Zambezi
1007 - The Intrigues - Just A Little Bit More / Let's Dance
1008 - Onyx - Something You're Trying To Hide / You Never Fail To Amaze Me
1009 - Florence De Vore - He Doesn't Love You / He's Got The Money Bags
1010 - The Intrigues - Tuck A Little Love Away / I Know There's Love
1011 - Florence De Vore - It Takes A Lot Of Love To Love Me / Look Out
1012 - The Intrigues - I Got Love / The Language Of Love
1013 - The Intrigues - Mojo Hannah / To Make A World

Yorktown

75 – The Miller Sisters – Looking Over My Life / Si Senor – 1965
1008 – Johnny Summers – I'm Still Yours / Prove It To Me – 1965
1009 – Johnny Summers – I Can't Let You Go – Tell It Like I Feel - 1965

Z

Z. Z. And Company

Z. Z. And Company (members Jessie Butler (lead), ...)

Columbus Records   Frjb-51679 - Gettin' Ready For The Getdown / Butt La Rose - 1979

Label Listing

Zell's

250 - Robert Copeland - I Could Never Deny / Will You Be My Girl - 1962
252/253 - Ada Ray - Give Our Love A Chance / I No Longer Believe In Miracles - 1962
256 - Taffie Lee - Stay Away From My Baby / The Trials Of Life Can Be Lonely - 1962
260/261 - Ada Ray - I Cried To Be Free / Oh Come Back Baby - 1962
4397 - Hartsy Maye - As The Years Go By / Heigh Ho The Merry O - 1962
711 - Henry Hodge - I Won't Ever Try To Change You / Sing Along With Henry Hodge
712 - The Relations - Crowd With The Phony Tattoo / Say You Love Me
1008/1009 - Jimmy Armstrong & The Pins - I Want To Be Close To You / Rise Sally, Come On To Me - 1963
1426 - Ada Ray - My Love Is Gone / Red Rose In The Snow - ?
1819 - Carolyn & Sam - Congratulations Honey / You Got Me Uptight - ?
3238 - Darlene Weeks - Soul Food Is What I Like / ? - ?
3377 - The Hearts - A Thousand Years From Today / I Feel So Good - 1970
3378 - The Hearts - Don't Let Me Down / Do You Remember - 1970
3379 - Miss Johnnie - Over The Mountain Across The Sea / Let Sleeping Dog's Lie - 1970
0004 - The Bates Family - God Bless Our Home / Let's Stand Up For Jesus - 1970
380 - Norman Gabel - God Knows (He's Got His Eyes On You) / The Bible: Yet It Lives
148 - Cross Bronx Expressway - Cross Bronx Expressway / Help Your Brothers - 1974

Zodiac

1001 - Ruby Andrews - Let's Get A Groove Going On / Part 2 - 1966
1002 - ?
1003 - Ruby Andrews - I Just Can't Get Enough / Johnny's Gone Away - 1967
1004 - Ruby Andrews - Casanova (Your Playing Days Are Over) / I Just Don't Believe It - 1967
1005 - The Creations - Footsteps / A Dream
1006 - Ruby Andrews - Hey Boy (Take A Chance On Love) / Come To Me - 1968
1007 - Ruby Andrews - You Can Run, But You Can't Hide / Wonderful Night - 1968

1008 - Freddy & Bobby - Come On Back / Mary's House - 1968
1009 - ?
1010 - Ruby Andrews - The Love I Need / Just Loving You - 1968
1011 - Billy Mize – Living Her Life In A Song / It Hurts To Know The Feeling's Gone - 1968
1012 - Ruby Andrews - I Let Him Take Me In His Arms / I Guess That Don't Make Me A Loser - 1969
1013 - ?
1014 - Chuck Bernard - Bessie Girl / Love Can Slip Away - 1969
1015 - Ruby Andrews - You Made A Believer Out Of Me / Where Have You Gone - 1969
1016 - Ruby Andrews - Help Yourself Lover / All The Way - 1970
1017 - Ruby Andrews - Can You Get Away / Everybody Saw You - 1970
1018 - Chuck Bernard - Everything Is Alright Now / The Other Side Of My Mind
1019 - Chuck Bernard - Deeper Than The Eyes Can See / Turn Her Loose
1020 - Ruby Andrews - You Ole Boo Boo You / Gotta Break Away -1971
1021 - Chuck Bernard - Love Bug / I'm Lonely - 1971
1022 - Ruby Andrews - Hound Dog / Away From The Crowd - 1971
1023 - Ruby Andrews - I Want To Be (Whatever It Takes To Please You) / Part 2 - 1971
1024 - Ruby Andrews - Good'n'plenty / My Love Is Coming Down - 1972
1025 - Chuck Bernard - Thank You Ma'am / Turn Her Loose - 1972
1026 - ?
1027 - ?
1028 - ?
1029 - ?
1030 - ?
1031 - Love Horn - If / Part 2
1032 - Ruby Andrews - You Got To Do The Same Thing / Didn't I Fool You - 1973
1050 - Chuck Bernard - Got To Get A Hold Of Myself / Everybody's Got Their Own Thing - 1973
1052 - Inner Drive - Party Man / Smell The Funk - 1974

www.soulfulkindamusic.net

CPSIA information can be obtained
at www.ICGtesting.com
Printed in the USA
LVHW081620211122
733717LV00006B/633

9 781530 552849